CONTEMPORARY ETHICAL
THEORY / *A Book of Readings*

CONSULTING EDITOR

V. C. Chappell

THE UNIVERSITY OF CHICAGO

CONTEMPORARY ETHICAL THEORY/*A Book of Readings*

Joseph Margolis

UNIVERSITY OF WESTERN ONTARIO

 RANDOM HOUSE / *New York*

Typography by Betty Binns

HAD THIS been a selection from the classical authors of philosophical ethics, no serious doubts could have arisen about what
the principal choices should be. The history of ethical theory
itself dictates what would have to be selected. Within a range
of very modest tolerance, everyone acquainted with the field
will agree on the most important writers on ethics between
Plato and G. E. Moore; problems of space and idiosyncrasy would
alone account for very nearly all the variations. But to attempt
a judicious selection from the enormous literature of ethics produced since Moore's time requires not so much the ability to
choose the most important writers as a sound conception of the
main lines of inquiry. And about this there is bound to be wide
disagreement.

I have restricted myself to two dozen selections from the
Anglo-American literature, chiefly from the professional journals,
that have appeared between the publication of Moore's *Principia
Ethica* and the present time. I cannot imagine anyone being
able to subscribe to the views of every entry included—many of
them are irreconcilably opposed to one another. Nor do I believe
that anyone else would have made exactly the same selections
I have made, in attempting to present the field fairly within the
same limits of space. The only justifications for my choices that
I can offer are that the range of selections includes a number of

the most influential writings of the period and that the sequence reveals a reasonable picture of the principal lines of inquiry during the period.

As I see it, there are at least three fundamentally distinct directions in which the main efforts of philosophers concerned with ethics have gone. In one, the earliest, questions have been raised about the cognitive status of judgments as to what is right and good and obligatory and about the logical properties of sentences that have ethical import. In the second, questions have been raised—granted that ethical judgments do obtain— about the grounds for ethical judgment and the nature of ethical argument, and about the role of rules and principles in ethical disputes. In the third, questions have been raised—once it is granted that men do act in accordance with ethical policies— about the nature of ethical conduct and about the psychological concepts that are presupposed when one speaks of ethically responsible agents.

The first of these lines of inquiry lends itself to an orderly sequence of presentation. The other two do not, and the selections there may be judged to be presented somewhat more arbitrarily. In order to offset some objections at least, since it was not possible to add to the number of selections, I have added at the end of the book a manageable list of suggested further readings.

CONTENTS

vii

CONTEMPORARY ETHICAL
THEORY / *A Book of Readings*

Part One / G. E. MOORE AND METAETHICS

IT is difficult now to appreciate, aside from historical retro-spect, the force exerted by G. E. Moore's attack on naturalistic ethics. Moore himself is partly responsible for this, in that his dramatic analysis of ethical terms, the exposure of the so-called Naturalistic Fallacy, and the formulation of the "open question" criterion have since been found to be seriously deficient and vague. It was characteristic of his way of working (and of the way in which his work was received) to isolate some telling puzzle on which the merits of an entire philosophical enter-prise were alleged to stand or fall. There is, in a sense, nothing left to Moore's work if these signal devices of his are defeated or neutralized—which is, I suggest, to say something at once terribly just and terribly unjust. Moore seems to dissolve, as it were, because he himself leaves no system behind and because his entire effort rests on the low peaks of single philosophical theses that later analysis (including, prominently, his own) has threatened to wash away.

Nevertheless, what Moore managed to do—although it was hardly his primary concern in dealing with ethics—was to oblige two generations of philosophers to undertake a reconsid-

eration, very nearly as if that were the sole issue in philosophical ethics, of the concepts of goodness, rightness, and obligation. To be sure, these concepts had always occupied philosophers; and very much in the spirit of Moore himself, they had already been the concern, thirty years earlier, of Henry Sidgwick. But the pre-occupations of most ethical studies from Moore's day almost to the present are altogether inconceivable except as responses to the enormous challenge his analyses had posed.

The distinctive character of much of the work in ethics during this interval, as a result, is the almost total neglect of a very wide range of issues that had been traditionally regarded as central to ethical theory (and were so regarded by Moore himself). Instead, there has been a collection of analytic tracts consciously opposed to accepting responsibility for providing ethical direction of any sort—not, at least, under some assumed authority of professional competence. The diversity among those who have followed Moore in this respect (ironically, this has run counter to his own ethical inclinations) cannot obscure their underlying unity of conviction on two points—namely, that data on ethical judgment and conduct may be presupposed for the sake of conceptual analysis and that such analysis may be undertaken in an ethically altogether neutral manner. No ethical consequences are expected to follow from these undertakings. On the contrary, we are told that what we may achieve philosophically is at most an accurate delineation of the ethical domain.

Here we find a confluence of the larger analytic endeavors of Moore and of Wittgenstein. Moore construed conceptual analysis as relatively independent (beyond minimal questions of usage) of the analysis of language; it has been said of him, for example, that his mode of analyzing a concept is a sort of introspective counterpart of the processes of chemical analysis. Wittgenstein, on the other hand, at least in the Investigations, *reduced the analysis of concepts to an analysis of the uses of linguistic expressions. I draw attention to these distinctions because they show how the vicissitudes of intellectual history sometimes tend to reinforce—from somewhat disparate sources at one and the same time—the dominance of particular philosophical*

currents. They also help to account for the inevitably mixed char-
acter of the analytic ventures of those who have sought to follow
Moore in his puzzles, although not necessarily in his methods.
The resultant somewhat eclectic way of considering ethical ques-
tions has been given the title of metaethics.

Very broadly speaking, the older strains of post-Moorean
ethical philosophy explore the possibilities of an intuitionist—
that is, cognitivist—theory (e.g., Prichard, Ross), which avoids
the old naturalism that Moore so effectively put on the defensive.
There are, to be sure, important writers on Ethics who persist in
subscribing to the naturalistic view (e.g., Dewey, Schlick, Perry),
although one has, in reading them, the definite sense that they
have not fully taken cognizance of Moore's challenge. The in-
herent difficulties of intuitionism, on the other hand—a doctrine
to which Moore himself seems clearly, although not altogether
explicitly, to incline—eventually discourage the continued em-
ployment of philosophical energies. This is not to say that the
champions of the intuitionist view have not themselves man-
aged to survive the accumulating criticisms against them (e.g.,
Ewing), but that the mainstream of the analysis of ethical con-
cepts has noticeably shifted its course away from them and the
direction of their endeavors.

The history of twentieth-century ethical thought displays
a certain inevitability. With the eclipse of naturalism and the
stalemate of intuitionism, philosophers understandably turned to
an examination of the possible noncognitive functions of ethical
sentences. Here, a positivistic flavor is dominant at first, gradu-
ally giving way to the linguistically subtler procedures initiated
by Wittgenstein and J. L. Austin (e.g., Ayer, Stevenson, Hare,
Nowell-Smith). Further, the earlier contributions to this litera-
ture tend to be strikingly devoted to the problems raised by
Moore's puzzles, whereas the later accounts begin once again to
take up the wider range of questions characteristic of the older,
traditional philosophical ethics. In a sense, the core of this shift
consists in turning from the analysis of "good" and "right" to the
analysis of sentence uses and thereby of a wider range of valua-
tional practices.

Finally, noncognitivism itself comes to seem anomalous, in the face of the obviously widespread practice of ethical judgment and the existence of ethical debate. Philosophy now turns to reexamine the defensibility of cognitivism, which is no longer formulated naïvely, as it had been by the old utilitarians, the hedonists, the eudaimonists. At the present moment, cognitivism of one sort or another dominates (although not exclusively) the ethical scene (e.g., Baier, Toulmin, Foot, Frankena, Brandt, Hampshire). Thus, the inquiry has spiraled—not circled!—back to Moore's original questions. And these most recent discussions inescapably show the effects of the philosophical discoveries made during the entire interval since the appearance of Moore's papers. The new cognitivism may perhaps best be characterized in terms of the following convictions: a) that the analysis of ethical judgments and arguments—in short, the analysis of ethical knowledge—may be undertaken without ipso facto posing the problem of the Naturalistic Fallacy; and b) that the resolution of that fallacy and the refinement of the "open question" criterion depend on a more powerful analysis of linguistic usage and meaning than has thus far been developed. We may consequently anticipate that, with the deepening interest in our own time in the philosophy of language, Moore's puzzles will again be revived and a second cycle of metaethical explorations will follow.

Section One / INTUITION AND NONNATURALISM

PREFACE TO *Principia Ethica* / G. E. Moore

IT APPEARS to me that in Ethics, as in all other philosophical studies, the difficulties and disagreements, of which its history is full, are mainly due to a very simple cause: namely to the attempt to answer questions, without first discovering precisely *what* question it is which you desire to answer. I do not know how far this source of error would be done away, if philosophers would *try* to discover what question they were asking, before they set about to answer it; for the work of analysis and distinction is often very difficult: we may often fail to make the necessary discovery, even though we make a definite attempt to do so. But I am inclined to think that in many cases a resolute attempt would be sufficient to ensure success; so that, if only this attempt were made, many of the most glaring difficulties and disagreements in philosophy would disappear. At all events, philosophers seem, in general, not to make the attempt; and, whether in consequence of this omission or not, they are constantly endeavouring to prove that 'Yes' or 'No' will answer questions, to which *neither* answer is correct, owing to the fact that what they

From G. E. Moore, *"Preface,"* Principia Ethica (*Cambridge: Cambridge University Press, 1903*), *pp. vii–x. Reprinted by permission of the publisher.*

have before their minds is not one question, but several, to some of which the true answer is 'No,' to others 'Yes.'

I have tried to distinguish clearly two kinds of question, which moral philosophers have always professed to answer, but which, as I have tried to shew, they have almost always confused both with one another and with other questions. These two questions may be expressed, the first in the form: What kind of things ought to exist for their own sakes? the second in the form: What kind of actions ought we to perform? I have tried to shew exactly what it is that we ask about a thing, when we ask whether it ought to exist for its own sake, is good in itself or has intrinsic value; and exactly what it is that we ask about an action, when we ask whether we ought to do it, whether it is a right action or a duty.

But from a clear insight into the nature of these two questions, there appears to me to follow a second most important result: namely, what is the nature of the evidence, by which alone any ethical proposition can be proved or disproved, confirmed or rendered doubtful. Once we recognise the exact meaning of the two questions, I think it also becomes plain exactly what kind of reasons are relevant as arguments for or against any particular answer to them. It becomes plain that, for answers to the *first* question, no relevant evidence whatever can be adduced: from no other truth, except themselves alone, can it be inferred that they are either true or false. We can guard against error only by taking care, that, when we try to answer a question of this kind, we have before our minds that question only, and not some other or others; but that there is great danger of such errors of confusion I have tried to shew, and also what are the chief precautions by the use of which we may guard against them. As for the *second* question, it becomes equally plain, that any answer to it *is* capable of proof or disproof—that, indeed, so many different considerations are relevant to its truth or falsehood, as to make the attainment of probability very difficult, and the attainment of certainty impossible. Nevertheless the *kind* of evidence, which is both necessary and alone relevant to such proof and disproof, is capable of exact definition. Such evidence must contain propositions of two kinds and of two kinds only: it must consist, in the first place, of truths with regard to the results of the action in question—of *causal* truths—but it must *also* contain ethical truths of our first or self-evident class. Many truths of both kinds are necessary to the proof that any action ought to be done; and any other kind of evidence is wholly irrelevant. It follows that, if any ethical philosopher offers for propositions of the first kind any evidence whatever, or if, for propositions of the second kind, he either fails to adduce both causal and ethical truths, or adduces truths that are neither, his reasoning has not the least tendency to establish his conclusions. But not only are his conclusions totally devoid of weight: we have, moreover, reason to suspect him of the error of confusion; since the offering of irrelevant evidence generally indicates that the philosopher who offers it has had before his mind, not the question which he professes to answer, but some other entirely different one. Ethical discussion, hitherto, has perhaps consisted chiefly in reasoning of this totally irrelevant kind.

One main object of this book may, then, be expressed by slightly changing one of Kant's famous titles. I have endeavoured to write 'Prolegomena to any future Ethics that can possibly pretend to be scientific.' In other words, I have endeavoured to discover what are the fundamental principles of ethical reasoning; and the establishment of these principles, rather than of any conclusions which may be attained by their use, may be regarded as my main object. I have, however, also attempted to present some conclusions, with regard to the proper answer of the question 'What is good in itself?' which are very different from any which have commonly been advocated by philosophers. I have tried to define the classes within which all great goods and evils fall; and I have maintained that very many different things are good and evil in themselves, and that neither class of things possesses any other property which is both common to all its members and peculiar to them.

In order to express the fact that ethical propositions of my *first* class are incapable of proof or disproof, I have sometimes followed Sidgwick's usage in calling them 'Intuitions.' But

I beg it may be noticed that I am not an 'Intuitionist,' in the ordinary sense of the term. Sidgwick himself seems never to have been clearly aware of the immense importance of the difference which distinguishes his Intuitionism from the common doctrine, which has generally been called by that name. The Intuitionist proper is distinguished by maintaining that propositions of my *second* class—propositions which assert that a certain action is *right* or a *duty*—are incapable of proof or disproof by any enquiry into the results of such actions. I, on the contrary, am no less anxious to maintain that propositions of *this* kind are *not* 'Intuitions,' than to maintain that propositions of my *first* class *are* Intuitions.

Again, I would wish it observed that, when I call such propositions 'Intuitions,' I mean *merely* to assert that they are incapable of proof; I imply nothing whatever as to the manner or origin of our cognition of them. Still less do I imply (as most Intuitionists have done) that any proposition whatever is true, *because* we cognise it in a particular way or by the exercise of any particular faculty: I hold, on the contrary, that in every way in which it is possible to cognise a true proposition, it is also possible to cognise a false one.

•   •   •

THE SUBJECT-MATTER OF
ETHICS / *G. E. Moore*

1. IT is very easy to point out some among our every-day judgments, with the truth of which Ethics is undoubtedly concerned.
Whenever we say, 'So and so is a good man,' or 'That fellow is a
villain'; whenever we ask, 'What ought I to do?' or 'Is it wrong
for me to do like this?'; whenever we hazard such remarks as
'Temperance is a virtue and drunkenness a vice'—it is undoubtedly the business of Ethics to discuss such questions and
such statements; to argue what is the true answer when we ask
what it is right to do, and to give reasons for thinking that our
statements about the character of persons or the morality of actions are true or false. In the vast majority of cases, where we
make statements involving any of the terms 'virtue,' 'vice,'
'duty,' 'right,' 'ought,' 'good,' 'bad,' we are making ethical judgments; and if we wish to discuss their truth, we shall be discussing a point of Ethics.

So much as this is not disputed; but it falls very far short
of defining the province of Ethics. That province may indeed be
defined as the whole truth about that which is at the same time
common to all such judgments and peculiar to them. But we
have still to ask the question: What is it that is thus common
and peculiar? And this is a question to which very different answers have been given by ethical philosophers of acknowledged

From G. E. Moore, "The Subject-Matter of Ethics," Principia Ethica (*Cambridge: Cambridge University Press, 1903*), *Ch. 1. Reprinted by permission of
the publisher.*

reputation, and none of them, perhaps, completely satisfactory.

2. If we take such examples as those given above, we shall not be far wrong in saying that they are all of them concerned with the question of 'conduct'—with the question, what, in the conduct of us, human beings, is good, and what is bad, what is right, and what is wrong. For when we say that a man is good, we commonly mean that he acts rightly; when we say that drunkenness is a vice, we commonly mean that to get drunk is a wrong or wicked action. And this discussion of human conduct is, in fact, that with which the name 'Ethics' is most intimately associated. It is so associated by derivation; and conduct is undoubtedly by far the commonest and most generally interesting object of ethical judgments.

Accordingly, we find that many ethical philosophers are disposed to accept as an adequate definition of 'Ethics' the statement that it deals with the question what is good or bad in human conduct. They hold that its enquiries are properly confined to 'conduct' or to 'practice'; they hold that the name 'practical philosophy' covers all the matter with which it has to do. Now, without discussing the proper meaning of the word (for verbal questions are properly left to the writers of dictionaries and other persons interested in literature; philosophy, as we shall see, has no concern with them), I may say that I intend to use 'Ethics' to cover more than this—a usage, for which there is, I think, quite sufficient authority. I am using it to cover an enquiry for which, at all events, there is no other word: the general enquiry into what is good.

Ethics is undoubtedly concerned with the question what good conduct is; but, being concerned with this, it obviously does not start at the beginning, unless it is prepared to tell us what is good as well as what is conduct. For 'good conduct' is a complex notion: all conduct is not good; for some is certainly bad and some may be indifferent. And on the other hand, other things, beside conduct, may be good; and if they are so, then, 'good' denotes some property, that is common to them and conduct; and if we examine good conduct alone of all good things, then we shall be in danger of mistaking for this property, some prop-

erty which is not shared by those other things: and thus we shall
have made a mistake about Ethics even in this limited sense; for
we shall not know what good conduct really is. This is a mistake
which many writers have actually made, from limiting their enquiry to conduct. And hence I shall try to avoid it by considering
first what is good in general; hoping, that if we can arrive at any
certainty about this, it will be much easier to settle the question
of good conduct: for we all know pretty well what 'conduct' is.
This, then, is our first question: What is good? and What is bad?
and to the discussion of this question (or these questions) I give
the name of Ethics, since that science must, at all events, include it.

   3. But this is a question which may have many meanings. If, for example, each of us were to say 'I am doing good
now' or 'I had a good dinner yesterday,' these statements would
each of them be some sort of answer to our question, although
perhaps a false one. So, too, when A asks B what school he ought
to send his son to, B's answer will certainly be an ethical judgment. And similarly all distribution of praise or blame to any
personage or thing that has existed, now exists, or will exist,
does give some answer to the question 'What is good?' In all
such cases some particular thing is judged to be good or bad: the
question 'What?' is answered by 'This.' But this is not the sense
in which a scientific Ethics asks the question. Not one, of all the
many million answers of this kind, which must be true, can form
a part of an ethical system; although that science must contain
reasons and principles sufficient for deciding on the truth of all
of them. There are far too many persons, things and events in
the world, past, present, or to come, for a discussion of their
individual merits to be embraced in any science. Ethics, therefore, does not deal at all with facts of this nature, facts that are
unique, individual, absolutely particular; facts with which such
studies as history, geography, astronomy, are compelled, in part
at least, to deal. And, for this reason, it is not the business of the
ethical philosopher to give personal advice or exhortation.

   4. But there is another meaning which may be given to
the question 'What is good?' 'Books are good' would be an an-

swer to it, though an answer obviously false; for some books are very bad indeed. And ethical judgments of this kind do indeed belong to Ethics; though I shall not deal with many of them. Such is the judgment 'Pleasure is good'—a judgment, of which Ethics should discuss the truth, although it is not nearly as important as that other judgment, with which we shall be much occupied presently—'Pleasure *alone* is good.' It is judgments of this sort, which are made in such books on Ethics as contain a list of 'virtues'—in Aristotle's 'Ethics' for example. But it is judgments of precisely the same kind, which form the substance of what is commonly supposed to be a study different from Ethics, and one much less respectable—the study of Casuistry. We may be told that Casuistry differs from Ethics, in that it is much more detailed and particular, Ethics much more general. But it is most important to notice that Casuistry does not deal with anything that is absolutely particular—particular in the only sense in which a perfectly precise line can be drawn between it and what is general. It is not particular in the sense just noticed, the sense in which this book is a particular book, and A's friend's advice particular advice. Casuistry may indeed be *more* particular and Ethics *more* general; but that means that they differ only in degree and not in kind. And this is universally true of 'particular' and 'general,' when used in this common, but inaccurate, sense. So far as Ethics allows itself to give lists of virtues or even to name constituents of the Ideal, it is indistinguishable from Casuistry. Both alike deal with what is general, in the sense in which physics and chemistry deal with what is general. Just as chemistry aims at discovering what are the properties of oxygen, *wherever it occurs,* and not only of this or that particular specimen of oxygen; so Casuistry aims at discovering what actions are good, *whenever they occur.* In this respect Ethics and Casuistry alike are to be classed with such sciences as physics, chemistry and physiology, in their absolute distinction from those of which history and geography are instances. And it is to be noted that, owing to their detailed nature, casuistical investigations are actually nearer to physics and to chemistry than are the investigations usually assigned to Ethics. For just as physics cannot rest content with the discovery that light is propagated by waves of ether, but must go on to discover the particular nature of the ether-waves corresponding to each several colour; so Casuistry, not content with the general law that charity is a virtue must attempt to discover the relative merits of every different form of charity. Casuistry forms, therefore, part of the ideal of ethical science: Ethics cannot be complete without it. The defects of Casuistry are not defects of principle; no objection can be taken to its aim and object. It has failed only because it is far too difficult a subject to be treated adequately in our present state of knowledge. The casuist has been unable to distinguish, in the cases which he treats, those elements upon which their value depends. Hence he often thinks two cases to be alike in respect of value, when in reality they are alike only in some other respect. It is to mistakes of this kind that the pernicious influence of such investigations has been due. For Casuistry is the goal of ethical investigation. It cannot be safely attempted at the beginning of our studies, but only at the end.

5. But our question 'What is good?' may have still another meaning. We may, in the third place, mean to ask, not what thing or things are good, but how 'good' is to be defined. This is an enquiry which belongs only to Ethics, not to Casuistry; and this is the enquiry which will occupy us first.

It is an enquiry to which most special attention should be directed; since this question, how 'good' is to be defined, is the most fundamental question in all Ethics. That which is meant by 'good' is, in fact, except its converse 'bad,' the *only* simple object of thought which is peculiar to Ethics. Its definition is, therefore, the most essential point in the definition of Ethics; and moreover a mistake with regard to it entails a far larger number of erroneous ethical judgments than any other. Unless this first question be fully understood, and its true answer clearly recognised, the rest of Ethics is as good as useless from the point of view of systematic knowledge. True ethical judgments, of the two kinds last dealt with, may indeed be made by those who do not know the answer to this question as well as by those who do; and it goes without saying that the two classes of people may lead equally good lives. But it is extremely unlikely that the *most general* ethical judgments will be equally valid, in the absence of a true answer to this question: I shall presently try to shew that the gravest errors have been largely due to beliefs in a false answer. And, in any case, it is impossible that, till the answer to this question be known, any one should know *what is the evidence* for any ethical judgment whatsoever. But the main object of Ethics, as a systematic science, is to give correct *reasons* for thinking that this or that is good; and, unless this question be answered, such reasons cannot be given. Even, therefore, apart from the fact that a false answer leads to false conclusions, the present enquiry is a most necessary and important part of the science of Ethics.

6. What, then, is good? How is good to be defined? Now, it may be thought that this is a verbal question. A definition does indeed often mean the expressing of one word's meaning in other words. But this is not the sort of definition I am asking for. Such a definition can never be of ultimate importance in any study except lexicography. If I wanted that kind of definition I should have to consider in the first place how people generally used the word 'good'; but my business is not with its proper usage, as established by custom. I should, indeed, be foolish, if I tried to use it for something which it did not usually denote: if, for instance, I were to announce that, whenever I used the word 'good,' I must be understood to be thinking of that object which is usually denoted by the word 'table.' I shall, therefore, use the word in the sense in which I think it is ordinarily used; but at the same time I am not anxious to discuss whether I am right in thinking that it is so used. My business is solely with that object or idea, which I hold, rightly or wrongly, that the word is generally used to stand for. What I want to discover is the nature of that object or idea, and about this I am extremely anxious to arrive at an agreement.

But, if we understand the question in this sense, my answer to it may seem a very disappointing one. If I am asked 'What is good?' my answer is that good is good, and that is the end of the matter. Or if I am asked 'How is good to be defined?'

my answer is that it cannot be defined, and that is all I have to say about it. But disappointing as these answers may appear, they are of the very last importance. To readers who are familiar with philosophic terminology, I can express their importance by saying that they amount to this: That propositions about the good are all of them synthetic and never analytic; and that is plainly no trivial matter. And the same thing may be expressed more popularly, by saying that, if I am right, then nobody can foist upon us such an axiom as that 'Pleasure is the only good' or that 'The good is the desired' on the pretence that this is 'the very meaning of the word.'

7. Let us, then, consider this position. My point is that 'good' is a simple notion, just as 'yellow' is a simple notion; that, just as you cannot, by any manner of means, explain to any one who does not already know it, what yellow is, so you cannot explain what good is. Definitions of the kind that I was asking for, definitions which describe the real nature of the object or notion denoted by a word, and which do not merely tell us what the word is used to mean, are only possible when the object or notion in question is something complex. You can give a definition of a horse, because a horse has many different properties and qualities, all of which you can enumerate. But when you have enumerated them all, when you have reduced a horse to his simplest terms, then you can no longer define those terms. They are simply something which you think of or perceive, and to any one who cannot think of or perceive them, you can never, by any definition, make their nature known. It may perhaps be objected to this that we are able to describe to others, objects which they have never seen or thought of. We can, for instance, make a man understand what a chimaera is, although he has never heard of one or seen one. You can tell him that it is an animal with a lioness's head and body, with a goat's head growing from the middle of its back, and with a snake in place of a tail. But here the object which you are describing is a complex object; it is entirely composed of parts, with which we are all perfectly familiar—a snake, a goat, a lioness; and we know, too, the manner in which those parts are to be put together, because we know

what is meant by the middle of a lioness's back, and where her tail is wont to grow. And so it is with all objects, not previously known, which we are able to define: they are all complex; all composed of parts, which may themselves, in the first instance, be capable of similar definition, but which must in the end be reducible to simplest parts, which can no longer be defined. But yellow and good, we say, are not complex: they are notions of that simple kind, out of which definitions are composed and with which the power of further defining ceases.

8. When we say, as Webster says, 'The definition of horse is "A hoofed quadruped of the genus Equus,"' we may, in fact, mean three different things. (1) We may mean merely: 'When I say "horse," you are to understand that I am talking about a hoofed quadruped of the genus Equus.' This might be called the arbitrary verbal definition: and I do not mean that good is indefinable in that sense. (2) We may mean, as Webster ought to mean: 'When most English people say "horse," they mean a hoofed quadruped of the genus Equus.' This may be called the verbal definition proper, and I do not say that good is indefinable in this sense either; for it is certainly possible to discover how people use a word: otherwise, we could never have known that 'good' may be translated by 'gut' in German and by 'bon' in French. But (3) we may, when we define horse, mean something much more important. We may mean that a certain object, which we all of us know, is composed in a certain manner: that it has four legs, a head, a heart, a liver, etc., etc., all of them arranged in definite relations to one another. It is in this sense that I deny good to be definable. I say that it is not composed of any parts, which we can substitute for it in our minds when we are thinking of it. We might think just as clearly and correctly about a horse, if we thought of all its parts and their arrangement instead of thinking of the whole: we could, I say, think how a horse differed from a donkey just as well, just as truly, in this way, as now we do, only not so easily; but there is nothing whatsoever which we could so substitute for good; and that is what I mean, when I say that good is indefinable.

9. But I am afraid I have still not removed the chief diffi-

culty which may prevent acceptance of the proposition that good is indefinable. I do not mean to say that *the* good, that which is good, is thus indefinable; if I did think so, I should not be writing on Ethics, for my main object is to help towards discovering that definition. It is just because I think there will be less risk of error in our search for a definition of 'the good,' that I am now insisting that *good* is indefinable. I must try to explain the difference between these two. I suppose it may be granted that 'good' is an adjective. Well 'the good,' 'that which is good,' must therefore be the substantive to which the adjective 'good' will apply: it must be the whole of that to which the adjective will apply, and the adjective must *always* truly apply to it. But if it is that to which the adjective will apply, it must be something different from that adjective itself; and the whole of that something different, whatever it is, will be our definition of *the* good. Now it may be that this something will have other adjectives, beside 'good,' that will apply to it. It may be full of pleasure, for example; it may be intelligent: and if these two adjectives are really part of its definition, then it will certainly be true, that pleasure and intelligence are good. And many people appear to think that, if we say 'Pleasure and intelligence are good,' or if we say 'Only pleasure and intelligence are good,' we are defining 'good.' Well, I cannot deny that propositions of this nature may sometimes be called definitions; I do not know well enough how the word is generally used to decide upon this point. I only wish it to be understood that that is not what I mean when I say there is no possible definition of good, and that I shall not mean this if I use the word again. I do most fully believe that some true proposition of the form 'Intelligence is good and intelligence alone is good' can be found; if none could be found, our definition of *the* good would be impossible. As it is, I believe *the* good to be definable; and yet I still say that good itself is indefinable.

10. 'Good,' then, if we mean by it that quality which we assert to belong to a thing, when we say that the thing is good, is incapable of any definition, in the most important sense of that word. The most important sense of 'definition' is that in which a definition states what are the parts which invariably compose a

certain whole; and in this sense 'good' has no definition because
it is simple and has no parts. It is one of those innumerable
objects of thought which are themselves incapable of definition,
because they are the ultimate terms by reference to which whatever *is* capable of definition must be defined. That there must be
an indefinite number of such terms is obvious, on reflection;
since we cannot define anything except by an analysis, which,
when carried as far as it will go, refers us to something, which is
simply different from anything else, and which by that ultimate
difference explains the peculiarity of the whole which we are
defining: for every whole contains some parts which are common to other wholes also. There is, therefore, no intrinsic difficulty in the contention that 'good' denotes a simple and indefinable quality. There are many other instances of such qualities.

Consider yellow, for example. We may try to define it, by
describing its physical equivalent; we may state what kind of
light-vibrations must stimulate the normal eye, in order that we
may perceive it. But a moment's reflection is sufficient to shew
that those light-vibrations are not themselves what we mean by
yellow. *They* are not what we perceive. Indeed we should never
have been able to discover their existence, unless we had first
been struck by the patent difference of quality between the
different colours. The most we can be entitled to say of those vi-
brations is that they are what corresponds in space to the yellow
which we actually perceive.

Yet a mistake of this simple kind has commonly been
made about 'good.' It may be true that all things which are good
are *also* something else, just as it is true that all things which are
yellow produce a certain kind of vibration in the light. And it is a
fact, that Ethics aims at discovering what are those other properties belonging to all things which are good. But far too many
philosophers have thought that when they named those other
properties they were actually defining good; that these properties, in fact, were simply not 'other,' but absolutely and entirely
the same with goodness. This view I propose to call the 'naturalistic fallacy' and of it I shall now endeavour to dispose.

11. Let us consider what it is such philosophers say. And

first it is to be noticed that they do not agree among themselves. They not only say that they are right as to what good is, but they endeavour to prove that other people who say that it is something else, are wrong. One, for instance, will affirm that good is pleasure, another, perhaps, that good is that which is desired; and each of these will argue eagerly to prove that the other is wrong. But how is that possible? One of them says that good is nothing but the object of desire, and at the same time tries to prove that it is not pleasure. But from his first assertion, that good just means the object of desire, one of two things must follow as regards his proof:

(1) He may be trying to prove that the object of desire is not pleasure. But, if this be all, where is his Ethics? The position he is maintaining is merely a psychological one. Desire is something which occurs in our minds, and pleasure is something else which so occurs; and our would-be ethical philosopher is merely holding that the latter is not the object of the former. But what has that to do with the question in dispute? His opponent held the ethical proposition that pleasure was the good, and although he should prove a million times over the psychological proposition that pleasure is not the object of desire, he is no nearer proving his opponent to be wrong. The position is like this. One man says a triangle is a circle: another replies 'A triangle is a straight line, and I will prove to you that I am right: *for*' (this is the only argument) 'a straight line is not a circle.' 'That is quite true,' the other may reply; 'but nevertheless a triangle is a circle, and you have said nothing whatever to prove the contrary. What is proved is that one of us is wrong, for we agree that a triangle cannot be both a straight line and a circle: but which is wrong, there can be no earthly means of proving, since you define triangle as straight line and I define it as circle.'—Well, that is one alternative which any naturalistic Ethics has to face; if good is *defined* as something else, it is then impossible either to prove that any other definition is wrong or even to deny such definition.

(2) The other alternative will scarcely be more welcome. It is that the discussion is after all a verbal one. When A says

'Good means pleasant' and B says 'Good means desired,' they may merely wish to assert that most people have used the word for what is pleasant and for what is desired respectively. And this is quite an interesting subject for discussion: only it is not a whit more an ethical discussion than the last was. Nor do I think that any exponent of naturalistic Ethics would be willing to allow that this was all he meant. They are all so anxious to persuade us that what they call the good is what we really ought to do. 'Do, pray, act so, because the word "good" is generally used to denote actions of this nature': such, on this view, would be the substance of their teaching. And in so far as they tell us how we ought to act, their teaching is truly ethical, as they mean it to be. But how perfectly absurd is the reason they would give for it! 'You are to do this, because most people use a certain word to denote conduct such as this.' 'You are to say the thing which is not, because most people call it lying.' That is an argument just as good!—My dear sirs, what we want to know from you as ethical teachers, is not how people use a word; it is not even, what kind of actions they approve, which the use of this word 'good' may certainly imply: what we want to know is simply what *is* good. We may indeed agree that what most people do think good, is actually so; we shall at all events be glad to know their opinions: but when we say their opinions about what *is* good, we do mean what we say; we do not care whether they call that thing which they mean 'horse' or 'table' or 'chair,' 'gut' or 'bon' or 'ἀγαθός'; we want to know what it is that they so call. When they say 'Pleasure is good,' we cannot believe that they merely mean 'Pleasure is pleasure' and nothing more than that.

12. Suppose a man says 'I am pleased'; and suppose that is not a lie or a mistake but the truth. Well, if it is true, what does that mean? It means that his mind, a certain definite mind, distinguished by certain definite marks from all others, has at this moment a certain definite feeling called pleasure. 'Pleased' *means* nothing but having pleasure, and though we may be more pleased or less pleased, and even, we may admit for the present, have one or another kind of pleasure; yet in so far as it is pleasure we have, whether there be more or less of it, and whether it

be of one kind or another, what we have is one definite thing,
absolutely indefinable, some one thing that is the same in all the
various degrees and in all the various kinds of it that there may
be. We may be able to say how it is related to other things: that,
for example, it is in the mind, that it causes desire, that we are
conscious of it, etc., etc. We can, I say, describe its relations to
other things, but define it we can *not*. And if anybody tried to
define pleasure for us as being any other natural object; if
anybody were to say, for instance, that pleasure *means* the sensation of red, and were to proceed to deduce from that that pleasure is a colour, we should be entitled to laugh at him and to dis-
trust his future statements about pleasure. Well, that would be
the same fallacy which I have called the naturalistic fallacy.
That 'pleased' does not mean 'having the sensation of red,' or
anything else whatever, does not prevent us from understanding
what it does mean. It is enough for us to know that 'pleased'
does mean 'having the sensation of pleasure,' and though pleasure is absolutely indefinable, though pleasure is pleasure and
nothing else whatever, yet we feel no difficulty in saying that we
are pleased. The reason is, of course, that when I say 'I am
pleased,' I do *not* mean that 'I' am the same thing as 'having
pleasure.' And similarly no difficulty need be found in my saying
that 'pleasure is good' and yet not meaning that 'pleasure' is
the same thing as 'good,' that pleasure *means* good, and that
good *means* pleasure. If I were to imagine that when I said 'I am
pleased,' I meant that I was exactly the same thing as 'pleased,'
I should not indeed call that a naturalistic fallacy, although it
would be the same fallacy as I have called naturalistic with reference to Ethics. The reason of this is obvious enough. When a
man confuses two natural objects with one another, defining the
one by the other, if for instance, he confuses himself, who is one
natural object, with 'pleased' or with 'pleasure' which are others,
then there is no reason to call the fallacy naturalistic. But if
he confuses 'good,' which is not in the same sense a natural
object, with any natural object whatever, then there is a reason
for calling that a naturalistic fallacy; its being made with regard
to 'good' marks it as something quite specific, and this specific

mistake deserves a name because it is so common. As for the reasons why good is not to be considered a natural object, they may be reserved for discussion in another place. But, for the present, it is sufficient to notice this: Even if it were a natural object, that would not alter the nature of the fallacy nor diminish its importance one whit. All that I have said about it would remain quite equally true: only the name which I have called it would not be so appropriate as I think it is. And I do not care about the name: what I do care about is the fallacy. It does not matter what we call it, provided we recognise it when we meet with it. It is to be met with in almost every book on Ethics; and yet it is not recognised: and that is why it is necessary to multiply illustrations of it, and convenient to give it a name. It is a very simple fallacy indeed. When we say that an orange is yellow, we do not think our statement binds us to hold that 'orange' means nothing else than 'yellow,' or that nothing can be yellow but an orange. Supposing the orange is also sweet! Does that bind us to say that 'sweet' is exactly the same thing as 'yellow,' that 'sweet' must be defined as 'yellow'? And supposing it be recognised that 'yellow' just means 'yellow' and nothing else whatever, does that make it any more difficult to hold that oranges are yellow? Most certainly it does not: on the contrary, it would be absolutely meaningless to say that oranges were yellow, unless yellow did in the end mean just 'yellow' and nothing else whatever—unless it was absolutely indefinable. We should not get any very clear notion about things, which are yellow—we should not get very far with our science, if we were bound to hold that everything which was yellow, *meant* exactly the same thing as yellow. We should find we had to hold that an orange was exactly the same thing as a stool, a piece of paper, a lemon, anything you like. We could prove any number of absurdities; but should we be the nearer to the truth? Why, then, should it be different with 'good'? Why, if good is good and indefinable, should I be held to deny that pleasure is good? Is there any difficulty in holding both to be true at once? On the contrary, there is no meaning in saying that pleasure is good, unless good is something different from pleasure. It is absolutely useless, so far as

Ethics is concerned, to prove, as Mr. Spencer tries to do, that increase of pleasure coincides with increase of life, unless good *means* something different from either life or pleasure. He might just as well try to prove that an orange is yellow by shewing that it always is wrapped up in paper.

13. In fact, if it is not the case that 'good' denotes something simple and indefinable, only two alternatives are possible: either it is a complex, a given whole, about the correct analysis of which there may be disagreement; or else it means nothing at all, and there is no such subject as Ethics. In general, however, ethical philosophers have attempted to define good, without recognising what such an attempt must mean. They actually use arguments which involve one or both of the absurdities considered in § 11. We are, therefore, justified in concluding that the attempt to define good is chiefly due to want of clearness as to the possible nature of definition. There are, in fact, only two serious alternatives to be considered, in order to establish the conclusion that 'good' does denote a simple and indefinable notion. It might possibly denote a complex, as 'horse' does; or it might have no meaning at all. Neither of these possibilities has, however, been clearly conceived and seriously maintained, as such, by those who presume to define good; and both may be dismissed by a simple appeal to facts.

(1) The hypothesis that disagreement about the meaning of good is disagreement with regard to the correct analysis of a given whole, may be most plainly seen to be incorrect by consideration of the fact that, whatever definition be offered, it may be always asked, with significance, of the complex so defined, whether it is itself good. To take, for instance, one of the more plausible, because one of the more complicated, of such proposed definitions, it may easily be thought, at first sight, that to be good may mean to be that which we desire to desire. Thus if we apply this definition to a particular instance and say 'When we think that A is good, we are thinking that A is one of the things which we desire to desire,' our proposition may seem quite plausible. But, if we carry the investigation further, and ask ourselves 'Is it good to desire to desire A?' it is apparent, on

a little reflection, that this question is itself as intelligible, as the original question 'Is A good?'—that we are, in fact, now asking for exactly the same information about the desire to desire A, for which we formerly asked with regard to A itself. But it is also apparent that the meaning of this second question cannot be correctly analysed into 'Is the desire to desire A one of the things which we desire to desire?': we have not before our minds anything so complicated as the question 'Do we desire to desire to desire to desire A?' Moreover any one can easily convince himself by inspection that the predicate of this proposition—'good' —is positively different from the notion of 'desiring to desire' which enters into its subject: 'That we should desire to desire A is good' is *not* merely equivalent to 'That A should be good is good.' It may indeed be true that what we desire to desire is always also good; perhaps, even the converse may be true: but it is very doubtful whether this is the case, and the mere fact that we understand very well what is meant by doubting it, shews clearly that we have two different notions before our minds.

(2) And the same consideration is sufficient to dismiss the hypothesis that 'good' has no meaning whatsoever. It is very natural to make the mistake of supposing that what is universally true is of such a nature that its negation would be self-contradictory: the importance which has been assigned to analytic propositions in the history of philosophy shews how easy such a mistake is. And thus it is very easy to conclude that what seems to be a universal ethical principle is in fact an identical proposition; that, if, for example, whatever is called 'good' seems to be pleasant, the proposition 'Pleasure is the good' does not assert a connection between two different notions, but involves only one, that of pleasure, which is easily recognised as a distinct entity. But whoever will attentively consider with himself what is actually before his mind when he asks the question 'Is pleasure (or whatever it may be) after all good?' can easily satisfy himself that he is not merely wondering whether pleasure is pleasant. And if he will try this experiment with each suggested definition in succession, he may become expert enough to recognise that in every case he has before his mind a unique

object, with regard to the connection of which with any other object, a distinct question may be asked. Every one does in fact understand the question 'Is this good?' When he thinks of it, his state of mind is different from what it would be, were he asked 'Is this pleasant, or desired, or approved?' It has a distinct meaning for him, even though he may not recognise in what respect it is distinct. Whenever he thinks of 'intrinsic value,' or 'intrinsic worth,' or says that a thing 'ought to exist,' he has before his mind the unique object—the unique property of things—which I mean by 'good.' Everybody is constantly aware of this notion, although he may never become aware at all that it is different from other notions of which he is also aware. But, for correct ethical reasoning, it is extremely important that he should become aware of this fact; and, as soon as the nature of the problem is clearly understood, there should be little difficulty in advancing so far in analysis.

14. 'Good,' then, is indefinable; and yet, so far as I know, there is only one ethical writer, Prof. Henry Sidgwick, who has clearly recognised and stated this fact. We shall see, indeed, how far many of the most reputed ethical systems fall short of drawing the conclusions which follow from such a recognition. At present I will only quote one instance, which will serve to illustrate the meaning and importance of this principle that 'good' is indefinable, or, as Prof. Sidgwick says, an 'unanalysable notion.' It is an instance to which Prof. Sidgwick himself refers in a note on the passage, in which he argues that 'ought' is unanalysable.[1]

'Bentham,' says Sidgwick, 'explains that his fundamental principle "states the greatest happiness of all those whose interest is in question as being the right and proper end of human action"'; and yet 'his language in other passages of the same chapter would seem to imply' that he *means* by the word "right" "conducive to the general happiness." Prof. Sidgwick sees that, if you take these two statements together, you get the absurd result that 'greatest happiness is the end of human action, which is conducive to the general happiness'; and so absurd does it seem

[1] *Methods of Ethics*, Bk. 1, Chap. III, §1 (6th edition).

to him to call this result, as Bentham calls it, 'the fundamental principle of a moral system,' that he suggests that Bentham cannot have meant it. Yet Prof. Sidgwick himself states elsewhere[2] that Psychological Hedonism is 'not seldom confounded with Egoistic Hedonism'; and that confusion, as we shall see, rests chiefly on that same fallacy, the naturalistic fallacy, which is implied in Bentham's statements. Prof. Sidgwick admits therefore that this fallacy is sometimes committed, absurd as it is; and I am inclined to think that Bentham may really have been one of those who committed it. Mill, as we shall see, certainly did commit it. In any case, whether Bentham committed it or not, his doctrine, as above quoted, will serve as a very good illustration of this fallacy, and of the importance of the contrary proposition that good is indefinable.

Let us consider this doctrine. Bentham seems to imply, so Prof. Sidgwick says, that the word 'right' *means* 'conducive to general happiness.' Now this, by itself, need not necessarily involve the naturalistic fallacy. For the word 'right' is very commonly appropriated to actions which lead to the attainment of what is good; which are regarded as *means* to the ideal and not as ends-in-themselves. This use of 'right,' as denoting what is good as a means, whether or not it be also good as an end, is indeed the use to which I shall confine the word. Had Bentham been using 'right' in this sense, it might be perfectly consistent for him to *define* right as 'conducive to the general happiness,' *provided only* (and notice this proviso) he had already proved, or laid down as an axiom, that general happiness was *the* good, or (what is equivalent to this) that general happiness alone was good. For in that case he would have already defined *the* good as general happiness (a position perfectly consistent, as we have seen, with the contention that 'good' is indefinable), and, since right was to be defined as 'conducive to *the* good,' it would actually *mean* 'conducive to general happiness.' But this method of escape from the charge of having committed the naturalistic fallacy has been closed by Bentham himself. For his fundamental principle is, we see, that the greatest happiness of all con-

2 *Methods of Ethics*, Bk. 1, Chap. IV, §1.

cerned is the *right* and proper *end* of human action. He applies the word 'right,' therefore, to the end, as such, not only to the means which are conducive to it; and, that being so, right can no longer be defined as 'conducive to the general happiness,' without involving the fallacy in question. For now it is obvious that the definition of right as conducive to general happiness can be used by him in support of the fundamental principle that general happiness is the right end; instead of being itself derived from that principle. If right, by definition, means conducive to general happiness, then it is obvious that general happiness is the right end. It is not necessary now first to prove or assert that general happiness is the right end, before right is defined as conducive to general happiness—a perfectly valid procedure; but on the contrary the definition of right as conducive to general happiness proves general happiness to be the right end—a perfectly invalid procedure, since in this case the statement that 'general happiness is the right end of human action' is not an ethical principle at all, but either, as we have seen, a proposition about the meaning of words, or else a proposition about the *nature* of general happiness, not about its rightness or goodness.

Now, I do not wish the importance I assign to this fallacy to be misunderstood. The discovery of it does not at all refute Bentham's contention that greatest happiness is the proper end of human action, if that be understood as an ethical proposition, as he undoubtedly intended it. That principle may be true all the same; we shall consider whether it is so in succeeding chapters. Bentham might have maintained it, as Prof. Sidgwick does, even if the fallacy had been pointed out to him. What I am maintaining is that the *reasons* which he actually gives for his ethical proposition are fallacious ones so far as they consist in a definition of right. What I suggest is that he did not perceive them to be fallacious; that, if he had done so, he would have been led to seek for other reasons in support of his Utilitarianism; and that, had he sought for other reasons, he *might* have found none which he thought to be sufficient. In that case he would have changed his whole system—a most important consequence. It is undoubtedly also possible that he would have thought other reasons to be sufficient, and in that case his ethical system, in its main results, would still have stood. But, even in this latter case, his use of the fallacy would be a serious objection to him as an ethical philosopher. For it is the business of Ethics, I must insist, not only to obtain true results, but also to find valid reasons for them. The direct object of Ethics is knowledge and not practice; and any one who uses the naturalistic fallacy has certainly not fulfilled this first object, however correct his practical principles may be.

My objections to Naturalism are then, in the first place, that it offers no reason at all, far less any valid reason, for any ethical principle whatever; and in this it already fails to satisfy the requirements of Ethics, as a scientific study. But in the second place I contend that, though it gives a reason for no ethical principle, it is a *cause* of the acceptance of false principles—it deludes the mind into accepting ethical principles, which are false; and in this it is contrary to every aim of Ethics. It is easy to see that if we start with a definition of right conduct as conduct conducive to general happiness; then, knowing that right conduct is universally conduct conducive to the good, we very easily arrive at the result that the good is general happiness. If, on the other hand, we once recognise that we must start our Ethics without a definition, we shall be much more apt to look about us, before we adopt any ethical principle whatever; and the more we look about us, the less likely are we to adopt a false one. It may be replied to this: Yes, but we shall look about us just as much, before we settle on our definition, and are therefore just as likely to be right. But I will try to shew that this is not the case. If we start with the conviction that a definition of good can be found, we start with the conviction that good *can mean* nothing else than some one property of things; and our only business will then be to discover what that property is. But if we recognize that, so far as the meaning of good goes, anything whatever may be good, we start with a much more open mind. Moreover, apart from the fact that, when we think we have a definition, we cannot logically defend our ethical princi-

ples in any way whatever, we shall also be much less apt to defend them well, even if illogically. For we shall start with the
conviction that good must mean so and so, and shall therefore be
inclined either to misunderstand our opponent's arguments or to
cut them short with the reply, 'This is not an open question: the
very meaning of the word decides it; no one can think otherwise
except through confusion.'

15. Our first conclusion as to the subject-matter of Ethics is, then, that there is a simple, indefinable, unanalysable object of thought by reference to which it must be defined. By what
name we call this unique object is a matter of indifference, so
long as we clearly recognise what it is and that it does differ
from other objects. The words which are commonly taken as the
signs of ethical judgments all do refer to it; and they are expressions of ethical judgments solely because they do so refer. But
they may refer to it in two different ways, which it is very important to distinguish, if we are to have a complete definition of the
range of ethical judgments. Before I proceeded to argue that
there was such an indefinable notion involved in ethical notions,
I stated (§4) that it was necessary for Ethics to enumerate all
true universal judgments, asserting that such and such a thing
was good, whenever it occurred. But, although all such judgments do refer to that unique notion which I have called 'good,'
they do not all refer to it in the same way. They may either assert
that this unique property does always attach to the thing in
question, or else they may assert only that the thing in question is *a cause or necessary condition* for the existence of other
things to which this unique property does attach. The nature of
these two species of universal ethical judgments is extremely
different; and a great part of the difficulties, which are met with
in ordinary ethical speculation, are due to the failure to distinguish them clearly. Their difference has, indeed, received expression in ordinary language by the contrast between the terms
'good as means' and 'good in itself,' 'value as a means' and
'intrinsic value.' But these terms are apt to be applied correctly
only in the more obvious instances; and this seems to be due to

the fact that the distinction between the conceptions which they denote has not been made a separate object of investigation. This distinction may be briefly pointed out as follows.

16. Whenever we judge that a thing is 'good as a means,' we are making a judgment with regard to its causal relations: we judge *both* that it will have a particular kind of effect, *and* that that effect will be good in itself. But to find causal judgments that are universally true is notoriously a matter of extreme difficulty. The late date at which most of the physical sciences became exact, and the comparative fewness of the laws which they have succeeded in establishing even now, are sufficient proofs of this difficulty. With regard, then, to what are the most frequent objects of ethical judgments, namely actions, it is obvious that we cannot be satisfied that any of our universal causal judgments are true, even in the sense in which scientific laws are so. We cannot even discover hypothetical laws of the form 'Exactly this action will always, under these conditions, produce exactly that effect.' But for a correct ethical judgment with regard to the effects of certain actions we require more than this in two respects. (1) We require to know that a given action will produce a certain effect, *under whatever circumstances it occurs*. But this is certainly impossible. It is certain that in different circumstances the same action may produce effects which are utterly different in all respects upon which the value of the effects depends. Hence we can never be entitled to more than a *generalisation*—to a proposition of the form 'This result *generally* follows this kind of action'; and even this generalisation will only be true, if the circumstances under which the action occurs are generally the same. This is in fact the case, to a great extent, within any one particular age and state of society. But, when we take other ages into account, in many most important cases the normal circumstances of a given kind of action will be so different, that the generalisation which is true for one will not be true for another. With regard then to ethical judgments which assert that a certain kind of action is good as a means to a certain kind of effect, none will be *universally* true; and many, though *generally* true at one period, will be generally false at

others. But (2) we require to know not only that *one* good effect will be produced, but that, among all subsequent events affected by the action in question, the balance of good will be greater than if any other possible action had been performed. In other words, to judge that an action is generally a means to good is to judge not only that it generally does *some* good, but that it generally does the greatest good of which the circumstances admit. In this respect ethical judgments about the effects of action involve a difficulty and a complication far greater than that involved in the establishment of scientific laws. For the latter we need only consider a single effect; for the former it is essential to consider not only this, but the effects of that effect, and so on as far as our view into the future can reach. It is, indeed, obvious that our view can never reach far enough for us to be certain that any action will produce the best possible effects. We must be content, if the greatest possible balance of good seems to be produced within a limited period. But it is important to notice that the whole series of effects within a period of considerable length is actually taken account of in our common judgments that an action is good as a means; and that hence this additional complication, which makes ethical generalisations so far more difficult to establish than scientific laws, is one which is involved in actual ethical discussions, and is of practical importance. The commonest rules of conduct involve such considerations as the balancing of future bad health against immediate gains; and even if we can never settle with any certainty how we shall secure the greatest possible total of good, we try at least to assure ourselves that probable future evils will not be greater than the immediate good.

17. There are, then, judgments which state that certain kinds of things have good effects; and such judgments, for the reasons just given, have the important characteristics (1) that they are unlikely to be true, if they state that the kind of thing in question *always* has good effects, and (2) that, even if they only state that it *generally* has good effects, many of them will only be true of certain periods in the world's history. On the other hand there are judgments which state that certain kinds of

things are themselves good; and these differ from the last in
that, if true at all, they are all of them universally true. It is,
therefore, extremely important to distinguish these two kinds of
possible judgments. Both may be expressed in the same language: in both cases we commonly say 'Such and such a thing is
good.' But in the one case 'good' will mean 'good as means,' i.e.
merely that the thing is a means to good—will have good
effects: in the other case it will mean 'good as end'—we shall be
judging that the thing itself has the property which, in the first
case, we asserted only to belong to its effects. It is plain that
these are very different assertions to make about a thing; it is
plain that either or both of them may be made, both truly and
falsely, about all manner of things; and it is certain that unless
we are clear as to which of the two we mean to assert, we shall
have a very poor chance of deciding rightly whether our assertion is true or false. It is precisely this clearness as to the meaning of the question asked which has hitherto been almost entirely
lacking in ethical speculation. Ethics has always been pre-
dominantly concerned with the investigation of a limited class
of actions. With regard to these we may ask *both* how far they
are good in themselves *and* how far they have a general tendency to produce good results. And the arguments brought forward in ethical discussion have always been of both classes—
both such as would prove the conduct in question to be good in
itself and such as would prove it to be good as a means. But that
these are the only questions which any ethical discussion can
have to settle, and that to settle the one is *not* the same thing as
to settle the other—these two fundamental facts have in general
escaped the notice of ethical philosophers. Ethical questions are
commonly asked in an ambiguous form. It is asked 'What is a
man's duty under these circumstances?' or 'Is it right to act in
this way?' or 'What ought we to aim at securing?' But all these
questions are capable of further analysis; a correct answer to
any of them involves both judgments of what is good in itself
and causal judgments. This is implied even by those who maintain that we have a direct and immediate judgment of absolute
rights and duties. Such a judgment can only mean that the

course of action in question is *the* best thing to do; that, by acting so, every good that *can* be secured will have been secured.
Now we are not concerned with the question whether such a
judgment will ever be true. The question is: What does it imply,
if it is true? And the only possible answer is that, whether true
or false, it implies both a proposition as to the degree of goodness of the action in question, as compared with other things,
and a number of causal propositions. For it cannot be denied
that the action will have consequences: and to deny that the
consequences matter is to make a judgment of their intrinsic
value, as compared with the action itself. In asserting that the
action is *the* best thing to do, we assert that it together with its
consequences presents a greater sum of intrinsic value than any
possible alternative. And this condition may be realised by any
of the three cases:—(*a*) If the action itself has greater intrinsic
value than any alternative, whereas both its consequences and
those of the alternatives are absolutely devoid either of intrinsic
merit or intrinsic demerit; or (*b*) if, though its consequences are
intrinsically bad, the balance of intrinsic value is greater than
would be produced by any alternative; or (*c*) if, its consequences being intrinsically good, the degree of value belonging
to them and it conjointly is greater than that of any alternative
series. In short, to assert that a certain line of conduct is, at a
given time, absolutely right or obligatory, is obviously to assert
that more good or less evil will exist in the world, if it be adopted
than if anything else be done instead. But this implies a judgment as to the value both of its own consequences and of those
of any possible alternative. And that an action will have such
and such consequences involves a number of causal judgments.

   Similarly, in answering the question 'What ought we to
aim at securing?' causal judgments are again involved, but in a
somewhat different way. We are liable to forget, because it is so
obvious, that this question can never be answered correctly except by naming something which *can* be secured. Not everything
can be secured; and, even if we judge that nothing which cannot
be obtained would be of equal value with that which can, the
possibility of the latter, as well as its value, is essential to its be-

ing a proper end of action. Accordingly neither our judgments as to what actions we ought to perform, nor even our judgments as to the ends which they ought to produce, are pure judgments of intrinsic value. With regard to the former, an action which is absolutely obligatory *may* have no intrinsic value whatsoever; that it is perfectly virtuous may mean merely that it causes the best possible effects. And with regard to the latter, these best possible results which justify our action can, in any case, have only so much intrinsic value as the laws of nature allow us to secure; and they in their turn *may* have no intrinsic value whatsoever, but may merely be a means to the attainment (in a still further future) of something that has such value. Whenever, therefore, we ask 'What ought we to do?' or 'What ought we to try to get?' we are asking questions which involve a correct answer to two others, completely different in kind from one another. We must know *both* what degree of intrinsic value different things have, *and* how these different things may be obtained. But the vast majority of questions which have actually been discussed in Ethics—*all* practical questions, indeed—involve this double knowledge; and they have been discussed without any clear separation of the two distinct questions involved. A great part of the vast disagreements prevalent in Ethics is to be attributed to this failure in analysis. By the use of conceptions which involve both that of intrinsic value and that of causal relation, as if they involved intrinsic value only, two different errors have been rendered almost universal. Either it is assumed that nothing has intrinsic value which is not possible, or else it is assumed that what is necessary must have intrinsic value. Hence the primary and peculiar business of Ethics, the determination what things have intrinsic value and in what degrees, has received no adequate treatment at all. And on the other hand a *thorough* discussion of means has been also largely neglected, owing to an obscure perception of the truth that it is perfectly irrelevant to the question of intrinsic values. But however this may be, and however strongly any particular reader may be convinced that some one of the mutually contradictory systems which hold the field has given a correct answer either to the question what has intrinsic value, or to the question what we ought to do, or to both, it must at least be admitted that the questions what is best in itself and what will bring about the best possible, are utterly distinct; that both belong to the actual subject-matter of Ethics; and that the more clearly distinct questions are distinguished, the better is our chance of answering both correctly.

18. There remains one point which must not be omitted in a complete description of the kind of questions which Ethics has to answer. The main division of those questions is, as I have said, into two; the question what things are good in themselves, and the question to what other things these are related as effects. The first of these, which is the primary ethical question and is presupposed by the other, includes a correct comparison of the various things which have intrinsic value (if there are many such) in respect of the degree of value which they have; and such comparison involves a difficulty of principle which has greatly aided the confusion of intrinsic value with mere 'goodness as a means.' It has been pointed out that one difference between a judgment which asserts that a thing is good in itself, and a judgment which asserts that it is a means to good, consists in the fact that the first, if true of one instance of the thing in question, is necessarily true of all; whereas a thing which has good effects under some circumstances may have bad ones under others. Now it is certainly true that all judgments of intrinsic value are in this sense universal; but the principle which I have now to enunciate may easily make it appear as if they were not so but resembled the judgment of means in being merely general. There is, as will presently be maintained, a vast number of different things, each of which has intrinsic value; there are also very many which are positively bad; and there is a still larger class of things, which appear to be indifferent. But a thing belonging to any of these three classes may occur as part of a whole, which includes among its other parts other things belonging both to the same and to the other two classes; and these wholes, as such, may also have intrinsic value. The paradox, to which it is necessary to call attention, is that *the value of such a whole bears no regular proportion to the sum of the val-*

ues of its parts. It is certain that a good thing may exist in such a relation to another good thing that the value of the whole thus formed is immensely greater than the sum of the values of the two good things. It is certain that a whole formed of a good thing and an indifferent thing may have immensely greater value than that good thing itself possesses. It is certain that two bad things or a bad thing and an indifferent thing may form a whole much worse than the sum of badness of its parts. And it seems as if indifferent things may also be the sole constituents of a whole which has great value, either positive or negative. Whether the addition of a bad thing to a good whole may increase the positive value of the whole, or the addition of a bad thing to a bad may produce a whole having positive value, may seem more doubtful; but it is, at least, possible, and this possibility must be taken into account in our ethical investigations. However we may decide particular questions, the principle is clear. *The value of a whole must not be assumed to be the same as the sum of the values of its parts.*

A single instance will suffice to illustrate the kind of relation in question. It seems to be true that to be conscious of a beautiful object is a thing of great intrinsic value; whereas the same object, if no one be conscious of it, has certainly compara tively little value, and is commonly held to have none at all. But the consciousness of a beautiful object is certainly a whole of some sort in which we can distinguish as parts the object on the one hand and the being conscious on the other. Now this latter factor occurs as part of a different whole, whenever we are conscious of anything; and it would seem that some of these wholes have at all events very little value, and may even be indifferent or positively bad. Yet we cannot always attribute the slightness of their value to any positive demerit in the object which differentiates them from the consciousness of beauty; the object itself may approach as near as possible to absolute neutrality. Since, therefore, mere consciousness does not always confer great value upon the whole of which it forms a part, even though its object may have no great demerit, we cannot attribute the great superiority of the consciousness of a beautiful thing over the beautiful thing itself to the mere addition of the value of consciousness to that of the beautiful thing. Whatever the intrinsic value of consciousness may be, it does not give to the whole of which it forms a part a value proportioned to the sum of its value and that of its object. If this be so, we have here an instance of a whole possessing a different intrinsic value from the sum of that of its parts; and whether it be so or not, what is meant by such a difference is illustrated by this case.

19. There are, then, wholes which possess the property that their value is different from the sum of the values of their parts; and the relations which subsist between such parts and the whole of which they form a part have not hitherto been distinctly recognised or received a separate name. Two points are especially worthy of notice. (1) It is plain that the existence of any such part is a necessary condition for the existence of that good which is constituted by the whole. And exactly the same language will also express the relation between a means and the good thing which is its effect. But yet there is a most important difference between the two cases, constituted by the fact that the part is, whereas the means is not, a part of the good thing for the existence of which its existence is a necessary condition. The necessity by which, if the good in question is to exist, the means to it must exist is merely a natural or causal necessity. If the laws of nature were different, exactly the same good might exist, although what is now a necessary condition of its existence did not exist. The existence of the means has no intrinsic value; and its utter annihilation would leave the value of that which it is now necessary to secure entirely unchanged. But in the case of a part of such a whole as we are now considering, it is otherwise. In this case the good in question cannot conceivably exist, unless the part exist also. The necessity which connects the two is quite independent of natural law. What is asserted to have intrinsic value is the existence of the whole; and the existence of the whole includes the existence of its part. Suppose the part removed, and what remains is *not* what was asserted to have intrinsic value; but if we suppose a means removed, what remains is just what *was* asserted to have intrinsic value. And yet (2) the

existence of the part may *itself* have no more intrinsic value than that of the means. It is this fact which constitutes the paradox of the relation which we are discussing. It has just been said that what has intrinsic value is the existence of the whole, and that this includes the existence of the part; and from this it would seem a natural inference that the existence of the part has intrinsic value. But the inference would be as false as if we were to conclude that, because the number of two stones was two, each of the stones was also two. The part of a valuable whole retains exactly the same value when it is, as when it is not, a part of that whole. If it had value under other circumstances, its value is not any greater, when it is part of a far more valuable whole; and if it had no value by itself, it has none still, however great be that of the whole of which it now forms a part. We are not then justified in asserting that one and the same thing is under some circumstances intrinsically good, and under others not so; as we are justified in asserting of a means that it sometimes does and sometimes does not produce good results. And yet we are justified in asserting that it is far more desirable that a certain thing should exist under some circumstances than under others; namely when other things will exist in such relations to it as to form a more valuable whole. *It* will not have more intrinsic value under these circumstances than under others; *it* will not necessarily even be a means to the existence of things having more intrinsic value: but it will, like a means, be a necessary condition for the existence of that which *has* greater intrinsic value, although, unlike a means, it will itself form a part of this more valuable existent.

20. I have said that the peculiar relation between part and whole which I have just been trying to define is one which has received no separate name. It would, however, be useful that it should have one; and there is a name, which might well be appropriated to it, if only it could be divorced from its present unfortunate usage. Philosophers, especially those who profess to have derived great benefit from the writings of Hegel, have latterly made much use of the terms 'organic whole,' 'organic unity,' 'organic relation.' The reason why these terms might

well be appropriated to the use suggested is that the peculiar relation of parts to whole, just defined, is one of the properties which distinguishes the wholes to which they are actually applied with the greatest frequency. And the reason why it is desirable that they should be divorced from their present usage is that, as at present used, they have no distinct sense and, on the contrary, both imply and propagate errors of confusion.

To say that a thing is an 'organic whole' is generally understood to imply that its parts are related to one another and to itself as means to end; it is also understood to imply that they have a property described in some such phrase as that they have 'no meaning or significance apart from the whole'; and finally such a whole is also treated as if it had the property to which I am proposing that the name should be confined. But those who use the term give us, in general, no hint as to how they suppose these three properties to be related to one another. It seems generally to be assumed that they are identical; and always, at least, that they are necessarily connected with one another. That they are not identical I have already tried to shew; to suppose them so is to neglect the very distinctions pointed out in the last paragraph; and the usage might well be discontinued merely because it encourages such neglect. But a still more cogent reason for its discontinuance is that, so far from being necessarily connected, the second is a property which can attach to nothing, being a self-contradictory conception; whereas the first, if we insist on its most important sense, applies to many cases, to which we have no reason to think that the third applies also, and the third certainly applies to many to which the first does not apply.

21. These relations between the three properties just distinguished may be illustrated by reference to a whole of the kind from which the name 'organic' was derived—a whole which is an organism in the scientific sense—namely the human body.

(1) There exists between many parts of our body (though not between all) a relation which has been familiarised by the fable, attributed to Menenius Agrippa, concerning the belly and its members. We can find in it parts such that the continued existence of the one is a necessary condition for the

continued existence of the other; while the continued existence of this latter is also a necessary condition for the continued existence of the former. This amounts to no more than saying that in the body we have instances of two things, both enduring for some time, which have a relation of mutual causal dependence on one another—a relation of 'reciprocity.' Frequently no more than this is meant by saying that the parts of the body form an 'organic unity,' or that they are mutually means and ends to one another. And we certainly have here a striking characteristic of living things. But it would be extremely rash to assert that this relation of mutual causal dependence was only exhibited by living things and hence was sufficient to define their peculiarity. And it is obvious that of two things which have this relation of mutual dependence, neither may have intrinsic value, or one may have it and the other lack it. They are not necessarily 'ends' to one another in any sense except that in which 'end' means 'effect.' And moreover it is plain that in this sense the whole cannot be an end to any of its parts. We are apt to talk of 'the whole' in contrast to one of its parts, when in fact we mean only *the rest* of the parts. But strictly the whole must include all its parts and no part can be a cause of the whole, because it cannot be a cause of itself. It is plain, therefore, that this relation of mutual causal dependence implies nothing with regard to the value of either of the objects which have it; and that, even if both of them happen also to have value, this relation between them is one which cannot hold between part and whole.

But (2) it may also be the case that our body as a whole has a value greater than the sum of values of its parts; and this may be what is meant when it is said that the parts are means to the whole. It is obvious that if we ask the question 'Why *should* the parts be such as they are?' a proper answer may be 'Because the whole they form has so much value.' But it is equally obvious that the relation which we thus assert to exist between part and whole is quite different from that which we assert to exist between part and part when we say 'This part exists, because that one could not exist without it.' In the latter case we assert the two parts to be causally connected; but, in the former, part and whole cannot be causally connected, and the relation which we assert to exist between them may exist even though the parts are not causally connected either. All the parts of a picture do not have that relation of mutual causal dependence, which certain parts of the body have, and yet the existence of those which do not have it may be absolutely essential to the value of the whole. The two relations are quite distinct in kind, and we cannot infer the existence of the one from that of the other. It can, therefore, serve no useful purpose to include them both under the same name; and if we are to say that a whole is organic because its parts are (in this sense) 'means' to the whole, we must *not* say that it is organic because its parts are causally dependent on one another.

22. But finally (3) the sense which has been most prominent in recent uses of the term 'organic whole' is one whereby it asserts the parts of such a whole to have a property which the parts of no whole can possibly have. It is supposed that just as the whole would not be what it is but for the existence of the parts, so the parts would not be what they are but for the exisence of the whole; and this is understood to mean not merely that any particular part could not exist unless the others existed too (which is the case where relation (1) exists between the parts), but actually that the part is no distinct object of thought —that the whole, of which it is a part, is in its turn a part of it. That this supposition is self-contradictory a very little reflection should be sufficient to shew. We may admit, indeed, that when a particular thing is a part of a whole, it does possess a predicate which it would not otherwise possess—namely that it is a part of that whole. But what cannot be admitted is that this predicate alters the nature or enters into the definition of the thing which has it. When we think of the part *itself*, we mean just *that which* we assert, in this case, to *have* the predicate that it is part of the whole; and the mere assertion that *it* is a part of the whole involves that it should itself be distinct from that which we assert of it. Otherwise we contradict ourselves since we assert that, not *it*, but something else—namely it together with that which we assert of it—has the predicate which we assert of it. In short, it

is obvious that no part contains analytically the whole to which it belongs, or any other parts of that whole. The relation of part to whole is *not* the same as that as whole to part; and the very definition of the latter is that it does contain analytically that which is said to be its part. And yet this very self-contradictory doctrine is the chief mark which shews the influence of Hegel upon modern philosophy—an influence which pervades almost the whole of orthodox philosophy. This is what is generally implied by the cry against falsification by abstraction: that a whole is always a part of its part! 'If you want to know the truth about a part,' we are told, 'you must consider *not* that part, but something else—namely the whole: *nothing* is true of the part, but only of the whole.' Yet plainly it must be true of the part at least that it is a part of the whole; and it is obvious that when we say it is, we do *not* mean merely that the whole is a part of itself. This doctrine, therefore, that a part can have 'no meaning or significance apart from its whole' must be utterly rejected. It implies itself that the statement 'This is a part of that whole' has a meaning; and in order that this may have one, both subject and predicate must have a distinct meaning. And it is easy to see how this false doctrine has arisen by confusion with the two relations (1) and (2) which may really be properties of wholes.

(*a*) The *existence* of a part may be connected by a natural or causal necessity with the existence of the other parts of its whole; and further what is a part of a whole and what has ceased to be such a part, although differing intrinsically from one another, may be called by one and the same name. Thus, to take a typical example, if an arm be cut off from the human body, we still call it an arm. Yet an arm, when it is a part of the body, undoubtedly differs from a dead arm: and hence we may easily be led to say 'The arm which is a part of the body would not be what it is, if it were not such a part,' and to think that the contradiction thus expressed is in reality a characteristic of things. But, in fact, the dead arm never was a part of the body; it is only *partially* identical with the living arm. Those parts of it which are identical with parts of the living arm are exactly the same, whether they belong to the body or not; and in them we have an undeniable instance of one and the same thing at one time forming a part, and at another not forming a part of the presumed 'organic whole.' On the other hand those properties which *are* possessed by the living, and *not* by the dead, arm, do not exist in a changed form in the latter: they simply do not exist there *at all*. By a causal necessity their existence depends on their having that relation to the other parts of the body which we express by saying that they form part of it. Yet, most certainly, *if* they ever did not form part of the body, they *would* be exactly what they are when they do. That they differ intrinsically from the properties of the dead arm and that they form part of the body are propositions not analytically related to one another. There is no contradiction in supposing them to retain such intrinsic differences and yet not to form part of the body.

But (*b*) when we are told that a living arm has no *meaning* or *significance* apart from the body to which it belongs, a different fallacy is also suggested. 'To have meaning or significance' is commonly used in the sense of 'to have importance'; and this again means 'to have value either as a means or as an end.' Now it is quite possible that even a living arm, apart from its body, would have no intrinsic value whatever; although the whole of which it is a part has great intrinsic value owing to its presence. Thus we may easily come to say that, *as* a part of the body, it has great value, whereas *by itself* it would have none; and thus that its whole 'meaning' lies in its relation to the body. But in fact the value in question obviously does not belong to *it* at all. To have value merely as a part is equivalent to having no value at all, but merely being a part of that which has it. Owing, however, to neglect of this distinction, the assertion that a part has value, *as a part*, which it would not otherwise have, easily leads to the assumption that it is also different, as a part, from what it would otherwise be; for it is, in fact, true that two things which have a different value must also differ in other respects. Hence the assumption that one and the same thing, because it is a part of a more valuable whole at one time than at another, therefore has more intrinsic value at one time than at another, has encouraged the self-contradictory belief that one and the same thing may be two different things, and that only in one of its forms is it truly what it is.

For these reasons, I shall, where it seems convenient, take the liberty to use the term 'organic' with a special sense. I shall use it to denote the fact that a whole has an intrinsic value different in amount from the sum of the values of its parts. I shall use it to denote this and only this. The term will not imply any causal relation whatever between the parts of the whole in question. And it will not imply either, that the parts are inconceivable except as parts of that whole, or that, when they form parts of such a whole, they have a value different from that which they would have if they did not. Understood in this special and perfectly definite sense the relation of an organic whole to its parts is one of the most important which Ethics has to recognise. A chief part of that science should be occupied in comparing the relative values of various goods; and the grossest errors will be committed in such comparison if it be assumed that wherever two things form a whole, the value of that whole is merely the sum of the values of those two things. With this question of 'organic wholes,' then, we complete the enumeration of the kind of problems, with which it is the business of Ethics to deal.

23. In this chapter I have endeavoured to enforce the following conclusions. (1) The peculiarity of Ethics is not that it investigates assertions about human conduct, but that it investigates assertions about the property of things which is denoted by the term 'good,' and the converse property denoted by the term 'bad.' It must, in order to establish its conclusions, investigate the truth of *all* such assertions, *except* those which assert the relation of this property only to a single existent (1–4). (2) This property, by reference to which the subject matter of Ethics must be defined, is itself simple and indefinable (5–14). And (3) all assertions about its relation to other things are of two, and only two, kinds: they either assert in what degree things themselves possess this property, or else they assert causal relations between other things and those which possess it (15–17). Finally, (4) in considering the different degrees in which things themselves possess this property, we have to take account of the

fact that a whole may possess it in a degree different from that which is obtained by summing the degrees in which its parts possess it (18–22).

DOES MORAL PHILOSOPHY REST ON A MISTAKE? / *H. A. Prichard*

PROBABLY to most students of Moral Philosophy there comes a time when they feel a vague sense of dissatisfaction with the whole subject. And the sense of dissatisfaction tends to grow rather than to diminish. It is not so much that the positions, and still more the arguments, of particular thinkers seem unconvincing, though this is true. It is rather that the aim of the subject becomes increasingly obscure. 'What,' it is asked, 'are we really going to learn by Moral Philosophy?' 'What are books on Moral Philosophy really trying to show, and when their aim is clear, why are they so unconvincing and artificial?' And again: 'Why is it so difficult to substitute anything better?' Personally, I have been led by growing dissatisfaction of this kind to wonder whether the reason may not be that the subject, at any rate as usually understood, consists in the attempt to answer an improper question. And in this article I shall venture to contend that the existence of the whole subject, as usually understood, rests on a mistake, and on a mistake parallel to that on which rests, as I think, the subject usually called the Theory of Knowledge.

If we reflect on our own mental history or on the history

From H. A. Prichard, "Does Moral Philosophy Rest on a Mistake?," Mind, XXI (1912), 487–499. Reprinted by permission of the Editor of Mind.

of the subject, we feel no doubt about the nature of the demand
which originates the subject. Any one who, stimulated by education, has come to feel the force of the various obligations in life,
at some time or other comes to feel the irksomeness of carrying
them out, and to recognize the sacrifice of interest involved; and,
if thoughtful, he inevitably puts to himself the question: 'Is
there really a reason why I should act in the ways in which hitherto I have thought I ought to act? May I not have been all the
time under an illusion in so thinking? Should not I really be
justified in simply trying to have a good time?' Yet, like Glau-
con, feeling that somehow he ought after all to act in these ways,
he asks for a *proof* that this feeling is justified. In other words,
he asks 'Why should I do these things?', and his and other people's moral philosophizing is an attempt to supply the answer,
i.e. to supply by a process of reflection a proof of the truth of
what he and they have prior to reflection believed immediately or
without proof. This frame of mind seems to present a close parallel to the frame of mind which originates the Theory of Knowledge. Just as the recognition that the doing of our duty often
vitally interferes with the satisfaction of our inclinations leads
us to wonder whether we really ought to do what we usually call
our duty, so the recognition that we and others are liable to mistakes in knowledge generally leads us, as it did Descartes, to
wonder whether hitherto we may not have been always mistaken. And just as we try to find a proof, based on the general
consideration of action and of human life, that we ought to act
in the ways usually called moral, so we, like Descartes, propose
by a process of reflection on our thinking to find a test of knowledge, i.e. a principle by applying which we can show that a certain condition of mind was really knowledge, a condition which
ex hypothesi existed independently of the process of reflection.

Now, how has the moral question been answered? So far
as I can see, the answers all fall, and fall from the necessities of
the case, into one of two species. *Either* they state that we ought
to do so and so, because, as we see when we fully apprehend the
facts, doing so will be for our good, i.e. really, as I would rather say, for our advantage, or, better still, for our happiness; *or*

they state that we ought to do so and so, because something realized either in or by the action is good. In other words, the reason
'why' is stated in terms either of the agent's happiness or of the
goodness of something involved in the action.

To see the prevalence of the former species of answer, we
have only to consider the history of Moral Philosophy. To take
obvious instances, Plato, Butler, Hutcheson, Paley, Mill, each in
his own way seeks at bottom to convince the individual that he
ought to act in so-called moral ways by showing that to do so will
really be for his happiness. Plato is perhaps the most significant
instance, because of all philosophers he is the one to whom we
are least willing to ascribe a mistake on such matters, and a mistake on his part would be evidence of the deep-rootedness of the
tendency to make it. To show that Plato really justifies morality
by its profitableness, it is only necessary to point out (1) that
the very formulation of the thesis to be met, viz. that justice is
ἀλλότριον ἀγαθόν [someone else's good] implies that any refutation
must consist in showing that justice is οἰκεῖον ἀγαθόν [one's own
good], i.e., really, as the context shows, one's own advantage, and
(2) that the term λυσιτελεῖν [to be profitable] supplies the key not
only to the problem but also to its solution.

The tendency to justify acting on moral rules in this way
is natural. For if, as often happens, we put to ourselves the question 'Why should we do so and so?', we are satisfied by being
convinced either that the doing so will lead to something which
we want (e.g. that taking certain medicine will heal our disease), or that the doing so itself, as we see when we appreciate
its nature, is something that we want or should like, e.g. playing
golf. The formulation of the question implies a state of unwill-
ingness or indifference towards the action, and we are brought
into a condition of willingness by the answer. And this process
seems to be precisely what we desire when we ask, e.g., 'Why
should we keep our engagements to our own loss?'; for it is just
the fact that the keeping of our engagements runs counter to the
satisfaction of our desires which produced the question.

The answer is, of course, not an answer, for it fails to
convince us that we ought to keep our engagements; even if suc-

cessful on its own lines, it only makes us *want* to keep them.
And Kant was really only pointing out this fact when he distinguished hypothetical and categorical imperatives, even though
he obscured the nature of the fact by wrongly describing his so-
called 'hypothetical imperatives' as imperatives. But if this answer be no answer, what other can be offered? Only, it seems, an
answer which bases the obligation to do something on the *goodness* either of something to which the act leads or of the act
itself. Suppose, when wondering whether we really ought to act
in the ways usually called moral, we are told as a means of resolving our doubt that those acts are right which produce happiness. We at once ask: 'Whose happiness?' If we are told 'Our
own happiness', then, though we shall lose our hesitation to act
in these ways, we shall not recover our sense that we ought to do
so. But how can this result be avoided? Apparently, only by
being told one of two things; *either* that anyone's happiness is a
thing good in itself, and that *therefore* we ought to do whatever
will produce it, *or* that working for happiness is itself good, and
that the intrinsic goodness of such an action is the reason why
we ought to do it. The advantage of this appeal to the goodness
of something consists in the fact that it avoids reference to desire, and, instead, refers to something impersonal and objective.
In this way it seems possible to avoid the resolution of obligation
into inclination. But just for this reason it is of the essence of the
answer, that to be effective it must neither include nor involve
the view that the apprehension of the goodness of anything necessarily arouses the desire for it. Otherwise the answer resolves
itself into a form of the former answer by substituting desire or
inclination for the sense of obligation, and in this way it loses
what seems its special advantage.

Now it seems to me that both forms of this answer break
down, though each for a different reason.

Consider the first form. It is what may be called Utilitarianism in the generic sense, in which what is good is not limited
to pleasure. It takes its stand upon the distinction between something which is not itself an action, but which can be produced by
an action, and the action which will produce it, and contends

that if something which is not an action is good, then we *ought* to undertake the action which will, directly or indirectly, originate it.[1]

But this argument, if it is to restore the sense of obligation to act, must presuppose an intermediate link, viz. the further thesis that what is good ought to be.[2] The necessity of this link is obvious. An 'ought', if it is to be derived at all, can only be derived from another 'ought'. Moreover, this link tacitly presupposes another, viz. that the apprehension that something good which is not an action ought to be involves just the feeling of imperativeness or obligation which is to be aroused by the thought of the action which will originate it. Otherwise the argument will not lead us to feel the obligation to produce it by the action. And, surely, both this link and its implication are false.[3] The word 'ought' refers to actions and to actions alone. The proper language is never 'So and so ought to be', but 'I ought to do so and so'. Even if we are sometimes moved to say that the world or something in it is not what it ought to be, what we really mean is that God or some human being has not made something what he ought to have made it. And it is merely stating another side of this fact to urge that we can only feel the imperativeness upon us of something which is in our power; for it is actions and actions alone which, directly at least, are in our power.

Perhaps, however, the best way to see the failure of this view is to see its failure to correspond to our actual moral convictions. Suppose we ask ourselves whether our sense that we ought to pay our debts or to tell the truth arises from our recognition that in doing so we should be orginating something good, e.g. material comfort in *A* or true belief in *B*, i.e. suppose we ask ourselves whether it is this aspect of the action which leads to our recognition that we ought to do it. We at once and without

---

[1] Cf. Dr. Rashdall's *Theory of Good and Evil*, Vol. I, p. 138.

[2] Dr. Rashdall, if I understand him rightly, supplies this link (cf. *ibid.*, pp. 135–136).

[3] When we speak of anything, e.g., of some emotion or of some quality of a human being, as good, we never dream in our ordinary consciousness of going on to say that therefore it ought to be.

hesitation answer 'No'. Again, if we take as our illustration our sense that we ought to act justly as between two parties, we have, if possible, even less hesitation in giving a similar answer; for the balance of resulting good may be, and often is, not on the side of justice.

At best it can only be maintained that there is this element of truth in the Utilitarian view, that unless we recognize that something which an act will originate is good, we should not recognize that we ought to do the action. Unless we thought knowledge a good thing, it may be urged, we should not think that we ought to tell the truth; unless we thought pain a bad thing, we should not think the infliction of it, without special reason, wrong. But this is not to imply that the badness of error is the reason why it is wrong to lie, or the badness of pain the reason why we ought not to inflict it without special cause.[4]

It is, I think, just because this form of the view is so plainly at variance with our moral consciousness that we are driven to adopt the other form of the view, viz. that the act is good in itself and that its intrinsic goodness is the reason why it ought to be done. It is this form which has always made the most serious appeal; for the goodness of the act itself seems more closely related to the obligation to do it than that of its mere consequences or results, and therefore, if obligation is to be based on the goodness of something, it would seem that this goodness should be that of the act itself. Moreover, the view gains plausibility from the fact that moral actions are most conspicuously those to which the term 'intrinsically good' is applicable.

Nevertheless this view, though perhaps less superficial, is equally untenable. For it leads to precisely the dilemma which faces everyone who tries to solve the problem raised by Kant's theory of the good will. To see this, we need only consider the

---

[4] It may be noted that if the badness of pain were the reason why we ought not to inflict pain on another, it would equally be a reason why we ought not to inflict pain on ourselves; yet, though we should allow the wanton infliction of pain on ourselves to be foolish, we should not think of describing it as wrong.

nature of the acts to which we apply the term 'intrinsically good'.

There is, of course, no doubt that we approve and even admire certain actions, and also that we should describe them as good, and as good in themselves. But it is, I think, equally unquestionable that our approval and our use of the term 'good' is always in respect of the motive and refers to actions which have been actually done and of which we think we know the motive. Further, the actions of which we approve and which we should describe as intrinsically good are of two and only two kinds. They are either actions in which the agent did what he did because he thought he ought to do it, or actions of which the motive was a desire prompted by some good emotion, such as gratitude, affection, family feeling, or public spirit, the most prominent of such desires in books on Moral Philosophy being that ascribed to what is vaguely called benevolence. For the sake of simplicity I omit the case of actions done partly from some such desire and partly from a sense of duty; for even if all good actions are done from a combination of these motives, the argument will not be affected. The dilemma is this. If the motive in respect of which we think an action good is the sense of obligation, then so far from the sense that we ought to do it being derived from our apprehension of its goodness, our apprehension of its goodness will presuppose the sense that we ought to do it. In other words, in this case the recognition that the act is good will plainly *presuppose* the recognition that the act is right, whereas the view under consideration is that the recognition of the goodness of the act *gives rise* to the recognition of its rightness. On the other hand, if the motive in respect of which we think an action good is some intrinsically good desire, such as the desire to help a friend, the recognition of the goodness of the act will equally fail to give rise to the sense of obligation to do it. For we cannot feel that we ought to do that the doing of which is *ex hypothesi* prompted solely by the desire to do it.[5]

5 It is, I think, on this latter horn of the dilemma that Martineau's view falls; cf. *Types of Ethical Theory*, Part II, Book I.

The fallacy underlying the view is that while to base the rightness of an act upon its intrinsic goodness implies that the goodness in question is that of the motive, in reality the rightness or wrongness of an act has nothing to do with any question of motives at all. For, as any instance will show, the rightness of an action concerns an action not in the fuller sense of the term in which we include the motive in the action, but in the narrower and commoner sense in which we distinguish an action from its motive and mean by an action merely the conscious origination of something, an origination which on different occasions or in different people may be prompted by different motives. The question 'Ought I to pay my bills?' really means simply 'Ought I to bring about my tradesmen's possession of what by my previous acts I explicitly or implicitly promised them?' There is, and can be, no question of whether I ought to pay my debts from a particular motive. No doubt we know that if we pay our bills we shall pay them with a motive, but in considering whether we ought to pay them we inevitably think of the act in abstraction from the motive. Even if we knew what our motive would be if we did the act, we should not be any nearer an answer to the question.

Moreover, if we eventually pay our bills from fear of the county court, we shall still have done *what* we ought, even though we shall not have done it *as* we ought. The attempt to bring in the motive involves a mistake similar to that involved in supposing that we can will to will. To feel that I ought to pay my bills is to be *moved towards* paying them. But what I can be moved towards must always be an action and not an action in which I am moved in a particular way, i.e. an action from a particular motive; otherwise I should be moved towards being moved, which is impossible. Yet the view under consideration involves this impossibility, for it really resolves the sense that I ought to do so and so, into the sense that I ought to be moved to do it in a particular way.[6]

[6] It is of course not denied here that an action done from a particular motive may be *good;* it is only denied that the *rightness* of an action depends on its being done with a particular motive.

So far my contentions have been mainly negative, but they form, I think, a useful, if not a necessary, introduction to what I take to be the truth. This I will now endeavour to state, first formulating what, as I think, is the real nature of our apprehension or appreciation of moral obligations, and then applying the result to elucidate the question of the existence of Moral Philosophy.

The sense of obligation to do, or of the rightness of, an action of a particular kind is absolutely underivative or immediate. The rightness of an action consists in its being the origination of something of a certain kind *A* in a situation of a certain kind, a situation consisting in a certain relation *B* of the agent to others or to his own nature. To appreciate its rightness two preliminaries may be necessary. We may have to follow out the consequences of the proposed action more fully than we have hitherto done, in order to realize that in the action we should originate *A*. Thus we may not appreciate the wrongness of telling a certain story until we realize that we should thereby be hurting the feelings of one of our audience. Again, we may have to take into account the relation *B* involved in the situation, which we had hitherto failed to notice. For instance, we may not appreciate the obligation to give *X* a present, until we remember that he has done us an act of kindness. But, given that by a process which is, of course, merely a process of general and not of moral thinking we come to recognize that the proposed act is one by which we shall originate *A* in a relation *B*, then we appreciate the obligation immediately or directly, the appreciation being an activity of *moral* thinking. We recognize, for instance, that this performance of a service to *X*, who has done us a service, just in virtue of its being the performance of a service to one who has rendered a service to the would-be agent, ought to be done by us. This apprehension is immediate, in precisely the sense in which a mathematical apprehension is immediate, e.g. the apprehension that this three-sided figure, in virtue of its being three-sided, must have three angles. Both apprehensions are immediate in the sense that in both insight into the nature of the subject directly leads us to recognize its possession of the predicate; and it is only stating this fact from the other side to say that in both cases the fact apprehended is self-evident.

The plausibility of the view that obligations are not self-evident but need proof lies in the fact that an act which is referred to as an obligation may be incompletely stated, what I have called the preliminaries to appreciating the obligation being incomplete. If, e.g., we refer to the act of repaying X by a present merely as giving X a present, it appears, and indeed is, necessary to give a reason. In other words, wherever a moral act is regarded in this incomplete way the question 'Why should I do it?' is perfectly legitimate. This fact suggests, but suggests wrongly, that even if the nature of the act is completely stated, it is still necessary to give a reason, or, in other words, to supply a proof.

The relations involved in obligations of various kinds are, of course, very different. The relation in certain cases is a relation to others due to a past act of theirs or ours. The obligation to repay a benefit involves a relation due to a past act of the benefactor. The obligation to pay a bill involves a relation due to a past act of ours in which we have either said or implied that we would make a certain return for something which we have asked for and received. On the other hand, the obligation to speak the truth implies no such definite act; it involves a relation consisting in the fact that others are trusting us to speak the truth, a relation the apprehension of which gives rise to the sense that communication of the truth is something owing by us to them. Again, the obligation not to hurt the feelings of another involves no special relation of us to that other, i.e. no relation other than that involved in our both being men, and men in one and the same world. Moreover, it seems that the relation involved in an obligation need not be a relation to another at all. Thus we should admit that there is an obligation to overcome our natural timidity or greediness, and that this involves no relations to others. Still there is a relation involved, viz. a relation to our own disposition. It is simply because we can and because others cannot directly modify our disposition that it is our business to improve it, and that it is not theirs, or, at least, not theirs to the same extent.

The negative side of all this is, of course, that we do not come to appreciate an obligation by an *argument*, i.e. by a process of non-moral thinking, and that, in particular, we do not do so by an argument of which a premise is the ethical but not moral activity of appreciating the goodness either of the act or of a consequence of the act; i.e. that our sense of the rightness of an act is not a conclusion from our appreciation of the goodness either of it or of anything else.

It will probably be urged that on this view our various obligations form, like Aristotle's categories, an unrelated chaos in which it is impossible to acquiesce. For, according to it, the obligation to repay a benefit, or to pay a debt, or to keep a promise, presupposes a previous act of another; whereas the obligation to speak the truth or not to harm another does not; and, again, the obligation to remove our timidity involves no relations to others at all. Yet, at any rate, an effective *argumentum ad hominem* is at hand in the fact that the various qualities which we recognize as good are equally unrelated; e.g. courage, humility, and interest in knowledge. If, as is plainly the case, ἀγαθά differ ᾗ ἀγαθά [Goods differ *qua* goods], why should not obligations equally differ *qua* their obligatoriness? Moreover, if this were not so there could in the end be only one obligation, which is palpably contrary to fact.[7]

7 Two other objections may be anticipated: (1) that obligations cannot be self-evident, since many actions regarded as obligations by some are not so regarded by others, and (2) that if obligations are self-evident, the problem of how we ought to act in the presence of conflicting obligations is insoluble.

To the first I should reply:

(*a*) That the appreciation of an obligation is, of course, only possible for a developed moral being, and that different degrees of development are possible.

(*b*) That the failure to recognize some particular obligation is usually due to the fact that, owing to a lack of thoughtfulness, what I have called the preliminaries to this recognition are incomplete.

(*c*) That the view put forward is consistent with the admission that, owing to a lack of thoughtfulness, even the best men are blind to many of their obligations, and that in the end our obligations are seen to be co-extensive with almost the whole of our life.

Certain observations will help to make the view clearer.

In the first place, it may seem that the view, being—as it is—avowedly put forward in opposition to the view that what is right is derived from what is good, must itself involve the opposite of this, viz. the Kantian position that what is good is based upon what is right, i.e. that an act, if it be good, is good because it is right. But this is not so. For, on the view put forward, the rightness of a right action lies solely in the origination in which the act consists, whereas the intrinsic goodness of an action lies solely in its motive; and this implies that a morally good action is morally good not simply because it is a right action but because it is a right action done because it is right, i.e. from a sense of obligation. And this implication, it may be remarked incidentally, seems plainly true.

In the second place, the view involves that when, or rather so far as, we act from a sense of obligation, we have no purpose or end. By a 'purpose' or 'end' we really mean something the existence of which we desire, and desire of the existence of which leads us to act. Usually our purpose is something which the act will originate, as when we turn round in order to look at a picture. But it may be the action itself, i.e. the origination of something, as when we hit a golf-ball into a hole or kill someone out of revenge.[8] Now if by a purpose we mean something the existence of which we desire and desire for which leads us to act, then plainly, so far as we act from a sense of obligation, we have no purpose, consisting either in the action or in anything which it will produce. This is so obvious that it scarcely seems worth pointing out. But I do so for two reasons. (1) If we fail to scrutinize the meaning of the terms 'end' and 'purpose', we are apt to assume uncritically that all deliberate

---

To the second objection I should reply that obligation admits of degrees, and that where obligations conflict, the decision of what we ought to do turns not on the question 'Which of the alternative courses of action will originate the greater good?' but on the question 'Which is the greater obligation?'

[8] It is no objection to urge that an action cannot be its own purpose, since the purpose of something cannot be the thing itself. For, speaking strictly, the purpose is not the *action's* purpose but *our* purpose, and there is no contradiction in holding that our purpose in acting may be the action.

action, i.e. action proper, must have a purpose; we then become puzzled both when we look for the purpose of an action done from a sense of obligation, and also when we try to apply to such an action the distinction of means and end, the truth all the time being that since there is no end, there is no means either. (2) The attempt to base the sense of obligation on the recognition of the goodness of something is really an attempt to find a purpose in a moral action in the shape of something good which, as good, we want. And the expectation that the goodness of something underlies an obligation disappears as soon as we cease to look for a purpose.

The thesis, however, that, so far as we act from a sense of obligation, we have no purpose must not be misunderstood. It must not be taken either to mean or to imply that so far as we so act we have no *motive*. No doubt in ordinary speech the words 'motive' and 'purpose' are usually treated as correlatives, 'motive' standing for the desire which induces us to act, and 'purpose' standing for the object of this desire. But this is only because, when we are looking for the motive of the action, say, of some crime, we are usually presupposing that the act in question is prompted by a desire and not by the sense of obligation. At bottom, however, we mean by a motive what moves us to act; a sense of obligation does sometimes move us to act; and in our ordinary consciousness we should not hesitate to allow that the action we were considering might have had as its motive a sense of obligation. Desire and the sense of obligation are co-ordinate forms or species of motive.

In the third place, if the view put forward be right, we must sharply distinguish morality and virtue as independent, though related, species of goodness, neither being an aspect of something of which the other is an aspect, nor again a form or species of the other, nor again something deducible from the other; and we must at the same time allow that it is possible to do the same act either virtuously or morally or in both ways at once. And surely this is true. An act, to be virtuous, must, as Aristotle saw, be done willingly or with pleasure; as such it is just not done from a sense of obligation but from some desire which is intrinsically good, as arising from some intrinsically good emotion. Thus, in an act of generosity the motive is the desire to help another arising from sympathy with that other; in an act which is courageous and no more, i.e. in an act which is not at the same time an act of public spirit or family affection or the like, we prevent ourselves from being dominated by a feeling of terror, desiring to do so from a sense of shame at being terrified. The goodness of such an act is different from the goodness of an act to which we apply the term moral in the strict and narrow sense, viz. an act done from a sense of obligation. Its goodness lies in the intrinsic goodness of the emotion and of the consequent desire under which we act, the goodness of this motive being different from the goodness of the moral motive proper, viz. the sense of duty or obligation. Nevertheless, at any rate in certain cases, an act can be done either virtuously or morally or in both ways at once. It is possible to repay a benefit either from desire to repay it, or from the feeling that we ought to do so, or from both motives combined. A doctor may tend his patients either from a desire arising out of interest in his patients or in the exercise of skill, or from a sense of duty, or from a desire and a sense of duty combined. Further, although we recognize that in each case the act possesses an intrinsic goodness, we regard that action as the best in which both motives are combined; in other words, we regard as the really best man the man in whom virtue and morality are united.

It may be objected that the distinction between the two kinds of motive is untenable, on the ground that the *desire* to repay a benefit, for example, is only the manifestation of that which manifests itself as the *sense of obligation* to repay whenever we think of something in the action which is other than the repayment and which we should not like, such as the loss or pain involved. Yet the distinction can, I think, easily be shown to be tenable. For, in the analogous case of revenge, the desire to return the injury and the sense that we ought not to do so, leading, as they do, in opposite directions, are plainly distinct; and the obviousness of the distinction here seems to remove any difficulty in admitting the existence of a parallel distinction between the desire to return a benefit and the sense that we ought to return it.[9]

Further, the view implies that an obligation can no more be based on or derived from a virtue than a virtue can be derived from an obligation, in which latter case a virtue would consist in carrying out an obligation. And the implication is surely true and important. Take the case of courage. It is untrue to urge that, since courage is a virtue, we ought to act courageously. It is and must be untrue, because, as we see in the end, to feel an obligation to act courageously would involve a contradiction. For, as I have urged before, we can only feel an obligation to *act;* we cannot feel an obligation to *act from a certain desire,* in this case the desire to conquer one's feelings of terror arising from the sense of shame which they arouse. Moreover, if the sense of obligation to act in a particular way leads to an action, the action will be an action done from a sense of obligation, and therefore not, if the above analysis of virtue be right, an act of courage.

The mistake of supposing that there can be an obligation to act courageously seems to arise from two causes. In the first place, there is often an obligation to do that which involves the conquering or controlling of our fear in the doing of it, e.g. the obligation to walk along the side of a precipice to fetch a doctor for a member of our family. Here the acting on the obligation is externally, though only externally, the same as an act of courage proper. In the second place there is an obligation to acquire courage, i.e. to do such things as will enable us afterwards to act courageously, and this may be mistaken for an obligation to act courageously. The same considerations can, of course, be applied, *mutatis mutandis,* to the other virtues.

[9] This sharp distinction of virtue and morality as co-ordinate and independent forms of goodness will explain a fact which otherwise it is difficult to account for. If we turn from books on Moral Philosophy to any vivid account of human life and action such as we find in Shakespeare, nothing strikes us more than the comparative remoteness of the discussions of Moral Philosophy from the facts of actual life. Is not this largely because, while Moral Philosophy has, quite rightly, concentrated its attention on the fact of obligation, in the case of many of those whom we admire most and whose lives are of the greatest interest, the sense of obligation, though it may be an important, is not a dominating factor in their lives?

The fact, if it be a fact, that virtue is no basis for morality will explain what otherwise it is difficult to account for, viz. the extreme sense of dissatisfaction produced by a close reading of Aristotle's *Ethics*. Why is the *Ethics* so disappointing? Not, I think, because it really answers two radically different questions as if they were one: (1) 'What is the happy life?', (2) 'What is the virtuous life?' It is, rather, because Aristotle does not do what we as moral philosophers want him to do, viz. to convince us that we really ought to do what in our nonreflective consciousness we have hitherto believed we ought to do, or if not, to tell us what, if any, are the other things which we really ought to do, and to prove to us that he is right. Now, if what I have just been contending is true, a systematic account of the virtuous character cannot possibly satisfy this demand. At best it can only make clear to us the details of one of our obligations, viz. the obligation to make ourselves better men; but the achievement of this does not help us to discover what we ought to do in life as a whole, and why; to think that it did would be to think that our only business in life was self-improvement. Hence it is not surprising that Aristotle's account of the good man strikes us as almost wholly of academic value, with little relation to our real demand, which is formulated in Plato's words: οὐ γὰρ περὶ τοῦ ἐπιτυχόντος ὁ λόγος, ἀλλὰ περὶ τοῦ ὄντινα τρόπον χρῆ ζῆν. [for no light matter is at stake, nothing less than the rule of human life].

I am not, of course, *criticizing* Aristotle for failing to satisfy this demand, except so far as here and there he leads us to think that he intends to satisfy it. For my main contention is that the demand cannot be satisfied, and cannot be satisfied because it is illegitimate. Thus we are brought to the question: 'Is there really such a thing as Moral Philosophy, and, if there is, in what sense?'

We should first consider the parallel case—as it appears to be—of the Theory of Knowledge. As I urged before, at some time or other in the history of all of us, if we are thoughtful, the frequency of our own and of others' mistakes is bound to lead to the reflection that possibly we and others have *always* been mistaken in consequence of some radical defect of our faculties. In consequence, certain things which previously we should have said without hesitation that we *knew*, as e.g. that $4 \times 7 = 28$, become subject to doubt; we become able only to say that we thought we knew these things. We inevitably go on to look for some general procedure by which we can ascertain that a given condition of mind is really one of knowledge. And this involves the search for a criterion of knowledge, i.e. for a principle by applying which we can settle that a given state of mind is really knowledge. The search for this criterion and the application of it, when found, is what is called the Theory of Knowledge. The search implies that instead of its being the fact that the knowledge that *A* is *B* is obtained directly by consideration of the nature of *A* and *B*, the knowledge that *A* is *B*, in the full or complete sense, can only be obtained by first knowing that *A* is *B*, and then knowing that we knew it by applying a criterion, such as Descartes's principle that what we clearly and distinctly conceive is true.

Now it is easy to show that the doubt whether *A* is *B*, based on this speculative or general ground, could, if genuine, never be set at rest. For if, in order really to know that *A* is *B*, we must first know that we knew it, then really, to know that we knew it, we must first know that we knew that we knew it. But— what is more important—it is also easy to show that this doubt is not a genuine doubt but rests on a confusion the exposure of which removes the doubt. For when we *say* we doubt whether our previous condition was one of knowledge, what we *mean*, if we mean anything at all, is that we doubt whether our previous *belief* was *true*, a belief which we should express as the *thinking* that *A* is *B*. For in order to doubt whether our previous condition was one of knowledge, we have to think of it not as knowledge but as only belief, and our only question can be 'Was this belief true?' But as soon as we see that we are thinking of our previous condition as only one of belief, we see that what we are now doubting is not what we first *said* we were doubting, viz. whether a previous condition of knowledge was really knowledge. Hence, to remove the doubt, it is only necessary to appreciate the real nature of our consciousness in apprehending, e.g. that

$7 \times 4 = 28$, and thereby see that it was no mere condition of believing but a condition of knowing, and then to notice that in our subsequent doubt what we are really doubting is not whether this consciousness was really knowledge, but whether a consciousness of another kind, viz. a belief that $7 \times 4 = 28$, was true. We thereby see that though a doubt based on speculative grounds is possible, it is not a doubt concerning what we believed the doubt concerned, and that a doubt concerning this latter is impossible.

Two results follow. In the first place, if, as is usually the case, we mean by the 'Theory of Knowledge' the knowledge which supplies the answer to the question 'Is what we have hitherto thought knowledge really knowledge?', there is and can be no such thing, and the supposition that there can is simply due to a confusion. There can be no answer to an illegitimate question, except that the question is illegitimate. Nevertheless the question is one which we continue to put until we realize the inevitable immediacy of knowledge. And it is positive knowledge that knowledge is immediate and neither can be, nor needs to be, improved or vindicated by the further knowledge that it was knowledge. This positive knowledge sets at rest the inevitable doubt, and, so far as by the 'Theory of Knowledge' is meant this knowledge, then even though this knowledge be the knowledge that there is no Theory of Knowledge in the former sense, to that extent the Theory of Knowledge exists.

In the second place, suppose we come genuinely to doubt whether, e.g., $7 \times 4 = 28$ owing to a genuine doubt whether we were right in believing yesterday that $7 \times 4 = 28$, a doubt which can in fact only arise if we have lost our hold of, i.e. no longer remember, the real nature of our consciousness of yesterday, and so think of it as consisting in believing. Plainly, the only remedy is to do the sum again. Or, to put the matter generally, if we do come to doubt whether it is true that A is B, as we once thought, the remedy lies not in any process of reflection but in such a reconsideration of the nature of A and B as leads to the knowledge that A is B.

With these considerations in mind, consider the parallel

which, as it seems to me, is presented—though with certain differences—by Moral Philosophy. The sense that we ought to do certain things arises in our unreflective consciousness, being an activity of moral thinking occasioned by the various situations in which we find ourselves. At this stage our attitude to these obligations is one of unquestioning confidence. But inevitably the appreciation of the degree to which the execution of these obligations is contrary to our interest raises the doubt whether after all these obligations are really obligatory, i.e. whether our sense that we ought not to do certain things is not illusion. We then want to have it *proved* to us that we ought to do so, i.e. to be convinced of this by a process which, as an argument, is different in kind from our original and unreflective appreciation of it. This demand is, as I have argued, illegitimate.

Hence, in the first place, if, as is almost universally the case, by Moral Philosophy is meant the knowledge which would satisfy this demand, there is no such knowledge, and all attempts to attain it are doomed to failure because they rest on a mistake, the mistake of supposing the possibility of proving what can only be apprehended directly by an act of moral thinking. Nevertheless the demand, though illegitimate, is inevitable until we have carried the process of reflection far enough to realize the self-evidence of our obligations, i.e. the immediacy of our apprehension of them. This realization of their self-evidence is positive knowledge, and so far, and so far only, as the term Moral Philosophy is confined to this knowledge and to the knowledge of the parallel immediacy of the apprehension of the goodness of the various virtues and of good dispositions generally, is there such a thing as Moral Philosophy. But since this knowledge may allay doubts which often affect the whole conduct of life, it is, though not extensive, important and even vitally important.

In the second place, suppose we come genuinely to doubt whether we ought, for example, to pay our debts, owing to a genuine doubt whether our previous conviction that we ought to do so is true, a doubt which can, in fact, only arise if we fail to remember the real nature of what we now call our past conviction. The only remedy lies in actually getting into a situation which occasions the obligation, or—if our imagination be strong enough—in imagining ourselves in that situation, and then letting our moral capacities of thinking do their work. Or, to put the matter generally, if we do doubt whether there is really an obligation to originate A in a situation B, the remedy lies not in any process of general thinking, but in getting face to face with a particular instance of the situation B, and then directly appreciating the obligation to originate A in that situation.

ETHICAL INTUITIONISM / P. F. Strawson

NORTH: What is the trouble about moral facts? When someone denies that there is an objective moral order, or asserts that ethical propositions are pseudo-propositions, cannot I refute him (rather as Moore refuted those who denied the existence of the external world) by saying: "You know very well that Brown did wrong in beating his wife. You know very well that you ought to keep promises. You know very well that human affection is good and cruelty bad, that many actions are wrong and some are right"?

WEST: Isn't the trouble about moral facts another case of trouble about knowing, about learning? We find out facts about the external world by looking and listening; about ourselves, by feeling; about other people, by looking and listening *and* feeling. When this is noticed, there arises a wish to say that the facts *are*

From P. F. Strawson, "Ethical Intuitionism," Philosophy, XXIV (1949), 347–357. Reprinted by permission of the Editor of Philosophy, and the author.

what is seen, what is heard, what is felt; and, consequently, that moral facts fall into one of these classes. So those who have denied that there are "objective moral characteristics" have not wanted to deny that Brown's action was wrong or that keeping promises is right. They have wanted to point out that rightness and wrongness are a matter of what is felt in the heart, not of what is seen with the eyes or heard with the ears. They have wanted to emphasize the way in which "Promise-keeping is right" resembles "Going abroad is exciting," "Stories about mothers-in-law are comic," "Bombs are terrifying"; and differs from "Roses are red" and "Sea-water is salt." This does not prevent you from talking about the moral order, or the moral world, if you want to; but it warns you not to forget that the only access to the moral world is through remorse and approval and so on; just as the only access to the world of comedy is through laughter; and the only access to the coward's world is through fear.

NORTH: I agree, of course, that we cannot see the goodness of something as we see its colour, or identify rightness by the sense of touch; though I think you should add that the senses are indispensable as a means of our becoming aware of those characteristics upon which moral characteristics depend. You may be partly right, too, in saying that access to the moral world is obtained through experience of the moral emotions; for it may be that only when our moral feelings have been strongly stirred do we first become clearly aware of the characteristics which evoke these feelings. But these feelings are not identical with that awareness. "Goodness" does not stand to "feeling approval," "guilt" to "feeling guilty," "obligation" to "feeling bound," as "excitingness" stands to "being excited" and "humorousness" to "feeling amused." To use the jargon for a moment: moral characteristics and relations are non-empirical, and awareness of them is neither sensory nor introspectual. It is a different kind of awareness, which the specialists call "intuition": and it is only empiricist prejudice which prevents your acknowledging its existence. Once acknowledged, it solves our problems: and we see that while "Promise-keeping is right" differs from "The sea is salt," this is not because it resembles "Detective-stories are exciting"; it differs from *both* in being the report neither of a sensible nor an introspectible experience, but of an intuition. We may, perhaps, know some moral characteristics mediately, through others. ("Obligation" is, perhaps, definable in terms of "goodness.") But at least one such characteristic—rightness or goodness—is unanalysable, and known by intuition alone. The fundamental cognitive situation in morals is that in which we intuit the rightness of a particular action or the goodness of a particular state of affairs. We see this moral characteristic as present in virtue of some other characteristics, themselves capable of being described in empirical terms, which the action or state of affairs possesses. (This is why I said that sense-perception is a necessary, though not a sufficient, condition of obtaining information about the moral order.) Our intuition, then, is not a bare intuition of the moral characteristic, but also the intuition of its dependence on some others: so that this fundamental situation yields us, by intuitive induction, knowledge of moral rules, generalizations regarding the right and the good, which we can apply in other cases, even when an actual intuition is lacking. So much do these rules become taken for granted, a part of our habitual moral life, that most of our everyday moral judgments involve merely an implicit reference to them[1]: a reference which becomes explicit only if the judgment is challenged or queried. Moral emotions, too, assume the character of habitual reactions. But emotions and judgments alike are grounded upon intuitions. Emotion may be the gatekeeper to the moral world; but intuition is the gate.

WEST: Not so fast. I understand you to say that at least one fundamental moral characteristic—rightness or goodness—is unanalysable. Perhaps both are. The experts are divided. In any case, the fundamental characteristic (or characteristics) can be known only by intuitive awareness of its presence in some particular contemplated action or state of affairs. There is, then, a kind of analogy between the word "right" (or "good") and the

1 Cf. D. Daiches Raphael, *The Moral Sense*, Chapters V and VI.

name of some simple sensible characteristic such as "red." [2]
Just as everybody who understands the word "red" has seen
some red things, so everybody who understands the word "right"
or the word "good" has intuited the character, rightness, in some
actions, or the character, goodness, in some states of affairs; and
nobody who has not intuited these characters understands the
words "right" or "good." But this is not quite enough, is it? In
order for me to know *now* the meaning of an indefinable word, it
is not enough that a certain perceptual or intuitional event
should have occurred at some particular point in my history; for
I might not only have forgotten the details of that event; I might
have forgotten what *kind* of an event it was; I might not know
now what it would be like for such an event to occur. If the word
"red" expresses an indefinable visual concept, then it is self-
contradictory to say: "I know what the word 'red' means, but I
can't remember ever *seeing* red and I don't know what it would
be *like* to see red." Similarly, if the word "right," or the word
"good," expresses an indefinable intuitive concept, then it is self-
contradictory to say: "I know what the word 'right' or the word
'good' means, but I can't remember ever *intuiting* rightness or
goodness, and I don't know what it would be *like* to intuit rightness or goodness." If your theory is true, then this statement is a
contradiction.

But it is not at all obvious to me that it is a contradiction.
I should be quite prepared to assert that I understood the words
"right" and "good," but that I couldn't remember ever intuiting
rightness or goodness and that I couldn't imagine what it would
be like to do so. And I think it is quite certain that I am not alone
in this, but that there are a large number of people who are to be
presumed capable of accurate reporting of their own cognitive
experience, and who would find nothing self-contradictory in
saying what I say. And if this is so, you are presented with a
choice of two possibilities. The first is that the words "right" and
"good" have quite a different meaning for one set of people from
the meaning which they have for another set. But neither
of us believes this. The second is that the intuitionist theory is a

[2] Cf. G. E. Moore, *Principia Ethica*, p. 7 *et seq.*

mistake; that the phrase "intuitional event having a moral characteristic as its object (or a part of its object)" is a phrase which
describes nothing at all; or describes misleadingly the kind of
emotional experience we both admit. There is no third possibility.
It is no good saying: "All people who succeed in learning the
meaning of moral words do as a matter of fact have moral intuitions, but unfortunately many people are inclined to forget
them, to be quite unable to remember what they are like." True,
there would be nothing self-contradictory in saying this: but it
would simply be a variant of the first possibility; for I cannot be
said to know *now* the meaning of a word expressing an intuitive
concept unless I know now what it would be like to intuit the
characteristic of which it is a concept. The trouble with your
intuitionist theory is that, if true, it should be a truism. There
should be no doubt about the occurrence of the distinctive experience of intuiting rightness (or goodness), and about its being
the only way to learn the meaning of the primary moral words;
just as there is no doubt about the occurrence of seeing red (or
blue), and about this being the only way to learn the meaning of
the primary colour words. But there *is* doubt; and over against
this doubt there rises a certainty: the certainty that we all know
what it is to *feel* guilty, to *feel* bound, to *feel* approving.

NORTH: What I have said *is* a truism; and that is its strength. It
is not I who am inventing a mythical faculty, but you, irritated,
perhaps, by the language of intuitionism, who are denying the
obvious. When you said that you couldn't *imagine* what it would
be like to have moral intuitions, isn't it clear that you wanted
"intuiting a moral characteristic" to be like seeing a colour or
hearing a sound? Naturally you couldn't *imagine* anything of the
sort. But I have already pointed out that moral characteristics
are dependent on others of which the presence *is* ascertainable
by looking and listening. You do not intuit rightness or goodness
independently of the other features of the situation. You intuit
that an action is (or would be) right, a state of affairs good,
because it has (or would have) certain other empirically ascertainable qualities. The total content of your intuition includes

the "because" clause. Of course, our ordinary moral judgments register unreflective reactions. Nevertheless "This act is right (or this state of affairs is good) because it has P, Q, R"—where "P, Q, R" stand for such empirically ascertainable qualities—expresses the type of fundamental cognitive situation in ethics, of which our normal judgments are copies, mediated by habit, but ready, if challenged, to become explicit as their original. Consider what happens when someone dissents from your opinion. You produce reasons. And this is not a matter of accounting for an emotional condition; but of bringing evidence in support of a verdict.

WEST: When the jury brings in a verdict of guilty on a charge of murder, they do so because the facts adduced in evidence are of the kind covered by the definition of "murder." When the chemical analyst concludes that the material submitted for analysis is a salt, he does so because it exhibits the defining properties of a salt. The evidence is the sort of thing that is *meant* by "murder," by "salt." But the fundamental moral word, or words, you say, cannot be defined; their concepts are unanalysable. So it cannot be in this way that the "because" clause of your ethical sentence functions as evidence. "X is a right action because it is a case of promise-keeping" does not work like "X is a salt because it is a compound of basic and acid radicals"; for, if "right" is indefinable, "X is right" does not *mean* "X is an act of promise-keeping or of relieving distress or of telling the truth or . . ."

When I say "It will be fine in the morning; for the evening sky is red," the evidence is of a different sort. For I might observe the fine morning without having noticed the state of the evening sky. But you have rightly stressed the point that there is no *independent* awareness of *moral* qualities: that they are always "seen" as dependent on those other features mentioned in the "because" clause. So it is not in this way, either, that the "because" clause of your ethical sentence functions as evidence. And there is no other way. Generally, we may say that whenever *q* is evidence for *p*, *either q* is the sort of thing we mean by "*p*" ("*p*" is definable in terms of "*q*") *or* we can have knowledge of the state of affairs described by "p" independently of knowledge of the state of affairs described by "q." But neither of these conditions is satisfied by the q, the "because" clause, of your ethical sentence.

The "because" clause, then, does not, as you said it did, constitute evidence for the ethical judgment. And this, it seems to me, should be a serious matter for you. For where is such evidence to be found? It is no good saying that, after all, the ethical judgments of other people (or your own at other times) may corroborate your own present judgment. They may agree with it: but their agreement strengthens the probability of your judgment only on the assumption that their moral intuitions tend on the whole to be correct. But the only possible evidence for the existence of a *tendency* to have correct intuitions is the correctness of *actual* intuitions. And it is precisely the correctness of actual intuitions for which we are seeking evidence, and failing to find it.

And evidence you must have, if your account of the matter is correct. You will scarcely say that ethical intuitions are infallible; for ethical disagreements may survive the resolution of factual disagreements. (You might, of course, say that *genuine* intuitions were infallible: then the problem becomes one of finding a criterion for distinguishing between the genuine ones and those false claimants that carry the same inner conviction.) So your use of the language of "unanalysable predicates ascribed in moral judgment to particular actions and states of affairs" leads to contradiction. For to call such a judgment "non-infallible" would be meaningless unless there were some way of checking it; of confirming or confuting it, by producing evidence for or against it. But I have just shown that your account of these judgments is incompatible with the possibility of producing evidence for or against them. So, if your account is true, these judgments are both corrigible and incorrigible; and this is absurd.

But the absurdity points to the solution. Of course these judgments are corrigible: but not in the way in which the diagnosis of a doctor is corrigible; rather in the way in which the musical taste of a child is corrigible. Correcting them is not a matter of *producing evidence* for them or their contraries, though it is (partly) a matter of *giving reasons* for them or their contraries. We say, warningly, that ethical judgments are corrigible, because ethical disagreement sometimes survives the resolution of factual disagreement. We say, encouragingly, that ethical judgments are corrigible, because the resolution of factual disagreement sometimes leads to the resolution of ethical disagreement. But the one kind of agreement leads (when it *does* lead) to the other, not in the way in which agreed evidence leads to an agreed conclusion, but in the way in which common experience leads to sympathy. The two kinds of agreement, the two kinds of judgment, are as different as chalk from cheese. Ordinary language can accommodate the difference without strain: it is the pseudo-precise philosophical use of "judgment" which slurs over the difference and raises the difficulty. Is it not clear, then, what people have meant when they said that ethical disagreements were like disagreements in taste, in choice, in practical attitude? [3] Of course, as you said, when we produce our reasons, we are not often simply giving the causes of our emotional condition. But neither are we producing evidence for a verdict, for a moral diagnosis. We are using the facts to back our attitudes, to appeal to the capacity of others to feel as we feel, to respond as we respond.

NORTH: I think I see now what you have been leaving out all the time. First, you accused me of inventing a mythical faculty to give us ethical knowledge. Then, when I pointed out that ethical qualities are not intuited out of all relation to other empirically ascertainable features of actions and states of affairs, but are intuited as dependent upon these, you twisted this dependence out of all recognition. You wanted to make it like the causal dependence of a psychological disposition upon some empirical feature of its object: as a child's fondness for strawberries depends upon their sweetness. But the connection between wrong-

[3] Cf. Charles Stevenson, *Ethics and Language*, Chapter 1.

ness and giving pain to others is not an accident of our constitution; nor does its perception require any special faculty—but
simply that which we use in all our reasoning. From the fact that
an action involves inflicting needless pain upon others, *it follows*
necessarily that the action is wrong, just as, from the fact that a
triangle is equilateral, it follows necessarily that its angles are
equal. This is the kind of dependence that we intuit; not an analytic dependence, but a synthetic entailment; and this is why the
"because" clause of my ethical sentence does, after all, constitute evidence for the ascription of the moral characteristic.

I can anticipate the obvious objection. No moral rule, you
will say, no moral generalization concerning the rightness of
acts or the goodness of conditions, holds without exception. It is
always possible to envisage circumstances in which the generalization breaks down. Or, if the generalization is so wide that no
counter-example can be found, if it can be so interpreted as to
cover every case, then it has become too wide: it has become
tautologous, like "It is always right to do that which will have the
best results on the whole," or intolerably vague, like "It is always
right to treat people as ends in themselves" or "The greatest good
is the greatest general welfare." It is plainly not with the help of
such recipes as these that we find out what is right, what is good,
in a particular case. There are no criteria for the meaning of
"treating a man as an end," for "the greatest general welfare,"
which do not presuppose the narrower criteria of rightness and
goodness of which I spoke and which seem always to have exceptions. All this is true. But it calls only for a trifling amendment to those narrower criteria. We cannot, for example, assert,
as a necessary synthetic proposition, "All acts of promise-keeping are right" or "All states of aesthetic enjoyment are good." But
we *can* assert, as a necessary synthetic proposition, "All acts of
promise-keeping *tend as such* to be right (or have *prima facie*
rightness)" [4] or "All states of aesthetic enjoyment *tend as such*
to be good." And we derive our knowledge of such general necessary connections from seeing, in particular cases, that the right-

4 Ross, *Foundations of Ethics*, pp. 83–86; Broad, "Some of the Main Problems
of Ethics," *Philosophy* (1946), p. 117.

ness of an action, the goodness of a state, *follows from* its being
an action or state of a certain kind.

WEST: Your "trifling amendment" is a destructive one. When
we say of swans that they tend to be white, we are not ascribing
a certain quality, namely "tending to be white," to each individual swan. We are saying that the number of swans which are
white exceeds the number of those which are not, that if anything is a swan, the chances are that it will be white. When we
say "Welshmen tend to be good singers," we mean that most
Welshmen sing well; and when we say, of an *individual* Welsh-
man, that *he* tends to sing well, we mean that he sings well more
often than not. In all such cases, we are talking of a *class* of
things or occasions or events; and saying, not that *all* members of
the class have the property of *tending-to-have* a certain characteristic, but that *most* members of the class do in fact have that
characteristic. Nobody would accept the claim that a sentence of
the form "*Most* As are Bs" expresses a necessary proposition. Is
the claim made more plausible by re-writing the proposition
in the form "*All* As *tend to be* Bs"?

But, waiving this point, there remains the difficulty that
the need for such an amendment to our moral generalizations is
incompatible with the account you gave of the way in which we
come to know both the moral characteristics of individual actions and states, and the moral generalizations themselves. You
said that we intuited the moral characteristic as *following from*
some empirically ascertainable features of the action or state.
True, if we did so, we should have implicitly learnt a moral generalization: but it would be one asserting *without qualification*
the entailment of the moral characteristic by these other features of the case. In other words, and to take your instance, if it
ever follows, from the fact that an act has the empirically ascertainable features described by the phrase "being an act of
promise-keeping," that the act is right, then it *always* follows,
from the fact that an act is of this kind, that it has this moral
quality. If, then, it is true that we intuit moral characteristics as
thus "following from" others, it is false that the implied generali-

zations require the "trifling amendment"; and if it is true that they require the amendment, it is false that we so intuit moral characteristics.[5]

And this is all that need be said of that rationalist superstition according to which a quasi-logical necessity binds moral predicates to others. "Le coeur a ses raisons, que la raison ne connaît pas": this is the whole truth of the matter: but your attention was so riveted to the first half of it that you forgot the second.

Looking for a logical nexus where there was none to be found, you overlooked the logical relations of the ethical words among themselves. And so you forgot what has often enough been pointed out: that for every expression containing the words "right" or "good," used in their ethical senses, it is always possible to find an expression with the same meaning, but containing, instead of these, the word "ought." The equivalences are various, and the variations subtle; but they are always to be found. For one to say, for example, "I know where the good lies, I know what the right course is; but I don't know the end I *ought* to aim at, the course I *ought* to follow" would be self-contradictory. "Right"-sentences, "good"-sentences are shorthand for "ought"-sentences. And this is enough in itself to explode the myth of unanalysable characteristics designated by the indefinable predicates, "right" and "good." For "ought" is a *relational* word; whereas "right" and "good" are *predicative*. The simplest sentences containing "ought" are syntactically more complicated than the simplest sentences containing "right" or "good." And

---

[5] One desperate expedient might occur to North. He might say that it is not the bare presence of the promise-keeping feature that entails the rightness of the act, but the presence of this feature, coupled with the absence of any features which would entail its wrongness. His general rules would then be, not of the form " 'x has ϕ' entails 'x is right,' " but of the form " 'x has ϕ and x has no Ψ such that "x has Ψ" entails "x is wrong" ' entails 'x is right.' " But the suggestion is inadmissible, since (i) the establishment of the general proposition "x has no Ψ, etc." would require the enumeration of all those features which would make it wrong to keep a promise, and (ii) any rule of the form " 'x has Ψ' entails 'x is wrong' " would require expansion in exactly the same way as the "right-making" rule; which would involve an infinite regress of such expansions. Besides having this *theoretical* defect, the suggested model is, of course, *practically* absurd.

hence, since the equivalences of meaning hold, the various ethical usages of "right" and "good" *are all definable:* variously definable in terms of "ought."

Of course this last consideration alone is not decisive against intuitionism. If this were all, you could still re-form the ranks: taking your stand on an intuited unanalysable non-natural *relation* of obligation, and admitting the definability of the ethical predicates in terms of this relation. But the objections I have already raised apply with equal force against this modified position; and, in other ways, its weakness is more obvious.[6]

NORTH: Well, then, suppose we agree to bury intuitionism. What have you to offer in its place? Has any analysis of moral judgments in terms of feeling ever been suggested which was not monstrously paradoxical or artificial? Even the simplest ethical sentence obstinately resists translation: and not in the way in which "Life, like a dome of many-coloured glass, Stains the white radiance of eternity" resists translation. For the ethical language is not the language of the poets, but the language of all the world. Somehow justice must be done both to this irreducible element of significance in ethical sentences, and to the commu-

---

[6] E.g. There was a certain plausibility in saying "My feeling morally obliged to pursue such a course (or end) presupposes my believing that it is right (or good)," and thence concluding that this belief cannot be "reduced to" the feeling which it arouses. (For examples of this sort of argument, see Ross, *op. cit.,* pp. 261–262, and Broad, *op. cit.,* p. 115.) But the weakness of the reasoning is more clearly exposed when the sentence is rewritten as "My feeling morally obliged to pursue such a course presupposes my believing that I *am* morally obliged to pursue it." The point is that "presupposes" and "believing" are both ambiguous. If "presupposes" means "causally requires" and "believing" is used in its ordinary sense, then it is obviously false that the beliefs which *occasion* such a feeling invariably include some belief which would be correctly described in these terms. (Compare: "My feeling frightened presupposes my believing that I am frightened.") But the argument begins to have weight against the "analysability" of beliefs correctly so described only if they are invariably present as occasioning factors. If, on the other hand, "presupposes" means "logically requires," then "believing" might be used in a queer sense such that the sentence is *tautologically* true. But this result is secured only by defining "believing" (used in this sense) in terms of feeling (compare the sense in which "thinking *x* funny" means "being amused by *x*"): and this was precisely the result which North sought to avoid.

nity of knowledge of their correct, their appropriate, use. Intuitionism, at any rate, was a way of attempting to do this.

WEST: Yes, intuitionism was a way of attempting to do this. It started from the fact that thousands and thousands of people can say, with perfect propriety: "I know that this is right, that is good"; and ended, as we have seen, by making it inexplicable how anybody could ever say such a thing. This was because of a failure to notice that the whole sentence, including the "I know," and not just the last word in the subordinate clause, is a unit of the ethical language; and, following upon this failure, a feverish ransacking of the drawers of a Theory of Knowledge for an "I know" which would fit. (Do I, perhaps, work it out like the answer to a sum?)

The man who attempts to provide a translation sees more than this. He sees, at any rate, that the sentence must be treated as a unit. His error is to think that he can find a substitute, in a different language, which will serve the same purpose. So long as he confines himself to describing how, in what sort of circumtances, the sentence is used, he does valuable work. He errs when he talks as if to say how a sentence is used is the same as to use it. The man who says he can translate ethical sentences into feeling sentences makes the same sort of mistake as some who said they could (if they had time) translate material-object sentences into sentences about actual and possible sense-experiences. What they *mean*—the commentary they are making on the use of the ethical language or the material-object language—is correct. And it is precisely because the commentary would be incorrect as a translation that it is useful as a commentary. For it brings out the fact that the irreducibility of these languages arises from the systematic vagueness of the notation they use in comparison with that of the commentary-languages, and not from their being used to talk of, to describe, different things from those of which the commentary-languages talk. This descriptive vagueness is no defect: it is what makes these languages useful for the kinds of communication (and persuasion) for which they are severally required. But by being mistaken for something more than it is, it leads to one kind of metaphysics: the metaphysics of substance (the thing-in-itself), or of intuited unanalysable ethical characteristics. And by being ignored altogether, it leads to another kind of metaphysics: the tough metaphysics of translation, the brutal suggestion that we could get along just as well without the ethical language. Neither metaphysics—neither the tender metaphysics of ultimacy, nor the tough metaphysics of reduction[7]—does justice to the facts: but the latter does them less injustice; for it doesn't seek to supplement them with a fairy-tale.

And so the alternative to intuitionism is not the provision of translations. For the communication and sharing of our moral experience, we must use the tools, the ethical language, we have. No sentences provided by the philosopher will take their place. His task is not to supply a new set of tools, but to describe what it is that is communicated and shared, and how the tools are used to do the work. And though the experience he describes is emotional experience, his descriptions are not like those of the psychologist. The psychologist is concerned with the relation of these experiences to others of a different sort; the philosopher is concerned with their relation to the ordinary use of ethical language. Of course, then, it would be absurd for the philosopher to deny that some actions are right (fair, legitimate, etc.) and others wrong (unfair, illegitimate, etc.), and that we know this; and absurd to claim that we can say what such sentences say without using such words. For this *is* the language we use in sharing and shaping our moral experience; and the occurrence of experience so shared, so shaped, is not brought into question.

We are in the position of the careful phenomenalist; who, for all his emphasis on sense-experience, neither denies that there is a table in the dining-room, nor claims to be able to assert this without using such words as "dining-room" and "table." A phenomenalism as careful as this has been said to forfeit the right to be called a "philosophical doctrine." [8] Then

[7] Cf. Wisdom, "Metaphysics and Verification," *Mind* (1938).
[8] Hardie, "The Paradox of Phenomenalism," *Proceedings of the Aristotelian Society* (1945–46), p. 150.

let the title be reserved for the productions of those who rest in myth or paradox, and fail to complete that journey, from the familiar to the familiar,[9] which is philosophical analysis.

[9] Wisdom.

Section Two / ANTINATURALISM AND NONCOGNITIVISM

THE EMOTIVE MEANING OF ETHICAL TERMS / C. L. Stevenson

[1]

ETHICAL questions first arise in the form "is so and so good?" or "is this alternative better than that?" These questions are difficult partly because we don't quite know what we are seeking. We are asking, "is there a needle in the haystack?" without even knowing just what a needle is. So the first thing to do is to examine the questions themselves. We must try to make them clearer, either by defining the terms in which they are expressed or by any other method that is available.

The present essay is concerned wholly with this preliminary step of making ethical questions clear. In order to help answer the question "is X good?" we must *substitute* for it a question that is free from ambiguity and confusion.

It is obvious that in substituting a clearer question we must not introduce some utterly different kind of question. It

From C. L. Stevenson, "The Emotive Meaning of Ethical Terms," Mind, XLVI (1938), 10–31. Reprinted by permission of the Editor of Mind. *This paper has been reprinted with additional footnotes in C. L. Stevenson,* Facts and Values *(New Haven: Yale University Press, 1963). The new footnotes are reprinted by permission of Yale University Press.*

won't do (to take an extreme instance of a prevalent fallacy) to substitute for "is X good?" the question "is X pink with yellow trimmings?" and then point out how easy the question really is. This would beg the original question, not help answer it. On the other hand, we must not expect the substituted question to be strictly "identical" with the original one. The original question may embody hypostatization, anthropomorphism, vagueness, and all the other ills to which our ordinary discourse is subject. If our substituted question is to be clearer it must remove these ills. The questions will be identical only in the sense that a child is identical with the man he later becomes. Hence we must not demand that the substitution strike us, on immediate introspection, as making no change in meaning.

Just how, then, must the substituted question be related to the original? Let us assume (inaccurately) that it must result from replacing "good" by some set of terms that define it. The question then resolves itself to this: How must the defined meaning of "good" be related to its original meaning?

I answer that it must be *relevant*. A defined meaning will be called "relevant" to the original meaning under these circumstances: Those who have understood the definition must be able to say all that they then want to say by using the term in the defined way. They must never have occasion to use the term in the old, unclear sense. (If a person did have to go on using the word in the old sense, then to this extent his meaning would not be clarified and the philosophical task would not be completed.) It frequently happens that a word is used so confusedly and ambiguously that we must give it *several* defined meanings, rather than one. In this case only the whole set of defined meanings will be called "relevant," and any one of them will be called "partially relevant." This is not a rigorous treatment of *relevance*, by any means, but it will serve for the present purposes.

Let us now turn to our particular task—that of giving a relevant definition of "good." Let us first examine some of the ways in which others have attempted to do this.

The word "good" has often been defined in terms of *approval*, or similar psychological attitudes. We may take as typical examples: "good" means *desired by me* (Hobbes); and "good" means *approved by most people* (Hume, in effect).[1] It will be convenient to refer to definitions of this sort as "interest theories," following R. B. Perry, although neither "interest" nor "theory" is used in the most usual way.[2]

Are definitions of this sort relevant?

It is idle to deny their *partial relevance.* The most superficial inquiry will reveal that "good" is exceedingly ambiguous. To maintain that "good" is *never* used in Hobbes' sense, and never in Hume's, is only to manifest an insensitivity to the complexities of language. We must recognize, perhaps, not only these senses, but a variety of similar ones, differing both with regard to the kind of interest in question and with regard to the people who are said to have the interest.

But that is a minor matter. The essential question is not whether interest theories are *partially* relevant, but whether they are *wholly* relevant. This is the only point for intelligent dispute. Briefly: Granted that some senses of "good" may relevantly be defined in terms of interest, is there some *other* sense which is *not* relevantly so defined? We must give this question careful attention. For it is quite possible that when philosophers (and many others) have found the question "is X good?" so difficult, they have been grasping for this *other* sense of "good" and not any sense relevantly defined in terms of interest. If we insist on defining "good" in terms of interest, and answer the question when thus interpreted, we may be begging *their* question entirely. Of course this *other* sense of "good" may not exist, or it

1 The definition ascribed to Hume is oversimplified, but not, I think, in a way that weakens the force of the observations that I am about to make. Perhaps the same should be said of Hobbes.

A more accurate account of Hume's Ethics is given in *Ethics and Language* (New Haven, 1944), pp. 273–276.

2 In *General Theory of Value* (New York, 1926) Perry used "interest" to refer to any sort of favoring or disfavoring, or any sort of disposition to be for or against something. And he used "theory" where he might, alternatively, have used "proposed definition," or "proposed analysis of a common sense meaning."

In most of the (chronologically) later essays in the present volume the term "interest" systematically gives place to the term "attitude." The purpose of the change was solely to provide a more transparent terminology: it was not intended to repudiate Perry's *conception* of interest.

may be a complete confusion; but that is what we must discover.

Now many have maintained that interest theories are *far* from being completely relevant. They have argued that such theories neglect the very sense of "good" that is most typical of ethics. And certainly, their arguments are not without plausibility.

Only—what *is* this typical sense of "good"? The answers have been so vague and so beset with difficulties that one can scarcely determine.

There are certain requirements, however, with which the typical sense has been expected to comply—requirements which appeal strongly to our common sense. It will be helpful to summarize these, showing how they exclude the interest theories:

In the first place, we must be able sensibly to *disagree* about whether something is "good." This condition rules out Hobbes' definition. For consider the following argument: "This is good." "That isn't so; it's not good." As translated by Hobbes, this becomes: "I desire this." "That isn't so, for *I* don't." The speakers are not contradicting one another, and think they are only because of an elementary confusion in the use of pronouns. The definition, "good" means *desired by my community,* is also excluded, for how could people from different communities disagree?[3]

In the second place, "goodness" must have, so to speak, a magnetism. A person who recognizes X to be "good" must ipso facto acquire a stronger tendency to act in its favor than he otherwise would have had. This rules out the Humian type of definition. For according to Hume, to recognize that something is "good" is simply to recognize that the majority approve of it. Clearly, a man may see that the majority approve of X without having, himself, a stronger tendency to favor it. This requirement excludes any attempt to define "good" in terms of the interest of people *other* than the speaker.[4]

In the third place, the "goodness" of anything must not be verifiable solely by use of the scientific method. "Ethics must not be psychology." This restriction rules out all of the tradi-

3 See G. E. Moore, *Philosophical Studies* (New York, 1922), pp. 332–334.
4 See G. C. Field, *Moral Theory* (London, 1921), pp. 52, 56–57.

tional interest theories without exception. It is so sweeping a restriction that we must examine its plausibility. What are the
methodological implications of interest theories which are here
rejected?

According to Hobbes' definition a person can prove his
ethical judgments with finality by showing that he is not making
an introspective error about his desires. According to Hume's
definition one may prove ethical judgments (roughly speaking)
by taking a vote. *This* use of the empirical method, at any rate,
seems highly remote from what we usually accept as proof and
reflects on the complete relevance of the definitions that imply it.

But are there not more complicated interest theories that
are immune from such methodological implications? No, for the
same factors appear; they are only put off for a while. Consider,
for example, the definition: "X is good" means *most people
would approve of X if they knew its nature and consequences.*
How, according to this definition, could we prove that a certain X
was good? We should first have to find out, empirically, just
what X was like and what its consequences would be. To this
extent the empirical method as required by the definition seems
beyond intelligent objection. But what remains? We should next
have to discover whether most people would approve of the sort
of thing we had discovered X to be. This could not be determined
by popular vote—but only because it would be too difficult to
explain to the voters, beforehand, what the nature and consequences of X really were. Apart from this, voting would be a
pertinent method. We are again reduced to counting noses as a
perfectly final appeal.

Now we need not scorn voting entirely. A man who rejected interest theories as irrelevant might readily make the following statement: "If I believed that X would be approved by the
majority, when they knew all about it, I should be strongly *led* to
say that X was good." But he would continue: "*Need* I say that X
was good, under the circumstances? Wouldn't my acceptance of
the alleged 'final proof' result simply from my being democratic? What about the more aristocratic people? They would
simply say that the approval of most people, even when they

knew all about the object of their approval, simply had nothing to do with the goodness of anything, and they would probably add a few remarks about the low state of people's interests." It would indeed seem, from these considerations, that the definition we have been considering has presupposed democratic ideals from the start; it has dressed up democratic propaganda in the guise of a definition.

The omnipotence of the empirical method, as implied by interest theories and others, may be shown unacceptable in a somewhat different way. G. E. Moore's familiar objection about the open question is chiefly pertinent in this regard. No matter what set of scientifically knowable properties a thing may have (says Moore, in effect), you will find, on careful introspection, that it is an open question to ask whether anything having these properties is *good*. It is difficult to believe that this recurrent question is a totally confused one, or that it seems open only because of the ambiguity of "good." Rather, we must be using some sense of "good" which is not definable, relevantly, in terms of anything scientifically knowable. That is, the scientific method is not sufficient for ethics.[5]

These, then, are the requirements with which the "typical" sense of "good" is expected to comply: (1) goodness must be a topic for intelligent disagreement; (2) it must be "magnetic"; and (3) it must not be discoverable solely through the scientific method.

[2]

I can now turn to my proposed analysis of ethical judgments. First let me present my position dogmatically, showing to what extent I vary from tradition.

I believe that the three requirements given above are perfectly sensible, that there is some *one* sense of "good" which satisfies all three requirements, and that no traditional interest theory satisfies them all. But this does not imply that "good"

[5] See G. E. Moore, *Principia Ethica* (Cambridge, 1903), Ch. 1. I am simply trying to preserve the spirit of Moore's objection and not the exact form of it.

must be explained in terms of a Platonic Idea, or of a categorical imperative, or of a unique, unanalyzable property. On the contrary, the three requirements can be met by a *kind* of interest theory. *But we must give up a presupposition that all the traditional interest theories have made.*

Traditional interest theories hold that ethical statements are *descriptive* of the existing state of interests—that they simply *give information* about interests. (More accurately, ethical judgments are said to describe what the state of interests is, was, or will be, or to indicate what the state of interests *would* be under specified circumstances.) It is this emphasis on description, on information, which leads to their incomplete relevance. Doubtless there is always *some* element of description in ethical judgments, but this is by no means all. Their major use is not to indicate facts but to *create an influence*. Instead of merely describing people's interests they *change* or *intensify* them. They *recommend* an interest in an object, rather than state that the interest already exists.

For instance: When you tell a man that he ought not to steal, your object is not merely to let him know that people disapprove of stealing. You are attempting, rather, to get *him* to disapprove of it. Your ethical judgment has a quasi-imperative force which, operating through suggestion and intensified by your tone of voice, readily permits you to begin to *influence,* to *modify,* his interests. If in the end you do not succeed in getting *him* to disapprove of stealing, you will feel that you have failed to convince him that stealing is wrong. You will continue to feel this, even though he fully acknowledges that you disapprove of it and that almost everyone else does. When you point out to him the consequences of his actions—consequences which you suspect he already disapproves of—these *reasons* which support your ethical judgment are simply a means of facilitating your influence. If you think you can change his interests by making vivid to him how others will disapprove of him, you will do so, otherwise not. So the consideration about other people's interest is just an additional means you may employ in order to move him and is not a part of the ethical judgment itself. Your ethical judgment does not merely describe interests to him, it directs his very interests. The difference between the traditional interest theories and my view is like the difference between describing a desert and irrigating it.

Another example: A munitions maker declares that war is a good thing. If he merely meant that he approved of it, he would not have to insist so strongly nor grow so excited in his argument. People would be quite easily convinced that he approved of it. If he merely meant that most people approved of war, or that most people would approve of it if they knew the consequences, he would have to yield his point if it were proved that this was not so. But he would not do this, nor does consistency require it. He is not *describing* the state of people's approval; he is trying to *change* it by his influence. If he found that few people approved of war, he might insist all the more strongly that it was good, for there would be more changing to be done.

This example illustrates how "good" may be used for what most of us would call bad purposes. Such cases are as pertinent as any others. I am not indicating the *good* way of using "good." I am not influencing people but am describing the way this influence sometimes goes on. If the reader wishes to say that the munitions maker's influence is bad—that is, if the reader wishes to awaken people's disapproval of the man, and to make him disapprove of his own actions—I should at another time be willing to join in this undertaking. But this is not the present concern. I am not using ethical terms but am indicating how they *are* used. The munitions maker, in his use of "good," illustrates the persuasive character of the word just as well as does the unselfish man who, eager to encourage in each of us a desire for the happiness of all, contends that the supreme good is peace.

Thus ethical terms are *instruments* used in the complicated interplay and readjustment of human interests. This can be seen plainly from more general observations. People from widely separated communities have different moral attitudes. Why? To a great extent because they have been subject to different social influences. Now clearly this influence does not operate through sticks and stones alone; words play a great part. People praise one another to encourage certain inclinations and blame one another to discourage others. Those of forceful personalities issue commands which weaker people, for complicated instinctive reasons, find it difficult to disobey, quite apart from fears of consequences. Further influence is brought to bear by writers and orators. Thus social influence is exerted, to an enormous extent, by means that have nothing to do with physical force or material reward. The ethical terms facilitate such influence. Being suited for use in *suggestion*, they are a means by which men's attitudes may be led this way or that. The reason, then, that we find a greater similarity in the moral attitudes of one community than in those of different communities is largely this: ethical judgments propagate themselves. One man says "this is good"; this may influence the approval of another person, who then makes the same ethical judgment, which in turn influences another person, and so on. In the end, by a process of mutual influence, people take up more or less the same attitudes. Between people of widely separated communities, of course, the influence is less strong; hence different communities have different attitudes.

These remarks will serve to give a general idea of my point of view. We must now go into more detail. There are several questions which must be answered: How does an ethical sentence acquire its power of influencing people—why is it suited to suggestion? Again, what has this influence to do with the *meaning* of ethical terms? And finally, do these considerations really lead us to a sense of "good" which meets the requirements mentioned in the preceding section?

Let us deal first with the question about *meaning*. This is far from an easy question, so we must enter into a preliminary inquiry about meaning in general. Although a seeming digression this will prove indispensable.

[3]

Broadly speaking, there are two different *purposes* which lead us to use language. On the one hand we use words (as in science) to record, clarify, and communicate *beliefs*. On the other hand we use words to give vent to our feelings (interjections), or to create moods (poetry), or to incite people to actions or attitudes (oratory).

The first use of words I shall call "descriptive," the second, "dynamic." Note that the distinction depends solely upon the *purpose* of the *speaker*.

When a person says "hydrogen is the lightest known gas," his purpose *may* be simply to lead the hearer to believe this, or to believe that the speaker believes it. In that case the words are used descriptively. When a person cuts himself and says "damn," his purpose is not ordinarily to record, clarify, or communicate any belief. The word is used dynamically. The two ways of using words, however, are by no means mutually exclusive. This is obvious from the fact that our purposes are often complex. Thus when one says "I want you to close the door," part of his purpose, ordinarily, is to lead the hearer to believe that he has this want. To that extent the words are used descriptively. But the major part of one's purpose is to lead the hearer to *satisfy* the want. To that extent the words are used dynamically.

It very frequently happens that the same sentence may have a dynamic use on one occasion and not on another, and that it may have different dynamic uses on different occasions. For instance: A man says to a visiting neighbor, "I am loaded down with work." His purpose may be to let the neighbor know how life is going with him. This would *not* be a dynamic use of words. He may make the remark, however, in order to drop a hint. This *would* be dynamic usage (as well as descriptive). Again, he may make the remark to arouse the neighbor's sympathy. This would be a *different* dynamic usage from that of hinting.

Or again, when we say to a man, "of course you won't make those mistakes any more," we *may* simply be making a prediction. But we are more likely to be using "suggestion," in order to encourage him and hence *keep* him from making mistakes. The first use would be descriptive, the second, mainly dynamic.

From these examples it will be clear that we can not determine whether words are used dynamically or not merely by reading the dictionary—even assuming that everyone is faithful to dictionary meanings. Indeed, to know whether a person is using a word dynamically we must note his tone of voice, his gestures, the general circumstances under which he is speaking, and so on.

We must now proceed to an important question: What has the dynamic use of words to do with their *meaning*? One thing is clear—we must not define "meaning" in a way that would make meaning vary with dynamic usage. If we did, we should have no use for the term. All that we could say about such "meaning" would be that it is very complicated and subject to constant change. So we must certainly distinguish between the dynamic use of words and their meaning.

It does not follow, however, that we must define "meaning" in some nonpsychological fashion. We must simply restrict the psychological field. Instead of identifying meaning with *all* the psychological causes and effects that attend a word's utterance, we must identify it with those that it has a *tendency* (causal property, dispositional property) to be connected with. The tendency must be of a particular kind, moreover. It must exist for all who speak the language; it must be persistent and must be realizable more or less independently of determinate circumstances attending the word's utterance. There will be further restrictions dealing with the interrelations of words in different contexts. Moreover, we must include, under the psychological responses which the words tend to produce, not only immediately introspectable experiences but *dispositions* to react in a given way with appropriate stimuli. I hope to go into these matters in a subsequent essay.[6] Suffice it now to say that I think "meaning" may be thus defined in a way to include "propositional" meaning as an important kind.

The definition will readily permit a distinction between meaning and dynamic use. For when words are accompanied by dynamic purposes, it does not follow that they *tend* to be accompanied by them in the way mentioned above. E.g. there need be no tendency realizable more or less independently of the determinate circumstances under which the words are uttered.

There will be a kind of meaning, however, in the sense above defined, which has an intimate relation to dynamic usage. I refer to "emotive" meaning (in a sense roughly like that employed by Ogden and Richards).[7] The emotive meaning of a word is a tendency of a word, arising through the history of its usage, to produce (result from) *affective* responses in people. It

6 The "subsequent essay" became, instead, Chapter 3 of *Ethics and Language*, which among other points defends those that follow:

(1) When used in a generic sense that emphasizes what C. W. Morris calls the *pragmatic* aspects of language, the term "meaning" designates a tendency of words to express or evoke states of mind in the people who use the words. The tendency is of a special kind, however, and many qualifications are needed (including some that bear on syntax) to specify its nature.

(2) When the states of mind in question are cognitive, the meaning can conveniently be called *descriptive;* and when they are feelings, emotions, or attitudes, the meanings can conveniently be called *emotive.*

(3) The states of mind (in a rough and tentative sense of that term) are normally quite complicated. They are not necessarily images or feelings but may in their turn be further tendencies—tendencies to respond to various stimuli that may subsequently arise. A word may have a constant meaning, accordingly, even though it is accompanied, at various times that it is used, by different images or feelings.

(4) Emotive meaning is sometimes more than a by-product of descriptive meaning. When a term has both sorts of meaning, for example, a change in its descriptive meaning may not be attended by a change in emotive meaning.

(5) When a speaker's use of emotive terms evokes an attitude in a hearer (as it sometimes may not, since it has only a *tendency* to do so), it must not be conceived as merely adding to the hearer's attitude in the way that a spark might add its heat to the atmosphere. For a more appropriate analogy, in many cases, we must think rather of a spark that ignites tinder.

7 See C. K. Ogden and I. A. Richards, *The Meaning of Meaning* (2nd ed., London, 1927). On p. 125 there is a passage on ethics which is the source of the ideas embodied in this essay.

is the immediate aura of feeling which hovers about a word.[8] Such tendencies to produce affective responses cling to words very tenaciously. It would be difficult, for instance, to express merriment by using the interjection "alas." Because of the persistence of such affective tendencies (among other reasons) it becomes feasible to classify them as "meanings."

Just *what* is the relation between emotive meaning and the dynamic use of words? Let us take an example. Suppose that a man tells his hostess, at the end of a party, that he thoroughly enjoyed himself, and suppose that he was in fact bored. If we consider his remark an innocent one, are we likely to remind him, later, that he "lied" to his hostess? Obviously not, or at least, not without a broad smile; for although he told her something that he believed to be false, and with the intent of making her believe that it was true—those being the ordinary earmarks of a lie—the expression, "you lied to her," would be emotively too strong for our purposes. It would seem to be a reproach, even if we intended it not to be a reproach. So it will be evident that such words as "lied" (and many parallel examples could be cited) become suited, on account of their emotive meaning, to a certain kind of dynamic use—so well suited, in fact, that the hearer is likely to be misled when we use them in any other way. The more pronounced a word's emotive meaning is, the less likely people are to use it purely descriptively. Some words are suited to encourage people, some to discourage them, some to quiet them, and so on.

---

[8] In *Ethics and Language* the phrase "aura of feeling" was expressly repudiated. If the present essay had been more successful in anticipating the analysis given in that later work, it would have introduced the notion of emotive meaning in some such way as this:

The emotive meaning of a word or phrase is a strong and persistent tendency, built up in the course of linguistic history, to give direct expression (quasi-interjectionally) to certain of the speaker's feelings or emotions or attitudes; and it is also a tendency to evoke (quasi-imperatively) corresponding feelings, emotions, or attitudes in those to whom the speaker's remarks are addressed. It is the emotive meaning of a word, accordingly, that leads us to characterize it as *laudatory* or *derogatory*—that rather generic characterization being of particular importance when we are dealing with terms like "good" and "bad" or "right and wrong." But emotive meanings are of great variety: they may yield terms that express or evoke horror, amazement, sadness, sympathy, and so on.

Even in these cases, of course, the dynamic purposes are
not to be identified with any sort of meaning; for the emotive
meaning accompanies a word much more persistently than do
the dynamic purposes. But there is an important contingent relation between emotive meaning and dynamic purpose: the former assists the latter. Hence if we define emotively laden terms
in a way that neglects their emotive meaning, we become seriously confused. *We lead people to think that the terms defined
are used dynamically less often than they are.*

[4]

Let us now apply these remarks in defining "good." This word
may be used morally or nonmorally. I shall deal with the non-
moral usage almost entirely, but only because it is simpler. The
main points of the analysis will apply equally well to either
usage.

As a preliminary definition let us take an inaccurate approximation. It may be more misleading than helpful but will do
to begin with. Roughly, then, the sentence "X is good" means *we
like X.* ("We" includes the hearer or hearers.)

At first glance this definition sounds absurd. If used, we
should expect to find the following sort of conversation: A. "This
is good." B. "But I *don't* like it. What led you to believe that I
did?" The unnaturalness of B's reply, judged by ordinary word
usage, would seem to cast doubt on the relevance of my definition.

B's unnaturalness, however, lies simply in this: he is assuming that "we like it" (as would occur implicitly in the use of
"good") is being used descriptively. This will not do. When "we
like it" is to take the place of "this is good," the former sentence
must be used not purely descriptively, but dynamically. More
specifically, it must be used to promote a very subtle (and for
the nonmoral sense in question, a very easily resisted) kind of
suggestion. To the extent that "we" refers to the hearer it must
have the dynamic use, essential to suggestion, of leading the
hearer to *make* true what is said, rather than merely to believe it.

And to the extent that "we" refers to the speaker, the sentence must have not only the descriptive use of indicating belief about the speaker's interest, but the quasi-interjectory, dynamic function of giving direct expression to the interest. (This immediate expression of feelings assists in the process of suggestion. It is difficult to disapprove in the face of another's enthusiasm.)

For an example of a case where "we like this" is used in the dynamic way that "this is good" is used, consider the case of a mother who says to her several children, "one thing is certain, *we all like to be neat.*" If she really believed this, she would not bother to say so. But she is not using the words descriptively. She is *encouraging* the children to like neatness. By telling them that they like neatness, she will lead them to *make* her statement true, so to speak. If, instead of saying "we all like to be neat" in this way, she had said "it's a good thing to be neat," the effect would have been approximately the same.

But these remarks are still misleading. Even when "we like it" is used for suggestion, it is not quite like "this is good." The latter is more subtle. With such a sentence as "this is a good book," for example, it would be practically impossible to use instead "we like this book." When the latter is used it must be accompanied by so exaggerated an intonation, to prevent its becoming confused with a descriptive statement, that the force of suggestion becomes stronger and ludicrously more overt than when "good" is used.

The definition is inadequate, further, in that the definiens has been restricted to dynamic usage. Having said that dynamic usage was different from meaning, I should not have to mention it in giving the *meaning* of "good."

It is in connection with this last point that we must return to emotive meaning. The word "good" has a laudatory emotive meaning that fits it for the dynamic use of suggesting favorable interest. But the sentence "we like it" has no such emotive meaning. Hence my definition has neglected emotive meaning entirely. Now to neglect emotive meaning serves to foster serious confusions, as I have previously intimated; so I have sought to make up for the inadequacy of the definition by letting the restriction about dynamic usage take the place of emotive meaning. What I should do, of course, is to find a definiens whose emotive meaning, like that of "good," simply does *lead* to dynamic usage.

Why did I not do this? I answer that it is not possible if the definition is to afford us increased clarity. No two words, in the first place, have quite the same emotive meaning. The most we can hope for is a rough approximation. But if we seek for such an approximation for "good," we shall find nothing more than synonyms, such as "desirable" or "valuable"; and these are profitless because they do not clear up the connection between "good" and favorable interest. If we reject such synonyms, in favor of nonethical terms, we shall be highly misleading. For instance "this is good" has something like the meaning of "I *do* like this; do so as well." But this is certainly not accurate. For the imperative makes an appeal to the conscious efforts of the hearer. Of course he cannot like something just by trying. He must be led to like it through suggestion. Hence an ethical sentence differs from an imperative in that it enables one to make changes in a much more subtle, less fully conscious way. Note that the ethical sentence centers the hearer's attention not on his interests but on the object of interest, and thereby facilitates suggestion. Because of its subtlety, moreover, an ethical sentence readily permits counter-suggestion and leads to the give and take situation that is so characteristic of arguments about values.

Strictly speaking, then, it is impossible to define "good" in terms of favorable interest if emotive meaning is not to be distorted. Yet it is possible to say that "this is good" is *about* the favorable interest of the speaker and the hearer or hearers, and that it has a laudatory emotive meaning which fits the words for use in suggestion. This is a rough description of meaning, not a definition. But it serves the same clarifying function that a definition ordinarily does, and that, after all, is enough.

A word must be added about the moral use of "good." This differs from the above in that it is about a different kind of interest. Instead of being about what the hearer and speaker *like,* it is about a stronger sort of approval. When a person *likes* something, he is pleased when it prospers and disappointed when it does not. When a person *morally approves* of something he experiences a rich feeling of security when it prospers and is indignant or "shocked" when it does not. These are rough and inaccurate examples of the many factors which one would have to mention in distinguishing the two kinds of interest. In the moral usage, as well as in the nonmoral, "good" has an emotive meaning which adapts it to suggestion.

And now, are these considerations of any importance? Why do I stress emotive meanings in this fashion? Does the omission of them really lead people into errors? I think, indeed, that the errors resulting from such omissions are enormous. In order to see this, however, we must return to the restrictions, mentioned in Section I, with which the typical sense of "good" has been expected to comply.

[5]

The first restriction, it will be remembered, had to do with disagreement. Now there is clearly some sense in which people disagree on ethical points, but we must not rashly assume that all disagreement is modeled after the sort that occurs in the natural sciences. We must distinguish between "disagreement in belief" (typical of the sciences) and "disagreement in interest." Disagreement in belief occurs when A believes *p* and B disbelieves it. Disagreement in interest occurs when A has a favorable interest in X and when B has an unfavorable one in it. (For a full-bodied disagreement, neither party is content with the discrepancy.)

Let me give an example of disagreement in interest. A. "Let's go to a cinema tonight." B. "I don't want to do that. Let's go to the symphony." A continues to insist on the cinema, B on the symphony. This is disagreement in a perfectly conventional sense. They cannot agree on where they want to go, and each is trying to redirect the other's interest. (Note that imperatives are used in the example.)

It is disagreement in *interest* which takes place in ethics. When C says "this is good," and D says "no, it's bad," we have a case of suggestion and counter-suggestion. Each man is trying to redirect the other's interest. There obviously need be no domineering, since each may be willing to give ear to the other's influence; but each is trying to move the other none the less. It is in this sense that they disagree. Those who argue that certain interest theories make no provision for disagreement have been misled, I believe, simply because the traditional theories, in leaving out emotive meaning, give the impression that ethical judgments are used descriptively only; and of course when judgments are used purely descriptively, the only disagreement that can arise is disagreement *in belief*. Such disagreement may be disagreement in belief *about* interests, but this is not the same as disagreement *in* interest. My definition does not provide for disagreement in belief about interests any more than does Hobbes'; but that is no matter, for there is no reason to believe, at least on common sense grounds, that this kind of disagreement exists. There is only disagreement *in* interest. (We shall see in a moment that disagreement in interest does not remove ethics from sober argument—that this kind of disagreement may often be resolved through empirical means.)

The second restriction, about "magnetism," or the connection between goodness and actions, requires only a word. This rules out only those interest theories that do *not* include the interest of the speaker in defining "good." My account does include the speaker's interest, hence is immune.

The third restriction, about the empirical method, may be met in a way that springs naturally from the above account of disagreement. Let us put the question in this way: When two people disagree over an ethical matter, can they completely resolve the disagreement through empirical considerations, assuming that each applies the empirical method exhaustively, consistently, and without error?

I answer that sometimes they can and sometimes they cannot, and that at any rate, even when they can, the relation between empirical knowledge and ethical judgments is quite different from the one that traditional interest theories seem to imply.

This can best be seen from an analogy. Let us return to the example where A and B could not agree on a cinema or a symphony. The example differed from an ethical argument in that imperatives were used, rather than ethical judgments, but was analogous to the extent that each person was endeavoring to modify the other's interest. Now how would these people argue the case, assuming that they were too intelligent just to shout at one another?

Clearly, they would give "reasons" to support their imperatives. A might say, "but you know, Garbo is at the Bijou." His hope is that B, who admires Garbo, will acquire a desire to go to the cinema when he knows what film will be there. B may counter, "but Toscanini is guest conductor tonight, in an all-Beethoven program." And so on. Each supports his imperative (*"let's* do so and so") by reasons which may be empirically established.

To generalize from this: disagreement in interest may be rooted to disagreement in belief. That is to say, people who disagree in interest would often cease to do so if they knew the precise nature and consequences of the object of their interest. To this extent disagreement in interest may be resolved by securing agreement in belief, which in turn may be secured empirically.

This generalization holds for ethics. If A and B, instead of using imperatives, had said, respectively, "it would be *better* to go to the cinema," and "it would be better to go to the symphony," the reasons which they would advance would be roughly the same. They would each give a more thorough account of the object of interest, with the purpose of completing the redirection of interest which was begun by the suggestive force of the ethical sentence. On the whole, of course, the suggestive force of the ethical statement merely exerts enough pressure to start such trains of reasons, since the reasons are much more essential in resolving disagreement in interest than the persuasive effect of the ethical judgment itself.

Thus the empirical method is relevant to ethics simply because our knowledge of the world is a determining factor to our interests. But note that empirical facts are not inductive grounds from which the ethical judgment problematically follows. (This is what traditional interest theories imply.) If someone said "close the door," and added the reason "we'll catch cold," the latter would scarcely be called an inductive ground of the former. Now imperatives are related to the reasons which support them in the same way that ethical judgments are related to reasons.

Is the empirical method *sufficient* for attaining ethical agreement? Clearly not. For empirical knowledge resolves disagreement in interest only to the extent that such disagreement is rooted in disagreement in belief. Not all disagreement in interest is of this sort. For instance: A is of a sympathetic nature and B is not. They are arguing about whether a public dole would be good. Suppose that they discovered all the consequences of the dole. Is it not possible, even so, that A will say that it is good and B that it is bad? The disagreement in interest may arise not from limited factual knowledge but simply from A's sympathy and B's coldness. Or again, suppose in the above argument that A was poor and unemployed and that B was rich. Here again the disagreement might not be due to different factual knowledge. It would be due to the different social positions of the men, together with their predominant self-interest.

When ethical disagreement is not rooted in disagreement in belief, is there *any* method by which it may be settled? If one means by "method" a *rational* method, then there is no method. But in any case there is a "way." Let us consider the above example again, where disagreement was due to A's sympathy and B's coldness. Must they end by saying, "well, it's just a matter of our having different temperaments"? Not necessarily. A, for instance, may try to *change* the temperament of his opponent. He may pour out his enthusiasms in such a moving way— present the sufferings of the poor with such appeal—that he will lead his opponent to see life through different eyes. He may build up by the contagion of his feelings an influence which will modify B's temperament and create in him a sympathy for the poor which did not previously exist. This is often the only way to obtain ethical agreement, if there is any way at all. It is persuasive, not empirical or rational; but that is no reason for neglecting it. There is no reason to scorn it, either, for it is only by such means that our personalities are able to grow, through our contact with others.

The point I wish to stress, however, is simply that the empirical method is instrumental to ethical agreement only to the extent that disagreement in interest is rooted in disagreement in belief. There is little reason to believe that all disagreements are of this sort. Hence the empirical method is not sufficient for ethics. In any case, ethics is not psychology, since psychology does not endeavor to *direct* our interests; it discovers facts about the ways in which interests are or can be directed, but that is quite another matter.

To summarize this section: my analysis of ethical judgments meets the three requirements for the typical sense of "good" that were mentioned in Section I. The traditional interest theories fail to meet these requirements simply because they neglect emotive meaning. This neglect leads them to neglect dynamic usage, and the sort of disagreement that results from such usage, together with the method of resolving the disagreement. I may add that my analysis answers Moore's objection about the open question. Whatever scientifically knowable properties a thing may have, it *is* always open to question whether a thing having these (enumerated) qualities is good. For to ask whether it is good is to ask for *influence*. And whatever I may know about an object, I can still ask, quite pertinently, to be influenced with regard to my interest in it.

[6]

And now, have I really pointed out the "typical" sense of "good"?

I suppose that many will still say "no," claiming that I have simply failed to set down *enough* requirements that this sense must meet, and that my analysis, like all others given in terms of interest, is a way of begging the issue. They will say: "When we ask 'is X good?' we don't want mere influence, mere advice. We decidedly don't want to be influenced through persuasion, nor are we fully content when the influence is supported by a wide scientific knowledge of X. The answer to our question will, of course, modify our interests. But this is only because a unique sort of truth will be revealed to us—a truth that must be apprehended a priori. We want our interests to be guided by this truth and by nothing else. To substitute for this special truth mere emotive meaning and mere factual truth is to conceal from us the very object of our search."

I can only answer that I do not understand. What is this truth to be *about*? For I recollect no Platonic Idea, nor do I know what to *try* to recollect. I find no indefinable property nor do I know what to look for. And the "self-evident" deliverances of reason, which so many philosophers have mentioned, seem on examination to be deliverances of their respective reasons only (if of anyone's) and not of mine.

I strongly suspect, indeed, that any sense of "good" which is expected both to unite itself in synthetic a priori fashion with other concepts and to influence interests as well, is really a great confusion. I extract from this meaning the power of influence alone, which I find the only intelligible part. If the rest is confusion, however, then it certainly deserves more than the shrug of one's shoulders. What I should like to do is to *account* for the confusion—to examine the psychological needs which have given rise to it and show how these needs may be satisfied in another way. This is *the* problem, if confusion is to be stopped at its source. But it is an enormous problem and my reflections on it, which are at present worked out only roughly, must be reserved until some later time.

I may add that if "X is good" has the meaning that I ascribe to it, then it is not a judgment that professional philosophers and only professional philosophers are qualified to make. To the extent that ethics predicates the ethical terms of anything, rather than explains their meaning, it becomes more than a purely intellectual study. Ethical judgments are social instruments. They are used in a cooperative enterprise that leads to a mutual readjustment of human interests. Philosophers have a part in this; but so too do all men.

'OUGHT' AND IMPERATIVES / *R. M. Hare*

1. SINCE a large part of my argument hinges on the assumption, hitherto not fully defended, that value-judgments, if they are action-guiding, must be held to entail imperatives, and since this assumption may very well be questioned, it is time to examine it. It might be held, for example, that I can without contradiction say 'You ought to do A, but don't', and that therefore there can be no question of entailment; entailment in any case is a very strong word, and though many might be found to agree that value-judgments are action-guiding in some sense, it might be held that they are action-guiding only in the sense in which even plain judgments of fact may be action-guiding. For example, if I say 'The train is just about to depart', this may guide a person who wants to catch the train to take his seat; or, to take a moral case, if I say to a person who is thinking of giving some money to a friend supposedly in distress, 'The story he has just told you is quite untrue', this may guide him to make a different moral decision from that which he would otherwise have made. And similarly it might be held that value-judgments are action-guiding in no stronger sense than these statements of fact. It might be urged that, just as the statement that the train is going

From R. M. Hare, " 'Ought' and Imperatives," The Language of Morals (Oxford: The Clarendon Press, 1952), pp. 163–179. Reprinted by permission of the Clarendon Press, Oxford.

to depart has no bearing upon the practical problems of someone who does not want to catch the train, and just as, if the man who is thinking of giving money to his friend does not recognize that the truth or otherwise of his friend's story has any bearing on the question, it may not affect his decision, so, if a man has no intention of doing what he ought, to tell him that he ought to do something may not be accepted by him as a reason for doing it. I have put as forcibly as possible this objection, which strikes at the root of my whole argument. The objection alleges, in brief, that 'ought'-sentences are not imperatives, neither do they entail imperatives without the addition of an imperative premiss. In answer to this, I have to show that 'ought'-sentences, at any rate in some of their uses, do entail imperatives.

It is necessary first to recall . . . the evaluative and descriptive forces of value-judgments. We noticed that it is possible for people who have acquired very stable standards of values to come to treat value-judgments more and more as purely descriptive, and to let their evaluative force get weaker. The limit of this process is reached when, as we described it, the value-judgment 'gets into inverted commas', and the standard becomes completely 'ossified'. Thus it is possible to say 'You ought to go and call on the So-and-sos' meaning by it no value-judgment at all, but simply the descriptive judgment that such an action is required in order to conform to a standard which people in general, or a certain kind of people not specified but well understood, accept. And certainly, if this is the way in which an 'ought'-sentence is being used, it does not entail an imperative; we can certainly say without contradiction 'You ought to go and call on the So-and-sos, but don't'. I do not wish to claim that all 'ought'-sentences entail imperatives, but only that they do so when they are being used evaluatively. It will subsequently become apparent that I am making this true by definition; for I should not say that an 'ought'-sentence *was* being used evaluatively, unless imperatives were held to follow from it; but more of that later.

Thus one answer which we can make to the objection is that the cases which appear to support it are not genuine value-judgments. In the example quoted, if a man has no intention of doing what he ought, and if, therefore, telling him what he ought to do is not taken by him as entailing an imperative, that merely shows that, in so far as he accepts that he ought to do so-and-so (and of course *no* premiss enables a conclusion to be drawn unless it is accepted), he accepts it only in a non-evaluative, inverted-commas sense, as meaning that so-and-so falls within a class of actions which is generally held (but not by him) to be obligatory in the evaluative, imperative-entailing sense. This is an answer which disposes of some awkward cases, but which will not be accepted as a complete answer unless we extend its scope considerably. For it may be held that there are some genuine value-judgments which do not entail imperatives.

2. Let us recall something else. . . . Practical principles, if they are accepted sufficiently long and unquestioningly, come to have the force of intuition. Thus our ultimate moral principles can become so completely accepted by us, that we treat them, not as universal imperatives, but as matters of fact; they have the same obstinate indubitability. And there is indeed a matter of fact to which it is very easy for us to take them as referring, namely, what we call our 'sense of obligation.' This is a concept that now requires investigation.

It is easy to see how, if we have been brought up from our earliest years in obedience to a principle, the thought of not obeying it becomes abhorrent to us. If we fail to obey it, we suffer remorse; when we do obey it, we feel at ease with ourselves. These feelings are reinforced by all those factors which psychologists have listed;[1] and the total result is what is generally called a feeling of obligation. It is a *fact* that we have this feeling of obligation—different people in different degrees, and with different contents. Judgments that I have a feeling of obligation to do X or Y are statements of empirical fact. This is not the place to argue about their interpretation; it is no doubt possible to dispute whether sentences like 'A is suffering from remorse' or 'B feels it is his duty to do Y' are reports of private mental events or are to be interpreted behaviouristically; but

---

[1] Cf. J. C. Flugel, *Man, Morals and Society*, especially Ch. III.

such controversies do not here concern us. Here it is important to point out a fact which has been singularly ignored by some moralists, that to say of someone that he has a feeling of obligation is not the same as to say that he has an obligation. To say the former is to make a statement of psychological fact; to say the latter is to make a value-judgment. A man who has been brought up in an Army family, but has become affected by pacifism, may well say 'I have a strong feeling that I ought to fight for my country, but I wonder whether I really ought'. Similarly, a Japanese brought up in accordance with Bushido might say 'I have a strong feeling that I ought to torture this prisoner in order to extract information which will be to my Emperor's advantage; but ought I really to do so?'

The confusion between psychological statements about a feeling or sense of obligation and value-judgments about obligation itself is not confined to professional philosophers. The ordinary man so very rarely questions the principles in which he has been brought up, that he is usually willing, whenever he has a feeling that he ought to do X, to say on this ground alone that he ought to do X; and therefore he often gives voice to this feeling by saying 'I ought to do X'. This sentence is not a statement that he has the feeling; it is a value-judgment made as a result of having the feeling. For those, however, who have not studied the logical behaviour of value-judgments, and have not reflected on such examples as those of the pacifist and the Japanese just given, it is easy to take this remark as a statement of fact to the effect that he has the feeling, or to confuse it in meaning with this statement. But anyone, except a professional philosopher maintaining at all costs a moral sense theory, could be got to see that the meaning is not the same, by being asked 'Wouldn't it be possible for you to feel just like that, although you really oughtn't to do X?' or 'Mightn't you feel like that and be wrong?'

The confusion, however, goes deeper than this. We have seen that there is a conscious inverted-commas use of value-words in which, for example, 'I ought to do X' becomes roughly equivalent to 'X is required in order to conform to a standard which people in general accept'. But it is also possible to use the

word 'ought' and other value-words, as it were, unconsciously in
inverted commas; for the standard which people in general accept may also be the standard which one has been brought up to
accept oneself, and therefore not only does one refer to this
standard by saying 'I ought to do X', but one has feelings of
obligation to conform to the standard.

It is then possible to treat 'I ought to do X' as a confused
mixture of three judgments.

(1) 'X is required in order to conform to the standard
which people generally accept' (statement of sociological fact);

(2) 'I have a feeling that I ought to do X' (statement of
psychological fact);

(3) 'I ought to do X' (value-judgment).

Even this tripartite division conceals the complexity of the
meaning of such sentences; for each of the three elements is
itself complex and can be taken in different senses. But even if
we confine ourselves to the three elements just given, it is usually impossible for an ordinary person, untrained in logical subtleties, to ask or to answer the question 'Which of these three
judgments are you making, just (1), or (1) and (2), or all
three, or some other combination?' The situation is very similar
to that of the scientist who is asked by the logician 'Is your statement that phosphorus melts at 44°C. analytic or synthetic;
if you found a substance which was in other respects just like
phosphorus, but which melted at another temperature, would
you say "It isn't really phosphorus" or would you say "Then after
all some phosphorus melts at other temperatures"?' [2] The scientist might well, as Mr. A. G. N. Flew has pointed out to me,
answer 'I don't know; I haven't yet come across the case which
would make me decide this question; I have got better things to
worry about.' Similarly, the ordinary person, making moral decisions on the basis of his accepted principles, very rarely has to
ask himself the question that we have just asked. So long as his
value-judgments correspond with the accepted standards, and
with his own feelings, he does not have to decide which he is

[2] See G. H. von Wright, *Logical Problem of Induction*, Ch. III.

saying, because, as we might put it, all three are as yet for him materially equivalent; that is to say, no occasion arises for saying one which is not also an occasion for saying the other two. He therefore does not ask himself 'As I am using the word "ought", are the sentences "I ought to do what I feel I ought" and "I ought to do what everybody would say I ought" analytic or synthetic?' It is the crucial case that makes him answer such a question; and in morals the crucial case comes when we are wondering whether to make a value-decision which is in disagreement with the accepted standards or with our own moral feelings—such cases as I have cited. It is these cases that really reveal the difference in meaning between the three judgments that I have listed.

My answer to the objection then is, that cases which are alleged to be value-judgments not entailing imperatives will always on examination be found to be cases where what is meant is not of type (3) above, but of type (1) or (2) or a mixture of both. This contention is, of course, impossible to prove or even to render plausible, unless we know when we are to count a judgment as of type (3); but I propose to get over this difficulty in the only possible way, by making it a matter of definition. I propose to say that the test, whether someone is using the judgment 'I ought to do X' as a value-judgment or not is, 'Does he or does he not recognize that if he assents to the judgment, he must also assent to the command "Let me do X"?' Thus I am not here claiming to prove anything substantial about the way in which we use language; I am merely suggesting a terminology which, if applied to the study of moral language, will, I am satisfied, prove illuminating. The substantial part of what I am trying to show is this, that, in the sense of 'value-judgment' just defined, we do make value-judgments, and that they are the class of sentences containing value-words which is of primary interest to the logician who studies moral language. Since what we are discussing is the logic of moral language and not that tangled subject known as moral psychology, I shall not here inquire farther into the fascinating problem, discussed by Aristotle, of *akrasia* or 'weakness of will'[3]—the problem presented by the person who thinks, or professes to think, that he ought to do something, but does not do it. The logical distinctions which I have been making shed considerable light on this question: but much more needs to be said, chiefly by way of a more thorough analysis of the phrase 'thinks that he ought'. For if we interpret my definition strictly, and take it in conjunction with . . . the criteria for 'sincerely assenting to a command', the familiar 'Socratic paradox' arises, in that it becomes analytic to say that everyone always[4] does what he thinks he ought to (in the evaluative sense). And this, to put Aristotle's objection in modern dress, is not how we use the word 'think'. The trouble arises because our criteria, in ordinary speech, for saying 'He thinks he ought' are exceedingly elastic. If a person does not do something, but the omission is accompanied by feelings of guilt, &c., we normally say that he has not done what he thinks he ought. It is therefore necessary to qualify the criterion given above for 'sincerely assenting to a command', and to admit that there are degrees of sincere assent, not all of which involve actually obeying the command. But the detailed analysis of this problem requires much more space than I can give it here, and must wait for another occasion.

3. The best way of establishing the primary logical interest of the evaluative sense of 'ought' is to show that, but for the existence of this sense, none of the familiar troubles generated by the word would arise. For of the three possible paraphrases of 'I ought to do X' given on p. 107, the first two are statements of fact. This is because, if they are expanded, it will be found that the word 'ought' in them always occurs in inverted commas or inside a subordinate clause beginning with 'that'. Thus (1) might be further paraphrased 'There is a principle of conduct which people generally accept, which says 'One ought to do X in circumstances of a certain kind; and I am now in circumstances of that kind'. Similarly, (2) might be further paraphrased 'The judgment "I ought to do X" evokes in me a

---

3 *Nicomachean Ethics*, VII. 1 ff.
4 Strictly, "always, if physically and psychologically able."

feeling of conviction' or 'I find myself unable to doubt the judgment "I ought to do X" ' (though the latter paraphrase is a good
deal too strong; for not all feelings are irresistible; there is indeed an infinite gradation from vague uneasy stirrings of conscience to what are often called 'moral intuitions'). Now the
fact, that when (1) and (2) are expanded the original judgment
which they paraphrase occurs within them inside inverted commas, shows that there must be some sense of that original judgment which is not exhausted by (1) and (2); for if there were
not, the sentence in the inverted commas would have in its turn
to be paraphrased by (1) or (2), and we should be involved in
an infinite regress. In the case of (1), I do not know any way of
getting over this difficulty; in the case of (2), it can be got over
temporarily by substituting for (2) some such paraphrase as 'I
have a certain recognizable feeling'. But the device is only temporary; for if we are asked what this feeling is, or how we recognize it, the reply can only be 'It is the feeling called "a feeling of
obligation"; it is the feeling you usually have when you say, and
mean "I ought to do so-and-so" '.

This means that neither (1) nor (2) can give the primary sense of 'I ought to do X'. Now let us suppose (as is not
the case) that (3) generates none of the logical puzzles of the
kind that we have been discussing; let us suppose, that is to say,
that (3) can be analysed naturalistically. If this were so, then
these puzzles would not arise in the cases of (1) or (2) either;
for since, besides the expression in inverted commas, there is
nothing else in the expansions of (1) and (2) that cannot be
analysed naturalistically, it would be possible to effect a completely naturalistic analysis of all uses of 'ought', and thus of
'good'. The fact that this is not possible is entirely due to the
intractably evaluative character of (3). It is due ultimately to
the impossibility of deriving imperatives from indicatives; for
(3), by definition, entails at least one imperative; but if (3)
were analysable naturalistically, this would mean that it was
equivalent to a series of indicative sentences; and this would
constitute a breach of the principle established. Thus it is this
fact, that in some of its uses 'ought' is used evaluatively (i.e. as

entailing at least one imperative) that makes a naturalistic analysis impossible, and hence generates all the difficulties that we have been considering. A logician who neglects these uses will make his task easy, at the cost of missing the essential purpose of moral language.

. . . For all the words discussed [earlier] have it as their distinctive function either to commend or in some other way to guide choices or actions; and it is this essential feature which defies any analysis in purely factual terms. But to guide choices or actions, a moral judgment has to be such that if a person assents to it, he must assent to some imperative sentence derivable from it; in other words, if a person does not assent to some such imperative sentence, that is knock-down evidence that he does not assent to the moral judgment in an evaluative sense—though of course he may assent to it in some other sense (e.g. one of those I have mentioned). This is true by my definition of the word evaluative. But to say this is to say that if he professes to assent to the moral judgment, but does not assent to the imperative, he must have misunderstood the moral judgment (by taking it to be non-evaluative, though the speaker intended it to be evaluative). We are therefore clearly entitled to say that the moral judgment entails the imperative; for to say that one judgment entails another is simply to say that you cannot assent to the first and dissent from the second unless you have misunderstood one or the other; and this 'cannot' is a logical 'cannot'—if someone assents to the first and not to the second, this is in itself a sufficient criterion for saying that he has misunderstood the meaning of one or the other. Thus to say that moral judgments guide actions, and to say that they entail imperatives, comes to much the same thing.

I do not in the least wish to deny that moral judgments are sometimes used non-evaluatively, in my sense. All I wish to assert is that they are sometimes used evaluatively, and that it is this use which gives them the special characteristics to which I have drawn attention; and that, if it were not for this use, it would be impossible to give a meaning to the other uses; and also that, if it were not for the logical difficulties connected with the evaluative use, the other uses could be analysed naturalistically. Ethics, as a special branch of logic, owes its existence to the function of moral judgments as a guide in answering questions of the form 'What shall I do?'

4. I am now in a position to answer an objection which may have occurred to some readers. Writers on ethics often condemn 'naturalism' or some related fallacy in others, only to commit it themselves in a subtler form. It may be alleged that I have done this. I have suggested that the term 'naturalist' should be reserved for such ethical theories as are open to refutation on lines similar to those marked out by Professor Moore. We must therefore ask whether any analogous refutation of my own theory can be constructed. Now it is true that I am not suggesting that moral judgments can be deduced from any statements of fact. In particular I am not suggesting the adoption of definitions of value-terms of the sort which Moore mistakenly attributed to Kant. Moore accused Kant of saying that 'This ought to be' means 'This is commanded'.[5] This definition would be naturalistic; for 'A is commanded' is a statement of fact; it is expansible into 'Someone [it is not disclosed who] has said "Do A" '. The fact that the imperative is in inverted commas prevents it affecting the mood of the complete sentence. Needless to say, I am not suggesting any such equivalence, either for 'good' or for 'ought' or for any other value-word, except perhaps when they are used in what I have called an 'inverted-commas' sense, or in some other purely descriptive way. But it might nevertheless be said that according to my treatment of moral judgments certain sentences would become analytic which in ordinary usage are not analytic—and this would be very like Moore's refutation. For example, consider sentences like the Psalmist's

Eschew evil and do good,[6]

or the line of John Wesley's hymn

In duty's path go on.[7]

5 *Principia Ethica*, pp. 127–128.
6 Ps. xxxiv, v. 14.
7 *Hymns Ancient and Modern* (1950), no. 310.

On my theory these would, it might be alleged, become analytic; for from 'A is evil' is deducible the imperative sentence 'Eschew A', and from 'Path P is the path of duty' is deducible the imperative sentence 'Go on in path P'.

Now it must be noticed that such sentences as those quoted are expansible into sentences in which a value-judgment occurs in a subordinate clause. Thus if, instead of the archaic 'Eschew evil' we write 'Do not do what is evil', this can be expanded into 'For all X, if X is evil, do not do X'. For this instruction to be applied, it is necessary that we should conjoin it with a minor premiss 'A is evil', and from the two premisses conclude 'Do not do A'. For this reasoning to be helpful, it is necessary that the minor premiss 'A is evil' should be a statement of fact; there must be a criterion for telling unambiguously whether it is true or false. This means that in this premiss the word 'evil' must have a descriptive meaning (whatever further meaning it may have). But if the reasoning is to be valid, the word 'evil' in the major premiss must have the same meaning as in the minor; there also, therefore, it must have a descriptive meaning. Now it is this descriptive content which prevents the major premiss being analytic. Sentences of the sort we are discussing are normally used by people who have firmly established value-standards, and whose value-words have, therefore, a large element of descriptive meaning. In the sentence 'Do not do what is evil', the evaluative content of 'evil' is for the moment neglected; the speaker, as it were, lets his support of the standard slip for a moment, only in order to ram it back into place with the imperative verb. This is a first-class exercise in the maintenance of our standards, and that is why it is so much in place in hymns and psalms. But it can only be performed by those who are in no doubt as to what the standard is.

Contrast with these cases others which are superficially similar. Suppose that I am asked 'What shall I do?' and answer 'Do whatever is best' or 'Do what you ought to do'. In most contexts such answers would be regarded as unhelpful. It would be as if a policeman were asked 'Where shall I park my car?' and replied 'Wherever it is legitimate to park it'. I am asked by the speaker to give definite advice as to what he is to do; he asks me, just because he does not know what standard to apply in his case. If, therefore, I reply by telling him to conform to some standard as to whose provisions he is quite in the dark, I do not give him any useful advice. Thus in such a context the sentence 'Do whatever is best' really *is* analytic; for because the standard is assumed to be unknown, 'best' has no descriptive meaning.

Thus my account of the meaning of value-words is not naturalistic; it does not result in sentences becoming analytic which are not so in our ordinary usage. Rather it shows, by doing full justice to both the descriptive and the evaluative elements in the meaning of value-words, how it is that they play in our ordinary usage the role that they do play. A somewhat similar difficulty is presented by Satan's famous paradox 'Evil be thou my good'. This yields to the same type of analysis, but for reasons of space I am compelled to leave the reader to unravel the problem himself.

5. It may be asked at this point 'Are you not assimilating moral judgments too much to the ordinary universal imperatives that exist in most languages?' It has indeed been objected to all imperative analyses of moral judgments, that they would make a moral judgment like 'You ought not to smoke (in this compartment)' the equivalent of the universal imperative 'No Smoking'. And they are clearly not equivalent, though both, according to the theory which I have been advocating, entail 'Do not smoke'. It is therefore necessary to state what it is that distinguishes 'You ought not to smoke' from 'No smoking'. I have already touched on this problem, but it requires further discussion.

The first thing to notice about 'No smoking' is that it is not a proper universal, because it implicitly refers to an individual; it is short for 'Do not ever smoke in *this* compartment'. The moral judgment 'You ought not to smoke in this compartment' also contains references to individuals; for the pronouns 'you' and 'this' occur in it. But . . . this is not the end of the matter. The moral judgment 'You ought not to smoke in this compartment' has to be made with some general moral principle in

mind, and its purpose must be either to invoke that general principle or to point to an instance of its application. The principle
might be 'One ought never to smoke in compartments in which
there are young children' or 'One ought never to smoke in compartments in which there is a "No Smoking" notice'. It is not
always easy to elicit just what the principle is; but it always
makes sense to ask what it is. The speaker cannot deny that
there is any such principle. The same point might be put another
way by saying that if we make a particular moral judgment, we
can always be asked to support it by reasons; the reasons consist
in the general principles under which the moral judgment is to
be subsumed. Thus the particular moral judgment 'You ought
not to smoke in this compartment' depends on a proper universal, even though it is not itself one. But this is not true of the
imperative 'Do not ever smoke in this compartment'. This in-
vokes no more general principle; it is itself as general as it requires to be, and this is not general enough to make it a proper
universal.

The difference in universality between 'Do not ever
smoke in this compartment' and 'You ought not to smoke in this
compartment' may be brought out in the following way. Suppose
that I say to someone 'You ought not to smoke in this compartment', and there are children in the compartment. The person
addressed is likely, if he wonders why I have said that he ought
not to smoke, to look around, notice the children, and so understand the reason. But suppose that, having ascertained everything that is to be ascertained about the compartment, he then
says 'All right; I'll go next door; there's another compartment
there just as good; in fact it is exactly like this one, and there are
children in it too'. I should think if he said this that he did not
understand the function of the word 'ought'; for 'ought' always
refers to some general principle; and if the next compartment is
really exactly like this one, every principle that is applicable to
this one must be applicable to the other. I might therefore reply
'But look here, if you oughtn't to smoke in this compartment,
and the other compartment is just like this one, has the same
sort of occupants, the same notices on the windows, &c., then

obviously you oughtn't to smoke in that one either'. On the other hand, when the Railway Executive is making the momentous decision, on which compartments to put notices saying 'No Smoking', nobody says 'Look here! You've put a notice on this compartment, so you must put one on the one next to it, because it's exactly like it'. This is because 'No Smoking' does not refer to a universal principle of which this compartment is an instance.

It is, in fact, almost impossible to frame a proper universal in the imperative mood. Suppose that we try to do this by generalizing the sentence 'Do not ever smoke in this compartment'. First we eliminate the implicit 'you' by writing 'No one is ever to smoke in this compartment'. We then have to eliminate the 'this'. A step towards this is taken by writing 'No one is ever to smoke in any compartment of British Railways'. But we still have left here the proper name 'British Railways'. We can only achieve a proper universal by excluding all proper names, for example by writing 'No one is ever to smoke in any railway compartment anywhere'. This is a proper universal; but it is a sentence which no one could ever have occasion to utter. Commands are always addressed to someone or to some individual set (not class) of people. It is not clear what could be meant by the sentence just quoted, unless it were a *moral* injunction or other value-judgment. Suppose that we imagine God issuing such a command. Then it becomes at once like the Ten Commandments in form. Historically speaking 'Honour thy father and thy mother' is supposed to have been said, not to everyone in general, but only to members of the chosen people, just as 'Render to no man evil for evil' was addressed to Christ's disciples, not to the world at large—though He intended that all men should become His disciples. But suppose that this were not so; suppose that 'Render to no man evil for evil' were addressed literally to the unlimited class 'every man'. Should we not say that it had become equivalent in meaning to the value-judgment 'One ought to render to no man evil for evil'? Similarly, a proverbial expression like 'Let sleeping dogs lie' may without much of a jolt be paraphrased by the (prudential) value-judgment 'One ought to let sleeping dogs lie'.

On the other hand, ordinary so-called universal imperatives like 'No Smoking' are distinguished from value-judgments by not being properly universal. We are thus able to discriminate between these two kinds of sentence, without in the least abandoning anything that I have said about the relation between value-judgments and imperatives. For both the complete universal and the incomplete entail the singular: 'Do not ever smoke in this compartment' entails 'Do not (now) smoke in this compartment'; and so does 'You ought not to smoke in this compartment', if it is used evaluatively. But the latter also entails, as the former does not, 'No one ought to smoke in any compartment exactly like this one', and this in its turn entails 'Do not smoke in any compartment exactly like this one'.

These considerations alone, however, would not be sufficient to account altogether for the complete difference in 'feel' between 'You ought not' and 'Do not ever'. This is reinforced by two other factors. The first has already been alluded to; the complete universality of the moral judgment means that we cannot 'get away from it'; and therefore its acceptance is a much more serious matter than the acceptance of an imperative from whose range of application we can escape. This would explain why imperatives such as those laws of a State, which are of very general application, and therefore very difficult to escape from, have a 'feel' much more akin to moral judgments than have the regulations of the Railway Executive. But a more important additional factor is that, partly because of their complete universality, moral principles have become so entrenched in our minds—in the ways already described—that they have acquired a quasi-factual character, and are indeed sometimes used non-evaluatively as statements of fact and nothing else, as we have seen. None of this is true of imperatives like 'No Smoking'; and this in itself would be quite enough to explain the difference in 'feel' between the two kinds of sentence. Since, however, I do not wish to deny that there are non-evaluative uses of moral judgments, but only to assert that there are evaluative uses, this difference in 'feel' in no way destroys my argument. It would indeed be absurd to pretend that 'No Smoking' is in all respects like 'You ought not to smoke'; I have been maintaining only that it is like it in one respect, that both entail singular imperatives such as 'Do not smoke (now)'.

'GOOD' / *P. H. Nowell-Smith*

[1]

'Good' in the Context of Choice

WE have seen that when 'good' is used in the context of choice there can be no logical gap between deciding that something is the best or better than its rivals and choosing it. This does not imply that there can be no discrepancy between the decision which is, on the face of it, not a performance of any kind but a judgment, and the choice; but it does imply that if there is such a discrepancy a special reason must be given for it. And we must now consider the role of such expressions as 'because it is a good one' and 'because it is the best' when they are used to explain why a man chose the thing he did.

The answer to the question 'Why did you choose that car?' might be a statement of fact ('because it has more leg-room') or an A-sentence ('because it is more comfortable'); and I have already discussed the contextual background in which such answers can be given and taken as logically complete explanations. In each case the car must have some A-

From P. H. Nowell-Smith, "Good," Ethics (Harmondsworth: Penguin Books, 1954), pp. 160–182. Reprinted by permission of the publisher.

property and some ordinary, empirical properties on which its A-property depends. While the factual answer says what the empirical properties are and contextually implies an A-property without specifying what it is, the A-sentence does the reverse. And each answer implies a pro-attitude towards the A-property concerned; otherwise it would not be an answer to the question.

The answer 'because it is the best' functions in a similar way, but with certain important differences. In the first place it does not just imply a pro-attitude; it expresses it. But it does not only do this. If this were all I wanted to do I should have to say 'because I happen to like it more than the others'. It contextually implies that I have reasons for my choice; but it does not say what they are and therefore does not explain my choice.

We are tempted to say that it gives the best possible reason. After all, what better reason could there be for choosing a car than the fact that it was the best available or the best that I could afford? What better reason could there be for doing anything than the belief that it is the best thing to do?

The trouble is that the reason is *too* good. It is like saying that I was frightened because it was a terrifying experience; and, as an explanation, it operates in much the same way. Just as 'because it was terrifying' shows that my fear was not an unusual one and contextually implies that the object had certain unspecified properties by which people are usually frightened, so 'because it was the best' shows that my choice was no passing whim, that it was considered more or less carefully, that the object had certain unspecified 'good-making' properties, and that my choice was not a peculiar one. Any of these contextual implications could be expressly withdrawn, especially, as we shall see, the last; but in default of such withdrawal my audience would be entitled to assume them. Just as a G-sentence showed more plainly than an A-sentence that advice was being given but was less explicit about the reasons, so 'because it was the best' shows more plainly that I was choosing but says even less about the reasons.

In fact it says nothing about them at all; it only implies that I have reasons. The goodness of something is not one of the properties for which I choose it. If it were, it would make sense to ask why its superior goodness was a reason for choosing it. To ask a man who chose a car because it was faster or more economical or had more leg-room why he chose it is to display ignorance of people's purchasing habits; to say to him "I know you thought it the best car; but why did you choose it?" is logically odd.

The same logical ties that bind goodness so closely to choosing bind it also to activities that are akin to choosing. A man who says that he voted for a certain proposal because he thought it good has not explained why he voted for it; he has merely guarded himself against accusations of flippancy, irresponsibility or indulging in complicated machinations. And it is logically odd to say 'I think it is an excellent proposal, but I shan't vote for it'. As we saw, reasons could be given for this discrepancy, and the logical nexus between thinking good and voting comes out in the fact that we should feel entitled to infer that there must be a special reason. To call something good is, in a way, already to vote for it, to side with it, to let others know where I stand. But it does more than this; it implies that I have reasons for casting my vote as I do.

'Good' in the Context of Advice

The considerations that apply to 'good' in the context of choice apply equally in the context of advice. And here again the subjectivist is right in connecting 'this is good' with the pro-attitude of the speaker. There is the same sort of absurdity in 'This is good, but I don't advise you to do it' as there is in 'This is the best course; but shall I take it?'. In the latter case the speaker both expresses a decision as to how he should act and in the same breath asks if he should; and in the former he gives advice and in the same breath retracts it. It would be equally odd if the hearer were to say "You have told me that it is the best course to take; but do you advise me to take it?".

The differences in the use of 'good' in advice and choice are due to the fact that the problem to be solved is now someone else's. The adviser is not making up his mind what to do, but helping someone else to make up his mind. And this difference brings with it another. The relevant pro-attitude is that of the audience. But in other respects the contextual implications are the same. To tell someone that something is the best thing for him to do is to advise him to do it, but not irresponsibly. The speaker implies that he has good reasons for his advice, that he knows what the problem is and that his advice is relevant. The same predictive and causal elements are present as in the case of A-sentences; and advice may, as before, be given disingenuously, improperly, mistakenly, or unfortunately if one or other of the contextual implications is absent.

[2]

Other Uses of 'Good'

I shall discuss the other uses of 'good' in the order in which they seem to diverge more and more from the fundamental use, which is to express or explain a preference.

(*a*) *Praising and applauding.* Like choosing, these are performances, not statements; and, although in primary uses they do express the speaker's pro-attitude, they have other contextual implications which will be examined later. They can be done with or without words; but the gestures, handclapping and the like, which are used for praising have conventional, symbolic meanings. They mean what they do in the way that words mean, not in the way that clouds mean rain or cobras in the garden mean trouble. Virtue-words are words of praise; and relatively specific words like 'brave', 'honest', and 'generous' are also descriptive; for they describe a person's behaviour and predict the way in which he can be relied upon to behave in certain sorts of situation. They both praise and give the reason, what the praise is *for*. But 'good' does not do this. In cases where there are recognized standards that a man must reach to be worthy of praise they contextually imply that he has reached those standards; but they do not say what the standards are. 'Because it is a good one' does not explain why I praise something; but it does imply that the thing has certain unspecified properties for which I praise it. My praise was not casual or capricious.

(b) *Commending.* The verb 'to commend' is used in two ways. It may mean 'entrust to the care of'; but this sense is irrelevant, since 'good' is not used to commend in this sense. In the sense in which 'good' is used for commending it is akin to praising but has a more hortatory force. To commend something to someone is to advise him to choose it. The Oxford Dictionary, as we saw, calls 'good' "the most general adjective of commendation" in English; but it goes on to add "implying the existence in a high or at least satisfactory degree of characteristic qualities which are either admirable in themselves or useful for some purpose".

The form of this definition is interesting, since it brings out the difference between the job that the word is used for and the conditions limiting its use in a way that philosophers' definitions of 'good' never do. The writer of the dictionary sees clearly that the word is used to do a job which is not 'stating' but commending and that the elements of objective fact which some philosophers insist on treating as part of its meaning are really part of the contextual background of its use. In the uses which follow this contextual background looms larger and larger, so that in some uses the word 'good' almost comes to be a descriptive word, though, as we shall see, it never quite does this and in moral contexts it can never wholly lose its gerundive force or its pro-force.

(c) *Verdicts and Appraisals.* . . . moral language is not only used for choosing and advising, but also making moral judgments, which are not decisions to do something but verdicts or appraisals of something or somebody. Now appraisals are *judgments*, not just expressions of a man's own taste or preference; and it is this point that the Consequential Property Theory tries to bring out, but in a misleading way. When we judge something to be good we always judge it to be good in respect of some property, and it is a question of empirical fact whether it has this property or not. Thus to judge a wine to be good is not just to express a preference for it—and we shall see that it need not be to do this at all—; the judgment must be backed by my belief that it has a certain bouquet, body, and flavour, and these are objective qualities, since a man who found that he disagreed markedly from all the experts on these points would admit himself to be wrong. It is an essential feature of judgments that they are made by reference to standards or criteria; but it is necessary to be extremely careful in discussing the way in which the criteria are related to the verdict or appraisal.

Let us assume for the moment that the criteria used by experts at wine-tastings, horse-shows, beauty contests, and school examinations are agreed to be the proper criteria, though this will have to be questioned later. We might be tempted to say that if the criteria for being a good X are that the X must have properties a, b, and c in some specifiable degree, then 'good X' simply means 'X which has the properties, a, b, and c in the requisite degree'. But this will not do. For it is possible to understand what 'good X' means without knowing what the criteria are. Thus, if I do not know the criteria used at Crufts I could not tell a good dog (in this sense of 'good') from a bad one or pick out the best dog from a group. But this does not mean that I cannot understand what 'good dog' means in the way that I could not understand what 'mangy dog' meant if I did not know what 'mangy' meant. For I do know that if it is a good dog it must have in a fairly high degree those properties which are mentioned in the list of criteria for judging dogs, although I do not know what these properties are or to what degree a dog must have them to rate as 'good'.

The next two uses are special cases of the appraising use.

(d) *Efficiency*. When 'good' is predicated of any object (natural or artificial, animate or inanimate) that is used for a purpose it implies the presence in a relatively high degree of those properties that the object must have to do its job. But again it would be a mistake to say that 'good knife' just *means* 'knife that is sharp, easily handled, durable, etc.'. The connection between the properties which a knife must have to be efficient and its efficiency is an empirical one. We know from experience that a knife which has not got these properties at all just won't cut and that its relative efficiency at cutting depends on the degree to which it has these properties. Nor can we even say that 'good knife' means 'knife which cuts efficiently', because we could understand what 'good' means in the expression 'good knife' without knowing what knives were for. But 'good knife' (in this sense of 'good') does mean 'knife which has those properties (whatever they are) which a knife must have if it is to do its job efficiently (whatever that is)'.

(e) *Skill.* When we call a man a good lawyer, scholar, cricketer or liar, the use is similar to the 'efficiency' use except for the fact that, since these are men, the purpose concerned is their purpose, not the purpose they are used for. Just as we could not use 'good' to imply efficiency unless we agreed about what the object concerned is for, so we could not use it to imply skill unless there was something that was agreed to constitute success at the activity concerned. But, just as we cannot say that 'good' means 'efficient' in the one sense, so we cannot say that it means 'successful' in the other. In activities involving skill there are rules for achieving success which are such that we know from experience that unless a man applies them he is unlikely to be successful. Thus, if we know the rules for success at bridge or cricket we can predict, in a very general way, what a good bridge-player or cricketer will do; and in calling a man 'good' we imply that he applies or follows the rules. This implication can, of course, be expressly withdrawn because we know that people sometimes achieve success in very unorthodox ways. But 'good' never quite loses its gerundive force and if we call a man a good cricketer without intending to imply that his methods ought to be imitated we mislead our audience.

(f) *The Descriptive Use.* Like most words, 'good' can be used to mean 'what most people would call good'. A man who uses it may not be choosing, advising, defending a choice or piece of advice, or appraising, but referring to an object which he or others would call good if they were doing one of these. Thus I may call a wine good even if I am not competent to apply the criteria, just because I have heard the experts praise it.

This use belongs to descriptive discourse because it is a question of historical fact whether people do or do not call the object good, and that is what is being asserted. It is necessarily a secondary use, since it would be impossible to use 'good' to mean 'what people call good' unless people called things good in primary ways. And 'good' is hardly ever used with this descriptive force alone. The speaker implies that he himself sides with those who call the thing good unless this implication is expressly withdrawn or obviously inadmissible in the context.

[3]

We must now consider the ways in which these uses of 'good' are connected with each other. It is clearly not an accident that the same word is used in all these different ways nor could this fact be explained in a purely historical or philological way. 'Good' is *the* Janus-word *par excellence;* it is often used to do more than one job on one occasion and the logical connections between the various jobs are what they are because the facts are what they are. It is also most emphatically an ordinary, non-technical word and it is a consequence of this that the logic of its use reflects empirical truths that hold only for the most part and admit of exceptions. For ordinary language, unlike mathematics, is not deliberately constructed by men who have a keen eye for consistency and rigour; it is not deliberately constructed at all but grows and changes in an environment in which the exceptional case can be and must be ignored. The contextual implications of any use of 'good' are many and varied and, on occasion, any of them can be withdrawn, a point which should make us suspicious of counter-examples. It is impossible to understand the actual uses of 'good' by considering artificial and exceptional situations because the logic of ordinary language does not cater for such situations.

But there is one element which seems to be common to all cases. Although a man need have no comparisons in mind when he calls something 'good', such comparisons are always implied. He must, if challenged, be able to produce examples of descriptively similar things that he would call not so good. For example, we always praise something with a certain degree of warmth which lies somewhere on a scale between mild commendation and hysterical adulation. The word 'good' can be used to express almost any degree of warmth, but it must be less than that expressed in the same context by 'excellent' or 'superb' and greater than that expressed by 'fair' or 'tolerable'.

It is not difficult to understand the connections between the more obviously performatory uses, praising, applauding, and commending; nor is it difficult to appreciate their intimate connection with preference and choice. To praise is not to choose; but it is connected with choosing in that it would be odd for a man to choose the thing he was prepared to praise less highly or not at all. He must have special reasons for this, modesty for example, a sense of unworthiness to possess the 'better' thing or a desire that someone else should have it. Again, if a man habitually praises one pianist more highly than another we expect to find him attending the recitals of the former more regularly and to be more annoyed when he is prevented from going. But he might have been told that the second is really a better pianist and be trying to cultivate a taste for his performance. Explanations can be given of discrepancies between praising and choice; but in default of an explanation the connection is contextually implied.

If, on a particular occasion, I call a man brave it would be logically odd to ask if I was in favour of what he did; for 'brave' is a praising word and by using it I show that I am in favour. Similarly, if I call courage a 'virtue' I show that I am, in a general way, in favour of courage, although I might not always want to praise a brave deed. It is an empirical fact that men are, for the most part, in favour of the modes of conduct that they call (descriptively) brave, honest, or generous. But this pro-attitude is so widespread that these words are not pure descriptive words; they are terms of praise and imply a pro-attitude unless this is expressly withdrawn.

Now praising and applauding are activities which are often performed with the special purpose of encouraging the person concerned to continue in the same style, and hissing and booing are used with the opposite intention. Although the words and gestures employed in praising owe their encouraging force to convention, they have, granted the convention, a natural effect on the people praised. For it is an empirical fact that, except in special circumstances—for example, if the praise is considered impertinent—people enjoy being praised and are therefore likely to go on doing what they are praised for. Praising is logically tied to approval; for if we heard a man praise something we could not wonder whether he approved of it or not unless we suspected him of being disingenuous or ironical; and it is logically tied in the same way to encouraging. But, although it is an empirical fact that men tend to encourage and try to promote that of which they approve, we must, as always, assume that men on the whole intend the natural consequences of their actions and therefore do not praise that which they would prefer to be otherwise. And this assumption is reflected in the fact that praising implies both approval and encouragement.

The same logical ties bind praising to advising; it would be logically odd to praise one candidate more highly than another and to go on to say that one was advising against his being given the job or the prize. Odd, but not impossible; for there might, as always, be special reasons for this.

The "characteristic qualities" which, according to the dictionary, are implied by the use of 'good' may be "either admirable in themselves or useful for some purpose". In contexts involving efficiency or skill it is the latter that we have in mind. In such contexts there need be no direct connection between the performatory uses, which are all variations of 'preferring' or 'being on the side of', and the usefulness implied by 'good'. We may have no pro-attitude whatsoever towards the purpose for which something is used or the activity at which a man is skilful, as when we speak of a 'good cosh' or a 'good liar'. But there is still an indirect link with the pro-attitudes since 'good' in these contexts implies success, and 'success' is a pro-word. A man is not a good liar unless he fairly consistently achieves his aim.

Preference and Appraisal

But it is the connections between the performatory uses and the verdict-giving, judging, or appraising use when the qualities on which the verdict is based are thought to be "admirable in themselves" that are the most important and the most difficult. I shall substitute 'preferable' for 'admirable', since admirable is itself a performance akin to praising and 'admirable' is therefore too narrow in scope to cover all appraisals other than those of efficiency or skill.

All the performatory uses contextually imply appraisal; for we have seen that it is improper to use 'good', at least in an impersonal formula, to express or defend a preference unless the preference is a considered one, based on reasons and not unusual. And to say that the preference is 'based on reasons' is to say that the speaker applied criteria or standards. It is not necessary that he should have done this deliberately; he may have done it automatically; but he must be able to defend his choice by an appeal to the standards which justify it.

But, although the performatory uses imply appraisal, it is not so clear that the converse is true. Indeed it is not true in any direct sense; appraisals often imply preference only in a roundabout way. For when 'good' is used to give a verdict it need neither express nor imply a pro-attitude on the part of the speaker. In such cases what a man is primarily doing with the word 'good' is *applying* those standards which are only contextually implied in the more subjective uses. Since 'good' is a Janus-word, he may, of course, be expressing his preferences or advising as well; but he need not be. The embittered schoolmaster may have no interest in the work of the examination candidates at all; he may even prefer stupidity to intelligence or have a private belief that the usual criteria for intelligence are quite wrong. Nevertheless he may still apply the grading words 'good', 'fair', 'poor', and so on in accordance with the accepted criteria either from conscientiousness or from habit or from fear of losing his job.

In the same way a professional taster of wine may dislike

all wine or prefer the less good to the better; his judgment is based solely on the presence of those "characteristic qualities" which, as an expert, he is able to detect and knows to be among the criteria for 'good wine'. But even in these cases there is an indirect reference to choosing and advising which comes out when we turn from the question "What are the criteria in fact used for grading Xs?" to the question "Why do we have the criteria that we do?". Professional wine-tasters are, after all, business men or the employees of business men and, though their job may be to taste wine, they only have this job because wine is to be bought and sold. It is no accident that the criteria for 'good Xs' are connected with the Xs that people prefer or approve of more highly. The professional wine-taster may not *like* Chateau Lafite; but he uses criteria for judging wine under which it gets high marks because people are prepared to pay highly for wine which rates highly under these criteria, and they do this because they like it.

[4]

Nature and Convention

The dictionary's phrase "admirable in themselves" is unfortunately ambiguous. In its context it is clear that 'in themselves' is contrasted with 'for a purpose', and that what the author has in mind is the familiar contrast between good-as-means and good-as-an-end. But 'in itself' is often used in philosophy with at least three other meanings. (a) It is sometimes used as a synonym for 'really' or 'objectively' to imply independence of human opinion or judgment of value. But, in discussing Moore's 'two worlds' argument I have already suggested that it is doubtful whether any sense can be given to the idea of something being good if there was no one to judge it good.

(b) It is sometimes used with a gerundive force. What is admirable or preferable in itself is what people ought to admire or prefer. But to use it in this way is not to comment on the use of 'good' but to make a value-judgment and, if the author of the dictionary were thought to be using it in this way, he must be thought to subscribe himself to all the value-judgments he cites as examples of 'good'. (c) But 'good-in-itself' could also be used to mean 'naturally good', to imply that the criteria or standards used for judging the goodness of something are not, like the criteria for a good postage stamp, dependent on human convention. It is this contrast that I propose to discuss.

We call a taste (or any other pro-attitude) a 'natural' one if (a) it is pretty general even among people of very different societies and if (b) most people do not have to learn to acquire it. It is important to notice that both these criteria for what is 'natural' are extremely vague and that they both admit of exceptions. A taste for strawberries does not cease to be natural because Jones happens not to like them or because Smith did not like them at first. Benevolence and love of life are natural pro-attitudes, even though there are misanthropes and suicides.

The criteria used for appraising are partly natural and partly conventional. In music, for example, the criteria which critics apply to a composition or performance are conventional in that they vary in different cultures and it is necessary to learn what they are; and musical taste is also partly conventional in that it is not natural to like or admire a Bach fugue in the way that it is natural to like sweets or to love one's children. It may well be that no criteria or tastes are wholly conventional. Correlations can be found between the criteria employed and the physiological facts of hearing; for example we know that the musical intervals and key-relationships on which all western music is based and which enter into the criteria used for judging a musical composition are of a mathematically simple kind. And even in the case of the criteria used for judging dogs at Crufts, which are highly artificial, it is possible to trace historical connections between the criteria now used and the criteria that were used when dogs were used for practical purposes; and these last were natural criteria in that the purposes, such as hunting and protection from wild animals, were based on natural pro-attitudes.

But in many cases the criteria now used are connected to natural criteria only through a long process of change and have become modified to such an extent that their original connection with natural pro-attitudes has been entirely lost. And in such cases it often happens that we do not use the criteria we do because people have the pro-attitudes they have, but we have the pro-attitudes we have because the criteria are what they are. It may be that no one can now remember exactly why certain criteria were originally chosen to be the standards of judging something to be good or bad of its kind and that people are now prepared to admire, praise, and pay highly for objects because they conform to the accepted criteria, rather than accepting the criteria as 'proper' ones because, under them, the things that they admire rate highly. Taste is dictated by fashion, not fashion by taste.

But such cases must (logically) be secondary cases and it would therefore be a mistake to cite them in proof of the contention that criteria are logically prior to pro-attitudes. For unless there were primary cases in which we adopted criteria *because* we already had a pro-attitude towards the objects that in fact rate highly under them, it would be impossible to understand how the same set of words could be used both in applying criteria and for choosing, praising, and advising. It is only because 'good' is used in applying criteria in cases where we use the criteria we do because our desires, interests, and tastes are what they are that men can come to acquire a taste for what counts as 'good' under the accepted criteria even in cases where the original connection between the criteria and the taste has been lost. Advertisers and propagandists, arbiters of taste and leaders of fashion could not (logically) stimulate new tastes and attitudes by the reiterated use of criterion-applying language unless this language was also used for applying criteria in cases where there are pre-existing tastes and attitudes. Without genuine enthusiasts there could be no snobs.

In many cases, therefore, the answer to the question 'Why do we use the criteria for judging so-and-sos that we do?' may be of a purely historical kind; the criteria are traditional; they have been concocted and moulded by interested parties, and so on. But this sort of answer cannot be given in all cases; there must be some cases in which we use a set of criteria because, as an empirical fact, they give higher ratings to those objects which we prefer.

In discussing appraisals I assumed that there was no difficulty about saying what the proper criteria for judging Xs are or about selecting the experts, leaders of fashion, or arbiters of taste; and it might seem that these assumptions involve a vicious circularity in the attempt to construe the grading-scale of good, fair, poor, and bad in terms of the standards used by experts. But this is not so for two reasons. (a) In some cases there are tests of competence which are purely objective and empirical. Some men, for example, have perfect pitch, can detect minute musical intervals, can recognize and accurately reproduce long and complicated tunes and so on, while others cannot; and these are matters of fact. In judging their expertise we must, of course, rely on the ability of other experts to assess their competence; but the judgments of these experts is 'objective' because they fulfil the requirements for objective language. It is possible that one man might have a finer ear than all other men, so that in a case in which he said that two notes were slightly different when everyone else said they were the same he would be right and they wrong. But if there were no indirect tests, such as the appeal to readings of scales and meters, for deciding whether he can really detect these differences or is only bluffing, and if those who honestly claimed to be able to make fine discriminations did not on the whole agree with each other, we could not call their judgments 'objective'.

Now from the fact that a man is able to make these fine discriminations or to perform better than others in these objectively testable ways, it does not, of course, follow that he is a good judge. For to say that he is a good judge is either to state that he is good at applying the accepted criteria for what is good (which is different from being good at passing the objective tests) or to express approval of his judgments, to praise him, to encourage others to accept his judgments, and so on; and in most cases it is to do all these things at once. But, once again, the reason why we allow that, in a general way, the most technically competent people are the best judges, lies in the facts. A man who is tone-deaf is unlikely to be able even to distinguish one piece of music from another and his value-judgments (if he makes them), are not likely to be consistent with each other; so that his value-judgments would be useless as a guide to others. A man who knows little Greek could not be a good judge of a piece of Greek prose. Consistency and fine discrimination are not sufficient conditions of good taste or moral insight, but they are necessary conditions if criteria are to be used for the purposes for which they are used.

(b) Secondly, the person who rejects the criteria usually employed or the verdict of the acknowledged experts may do so in two ways. He may simply refuse to be guided by them on the grounds that he happens not to like what is usually called good. But, if he goes further and says that the usual criteria are not *good* criteria, he is not just rejecting them; he is himself using criterion-applying language and he implies that he has second-order criteria for judging (and condemning) the usual first-order criteria.

To the questioning of criteria there is no end; but if we ask whether the criteria for judging Xs are *good* criteria we must, at whatever level we have reached, use criteria for deciding whether they are good or not. It is logically absurd to ask a question without knowing how the answers to it are to be judged to be good or bad answers. The appeal to criteria accepted by experts is not circular, but regressive; and the regress is not a vicious one since, although we *can* always question the criteria, there is no practical or logical necessity to do so. The self-guaranteeing criteria so vainly sought by some moralists are neither possible nor necessary.

[5]

Non-practical Appraisals

We often make appraisals in contexts where there is clearly no question of choosing or advising, for example moral judgments about historical or fictional characters. And this seems to involve

a difficulty for theories which make appraisals logically dependent on pro-attitudes. Hutcheson and Hume, for example, tried to
reduce moral judgments to expressions of feeling. They were not
guilty of the Naturalistic Fallacy, since they were prepared to
allow that moral approval and sympathy are special, moral feelings distinct from other types of feeling. But even this concession to the peculiarity of the moral use of language does not save
them from an important objection that seems at first sight fatal
to their case. Sentiments, as Hume noticed, seem to vary in
rough proportion to the propinquity of their objects. We are not
moved by the iniquity of remote historical characters as we are
by those closer to us; and we feel more approval for and sympathy with those near to us than with those who are more remote.
Yet our moral judgments do not vary in the same way. "We read
Cicero now without emotion, yet we can still judge Verres to be a
villain. According to Hume's theory our judgment must change
as do our feelings. I do not feel indignation as strongly now
about the German invasion of Czechoslovakia as I did at the
time it happened; yet I do not judge the action to be less wrong
than I did then, or the agents less criminal. . . . It is but a
weak subterfuge to say we transport ourselves by the force of
imagination into distant ages and countries, and consider the
passions which we should have felt on contemplating these
characters had we been contemporaries and had commerce with
the persons. . . . I now feel completely indifferent to Verres,
and know it. Yet, Hume tells me, when I judge Verres to have
been a villain, I am so deceived by my imagination that I talk as
if I felt a strong feeling of anger." [1]

  Dr. Raphael's criticism is fatal to the theory that a man
who makes a moral appraisal is always expressing a feeling; and
a similar criticism could also be made of any theory which says
that to appraise is always to praise, advise, commend, etc. On
some occasions a man may be simply *applying* the criteria that
he and others customarily use for these purposes. To call Verres
a villain is to pass a verdict on him, to condemn him. Now the

[1] D. D. Raphael, *The Moral Sense*, pp. 88 and 91.

Moral Sense School were, I think, mistaken in construing moral approval and disapproval as *feelings,* since this suggests too strongly the analogy with itches, aches, and tickles. But they were right to connect moral appraisals and verdicts with approval and disapproval. For although a man who passes a verdict need not be expressing a pro- or con-attitude, we have seen that the criteria he uses are directly or indirectly linked with these attitudes; and in the case of moral judgments they must be linked in a special way that may be absent in other cases.

I said earlier that, although in other cases 'good' might lose its gerundive force, it cannot wholly do so when used to make moral appraisals. The reason is that, whatever may be the case with other types of appraisal, moral appraisals must be universal. Anyone who makes a moral appraisal even of a remote character must be willing to apply the same criteria universally. And it follows from this that he must be willing to apply them in practical contexts. If I am not prepared to condemn anyone whose behaviour is like that of Verres in all relevant respects then, in calling Verres a villain, I am not making a genuine moral judgment; and the relevant respects are all of an empirical, objective kind. It would, of course, be trivial to include among them an objective property of villainy or moral turpitude; all that is necessary is that I should be prepared to condemn anyone who did the sort of thing that Verres is called a villain for having done, anyone who oppressed the poor, robbed the rich, took bribes, and cheated the treasury, and all for his own personal profit.

Moral appraisals are therefore connected with choosing and advising in a way that non-moral appraisals need not be. It is not logically odd to say "This is the better wine, but I prefer that"; but it is logically odd to say "This is the (morally) better course; but I shall do that".[2] And a man cannot be making a genuine moral judgment about Verres if he would himself be prepared to act on the same principles on which Verres acted

---

[2] This may sound surprising. We all know what it is to take what we know to be the morally worse course.

and prepared to exhort others to do so. In condemning Verres he is not expressing any emotion; but he is affirming his own moral principles.

[6]

Objective-Subjective

. . . the distinction between "For what job is the word '. . .' used?" and "Under what conditions is it proper to use that word for that job?" throws light on the objective-subjective dispute.

As we should expect, both parties are right. Just as the subjectivists are right in denying that A-words stand for special properties and explaining them in terms of people's reactions, so they are also right in connecting 'good' and 'bad' with people's desires, tastes, interests, approvals, and disapprovals. There is a logical absurdity about calling a play 'amusing' if the speaker believes that it never has amused anyone and never will; and there is the same logical absurdity in calling something 'good' without any direct or indirect reference to a pro-attitude. If the connection between 'good' and the pro-attitude that is contextually relevant were not a logical one, a gap would emerge between calling something good on the one hand and deciding to choose it, choosing it or advising others to choose it on the other which would make these activities unintelligible. Moreover, the subjectivists are also right in connecting 'good' with the pro-attitudes of the speaker, at least in moral cases.

But the objectivists are also right. They are mistaken in denying the points made by the subjectivists above and in thinking that goodness must be a unique, non-natural property. It is sometimes argued that if there were no such property we could not account for the fact that we use the impersonal form 'this is good' rather than the personal form 'I approve of this', and those who use this argument are inclined to forget that we have an impersonal form 'this is nice' as well as the personal form 'I like it', so that niceness would have to be an objective property too.

It would indeed be puzzling to understand why we use

these impersonal forms if we were just talking about or expressing our own approvals; but this argument does not show that we are talking about something else, still less that this must be a unique property. We can account for the objective formula, as we did in the case of 'nice', by saying (a) that 'X is good' is not only used in the context of choice and (b) that, when it is so used, it implies a great deal that is not implied by 'I approve of X' and is expressly denied by 'I happen to approve of X'. It implies that my approval is not an unusual one and that I could give reasons for it. It implies also—what is a matter of objective fact—that the object conforms to certain standards which are generally accepted.

It is sometimes argued that 'this is good' cannot just mean 'I approve of this' on the ground that we can say "I approve of this because it is good". Approval must therefore be an intellectual emotion which arises in us only when we recognize something to have the objective property 'goodness'. But it has never been clear what the connection between the approval and the recognition of the property is supposed to be. Is it logically necessary that anyone who recognizes the property should feel approval or is it just an empirical fact that people who notice the property, and only they, have the feeling? Each of these answers involves insuperable difficulties; but if neither is correct we must find some other way of explaining the 'because' in 'I approve of X because it is good'.

The need for such an explanation vanishes when we see that this is not a reason-giving 'because' like that in 'I approve of Jones because he is kind to children' but more like 'I like Jones because he is likeable'. It rebuts the suggestion that I just 'happen to' approve of X and it implies that X has certain properties which make it worthy of my approval and that it conforms to the known standards for Xs.

The objectivist is right in drawing attention to the factual background which makes impersonal appraisals possible; but the facts which it contains are ordinary, empirical facts, not special, non-natural facts. Unlike the subjectivist (who tends to ignore the background altogether), he tries to include the background in the meaning of the word; and this, combined with the mistake of confusing practical and descriptive discourse, leads him into the vain pursuit of a single ingredient to which we always refer when we call something good.

[7]
The Naturalistic Fallacy

We are now in a position to see why the moral philosophers of the past subordinated the critical or appraising uses of moral language to the practical uses. Each presupposes the other, but in a different way. The practical uses presuppose the appraising use in that we could not use 'good' as we do for choosing, advising, and praising if we did not employ criteria or standards; since we only use 'good' for these purposes *when* we are employing standards. Nevertheless people who did not know what standards were could do things recognizably like what we, who have standards, call choosing, advising, and praising. They would be very rudimentary performances, hardly deserving the names of choice, advice, and praise; but they could occur. We draw a distinction between 'good' and 'happen to like' which people without standards could not draw; and we, who have the distinction, would describe their activities in terms of what they 'happen to like', because they could not do anything that we would call 'choosing the best'. In this way the practical uses of 'good' imply the appraising use.

But the practical uses are logically prior to the appraising use in a much more fundamental way. Unless men had pro-attitudes, there could not be even rudimentary analogues of what we know as appraising, judging, or passing a verdict. For these involve the use of standards; and without pro-attitudes we should neither have any use for standards nor even be able to understand what a 'standard' was. We can imagine a world in which there was choosing, but no appraising and also a world in which there was classifying, sorting, and ordering (for example by size) but no choosing; but, in a world in which there was no choosing, there could be no such thing as appraising or grading.

Ethical Naturalism is the attempt to trace logical connections between moral appraisals and the actual pro- and con-attitudes of men, their desires and aversions, hopes and fears, joys and sorrows. One-track naturalistic theories always fail to do justice to the complexity both of the facts and of the logical connections, since they suggest that there is only one thing towards which men have a pro-attitude, pleasure, or that all pro-attitudes are desires. And these theories are both psychologically and logically misleading.

Opponents of the Naturalistic Fallacy have pointed out the logical errors. It is true that gerundive and deontological words cannot be defined in terms of pleasure, desire, or even purpose; and I shall try to show how they are connected with these teleological concepts later. It is also true that gerundive judgments and value-judgments do not follow logically from descriptive statements about what men like, enjoy, and approve of. But the reason for this is not that gerundive words and value words refer to special entities or qualities, but that a person who *uses* them is not, except in certain secondary cases, describing anything at all. He is not doing what psychologists do, which is to describe, explain, and comment on what people like, enjoy, and approve of; and he is not doing what moral philosophers do, which is to describe, explain, and comment on the way in which people use moral words; he is himself using moral language, expressing approval, praising, advising, exhorting, commending, or appraising.

The attack on the Naturalistic Fallacy is thus far justified. But the conclusion which is commonly drawn, that moral concepts are a special sort of concept which must be purged of all association with the 'merely empirical or phenomenal' concepts of enjoying, wanting, and approval is not justified. Psychology is not as irrelevant to ethics as some modern philosophers insist; for, although moral judgments do not follow from psychological statements, we cannot understand what the terms used in moral judgments mean unless we examine them in the context of their use; and they are used either directly to express a pro- or con-attitude or to perform some other task which beings

who had no pro- or con-attitudes could not perform or even understand. The various ways in which 'good' is used are unintelligible unless they are directly or indirectly connected with
choice; and I shall try to show later that the same applies to
'ought'.

Moral philosophy does not, therefore, 'rest on a mistake'.
For the great philosophers were not primarily interested in the
question whether deontological words could be analysed in
terms of 'merely empirical' or 'natural' concepts. They believed
that, human beings being what they are, there are certain types
of activity that are in fact satisfactory to them and that it is
possible empirically to discover what these are. No doubt they
often made mistakes of fact, for example that of supposing that
what is satisfactory to one man would be satisfactory to another;
and they made mistakes of logic, for example that of supposing
that 'good' could be extracted from its context and be said to
mean the same as 'satisfactory'. But they do not seem to have
been mistaken in their basic assumptions that the language of
obligation is intelligible only in connection with the language of
purpose and choice, that men choose to do what they do because
they are what they are, and that moral theories which attempt to
exclude all consideration of human nature as it is do not even
begin to be moral theories.

THE NATURALISTIC FALLACY /
W. K. Frankena

THE FUTURE HISTORIAN of "thought and expression" in the twentieth century will no doubt record with some amusement the ingenious trick, which some of the philosophical controversialists
of the first quarter of our century had, of labelling their opponents' views "fallacies." He may even list some of these alleged
fallacies for a certain sonority which their inventors embodied in
their titles: the fallacy of initial predication, the fallacy of
simple location, the fallacy of misplaced concreteness, the naturalistic fallacy.

Of these fallacies, real or supposed, perhaps the most famous is the naturalistic fallacy. For the practitioners of a certain
kind of ethical theory, which is dominant in England and cap-
ably represented in America, and which is variously called ob-
jectivism, non-naturalism, or intuitionism, have frequently
charged their opponents with committing the naturalistic fallacy. Some of these opponents have strongly repudiated the
charge of fallacy, others have at least commented on it in passing, and altogether the notion of a naturalistic fallacy has had a

From *W. K. Frankena*, "*The Naturalistic Fallacy*," Mind, XLVIII (*1939*), *103–
114. Reprinted by permission of the Editor of* Mind.

considerable currency in ethical literature. Yet, in spite of its repute, the naturalistic fallacy has never been discussed at any length, and, for this reason, I have elected to make a study of it in this paper. I hope incidentally to clarify certain confusions which have been made in connection with the naturalistic fallacy, but my main interest is to free the controversy between the intuitionists and their opponents of the notion of a logical or quasi-logical fallacy, and to indicate where the issue really lies.

The prominence of the concept of a naturalistic fallacy in recent moral philosophy is another testimony to the great influence of the Cambridge philosopher, Mr. G. E. Moore, and his book, *Principia Ethica*. Thus Mr. Taylor speaks of the "vulgar mistake" which Mr. Moore has taught us to call "the naturalistic fallacy," [1] and Mr. G. S. Jury, as if to illustrate how well we have learned this lesson, says, with reference to naturalistic definitions of value, "All such definitions stand charged with Dr. Moore's 'naturalistic fallacy.' " [2] Now, Mr. Moore coined the notion of the naturalistic fallacy in his polemic against naturalistic and metaphysical systems of ethics. "The naturalistic fallacy is a fallacy," he writes, and it "must not be committed." All naturalistic and metaphysical theories of ethics, however, "are *based* on the naturalistic fallacy, in the sense that the commission of this fallacy has been the main cause of their wide acceptance." [3] The best way to dispose of them, then, is to expose this fallacy. Yet it is not entirely clear just what is the status of the naturalistic fallacy in the polemics of the intuitionists against other theories. Sometimes it is used as a weapon, as when Miss Clarke says that if we call a thing good simply because it is liked we are guilty of the naturalistic fallacy. [4] Indeed, it presents this aspect to the reader in many parts of *Principia Ethica* itself. Now, in taking it as a weapon, the intuitionists use the naturalistic fallacy as if it were a logical fallacy on all fours with the fallacy of composition, the revelation of which disposes of naturalistic and meta-

[1] A. E. Taylor, *The Faith of a Moralist*, Vol. I, p. 104 n.
[2] *Value and Ethical Objectivity*, p. 58.
[3] *Principia Ethica*, pp. 38, 64.
[4] M. E. Clarke, "Cognition and Affection in the Experience of Value," *Journal of Philosophy* (1938).

physical ethics and leaves intuitionism standing triumphant. That is, it is taken as a fallacy in advance, for use in controversy. But there are signs in *Principia Ethica* which indicate that the naturalistic fallacy has a rather different place in the intuitionist scheme, and should not be used as a weapon at all. In this aspect, the naturalistic fallacy must be proved to be a fallacy. It cannot be used to settle the controversy, but can only be asserted to be a fallacy when the smoke of battle has cleared. Consider the following passages: (*a*) "the naturalistic fallacy consists in the contention that good *means* nothing but some simple or complex notion, that can be defined in terms of natural qualities"; (*b*) "the point that good is indefinable and that to deny this involves a fallacy, is a point capable of strict proof." [5] These passages seem to imply that the fallaciousness of the naturalistic fallacy is just what is at issue in the controversy between the intuitionists and their opponents, and cannot be wielded as a weapon in that controversy. One of the points I wish to make in this paper is that the charge of committing the naturalistic fallacy can be made, if at all, only as a conclusion from the discussion and not as an instrument of deciding it.

The notion of a naturalistic fallacy has been connected with the notion of a bifurcation between the 'ought' and the 'is,' between value and fact, between the normative and the descriptive. Thus Mr. D. C. Williams says that some moralists have thought it appropriate to chastise as the naturalistic fallacy the attempt to derive the Ought from the Is.[6] We may begin, then, by considering this bifurcation, emphasis on which, by Sidgwick, Sorley, and others, came largely as a reaction to the procedures of Mill and Spencer. Hume affirms the bifurcation in his *Treatise:* "I cannot forbear adding to these reasonings an observation, which may, perhaps, be found of some importance. In every system of morality which I have hitherto met with, I have always remarked, that the author proceeds for some time in the ordinary way of reasoning, and establishes

---

[5] *Principia Ethica*, pp. 73, 77. See also p. xix.
[6] "Ethics as Pure Postulate," *Philosophical Review* (1933). See also T. Whittaker, *The Theory of Abstract Ethics*, pp. 19 f.

the being of a God, or makes observations concerning human affairs; when of a sudden I am surprised to find, that instead of the usual copulations of propositions, *is,* and *is not,* I meet with no proposition that is not connected with an *ought,* or an *ought not.* This change is imperceptible; but is, however, of the last consequence. For as this *ought,* or *ought not,* expresses some new relation or affirmation, it is necessary that it should be observed and explained; and at the same time that a reason should be given, for what seems altogether inconceivable, how this new relation can be a deduction from others, which are entirely different from it. But as authors do not commonly use this precaution, I shall presume to recommend it to the readers; and am persuaded, that this small attention would subvert all the vulgar systems of morality, and let us see that the distinction of vice and virtue is not founded merely on the relations of objects, nor is perceived by reason." [7]

Needless to say, the intuitionists *have* found this observation of some importance.[8] They agree with Hume that it subverts all the vulgar systems of morality, though, of course, they deny that it lets us see that the distinction of virtue and vice is not founded on the relations of objects, nor is perceived by reason. In fact, they hold that a small attention to it subverts Hume's own system also, since this gives naturalistic definitions of virtue and vice and of good and evil.[9]

Hume's point is that ethical conclusions cannot be drawn validly from premises which are non-ethical. But when the intuitionists affirm the bifurcation of the 'ought' and the 'is,' they mean more than that ethical propositions cannot be deduced from non-ethical ones. For this difficulty in the vulgar systems of morality could be remedied, as we shall see, by the introduction of definitions of ethical notions in non-ethical terms. They mean, further, that such definitions of ethical notions in non-ethical terms are impossible. "The essential point," says Mr. Laird, "is

---

[7] Book III, Part II, Section I.
[8] See J. Laird, *A Study in Moral Theory*, pp. 16 f.; Whittaker, *op. cit.*, p. 19.
[9] See C. D. Broad, *Five Types of Ethical Theory*, Ch. IV.

the irreducibility of values to non-values." [10] But they mean still more. Yellow and pleasantness are, according to Mr. Moore, indefinable in non-ethical terms, but they are natural qualities and belong on the 'is' side of the fence. Ethical properties, however, are not, for him, mere indefinable natural qualities, descriptive or expository. They are properties of a different *kind*—nondescriptive or non-natural. [11] The intuitionist bifurcation consists of three statements:—

(1) Ethical propositions are not deducible from non-ethical ones. [12]

(2) Ethical characteristics are not definable in terms of non-ethical ones.

(3) Ethical characteristics are different in kind from non-ethical ones.

Really it consists of but one statement, namely, (3) since (3) entails (2) and (2) entails (1). It does not involve saying that any ethical characteristics are absolutely indefinable. That is another question, although this is not always noticed.

What, now, has the naturalistic fallacy to do with the bifurcation of the 'ought' and the 'is'? To begin with, the connection is this: many naturalistic and metaphysical moralists proceed as if ethical conclusions can be deduced from premises all of which are non-ethical, the classical examples being Mill and Spencer. That is, they violate (1). This procedure has lately been referred to as the "factualist fallacy" by Mr. Wheelwright and as the "valuational fallacy" by Mr. Wood. [13] Mr. Moore sometimes seems to identify it with the naturalistic fallacy, but in the main he holds only that it involves, implies, or rests upon this fallacy. [14] We may now consider the charge that the procedure in question is or involves a fallacy.

[10] *A Study in Moral Theory*, p. 94 n.

[11] See his *Philosophical Studies*, pp. 259, 273 f.

[12] See J. Laird, *op. cit.*, p. 318. Also pp. 12 ff.

[13] P. E. Wheelwright, *A Critical Introduction to Ethics*, pp. 40–51, 91 f.; L. Wood, "Cognition and Moral Value," *Journal of Philosophy* (1937), p. 237.

[14] See *Principia Ethica*, pp. 114, 57, 43, 49. Whittaker identifies it with the naturalistic fallacy and regards it as a "logical" fallacy, *op. cit.*, pp. 19 f.

It may be noted at once that, even if the deduction of ethical conclusions from non-ethical premises is in no way a fallacy, Mill certainly did commit a fallacy in drawing an analogy between visibility and desirability in his argument for hedonism; and perhaps his committing *this* fallacy, which, as Mr. Broad has said, we all learn about at our mothers' knees, is chiefly responsible for the notion of a naturalistic *fallacy*. But is it a fallacy to deduce ethical conclusions from non-ethical premises? Consider the Epicurean argument for hedonism which Mill so unwisely sought to embellish: pleasure is good, since it is sought by all men. Here an ethical conclusion is being derived from a non-ethical premise. And, indeed, the argument, taken strictly as it stands, *is* fallacious. But it is not fallacious because an *ethical* term occurs in the conclusion which does not occur in the premise. It is fallacious because any argument of the form "A is B, therefore A is C" is invalid, if taken strictly as it stands. For example, it is invalid to argue that Croesus is rich because he is wealthy. Such arguments are, however, not intended to be taken strictly as they stand. They are enthymemes and contain a suppressed premise. And, when this suppressed premise is made explicit, they are valid and involve no logical fallacy.[15] Thus the Epicurean inference from psychological to ethical hedonism is valid when the suppressed premise is added to the effect that what is sought by all men is good. Then the only question left is whether the premises are true.

It is clear, then, that the naturalistic fallacy is not a logical fallacy, since it may be involved even when the argument is valid. How does the naturalistic fallacy enter such "mixed ethical arguments"[16] as that of the Epicureans? Whether it does or not depends on the nature of the suppressed premise. This may be either an induction, an intuition, a deduction from a "pure ethical argument," a definition, or a proposition which is true by definition. If it is one of the first three, then the naturalistic fallacy does not enter at all. In fact, the argument does not then

---

15 See *ibid.*, pp. 50, 139; Wheelwright, *loc. cit.*

16 See C. D. Broad, *The Mind and Its Place in Nature*, pp. 488 f.; Laird, *loc. cit.*

involve violating (1), since one of its premises will be ethical. But if the premise to be supplied is a definition or a proposition which is true by definition, as it probably was for the Epicureans, then the argument, while still valid, involves the naturalistic fallacy, and will run as follows:—

> (a) Pleasure is sought by all men.
> (b) What is sought by all men is good (definition).
> (c) Therefore, pleasure is good.

Now I am not greatly interested in deciding whether the argument as here set up violates (1). If it does not, then no 'mixed ethical argument' actually commits any factualist or valuational fallacy, except when it is unfairly taken as complete in its enthymematic form. If it does, then a valid argument may involve the deduction of an ethical conclusion from non-ethical premises and the factualist or valuational fallacy is not really a fallacy. The question depends on whether or not (b) and (c) are to be regarded as ethical propositions. Mr. Moore refuses so to regard them, contending that, by hypothesis, (b) is analytic or tautologous, and that (c) is psychological, since it really says only that pleasure is sought by all men.[17] But to say that (b) is analytic and not ethical and that (c) is not ethical but psychological is to prejudice the question whether 'good' can be defined; for the Epicureans would contend precisely that if their definition is correct then (b) is ethical but analytic and (c) ethical though psychological. Thus, unless the question of the definability of goodness is to be begged, (b) and (c) must be regarded as ethical, in which case our argument does not violate (1). However, suppose, if it be not nonsense, that (b) is non-ethical and (c) ethical, then the argument will violate (1), but it will still obey all of the canons of logic, and it is only confusing to talk of a 'valuational logic' whose basic rule is that an evaluative conclusion cannot be deduced from non-evaluative premises.[18]

For the only way in which either the intuitionists or pos-

---

17 See *op. cit.*, pp. 11 f.; 19, 38, 73, 139.
18 See L. Wood, *loc. cit.*

tulationists like Mr. Wood can cast doubt upon the conclusion of the argument of the Epicureans (or upon the conclusion of any parallel argument) is to attack the premises, in particular (b). Now, according to Mr. Moore, it is due to the presence of (b) that the argument involves the naturalistic fallacy. (b) involves the identification of goodness with 'being sought by all men,' and to make this or any other such identification is to commit the naturalistic fallacy. The naturalistic fallacy is not the procedure of violating (1). It is the procedure, implied in many mixed ethical arguments and explicitly carried out apart from such arguments by many moralists, of defining such characteristics as goodness or of substituting some other characteristic for them. To quote some passages from *Principia Ethica:*—

(a) . . . far too many philosophers have thought that when they named those other properties [belonging to all things which are good] they were actually defining good; that these properties, in fact, were simply not 'other,' but absolutely and entirely the same with goodness. This view I propose to call the 'naturalistic fallacy.' . . .[19]

(b) I have thus appropriated the name Naturalism to a particular method of approaching Ethics. . . . This method consists in substituting for 'good' some one property of a natural object or of a collection of natural objects. . . .[20]

(c) . . . the naturalistic fallacy [is] the fallacy which consists in identifying the simple notion which we mean by 'good' with some other notion.[21]

Thus, to identify 'better' and 'more evolved,' 'good' and 'desired,' etc., is to commit the naturalistic fallacy.[22] But just why is such a procedure fallacious or erroneous? And is it a fallacy only when applied to good? We must now study Section 12 of *Principia Ethica*. Here Mr. Moore makes some interesting statements:—

[19] p. 10.
[20] p. 40.
[21] p. 58, cf. pp. xiii, 73.
[22] Cf. pp. 49, 53, 108, 139.

. . . if anybody tried to define pleasure for us as being any other natural object; if anybody were to say, for instance, that pleasure *means* the sensation of red. . . . Well, that would be the same fallacy which I have called the naturalistic fallacy. . . . I should not indeed call that a naturalistic fallacy, although it is the same fallacy as I have called naturalistic with reference to Ethics. . . . When a man confuses two natural objects with one another, defining the one by the other . . . then there is no reason to call the fallacy naturalistic. But if he confuses 'good,' which is not . . . a natural object, with any natural object whatever, then there is a reason for calling that a naturalistic fallacy. . . .[23]

Here Mr. Moore should have added that, when one confuses 'good,' which is not a metaphysical object or quality, with any metaphysical object or quality, as metaphysical moralists do, according to him, then the fallacy should be called the metaphysical fallacy. Instead he calls it a naturalistic fallacy in this case too, though he recognises that the case is different since metaphysical properties are non-natural [24]—a procedure which has misled many readers of *Principia Ethica*. For example, it has led Mr. Broad to speak of "theological naturalism." [25]

To resume: "Even if [goodness] were a natural object, that would not alter the nature of the fallacy nor diminish its importance one whit." [26]

From these passages it is clear that the fallaciousness of the procedure which Mr. Moore calls the naturalistic fallacy is not due to the fact that it is applied to good or to an ethical or non-natural characteristic. When Mr. R. B. Perry defines 'good' as 'being an object of interest' the trouble is not merely that he is defining *good*. Nor is the trouble that he is defining an *ethical* characteristic in terms of *non-ethical* ones. Nor is the trouble that he is regarding a *non-natural* characteristic as a *natural* one. The trouble is more generic than that. For clarity's sake I shall speak of the definist fallacy as the generic fallacy which underlies the naturalistic fallacy. The naturalistic fallacy will

[23] p. 13.
[24] See pp. 38–40, 110–112.
[25] *Five Types of Ethical Theory*, p. 259.
[26] p. 14.

then, by the above passages, be a species or form of the definist fallacy, as would the metaphysical fallacy if Mr. Moore had given that a separate name.[27] That is, the naturalistic fallacy, as illustrated by Mr. Perry's procedure, is a fallacy, not because it is naturalistic or confuses a non-natural quality with a natural one, but solely because it involves the definist fallacy. We may, then, confine our attention entirely to an understanding and evaluation of the definist fallacy.

To judge by the passages I have just quoted, the definist fallacy is the process of confusing or identifying two properties, of defining one property by another, or of substituting one property for another. Furthermore, the fallacy is always simply that two properties are being treated as one, and it is irrelevant, if it be the case, that one of them is natural or non-ethical and the other non-natural or ethical. One may commit the definist fallacy without infringing on the bifurcation of the ethical and the non-ethical, as when one identifies pleasantness and redness or rightness and goodness. But even when one infringes on that bifurcation in committing the definist fallacy, as when one identifies goodness and pleasantness or goodness and satisfaction, then the *mistake* is still not that the bifurcation is being infringed on, but only that two properties are being treated as one. Hence, on the present interpretation, the definist *fallacy* does not, in any of its forms, consist in violating (3), and has no essential connection with the bifurcation of the 'ought' and the 'is.'

This formulation of the definist fallacy explains or reflects the motto of *Principia Ethica,* borrowed from Bishop Butler: "Everything is what it is, and not another thing." It follows from this motto that goodness is what it is and not another thing. It follows that views which try to identify it with something else are making a mistake of an elementary sort. For it *is* a mistake to confuse or identify two properties. If the properties really are two, then they simply are not identical. But do those who define ethical notions in non-ethical terms make this mistake? They will reply to Mr. Moore that they are not identifying

27 As Whittaker has, *loc. cit.*

two properties; what they are saying is that two words or sets of words stand for or mean one and the same property. Mr. Moore was being, in part, misled by the material mode of speech, as Mr. Carnap calls it, in such sentences as "Goodness is pleasantness," "Knowledge is true belief," etc. When one says instead, "The word 'good' and the word 'pleasant' mean the same thing," etc., it is clear that one is not identifying two things. But Mr. Moore kept himself from seeing this by his disclaimer that he was interested in any statement about the use of words.[28]

The definist fallacy, then, as we have stated it, does not rule out any naturalistic or metaphysical definitions of ethical terms. Goodness is not identifiable with any 'other' characteristic (if it is a characteristic at all). But the question is: *which* characteristics are other than goodness, which names stand for characteristics other than goodness? And it is begging the question of the definability of goodness to say out of hand that Mr. Perry, for instance, is identifying goodness with something else. The point is that goodness is what it is, even if it is definable. That is why Mr. Perry can take as the motto of his naturalistic *Moral Economy* another sentence from Bishop Butler: "Things and actions are what they are, and the consequences of them will be what they will be; why then should we desire to be deceived?" The motto of *Principia Ethica* is a tautology, and should be expanded as follows: Everything is what it is, and not another thing, unless it is another thing, and even then it is what it is.

On the other hand, if Mr. Moore's motto (or the definist fallacy) rules out any definitions, for example of 'good,' then it rules out all definitions of any term whatever. To be effective at all, it must be understood to mean, "Every term means what it means, and not what is meant by any other term." Mr. Moore seems implicitly to understand his motto in this way in Section 13, for he proceeds as if 'good' has no meaning, if it has no unique meaning. If the motto be taken in this way, it will follow that 'good' is an indefinable term, since no synonyms can be found. But it will also follow that no term is definable. And then

28 See *op. cit.*, pp. 6, 8, 12.

the method of analysis is as useless as an English butcher in a world without sheep.

Perhaps we have misinterpreted the definist fallacy. And, indeed, some of the passages which I quoted earlier in this paper seem to imply that the definist fallacy is just the error of defining an indefinable characteristic. On this interpretation, again, the definist fallacy has, in all of its forms, no essential connection with the bifurcation of the ethical and the non-ethical. Again, one may commit the definist fallacy without violating that bifurcation, as when one defines pleasantness in terms of redness or goodness in terms of rightness (granted Mr. Moore's belief that pleasantness and goodness are indefinable). But even when one infringes on that bifurcation and defines goodness in terms of desire, the *mistake* is not that one is infringing on the bifurcation by violating (3), but only that one is defining an indefinable characteristic. This is possible because the proposition that goodness is indefinable is logically independent of the proposition that goodness is non-natural: as is shown by the fact that a characteristic may be indefinable and yet natural, as yellowness is; or non-natural and yet definable, as rightness is (granted Mr. Moore's views about yellowness and rightness).

Consider the definist fallacy as we have just stated it. It is, of course, an error to define an indefinable quality. But the question, again, is: which qualities are indefinable? It is begging the question in favour of intuitionism to say in advance that the quality goodness is indefinable and that, therefore, all naturalists commit the definist fallacy. One must know that goodness is indefinable before one can argue that the definist fallacy *is* a fallacy. Then, however, the definist fallacy can enter only at the end of the controversy between intuitionism and definism, and cannot be used as a weapon in the controversy.

The definist fallacy may be stated in such a way as to involve the bifurcation between the 'ought' and the 'is.' [29] It would then be committed by anyone who offered a definition of any ethical characteristic in terms of non-ethical ones. The trouble with such a definition, on this interpretation, would be that

29 See J. Wisdom, *Mind* (1931), p. 213, note 1.

an *ethical* characteristic is being reduced to a *non-ethical* one, a *non-natural* one to a *natural* one. That is, the definition would be ruled out by the fact that the characteristic being defined is ethical or non-natural and therefore cannot be defined in non-ethical or natural terms. But on this interpretation, too, there is danger of a *petitio* in the intuitionist argumentation. To assume that the ethical characteristic is exclusively ethical is to beg precisely the question which is at issue when the definition is offered. Thus, again, one must know that the characteristic is non-natural and indefinable in natural terms before one can say that the definists are making a mistake.

Mr. Moore, McTaggart, and others formulate the naturalistic fallacy sometimes in a way somewhat different from any of those yet discussed. They say that the definists are confusing a universal synthetic proposition about *the good* with a definition of *goodness*.[30] Mr. Abraham calls this the "fallacy of misconstrued proposition." [31] Here again the difficulty is that, while it is true that it is an error to construe a universal synthetic proposition as a definition, it is a *petitio* for the intuitionists to say that what the definist is taking for a definition is really a universal synthetic proposition.[32]

At last, however, the issue between the intuitionists and the definists (naturalistic or metaphysical) is becoming clearer. The definists are all holding that certain propositions involving ethical terms are analytic, tautologous, or true by definition, e.g., Mr. Perry so regards the statement, "All objects of desire are good." The intuitionists hold that such statements are synthetic. What underlies this difference of opinion is that the intuitionists claim to have at least a dim awareness of a simple unique quality or relation of goodness or rightness which appears in the region which our ethical terms roughly indicate whereas the definists claim to have no awareness of any such quality or relation in that region, which is different from all other qualities and

[30] See *Principia Ethica*, pp. 10, 16, 38; *The Nature of Existence*, Vol. II, p. 398.

[31] Leo Abraham, "The Logic of Intuitionism," *International Journal of Ethics* (1933).

[32] As Mr. Abraham points out, *loc. cit.*

relations which belong to the same context but are designated
by words other than 'good' and 'right' and their obvious
synonyms.[33] The definists are in all honesty claiming to find but
one characteristic where the intuitionists claim to find two, as
Mr. Perry claims to find only the property of being desired where
Mr. Moore claims to find both it and the property of being good.
The issue, then, is one of inspection or intuition, and concerns the awareness or discernment of qualities and relations.[34]
That is why it cannot be decided by the use of the notion of a
fallacy.

If the definists may be taken at their word, then they are
not actually confusing two characteristics with each other, nor
defining an indefinable characteristic, nor confusing definitions
and universal synthetic propositions—in short they are not committing the naturalistic or definist fallacy in any of the interpretations given above. Then the only fallacy which they commit—
the real naturalistic or definist fallacy—is the failure to descry
the qualities and relations which are central to morality. But this
is neither a logical fallacy nor a logical confusion. It is not even,
properly speaking, an error. It is rather a kind of blindness,
analogous to colour-blindness. Even this moral blindness can be
ascribed to the definists only if they are correct in their claim to
have no awareness of any unique ethical characteristics and if
the intuitionists are correct in affirming the existence of such
characteristics, but certainly to call it a 'fallacy,' even in a loose
sense, is both unamiable and profitless.

On the other hand, of course, if there are no such characteristics in the objects to which we attach ethical predicates,
then the intuitionists, if we may take them at their word, are
suffering from a corresponding moral hallucination. Definists
might then call this the intuitionistic or moralistic fallacy, except that it is no more a 'fallacy' than is the blindness just
described. Anyway, they do not believe the claim of the intuitionists to be aware of unique ethical characteristics, and conse-

[33] See R. B. Perry, *General Theory of Value*, p. 30; cf. *Journal of Philosophy*
(1931), p. 520.
[34] See H. Osborne, *Foundations of the Philosophy of Value*, pp. 15, 19, 70.

quently do not attribute to them this hallucination. Instead, they simply deny that the intuitionists really do find such unique qualities or relations, and then they try to find some plausible way of accounting for the fact that very respectable and trustworthy people think they find them.[35] Thus they charge the intuitionists with verbalism, hypostatisation, and the like. But this half of the story does not concern us now.

What concerns us more is the fact that the intuitionists do not credit the claim of the definists either. They would be much disturbed, if they really thought that their opponents were morally blind, for they do not hold that we must be regenerated by grace before we can have moral insight, and they share the common feeling that morality is something democratic even though not all men are good. Thus they hold that "we are all aware" of certain unique characteristics when we use the terms 'good,' 'right,' etc., only due to a lack of analytic clearness of mind, abetted perhaps by a philosophical prejudice, we may not be aware at all that they are different from other characteristics of which we are also aware.[36] Now, I have been arguing that the intuitionists cannot charge the definists with committing any fallacy unless and until they have shown that we are all, the definists included, aware of the disputed unique characteristics. If, however, they were to show this, then, at least at the end of the controversy, they could accuse the definists of the error of confusing two characteristics, or of the error of defining an indefinable one, and these errors might, since the term is somewhat loose in its habits, be called 'fallacies,' though they are not logical fallacies in the sense in which an invalid argument is. The fallacy of misconstrued proposition depends on the error of confusing two characteristics, and hence could also on our present supposition, be ascribed to the definists, but it is not really a *logical* confusion,[37] since it does not actually involve being confused about the difference between a proposition and a definition.

[35] Cf. R. B. Perry, *Journal of Philosophy* (1931), pp. 520 ff.
[36] *Principia Ethica*, pp. 17, 38, 59, 61.
[37] But see H. Osborne, *op. cit.*, pp. 18 f.

Only it is difficult to see how the intuitionists can prove that the definists are at least vaguely aware of the requisite unique characteristics.[38] The question must surely be left to the inspection or intuition of the definists themselves, aided by whatever suggestions the intuitionists may have to make. If so, we must credit the verdict of their inspection, especially of those among them who have read the writings of the intuitionists reflectively, and, then, as we have seen, the most they can be charged with is moral blindness.

Besides trying to discover just what is meant by the naturalistic fallacy, I have tried to show that the notion that a logical or quasi-logical fallacy is committed by the definists only confuses the issue between the intuitionists and the definists (and the issue between the latter and the emotists or postulationists), and misrepresents the way in which the issue is to be settled. No logical fallacy need appear anywhere in the procedure of the definists. Even fallacies in any less accurate sense cannot be implemented to decide the case against the definists; at best they can be ascribed to the definists only after the issue has been decided against them on independent grounds. But the only defect which can be attributed to the definists, *if* the intuitionists are right in affirming the existence of unique indefinable ethical characteristics, is a peculiar moral blindness, which is not a fallacy even in the looser sense. The issue in question must be decided by whatever method we may find satisfactory for determining whether or not a word stands for a characteristic at all, and, if it does, whether or not it stands for a unique characteristic. What method is to be employed is, perhaps, in one form or another, the basic problem of contemporary philosophy, but no generally satisfactory solution of the problem has yet been reached. I shall venture to say only this: it does seem to me that the issue is not to be decided against the intuitionists by the application *ab extra* to ethical judgments of any empirical or ontological meaning dictum.[39]

[38] For a brief discussion of their arguments, see *ibid.*, p. 67; L. Abraham, *op. cit.* I think they are all inconclusive, but cannot show this here.

[39] See *Principia Ethica*, pp. 124 f., 140.

FALLACIES IN MORAL PHILOSOPHY /
Stuart Hampshire

1. IN 1912 there appeared in *Mind* an article by the late Professor Prichard entitled "Does Moral Philosophy Rest on a Mistake?" I wish to ask the same question about contemporary
moral philosophy, but to suggest different reasons for an affirmative answer. Most recent academic discussions of moral
philosophy have directly or indirectly reflected the conception
of the subject-matter of moral philosophy which is stated or
implied in Professor Prichard's article; and this conception of
the subject was in turn directly derived from Kant. Kant's influence has been so great, that it is now difficult to realise how
revolutionary it was; yet I think that his main thesis, now generally accepted without question by philosophers as the starting-
point of moral philosophy, had not been advocated, or even seriously entertained, by any philosopher who preceded him. I shall
suggest that the *unbridgeable* separation between moral judgments and factual judgments, which Kant introduced, has had
the effect, in association with certain logical assumptions, of
leading philosophers away from the primary and proper questions of moral philosophy.[1]

What I shall summarily call the post-Kantian thesis, now
so widely accepted without question, is: there is an unbridgeable

From Stuart Hampshire, "Fallacies in Moral Philosophy," Mind, *LVIII (1949),*
466–482. Reprinted by permission of the Editor of Mind.

[1] Hume never denied that our moral judgments are based on arguments about
matters of fact; he only showed that these arguments are not logically conclusive
or deductive arguments.

logical gulf between sentences which express statements of fact and sentences which express judgments of value and particularly moral judgments; this absolute logical independence, ignored or not clearly stated by Aristotle, must be the starting-point of moral philosophy, and constitutes its peculiar problem. Post-Kantian philosophers of different logical persuasions have, of course, given very different accounts of the logic and use of value judgments; but they have generally agreed in regarding the logical independence of moral and empirical beliefs as defining the main problem of ethics.

If one reads the Nichomachean Ethics after reading the works of (for example) Professor G. E. Moore or Sir David Ross or Professor Stevenson, one has the impression of confronting a wholly different subject. The first point of difference can be tentatively expressed by saying that Aristotle is almost entirely concerned to analyse the problems of the moral *agent*, while most contemporary moral philosophers seem to be primarily concerned to analyse the problems of the moral *judge* or critic. Aristotle describes and analyses the processes of thought, or types of argument, which lead up to the *choice* of one course of action, or way of life, in preference to another, while most contemporary philosophers describe the arguments (or lack of arguments) which lead up to the acceptance or rejection of a moral *judgment about actions*. Aristotle's Ethics incidentally mentions the kind of arguments we use as spectators in justifying sentences which express moral praise and blame of actions already performed, while many contemporary moral philosophers scarcely mention any other kind of argument. Aristotle's principal question is—What sort of arguments do we use in practical deliberation about policies and courses of action and in choosing one kind of life in preference to another? What are the characteristic differences between moral and theoretical problems? The question posed by most contemporary moral philosophers seems to be—What do we mean by, and how (if at all) do we establish the truth of, sentences used to express moral judgments about our own or other people's actions?

The difference between these two approaches to the problems of moral philosophy emerges most clearly from the analogy between aesthetics and ethics to which allusion is made both in Aristotle's Ethics and also in most modern discussions of so-called value judgments (e.g. by Sir David Ross in 'The Right and the Good' and by Professor Ayer in 'Language, Truth and Logic'). For Aristotle (as for Plato) the aesthetic analogy which illuminates the problem of moral philosophy is the analogy between the artist or craftsman's characteristic procedures in designing and executing his work and the similar, but also different, procedures which we all use in designing and executing practical policies in ordinary life. For contemporary moral philosophers, largely preoccupied with elucidating sentences which express moral praise or blame (moral 'judgments' in the sense in which a judge gives judgments), the relevant analogy is between sentences expressing moral praise or condemnation and sentences expressing aesthetic praise or condemnation. As aesthetics has become the study of the logic and language of aesthetic *criticism*, so moral philosophy has become largely the study of the logic and language of moral criticism.

No one will be inclined to dispute that the processes of thought which are characteristic of the artist or craftsman in conceiving and executing his designs, are essentially different from the processes of the critic who passes judgment on the artist's work; it is notorious that the processes involved in, and the gifts and training required for, the actual making of a work of art are different from those which are required for the competent appraisal of the work; the artist's problem is not the critic's problem. An aesthetician may choose—and in fact most modern aestheticians have chosen—to confine himself to an analysis of the characteristic arguments involved in arriving at a judgment about a work of art (theories of a special aesthetic emotion, of objective standards of taste, etc.). Alternatively he may analyse and characterise the creative process itself (theories of imagination, the relation of technique to conception, the formation of style, the nature of inspiration, etc.). He may decide that the two inquiries, though certainly distinguishable and separable, are in some respects complementary, or at least that there are some questions contained within the first which cannot be answered without a prior answer to the second. But, however complementary they may be, the first inquiry certainly does not include the second. Those who wish to distinguish more clearly the peculiar characteristics of artistic activity, will learn little or nothing from the typical aestheticians' discussions of the objective and subjective interpretations of critical aesthetic judgments. But it seems now to be generally assumed that to ask whether sentences expressing moral praise or blame are to be classified as true or false statements, or alternatively as mere expressions of feeling, is somehow a substitute for the analysis of the processes of thought by which as moral agents we decide what we ought to do and how we ought to behave. Unless this is the underlying assumption, it is difficult to understand why moral philosophers should concentrate attention primarily on the analysis of ethical terms as they are used in sentences expressing moral praise and blame; for we are not primarily interested in moral criticism, or even self-criticism, except in so far as it is directly or indirectly an aid to the solution of practical problems, to deciding what we ought to do in particular situations or types of situation; we do not normally perplex ourselves deeply in moral appraisal for its own sake, in allotting moral marks to ourselves or to other people. The typical moral problem is not a spectator's problem or a problem of classifying or describing conduct, but a problem of practical choice and decision.

But the aesthetic analogy may be misleading, in that the relation of the value judgments of the art critic to the characteristic problems of the artist or craftsman cannot be assumed to be the same as the relation of the sentences expressing moral praise or blame to the problems of the moral agent.[2] To press

2 In so far as we now distinguish between the creative artist and the mere craftsman, a work of art by definition is not the answer to any problem; the artist is only said to have problems when conceived as a craftsman, that is, as having technical problems of devising means towards a given or presumed end. Where there is no problem posed, there can be no question of a right or wrong solution of it. Therefore the critic of poetry cannot be expected to show how the poem should be re-written; he describes, but he does not prescribe or make a practical judgment, as does the critic of conduct or technique. So the aesthetic analogy misleads in at least this respect; the valued critic of art excels in de-

the analogy would be question-begging, although the validity of the analogy between the problems of ethics and aesthetics is so often assumed. Leaving aside the analogy, the issue is—Is the answer to the question 'What are the distinguishing characteristics of sentences expressing moral praise or blame?' necessarily the same as the answer to the question 'What are the distinguishing characteristics of moral problems as they present themselves to us as practical agents?'? Unless these two questions are identical, or unless the first includes the second, much of contemporary moral philosophy is concerned with a relatively trivial side-issue, or is at the very least incomplete. My thesis is that the answer to the second question must contain the answer to the first, but that, if one tries to answer the first question without approaching it as part of the second, the answer will tend to be, not only incomplete, but positively misleading; and that the now most widely accepted philosophical interpretations of moral judgments, their logical status and peculiarities, are radically misleading for this reason. They purport to be logical characterisations of moral judgments and of the distinguishing features of moral arguments, but in these characterisations the *primary* use of moral judgments (= decisions) is largely or even entirely ignored.

2. Suppose (what probably occurs occasionally in most people's experience) one is confronted with a difficult and untrivial situation in which one is in doubt what one ought to do, and then, after full consideration of the issues involved, one arrives at a conclusion. One's conclusion, reached after deliberation, expressed in the sentence 'x is the best thing to do in these circumstances,' is a pure or primary moral judgment (the solution of a practical problem). It is misleading to the point of absurdity to describe this sentence, as used in such a context, as meaningful only in the sense in which an exclamation is meaningful, or as having no literal significance, or as having the function merely of expression and evoking feeling. It is also misleading to describe it as a statement about the agent's feeling or

scription and classification; he is not the artist's adviser, while moral or technical criticism is necessarily the giving of practical advice.

attitude; for such a description suggests that the judgment would be defended, if attacked, primarily by an appeal to introspection. It is surely misleading to describe the procedure by which such a judgment or decision is established as right as one of comparing degrees of moral emotion towards alternative courses of action. I am supposing (what is normal in such cases) that the agent has reasoned and argued about the alternatives, and am asserting that he would then justify his conclusion, if it were attacked, by reference to these arguments; and a statement about his own moral feelings or attitudes would not be, within the ordinary use of language, either a necessary or sufficient justification. Therefore the characterisation of such judgments as purely, or even largely, reports of feelings or attitudes is at the least incomplete and misleadingly incomplete, because in this characterisation the typical procedures of deliberation on which the judgment is based are suppressed or ignored. It is also paradoxical and misleading to introduce the word 'intuition', as another group of post-Kantian philosophers have done, in describing the procedure by which such a judgment is arrived at, or by which it is justified and defended; for the force of the word 'intuition' is to suggest that the conclusion is not established by any recognised form of argument, by any ratiocinative process involving a succession of steps which are logically criticisable; the word 'intuition' carries the suggestion that we do not, or even cannot, deliberate and calculate in deciding what we ought to do; but we always can and often actually do deliberate and calculate.

If the procedure of practical deliberation does not conform, either in its intermediate steps or in the form of its conclusions, with any forms of argument acknowledged as respectable in logical text-books, this is a deficiency of the logical text-books. Or rather it is a mistake in the *interpretation* of text books of logic to assume that they provide, or that they are intended to provide, patterns of all forms of reasoning or argument which can properly be described as rational argument. Arguments may be, in the ordinary and wider sense, rational, without being included among the types of argument which are ordinarily studied by logicians, since logicians are generally concerned exclusively with the types of argument which are characteristic of the *a priori* and empirical sciences. There are other patterns of argument habitually used outside the sciences, which may be described as more or less rational in the sense that they are more or less strictly governed by recognised (though not necessarily formulated) rules of relevance. If one criticises a sequence of sentences by saying that assertion or denial of the earlier members of the sequence is irrelevant to acceptance or rejection of their successors, then this sequence is being regarded as constituting an argument. Aristotle at least remarks that not all arguments are theoretical arguments, terminating in a conclusion which is intended as a statement, either factual or logically true; there are also practical arguments—he naturally says 'syllogisms'—the form of which is similar in many respects to some types of theoretical argument, but which are also characteristically different in their form; in particular they differ in the form of their conclusion, which is not a theoretical or true-or-false statement, but has the distinctive form of a practical judgment, e.g. 'this is the right action' or 'this is the best thing to do', or 'this ought to be done'.

Even when sentences containing moral terms are used by spectators (not agents) in contexts in which they seem to be in fact associated with a purely emotional reaction to a decision or action, it is misleadingly incomplete to characterise them as having the logical force only, or largely, of expressions of, or statements about, the speaker's or writer's feelings or attitudes. If a purely critical and apparently emotional moral judgment of this kind is challenged and needs to be defended and justified, it will be justified by the same kind of arguments which one would have used as an agent in practical deliberation. If I am not prepared to produce such practical arguments, pointing to what ought to have been done, I shall admit that I am not making a genuine moral judgment, but merely expressing or reporting my own feelings; and I shall admit that it was misleading to use the form of sentence ordinarily associated with moral judgments, and not with expressions of feeling. Doubtless many sentences containing moral terms are ambiguous, and may be normally used both as expressions of practical judgments and as expressions of feeling; but the important point is that, if challenged about our intentions, we are required to *distinguish* between such uses; and our languages, by providing the distinctive quasi-imperative form of the practical judgment, enable us to distinguish. But moral philosophers, tacitly assuming that moral judgments must be descriptive statements, have represented a moral problem as a critic's or spectator's problem of proper classification and description.

If, following Aristotle, one begins by describing how moral problems differ both from technical and theoretical problems, one will have begun to answer the question about the distinctive nature of moral judgments, even in their purely critical use. But if one begins by separating them from their context in practical deliberation, and considers them as quasi-theoretical [3] expressions of moral praise and condemnation, the resulting characterisation of them must be misleadingly incomplete.

3. The fact that moral judgments, in spite of the peculiarity of their form as practical judgments, are established by familiar patterns of argument, has been under-emphasised by post-Kantian moral philosophers as a consequence of three connected logical doctrines: (a) the doctrine that so-called value judgments cannot be derived from factual judgments: (b) the doctrine that, although we deliberate and argue about the facts of moral situations (e.g. about the probable consequences of various possible actions), no further argument is possible when once the facts of the situation have been determined; we are thus left in every case of practical deliberation with (c) an ultimate moral judgment, which cannot be replaced by any statement of fact, or by an empirical statement of any kind, and which cannot itself be defended by further argument. From no consideration of facts, or accumulation of factual knowledge, can we ever deduce a moral judgment of the form 'this ought to be done' or 'this is the right action in these circumstances'.

---

[3] To pose the problem of ethics as the problem of 'ethical predicates' or 'non-natural characteristics', is at the outset to suggest that moral judgments are to be interpreted as a peculiar kind of descriptive statement.

Therefore all appeal to the procedure of deliberation is irrelevant to the real problem, which is the analysis or characterisation of these *ultimate* moral judgments.

The fallacy in this position, as I have stated it, emerges in the words 'derive' and 'deduce'. It is only in limiting cases that, in describing the logic of any class of sentences of ordinary discourse, one can reasonably expect to find another class of sentences from which the problem-sentences are logically deducible. Statements about physical things cannot be deduced, or logically derived, from statements about sensations; statements about people's character or dispositions cannot be deduced, or logically derived from, statements about their behaviour; yet in both cases the truth of the first kind of statement is established exclusively by reference to the second kind. In general, one kind of sentence may be established and defended exclusively by reference to another kind, without the first kind being deducible, or logically derivable, from the second. When as philosophers we ask how a particular kind of sentence is to be categorised or described, we are asking ourselves by what sort of arguments it is established and how we justify its use if it is disputed; to explain its logic and meaning is generally to describe and illustrate by examples the kind of sentences which are conventionally accepted as sufficient grounds for its assertion or rejection. So we may properly eludicate moral or practical judgments by saying that they are established and supported by arguments consisting of factual judgments of a particular range, while admitting that they are never strictly deducible, or in this sense logically derivable, from any set of factual judgments.

Certainly no practical judgment is logically deducible from any set of statements of fact; for if practical judgments were so deducible, they would be redundant; we could confine ourselves simply to factual or theoretical judgments; this is in effect what strict Utilitarians, such as Bentham, proposed that we should do. Bentham recommended the removal of distinctively moral terms from the language, so that moral problems would be replaced by technical problems, or problems of applied science. He made this proposal quite self-consciously and deliberately, wishing to introduce a science of morals, in which all moral problems would be experimentally decidable as technical problems. The distinctive form in which moral problems are posed and moral conclusions expressed disappears in his usage, precisely because he makes arguments about matters of fact *logically conclusive* in settling moral problems; and it is precisely to this *replacement* of moral terms that critics of strict Utilitarians have always objected (e.g. Professor G. E. Moore in *Principia Ethica*); they have argued that Utilitarians confuse the reasons on which moral judgments may be based with those judgments themselves; and this confusion arises from supposing that the reasons must be logically conclusive reasons, so that to accept the empirical premises and to deny the moral conclusion is self-contradictory. But it does not follow from the fact that moral or practical judgments are not in their normal use so deducible that they must be described as ultimate, mysterious, and removed from the sphere of rational discussion. All argument is not deduction, and giving reasons in support of a judgment or statement is not necessarily, or even generally, giving logically conclusive reasons.

Once this assumption is removed, it is possible to reconsider, without philosophical prejudice, what is the difference and the relation between ordinary empirical statements and moral judgments as we actually use them when we are arguing with ourselves, or with others, about what we ought to do. It is important to consider examples of practical or moral problems which are neither trivial in themselves nor abstractly described; for it is only by reflecting on our procedure when confronted with what would ordinarily be called a genuine moral problem that the characteristic types of argument can be seen clearly deployed. A simplified variant of the situation presented in a recent novel [4] may serve the purpose. Suppose that I am convinced that if I continue to live, I cannot avoid inflicting great and indefinitely prolonged unhappiness on one or both of two people, and at the same time on myself; by committing suicide without

4 *The Heart of the Matter*, by Graham Greene.

detection I can avoid this accumulation of unhappiness; I therefore decide, after careful deliberation, that the right or best thing to do is to commit suicide. This is a moral judgment of the primary kind. (Having reached this conclusion, I may of course in any particular case fail to act in accordance with it; as Aristotle points out, deciding *that* x is the best thing to do and deciding *to* do x are both distinguishable and separable.) Suppose that in this case the moral judgment, which is the conclusion of my deliberation, is challenged by someone who at the same time agrees with me in my assessment of all the facts of the situation; that is, he agrees with me about the probable consequences of all the possible courses of action, but does not agree with my conclusion that it is right to commit suicide. An argument develops; we each give our reasons for saying that suicide under these circumstances is right or wrong. However the argument may develop in detail, it will generally exhibit the following features. (1) Although it is assumed that my disputant agrees with me about the facts of this particular situation (probable consequences of various actions etc.), he will in his argument appeal to other facts or beliefs about the world, which are not strictly describable as beliefs about the facts of this particular situation. For instance, we might both recognise as relevant a dispute, partly empirical and partly logical, about whether there is life after death, and whether the Christian dogmas on this subject are true or significant; or we may become involved in a largely historical argument about the social effects of suicide; and it would be recognised as pertinent to produce psychological arguments to the effect that intense unhappiness is often preferred to mere loneliness and *therefore* (and this 'therefore' is not the sign of an entailment) it would be better not to desert the other two people involved. *The point is that it does not follow from the fact that two people are in agreement about the facts of a particular situation, but disagree in their moral judgment, that their disagreement is ultimate and admits of no further rational argument;* hence (2) our disagreement about the moral or practical conclusion, which is not a disagreement about the facts of the particular situation, is nevertheless, a disagreement to which empirical arguments, beliefs about an indefinitely wide range of matters of fact, are recognised to be relevant. If we are deliberating or arguing about whether suicide is right or wrong in these particular circumstances (or in any circumstances), then our psychological, historical and religious beliefs are always taken to be relevant parts of the argument. By representing so-called value judgments as ultimate and logically divorced from ordinary factual judgments, philosophers have implicitly or explicitly suggested that such sentences as 'suicide is always wrong' or 'suicide is wrong in these circumstances' cannot be defended or refuted by appeals to facts or to the empirical sciences. This paradox is a legacy of Kant's anxiety to underline as strongly as possible the difference between practical problems which are moral problems and those which are purely technical problems. Almost all previous philosophers— and most people without Kantian or other philosophical prejudices—have assumed accumulating knowledge, or changing beliefs arising out of the study of history, psychology, anthropology and other empirical sciences, to be relevant to their moral judgments; to be relevant, not in the sense that the falsity of moral judgments previously accepted as true can be *deduced* from some empirical propositions of history, psychology or any natural science, but in the sense in which (for example) propositions about somebody's conduct are relevant to propositions about his character; that is, previous moral judgments are shown to be groundless, the empirical propositions on which they were based having been contradicted as scientific or historical knowledge increases. The conflicting moral conclusions of a Marxist and a Christian Fundamentalist, or the differences which may arise even between two contemporary and similarly educated liberal unbelievers, will generally (but not always or necessarily) be shown in argument to rest on different empirical or at least corrigible beliefs about the constitution of the universe. Whenever we argue about any moral question which is not trivial, our beliefs and assumptions, however rudimentary and half-formulated, about psychological, sociological and probably theological questions are recognised as relevant, as logically involved in the nature of the dispute.

The result of the supposed argument about my judgment that suicide is the right policy in this particular circumstance might be that I am convinced that my judgment was wrong, and am persuaded that suicide is not the right policy. I might be persuaded to withdraw my original judgment, either because I have been made to recognise a fault in the logic of my previous argument, or because I have been persuaded to abandon admittedly relevant beliefs about matters of fact, or because my attention has been directed to new facts as being relevant to the decision, facts which I had known but the relevance of which I had previously overlooked. To direct attention to further known facts as relevant to a judgment is perhaps the most important effect and function of moral arguments or practical deliberation (e.g. of giving practical advice). It is misleading to speak of 'the facts of a situation' in such a way as to suggest that there must be a closed set of propositions which, once established, precisely determine the situation.[5] The situations in which we must act or abstain from acting, are 'open' in the sense that they cannot be uniquely described and finally circumscribed. Situations do not present themselves with their labels attached to them; if they did, practical problems would be conclusively soluble theoretical problems, the philosopher's dream; but ἐν τῇ αἰσθήσει ἡ κρίσις— the crux is in the labelling, or the decision depends on how we see the situation.

For these reasons the logical divorce between so-called judgments of value and factual judgments is misleading; for arguments about practical conclusions are arguments about facts. Our moral or practical judgments—'*x* is the right or best course of action (in these or in all circumstances)'—are corrigible by

[5] The word 'fact', here as always, is treacherous, involving the old confusion between the actual situation and the description of it; the situation is given, but not 'the facts of the situation'; to state the facts is to analyse and interpret the situation. And just this is the characteristic difficulty of actual practical decisions, which disappears in the text-book cases, where the 'relevant facts' are pre-selected. So the determining arguments are cut out of the text-book, and the gap is filled by 'intuition' or feeling.

experience and observation; we feel certain about some, and very doubtful about others.

4. Certainly there may (logically) be cases in which we cannot attribute conflicting solutions of practical moral problems to conflicting beliefs about matters of fact; that is, two disputants, in giving their reasons for conflicting moral judgments, may be unable to find among their reasons any empirical proposition which is accepted by one of them and rejected by the other. It is logically possible that A and B should agree entirely e.g. about the effects of capital punishment, and furthermore should find no relevant differences in their general psychological or sociological or other beliefs, and yet disagree as to whether capital punishment should or should not now be abolished. However rare such situations may be (and I believe them to be much more rare than is commonly allowed) such so-called 'ultimate' moral differences may occur. Both A and B, if they can claim to be making a moral judgment and not merely expressing their own feelings about, or attitudes towards, capital punishment, will be able to give the reasons which seem to them sufficient to justify their conclusion; but what is accepted by A as a sufficient reason for a practical conclusion is not accepted by B as a sufficient reason and *vice versa*. They may then argue further to ensure that each does recognise the reason which he is claiming to be sufficient in this case as sufficient in other cases; but, when this consistency of use is once established, the argument must terminate. How is such an 'ultimate' or irresoluble difference about a moral judgment properly described?

Compare this ultimate difference about the practical judgment with a similar ultimate difference about a theoretical judgment: if A and B were to disagree about whether somebody is intelligent, and yet find that they did not disagree about the facts (actual behaviour) or probabilities (how he is likely to behave under hypothetical conditions) on which their judgment is based, they would describe their difference as a difference in the use of the word 'intelligent'; they would say 'you use a different criterion of intelligence, and so do not mean by "intelligent" ex-

actly what I mean'.[6] Similarly when it has been shown that A
and B generally apply wholly or largely different tests in deciding whether something ought or ought not to be done, they might
properly describe their so-called ultimate difference by saying
that they do not both mean the same, or exactly the same, thing
when they say that something ought or ought not to be done; and
in most such cases of ultimate or irresoluble moral differences
this is in fact what we do say—that different societies (and even
different individuals within the same society) may have more or
less different moral terminologies, which are not mutually trans-
latable. But of practical judgments one cannot say that differences which are in principle irresoluble are *simply* terminological misunderstandings and in *no* sense genuine contradictions;
for it is the distinguishing characteristic of practical judgments
that they have a prescriptive or quasi-imperative force as part of
their meaning. There is therefore one sense in which, when A
says that capital punishment ought to be abolished and B says
that it ought not, they are contradicting each other; their judgments contradict each other in the sense in which two conflicting commands or recommendations may be said to contradict
each other. They can only argue about which of their prescriptions is right if they can agree on some common criteria of rightness. A, following the practice of all reforming moralists and
many moral philosophers, may try to influence B's actions by
giving moral reasons for preferring his own criteria of use to B's
use; but in his advocacy of his own use of moral terms, he will
be using his moral terms in his own way. The argument might
have shown B that his conclusion was wrong in A's sense of
'wrong' or even in his own sense of 'wrong'; but no argument
can show that B *must* use the criteria which A uses and so must
attach the same meaning (in this sense) to moral terms as A.

[6] 'What do you mean by saying that he is intelligent?' is ordinarily interpreted as the same question as 'what are your reasons for saying or why do
you say, that he is intelligent?' Similarly, 'What do you mean by saying that
that was a wrong decision?' is the same question as '*Why* do you say that that
was a wrong decision?' To find the different reasons in different cases is to find
the meaning of 'wrong', although no *one* set of reasons is *the* meaning.

Between two consistently applied terminologies, whether in theoretical science or in moral decision, ultimately we must simply
choose; we can give reasons for our choice, but not reasons for
reasons for . . . *ad infinitum.*

5. We may find that many people do not deliberate and
so can scarcely be said to make moral judgments, but simply act
as they have been conditioned to act, and, when challenged, repeat the moral sentences which they have been taught to repeat
or merely state or express personal feelings or attitudes. A second, and much smaller class, act generally, and even wholly, on
impulse, in the sense that they do not propose practical problems
to themselves or choose policies, but simply do whatever they
feel inclined to do—and such people are to be distinguished
from those who have *decided that* to act on impulse, or to do
what one feels inclined to do, is the right policy; for this is to
make a moral judgment. But the great majority of people for
some part of their lives are thinking about what is the best thing
to do, sometimes reaching a conclusion and failing to act on it,
sometimes reaching a conclusion which, in the light of correc-
tions of their empirical beliefs or their logic, they later recognise
to have been a wrong conclusion, and sometimes reaching a conclusion which they are prepared to defend by argument and acting in accordance with it.

'Thinking what is the best thing to do' describes a procedure which it is unprofitable, if not impossible, to analyse, or
find a paraphrase for, in general terms without constant reference to specific cases. Aristotle begins by describing it as calculating means to a vaguely conceived end (happiness or well-
doing), the nature of the end being more precisely determined
by the means chosen as involved in its realisation. But he progressively qualifies and complicates this schematic account in
such a way as to suggest that to make a moral decision is not to
choose means to an already decided end, but to choose a policy
of means-to-end which is judged right or wrong as a whole. Practical problems are (as Kant emphasised and over-emphasised)
sub-divisible into moral and purely technical problems; the
choice of the most efficient means to an already determined end

is not called a moral choice. It is the defining characteristic of a moral problem, that it requires an unconditional decision, the choice of an action or policy as a whole.

6. There is another and related logical fallacy, often implicitly assumed and not explicitly stated, which has led philosophers to describe moral or practical judgments as expressions or reports of feeling or as established by *a priori* intuitions, and to neglect their normal occurrence as the corrigible conclusions of arguments involving the facts of a particular situation and our general beliefs about the world; this is the fallacy of assuming that all literally significant sentences must correspond to something, or describe something. As ordinary empirical statements were said to correspond to facts, so some philosophers have introduced the word 'values' in order that there should be something to which moral (and aesthetic) judgments can be said to correspond; we are said to 'intuit' or to 'apprehend' these values, these words being used to suggest an analogy with sense-perception. Other philosophers, wishing to define the world as the totality of facts, or as the objects of sense and introspection, have inferred that, as moral judgments cannot be said to correspond to anything in the external world, they must either correspond to something in the internal world (i.e. to feelings) or, failing that, that they cannot be admitted to be literally significant. The question 'what do moral judgments correspond to?' or 'what do they describe?' suggests itself particularly to those who are preoccupied with the critical use of these judgments as expressions of retrospective praise or blame; in so far as we relate them to practical deliberations and decisions, we come to recognise them as not descriptions of, but prescriptions for, actions. Practical judgments, no less than theoretical or descriptive statements, are in the natural sense of the words, literally significant, although they do not in the normal sense describe. If I say 'this is (or would have been) the right action in these circumstances', this judgment can be significantly denied; but, as it is not a descriptive statement or statement of fact, the denial is not normally expressed in the form 'it is *false* that this is the best action in these circumstances'; 'true' and 'false' are more

naturally used with theoretical judgments and statements of fact.[7] Of course this distinction between true or false descriptive statements and right or wrong practical judgments is not absolute and clear; many sentences are partly descriptive and are partly expressions of practical judgments. But there is a distinction which emerges clearly in simple cases of pure moral judgments and purely descriptive statements. One *can* describe somebody's behaviour or character without making any moral judgment (i.e. prescription), even if in fact prescriptions and descriptions are often almost inextricably combined.

7. There is (I think) a widespread impression that the concentration of academic moral philosophers on the attempt to *define* ethical expressions—'good', 'right', 'ought', etc.,—as being the principal problem of moral philosophy has tended to make the subject sterile and unenlightening. One is inclined to say that it does not *matter* whether 'right', as ordinarily used, is definable in terms of 'good' or not. There is the feeling that the clarifications which one expects from the moral philosopher cannot be answered by verbal definitions or the discovery of paraphrases. And I think this apparently philistine impatience with the search for verbal definitions or equivalences has good logical grounds. If we wish to clarify our own or somebody else's use of moral terms, the discovery of verbal equivalences or paraphrases among these terms is not an answer, but, at the most, a preliminary step towards an answer. I can become clear about what somebody means by saying 'this is the right action in these circumstances' only by finding out under what conditions he makes this judgment, and what reasons (and there may be many) he regards as sufficient to justify it. What we want to know, in clarifications of differences in our use of moral (or aesthetic) terms, is—What makes me (in the logical, not the causal sense) decide that this is the right action? There is no reason to expect a simple answer in terms of a single formula, e.g. 'it is likely to increase happiness'. But to search only for definitions

---

7 Although we can speak of believing that this is the right action we cannot speak of evidence that it is right. 'Evidence' is tied to statements which are true or false.

or verbal equivalences is to assume that there must be a single sufficient reason from which I always and necessarily derive my judgment. This is another expression of the fundamental fallacy of thinking of analysis or clarification of the standard use of words or sentences as necessarily a matter of exhibiting deducibilities or entailments. If I am asked what I mean by saying of someone that he is intelligent, I explain my use of the word by describing specimens of the type of behaviour to which I apply the word; I give some specimens of the types of statements about his behaviour which would be taken as sufficient grounds for asserting or denying that he is intelligent. Similarly, one can only clarify the use of the principal moral (or aesthetic) terms —'good', 'right', 'ought', etc.—by describing specimens of conduct to which they are applied, that is, by quoting the different characteristics of actions which are normally and generally taken to be sufficient grounds for deciding that they are the right actions. The type of analysis which consists in defining, or finding synonyms for the moral terms of a particular language cannot illuminate the nature of moral decisions or practical problems; it is no more than local dictionary-making, or the elimination of redundant terms, which is useful only as a preliminary to the study of typical moral arguments. An informative treatise on ethics—or on the ethics of a particular society or person—would contain an accumulation of examples selected to illustrate the kind of decisions which are said to be right in various circumstances, and the reasons given and the arguments used in concluding that they are right. An uninformative treatise on ethics consists of specimens of moral sentences, separated from actual or imaginable contexts of argument about particular practical problems, and treated as texts for the definition of moral terms; and many academic text-books follow this pattern.

Summary

The four logically related fallacies underlying the typical post-Kantian approach to moral philosophy are (*a*) The assimilation of moral or practical judgments to descriptive statements, which is associated with concentration on the use of moral terms in sentences expressing a spectator's praise or blame; (b) the inference from the fact that moral or practical judgment cannot be logically derived from statements of fact that they cannot be based on, or established exclusively by reference to, beliefs about matters of fact; hence theories that moral judgments must be ultimate and irrational, that they are established by intuition or are not literally significant; (c) the assumption that all literally significant sentences must correspond to or describe something; moral decisions do not correspond to or describe anything, but they may, nevertheless, be said to be rational or irrational, right or wrong.[8] (d) The confusion between clarifying the use of ethical terms with discovering definitions of, or verbal equivalences between, these terms; the search for definitions is another expression of the old obsession of philosophers with entailment and deducibility as the only admissible relation between sentences in rational argument. To interpret 'rational argument' so narrowly is, although misleading, not in itself fallacious; but if, on the basis of this arbitrary restriction, moral judgments are relegated to a logical limbo, labelled 'emotive', the study of the characteristic logic of these sentences, and of the types of argument in which they occur, is obscured and suppressed.

MORAL ARGUMENTS / *Philippa Foot*

THOSE who are influenced by the emotivist theory of ethics, and

8 'I decided that x was the right thing to do' is a descriptive statement, true or false; but 'x was the right thing to do' is a practical or moral judgment, right or wrong.

From Philippa Foot, "Moral Arguments," Mind, LXVII (1958), 502–513. Reprinted by permission of the Editor of Mind.

yet wish to defend what Hare has called "the rationality of moral discourse", generally talk a lot about "giving reasons" for saying that one thing is right, and another wrong. The fact that moral judgements need defence seems to distinguish the impact of one man's moral views upon others from mere persuasion or coercion, and the judgements themselves from mere expressions of likes and dislikes. Yet the version of argument in morals currently accepted seems to say that, while reasons must be given, no one need accept them unless he happens to hold particular moral views. It follows that disputes about what is right and wrong can be resolved only if certain contingent conditions are fulfilled; if they are not fulfilled, the argument breaks down, and the disputants are left face to face in an opposition which is merely an expression of attitude and will. Much energy is expended in trying to show that no sceptical conclusion can be drawn. It is suggested, for instance, that anyone who has considered all the facts which could bear on his moral position has *ipso facto* produced a 'well founded' moral judgement; in spite of the fact that anyone else who has considered the same facts may well come to the opposite conclusion. How 'x is good' can be a well founded moral judgement when 'x is bad' can be equally well founded it is not easy to see.

The statement that moral arguments 'may always break down' is often thought of as something that has to be accepted, and it is thought that those who deny it fail to take account of what was proved once for all by Hume, and elaborated by Stevenson, by Ayer, and by Hare. This article is an attempt to expose the assumptions which give the 'breakdown' theory so tenacious a hold, and to suggest an alternative view.

Looked at in one way, the assertion that moral arguments "may always break down" appears to make a large claim. What is meant is that they may break down in a way in which other arguments may not. We are therefore working on a model on which such factors as shortage of time or temper are not shown; the suggestion is not that A's argument with B may break down because B refuses for one reason or another to go on with it, but that their positions as such are irreconcilable. Now the question is: how can we assert that any disagreement about what is right and wrong may end like this? How do we know, without consulting the details of each argument, that there is always an impregnable position both for the man who says that X is right, or good, or what he ought to do, and for the man who denies it? How do we know that each is able to deal with every argument the other may bring?

Thus, when Hare describes someone who listens to all his adversary has to say and then at the end simply rejects his conclusion, we want to ask "How can he?" Hare clearly supposes that he can, for he says that at this point the objector can only be asked to make up his mind for himself.[1] No one would ever paint such a picture of other kinds of argument—suggesting, for instance, that a man might listen to all that could be said about the shape of the earth, and then ask why he should believe that it was round. We should want, in such a case, to know how he met the case put to him; and it is remarkable that in ethics this question is thought not to be in place.

If a man making a moral judgement is to be invulnerable to criticism, he must be free from reproach on two scores: (*a*) he must have brought forward evidence, where evidence is needed; and (*b*) he must have disposed of any contrary evidence offered. It is worth showing why writers who insist that moral arguments may always break down assume, for both sides in a moral dispute, invulnerability on both counts. The critical assumption appears in different forms because different descriptions of moral arguments are given; and I shall consider briefly what has been said by Stevenson and by Hare.

I. Stevenson sees the process of giving reasons for ethical conclusions as a special process of non-deductive inference, in which statements expressing beliefs (R) form the premises and emotive (evaluative) utterances (E) the conclusion. There are no rules validating particular inferences, but only causal connections between the beliefs and attitudes concerned. "Suppose", he writes, "that a theorist should *tabulate* the 'valid' inferences from R's to E's. It is difficult to see how he could be doing any-

1 *The Language of Morals*, p. 69.

thing more than specify what R's he thereby resolves to *accept* as supporting the various E's. . . . Under the name of 'validity' he will be selecting those inferences to which he is psychologically disposed to give assent, and perhaps inducing others to give a similar assent to them." [2] It follows that disputes in which each man backs up his moral judgement with "reasons" may always break down, and this is an implication on which Stevenson insists. So long as he does not contradict himself and gets his facts right, a man may argue as he chooses, or as he finds himself psychologically disposed. He alone says which facts are relevant to ethical conclusions, so that he is invulnerable on counts (*a*) and (*b*): he can simply assert that what he brings forward is evidence, and can simply deny the relevance of any other. His argument may be ineffective, but it cannot be said to be wrong. Stevenson speaks of ethical "inference" and of giving "reasons", but the process which he describes is rather that of trying to produce a result, an attitude, by means of a special kind of adjustment, an alteration in belief. All that is needed for a breakdown is for different attitudes in different people to be causally connected to the same beliefs. Then even complete agreement in belief will not settle a moral dispute.

II. Hare gives a picture of moral reasoning which escapes the difficulties of a special form of inference without rules of validity. He regards an argument to a moral conclusion as a syllogistic inference, with the ordinary rules. The facts, such as "this is stealing", which are to back up a moral judgement are to be stated in a "descriptive" minor premise, and their relevance is to be guaranteed by an "evaluative" major premise in which that kind of thing is said to be good or bad. There is thus no difficulty about the validity of the argument; but one does arise about the status of the major premise. We are supposed to say that a particular action is bad because it is a case of stealing, and because stealing is wrong; but if we ask why stealing is wrong, we can only be presented with another argument of the same form, with another exposed moral principle as its major premise. In the end everyone is forced back to some moral principle which he simply

[2] *Ethics and Language*, pp. 170–171.

asserts—and which someone else may simply deny. It can therefore be no reproach to anyone that he gives no reasons for a
statement of moral principle, since any moral argument must
contain some undefended premise of this kind. Nor can he be
accused of failing to meet arguments put forward by opponents
arguing from different principles; for by denying their ultimate
major premises he can successfully deny the relevance of anything they say.

Both these accounts of moral argument are governed by
the thought that there is no logical connection between statements of fact and statements of value, so that each man makes
his own decision as to the facts about an action which are relevant to its evaluation. To oppose this view we should need to
show that, on the contrary, it is laid down that some things do,
and some things do not, count in favour of a moral conclusion,
and that a man can no more decide for himself what is evidence
for rightness and wrongness than he can decide what is evidence for monetary inflation or a tumour on the brain. If such
objective relations between facts and values existed, they could
be of two kinds: descriptive, or factual premises might *entail*
evaluative conclusions, or they might count as *evidence* for
them. It is the second possibility which chiefly concerns me, but
I shall nevertheless consider the arguments which are supposed
to show that the stronger relationship cannot exist. For I want to
show that the arguments usually brought forward do not *even*
prove this. I want to say that it has not even been proved that
moral conclusions cannot be entailed by factual or descriptive
premises.

It is often thought that Hume showed the impossibility of
deducing "ought", from "is", but the form in which this view is
now defended is, of course, that in which it was rediscovered by
G. E. Moore at the beginning of the present century, and developed by such other critics of "naturalistic" ethics as Stevenson,
Ayer and Hare. We need therefore to look into the case against
naturalism to see exactly what was proved.

Moore tried to show that goodness was a non-natural
property, and thus not to be defined in terms of natural prop-

erties; the problem was to explain the concept of a "natural property", and to prove that no ethical definition in terms of natural properties could be correct. As Frankena[3] and Prior[4] pointed out, the argument against naturalism was always in danger of degenerating into a truism. A natural property tended to become one not identical with goodness, and the naturalistic fallacy that of identifying goodness with "some other thing".

What was needed to give the attack on naturalism new life was the identification of some deficiency common to the whole range of definitions rejected by Moore, a reason why they all failed. This was provided by the theory that value terms in general, and moral terms in particular, were used for a special function—variously identified as expressing feelings, expressing and inducing attitudes, or commending. Now it was said that words with emotive or commendatory force, such as "good", were not to be defined by the use of words whose meaning was merely "descriptive". This discovery tended to appear greater than it was, because it looked as if the two categories of fact and value had been identified separately and found never to coincide, whereas actually the factual or descriptive was defined by exclusion from the realm of value. In the ordinary sense of "descriptive" the word "good" is a descriptive word and in the ordinary sense of "fact" we say that it is a fact about so and so that he is a good man, so that the words must be used in a special sense in moral philosophy. But a special philosopher's sense of these words has never, so far as I know, been explained except by contrasting value and fact. A word or sentence seems to be called "descriptive" on account of the fact that it is *not* emotive, does *not* commend, does *not* entail an imperative, and so on according to the theory involved. This might seem to reduce the case against naturalism once more to an uninteresting tautology, but it does not do so. For if the non-naturalist has discovered a special feature found in all value judgements, he can no longer be accused of saying merely that nothing is a definition of "good" unless it is a definition of "good" and not "some other thing". His

3 W. K. Frankena, "The Naturalistic Fallacy", *Mind* (1939).
4 A. N. Prior, *Logic and the Basis of Ethics*, Chap. I.

part is now to insist that any definition which fails to allow for the special feature of value judgements must be rejected, and to label as "naturalistic" all the definitions which fail to pass this test.

I shall suppose, for the sake of argument, that the non-naturalist really has identified some characteristic (let us call it f) essential to evaluative words; that he is right in saying that evaluations involve emotions, attitudes, the acceptance of imperatives, or something of the kind. He is therefore justified in insisting that no word or statement which does not have the property f can be taken as equivalent to any evaluation, and that no account of the use of an evaluative term can leave out f and yet be complete. What, if anything, follows about the relation between premises and conclusion in an argument designed to support an evaluation?

It is often said that what follows is that evaluative conclusion cannot be deduced from descriptive premises, but how is this to be shown? Of course if a descriptive premise is redefined, as one which does not entail an evaluative conclusion, the non-naturalist will once more have bought security at the price of becoming a bore. He can once more improve his position by pointing to the characteristic f belonging to all evaluations, and asserting that no set of premises which do not entail an f proposition can entail an evaluation. If he takes this course he will be more like the man who says that a proposition which entails a proposition about a dog must be one which entails a proposition about an animal; he is telling us what to look out for in checking the entailment. What he is not so far telling us is that we can test for the entailment by looking to see whether the premise itself has the characteristic f. For all that has yet been shown it might be possible for a premise which is not f to entail a conclusion which is f, and it is obviously this proposition which the non-naturalist wants to deny.

Now it may seem obvious that a non-evaluative premise could not entail an evaluative conclusion, but it remains unclear how it is supposed to be proved.

In one form, the theory that an evaluative conclusion of a

deductive argument needs evaluative premises is clearly unwarrantable; I mention it only to get it out of the way. We cannot possibly say that at least one of the premises must be evaluative if the conclusion is to be so; for there is nothing to tell us that whatever can truly be said of the conclusion of a deductive argument can truly be said of any one of the premises. It is not necessary that the evaluative element should "come in whole", so to speak. If f has to belong to the premises it can only be necessary that it should belong to the premises *together*, and it may be no easy matter to see whether a set of propositions has the property f.

How in any case is it to be proved that if the conclusion is to have the characteristic f the premises taken together must also have it? Can it be said that unless this is so it will always be possible to assert the premises and yet deny the conclusion? I shall try to show that this at least is false, and in order to do so I shall consider the case of arguments designed to show that a certain piece of behaviour is or is not rude.

I think it will be agreed that in the wide sense in which philosophers speak of evaluation, "rude" is an evaluative word. At any rate it has the kind of characteristics upon which nonnaturalists fasten: it expresses disapproval, is meant to be used when action is to be discouraged, implies that other things being equal the behaviour to which it is applied will be avoided by the speaker, and so on. For the purpose of this argument I shall ignore the cases in which it is admitted that there are reasons why something should be done in spite of, or even because of, the fact that it is rude. Clearly there are occasions when a little rudeness is in place, but this does not alter the fact that "rude" is a condemnatory word.

It is obvious that there is something else to be said about the word "rude" besides the fact that it expresses, fairly mild, condemnation: it can only be used where certain descriptions apply. The right account of the situation in which it is correct to say that a piece of behaviour is rude, is, I think, that this kind of behaviour causes offence by indicating lack of respect. Sometimes it is merely conventional that such behaviour does indicate lack of respect (*e.g.* when a man keeps his hat on in someone else's house); sometimes the behaviour is naturally disrespectful, as when one man pushes another out of the way. (It should be mentioned that rudeness and the absence of rudeness do not exhaust the subject of etiquette; some things are not rude, and yet are "not done." It is rude to wear flannels at a formal dinner party, but merely not done to wear a dinner jacket for tennis.)

Given that this reference to offence is to be included in any account of the concept of rudeness, we may ask what the relation is between the assertion that these conditions of offence are fulfilled—let us call it O—and the statement that a piece of behaviour is rude—let us call it R. Can someone who accepts the proposition O (that this kind of offence is caused) deny the proposition R (that the behaviour is rude)? I should have thought that this was just what he could not do, for if he says that it is not rude, we shall stare, and ask him what sort of behaviour would be rude; and what is he to say? Suppose that he were to answer "a man is rude when he behaves conventionally", or "a man is rude when he walks slowly up to a front door", and this not because he believes that such behaviour causes offence, but with the intention of leaving behind entirely the usual criteria of rudeness. It is evident that with the usual criteria of rudeness he leaves behind the concept itself; he may say the words "I think this rude", but it will not on that account be right to describe him as "thinking it rude". If I *say* "I am sitting on a pile of hay" and bring as evidence the fact that the object I am sitting on has four wooden legs and a hard wooden back, I shall hardly be described as thinking, even mistakenly, that I am sitting on a pile of hay; all I am doing is to use the *words* "pile of hay".

It might be thought that the two cases were not parallel, for while the meaning of "pile of hay" is given by the characteristics which piles of hay must possess, the meaning of "rude" is given by the attitude it expresses. The answer is that if "thinking a thing rude" is to be described as having a particular attitude to it, then having an attitude presupposes, in this case, believing that certain conditions are fulfilled. If "attitudes" were solely a matter of reactions such as wrinkling the nose, and tendencies to such things as making resolutions and scolding, then thinking something rude would not be describable solely in terms of attitudes. Either thinking something rude is not to be described in terms of attitudes, or attitudes are not to be described in terms of such things. Even if we could suppose that a particular individual could react towards conventional behaviour, or to walking slowly up to an English front door, *exactly* as most people react to behaviour which gives offence, this would not mean that he was to be described as thinking these things rude. And in any case the supposition is nonsense. Although he could behave in some ways as if he thought them rude, e.g. by scolding conventional or slow-walking children, but not turning daughters with these proclivities out of doors, his behaviour could not be just as if he thought them rude. For as the social reaction to conventional behaviour is not the same as the social reaction to offensive behaviour, he could not act in just the same way. He could not for instance apologise for what he would call his "rudeness", for he would have to admit that it had caused no offence.

I conclude that whether a man is speaking of behaviour as rude or not rude, he must use the same criteria as anyone else, and that since the criteria are satisfied if O is true, it is impossible for him to assert O while denying R. It follows that if it is a sufficient condition of P's entailing Q that the assertion of P is inconsistent with the denial of Q, we have here an example of a non-evaluative premise from which an evaluative conclusion can be deduced.

It is of course possible to admit O while refusing to assert R, and this will not be like the refusal to say about prunes what one has already admitted about dried plums. Calling an action 'rude' is using a concept which a man might want to reject, rejecting the whole practice of praising and blaming embodied in terms such as 'polite' and 'rude'. Such a man would refuse to discuss points of etiquette, and arguments with him about what is rude would not so much break down as never begin. But once he did accept the question "Is this rude?", he would have to abide by the rules of this kind of argument; he could not bring forward any evidence he liked, and he could not deny the relevance of any piece of evidence brought forward by his opponent. Nor could he say that he was unable to move from O to R on this occasion because the belief in O had not induced in him feelings or attitudes warranting the assertion of R. If he had agreed to discuss rudeness he had committed himself to accepting O as evidence for R, and evidence is not a sort of medicine which is taken in the hope that it will work. To suggest that he could refuse to admit that certain behaviour was rude because the right psychological state had not been induced, is as odd as to suppose that one might refuse to speak of the world as round because in spite of the good evidence of roundness a feeling of confidence in the proposition had not been produced. When given good evidence it is one's business to act on it, not to hang around waiting for the right state of mind. It follows that if a man is prepared to discuss questions of rudeness, and hence to accept as evidence the fact that behaviour causes a certain kind of offence, he cannot refuse to admit R when O has been proved.

The point of considering this example was to show that there may be the strictest rules of evidence even where an evaluative conclusion is concerned. Applying this principle to the case of moral judgements, we see that—for all that the non-naturalist has proved to the contrary—Bentham, for instance, may be right in saying that when used in conjunction with the principle of utility "the words *ought* and *right* and *wrong,* and others of that stamp, have a meaning: when otherwise they have none".[5] Anyone who uses moral terms at all, whether to assert or deny a moral proposition, must abide by the rules for their use, including the rules about what shall count as evidence for or against the moral judgement concerned. For anything that has yet been shown to the contrary these rules could be entailment rules, forbidding the assertion of factual propositions in conjunction with the denial of moral propositions. The only recourse of the man who refused to accept the things which counted in favour of a moral proposition as giving him a reason to do certain things or to take up a particular attitude, would be to leave the moral discussion and abjure altogether the use of moral terms.

5 *Principles of Morals in Legislation,* Chap. I, x.

To say what Bentham said is not, then, to commit any sort of "naturalistic fallacy". It is open to us to enquire whether moral terms do lose their meaning when divorced from the pleasure principle, or from some other set of criteria, as the word "rude" loses its meaning when the criterion of offensiveness is dropped. To me it seems that this is clearly the case; I do not know what could be meant by saying that it was someone's duty to do something unless there was an attempt to show why it mattered if this sort of thing was not done. How can questions such as "what does it matter?", "what harm does it do?", "what advantage is there in . . . ?", "why is it important?", be set aside here? Is it even to be suggested that the harm done by a certain trait of character could be taken, by some extreme moral eccentric, to be just what made it a virtue? I suggest that such a man would not even be a moral eccentric, any more than the man who used the word "rude" of conventional behaviour was putting forward strange views about what was rude. Both descriptions have their proper application, but it is not here. How exactly the concepts of harm, advantage, benefit, importance, etc., are related to the different moral concepts, such as rightness, obligation, goodness, duty and virtue, is something that needs the most patient investigation, but that they are so related seems undeniable, and it follows that a man cannot make his own personal decision about the considerations which are to count as evidence in morals.

Perhaps it will be argued that this kind of freedom of choice is not ruled out after all, because a man has to decide for himself what is to count as advantage, benefit, or harm. But is this really plausible? Consider the man described by Hare as thinking that torturing is morally permissible.[6] Apparently he is not supposed to be arguing that in spite of everything torture is justifiable as a means of extracting confessions from enemies of the state, for the argument is supposed to be at an end when he has said that torturing people is permissible, and his opponent has said that it is not. How is he supposed to have answered the objection that to inflict torture is to do harm? If he is supposed

[6] *Universalisbility*, *P.A.S.* 1954–1955, p. 304.

to have said that pain is good for a man in the long run, rather than bad, he will have to show the benefits involved, and he can no more choose what shall count as a benefit than he could have chosen what counted as harm. Is he supposed perhaps to count as harm only harm to himself? In this case he is guilty of *igno-ratio elenchi*. By refusing to count as harm anything except harm to himself, he puts himself outside the pale of moral discussion, and should have explained that this was his position. One might compare his case to that of a man who in some discussion of common policy says "this will be the best thing to do", and announces afterwards that *he* meant best for himself. This is not what the word "best" does mean in the context of such a discussion.

It may be objected that these considerations about the evidence which must be brought for saying that one thing is good and another bad, could not in any case be of the least importance; such rules of evidence, even if they exist, only reflecting the connection between our existing moral code and our existing moral terms; if there are no "free" moral terms in our language, it can always be supposed that some have been invented—as indeed they will have to be invented if we are to be able to argue with people who subscribe to a moral code entirely different from our own. This objection rests on a doubtful assumption about the concept of *morality*. It assumes that even if there are rules about the grounds on which actions can be called good, right, or obligatory, there are no rules about the grounds on which a principle which is to be called a moral principle may be asserted. Those who believe this must think it possible to identify an element of feeling or attitude which carries the meaning of the word "moral". It must be supposed, for instance, that if we describe a man as being for or against certain actions, bringing them under universal rules, adopting these rules for himself, and thinking himself bound to urge them on others, we shall be able to identify him as holding moral principles, whatever the content of the principle at which he stops. But why should it be supposed that the concept of morality is to be caught in this particular kind of net? The consequences of such an assumption are very hard to stomach; for it follows that a rule which was admitted by those who obeyed it to be completely pointless could yet be recognised as a moral rule. If people happened to insist that no one should run round trees left handed, or look at hedgehogs in the light of the moon, this might count as a basic moral principle about which nothing more need be said.

I think that the main reason why this view is so often held in spite of these difficulties, is that we fear the charge of making a verbal decision in favour of our own moral code. But those who bring that charge are merely begging the question against arguments such as those given above. Of course if the rules we are refusing to call moral rules can really be given this name, then we are merely legislating against alien *moral codes*. But the suggestion which has been put forward is that this could not be the right description for rules of behaviour for which an entirely different defence is offered from that which we offer for our moral beliefs. If this suggestion is right, the difference between ourselves and the people who have these rules is not to be described as a difference of moral outlook, but rather as a difference between a moral and a non-moral point of view. The example of etiquette is again useful here. No one is tempted to say that the ruling out, *a priori*, of rules of etiquette which each man decides on for himself when he feels so inclined, represents a mere verbal decision in favour of our kind of socially determined standards of etiquette. On what grounds could one call a rule which someone was allowed to invent for himself a rule of *etiquette*? It is not just a fact about the use of our words "rude", "not done", etc., that they could not be applied in such a case; it is also a fact about etiquette that if terms in another language did appear in such situations they would not be terms of etiquette. We can make a similar point about the terms "legal" and "illegal" and the concept of law. If any individual was allowed to apply a certain pair of terms expressing approval and disapproval off his own bat, without taking notice of any recognised authority, such terms could not be legal terms. Similarly it is a fact about etiquette and law that they are both conventional as morality is not.

It may be that in attempting to state the rules which govern the assertion of moral propositions we shall legislate against a moral system radically opposed to our own. But this is only to say that we may make a mistake. The remedy is to look more carefully at the rules of evidence, not to assume that there cannot be any at all. If a moral system such as Nietzsche's has been refused recognition as a moral system, then we have got the criteria wrong. The fact that Nietzsche was a moralist cannot, however, be quoted in favour of the private enterprise theory of moral criteria. Admittedly Nietzsche said "You want to decrease suffering; I want precisely to increase it" but he did not *just* say this. Nor did he offer as a justification the fact that suffering causes a tendency to absentmindedness, or lines on the human face. We recognise Nietzsche as a moralist because he tries to justify an increase in suffering by connecting it with strength as opposed to weakness, and individuality as opposed to conformity. That strength is a good thing can only be denied by someone who can show that the strong man overreaches himself, or in some other way brings harm to himself or other people. That individuality is a good thing is something that has to be shown, but in a vague way we connect it with originality, and with courage, and hence there is no difficulty in conceiving Nietzsche as a moralist when he appeals to such a thing.

In conclusion it is worth remarking that moral arguments break down more often than philosophers tend to think, but that the breakdown is of a different kind. When people argue about what is right, good, or obligatory, or whether a certain character trait is or is not a virtue, they do not confine their remarks to the adducing of facts which can be established by simple observation, or by some clear-cut technique. What is said may well be subtle or profound, and in this sort of discussion as in others, in the field of literary criticism for instance, or the discussion of character, much depends on experience and imagination. It is quite common for one man to be unable to see what the other is getting at, and this sort of misunderstanding will not always be resolvable by anything which could be called argument in the ordinary sense.

Part Two / DUTY, SELF-INTEREST, AND WELFARE

THE *fascination of the metaethical questions posed by Moore and those who followed him lies precisely in the threat these questions entail for the ultimate coherence of ethical discourse. The tradition from Plato up to Moore had hardly hinted at the puzzles inherent in speaking of what is right and what is good in terms of knowledge itself. The alternative positions taken in the history of ethical thought strongly disagree with one another about the nature of ethical knowledge and about the cognitive grounds on which conduct may be justified or condemned; but the assumption is everywhere made that acts, preferences, choices may be assessed on the basis of relevant knowledge. The ethical tradition begins in some form of cognitivism and it has more or less consistently cleaved to it. In fact, Moore's own analytic efforts were not essentially designed to draw this matter into doubt. Considered historically, a radical noncognitivism in ethics has been a comparatively rare development. Even those who have committed themselves to the view that ethical sentences have important noncognitive (for instance, persuasive or emotive) functions have characteristically been unwilling to deny altogether that ethical sentences also make claims of a relevant sort and therefore require defense and support of a logically appropriate kind.*

In a word, the ethical tradition has never altogether lost sight of the venerable inquiry into the nature of the reasons that may be given in defending some particular action or other. The disputes that inevitably developed around this question were pursued all during that very interval in which metaethical quarrels were being most heatedly and absorbingly explored. Hence, the restoration of cognitivism took place almost simultaneously with the emergence of advanced views on the nature of ethical arguments (e.g., Rawls, Hare, Gellner, Harrison, Baier, Foot, Singer).

There is, it may also be noted, a natural connection between the concepts of ethical judgment and ethical behavior, which serves to broaden significantly the range of relevant philosophical interests. The connection is this: an ethically responsible agent, we must suppose, is one who acts either in accordance with appropriate justificatory reasons or under their impetus. Consequently, there is a sense in which the analysis of an evaluation by an ethical critic corresponds with the analysis of the conscious reflection and behavior of an ethical agent. Even the discrepancies between the conclusions arrived at by way of the employment of these two points of view, as in regard to excuses and extenuating circumstances (e.g., J. L. Austin, Hart, Anscombe), reveal themselves as fundamental aspects of the nature of ethical reasons and arguments. One must hold, at the very least, that the kinds of reasons that are found to be compelling from the critic's point of view must be in accord with, and to some extent overlap, the kinds of reasons by which an ethically responsible agent would be guided. This is a logical condition, not a psychological one; the literature, in this respect, moves easily —sometimes, perhaps, misleadingly—between the point of view of those who make ethical judgments and that held by those who conduct themselves in an ethically responsible way.

The crucial issue here, around which cluster many subsidiary questions, has to do with the logical relations between particular actions, the rules for judging actions, and the prin-

*ciples and purposes that ethical conduct and judgment are al-
leged to subserve. Historically, the modern version of the question has taken the form of a debate between the deontological
and utilitarian alternatives. Ross's criticism of utilitarian arguments provides, without a doubt, the most convenient introduction to the issues. What he shows conclusively is that utilitarian
reasons cannot appropriately be brought to bear on the ethical
assessment of particular acts, which we must judge in terms of
rightness and wrongness. What Ross thereby manages to point
up, in a single stroke, is the fundamental difference between considerations of goodness and considerations of rightness and, at
the same time, the problematic nature of the alleged rules by
which particular acts are judged to be right or wrong. The subsequent development of ethical theory pursues both the possibility
of reconciling questions of rightness with questions of goodness
and the logical problems suggested by the concept of a moral
rule. It may be said not unfairly that, if Ross's analysis represents the first step in the argument, Rawls's account represents the second. What Rawls attempts to show is the possibility
of reestablishing the utilitarian position (without committing
himself to utilitarianism), compatibly with Ross's criticism; in
doing so, Rawls addresses himself to the relationship between
considerations of rightness and of goodness as well as to the distinction between rules and principles. The most recent contributions to this literature have attempted to deal with detailed problems regarding the nature of rules (e.g., Hart) and the nature
of principles (e.g., Hare, Gellner, Singer, Urmson).*

*The possibility of a discrepancy between what is right and
what is good—a question which fascinated such classical authors
as Butler and Hume and Kant—continues to command attention
along certain well-defined lines of inquiry—for instance, along
the lines of the intelligibility of the repudiation of obligations to
others (e.g., Broad, Brunton, Baier, Medlin); or along the lines
of an analysis of the nature of blame and obligation (e.g., Frankena, Brandt, Hart, Falk, Rees); or along the lines of a reconciliation between personal and other-regarding concerns, especially
in terms of justice and personal rights (e.g., Rawls, Baier, Toul-*

min, Hart, Melden). At the bottom of all such inquiries, however, lies the master question—whether the entire range of what we call ethical matters can be coherently and convincingly systematized in terms of some comprehensive first principle, which guides or governs all moral judgment and conduct. Some form of utilitarianism has been the chief candidate for that post, but there are relevant reasons for thinking that even the best formulations fall significantly short of their goal and that, perhaps, the domain of ethics does not entirely lend itself to such systematization.

WHAT MAKES RIGHT ACTS RIGHT? / *W. D. Ross*

THE real point at issue between hedonism and utilitarianism on the one hand and their opponents on the other is not whether 'right' means 'productive of so and so'; for it cannot with any plausibility be maintained that it does. The point at issue is that to which we now pass, viz. whether there is any general character which makes right acts right, and if so, what it is. Among the main historical attempts to state a single characteristic of all right actions which is the foundation of their rightness are those made by egoism and utilitarianism. But I do not propose to discuss these, not because the subject is unimportant, but because it has been dealt with so often and so well already, and because there has come to be so much agreement among moral philosophers that neither of these theories is satisfactory. A much more attractive theory has been put forward by Professor Moore: that what makes actions right is that they are productive of more *good* than could have been produced by any other action open to the agent.[1]

From W. D. Ross, "*What Makes Right Acts Right?*" The Right and the Good (*Oxford: The Clarendon Press, 1930*), *pp. 16–47. Reprinted by permission of the Clarendon Press, Oxford.*

[1] I take the theory which, as I have tried to show, seems to be put forward in

This theory is in fact the culmination of all the attempts to base rightness on productivity of some sort of result. The first form this attempt takes is the attempt to base rightness on conduciveness to the advantage or pleasure of the agent. This theory comes to grief over the fact, which stares us in the face, that a great part of duty consists in an observance of the rights and a furtherance of the interests of others, whatever the cost to ourselves may be. Plato and others may be right in holding that a regard for the rights of others never in the long run involves a loss of happiness for the agent, that 'the just life profits a man'. But this, even if true, is irrelevant to the rightness of the act. As soon as a man does an action *because* he thinks he will promote his own interests thereby, he is acting not from a sense of its rightness but from self-interest.

To the egoistic theory hedonistic utilitarianism supplies a much-needed amendment. It points out correctly that the fact that a certain pleasure will be enjoyed by the agent is no reason why he *ought* to bring it into being rather than an equal or greater pleasure to be enjoyed by another, though, human nature being what it is, it makes it not unlikely that he *will* try to bring it into being. But hedonistic utilitarianism in its turn needs a correction. On reflection it seems clear that pleasure is not the only thing in life that we think good in itself, that for instance we think the possession of a good character, or an intelligent understanding of the world, as good or better. A great advance is made by the substitution of 'productive of the greatest good' for 'productive of the greatest pleasure'.

Not only is this theory more attractive than hedonistic utilitarianism, but its logical relation to that theory is such that the latter could not be true unless *it* were true, while it might be true though hedonistic utilitarianism were not. It is in fact one of the logical bases of hedonistic utilitarianism. For the view that what produces the maximum pleasure is right has for its bases the views (1) that what produces the maximum good is

---

Ethics rather than the earlier and less plausible theory put forward in *Principia Ethica*. For the difference, cf. Ross, *The Right and the Good* (Oxford: 1930), pp. 8–11.

right, and (2) that pleasure is the only thing good in itself. If they were not assuming that what produces the maximum *good* is right, the utilitarians' attempt to show that pleasure is the only thing good in itself, which is in fact the point they take most pains to establish, would have been quite irrelevant to their attempt to prove that only what produces the maximum *pleasure* is right. If, therefore, it can be shown that productivity of the maximum good is not what makes all right actions right, we shall *a fortiori* have refuted hedonistic utilitarianism.

When a plain man fulfills a promise because he thinks he ought to do so, it seems clear that he does so with no thought of its total consequences, still less with any opinion that these are likely to be the best possible. He thinks in fact much more of the past than of the future. What makes him think it right to act in a certain way is the fact that he has promised to do so—that and, usually, nothing more. That his act will produce the best possible consequences is not his reason for calling it right. What lends colour to the theory we are examining, then, is not the actions (which form probably a great majority of our actions) in which some such reflection as 'I have promised' is the only reason we give ourselves for thinking a certain action right, but the exceptional cases in which the consequences of fulfilling a promise (for instance) would be so disastrous to others that we judge it right not to do so. It must of course be admitted that such cases exist. If I have promised to meet a friend at a particular time for some trivial purpose, I should certainly think myself justified in breaking my engagement if by doing so I could prevent a serious accident or bring relief to the victims of one. And the supporters of the view we are examining hold that my thinking so is due to my thinking that I shall bring more good into existence by the one action than by the other. A different account may, however, be given of the matter, an account which will, I believe, show itself to be the true one. It may be said that besides the duty of fulfilling promises I have and recognize a duty of relieving distress,[2] and that when I think it right to do

[2] These are not strictly speaking duties, but things that tend to be our duty, or *prima facie* duties. Cf. Ross, *op. cit.*, pp. 19–20 [pp. 198–200].

the latter at the cost of not doing the former, it is not because I think I shall produce more good thereby but because I think it the duty which is in the circumstances more of a duty. This account surely corresponds much more closely with what we really think in such a situation. If, so far as I can see, I could bring equal amounts of good into being by fulfilling my promise and by helping some one to whom I had made no promise, I should not hesitate to regard the former as my duty. Yet on the view that what is right is right because it is productive of the most good I should not so regard it.

There are two theories, each in its way simple, that offer a solution of such cases of conscience. One is the view of Kant, that there are certain duties of perfect obligation, such as those of fulfilling promises, of paying debts, of telling the truth, which admit of no exception whatever in favour of duties of imperfect obligation, such as that of relieving distress. The other is the view of, for instance, Professor Moore and Dr. Rashdall, that there is only the duty of producing good, and that all 'conflicts of duties' should be resolved by asking 'by which action will most good be produced?' But it is more important that our theory fit the facts than that it be simple, and the account we have given above corresponds (it seems to me) better than either of the simpler theories with what we really think, viz. that normally promise-keeping, for example, should come before benevolence, but that when and only when the good to be produced by the benevolent act is very great and the promise comparatively trivial, the act of benevolence becomes our duty.

In fact the theory of 'ideal utilitarianism', if I may for brevity refer so to the theory of Professor Moore, seems to simplify unduly our relations to our fellows. It says, in effect, that the only morally significant relation in which my neighbours stand to me is that of being possible beneficiaries by my action.[3] They do stand in this relation to me, and this relation is morally significant. But they may also stand to me in the relation of

3 Some will think it, apart from other considerations, a sufficient refutation of this view to point out that I also stand in that relation to myself, so that for this view the distinction of oneself from others is morally insignificant.

promisee to promiser, of creditor to debtor, of wife to husband, of child to parent, of friend to friend, of fellow countryman to fellow countryman, and the like; and each of these relations is the foundation of a *prima facie* duty, which is more or less incumbent on me according to the circumstances of the case. When I am in a situation, as perhaps I always am, in which more than one of these *prima facie* duties is incumbent on me, what I have to do is to study the situation as fully as I can until I form the considered opinion (it is never more) that in the circumstances one of them is more incumbent than any other; then I am bound to think that to do this *prima facie* duty is my duty *sans phrase* in the situation.

I suggest '*prima facie* duty' or 'conditional duty' as a brief way of referring to the characteristic (quite distinct from that of being a duty proper) which an act has, in virtue of being of a certain kind (e.g. the keeping of a promise), of being an act which would be a duty proper if it were not at the same time of another kind which is morally significant. Whether an act is a duty proper or actual duty depends on *all* the morally significant kinds it is an instance of. The phrase '*prima facie* duty' must be apologized for, since (1) it suggests that what we are speaking of is a certain kind of duty, whereas it is in fact not a duty, but something related in a special way to duty. Strictly speaking, we want not a phrase in which duty is qualified by an adjective, but a separate noun. (2) '*Prima*' *facie* suggests that one is speaking only of an appearance which a moral situation presents at first sight, and which may turn out to be illusory; whereas what I am speaking of is an objective fact involved in the nature of the situation, or more strictly in an element of its nature, though not, as duty proper does, arising from its *whole* nature. I can, however, think of no term which fully meets the case. 'Claim' has been suggested by Professor Prichard. The word 'claim' has the advantage of being quite a familiar one in this connection, and it seems to cover much of the ground. It would be quite natural to say, 'a person to whom I have made a promise has a claim on me', and also, 'a person whose distress I could relieve (at the cost of breaking the promise) has a claim on me'. But

(1) while 'claim' is appropriate from *their* point of view, we want a word to express the corresponding fact from the agent's point of view—the fact of his being subject to claims that can be made against him; and ordinary language provides us with no such correlative to 'claim'. And (2) (what is more important) 'claim' seems inevitably to suggest two persons, one of whom might make a claim on the other; and while this covers the ground of social duty, it is inappropriate in the case of that important part of duty which is the duty of cultivating a certain kind of character in oneself. It would be artificial, I think, and at any rate metaphorical, to say that one's character has a claim on oneself.

There is nothing arbitrary about these *prima facie* duties. Each rests on a definite circumstance which cannot seriously be held to be without moral significance. Of *prima facie* duties I suggest, without claiming completeness or finality for it, the following division.[4]

(1) Some duties rest on previous acts of my own. These duties seem to include two kinds, (*a*) those resting on a promise or what may fairly be called an implicit promise, such as the implicit undertaking not to tell lies which seems to be implied in the act of entering into conversation (at any rate by civilized men), or of writing books that purport to be history and not fiction. These may be called the duties of fidelity. (*b*) Those resting on a previous wrongful act. These may be called the duties of reparation. (2) Some rest on previous acts of other men, i.e. services done by them to me. These may be loosely described as

---

4 I should make it plain at this stage that I am *assuming* the correctness of some of our main convictions as to *prima facie* duties, or, more strictly, am claiming that we *know* them to be true. To me it seems as self-evident as anything could be, that to make a promise, for instance, is to create a moral claim on us in someone else. Many readers will perhaps say that they do *not* know this to be true. If so, I certainly cannot prove it to them; I can only ask them to reflect again, in the hope that they will ultimately agree that they also know it to be true. The main moral convictions of the plain man seem to me to be, not opinions which it is for philosophy to prove or disprove, but knowledge from the start; and in my own case I seem to find little difficulty in distinguishing these essential convictions from other moral convictions which I also have, which are merely fallible opinions based on an imperfect study of the working for good or evil of certain institutions or types of action.

the duties of gratitude.[5] (3) Some rest on the fact or possibility of a distribution of pleasure or happiness (or of the means thereto) which is not in accordance with the merit of the persons concerned; in such cases there arises a duty to upset or prevent such a distribution. These are the duties of justice. (4) Some rest on the mere fact that there are other beings in the world whose condition we can make better in respect of virtue, or of intelligence, or of pleasure. These are the duties of beneficence. (5) Some rest on the fact that we can improve our own condition in respect of virtue or of intelligence. These are the duties of self-improvement. (6) I think that we should distinguish from (4) the duties that may be summed up under the title of 'not injuring others'. No doubt to injure others is incidentally to fail to do them good; but it seems to me clear that non-maleficence is apprehended as a duty distinct from that of beneficence, and as a duty of a more stringent character. It will be noticed that this alone among the types of duty has been stated in a negative way. An attempt might no doubt be made to state this duty, like the others, in a positive way. It might be said that it is really the duty to prevent ourselves from acting either from an inclination to harm others or from an inclination to seek our own pleasure, in doing which we should incidentally harm them. But on reflection it seems clear that the primary duty here is the duty not to harm others, this being a duty whether or not we have an inclination that if followed would lead to our harming them; and that when we have such an inclination the primary duty not to harm others gives rise to a consequential duty to resist the inclination. The recognition of this duty of non-maleficence is the first step on the way to the recognition of the duty of beneficence; and that accounts for the prominence of the commands 'thou shalt not kill', 'thou shalt not commit adultery', 'thou shalt not steal', 'thou shalt not bear false witness', in so early a code as the Decalogue. But even when we have come to recognize the duty of beneficence, it appears to me that the duty of non-maleficence is recognized as a distinct one, and as *prima facie* more binding. We should not in general consider

5 For a needed correction of this statement, cf. Ross, *op. cit.*, pp. 22–3 [p. 202].

it justifiable to kill one person in order to keep another alive, or to steal from one in order to give alms to another.

The essential defect of the 'ideal utilitarian' theory is that it ignores, or at least does not do full justice to, the highly personal character of duty. If the only duty is to produce the maximum of good, the question who is to have the good—whether it is myself, or my benefactor, or a person to whom I have made a promise to confer that good on him, or a mere fellow man to whom I stand in no such special relation—should make no difference to my having a duty to produce that good. But we are all in fact sure that it makes a vast difference.

One or two other comments must be made on this provisional list of the divisions of duty. (1) The nomenclature is not strictly correct. For by 'fidelity' or 'gratitude' we mean, strictly, certain states of motivation; and, as I have urged, it is not our duty to have certain motives, but to do certain acts. By 'fidelity', for instance, is meant, strictly, the disposition to fulfill promises and implicit promises *because we have made them*. We have no general word to cover the actual fulfillment of promises and implicit promises *irrespective of motive;* and I use 'fidelity', loosely but perhaps conveniently, to fill this gap. So too I use 'gratitude' for the returning of services, irrespective of motive. The term 'justice' is not so much confined, in ordinary usage, to a certain state of motivation, for we should often talk of a man as acting justly even when we did not think his motive was the wish to do what was just simply for the sake of doing so. Less apology is therefore needed for our use of 'justice' in this sense. And I have used the word 'beneficence' rather than 'benevolence', in order to emphasize the fact that it is our duty to do certain things, and not to do them from certain motives.

(2) If the objection be made, that this catalogue of the main types of duty is an unsystematic one resting on no logical principle, it may be replied, first, that it makes no claim to being ultimate. It is a *prima facie* classification of the duties which reflection on our moral convictions seems actually to reveal. And if these convictions are, as I would claim that they are, of the nature of knowledge, and if I have not misstated them, the list

will be a list of authentic conditional duties, correct as far as it goes though not necessarily complete. The list of *goods* put forward by the rival theory is reached by exactly the same method —the only sound one in the circumstances—viz. that of direct reflection on what we really think. Loyalty to the facts is worth more than a symmetrical architectonic or a hastily reached simplicity. If further reflection discovers a perfect logical basis for this or for a better classification, so much the better.

(3) It may, again, be objected that our theory that there are these various and often conflicting types of *prima facie* duty leaves us with no principle upon which to discern what is our actual duty in particular circumstances. But this objection is not one which the rival theory is in a position to bring forward. For when we have to choose between the production of two heterogeneous goods, say knowledge and pleasure, the 'ideal utilitarian' theory can only fall back on an opinion, for which no logical basis can be offered, that one of the goods is the greater; and this is no better than a similar opinion that one of two duties is the more urgent. And again, when we consider the infinite variety of the effects of our actions in the way of pleasure, it must surely be admitted that the claim which *hedonism* sometimes makes, that it offers a readily applicable criterion of right conduct, is quite illusory.

I am unwilling, however, to content myself with an *argumentum ad hominem*, and I would contend that in principle there is no reason to anticipate that every act that is our duty is so for one and the same reason. Why should two sets of circumstances, or one set of circumstances, *not* possess different characteristics, any one of which makes a certain act our *prima facie* duty? When I ask what it is that makes me in certain cases sure that I have a *prima facie* duty to do so and so, I find that it lies in the fact that I have made a promise; when I ask the same question in another case, I find the answer lies in the fact that I have done a wrong. And if on reflection I find (as I think I do) that neither of these reasons is reducible to the other, I must not on any *a priori* ground assume that such a reduction is possible.

An attempt may be made to arrange in a more systematic

way the main types of duty which we have indicated. In the first place it seems self-evident that if there are things that are intrinsically good, it is *prima facie* a duty to bring them into existence rather than not to do so, and to bring as much of them into existence as possible. . . . there are three main things that are intrinsically good—virtue, knowledge, and, with certain limitations, pleasure. And since a given virtuous disposition, for instance, is equally good whether it is realized in myself or in another, it seems to be my duty to bring it into existence whether in myself or in another. So too with a given piece of knowledge.

The case of pleasure is difficult; for while we clearly recognize a duty to produce pleasure for others, it is by no means so clear that we recognize a duty to produce pleasure for ourselves. This appears to arise from the following facts. The thought of an act as our duty is one that presupposes a certain amount of reflection about the act; and for that reason does not normally arise in connection with acts towards which we are already impelled by another strong impulse. So far, the cause of our not thinking of the promotion of our own pleasure as a duty is analogous to the cause which usually prevents a highly sympathetic person from thinking of the promotion of the pleasure of others as a duty. He is impelled so strongly by direct interest in the well-being of others towards promoting their pleasure that he does not stop to ask whether it is his duty to promote it; and we are all impelled so strongly towards the promotion of our own pleasure that we do not stop to ask whether it is a duty or not. But there is a further reason why even when we stop to think about the matter it does not usually present itself as a duty: viz. that, since the performance of most of our duties involves the giving up of some pleasure that we desire, the doing of duty and the getting of pleasure for ourselves come by a natural association of ideas to be thought of as incompatible things. This association of ideas is in the main salutary in its operation, since it puts a check on what but for it would be much too strong, the tendency to pursue one's own pleasure without thought of other considerations. Yet if pleasure is good, it seems in the long run clear that it is right to get it for ourselves as well as to produce it for others, when this does not involve the failure to discharge some more stringent *prima facie* duty. The question is a very difficult one, but it seems that this conclusion can be denied only on one or other of three grounds: (1) that pleasure is not *prima facie* good (i.e. good when it is neither the actualization of a bad disposition nor undeserved), (2) that there is no *prima facie* duty to produce as much that is good as we can, or (3) that though there is a *prima facie* duty to produce other things that are good, there is no *prima facie* duty to produce pleasure which will be enjoyed by ourselves. . . . The second hardly admits of argument but seems to me plainly false. The third seems plausible only if we hold that an act that is pleasant or brings pleasure to ourselves must for that reason not be a duty; and this would lead to paradoxical consequences, such as that if a man enjoys giving pleasure to others or working for their moral improvement, it cannot be his duty to do so. Yet it seems to be a very stubborn fact, that in our ordinary consciousness we are not aware of a duty to get pleasure for ourselves; and by way of partial explanation of this I may add that though, as I think, one's own pleasure is a good and there is a duty to produce it, it is only if we *think* of our own pleasure not as simply our own pleasure, but as an objective good, something that an impartial spectator would approve, that we can think of the getting it as a duty; and we do not habitually think of it in this way.

If these contentions are right, what we have called the duty of beneficence and the duty of self-improvement rest on the same ground. No different principles of duty are involved in the two cases. If we feel a special responsibility for improving our own character rather than that of others, it is not because a special principle is involved, but because we are aware that the one is more under our control than the other. It was on this ground that Kant expressed the practical law of duty in the form 'seek to make yourself good and other people happy'. He was so persuaded of the internality of virtue that he regarded any attempt by one person to produce virtue in another as bound to produce, at most, only a counterfeit of virtue, the doing of externally right acts not from the true principle of virtuous action but out of regard to another person. It must be admitted that one man cannot compel another to be virtuous; compulsory virtue would just not be virtue. But experience clearly shows that Kant overshoots the mark when he contends that one man cannot do anything to *promote* virtue in another, to bring such influences to bear upon him that his own response to them is more likely to be virtuous than his response to other influences would have been. And our duty to do this is not different in kind from our duty to improve our own characters.

It is equally clear, and clear at an earlier stage of moral development, that if there are things that are bad in themselves we ought, *prima facie,* not to bring them upon others; and on this fact rests the duty of non-maleficence.

The duty of justice is particularly complicated, and the word is used to cover things which are really very different— things such as the payment of debts, the reparation of injuries done by oneself to another, and the bringing about of a distribution of happiness between other people in proportion to merit. I use the word to denote only the last of these three. [Later] I shall try to show that besides the three (comparatively) simple goods, virtue, knowledge, and pleasure, there is a more complex good, not reducible to these, consisting in the proportionment of happiness to virtue. The bringing of this about is a duty which we owe to all men alike, though it may be reinforced by special responsibilities that we have undertaken to particular men. This, therefore, with beneficence and self-improvement, comes under the general principle that we should produce as much good as possible, though the good here involved is different in kind from any other.

But besides this general obligation, there are special obligations. These may arise, in the first place, incidentally, from acts which were not essentially meant to create such an obligation, but which nevertheless create it. From the nature of the case such acts may be of two kinds—the infliction of injuries on others, and the acceptance of benefits from them. It seems clear that these put us under a special obligation to other men, and that only these acts can do so incidentally. From these arise the twin duties of reparation and gratitude.

And finally there are special obligations arising from acts the very intention of which, when they were done, was to put us under such an obligation. The name for such acts is 'promises'; the name is wide enough if we are willing to include under it implicit promises, i.e. modes of behaviour in which without explicit verbal promise we intentionally create an expectation that we can be counted on to behave in a certain way in the interest of another person.

These seem to be, in principle, all the ways in which *prima facie* duties arise. In actual experience they are compounded together in highly complex ways. Thus, for example, the duty of obeying the laws of one's country arises partly (as Socrates contends in the *Crito*) from the duty of gratitude for the benefits one has received from it; partly from the implicit promise to obey which seems to be involved in permanent residence in a country whose laws we know we are *expected* to obey, and still more clearly involved when we ourselves invoke the protection of its laws (this is the truth underlying the doctrine of the social contract); and partly (if we are fortunate in our country) from the fact that its laws are potent instruments for the general good.

Or again, the sense of a general obligation to bring about (so far as we can) a just apportionment of happiness to merit is often greatly reinforced by the fact that many of the existing injustices are due to a social and economic system which we have, not indeed created, but taken part in and assented to; the duty of justice is then reinforced by the duty of reparation.

It is necessary to say something by way of clearing up the relation between *prima facie* duties and the actual or absolute duty to do one particular act in particular circumstances. If, as almost all moralists except Kant are agreed, and as most plain men think, it is sometimes right to tell a lie or to break a promise, it must be maintained that there is a difference between *prima facie* duty and actual or absolute duty. When we think ourselves justified in breaking, and indeed morally obliged to break, a promise in order to relieve some one's distress, we do not for a moment cease to recognize a *prima facie* duty to keep our promise, and this leads us to feel, not indeed shame or repentance, but certainly compunction, for behaving as we do; we recognize, further, that it is our duty to make up somehow to the promisee for the breaking of the promise. We have to distinguish from the characteristic of being our duty that of tending to be our duty. Any act that we do contains various elements in virtue of which it falls under various categories. In virtue of being the breaking of a promise, for instance, it tends to be wrong; in virtue of being an instance of relieving distress it tends to be right. Tendency to be one's duty may be called a parti-resultant attribute, i.e. one which belongs to an act in virtue of some one component in its nature. *Being* one's duty is a toti-resultant attribute, one which belongs to an act in virtue of its whole nature and of nothing less than this.[6] This distinction between parti-resultant and toti-resultant attributes is one which we shall meet in another context also.

Another instance of the same distinction may be found in the operation of natural laws. *Qua* subject to the force of gravitation towards some other body, each body tends to move in a particular direction with a particular velocity; but its actual movement depends on *all* the forces to which it is subject. It is only by recognizing this distinction that we can preserve the absoluteness of laws of nature, and only by recognizing a corresponding distinction that we can preserve the absoluteness of the general principles of morality. But an important difference between the two cases must be pointed out. When we say that in virtue of gravitation a body tends to move in a certain way, we are referring to a causal influence actually exercised on it by another body or other bodies. When we say that in virtue of being deliberately untrue a certain remark tends to be wrong, we are referring to no causal relation, to no relation that involves succession in time, but to such a relation as connects the various attributes of a mathematical figure. And if the word 'tendency' is thought to suggest too much a causal relation, it is better to

6 But cf. the qualification in p. 213, n. 8.

talk of certain types of act as being *prima facie* right or wrong
(or of different persons as having different and possibly conflicting claims upon us), than of their tending to be right or wrong.

Something should be said of the relation between our apprehension of the *prima facie* rightness of certain types of act
and our mental attitude towards particular acts. It is proper to
use the word 'apprehension' in the former case and not in the
latter. That an act, *qua* fulfilling a promise, or *qua* effecting a
just distribution of good, or *qua* returning services rendered, or
qua promoting the good of others, or *qua* promoting the virtue or
insight of the agent, is *prima facie* right, is self-evident; not in
the sense that it is evident from the beginning of our lives, or as
soon as we attend to the proposition for the first time, but in the
sense that when we have reached sufficient mental maturity and
have given sufficient attention to the proposition it is evident
without any need of proof, or of evidence beyond itself. It is self-
evident just as a mathematical axiom, or the validity of a form
of inference, is evident. The moral order expressed in these
propositions is just as much part of the fundamental nature of
the universe (and, we may add, of any possible universe in
which there were moral agents at all) as is the spatial or numerical structure expressed in the axioms of geometry or arithmetic. In our confidence that these propositions are true there is
involved the same trust in our reason that is involved in our
confidence in mathematics; and we should have no justification
for trusting it in the latter sphere and distrusting it in the former. In both cases we are dealing with propositions that cannot
be proved, but that just as certainly need no proof.

Some of these general principles of *prima facie* duty may
appear to be open to criticism. It may be thought, for example,
that the principle of returning good for good is a falling off from
the Christian principle, generally and rightly recognized as expressing the highest morality, of returning good for evil. To this
it may be replied that I do not suggest that there is a principle
commanding us to return good for good and forbidding us to
return good for evil, and that I do suggest that there is a positive
duty to seek the good of all men. What I maintain is that an act

in which good is returned for good is recognized as *specially* binding on us just because it is of that character, and that *ceteris paribus* any one would think it his duty to help his benefactors rather than his enemies, if he could not do both; just as it is generally recognized that *ceteris paribus* we should pay our debts rather than give our money in charity, when we cannot do both. A benefactor is not only a man, calling for our effort on his behalf on that ground, but also our benefactor, calling for our *special* effort on *that* ground.

Our judgments about our actual duty in concrete situations have none of the certainty that attaches to our recognition of the general principles of duty. A statement is certain, i.e. is an expression of knowledge, only in one or other of two cases: when it is either self-evident, or a valid conclusion from self-evident premises. And our judgments about our particular duties have neither of these characters. (1) They are not self-evident. Where a possible act is seen to have two characteristics, in virtue of one of which it is *prima facie* right, and in virtue of the other *prima facie* wrong, we are (I think) well aware that we are not certain whether we ought or ought not to do it; that whether we do it or not, we are taking a moral risk. We come in the long run, after consideration, to think one duty more pressing than the other, but we do not feel certain that it is so. And though we do not always recognize that a possible act has two such characteristics, and though there *may* be cases in which it has not, we are never certain that any particular possible act has not, and therefore never certain that it is right, nor certain that it is wrong. For, to go no further in the analysis, it is enough to point out that any particular act will in all probability in the course of time contribute to the bringing about of good or of evil for many human beings, and thus have a *prima facie* rightness or wrongness of which we know nothing. (2) Again, our judgments about our particular duties are not logical conclusions from self-evident premises. The only possible premises would be the general principles stating their *prima facie* rightness or wrongness *qua* having the different characteristics they do have; and even if we could (as we cannot) apprehend the extent to which an act will tend on the one hand, for example, to bring about advantages for our benefactors, and on the other hand to bring about disadvantages for fellow men who are not our benefactors, there is no principle by which we can draw the conclusion that it is on the whole right or on the whole wrong. In this respect the judgment as to the rightness of a particular act is just like the judgment as to the beauty of a particular natural object or work of art. A poem is, for instance, in respect of certain qualities beautiful and in respect of certain others not beautiful; and our judgment as to the degree of beauty it possesses on the whole is never reached by logical reasoning from the apprehension of its particular beauties or particular defects. Both in this and in the moral case we have more or less probable opinions which are not logically justified conclusions from the general principles that are recognized as self-evident.

There is therefore much truth in the description of the right act as a fortunate act. If we cannot be certain that it is right, it is our good fortune if the act we do is the right act. This consideration does not, however, make the doing of our duty a mere matter of chance. There is a parallel here between the doing of duty and of what will be to our personal advantage. We never *know* what act will in the long run be to our advantage. Yet it is certain that we are more likely in general to secure our advantage if we estimate to the best of our ability the probable tendencies of our actions in this respect, than if we act on caprice. And similarly we are more likely to do our duty if we reflect to the best of our ability on the *prima facie* rightness or wrongness of various possible acts in virtue of the characteristics we perceive them to have, than if we act without reflection. With this greater likelihood we must be content.

Many people would be inclined to say that the right act for me is not that whose general nature I have been describing, viz. that which if I were omniscient I should see to be my duty, but that which on all the evidence available to me I should think to be my duty. But suppose that from the state of partial knowledge in which I think act A to be my duty, I could pass to a state of perfect knowledge in which I saw act B to be my duty, should

I not say 'act B was the right act for me to do'? I should no doubt add 'though I am not to be blamed for doing act A'. But in adding this, am I not passing from the question 'what is right' to the question 'what is morally good'? At the same time I am not making the *full* passage from the one notion to the other; for in order that the act should be morally good, or an act I am not to be blamed for doing, it must not merely be the act which it is reasonable for me to think my duty; it must also be done for that reason, or from some other morally good motive. Thus the conception of the right act as the act which it is reasonable for me to think my duty is an unsatisfactory compromise between the true notion of the right act and the notion of the morally good action.

The general principles of duty are obviously not self-evident from the beginning of our lives. How do they come to be so? The answer is, that they come to be self-evident to us just as mathematical axioms do. We find by experience that this couple of matches and that couple make four matches, that this couple of balls on a wire and that couple make four balls; and by reflection on these and similar discoveries we come to see that it is of the nature of two and two to make four. In a precisely similar way, we see the *prima facie* rightness of an act which would be the fulfillment of a particular promise, and of another which would be the fulfillment of another promise, and when we have reached sufficient maturity to think in general terms, we apprehend *prima facie* rightness to belong to the nature of any fulfillment of promise. What comes first in time is the apprehension of the self-evident *prima facie* rightness of an individual act of a particular type. From this we come by reflection to apprehend the self-evident general principle of *prima facie* duty. From this, too, perhaps along with the apprehension of the self-evident *prima facie* rightness of the same act in virtue of its having another characteristic as well, and perhaps in spite of the apprehension of its *prima facie* wrongness in virtue of its having some third characteristic, we come to believe something not self-evident at all, but an object of probable opinion, viz. that this particular act is (not *prima facie* but) actually right.

In this respect there is an important difference between

rightness and mathematical properties. A triangle which is isosceles necessarily has two of its angles equal, whatever other characteristics the triangle may have—whatever, for instance, be its area, or the size of its third angle. The equality of the two angles is a parti-resultant attribute.[7] And the same is true of all mathematical attributes. It is true, I may add, of *prima facie* rightness. But no act is ever, in virtue of falling under some general description, necessarily actually right; its rightness depends on its whole nature[8] and not on any element in it. The reason is that no mathematical object (no figure, for instance, or angle) ever has two characteristics that tend to give it opposite resultant characteristics, while moral acts often (as everyone knows) and indeed always (as on reflection we must admit) have different characteristics that tend to make them at the same time *prima facie* right and *prima facie* wrong; there is probably no act, for instance, which does good to anyone without doing harm to someone else, and *vice versa*.

Supposing it to be agreed, as I think on reflection it must, that no one *means* by 'right' just 'productive of the best possible consequences', or 'optimific', the attributes 'right' and 'optimific' might stand in either of two kinds of relation to each other. (1) They might be so related that we could apprehend *a priori*, either immediately or deductively, that any act that is optimific is right and any act that is right is optimific, as we can apprehend that any triangle that is equilateral is equiangular and *vice versa*. Professor Moore's view is, I think, that the coextensiveness of 'right' and 'optimific' is apprehended immediately.[9] He rejects the possibility of any proof of it. Or (2) the two attributes might be such that the question whether they are

[7] Cf. Ross, *op. cit.*, pp. 28 [pp. 207–208], 122–123.

[8] To avoid complicating unduly the statement of the general view I am putting forward, I have here rather overstated it. Any act is the origination of a great variety of things many of which make no difference to its rightness or wrongness. But there are always many elements in its nature (i.e. in what it is the origination of) that make a difference to its rightness or wrongness, and no element in its nature can be dismissed without consideration as indifferent.

[9] *Ethics*, p. 181.

invariably connected had to be answered by means of an inductive inquiry. Now at first sight it might seem as if the constant
connection of the two attributes could be immediately apprehended. It might seem absurd to suggest that it could be right for
anyone to do an act which would produce consequences less
good than those which would be produced by some other act in
his power. Yet a little thought will convince us that this is not
absurd. The type of case in which it is easiest to see that this is
so is, perhaps, that in which one has made a promise. In such a
case we all think that *prima facie* it is our duty to fulfill the
promise irrespective of the precise goodness of the total consequences. And though we do not think it is necessarily our actual
or absolute duty to do so, we are far from thinking that any, even
the slightest, gain in the value of the total consequences will necessarily justify us in doing something else instead. Suppose, to
simplify the case by abstraction, that the fulfillment of a
promise to A would produce 1,000 units of good [10] for him, but
that by doing some other act I could produce 1,001 units of good
for B, to whom I have made no promise, the other consequences
of the two acts being of equal value; should we really think it
self-evident that it was our duty to do the second act and not the
first? I think not. We should, I fancy, hold that only a much
greater disparity of value between the total consequences would
justify us in failing to discharge our *prima facie* duty to A. After
all, a promise is a promise, and is not to be treated so lightly as
the theory we are examining would imply. What, exactly, a promise is, is not so easy to determine, but we are surely agreed that it
constitutes a serious moral limitation to our freedom of action.
To produce the 1,001 units of good for B rather than fulfill our
promise to A would be to take, not perhaps our duty as philan-
thropists too seriously, but certainly our duty as makers of promises too lightly.

   Or consider another phase of the same problem. If I have

---

10 I am assuming that good is objectively quantitative, but not that we can
accurately assign an exact quantitative measure to it. Since it is of a definite
amount, we can make the *supposition* that its amount is so-and-so, though we
cannot with any confidence *assert* that it is.

promised to confer on *A* a particular benefit containing 1,000 units of good, is it self-evident that if by doing some different act I could produce 1,001 units of good for *A* himself (the other consequences of the two acts being supposed equal in value), it would be right for me to do so? Again, I think not. Apart from my general *prima facie* duty to do *A* what good I can, I have another *prima facie* duty to do him the particular service I have promised to do him, and this is not to be set aside in consequence of a disparity of good of the order of 1,001 to 1,000, though a much greater disparity might justify me in so doing.

Or again, suppose that *A* is a very good and *B* a very bad man, should I then, even when I have made no promise, think it self-evidently right to produce 1,001 units of good for *B* rather than 1,000 for *A*? Surely not. I should be sensible of a *prima facie* duty of justice, i.e. of producing a distribution of goods in proportion to merit, which is not outweighed by such a slight disparity in the total goods to be produced.

Such instances—and they might easily be added to—make it clear that there is no self-evident connection between the attributes 'right' and 'optimific'. The theory we are examining has a certain attractiveness when applied to our decision that a particular act is our duty (though I have tried to show that it does not agree with our actual moral judgments even here). But it is not even plausible when applied to our recognition of *prima facie* duty. For if it were self-evident that the right coincides with the optimific, it should be self-evident that what is *prima facie* right is *prima facie* optimific. But whereas we are certain that keeping a promise is *prima facie* right, we are not certain that it is *prima facie* optimific (though we are perhaps certain that it is *prima facie* bonific). Our certainty that it is *prima facie* right depends not on its consequences but on its being the fulfillment of a promise. The theory we are examining involves too much difference between the evident ground of our conviction about *prima facie* duty and the alleged ground of our conviction about actual duty.

The coextensiveness of the right and the optimific is, then, not self-evident. And I can see no way of proving it deductively; nor, so far as I know, has anyone tried to do so. There remains the question whether it can be established inductively. Such an inquiry, to be conclusive, would have to be very thorough and extensive. We should have to take a large variety of the acts which we, to the best of our ability, judge to be right. We should have to trace as far as possible their consequences, not only for the persons directly affected but also for those indirectly affected, and to these no limit can be set. To make our inquiry thoroughly conclusive, we should have to do what we cannot do, viz. trace these consequences into an unending future. And even to make it reasonably conclusive, we should have to trace them far into the future. It is clear that the most we could possibly say is that a large variety of typical acts that are judged right appear, so far as we can trace their consequences, to produce more good than any other acts possible to the agents in the circumstances. And such a result falls far short of proving the constant connection of the two attributes. But it is surely clear that no inductive inquiry justifying even this result has ever been carried through. The advocates of utilitarian systems have been so much persuaded either of the identity or of the self-evident connection of the attributes 'right' and 'optimific' (or 'felicific') that they have not attempted even such an inductive inquiry as is possible. And in view of the enormous complexity of the task and the inevitable inconclusiveness of the result, it is worth no one's while to make the attempt. What, after all, would be gained by it? If, as I have tried to show, for an act to be right and to be optimific are not the same thing, and an act's being optimific is not even the ground of its being right, then if we could ask ourselves (though the question is really unmeaning) which we ought to do, right acts because they are right or optimific acts because they are optimific, our answer must be 'the former'. If they are optimific as well as right, that is interesting but not morally important; if not, we still ought to do them (which is only another way of saying that they *are* the right acts), and the question whether they are optimific has no importance for moral theory.

There is one direction in which a fairly serious attempt

has been made to show the connection of the attributes 'right' and 'optimific'. One of the most evident facts of our moral consciousness is the sense which we have of the sanctity of promises, a sense which does not, on the face of it, involve the thought that one will be bringing more good into existence by fulfilling the promise than by breaking it. It is plain, I think, that in our normal thought we consider that the fact that we have made a promise is in itself sufficient to create a duty of keeping it, the sense of duty resting on remembrance of the past promise and not on thoughts of the future consequences of its fulfillment. Utilitarianism tries to show that this is not so, that the sanctity of promises rests on the good consequences of the fulfillment of them and the bad consequences of their non-fulfillment. It does so in this way: it points out that when you break a promise you not only fail to confer a certain advantage on your promisee but you diminish his confidence, and indirectly the confidence of others, in the fulfillment of promises. You thus strike a blow at one of the devices that have been found most useful in the relations between man and man—the device on which, for example, the whole system of commercial credit rests —and you tend to bring about a state of things wherein each man, being entirely unable to rely on the keeping of promises by others, will have to do everything for himself, to the enormous impoverishment of human well-being.

To put the matter otherwise, utilitarians say that when a promise ought to be kept it is because the total good to be produced by keeping it is greater than the total good to be produced by breaking it, the former including as its main element the maintenance and strengthening of general mutual confidence, and the latter being greatly diminished by a weakening of this confidence. They say, in fact, that the case I put some pages back[11] never arises—the case in which by fulfilling a promise I shall bring into being 1,000 units of good for my promisee, and by breaking it 1,001 units of good for someone else, the other effects of the two acts being of equal value. The other effects, they say, never are of equal value. By keeping my promise I am

[11] pp. 213–214.

helping to strengthen the system of mutual confidence; by breaking it I am helping to weaken this; so that really the first act
produces $1,000 + x$ units of good, and the second $1,001 - y$
units, and the difference between $+ x$ and $- y$ is enough to
outweigh the slight superiority in the *immediate* effects of the
second act. In answer to this it may be pointed out that there
must be *some* amount of good that exceeds the difference between $+ x$ and $- y$ (i.e. exceeds $x + y$); say, $x + y + z$. Let
us suppose the *immediate* good effects of the second act to be
assessed not at $1,001$ but at $1,000 + x + y + z$. Then its *net*
good effects are $1,000 + x + z$, i.e. greater than those of the
fulfillment of the promise; and the utilitarian is bound to say
forthwith that the promise should be broken. Now, we may ask
whether that is really the way we think about promises? Do we
really think that the production of the slightest balance of good,
no matter who will enjoy it, by the breach of a promise frees us
from the obligation to keep our promise? We need not doubt that
a system by which promises are made and kept is one that has
great advantages for the general well-being. But that is not the
whole truth. To make a promise is not merely to adapt an ingenious device for promoting the general well-being; it is to put oneself in a new relation to one person in particular, a relation
which creates a specifically new *prima facie* duty to him, not
reducible to the duty of promoting the general well-being of society. By all means let us try to foresee the net good effects of
keeping one's promise and the net good effects of breaking it, but
even if we assess the first at $1,000 + x$ and the second at
$1,000 + x + z$, the question still remains whether it is not our
duty to fulfill the promise. It may be suspected, too, that the
effect of a single keeping or breaking of a promise in strengthening or weakening the fabric of mutual confidence is greatly
exaggerated by the theory we are examining. And if we suppose
two men dying together alone, do we think that the duty of one
to fulfill before he dies a promise he has made to the other would
be extinguished by the fact that neither act would have any
effect on the general confidence? Anyone who holds this may be
suspected of not having reflected on what a promise is.

I conclude that the attributes 'right' and 'optimific' are not identical, and that we do not know either by intuition, by deduction, or by induction that they coincide in their application, still less that the latter is the foundation of the former. It must be added, however, that if we are ever under no special obligation such as that of fidelity to a promisee or of gratitude to a benefactor, we ought to do what will produce most good; and that even when we are under a special obligation the tendency of acts to promote general good is one of the main factors in determining whether they are right.

In what has preceded, a good deal of use has been made of 'what we really think' about moral questions; a certain theory has been rejected because it does not agree with what we really think. It might be said that this is in principle wrong; that we should not be content to expound what our present moral consciousness tells us but should aim at a criticism of our existing moral consciousness in the light of theory. Now I do not doubt that the moral consciousness of men has in detail undergone a good deal of modification as regards the things we think right, at the hands of moral theory. But if we are told, for instance, that we should give up our view that there is a special obligatoriness attaching to the keeping of promises because it is self-evident that the only duty is to produce as much good as possible, we have to ask ourselves whether we really, when we reflect, *are* convinced that this is self-evident, and whether we really *can* get rid of our view that promise-keeping has a bindingness independent of productiveness of maximum good. In my own experience I find that I cannot, in spite of a very genuine attempt to do so; and I venture to think that most people will find the same, and that just because they cannot lose the sense of special obligation, they cannot accept as self-evident, or even as true, the theory which would require them to do so. In fact it seems, on reflection, self-evident that a promise, simply as such is something that *prima facie* ought to be kept, and it does *not*, on reflection, seem self-evident that production of maximum good is the only thing that makes an act obligatory. And to ask us to give up at the bidding of a theory our actual apprehension of what is right and what is wrong seems like asking people to repudiate their actual experience of beauty, at the bidding of a theory which says 'only that which satisfies such and such conditions can be beautiful'. If what I have called our actual apprehension is (as I would maintain that it is) truly an apprehension, i.e. an instance of knowledge, the request is nothing less than absurd.

I would maintain, in fact, that what we are apt to describe as 'what we think' about moral questions contains a considerable amount that we do not think but know, and that this forms the standard by reference to which the truth of any moral theory has to be tested, instead of having itself to be tested by reference to any theory. I hope that I have in what precedes indicated what in my view these elements of knowledge are that are involved in our ordinary moral consciousness.

It would be a mistake to found a natural science on 'what we really think', i.e. on what reasonably thoughtful and well-educated people think about the subjects of the science before they have studied them scientifically. For such opinions are interpretations, and often misinterpretations, of sense-experience; and the man of science must appeal from these to sense-experience itself, which furnishes his real data. In ethics no such appeal is possible. We have no more direct way of access to the facts about rightness and goodness and about what things are right or good, than by thinking about them; the moral convictions of thoughtful and well-educated people are the data of ethics just as sense-perceptions are the data of a natural science. Just as some of the latter have to be rejected as illusory, so have some of the former; but as the latter are rejected only when they are in conflict with other more accurate sense-perceptions, the former are rejected only when they are in conflict with other convictions which stand better the test of reflection. The existing body of moral convictions of the best people is the cumulative product of the moral reflection of many generations, which has developed an extremely delicate power of appreciation of moral distinctions; and this the theorist cannot afford to treat with anything other than the greatest respect. The verdicts of the moral consciousness of the best people are the foundation on which he must build; though he must first compare them with one another and eliminate any contradictions they may contain.

It is worth while to try to state more definitely the nature of the acts that are right. We may try to state first what (if anything) is the universal nature of *all* acts that are right. It is obvious that any of the acts that we do has countless effects, directly or indirectly, on countless people, and the probability is that any act, however right it be, will have adverse effects (though these may be very trivial) on some innocent people. Similarly, any wrong act will probably have beneficial effects on some deserving people. Every act therefore, viewed in some aspects, will be *prima facie* right, and viewed in others, *prima facie* wrong, and right acts can be distinguished from wrong acts only as being those which, of all those possible for the agent in the circumstances, have the greatest balance of *prima facie* rightness, in those respects in which they are *prima facie* right, over their *prima facie* wrongness, in those respects in which they are *prima facie* wrong—*prima facie* rightness and wrongness being understood in the sense previously explained. For the estimation of the comparative stringency of these *prima facie* obligations no general rules can, so far as I can see, be laid down. We can only say that a great deal of stringency belongs to the duties of 'perfect obligation'—the duties of keeping our promises, of repairing wrongs we have done, and of returning the equivalent of services we have received. For the rest, ἐν τῇ αἰσθήσει ἡ κρίσις.[12] This sense of our particular duty in particular circumstances, preceded and informed by the fullest reflection we can bestow on the act in all its bearings, is highly fallible, but it is the only guide we have to our duty.

When we turn to consider the nature of individual right acts, the first point to which attention should be called is that any act may be correctly described in an indefinite, and in principle infinite, number of ways. An act is the production of a change in the state of affairs (if we ignore, for simplicity's sake,

---

[12] 'The decision rests with perception'. Arist. *Nic. Eth.* 1109 b 23, 1126 b 4.

the comparatively few cases in which it is the maintenance of an existing state of affairs; cases which, I think, raise no special difficulty). Now the only changes we can *directly* produce are changes in our own bodies or in our own minds. But these are not, as such, what as a rule we think it our duty to produce. Consider some comparatively simple act, such as telling the truth or fulfilling a promise. In the first case what I produce directly is movements of my vocal organs. But what I think it my duty to produce is a true view in someone else's mind about some fact, and between my movement of my vocal organs and this result there intervenes a series of physical events and events in his mind. Again, in the second case, I may have promised, for instance, to return a book to a friend. I may be able, by a series of movements of my legs and hands, to place it in his hands. But what I am just as likely to do, and to think I have done my duty in doing, is to send it by a messenger or to hand it to his servant or to send it by post; and in each of these cases what I *do* directly is worthless in itself and is connected by a series of intermediate links with what I do think it is my duty to bring about, viz. his receiving what I have promised to return to him. This being so, it *seems* as if what I *do* has no obligatoriness in itself and as if one or other of three accounts should be given of the matter, each of which makes rightness not belong to what I do, considered in its own nature.

(1) One of them would be that what is obligatory is not *doing* anything in the natural sense of producing any change in the state of affairs, but *aiming at* something—at, for instance, my friend's reception of the book. But this account will not do. For (*a*) to aim at something is to act from a motive consisting of the wish to bring that thing about. But . . . motive never forms part of the content of our duty; if anything is certain about morals, that, I think, is certain. And (*b*) if I have promised to return the book to my friend, I obviously do not fulfill my promise and do my duty merely by aiming at his receiving the book; I must see that he actually receives it. (2) A more plausible account is that which says I must do that which is likely to produce the result. But this account is open to the second of these objections,

and probably also to the first. For in the first place, however likely my act may seem, even on careful consideration, and even however likely it may in fact be, to produce the result, if it does not produce it I have not done what I promised to do, i.e. have not done my duty. And secondly, when it is said that I ought to do what is likely to produce the result, what is *probably* meant is that I ought to do a certain thing as a result of the wish to produce a certain result, and of the thought that my act is likely to produce it; and this again introduces motive into the content of duty. (3) Much the most plausible of the three accounts is that which says, 'I ought to do that which will actually produce a certain result.' This escapes objection (*b*). Whether it escapes objection (*a*) or not depends on what exactly is meant. If it is meant that I ought to do a certain thing from the wish to produce a certain result and the thought that it will do so, the account is still open to objection (*a*). But if it is meant simply that I ought to do a certain thing, and that the reason why I ought to do it is that it will produce a certain result, objection (*a*) is avoided. Now this account in its second form is that which utilitarianism gives. It says what is right is certain acts, not certain acts motivated in a certain way; and it says that acts are never right by their own nature but by virtue of the goodness of their actual results. And this account is, I think, clearly nearer the truth than one which makes the rightness of an act depend on the goodness of either the *intended* or the *likely* results.

Nevertheless, this account appears not to be the true one. For it implies that what we consider right or our duty is what we do *directly*. It is this, e.g. the packing up and posting of the book, that derives its moral significance not from its own nature but from its consequences. But this is *not* what we should describe, strictly, as our duty; our duty is to fulfill our promise, i.e. to put the book into our friend's possession. This we consider obligatory in its own nature, just because it is a fulfillment of promise, and not because of *its* consequences. But, it might be replied by the utilitarian, I do not do this; I only do something that leads up to this, and what I do has no moral significance in itself but only because of its consequences. In answer to this, however, we may point out that a cause produces not only its immediate, but also its remote consequences, and the latter no less than the former. I, therefore, not only produce the immediate movements of parts of my body but also my friend's reception of the book, which results from these. Or, if this be objected to on the grounds that I can hardly be said to have produced my friend's reception of the book when I have packed and posted it, owing to the time that has still to elapse before he receives it, and that to say I have produced the result hardly does justice to the part played by the Post Office, we may at least say that I have *secured* my friend's reception of the book. What I do is as truly describable in this way as by saying that it is the packing and posting of a book. (It is equally truly describable in many other ways; e.g. I have provided a few moments' employment for Post Office officials. But this is irrelevant to the argument.) And if we ask ourselves whether it is *qua* the packing and posting of a book, or *qua* the securing of my friend's getting what I have promised to return to him, that my action is right, it is clear that it is in the second capacity that it is right; and in this capacity, the only capacity in which it is right, it is right by its own nature and not because of its consequences.

This account may no doubt be objected to, on the ground that we are ignoring the freedom of will of the other agents—the sorter and the postman, for instance—who are equally responsible for the result. Society, it may be said, is not like a machine, in which event follows event by rigorous necessity. Someone may, for instance, in the exercise of his freedom of will, steal the book on the way. But it is to be observed that I have excluded that case, and any similar case. I am dealing with the case in which I secure my friend's receiving the book; and if he does not receive it I have not secured his receiving it. If on the other hand the book reaches its destination, that alone shows that, the system of things being what it is, the trains by which the book travels and the railway lines along which it travels being such as they are and subject to the laws they are subject to, the postal officials who handle it being such as they are, having the motives they have and being subject to the psychological laws they are subject to, my posting the book was the one further thing which was sufficient to procure my friend's receiving it. If it had not been sufficient, the result would not have followed. The attainment of the result proves the sufficiency of the means. The objection in fact rests on the supposition that there can be unmotived action, i.e. an event without a cause, and may be refuted by reflection on the universality of the law of causation.

It is equally true that non-attainment of the result proves the insufficiency of the means. If the book had been destroyed in a railway accident or stolen by a dishonest postman, that would prove that my immediate act was not sufficient to produce the desired result. We get the curious consequence that however carelessly I pack or dispatch the book, if it comes to hand I have done my duty, and however carefully I have acted, if the book does not come to hand I have not done my duty. Success and failure are the only test, and a sufficient test, of the performance of duty. Of course, I should deserve more praise in the second case than in the first; but that is an entirely different question; we must not mix up the question of right and wrong with that of the morally good and the morally bad. And that our conclusion is not as strange as at first sight it might seem is shown by the fact that if the carelessly dispatched book comes to hand, it is not my duty to send another copy, while if the carefully dispatched book does not come to hand I must send another copy to replace it. In the first case I have not my duty still to do, which shows that I have done it; in the second I have it still to do, which shows that I have not done it.

We have reached the result that my act is right *qua* being an ensuring of one of the particular states of affairs of which it is an ensuring, viz. in the case we have taken, of my friend's receiving the book I have promised to return to him. But this answer requires some correction; for it refers only to the *prima facie* rightness of my act. If to be a fulfillment of promise were a sufficient ground of the rightness of an act, all fulfillments of promises would be right, whereas it seems clear that there are cases in which some other *prima facie* duty overrides the *prima facie* duty of fulfilling a promise. The more correct answer would be that the ground of the actual rightness of the act is that, of all acts possible for the agent in the circumstances, it is that whose *prima facie* rightness in the respects in which it is *prima facie* right most outweighs its *prima facie* wrongness in any respects in which it is *prima facie* wrong. But since its *prima facie* rightness is mainly due to its being a fulfillment of promise, we may call its being so the salient element in the ground of its rightness.

Subject to this qualification, then, it is as being the production (or if we prefer the word, the securing or ensuring) of the reception by my friend of what I have promised him (or in other words as the fulfillment of my promise) that my act is right. It is not right as a packing and posting of a book. The packing and posting of the book is only incidentally right, right only because it is a fulfillment of promise, which is what is directly or essentially right.

Our duty, then, is not to do certain things which will produce certain results. Our acts, at any rate our acts of special obligation, are not right because they will produce certain results —which is the view common to all forms of utilitarianism. To say that is to say that in the case in question what is essentially right is to pack and post a book, whereas what is essentially right is to secure the possession by my friend of what I have promised to return to him. An act is not right because it, being one thing, produces good results different from itself; it is right because it is itself the production of a certain state of affairs. Such production is right in itself, apart from any consequence.

But, it might be said, this analysis applies only to acts of special obligation; the utilitarian account still holds good for the acts in which we are not under a special obligation to any person or set of persons but only under that of augmenting the general good. Now merely to have established that there *are* special obligations to do certain things irrespective of their consequences would be already to have made a considerable breach in the utilitarian walls; for according to utilitarianism there is no such thing, there is only the single obligation to promote the general good. But, further, on reflection it is clear that just as (in the case we have taken) my act is not only the packing and posting of a book but the fulfilling of a promise, and just as it is in the latter capacity and not in the former that it is my duty, so an act whereby I augment the general good is not only, let us say, the writing of a begging letter on behalf of a hospital, but the producing (or ensuring) of whatever good ensues therefrom, and it is in the latter capacity and not in the former that it is right, if it *is* right. That which is right is right not because it is an act, one thing, which will produce another thing, an increase of the general welfare, but because it is itself the producing of an increase in the general welfare. Or, to qualify this in the necessary way, its being the production of an increase in the general welfare is the salient element in the ground of its rightness. Just as before we were led to recognize the *prima facie* rightness of the fulfillment of promises, we are now led to recognize the *prima facie* rightness of promoting the general welfare. In both cases we have to recognize the *intrinsic* rightness of a certain type of act, not depending on its consequences but on its own nature.

ETHICS AND LOGIC / *E. A. Gellner*

THERE are ethical theories which surprisingly tie up moral validity with classifications of logical form such as universality or particularity. Kantian ethics make use of the first of the logical terms mentioned, and Existentialist ethics of the second. I shall not in this paper be concerned with either Kantian exegesis or with describing any of the actual forms of Existentialism,

From E. A. Gellner, "Ethics and Logic," Proceedings of the Aristotelian Society, *LV (1954–1955), 157–178. Reprinted by courtesy of the Editor of The Aristotelian Society.*

though I shall use a possibly simplified form of either theory to discuss why there appears to be a connection between logical form and ethics, and with what reason. If my simplified types turn out to be caricatures, I only hope they are illuminating ones.

My general argument could perhaps be summarised in the following way: when people act they are also prepared to give reasons for their actions. The reasons they will offer will have a logical form, which will tend to be one of two kinds. Either the reasons employed will be of an impersonal, general, abstracted kind, or they will include a so to speak biassed reference to some privileged person, thing or event, privileged in the sense that quite similar but not numerically identical persons, things or events would not by the agent be counted as equally good grounds for the relevant action. Naturally, such a privileged particular would have to be *named* and not just described in the justification of the action, for a description would apply equally to the similar particulars which, *ex hypothesi*, would not count as grounds and thus should not be covered by a genuine justification which really told us the reasons the agent has for acting in the way he does.

Thus we have two kinds of justifications of action, those which employ only descriptions and thus constitute open rules, and those which contain logically proper names and thus are not open. Ethical theories have been built round this distinction, to the effect that we should act in such a way that our possible justifications should be of one or the other kind. My aim is both to describe how these theories arise out of our habitual modes of justifying our conduct, and to discuss what philosophical reasons can be offered in defence of either theory.

For purposes of this discussion I assume it to be analytically true that all actions are based on a rule or a maxim.[1] This assumption, which in the appropriate sense seems to me justified, is obviously necessary if the suggestion that there is a connection between logical form and ethics is to make sense. For actions in the sense of events cannot have a "logical form",

[1] I have tried to show this in "Maxims," *Mind* (1951).

though the maxims on which they are based can and must. The required thesis can perhaps be put in the following way: with regard to any action, a command can be constructed such that it enjoins that particular action and no other. If one then appends reasons specifying why each of the various features of the action is required to be what it is, we have a rule or maxim in the desired sense.

I shall begin by discussing the apparently irrelevant question whether there is such a thing as "love at first sight" or not. This question is, if my reading in dentists' waiting rooms is at all representative, frequently and with interest discussed in the pages of women's journals. The tone of the articles on this subject, the way examples are brought up and so on suggests that the authors are under the impression that they are discussing an empirical question; that, in fact, they know by what tests l.a.f.s. could be recognised, the issue thus being merely whether anything satisfying those tests actually occurs. But a more careful reading would I think show that this is a superficial analysis, and that the question is in part or wholly logical, about whether anything *could* count as l.a.f.s.

Consider the following possible *a priori* grounds for denying the existence of l.a.f.s.: for X to fall in love at first sight with Y, X must after his first encounter with Y develop an attitude or feeling towards Y which, *ex hypothesi*, he has towards no one else. But assume, as is plausible, that X could only have noticed a finite set S of Y's characteristics[2] during that first encounter. If now X encounters a person other than Y who however like Y is characterised by S, two possibilities arise: either X manifests towards the new possessor of S the same attitude or emotion as he manifested towards Y, or he does not. Either of these two (exhaustive) alternatives can be taken to be conclusive evidence of the absence of love, and thus jointly to constitute an *a priori* case against its possibility.

In the former case, the fact that X does not really love Y

---

2 Of some one appropriate logical type, if you are pedantic about counting such things as "characteristics". Professor Popper has pointed out to me that the argument does not depend on this finitude, anyway.

is shown by the very recurrence towards someone who is not Y, for "love" (or perhaps "romantic love") is defined in such a way that it can only have one object. It might pertinently be objected at this point that uniqueness, or primacy for that matter, are not, as existence is not, logical predicates, in other words that they cannot legitimately be included in definitions. This may be so, but, for better or for worse (for worse as I shall argue), some concepts with which we operate *are* defined in terms of uniqueness, in conjunction with other characteristics. For instance: Y is considered X's "beloved", but when it is found that X has a relationship towards Z similar to the one he has to Y, some people at any rate will withdraw the description of "X's beloved" from Y, without indeed granting it to Z either, thus showing that for them *uniqueness* is a part of the definition of "beloved".

The alternative is that X does *not* have the same attitude or feelings towards the new possessor of S as he had towards Y. But this equally constitutes conclusive evidence for X not really loving Y. For S is all he knows of Y; if, consequently, on reën-countering S the original emotion or attitude is not reëvoked, this shows that it had not really been connected with its apparent stimulus and object, that it had been accidental, arbitrary, and without any of the significance which one normally attributes to emotions or attitudes of that kind.

With regard to either alternative, then, decisive considerations show the impossibility of correctly predicating "love". In practice, of course, we avoid the paradox with the help of the notion of primacy, or some similar expedient. S in conjunction with primacy does give us uniqueness. But primacy of encounter is not a characteristic of Y. It only tells us something about the history of X himself. Much will be made to hinge in this argument on the fact that certain classes of action and attitudes must include in their maxims such autobiographical, agent-mentioning clauses.

I have chosen l.a.f.s. only because the point emerges with particular clarity, owing to the fact that here the limitation of the information available about the object of the emotion, and the possibility of that information also holding of some other object, emerge very noticeably. There is a number of attitudes, dispositions to act, for instance loyalty, patriotism, devotion to some specific tradition or leader, which are all logically similar. They all involve the agent in having some specific attitude towards some one object and that not merely or at all in virtue of the properties of the object in question: if, for instance, a country is discovered possessing all the characteristics of the patriot's country which he was ever aware of, this will probably not induce him to extend his loyalty and share it equally between the two countries, as would in a way be logical in view of his inability to distinguish in any important way between them. But such is the logic of patriotism. Similar problems have hitherto only been noticed in connection with identity and the use of logically proper names; how can we use a proper name seeing that no characteristics of the nominee are parts of the definiens of the name, so that they can all cease to be true of him or become true of someone else, without this warranting either a restriction or an extension of the use of that name? My point is that there are dispositions or attitudes which select their objects in a similarly puzzling manner. I shall call these E-type preferences or valuations. Behaviour manifesting an E-type valuation cannot be universalised, i.e., its maxim cannot be deduced (in the sense in which an exemplification is deduced from the rule it exemplifies) from an open rule formulated with the help of only property words and variables, but, of course, no proper names. All this has already been shown: an agent acting in accordance with an E-type preference cannot be said to be acting in accordance with some rule from which his preference follows as an instance, for he would not act in accordance with that rule with regard to another instance if one turned up; *that* has been made the defining property of E-type preferences.

The point is that an object of, for instance, love, must by definition be unique (and the same goes for object of loyalty, etc.); whilst there is at the same time no guarantee that these objects are objectively unique, that they possess distinguishing characteristics not shared by such objects as have not been singled out for that attitude. There are of course, as already mentioned, certain relational characteristics which can always be found to help single out the object uniquely; primacy of encounter, *accident* of birth, and so on. Amongst civilised and liberal-minded people a certain shame tends to attach to being influenced by such subjective or accidental factors, to selecting the objects of one's important attitudes (such as loyalty, worship or devotion), in a non-universalisable way, without a rule which one would be prepared to see applied in all analogous situations.

It might be contended that with the help of the kind of relational characteristics mentioned above the important attitudes under discussion *could* be universalised; but this would, I think, be mistaken. The genuine patriot does not wish to see others equally devoted to their country of birth or ancestry to the possible detriment of other countries, possibly his own. Such an attitude characterises only the games-player, to whom, logically, the continuation and quality of the game must be a more genuine consideration than victory; but I take it that genuine patriots do not see international conflicts in which their countries are involved as games.[3] Similarly, the genuine lover cannot admit that his love would have had a different object had the order of his encounters been different. Similarly the believer with the "Credo quia absurdum" attitude is not condoning the belief in *other* scandalously absurd religions. If, as often happens, the awareness of the asymmetrical, arbitrary nature of one's position is accompanied by a tolerant willingness for others (or oneself had things gone differently) to have their rival accident-biassed attitude, that is equivalent within my system of definitions to a cynicism incompatible with *genuinely* loving, believing, etc. And this surely corresponds to our notion of the real romantic lover or the convinced believer, neither of whom can abandon the conviction of the unique appropriateness of the object of his particular attitude.

It is sometimes suggested that we have access to "Being"

---

3 In actual fact the attitude of what I describe as genuine patriotism, and that of the abstracted, so to speak aesthetic enjoyment of the games-connoisseur frequently co-exist, with the help of some double-think. I am talking of simplified types, and in saying what they can and cannot do am discussing what is and is not compatible with their definitions, and not of psychological possibility.

through the fact of our own existence, inwardly experienced, and that this, rather than the subject-predicate form of language, is responsible for the psychological resistance to phenomenalism or the "applicability of a predicate" analysis of "existence": for the feeling that "to exist" somehow must amount to more than that. This metaphysical feeling seems to me to spring from this: my "being myself" seems to me independent of the predicates which apply to me and to be something that would survive the replacement of all of them by others. Hence the "exist" in "I exist" cannot be accounted for by the predicate-applicability analysis with even such plausibility as attaches to it elsewhere. (It would also follow that Identity of Indiscernibles does not apply to self-conscious beings.) This feeling may be totally unjustified, and I bring it in not to defend it but as prima facie evidence that "awareness of oneself" as we normally think of it is an E-type attitude.

Given that I have clarified what I mean by E-type valuations, I should also show that they occur, that actual instances of purposeful behaviour are based on them. But I can only plead that this be accepted as a highly reasonable and plausible hypothesis, for the experiments that would be required to *prove* it are in practice almost or totally impossible to arrange. We cannot build a country resembling closely that of our hypothetical patriot, nor re-arrange the temporal order of the lover's experiences, to test whether indeed their conduct is inspired by an E-type preference. I am confident that this is so, but for anyone not sharing this conviction the subsequent argument can be of little interest.

There is an alternative kind of valuation which I shall call type U. For instance: a judge ideally applies a rule wholly devoid of any personal reference, a rule containing merely predicates (descriptions) and logical terms. This, I suppose, is at least a part of what is meant by the ideals of the "rule of law" and "equality before the law", which suggest the desirability in some sphere of completely impersonal decisions, i.e., decisions formally deduced from abstract premises and consequently not varying in application from person to person, except, of course, in the manner prescribed by those abstract premises. But judicial impartiality is not the only instance of U-type valuation. Type-U valuation is equivalent with one possible and important sense of "rational", corresponding roughly to the common notion of "acting on principle". It is this sense of "rational" which is relevant to the Kantian connection between rationality and morality, and to the fact that E-type valuations and cults such as that of loyalty, the Fuehrerprinzip, "credo quia absurdum" and so on are patently incompatible with Kantianism, and with the vaguer class of attitudes describable as liberalism or rationalism in general.

Having established my dichotomy between E-type and U-type valuations two problems concerning the classification of valuations as one or the other arise:

(i) Whether an action or tendency, or, more precisely, the valuation "on which it is based", falls into category U or not depends on whether it is derivable from an open rule or not. The identification of this rule is indeed a matter of speculation concerning what the agent would do in other circumstances, and not of recording on an intra-cranially located dictaphone such verbal accompaniments as the action may have. Now just as a phenomenon may be subsumable under a number of mutually compatible theories of differing generality, and may be subsumable under some theory of smaller generality and not under any theory of more than a certain degree of abstractness, similarly a valuation may be derivable from a less general open rule but not from a more general one. This being so, we do not know whether to consign it to type E or U, for with regard to different levels of abstractness it satisfies the criteria of entry of either. This point is crucial and will be discussed later.

(ii) Is the use of the first person singular in the maxim to count as the kind of asymmetry which consigns the relevant act to type E? It might be argued that a person biassed in his own favour is not irrational in the same sense, if indeed irrational at all, which the person drawing a distinction in his conduct where there is none in the facts, so to speak, *is* irrational. In other words, is intelligent egoism irrational? This is a merely terminological matter. Intelligent egoism is not universalisable in the same way as I have shown that genuine patriotism or romantic love are not; it is *not* rational in the sense of "being influenced only by considerations which one is prepared to see operative generally and not by merely local factors", and consequently must be consigned to type E, despite the fact that there is a perfectly good sense of "rational" equivalent to "intelligently selfish".

Roughly speaking, my distinction is between actions based on rules and those which are not. I shall go on to suggest that Kant's mysterious universalisation recommendation can be stated as requiring that our actions be based on rules or plans of action that can be formulated with the help of a symbolism employing only predicates, individual *variables,* operators and logical connectives; and that this second order rule or general plan itself employs in addition to the items mentioned above only predicate *variables* instead of actual predicates.[4] Given that, I am trying to show how Kant's recommendation is an exaggeration and development of the actually effective U-type valuations, why and whether he thought that the formal recommendation actually had concrete entailments with regard to conduct, and what general reasons, with what merit, could be put forward for the validity and bindingness of that recommendation.

The recommendation of the alternative logical form to our programmes of action, namely of particularity, also elaborates or rather makes explicit the logic of a class of actually effective valuations, those earlier described as of type E. This doctrine also has certain difficulties of application such as those mentioned with regard to Kantianism, and general reasons can be offered in justification of its validity.

Historically, E-type valuations occur twice: once as all the old, non-universalistic, loyalty type of ethics, and the second time in the reaction to the rationalistic, universalistic ethics, in

---

[4] All these rules would of course be only formulable in a symbolism designed to accommodate imperatives as well as indicative statements. I am just assuming that such a symbolism is possible and that it would be fairly similar in its logic to the familiar symbolisms. I have not attempted to work it out.

those cults of the *acte gratuit*, of the unbacked decision, of blind
self-assertion which are often lumped together as modern irra-
tionalism. Philosophically, as politically, extreme traditionalism
and a cult of unreason based on some acquaintance with and
rejection of open ethics may combine. Hitler and Petain were
not accidental allies. There is no corresponding cleavage within
rationalistic, U-type values.

A further historical point seems to me to be worth making: it may seem odd to pit a simplified Kant, of the *Grundle-
gung*, against a simplified Kierkegaard, of *Fear and Trembling*
(for this is what in effect I have been doing), in view of the fact
that Kierkegaard was reacting not against Kant but against
Hegel. (In fact Kierkegaard might equally well have made
Goethe the object of his invective and ridicule. Goethe's omnivo-
rous determination to make the best of all alternative worlds re-
minds one of the dialectic of opposites and mediation making
sure that nothing was left out. Such proceedings do indeed satisfy something in us. We feel a regret every time some choice
makes us abandon irrevocably one alternative, and feel wistfully
that in an ideal world we should be able to enjoy *all* possibilities
in a perfect synthesis, or, in English, have our cake and eat it.
Goethe tried to do this by being his own Cunning of Reason.)
But to return to the justification of opposing Kierkegaard to Kant
rather than Hegel. Hegel located by means of an ingenious and
ultimately tautologous system, the rationality which Kant had in
a sense exiled to the noumenal, in historical development and
the national whole.[5] But this historicist and immanentist side of
Hegel, important though it may be for other purposes, seems
irrelevant to the central Universalist-Existentialist quarrel, and
is therefore ignored in this discussion. The Universalist (or Rationalist, or Essentialist) case is therefore being represented by
streamlined or if you like, stylised Kant, rather than by a Kant
rewritten for an immanentist, holistic and historicist mind,.
which from one aspect is what Hegelianism amounts to.

[5] For an interpretation of Hegel supporting these contentions see J. Hyppolite,.
Introduction à la Philosophie de l'Histoire de Hegel, M. Riviere et Cie., Paris,.
1948.

Having shown both theories to be ideal and exaggerated types elicited by philosophers from kinds of valuations actually operative, let us examine the fundamental reasons for advocating the *validity* of these types. In both cases these reasons are connected with a theory of freedom (this being clearer with regard to Kant) and with "being really oneself" (this being clearer with regard to Existentialism and indeed being connected with its name).

The possibly camouflaged universality has of course often been noticed in ethical judgments; what recent perceptions have lacked—apart from seeing that some moral judgments are of type E—has been any kind of justification of moral judgments having this form, any attempt to tie up this form of theirs, as Kant did, with their obligatoriness. Recent discussions in particular seem to make the "analysis of moral judgments" a purely *de facto* matter, with the answer having a purely contingent status. The analysis of the German word "schimmel" is "horse, and white", but there is no necessity for a language to contain such a word—indeed English doesn't. Similarly, some "analyses of ethics" make the answer sound similarly accidental. But this simply won't do, for the question concerning the correct analysis of ethical statements is itself ethical; by which I mean that when we ask it, we wish to know not how the inhabitants of Huddersfield or of Bongo Bongo use them, but how they should. (This criticism does not apply to the "Emotive Theory", whose analysis does tie up with obligatoriness—by denying it— and which is not a mere *de facto* theory, for it really concludes that ethical judgments must be emotive because there is no other logical pigeon hole for them to fit. The fact that it is thus deduced from a general position rather than based on a direct examination of ethical judgments is sometimes used as a basis for attacking it—but it seems to me to be, on the contrary, a merit. To show that ethical judgments cannot but be of a certain kind is a way of showing that they must and ought to be of that kind—perhaps the only way.)

According to Kant, a man making an U-type valuation and attempting to act in accordance with it *because* it is of that type is *therefore* free, and only such a man is free.[6] This appears to him to be so because the only alternative to being influenced [7] by the form of one's maxim, by the fact that it is deducible from an open rule which in turn could be schematised with the help of individual and predicate variables alone, is to be influenced by the content of the maxim, by the empirical, "it so happens" preferences specified in it. But the content of the maxims refers only to the preferences which, as a matter of empirical psychology, we happen to have. But to be influenced by these empirical contents of one's maxims, or, more accurately, by the empirical inclinations corresponding to the concrete ends specified in those maxims, is to be determined by something which in view of the arguments of the Second Analogy of the C.P.R. is part of the mechanism of nature; it is, consequently, to be unfree. But that being moved by the form of the rule, by the fact that it is of type U, is to be exempt from the causal system of nature, follows for Kant from the fact that our faculty of generalising, of conceiving or operating with open rules whether in the indicative ("theoretical") or in the imperative ("practical") mood, is not a part of nature. It is for him not continuous with and a refinement of ("passive") sensibility, but radically distinct from it and somehow "spontaneous". I do not propose to discuss here his doctrine of "spontaneity", the doctrine that valid rules of thought can be effective in our thinking because of their validity and independently of whether the psychological laws which happen to be operative luckily coalesce with them or not. But it is worth remarking that the arguments in favour of this doctrine, based on the conditions under which we can sensibly attribute validity to our thinking, are equally effective with regard to Theoretical Reason and Practical Reason, or, if you prefer, with re-

---

[6] This is notoriously a tricky piece of Kantian interpretation. I am for the sake of simplicity assuming the validity of the interpretation of Kant which makes him say that we are only free when doing our duty; an interpretation which is in accordance with *one* at any rate of Kant's uses of "free".

[7] This means something like "varying one's behaviour in accordance with . . ." and *not* "pushes, in billiard ball fashion". It is sometimes argued that Kantian ethics presuppose a philosophy of mind construing motives as efficient causes, and that this invalidates his ethical theory. Neither the premiss nor the inference of this argument is valid.

gard to inferences in the indicative and imperative moods. In a period such as ours when genuinely felt scepticism is far more widespread with regard to ethics than with regard to science, the argument can of course be far more persuasively formulated with regard to Theoretical rather than Practical Reason.

A number of things is presupposed if the Kantian model is to work. To begin with, we have the puzzling claim that logical form, or validity, can be causally, psychologically effective, a claim which Kant partly tried to make plausible with the help of the doctrine of the "self-wrought" feeling of respect for law, and which in the end he declares to be an intrinsically irresoluble mystery. This claim I do not propose to discuss.

Another gap in the Kantian argument is this: suppose we accept that criterion and justification of validity of moral commands lies in their "form" rather than content, this by itself does not single out which form; and if "universal" and "particular" are kinds of forms, then both are so equally. In other words, why single out universality as the ethically important logical form? I do not think Kant could offer a very good answer, for it follows from his general position that a merely sentient being, without the rational faculties, would be as little capable of making singular or particular judgments as of making universal ones. Still, psychologically one can see what led him to this assumption: somehow, universal judgments seem further removed from mere "anschauungen" than the others.

But furthermore, the argument presupposes that the privileged logical form of moral commands by itself determines a specific class of commands. This presupposition can usefully be split into two: that it uniquely determines one command in any given situation, in other words that it is a sufficient criterion of duty,[8] and, less ambitiously, that this form is at least

---

[8] *Which* of these represents what Kant intended to say is, again, a matter of controversial Kantian interpretation. The weaker and second interpretation gives rise to fewer difficulties and can be defended with reference to the text, but I nevertheless prefer the first as being more interesting, illuminating and characteristically Kantian, in that it follows obviously from typical Kantian premises and shows us where they lead. If Kant were merely another intuitionist, he would hardly deserve the attention he receives.

compatible with some commands, though possibly mutually incompatible ones, so that additional premisses, presumably intuitive "moral laws" of the commandment type, are required before duty can be determined.

To begin with, the formal recipe prescribing that our maxims be of type U fails to determine uniquely a line of conduct. With regard to any course of action whatever, it will be possible to devise a maxim which will be universalisable, i.e., one which will be of type U and which will be, in that form, approved by the agent. After all, all that is required from a maxim for it to receive grading U is for it to be expressed solely with the help of predicates, etc., eschewing any proper names or personal pronouns. But we can, with the help of these quite impersonal predicates, include so much detail in the maxim that in effect, though not as a matter of logical necessity, it will only have a unique object, i.e., the immediate situation in which the agent wishes to apply it. In effect, its application will be as limited as if the agent had as his maxim the patently E-type plan "I, now, wish to do such and such though I do not approve of anyone else, or myself at other times, doing so; I am quite happily making an exception in my own favour, or in favour of the present moment." But having used an U-type rule, he will in fact have no need of making "an exception in his own favour": for he will be able happily to subscribe to the open U-type rule, knowing that thanks to the plethora of detail included, a sufficiently similar situation will not arise. If I put in enough details about myself, though formulated in an impersonal way so that those details could characterise someone else, then in practice that someone else would have to *be* I before the situation would become adequately similar and the maxim be re-applicable. This is really the force of "Tout comprendre c'est tout pardonner", which becomes analytic, for "Tout comprendre" becomes equivalent to *"being* the other chap."

Similarly, if too few details are included in the maxims, it will be difficult to find *any* that will be universalisable at all (as opposed to the situation where, with too much detail included, *any* maxim ever acted upon *was* universalisable). If we progressively eliminate more and more from the details specified in the initial conditions of the rule of action, the number of occasions on which the act specified in the apodosis of the maxim becomes ordained correspondingly increases (at any rate, it cannot *de*crease, and the circumstances under which it would fail to *in*crease would have to be very exceptional ones), and a point is bound to be reached where we should no longer subscribe to the now modified maxim in its U-form, for doing so would commit us to repeat the relevant act in circumstances in which in fact we should not wish to do so. If *all* the conditions specified in the protasis of the maxim were eliminated, we should have an absurd kind of categorical imperative enjoining some specific act completely irrespective of any conditions, in other words to be endlessly repeated under all conditions: and a maxim universalised in such an absurd way we should *not* accept. (This might conceivably make sense if that act is described in a sufficiently abstract manner, thus allowing variation in application: for instance, if the categorical rule in this sense, were, for instance, "Be benevolent" or "Act beneficently", or something of the kind. It is by means of this kind of abstractness that commandment-type ethics manage to be acceptable.) But this was not the kind of categorical imperative that Kant intended. The Kantian categorical imperative is not co-ordinate with the ordinary maxims, but is a second-order rule enjoining that those maxims have a certain form, namely that they be universalisable. There is indeed an analogy between this and the manner in which the universal applicability of the categories is not co-ordinate with ordinary scientific truths.

The important consequence of this argument is that any action whatever is or is not "universalisable", as we please, according to the quantity of detail we choose to put into the "maxim". It follows that the Kantian recommendation does not uniquely or in any way determine duty, or even the field of what is permissible.

Something of this is sometimes realised but formulated in the following highly misleading way: "Of course the formal principle of morality does not enable us to determine what the duty of a specific agent in a given situation is; to do *that* we'd have to know just what the *relevant* circumstances were (i.e., the ones to be included in the maxim), and perhaps only the agent himself can do that, and surely no one else can do it with confidence". But this makes it sound as if the specification of the relevant details was merely a practical difficulty, which some favourably placed person, possibly the agent, can hope to some degree at any rate to solve. But it seems to me that the above argument makes clear that the indeterminacy of boundaries of relevance are objectively there, and no amount of intimate acquaintance with the circumstances of the action such as may be granted, sometimes, to the agent, can avail against it.

An alternative way sometimes adopted as a means of coping with this difficulty of Kantian theory is to say that the formal principle of morality was not meant to be a sufficient criterion of morality, that Kant meant it to be supplemented by "moral laws" of the ordinary, commandment type. This interpretation, which is perhaps tenable as far as mere textual evidence goes, can be nevertheless rejected on a number of grounds: first, that if an interpretation of a great philosopher is possible which makes his doctrine both commonplace and silly, it should not be adopted unless we wish to use that interpretation as grounds for discontinuing the study of that philosopher. Had Kant been merely another dogmatic intuitionist, surely there would be no justification for studying that doctrine in his difficult writings, seeing we can find the unexciting falsehoods of which it consists in more accessible places. What people who adopt this interpretation forget is that Kant called his philosophy Critical, not Uncritical. Had he considered a supplementation of the formal principle by a set of moral laws of the commandment type necessary, he would presumably in accordance with his method have asked how they were "possible", in the special sense he gives to this query, and have perhaps written a Critique of them. Furthermore, these supplementary moral laws would make the formal principle redundant.

I wish now to return to an earlier theme, namely that the

Kantian recommendation is an exaggeration of features found in certain types of valuation, notably in the imperatives of an impartial, egalitarian legal code. If, as is claimed in the preceding paragraph, the formal Kantian recommendation has no entailments such as he thought it had, can it also be maintained that a specific type of valuation approaches it more closely than alternative kinds?

The answer is that although, as maintained above, all courses of action are universalisable, some are more so than others: though all are universalisable (i.e., an U-type maxim can be found for them) if we try hard enough by means of piling on the conditions specified in the apodosis of the maxim, with some we need to try less hard than with others (the amount of detail to be added being less), and what we do add may come more naturally.[9] The man who cheats in an exam may universalise his procedure by including so many impersonally stated autobiographical data into the apodosis of his maxim that the maxim would never in fact apply in any other case. He would in fact be indulging in sophistry, though this could never be strictly demonstrated, for whether he honestly adopts the queer overburdened maxim or not could only be tested in the situation where it became re-applicable without this time serving his interests, and, thanks to precisely this over-burdening, such a case is most unlikely to arise (which indeed was the object of the sophistry). But a genuinely moral (by Kantian standards) course of conduct, inspired by considerations in which the fact that the agent *is* the agent, so to speak, does not figure, the agent having in a

[9] Not much should be made of this naturalness, for it will be relative to the language employed, i.e., to the kind of action-concepts occurring in it. When definitions of action-concepts are constructed, the definiens will be a concatenation of characteristics which, suitably phrased, can become parts of a maxim. But, as shown, the possibility of universalisation depends on which elements are included in the maxim. When we wish to include a particular set of these in a maxim, we can of course do this very simply if that set happens to correspond to the definiens of some natural action-word, by just including the name of that action. Otherwise we must either invent a name and construct its definition, or include all the features which would have figured in that definition in the maxim itself.

way abstracted himself and not allowed his bias in his own favour to influence him, is much more obviously and genuinely
universalisable.

But whilst the considerations expressed in the general
precepts of an egalitarian, universalistic ethic *are* highly impersonal, in the sense of not being loaded in favour of any group or
individual, they are not *totally* formal. All proper names and
most descriptive predicates have been eliminated from the maxims of a man acting in accordance with such an ethic: but only
most, and not all, the predicates. And this in-eliminable empirical content of the maxim, however abstract and general, makes
the Kantian model of moral action ultimately unworkable. For
either it must be eliminated—but then from the *mere* form of
the moral law no concrete directives can be deduced, for, as
shown above, many directives, given a little ingenuity, will fit
into it equally; or it remains as an independent element present
not in virtue of being the sole contents compatible with the form,
but *chosen* for some independent, and, necessarily, empirical
reasons.[10] And to say that the maxim contains empirical elements, especially specifications of aims, *not* entailed by the mere
form of the moral law for the sake of which alone the moral man
can act, is to say in more ordinary language, that he is acting at
least partly (namely, with regard to his choice of just those empirical elements as against possible alternatives) not from duty
but from inclination.[11]

This is the appropriate point at which to shift our atten-

[10] Necessarily, for in the Kantian scheme there are only two alternatives for
the groundings of a part or whole of the contents of a maxim; either to be entailed by the very form of the moral law, or to be empirically founded.

[11] It is of course not made unambiguously clear in Kant's ethics whether he
meant the formal principle to determine all the important details, or not. It
really amounts to whether he meant to expound an ethic of obligation or one of
permissibility, whether he thought that morality was like Italy, where everything not forbidden is allowed, or like Germany, where everything not allowed
was forbidden. I feel inclined to say that he tried at least to be on the German
side, mainly because that makes for an interpretation which is simultaneously
more difficult to defend philosophically and (a frequent conjunction, this, in
issues of Kantian exegesis) more interesting, in that it more clearly follows
from the general theses inspiring Kantian ethics, such as that of the "heteronomy" of all empirically motivated conduct.

tion to the logic of Existentialist ethics, for the decisive starting point for Existentialism is precisely that irreducible element which resists Kantian Essentialism, so to speak, and which can neither be dispensed with nor deduced from the purely formal principle.

Frequently, one hears accounts of Existentialism in roughly the following terms: Existentialism rejects abstract descriptions of the world and life, and concentrates on the concrete stuff of human experience of life. This kind of account reduces Existentialism to a preference for journalistic sketches as against statistics and analysis, or for impressionistic painting as against diagrams. But that is not Existentialism.

Existentialism is the doctrine that choice (whether of faith or behaviour) ought to be or is bound to be (vacillation between these two positions is inherent in the doctrine) based on an ungrounded "leap" and cannot or should not be deduced from a formal, and consequently blessedly non-arbitrary rule such as the one Kant hoped for (though, as already stated, owing to what essentially is no more than an historical accident the founder of Existentialism was reacting not against Kantian Essentialism, but against Hegel's historicised version of it). The negative clause in my above definition is much more important than the positive one, and consequently it does not matter that the positive one is metaphorical. The ultimate weakness of Kantian Essentialism was that *no* actual valuation, or attitude (= set of valuations) *could* fit the rigour of pure formality (be completely of type U), that no actual specific valuation was entailed in the formal moral principle. The weakness of Existentialism is that no valuation can possibly escape being of the kind enjoined by the doctrine, at least to the extent of containing the irreducibly arbitrary (in the sense of not deducible from formal considerations) element. This fact is responsible for the incontestably true aspect of Existentialism, its indicative formulation to the effect that to some extent at least all our valuations are of type E. It is equally responsible for the failure of the doctrine in its imperative formulation: for to the extent of possessing *an* arbitrary element all valuations are of type E, and consequently *that* cannot be made into a principle of selection; and as for the recommendation to make our valuation as much of type E as possible (the cult of the *acte gratuit* aspect of Existentialism), *that* second order recommendation can neither be justified nor is it itself, with its great generality and abstractness, particularly of type E. On the contrary, it paradoxically provides a general open premiss for E-type maxims, thus in a way undermining their E status. If one embarks on a policy of inconsequentiality one *has* acquired a kind of general policy. In any case, I do not think it makes much sense to attach numerical indices to the arbitrariness-saturation of valuation, a miss in this context being as good as a mile; and this is another reason why Existentialism fails to become a recommendation by being necessarily and universally followed anyway.

It remains to discuss what the appeal of the E-type of valuation and its generalisation and erection into a principle, corresponding to the "Escape from heteronomy and arbitrariness" appeal of Essentialist ethics. Ultimately, in both a logical and a factual sense, choices and decisions are made by concrete, here-now people and not by principles. The logical sense has been elucidated earlier: it amounts to saying that formal principles are not, contrary to certain metaphysical doctrines, strong enough to entail valuations. The factual sense amounts to this: that even if the formal principles were strong enough to entail valuations, these would nevertheless only in fact be *made* thanks to and *in* the concrete *existenz* of individual men, choosing or preferring to adopt them.

If the universal principles are somehow built into the world-process as forces in the "historicist" way, the performance of an arbitrary, E-type action becomes the only way of asserting or attaining one's freedom—like making a face at an otherwise all-powerful headmaster. (Cf. Dostoevski's "Notes from Underground" for this appeal of the unreasonable act.)

There is something paradoxical about the recent revival of interest in Kierkegaard, in view of the fact that he considered himself to be primarily combatting Hegel. The reputation and attention devoted to Hegel having at the present time reached an all time low, the enthusiastic exhumation of Kierkegaard would seem superfluous. This paradox supplies a clue to a radical difference between Kierkegaard's and latter-day Existentialism. The contemporary version is really a *faute de mieux* Existentialism, a more or less regretful recognition of the fact that there is no, and could not be, immanent, or transcendent, Reason, this entity being envisaged as a combination of the hypostatised criteria of validity and an actually operative force ensuring that thoughts or even things will satisfy those criteria. Kierkegaard's attitude was totally different: he did not regret its absence, on the contrary he feared the possibility of its not being absent, wishing as he did a universe in which the burden of selecting what is valid in belief and action remained on the shoulders of the individual.[12] For that reason he seemed positively to relish the absurdities of religion: the more scandalous the absurdity, the lesser the danger that it might be incorporated in a rational system guaranteeing its validity.

I have tried to show that the recommendations of both Kantian and Existentialist ethics fail in their respective ways to be satisfactory, the one through being impossible to comply with, the other inescapably operative anyway. I have also tried to show that these two theories are not accidental fallacies or confusions, but naturally arise out of the fact that human beings not merely act but have statable reasons for their actions. The two theories under discussion arise through the exaggeration of certain features of the logic of giving reasons for a course of conduct. They arise "naturally" rather in the way in which Kant tried to show in the Transcendental Dialectic of the C.P.R. that certain metaphysical doctrines were natural by-products of human thinking. Given a tendency, inspired by considerations concerning the possibility of attributing validity to our thinking, towards transcendentalism with regard to our thinking faculties, *that* in conjunction with the fact that some of our valuations are of a certain kind, namely type U, will naturally lead to a Kantian ethical theory; given, as a philosophical reaction, an emotively charged

---

[12] In a way, Kierkegaard was to metaphysical optimism what "Brave New World" is to scientific optimism.

insistence on immanence and concreteness (consider the "Existence precedes essence" slogan), *that* in conjunction with the fact that some of our valuations are of a different type, namely type E, will naturally lead to Existentialist theories of conduct.

One might ask, in the end, whether, although the two extreme recommendations fail to be serviceable signposts, we could not after all extract an ethic from the logical form of maxims by adopting as a general recommendation that we should universalise as much as possible, that, even if complete derivation of the content of the maxim from its law-like form is impossible, that we should strive to retain as few underived, arbitrary elements in our maxims as possible. (*Perhaps* this is all Kant intended to say, and my criticisms of Kantianism have missed the mark.) Similarly, a modified (though hardly moderated!) Existentialism might maintain that although we all indulge in the *leap* anyway, we should do so as much as possible, that we should minimise the extent to which we justify our behaviour by more general grounds.

I think that both these attitudes are, as a matter of historical fact, operative, and influential at least partly in consequence of the philosophical reasons adduced in their favour; but I do not see by what standard external to both one could choose between them. This very fact would seem to give the victory to the Existentialist side; but this should not obscure the fact that we can also choose to be Kantians.

TWO CONCEPTS OF RULES / *John Rawls*

IN THIS paper I want to show the importance of the distinction between justifying a practice[1] and justifying a particular action falling under it, and I want to explain the logical basis of this distinction and how it is possible to miss its significance. While the distinction has frequently been made,[2] and is now becoming commonplace, there remains the task of explaining the tendency

From John Rawls, *"Two Concepts of Rules,"* The Philosophical Review, *LXIV* (*1955*), *3–32. Reprinted by permission of the Editors of* The Philosophical Review, *and the author.*

[1] I use the word "practice" throughout as a sort of technical term meaning any form of activity specified by a system of rules which defines offices, roles, moves, penalties, defenses, and so on, and which gives the activity its structure. As examples one may think of games and rituals, trials and parliaments.

[2] The distinction is central to Hume's discussion of justice in *A Treatise of Human Nature*, Bk. III, Pt. II, esp. secs. 2–4. It is clearly stated by John Austin in the second lecture of *Lectures on Jurisprudence* (4th ed.; London, 1873), I, 116 ff. (1st ed., 1832). Also it may be argued that J. S. Mill took it for granted in *Utilitarianism;* on this point cf. J. O. Urmson, "The Interpretation of the Moral Philosophy of J. S. Mill," *Philosophical Quarterly*, Vol. III (1953). In addition to the arguments given by Urmson there are several clear statements of the distinction in *A System of Logic* (8th ed.; London, 1872), Bk. VI, Ch. XII, pars. 2, 3, 7. The distinction is fundamental to J. D. Mabbott's important paper, "Punishment," *Mind*, n.s., Vol. XLVIII (April, 1939). More recently the distinction has been stated with particular emphasis by S. E. Toulmin in *The Place of Reason in Ethics* (Cambridge, 1950), see esp. Ch. XI, where it plays a major part in his account of moral reasoning. Toulmin doesn't explain the basis of the distinction, nor how one might overlook its importance, as I try to in this paper, and in my review of his book (*Philosophical Review*, Vol. LX [October, 1951]), as some of my criticisms show, I failed to understand the force of it. See also H. D. Aiken, "The Levels of Moral Discourse," *Ethics*, Vol. LXII (1952), A. M. Quinton, "Punishment," *Analysis*, Vol. XIV (June, 1954), and P. H. Nowell-Smith, *Ethics* (London, 1954), pp. 236–239, 271–273.

either to overlook it altogether, or to fail to appreciate its importance.

To show the importance of the distinction I am going to defend utilitarianism against those objections which have traditionally been made against it in connection with punishment and the obligation to keep promises. I hope to show that if one uses the distinction in question then one can state utilitarianism in a way which makes it a much better explication of our considered moral judgments than these traditional objections would seem to admit.[3] Thus the importance of the distinction is shown by the way it strengthens the utilitarian view regardless of whether that view is completely defensible or not.

To explain how the significance of the distinction may be overlooked, I am going to discuss two conceptions of rules. One of these conceptions conceals the importance of distinguishing between the justification of a rule or practice and the justification of a particular action falling under it. The other conception makes it clear why this distinction must be made and what is its logical basis.

[1]

The subject of punishment, in the sense of attaching legal penalties to the violation of legal rules, has always been a troubling moral question.[4] The trouble about it has not been that people disagree as to whether or not punishment is justifiable. Most people have held that, freed from certain abuses, it is an acceptable institution. Only a few have rejected punishment entirely, which is rather surprising when one considers all that can be said against it. The difficulty is with the justification of punishment: various arguments for it have been given by moral philos-

---

3 On the concept of explication see the author's paper, *Philosophical Review*, Vol. LX (April, 1951).

4 While this paper was being revised, Quinton's appeared; footnote 2 supra. There are several respects in which my remarks are similar to his. Yet as I consider some further questions and rely on somewhat different arguments, I have retained the discussion of punishment and promises together as two test cases for utilitarianism.

ophers, but so far none of them has won any sort of general acceptance; no justification is without those who detest it. I hope to show that the use of the aforementioned distinction enables one to state the utilitarian view in a way which allows for the sound points of its critics.

For our purposes we may say that there are two justifications of punishment. What we may call the retributive view is that punishment is justified on the grounds that wrongdoing merits punishment. It is morally fitting that a person who does wrong should suffer in proportion to his wrongdoing. That a criminal should be punished follows from his guilt, and the severity of the appropriate punishment depends on the depravity of his act. The state of affairs where a wrongdoer suffers punishment is morally better than the state of affairs where he does not; and it is better irrespective of any of the consequences of punishing him.

What we may call the utilitarian view holds that on the principle that bygones are bygones and that only future consequences are material to present decisions, punishment is justifiable only by reference to the probable consequences of maintaining it as one of the devices of the social order. Wrongs committed in the past are, as such, not relevant considerations for deciding what to do. If punishment can be shown to promote effectively the interest of society it is justifiable, otherwise it is not.

I have stated these two competing views very roughly to make one feel the conflict between them: one feels the force of *both* arguments and one wonders how they can be reconciled. From my introductory remarks it is obvious that the resolution which I am going to propose is that in this case one must distinguish between justifying a practice as a system of rules to be applied and enforced, and justifying a particular action which falls under these rules; utilitarian arguments are appropriate with regard to questions about practices, while retributive arguments fit the application of particular rules to particular cases.

We might try to get clear about this distinction by imagining how a father might answer the question of his son. Suppose the son asks, "Why was *J* put in jail yesterday?" The father answers, "Because he robbed the bank at *B*. He was duly tried and found guilty. That's why he was put in jail yesterday." But suppose the son had asked a different question, namely, "Why do people put other people in jail?" Then the father might answer, "To protect good people from bad people" or "To stop people from doing things that would make it uneasy for all of us; for otherwise we wouldn't be able to go to bed at night and sleep in peace." There are two very different questions here. One question emphasizes the proper name: it asks why *J* was punished rather than someone else, or it asks what he was punished for. The other question asks why we have the institution of punishment: why do people punish one another rather than, say, always forgiving one another?

Thus the father says in effect that a particular man is punished, rather than some other man, because he is guilty, and he is guilty because he broke the law (past tense). In his case the law looks back, the judge looks back, the jury looks back, and a penalty is visited upon him for something he did. That a man is to be punished, and what his punishment is to be, is settled by its being shown that he broke the law and that the law assigns that penalty for the violation of it.

On the other hand we have the institution of punishment itself, and recommend and accept various changes in it, because it is thought by the (ideal) legislator and by those to whom the law applies that, as a part of a system of law impartially applied from case to case arising under it, it will have the consequence, in the long run, of furthering the interests of society.

One can say, then, that the judge and the legislator stand in different positions and look in different directions: one to the past, the other to the future. The justification of what the judge does, *qua* judge, sounds like the retributive view; the justification of what the (ideal) legislator does, *qua* legislator, sounds like the utilitarian view. Thus both views have a point (this is as it should be since intelligent and sensitive persons have been on both sides of the argument); and one's initial confusion disappears once one sees that these views apply to persons holding different offices with different duties, and situated differently with respect to the system of rules that make up the criminal law.[5]

One might say, however, that the utilitarian view is more fundamental since it applies to a more fundamental office, for the judge carries out the legislator's will so far as he can determine it. Once the legislator decides to have laws and to assign penalties for their violation (as things are there must be both the law and the penalty) an institution is set up which involves a retributive conception of particular cases. It is part of the concept of the criminal law as a system of rules that the application and enforcement of these rules in particular cases should be justifiable by arguments of a retributive character. The decision whether or not to use law rather than some other mechanism of social control, and the decision as to what laws to have and what penalties to assign, may be settled by utilitarian arguments; but if one decides to have laws then one has decided on something whose working in particular cases is retributive in form.[6]

The answer, then, to the confusion engendered by the two views of punishment is quite simple: one distinguishes two offices, that of the judge and that of the legislator, and one distinguishes their different stations with respect to the system of rules which make up the law; and then one notes that the different sorts of considerations which would usually be offered as reasons for what is done under the cover of these offices can be paired off with the competing justifications of punishment. One reconciles the two views by the time-honored device of making them apply to different situations.

But can it really be this simple? Well, this answer allows for the apparent intent of each side. Does a person who advocates the retributive view necessarily advocate, as an *institution*, legal machinery whose essential purpose is to set up and preserve a correspondence between moral turpitude and suffering?

[5] Note the fact that different sorts of arguments are suited to different offices. One way of taking the differences between ethical theories is to regard them as accounts of the reasons expected in different offices.

[6] In this connection see Mabbott, *op. cit.*, pp. 163–164.

Surely not.[7] What retributionists have rightly insisted upon is
that no man can be punished unless he is guilty, that is, unless
he has broken the law. Their fundamental criticism of the utilitarian account is that, as they interpret it, it sanctions an innocent person's being punished (if one may call it that) for the
benefit of society.

On the other hand, utilitarians agree that punishment is
to be inflicted only for the violation of law. They regard this
much as understood from the concept of punishment itself.[8]
The point of the utilitarian account concerns the institution as a
system of rules: utilitarianism seeks to limit its use by declaring
it justifiable only if it can be shown to foster effectively the good
of society. Historically it is a protest against the indiscriminate
and ineffective use of the criminal law.[9] It seeks to dissuade us
from assigning to penal institutions the improper, if not sacri-
legious, task of matching suffering with moral turpitude. Like
others, utilitarians want penal institutions designed so that, as
far as humanly possible, only those who break the law run afoul
of it. They hold that no official should have discretionary power
to inflict penalties whenever he thinks it for the benefit of society; for on utilitarian grounds an institution granting such
power could not be justified.[10]

[7] On this point see Sir David Ross, *The Right and the Good* (Oxford, 1930),
pp. 57–60.

[8] See Hobbes's definition of punishment in *Leviathan*, Ch. XXVIII; and Bentham's definition in *The Principle of Morals and Legislation*, Ch. XII, par. 36,
Ch. XV, par. 28, and in *The Rationale of Punishment* (London, 1830), Bk. I,
Ch. I. They could agree with Bradley that: "Punishment is punishment only
when it is deserved. We pay the penalty, because we owe it, and for no other
reason; and if punishment is inflicted for any other reason whatever than because it is merited by wrong, it is a gross immorality, a crying injustice, an
abominable crime, and not what it pretends to be." *Ethical Studies* (2nd ed.;
Oxford, 1927), pp. 26–27. Certainly by definition it isn't what it pretends to be.
The innocent can only be punished by mistake; deliberate "punishment" of the
innocent necessarily involves fraud.

[9] Cf. Leon Radzinowicz, *A History of English Criminal Law: The Movement
for Reform 1750–1833* (London, 1948), esp. Ch. XI on Bentham.

[10] Bentham discusses how corresponding to a punitory provision of a criminal
law there is another provision which stands to it as an antagonist and which
needs a name as much as the punitory. He calls it, as one might expect, the
anaetiosostic, and of it he says: "The punishment of guilt is the object of the

The suggested way of reconciling the retributive and the utilitarian justifications of punishment seems to account for what both sides have wanted to say. There are, however, two further questions which arise, and I shall devote the remainder of this section to them.

First, will not a difference of opinion as to the proper criterion of just law make the proposed reconciliation unacceptable to retributionists? Will they not question whether, if the utilitarian principle is used as the criterion, it follows that those who have broken the law are guilty in a way which satisfies their demand that those punished deserve to be punished? To answer this difficulty, suppose that the rules of the criminal law are justified on utilitarian grounds (it is only for laws that meet his criterion that the utilitarian can be held responsible). Then it follows that the actions which the criminal law specifies as offenses are such that, if they were tolerated, terror and alarm would spread in society. Consequently, retributionists can only deny that those who are punished deserve to be punished if they deny that such actions are wrong. This they will not want to do.

The second question is whether utilitarianism doesn't justify too much. One pictures it as an engine of justification which, if consistently adopted, could be used to justify cruel and arbitrary institutions. Retributionists may be supposed to concede that utilitarians *intend* to reform the law and to make it more humane; that utilitarians do not *wish* to justify any such thing as punishment of the innocent; and that utilitarians may appeal to the fact that punishment presupposes guilt in the sense that by punishment one understands an institution attaching penalties to the infraction of legal rules, and therefore that it is logically absurd to suppose that utilitarians in justifying *pun-*

---

former one: the preservation of innocence that of the latter." In the same connection he asserts that it is never thought fit to give the judge the option of deciding whether a thief (that is, a person whom he believes to be a thief, for the judge's belief is what the question must always turn upon) should hang or not, and so the law writes the provision: "The judge shall not cause a thief to be hanged unless he have been duly convicted and sentenced in course of law" (*The Limits of Jurisprudence Defined*, ed. C. W. Everett [New York, 1945], pp. 238–239).

ishment might also have justified punishment (if we may call it that) of the innocent. The real question, however, is whether the utilitarian, in justifying punishment, hasn't used arguments which commit him to accepting the infliction of suffering on innocent persons if it is for the good of society (whether or not one calls this punishment). More generally, isn't the utilitarian committed in principle to accepting many practices which he, as a morally sensitive person, wouldn't want to accept? Retributionists are inclined to hold that there is no way to stop the utilitarian principle from justifying too much except by adding to it a principle which distributes certain rights to individuals. Then the amended criterion is not the greatest benefit of society *simpliciter*, but the greatest benefit of society subject to the constraint that no one's rights may be violated. Now while I think that the classical utilitarians proposed a criterion of this more complicated sort, I do not want to argue that point here.[11] What I want to show is that there is *another* way of preventing the utilitarian principle from justifying too much, or at least of making it much less likely to do so: namely, by stating utilitarianism in a way which accounts for the distinction between the justification of an institution and the justification of a particular action falling under it.

I begin by defining the institution of punishment as follows: a person is said to suffer punishment whenever he is legally deprived of some of the normal rights of a citizen on the ground that he has violated a rule of law, the violation having been established by trial according to the due process of law, provided that the deprivation is carried out by the recognized legal authorities of the state, that the rule of law clearly specifies both the offense and the attached penalty, that the courts construe statutes strictly, and that the statute was on the books prior to the time of the offense.[12] This definition specifies what I shall understand by punishment. The question is whether utilitarian

11 By the classical utilitarians I understand Hobbes, Hume, Bentham, J. S. Mill, and Sidgwick.

12 All these features of punishment are mentioned by Hobbes; cf. *Leviathan*, Ch. XXVIII.

arguments may be found to justify institutions widely different from this and such as one would find cruel and arbitrary.

This question is best answered, I think, by taking up a particular accusation. Consider the following from Carritt:

> . . . the utilitarian must hold that we are justified in inflicting pain always and only to prevent worse pain or bring about greater happiness. This, then, is all we need to consider in so-called punishment, which must be purely preventive. But if some kind of very cruel crime becomes common, and none of the criminals can be caught, it might be highly expedient, as an example, to hang an innocent man, if a charge against him could be so framed that he were universally thought guilty; indeed this would only fail to be an ideal instance of utilitarian 'punishment' because the victim himself would not have been so likely as a real felon to commit such a crime in the future; in all other respects it would be perfectly deterrent and therefore felicific.[13]

Carritt is trying to show that there are occasions when a utilitarian argument would justify taking an action which would be generally condemned; and thus that utilitarianism justifies too much. But the failure of Carritt's argument lies in the fact that he makes no distinction between the justification of the general system of rules which constitutes penal institutions and the justification of particular applications of these rules to particular cases by the various officials whose job it is to administer them. This becomes perfectly clear when one asks who the "we" are of whom Carritt speaks. Who is this who has a sort of absolute authority on particular occasions to decide that an innocent man shall be "punished" if everyone can be convinced that he is guilty? Is this person the legislator, or the judge, or the body of private citizens, or what? It is utterly crucial to know who is to decide such matters, and by what authority, for all of this must be written into the rules of the institution. Until one knows these things one doesn't know what the institution is whose justification is being challenged; and as the utilitarian principle applies to the institution one doesn't know whether it is justifiable on utilitarian grounds or not.

[13] *Ethical and Political Thinking* (Oxford, 1947), p. 65.

Once this is understood it is clear what the countermove to Carritt's argument is. One must describe more carefully what the *institution* is which his example suggests, and then ask oneself whether or not it is likely that having this institution would be for the benefit of society in the long run. One must not content oneself with the vague thought that, when it's a question of *this* case, it would be a good thing if *somebody* did something even if an innocent person were to suffer.

Try to imagine, then, an institution (which we may call "telishment") which is such that the officials set up by it have authority to arrange a trial for the condemnation of an innocent man whenever they are of the opinion that doing so would be in the best interests of society. The discretion of officials is limited, however, by the rule that they may not condemn an innocent man to undergo such an ordeal unless there is, at the time, a wave of offenses similar to that with which they charge him and telish him for. We may imagine that the officials having the discretionary authority are the judges of the higher courts in consultation with the chief of police, the minister of justice, and a committee of the legislature.

Once one realizes that one is involved in setting up an *institution*, one sees that the hazards are very great. For example, what check is there on the officials? How is one to tell whether or not their actions are authorized? How is one to limit the risks involved in allowing such systematic deception? How is one to avoid giving anything short of complete discretion to the authorities to telish anyone they like? In addition to these considerations, it is obvious that people will come to have a very different attitude towards their penal system when telishment is adjoined to it. They will be uncertain as to whether a convicted man has been punished or telished. They will wonder whether or not they should feel sorry for him. They will wonder whether the same fate won't at any time fall on them. If one pictures how such an institution would actually work, and the enormous risks involved in it, it seems clear that it would serve no useful purpose. A utilitarian justification for this institution is most unlikely.

It happens in general that as one drops off the defining features of punishment one ends up with an institution whose utilitarian justification is highly doubtful. One reason for this is that punishment works like a kind of price system: by altering the prices one has to pay for the performance of actions it supplies a motive for avoiding some actions and doing others. The defining features are essential if punishment is to work in this way; so that an institution which lacks these features, e.g., an institution which is set up to "punish" the innocent, is likely to have about as much point as a price system (if one may call it that) where the prices of things change at random from day to day and one learns the price of something after one has agreed to buy it.[14]

If one is careful to apply the utilitarian principle to the institution which is to authorize particular actions, then there is *less* danger of its justifying too much. Carritt's example gains plausibility by its indefiniteness and by its concentration on the particular case. His argument will only hold if it can be shown that there are utilitarian arguments which justify an institution whose publicly ascertainable offices and powers are such as to permit officials to exercise that kind of discretion in particular cases. But the requirement of having to build the arbitrary fea-

---

[14] The analogy with the price system suggests an answer to the question how utilitarian considerations insure that punishment is proportional to the offense. It is interesting to note that Sir David Ross, after making the distinction between justifying a penal law and justifying a particular application of it, and after stating that utilitarian considerations have a large place in determining the former, still holds back from accepting the utilitarian justification of punishment on the grounds that justice requires that punishment be proportional to the offense, and that utilitarianism is unable to account for this. Cf. *The Right and the Good*, pp. 61–62. I do not claim that utilitarianism can account for this requirement as Sir David might wish, but it happens, nevertheless, that if utilitarian considerations are followed penalties will be proportional to offenses in this sense: the order of offenses according to seriousness can be paired off with the order of penalties according to severity. Also the absolute level of penalties will be as low as possible. This follows from the assumption that people are rational (i.e., that they are able to take into account the "prices" the state puts on actions), the utilitarian rule that a penal system should provide a motive for preferring the less serious offense, and the principle that punishment as such is an evil. All this was carefully worked out by Bentham in *The Principles of Morals and Legislation*, Chs. XIII–XV.

tures of the particular decision into the institutional practice makes the justification much less likely to go through.

[II]

I shall now consider the question of promises. The objection to utilitarianism in connection with promises seems to be this: it is believed that on the utilitarian view when a person makes a promise the only ground upon which he should keep it, if he should keep it, is that by keeping it he will realize the most good on the whole. So that if one asks the question "Why should I keep *my* promise?" the utilitarian answer is understood to be that doing so in *this* case will have the best consequences. And this answer is said, quite rightly, to conflict with the way in which the obligation to keep promises is regarded.

Now of course critics of utilitarianism are not unaware that one defense sometimes attributed to utilitarians is the consideration involving the practice of promise-keeping.[15] In this connection they are supposed to argue something like this: it must be admitted that we feel strictly about keeping promises, more strictly than it might seem our view can account for. But when we consider the matter carefully it is always necessary to take into account the effect which our action will have on the practice of making promises. The promisor must weigh, not only the effects of breaking his promise on the particular case, but also the effect which his breaking his promise will have on the practice itself. Since the practice is of great utilitarian value, and since breaking one's promise always seriously damages it, one will seldom be justified in breaking one's promise. If we view our individual promises in the wider context of the practice of promising itself we can account for the strictness of the obli-

15 Ross, *The Right and the Good*, pp. 37–39, and *Foundations of Ethics* (Oxford, 1939), pp. 92–94. I know of no utilitarian who has used this argument except W. A. Pickard-Cambridge in "Two Problems about Duty," *Mind*, n.s., XLI (April, 1932), 153–157, although the argument goes with G. E. Moore's version of utilitarianism in *Principia Ethica* (Cambridge, 1903). To my knowledge it does not appear in the classical utilitarians; and if one interprets their view correctly this is no accident.

gation to keep promises. There is always one very strong utilitarian consideration in favor of keeping them, and this will insure that when the question arises as to whether or not to keep a promise it will usually turn out that one should, even where the facts of the particular case taken by itself would seem to justify one's breaking it. In this way the strictness with which we view the obligation to keep promises is accounted for.

Ross has criticized this defense as follows:[16] however great the value of the practice of promising, on utilitarian grounds, there must be some value which is greater, and one can imagine it to be obtainable by breaking a promise. Therefore there might be a case where the promisor could argue that breaking his promise was justified as leading to a better state of affairs on the whole. And the promisor could argue in this way no matter how slight the advantage won by breaking the promise. If one were to challenge the promisor his defense would be that what he did was best on the whole in view of all the utilitarian considerations, which in this case *include* the importance of the practice. Ross feels that such a defense would be unacceptable. I think he is right insofar as he is protesting against the appeal to consequences in general and without further explanation. Yet it is extremely difficult to weigh the force of Ross's argument. The kind of case imagined seems unrealistic and one feels that it needs to be described. One is inclined to think that it would either turn out that such a case came under an exception defined by the practice itself, in which case there would not be an appeal to consequences in general on the particular case, or it would happen that the circumstances were so peculiar that the conditions which the practice presupposes no longer obtained. But certainly Ross is right in thinking that it strikes us as wrong for a person to defend breaking a promise by a general appeal to consequences. For a general utilitarian defense is not open to the promisor: it is not one of the defenses allowed by the practice of making promises.

Ross gives two further counterarguments:[17] First, he

16 Ross, *The Right and the Good*, pp. 38–39.
17 Ross, *ibid.*, p. 39. The case of the nonpublic promise is discussed again in

holds that it overestimates the damage done to the practice of promising by a failure to keep a promise. One who breaks a promise harms his own name certainly, but it isn't clear that a broken promise always damages the practice itself sufficiently to account for the strictness of the obligation. Second, and more important, I think, he raises the question of what one is to say of a promise which isn't known to have been made except to the promisor and the promisee, as in the case of a promise a son makes to his dying father concerning the handling of the estate.[18] In this sort of case the consideration relating to the practice doesn't weigh on the promisor at all, and yet one feels that this sort of promise is as binding as other promises. The question of the effect which breaking it has on the practice seems irrelevant. The only consequence seems to be that one can break the promise without running any risk of being censured; but the obligation itself seems not the least weakened. Hence it is doubtful whether the effect on the practice ever weighs in the particular case; certainly it cannot account for the strictness of the obligation where it fails to obtain. It seems to follow that a utilitarian account of the obligation to keep promises cannot be successfully carried out.

From what I have said in connection with punishment, one can foresee what I am going to say about these arguments and counterarguments. They fail to make the distinction between the justification of a practice and the justification of a particular action falling under it, and therefore they fall into the mistake of taking it for granted that the promisor, like Carritt's official, is entitled without restriction to bring utilitarian considerations to bear in deciding whether to keep *his* promise. But if

---

Foundations of Ethics, pp. 95–96, 104–105. It occurs also in Mabbott, "Punishment," *op. cit.*, pp. 155–157, and in A. I. Melden, "Two Comments on Utilitarianism," *Philosophical Review*, LX (October, 1951), 519–523, which discusses Carritt's example in *Ethical and Political Thinking*, p. 64.

18 Ross's example is described simply as that of two men dying alone where one makes a promise to the other. Carritt's example (cf. n. 17 supra) is that of two men at the North Pole. The example in the text is more realistic and is similar to Mabbott's. Another example is that of being told something in confidence by one who subsequently dies. Such cases need not be "desert-island arguments" as Nowell-Smith seems to believe (cf. his *Ethics*, pp. 239–244).

one considers what the practice of promising is one will see, I think, that it is such as not to allow this sort of general discretion to the promisor. Indeed, the point of the practice is to abdicate one's title to act in accordance with utilitarian and prudential considerations in order that the future may be tied down and plans coordinated in advance. There are obvious utilitarian advantages in having a practice which denies to the promisor, as a defense, any general appeal to the utilitarian principle in accordance with which the practice itself may be justified. There is nothing contradictory, or surprising, in this: utilitarian (or aesthetic) reasons might properly be given in arguing that the game of chess, or baseball, is satisfactory just as it is, or in arguing that it should be changed in various respects, but a player in a game cannot properly appeal to such considerations as reasons for his making one move rather than another. It is a mistake to think that if the practice is justified on utilitarian grounds then the promisor must have complete liberty to use utilitarian arguments to decide whether or not to keep his promise. The practice forbids this general defense; and it is a purpose of the practice to do this. Therefore what the above arguments presuppose—the idea that if the utilitarian view is accepted then the promisor is bound if, and only if, the application of the utilitarian principle to his own case shows that keeping it is best on the whole—is false. The promisor is bound because he promised: weighing the case on its merits is not open to him.[19]

Is this to say that in particular cases one cannot deliberate whether or not to keep one's promise? Of course not. But to do so is to deliberate whether the various excuses, exceptions and defenses, which are understood by, and which constitute an important part of, the practice, apply to one's own case.[20] Various defenses for not keeping one's promise are allowed, but among them there isn't the one that, on general utilitarian grounds, the promisor (truly) thought his action best on the

[19] What I have said in this paragraph seems to me to coincide with Hume's important discussion in the *Treatise of Human Nature*, Bk. III, Pt. II, sec. 5; and also sec. 6, par. 8.

[20] For a discussion of these, see H. Sidgwick, *The Methods of Ethics* (6th ed., London, 1901), Bk. III, Ch. VI.

whole, even though there may be the defense that the consequences of keeping one's promise would have been *extremely* severe. While there are too many complexities here to consider all the necessary details, one can see that the general defense isn't allowed if one asks the following question: what would one say of someone who, when asked why he broke his promise, replied simply that breaking it was best on the whole? Assuming that his reply is sincere, and that his belief was reasonable (i.e., one need not consider the possibility that he was mistaken), I think that one would question whether or not he knows what it means to say "I promise" (in the appropriate circumstances). It would be said of someone who used this excuse without further explanation that he didn't understand what defenses the practice, which defines a promise, allows to him. If a child were to use this excuse one would correct him; for it is part of the way one is taught the concept of a promise to be corrected if one uses this excuse. The point of having the practice would be lost if the practice did allow this excuse.

It is no doubt part of the utilitarian view that every practice should admit the defense that the consequences of abiding by it would have been extremely severe; and utilitarians would be inclined to hold that some reliance on people's good sense and some concession to hard cases is necessary. They would hold that a practice is justified by serving the interests of those who take part in it; and as with any set of rules there is understood a background of circumstances under which it is expected to be applied and which need not—indeed which cannot—be fully stated. Should these circumstances change, then even if there is no rule which provides for the case, it may still be in accordance with the practice that one be released from one's obligation. But this sort of defense allowed by a practice must not be confused with the general option to weigh each particular case on utilitarian grounds which critics of utilitarianism have thought it necessarily to involve.

The concern which utilitarianism raises by its justification of punishment is that it may justify too much. The question in connection with promises is different: it is how utilitarianism can account for the obligation to keep promises at all. One feels that the recognized obligation to keep one's promise and utilitarianism are incompatible. And to be sure, they are incompatible if one interprets the utilitarian view as necessarily holding that each person has complete liberty to weigh every particular action on general utilitarian grounds. But must one interpret utilitarianism in this way? I hope to show that, in the sorts of cases I have discussed, one cannot interpret it in this way.

[III]

So far I have tried to show the importance of the distinction between the justification of a practice and the justification of a particular action falling under it by indicating how this distinction might be used to defend utilitarianism against two long-standing objections. One might be tempted to close the discussion at this point by saying that utilitarian considerations should be understood as applying to practices in the first instance and not to particular actions falling under them except insofar as the practices admit of it. One might say that in this modified form it is a better account of our considered moral opinions and let it go at that. But to stop here would be to neglect the interesting question as to how one can fail to appreciate the significance of this rather obvious distinction and can take it for granted that utilitarianism has the consequence that particular cases may always be decided on general utilitarian grounds.[21] I want to argue that

21 So far as I can see it is not until Moore that the doctrine is expressly stated in this way. See, for example, *Principia Ethica*, p. 147, where it is said that the statement "I am morally bound to perform this action" is identical with the statement "*This* action will produce the greatest possible amount of good in the Universe" (my italics). It is important to remember that those whom I have called the classical utilitarians were largely interested in social institutions. They were among the leading economists and political theorists of their day, and they were not infrequently reformers interested in practical affairs. Utilitarianism historically goes together with a coherent view of society, and is not simply an ethical theory, much less an attempt at philosophical analysis in the modern sense. The utilitarian principle was quite naturally thought of, and used, as a criterion for judging social institutions (practices) and as a basis for urging reforms. It is not clear, therefore, how far it is necessary to amend utilitarianism in its classical form. For a discussion of utilitarianism as an in-

this mistake may be connected with misconceiving the logical status of the rules of practices; and to show this I am going to examine two conceptions of rules, two ways of placing them within the utilitarian theory.

The conception which conceals from us the significance of the distinction I am going to call the summary view. It regards rules in the following way: one supposes that each person decides what he shall do in particular cases by applying the utilitarian principle; one supposes further that different people will decide the same particular case in the same way and that there will be recurrences of cases similar to those previously decided. Thus it will happen that in cases of certain kinds the same decision will be made either by the same person at different times or by different persons at the same time. If a case occurs frequently enough one supposes that a rule is formulated to cover that sort of case. I have called this conception the summary view because rules are pictured as summaries of past decisions arrived at by the *direct* application of the utilitarian principle to particular cases. Rules are regarded as reports that cases of a certain sort have been found on *other* grounds to be properly decided in a certain way (although, of course, they do not *say* this).

There are several things to notice about this way of placing rules within the utilitarian theory.[22]

---

tegral part of a theory of society, see L. Robbins, *The Theory of Economic Policy in English Classical Political Economy* (London, 1952).

22 This footnote should be read after sec. 3 and presupposes what I have said there. It provides a few references to statements by leading utilitarians of the summary conception. In general it appears that when they discussed the logical features of rules the summary conception prevailed and that it was typical of the way they talked about moral rules. I cite a rather lengthy group of passages from Austin as a full illustration.

John Austin in his *Lectures on Jurisprudence* meets the objection that deciding in accordance with the utilitarian principle case by case is impractical by saying that this is a misinterpretation of utilitarianism. According to the utilitarian view " . . . our conduct would conform to *rules* inferred from the tendencies of actions, but would not be determined by a direct resort to the principle of general utility. Utility would be the test of our conduct, ultimately, but not immediately: the immediate test of the rules to which our conduct would conform, but not the immediate test of specific or individual actions. Our rules would be fashioned on utility; our conduct, on our rules" (Vol. I, p. 116). As to how one decides on the tendency of an action he says: "If we would try the

1. The point of having rules derives from the fact that similar cases tend to recur and that one can decide cases more quickly if one records past decisions in the form of rules. If similar cases didn't recur, one would be required to apply the utilitarian principle directly, case by case, and rules reporting past decisions would be of no use.

2. The decisions made on particular cases are logically prior to rules. Since rules gain their point from the need to apply the utilitarian principle to many similar cases, it follows that a particular case (or several cases similar to it) may exist whether or not there is a rule covering that case. We are pictured as recognizing particular cases prior to there being a rule which covers them, for it is only if we meet with a number of cases of a cer-

---

tendency of a specific or individual act, we must not contemplate the act as if it were single and insulated, but must look at the class of acts to which it belongs. We must suppose that acts of the class were generally done or omitted, and consider the probable effect upon the general happiness or good. We must guess the consequences which would follow, if the class of acts were general; and also the consequences which would follow, if they were generally omitted. We must then compare the consequences on the positive and negative sides, and determine on which of the two the *balance* of advantage lies. . . . If we truly try the tendency of a specific or individual act, we try the tendency of the class to which that act belongs. The *particular* conclusion which we draw, with regard to the single act, implies a *general* conclusion embracing all similar acts. . . . To the rules thus inferred, and lodged in the memory, our conduct would conform *immediately* if it were truly adjusted to utility" (*ibid.*, p. 117). One might think that Austin meets the objection by stating the practice conception of rules; and perhaps he did intend to. But it is not clear that he has stated this conception. Is the generality he refers to of the statistical sort? This is suggested by the notion of tendency. Or does he refer to the utility of setting up a practice? I don't know; but what suggests the summary view is his subsequent remarks. He says: "To consider the specific consequences of single or individual acts, would *seldom* [my italics] consist with that ultimate principle" (*ibid.*, p. 117). But would one ever do this? He continues: " . . . this being admitted, the necessity of pausing and calculating, which the objection in question supposes, is an imagined necessity. To preface each act or forbearance by a conjecture and comparison of consequences, were clearly *superfluous* [my italics] and mischievous. It were clearly superfluous, inasmuch as the *result of that process* [my italics] would be embodied in a known *rule*. It were clearly mischievous, inasmuch as the *true* result would be expressed by that rule, whilst the process would probably be faulty, if it were done on the spur of the occasion" (*ibid.*, pp. 117–118). He goes on: "If our experience and observation of particulars were not *generalized*, our experience and observation of particulars would seldom avail us in *practice*. . . . The inferences suggested to our minds by

tain sort that we formulate a rule. Thus we are able to describe a particular case as a particular case of the requisite sort whether there is a rule regarding *that* sort of case or not. Put another way: what the *A*'s and the *B*'s refer to in rules of the form 'Whenever *A* do *B*' may be described as *A*'s and *B*'s whether or not there is the rule 'Whenever *A* do *B*', or whether or not there is any body of rules which make up a practice of which that rule is a part.

To illustrate this consider a rule, or maxim, which could arise in this way: suppose that a person is trying to decide whether to tell someone who is fatally ill what his illness is when he has been asked to do so. Suppose the person to reflect and then decide, on utilitarian grounds, that he should not answer

---

repeated experience and observation are, therefore, drawn into *principles*, or compressed into *maxims*. These we carry about us ready for use, and apply to individual cases promptly . . . without reverting to the process by which they were obtained; or without recalling, and arraying before our minds, the numerous and intricate considerations of which they are *handy abridgments* [my italics]. . . . True theory is a *compendium* of particular truths. . . . Speaking then, generally, human conduct is inevitably *guided* [my italics] by *rules*, or by *principles* or *maxims*" (*ibid.*, pp. 117–118). I need not trouble to show how all these remarks incline to the summary view. Further, when Austin comes to deal with cases "of comparatively rare occurrence" he holds that specific considerations may outweigh the general. "Looking at the reasons from which we had inferred the rule, it were absurd to think it inflexible. We should therefore dismiss the *rule;* resort directly to the *principle* upon which our rules were fashioned; and calculate *specific* consequences to the best of our knowledge and ability" (*ibid.*, pp. 120–121). Austin's view is interesting because it shows how one may come close to the practice conception and then slide away from it.

In *A System of Logic*, Bk. VI, Ch. XII, par. 2, Mill distinguishes clearly between the position of judge and legislator and in doing so suggests the distinction between the two concepts of rules. However, he distinguishes the two positions to illustrate the difference between cases where one is to apply a rule already established and cases where one must formulate a rule to govern subsequent conduct. It's the latter case that interests him and he takes the "maxim of policy" of a legislator as typical of rules. In par. 3 the summary conception is very clearly stated. For example, he says of rules of conduct that they should be taken provisionally, as they are made for the most numerous cases. He says that they "point out" the manner in which it is least perilous to act; they serve as an "admonition" that a certain mode of conduct has been found suited to the most common occurrences. In *Utilitarianism*, Ch. II, par. 24, the summary conception appears in Mill's answer to the same objection Austin considered. Here he speaks of rules as "corollaries" from the principle of utility; these "secondary" rules are compared to "landmarks" and "direction-posts." They are

truthfully; and suppose that on the basis of this and other like occasions he formulates a rule to the effect that when asked by someone fatally ill what his illness is, one should not tell him. The point to notice is that someone's being fatally ill and asking what his illness is, and someone's telling him, are things that can be described as such whether or not there is this rule. The performance of the action to which the rule refers doesn't require the stage-setting of a practice of which this rule is a part. This is what is meant by saying that on the summary view particular cases are logically prior to rules.

3. Each person is in principle always entitled to reconsider the correctness of a rule and to question whether or not it

---

based on long experience and so make it unnecessary to apply the utilitarian principle to each case. In par. 25 Mill refers to the task of the utilitarian principle in adjudicating between competing moral rules. He talks here as if one then applies the utilitarian principle directly to the particular case. On the practice view one would rather use the principle to decide which of the ways that make the practice consistent is the best. It should be noted that while in par. 10 Mill's definition of utilitarianism makes the utilitarian principle apply to morality, i.e., to the rules and precepts of human conduct, the definition in par. 2 uses the phrase "actions are right in *proportion* as they *tend* to promote happiness" [my italics] and this inclines towards the summary view. In the last paragraph of the essay "On the Definition of Political Economy," *Westminster Review* (October, 1836), Mill says that it is only in art, as distinguished from science, that one can properly speak of exceptions. In a question of practice, if something is fit to be done "in the majority of cases" then it is made the rule. "We may . . . in talking of art *unobjectionably* speak of the *rule* and the *exception*, meaning by the rule the cases in which there exists a preponderance . . . of inducements for acting in a particular way; and by the exception, the cases in which the preponderance is on the contrary side." These remarks, too, suggest the summary view.

In Moore's *Principia Ethica*, Ch. V, there is a complicated and difficult discussion of moral rules. I will not examine it here except to express my suspicion that the summary conception prevails. To be sure, Moore speaks frequently of the utility of rules as generally followed, and of actions as generally practiced, but it is possible that these passages fit the statistical notion of generality which the summary conception allows. This conception is suggested by Moore's taking the utilitarian principle as applying directly to particular actions (pp. 147–148) and by his notion of a rule as something indicating which of the few alternatives likely to occur to anyone will generally produce a greater total good in the immediate future (p. 154). He talks of an "ethical law" as a prediction, and as a generalization (pp. 146, 155). The summary conception is also suggested by his discussion of exceptions (pp. 162–163) and of the force of examples of breaching a rule (pp. 163–164).

is proper to follow it in a particular case. As rules are guides and aids, one may ask whether in past decisions there might not have been a mistake in applying the utilitarian principle to get the rule in question, and wonder whether or not it is best in this case. The reason for rules is that people are not able to apply the utilitarian principle effortlessly and flawlessly; there is need to save time and to post a guide. On this view a society of rational utilitarians would be a society without rules in which each person applied the utilitarian principle directly and smoothly, and without error, case by case. On the other hand, ours is a society in which rules are formulated to serve as aids in reaching these ideally rational decisions on particular cases, guides which have been built up and tested by the experience of generations. If one applies this view to rules, one is interpreting them as maxims, as "rules of thumb"; and it is doubtful that anything to which the summary conception did apply would be called a *rule*. Arguing as if one regarded rules in this way is a mistake one makes while doing philosophy.

4. The concept of a *general* rule takes the following form. One is pictured as estimating on what percentage of the cases likely to arise a given rule may be relied upon to express the correct decision, that is, the decision that would be arrived at if one were to correctly apply the utilitarian principle case by case. If one estimates that by and large the rule will give the correct decision, or if one estimates that the likelihood of making a mistake by applying the utilitarian principle directly on one's own is greater than the likelihood of making a mistake by following the rule, and if these considerations held of persons generally, then one would be justified in urging its adoption as a general rule. In this way *general* rules might be accounted for on the summary view. It will still make sense, however, to speak of applying the utilitarian principle case by case, for it was by trying to foresee the results of doing this that one got the initial estimates upon which acceptance of the rule depends. That one is taking a rule in accordance with the summary conception will show itself in the naturalness with which one speaks of the rule as a guide, or as a maxim, or as a generalization from experi-

ence, and as something to be laid aside in extraordinary cases where there is no assurance that the generalization will hold and the case must therefore be treated on its merits. Thus there goes with this conception the notion of a particular exception which renders a rule suspect on a particular occasion.

The other conception of rules I will call the practice conception. On this view rules are pictured as defining a practice. Practices are set up for various reasons, but one of them is that in many areas of conduct each person's deciding what to do on utilitarian grounds case by case leads to confusion, and that the attempt to coordinate behavior by trying to foresee how others will act is bound to fail. As an alternative one realizes that what is required is the establishment of a practice, the specification of a new form of activity; and from this one sees that a practice necessarily involves the abdication of full liberty to act on utilitarian and prudential grounds. It is the mark of a practice that being taught how to engage in it involves being instructed in the rules which define it, and that appeal is made to those rules to correct the behavior of those engaged in it. Those engaged in a practice recognize the rules as defining it. The rules cannot be taken as simply describing how those engaged in the practice in fact behave: it is not simply that they act as if they were obeying the rules. Thus it is essential to the notion of a practice that the rules are publicly known and understood as definitive; and it is essential also that the rules of a practice can be taught and can be acted upon to yield a coherent practice. On this conception, then, rules are not generalizations from the decisions of individuals applying the utilitarian principle directly and independently to recurrent particular cases. On the contrary, rules define a practice and are themselves the subject of the utilitarian principle.

To show the important differences between this way of fitting rules into the utilitarian theory and the previous way, I shall consider the differences between the two conceptions on the points previously discussed.

1. In contrast with the summary view, the rules of practices are logically prior to particular cases. This is so because

there cannot be a particular case of an action falling under a rule of a practice unless there is the practice. This can be made clearer as follows: in a practice there are rules setting up offices, specifying certain forms of action appropriate to various offices, establishing penalties for the breach of rules, and so on. We may think of the rules of a practice as defining offices, moves, and offenses. Now what is meant by saying that the practice is logically prior to particular cases is this: given any rule which specifies a form of action (a move), a particular action which would be taken as falling under this rule given that there is the practice would not be *described as* that sort of action unless there was the practice. In the case of actions specified by practices it is logically impossible to perform them outside the stage-setting provided by those practices, for unless there is the practice, and unless the requisite proprieties are fulfilled, whatever one does, whatever movements one makes, will fail to count as a form of action which the practice specifies. What one does will be described in some *other* way.

One may illustrate this point from the game of baseball. Many of the actions one performs in a game of baseball one can do by oneself or with others whether there is the game or not. For example, one can throw a ball, run, or swing a peculiarly shaped piece of wood. But one cannot steal base, or strike out, or draw a walk, or make an error, or balk; although one can do certain things which appear to resemble these actions such as sliding into a bag, missing a grounder and so on. Striking out, stealing a base, balking, etc., are all actions which can only happen in a game. No matter what a person did, what he did would not be described as stealing a base or striking out or drawing a walk unless he could also be described as playing baseball, and for him to be doing this presupposes the rule-like practice which constitutes the game. The practice is logically prior to particular cases: unless there is the practice the terms referring to actions specified by it lack a sense.[23]

23 One might feel that it is a mistake to say that a practice is logically prior to the forms of action it specifies on the grounds that if there were never any instances of actions falling under a practice then we should be strongly inclined to say that there wasn't the practice either. Blue-prints for a practice do not

2. The practice view leads to an entirely different conception of the authority which each person has to decide on the propriety of following a rule in particular cases. To engage in a practice, to perform those actions specified by a practice, means to follow the appropriate rules. If one wants to do an action which a certain practice specifies then there is no way to do it except to follow the rules which define it. Therefore, it doesn't make sense for a person to raise the question whether or not a rule of a practice correctly applies to *his* case where the action he contemplates is a form of action defined by a practice. If someone were to raise such a question, he would simply show that he didn't understand the situation in which he was acting. If one wants to perform an action specified by a practice, the only legitimate question concerns the nature of the practice itself ("How do I go about making a will?").

This point is illustrated by the behavior expected of a player in games. If one wants to play a game, one doesn't treat the rules of the game as guides as to what is best in particular cases. In a game of baseball if a batter were to ask "Can I have four strikes?" it would be assumed that he was asking what the rule was; and if, when told what the rule was, he were to say that he meant that on this occasion he thought it would be best on the whole for him to have four strikes rather than three, this would be most kindly taken as a joke. One might contend that baseball would be a better game if four strikes were allowed instead of three; but one cannot picture the rules as guides to what is best on the whole in particular cases, and question their applicability to particular cases as particular cases.

3 and 4. To complete the four points of comparison with the summary conception, it is clear from what has been said that rules of practices are not guides to help one decide particular

---

make a practice. That there is a practice entails that there are instances of people having been engaged and now being engaged in it (with suitable qualifications). This is correct, but it doesn't hurt the claim that any given particular instance of a form of action specified by a practice presupposes the practice. This isn't so on the summary picture, as each instance must be "there" prior to the rules, so to speak, as something from which one gets the rule by applying the utilitarian principle to it directly.

cases correctly as judged by some higher ethical principle. And neither the quasi-statistical notion of generality, nor the notion of a particular exception, can apply to the rules of practices. A more or less general rule of a practice must be a rule which according to the structure of the practice applies to more or fewer of the kinds of cases arising under it; or it must be a rule which is more or less basic to the understanding of the practice. Again, a particular case cannot be an exception to a rule of a practice. An exception is rather a qualification or a further specification of the rule.

It follows from what we have said about the practice conception of rules that if a person is engaged in a practice, and if he is asked why *he* does what *he* does, or if he is asked to defend what he does, then his explanation, or defense, lies in referring the questioner to the practice. He cannot say of *his* action, if it is an action specified by a practice, that he does it rather than some other because he thinks it is best on the whole.[24] When a man engaged in a practice is queried about his action he must assume that the questioner either doesn't know that he is engaged in it ("Why are you in a hurry to pay him?" "I promised to pay him today") or doesn't know what the practice is. One doesn't so much justify one's particular action as explain, or show, that it is in accordance with the practice. The reason for this is that it is only against the stage-setting of the practice that one's particular action is described as it is. Only by reference to the practice can one *say* what one is doing. To explain or to defend one's own action, as a particular action, one fits it into the practice which defines it. If this is not accepted it's a sign that a different question is being raised as to whether one is justified in accepting the practice, or in tolerating it. When the challenge is to the practice, citing the rules (saying what the practice is) is naturally to no avail. But when the challenge is to the particular action defined by the practice, there is nothing one can do but refer to the rules. Concerning particular actions there

---

24 A philosophical joke (in the mouth of Jeremy Bentham): "When I run to the other wicket after my partner has struck a good ball I do so because it is best on the whole."

is only a question for one who isn't clear as to what the practice is, or who doesn't know that it is being engaged in. This is to be contrasted with the case of a maxim which may be taken as pointing to the correct decision on the case as decided on *other* grounds, and so giving a challenge on the case a sense by having it question whether these other grounds really support the decision on this case.

If one compares the two conceptions of rules I have discussed, one can see how the summary conception misses the significance of the distinction between justifying a practice and justifying actions falling under it. On this view rules are regarded as guides whose purpose it is to indicate the ideally rational decision on the given particular case which the flawless application of the utilitarian principle would yield. One has, in principle, full option to use the guides or to discard them as the situation warrants without one's moral office being altered in any way: whether one discards the rules or not, one always holds the office of a rational person seeking case by case to realize the best on the whole. But on the practice conception, if one holds an office defined by a practice then questions regarding one's actions in this office are settled by reference to the rules which define the practice. If one seeks to question these rules, then one's office undergoes a fundamental change: one then assumes the office of one empowered to change and criticize the rules, or the office of a reformer, and so on. The summary conception does away with the distinction of offices and the various forms of argument appropriate to each. On that conception there is one office and so no offices at all. It therefore obscures the fact that the utilitarian principle must, in the case of actions and offices defined by a practice, apply to the practice, so that general utilitarian arguments are not available to those who act in offices so defined.[25]

---

[25] How do these remarks apply to the case of the promise known only to father and son? Well, at first sight the son certainly holds the office of promisor, and so he isn't allowed by the practice to weigh the particular case on general utilitarian grounds. Suppose instead that he wishes to consider himself in the office of one empowered to criticize and change the practice, leaving aside the question as to his right to move from his previously assumed office to another.

Some qualifications are necessary in what I have said. First, I may have talked of the summary and the practice conceptions of rules as if only one of them could be true of rules, and if true of any rules, then necessarily true of *all* rules. I do not, of course, mean this. (It is the critics of utilitarianism who make this mistake insofar as their arguments against utilitarianism presuppose a summary conception of the rules of practices.) Some rules will fit one conception, some rules the other; and so there are rules of practices (rules in the strict sense), and maxims and "rules of thumb."

Secondly, there are further distinctions that can be made in classifying rules, distinctions which should be made if one were considering other questions. The distinctions which I have drawn are those most relevant for the rather special matter I have discussed, and are not intended to be exhaustive.

Finally, there will be many border-line cases about which it will be difficult, if not impossible, to decide which conception of rules is applicable. One expects border-line cases with any concept, and they are especially likely in connection with such involved concepts as those of a practice, institution, game, rule, and so on. Wittgenstein has shown how fluid these notions are.[26] What I have done is to emphasize and sharpen two conceptions for the limited purpose of this paper.

[IV]

What I have tried to show by distinguishing between two conceptions of rules is that there is a way of regarding rules which allows the option to consider particular cases on general utilitarian grounds; whereas there is another conception which does not admit of such discretion except insofar as the rules themselves

---

Then he may consider utilitarian arguments as applied to the practice; but once he does this he will see that there are such arguments for not allowing a general utilitarian defense in the practice for this sort of case. For to do so would make it impossible to ask for and to give a kind of promise which one often wants to be able to ask for and to give. Therefore he will not want to change the practice, and so as a promisor he has no option but to keep his promise.

26 *Philosophical Investigations* (Oxford, 1953), I, pars. 65–71, for example.

authorize it. I want to suggest that the tendency while doing philosophy to picture rules in accordance with the summary conception is what may have blinded moral philosophers to the significance of the distinction between justifying a practice and justifying a particular action falling under it; and it does so by misrepresenting the logical force of the reference to the rules in the case of a challenge to a particular action falling under a practice, and by obscuring the fact that where there is a practice, it is the practice itself that must be the subject of the utilitarian principle.

It is surely no accident that two of the traditional test cases of utilitarianism, punishment and promises, are clear cases of practices. Under the influence of the summary conception it is natural to suppose that the officials of a penal system, and one who has made a promise, may decide what to do in particular cases on utilitarian grounds. One fails to see that a general discretion to decide particular cases on utilitarian grounds is incompatible with the concept of a practice; and that what discretion one does have is itself defined by the practice (e.g., a judge may have discretion to determine the penalty within certain limits). The traditional objections to utilitarianism which I have discussed presuppose the attribution to judges, and to those who have made promises, of a plenitude of moral authority to decide particular cases on utilitarian grounds. But once one fits utilitarianism together with the notion of a practice, and notes that punishment and promising are practices, then one sees that this attribution is logically precluded.

That punishment and promising are practices is beyond question. In the case of promising this is shown by the fact that the form of words "I promise" is a performative utterance which presupposes the stage-setting of the practice and the proprieties defined by it. Saying the words "I promise" will only be promising given the existence of the practice. It would be absurd to interpret the rules about promising in accordance with the summary conception. It is absurd to say, for example, that the rule that promises should be kept could have arisen from its being found in past cases to be best on the whole to keep one's promise; for unless there were already the understanding that one keeps one's promises as part of the practice itself there couldn't have been any cases of promising.

It must, of course, be granted that the rules defining promising are not codified, and that one's conception of what they are necessarily depends on one's moral training. Therefore it is likely that there is considerable variation in the way people understand the practice, and room for argument as to how it is best set up. For example, differences as to how strictly various defenses are to be taken, or just what defenses are available, are likely to arise amongst persons with different backgrounds. But irrespective of these variations it belongs to the concept of the practice of promising that the general utilitarian defense is not available to the promisor. That this is so accounts for the force of the traditional objection which I have discussed. And the point I wish to make is that when one fits the utilitarian view together with the practice conception of rules, as one must in the appropriate cases, then there is nothing in that view which entails that there must be such a defense, either in the practice of promising, or in any other practice.

Punishment is also a clear case. There are many actions in the sequence of events which constitute someone's being punished which presuppose a practice. One can see this by considering the definition of punishment which I gave when discussing Carritt's criticism of utilitarianism. The definition there stated refers to such things as the normal rights of a citizen, rules of law, due process of law, trials and courts of law, statutes, etc., none of which can exist outside the elaborate stage-setting of a legal system. It is also the case that many of the actions for which people are punished presuppose practices. For example, one is punished for stealing, for trespassing, and the like, which presuppose the institution of property. It is impossible to say what punishment is, or to describe a particular instance of it, without referring to offices, actions, and offenses specified by practices. Punishment is a move in an elaborate legal game and presupposes the complex of practices which make up the legal order. The same thing is true of the less formal sorts of punishment: a parent or guardian or someone in proper authority may punish a child, but no one else can.

There is one mistaken interpretation of what I have been saying which it is worthwhile to warn against. One might think that the use I am making of the distinction between justifying a practice and justifying the particular actions falling under it involves one in a definite social and political attitude in that it leads to a kind of conservatism. It might seem that I am saying that for each person the social practices of his society provide the standard of justification for his actions; therefore let each person abide by them and his conduct will be justified.

This interpretation is entirely wrong. The point I have been making is rather a logical point. To be sure, it has consequences in matters of ethical theory; but in itself it leads to no particular social or political attitude. It is simply that where a form of action is specified by a practice there is no justification possible of the particular action of a particular person save by reference to the practice. In such cases the action is what it is in virtue of the practice and to explain it is to refer to the practice. There is no inference whatsoever to be drawn with respect to whether or not one should accept the practices of one's society. One can be as radical as one likes but in the case of actions specified by practices the objects of one's radicalism must be the social practices and people's acceptance of them.

I have tried to show that when we fit the utilitarian view together with the practice conception of rules, where this conception is appropriate,[27] we can formulate it in a way which saves it from several traditional objections. I have further tried to show how the logical force of the distinction between justifying a practice and justifying an action falling under it is connected

---

[27] As I have already stated, it is not always easy to say where the conception is appropriate. Nor do I care to discuss at this point the general sorts of cases to which it does apply except to say that one should not take it for granted that it applies to many so-called "moral rules." It is my feeling that relatively few actions of the moral life are defined by practices and that the practice conception is more relevant to understanding legal and legal-like arguments than it is to the more complex sort of moral arguments. Utilitarianism must be fitted to different conceptions of rules depending on the case, and no doubt the failure to do this has been one source of difficulty in interpreting it correctly.

with the practice conception of rules and cannot be understood as long as one regards the rules of practices in accordance with the summary view. Why, when doing philosophy, one may be inclined to so regard them, I have not discussed. The reasons for this are evidently very deep and would require another paper.

EGOISM AND MORALITY /
J. A. Brunton

A GOOD deal of interest has been shown of late, in articles and discussions, in what might be regarded as the minimum requirements for a moral system. What, for instance, is it to call a principle a moral principle, irrespective of one's own penchant for Utilitarianism, Intuitionism, Kantianism, or, generally speaking, one's own choice of a way of life? In these discussions it is fairly widely agreed that Egoism does not satisfy these minimum conditions and that therefore, even on purely formal grounds, it does not qualify as a moral theory. Mr. Gellner, indeed, seems to imply in his *Ethics and Logic* (*Proc. Arist. Soc.*, 1954–5, pp. 157 ff.) that Egoism could be a moral theory of what he calls type 'E', but Mr. Hare would, I should imagine, have much wider support for the opposite view expressed in his *Universalisability* (*Proc. Arist. Soc.*, 1954–5, pp. 295 ff.). Rather than put Egoism either outside or inside the moral pale, however, it would seem

From J. A. Brunton, "Egoism and Morality," The Philosophical Quarterly, VI (*1956*), *289–303*. Reprinted by permission of the Editor of The Philosophical Quarterly.

to be more helpful, if we are to fix its place on the logical map, to examine in what ways it is like and in what ways it is unlike a "moral" system in the accepted minimum sense. We may then draw our own conclusions.

In order to cast the net fairly wide I shall not make any assumptions about what are generally regarded as minimum requirements for a moral system. Let us label these requirements as over-ridingness, comprehensiveness, and the acceptance of rules of behaviour. Let us, that is, say (1) that it is logically odd to defend a course of action sincerely on moral grounds and at the same time to admit that there are over-riding grounds of a non-moral nature that rule out the performance of the action (cases of compulsion neurosis, etc., are automatically ruled out from consideration if one accepts 'ought implies can' as axiomatic); (2) that a principle which is so frivolous as to have no relation to or connection with parts of one's life other than those for which the principle itself has been tailor-made shall not count as a moral principle; and (3) that although *which* rules we accept cannot be formally decided, the acceptance of *some* rules is entailed by the use of such words as 'principle' and 'system'. Even on these three points there may be disagreement but the first two are of no great concern to us since, if they *are* accepted as minimum requirements, then Egoism fulfils them. The Egoist certainly has a principle of life which he regards as over-riding and in some sense permeating all his deliberate actions. Much more must be said, however, about the third condition, for it is here that the sting of the attack on Egoism lies.

My argument will fall roughly into three sections. First I shall try to establish in what sense the Egoist can be said to observe rules of behaviour and in what sense he cannot. Secondly I shall try to examine the logical peculiarities of the Egoist's 'Individualistic' axiom (the principle that I ought to do X simply because 'I am I' is at the heart of the whole controversy). And lastly, I shall attempt to show why, for the moral philosopher, the attempt to put Egoism in its correct place on the logical map is by no means a frivolous procedure of merely academic interest.

[1]

To return to the third condition mentioned above—the acceptance of rules of behaviour. The argument usually goes something
like this, or perhaps it would be more accurate to say that this is
one way of putting the matter. The word 'ought' or its equivalent in other languages is obviously a word of central importance
in the language of morals. This word differs in its uses from
straightforward imperatives. It would make sense to give an
order without implying that there were good reasons for the
order or without implying that the same order must be given on
a suitably similar occasion. This is not so when the word 'ought'
is used. One can logically demand reasons for 'ought' statements. One can also logically demand that if an 'ought' statement fills the bill in one situation the same 'ought' statement
should fill the bill in another situation of a sufficiently similar
kind. To take these two criteria together (i.e. (i) 'ought' implies
reasons and (ii) indifference to mere particularity) is, it is argued, equivalent to an admission that morality demands rules.
To give reasons and to rule out particularity is what the acceptance and observation of rules of behaviour means.

It is important to keep the two criteria separate. If we
make a distinction between (a) subsidiary and (b) ultimate
principles of action (roughly analogous to Kant's distinction between hypothetical and categorical imperatives), reasons can be
demanded for (a) but not for (b). Ultimate principles are 'reasonable' in the different sense outlined above, namely, that they
rule out merely particular considerations. An example will perhaps make this point clear.

'You ought to return that book to Jones'. 'Why?' 'Because you promised to'. This illustrates (a).

'Other things being equal one ought to keep one's promises'. Here the question 'Why?' is out of place, but the neutral
use of the word 'one' makes this a rational principle rather than
a private whim.

Now, to return to the Egoist. He seems to be in little diffi-

culty when asked for reasons for his actions or when asked to
supply the rule which guides them so long as the second question, whether his rule and his reasons are neutral as between different agents, is kept in the background. As is generally recognised, one can have a policy of Prudence. Kant saw well enough
that the Egoist is in a sense entitled to the use of words like
'rational', 'ought', 'principle', etc., because he can have a plan of
life (and must if he is to be consistent) which rules out, or at
least makes subordinate, the language of wants and desires. It
might, of course, be said that the Egoist's whole aim in life is to
satisfy his wants and desires, but Egoism need neither be crudely
formulated nor stupidly observed. (In what sense was Iago an
Altruist? Yet he could hardly be called an undisciplined man.)
No, the Egoist can certainly give reasons and a rule for his individual acts. He can always say, this act in my estimation serves
my own best interests; therefore I *ought* to do it. All this is indeed
commonplace and would hardly be questioned by any philosopher.

It would seem then that the whole charge against the
Egoist on formal or quasi-formal grounds is that his use of words
like 'ought', 'principle', 'rule', 'reason', is logically vicious in
that all these words entail what I shall call the 'Neutrality' principle [namely the principle that these words are always applicable without change (i.e. without the adoption of a negative or
some similar device) in suitably similar situations], whereas the
Egoist adopts what I have already called the 'Individualistic'
axiom.

A simple way out of this impasse might appear to offer
itself in the device of endowing the Egoist with a 'neutral' attitude towards his own philosophy of life. He might universalise
his Egoism by admitting and indeed sponsoring the right or the
duty of everyone else to be an Egoist. This way out, however, is
blocked. A state of affairs is indeed conceivable in which a whole
society of Egoists might satisfy their own best interests without
interfering with those of anyone else, all of them at the same
time being highly delighted with each other's way of life. Some
sort of quasi-moral terminology could indeed still be used in

such a society: one of a group of such Egoists might, for instance, say 'I ought not to eat so many peaches, since being unnecessarily sick offends against my policy of life'. But, as Kant
saw, if we are to discuss the normal use of words in a moral
context we cannot use as our basis highly artificial and imagi-
nary societies in which such words would have an artificial and
attenuated use. Just as 'Holy' wills would have no use for the
concept of Duty, so a society of particularly fortunate Egoists
would have small use for it either. If we are fairly to discuss the
moral status of a society of rational Egoists we must at least assume the possibility of a clash of interests, since it is perfectly
legitimate to ask how their 'moral' system would stand in the
face of circumstances normally encountered by anyone who uses
moral discourse. And it is here of course that the trouble begins.
To reduce the issue to a simple example. The Egoist A could
hardly say 'I ought to murder my neighbour B because I covet his
wife' and at the same time admit that his neighbour B was in all
essential respects his (A's) natural and moral twin, and that
therefore B ought to murder A because B coveted A's equally desirable wife (polygamy being granted for the purposes of the example). The Egoist must be unwaveringly self-centred if he is to
carry out his policy of life, and he cannot welcome a similar
policy on the part of others which might (logically) and probably
would (empirically) interfere with his own plan.

Another favourite refuge of the Egoist is to insist on his
own difference from everyone else by claiming that he has special characteristics not shared by others. He then argues that the
situation never *is* the same for others because he himself is a
unique factor in any situation. This position is perhaps formally
irrefutable but I shall not dwell on it since it does not seem to me
to go to the heart of the matter or raise the really interesting
issues. To such an Egoist one could say two things. One could
accuse him of hypocrisy (Bishop Butler's self-partiality) and
argue that therefore his glorification of himself was bogus and
not a genuine moral consideration. One could alternatively suggest that the man was a fool, seeing characteristics in himself
that did not exist or over-estimating the particularising impor-

tance of those which did. This alternative answer would obviously not be a formal refutation since a man's ability to weigh the importance and uniqueness of his own individualising characteristics is not a formal matter.[1]

We are thus at length brought face to face with the really interesting case of the Egoist who makes an exception of himself simply because he is himself and not because of any distinguishing characteristics of himself which he regards as morally relevant to the issue. Such a man would seem to use words normally employed in moral (and essentially inter-personal) discourse for his own personal prudential policies whilst at the same time being unable to allow others like himself to use the same words in the same contexts. The Egoist would indeed seem to be accepting a very strange rule of life, if indeed it is to be called a rule at all.

Before I come, however, to the second part of my paper and a discussion of the Egoist's 'individualistic' axiom, more must be said about the use of the word 'ought'. The distinction I have made between ultimate and subsidiary principles of action is not one that has been ignored in recent controversy. I am not so sure, however, that it has always been fully realised that, in the light of this distinction, one must admit that the word 'ought' is used in possibly analogous but certainly different ways. To put the matter perhaps rather cryptically, it has both its vertical and its lateral uses. It is one thing to say that one ought to do a particular action and to refer back to a principle in justification of one's 'ought'. It is quite another to say that one ought to accept the principle when no further principle can be adduced to justify the use of the word 'ought'. The first 'ought' refers back (vertically) to the principle on which it is based. The second 'ought' refers (laterally) to the universal validity of the recommended principle.

Now within the context of suggested minimum requirements for the use of words in moral discourse (and it is within

---

[1] That personal characteristics matter up to a point is generally conceded. A Prime Minister has not the same duty as a private soldier to expose himself to enemy fire.

this context that this paper is being written) it is usually accepted that ultimate principles are (roughly speaking) a matter of choice. Mr. Hare, for instance, in his *Universalisability* quite rightly rebuts charges of arbitrariness and of making first-order principles a mere matter of inclination. This does not alter the fact, however, that he regards the logic of ultimate 'ought' statements as being ultimately connected with the logic of choice.

Now, as Kant saw, when he suggested that we are under no direct obligation to promote virtue in others, there is something logically odd in the suggestion that one can choose other people's ways of life. One can, of course, approve of them but not choose them. Might not then the Egoist argue unashamedly on these lines: I have chosen a way of life. It happens to suit my book that others should choose a different way of life. I am under no obligation, however, to say that they *ought* to choose one or the other?

A partial analogy might be offered by the following example. Imagine A, a Euclidean geometer, and B, a non-Euclidean geometer. B might be very jealous of his own technique and might resent any attempt of A's to copy him. B could certainly not call A a fool if A changed techniques but he would be under no obligation positively to sponsor A's change. Similarly an Egoist could not condemn anyone who looked at conduct in a similar way to his own but he is under no obligation positively to foster in others his own approach to morality. And if this non-parallelism between A's attitude to his own choice of a way of life and his attitude to that of others appears logically suspicious, it is perhaps worth while pointing out that an analogous non-parallelism exists in the philosophies of non-egoistic moral philosophers of high repute. Kant has already been mentioned. He certainly accepted an analogous non-parallelism when he suggested (*a*) that we have a duty to be virtuous but no direct duty to promote virtues in others, and (*b*) that we have no direct duty to make ourselves happy but that we have a duty to promote the happiness of others. W. D. Ross, I would suggest, has also held the view that it might very well be moral to give someone pleasure and not moral at all to give the same amount of pleasure to oneself, even though it be admitted that oneself and the other person in question have both equal need for and an equal right to accept from others just that amount of pleasure.

I do not, of course, wish to push this analogy too far. If I did, the obvious critical retort would be that Kant wished the non-parallelism between an agent's duty to himself and his duty to others to be universally accepted. The Egoist wishes the distinction between himself and others to be observed only by himself. That there is a distinction in kind, however, in many moral systems, between one's duty to oneself and one's duty to others is, I think, sufficient to give some kind of rationale to the Egoist's divided attitude.

To sum up this part of my paper; it would seem that there are various ways in which the Egoist cannot be formally shown to be wrong. He accepts an over-riding and comprehensive policy of life. He can give an ultimate reason for all his deliberate acts and can thus regard his life as being lived according to a plan. This would seem to give him a *prima facie* right to use words like 'ought' to enable him to distinguish between his ephemeral desires and his more settled policy of enlightened Egoism. He seems to fail when tested by the 'Neutrality' or the 'Valid for one, valid for all' principle. If, however, it is true that ultimate 'ought' statements logically represent choices rather than propositional truths it would seem that this principle is not perhaps quite so much implicit in the connotation of the word 'ought' and similar words as has hitherto been supposed.

No amount of apologetics will, however, slur over the logical oddity of the 'Individualistic' axiom and this must now be discussed.

[II]

Mr. Hare in his *Universalisability* (p. 305) makes an interesting point which I should like to quote *in extenso:*

> EXISTENTIALIST: You oughtn't to do that.
> KANTIAN: So you think that one oughtn't to do that kind of thing?

E.:   I think nothing of the kind; I say only that
           you oughtn't to do *that*.

K.:   Don't you even imply that a person like me
           in circumstances of this kind oughtn't to
           do that kind of thing when the other peo-
           ple involved are the sort of people that
           they are?

E.:   No; I say only that *you* oughtn't to do *that*.

K.:   Are you making a moral judgment?

E.:   Yes.

K.:   In that case I fail to understand your use of
           the word 'moral.'

Now to make this conversation fit the Egoist it would
have to begin with 'I ought to do that' and the pronouns would
have to be suitably altered. Even this alteration of pronouns is
not strictly necessary, however, if the concession which I have
already granted in Part I of my paper be observed. I have already, that is, admitted that an Egoist could not logically blame
another Egoist; but I have tried to make something of the point
that if an Egoist admits the validity of Egoism for others he is
still far from actively supporting the choice by others of his own
principle.

Keeping this in mind, Hare's conversation would now
run something like this:

EGOIST: If you have chosen Egoism you oughtn't to do that.

K.:   So you think that one oughtn't to do that kind of
           thing?

E.:   I think nothing of the kind. I say only that, if you
           have chosen Egoism, *you* oughtn't to do *that*.

The rest of the amended conversation can easily be supplied by
the reader. This amended version might, however, seem to give
the game away as it would imply some kind of universal principle, namely, All who are Egoists should behave in such and such
a way. I maintain, however, that the game is only partly given
away, since the Egoist A could still admit that a person B was
exactly like himself in personal characteristics, situation, and
his relationship to others, and yet be able to maintain that B's

behaviour depended entirely on his choice of a principle of life. If we are to take Hare seriously when he writes (*Universalisability*, p. 303) 'if I am trying to decide what my ultimate moral principles are to be I cannot deduce the answer from anything whatsoever', then it must be a theoretical possibility for two people who are (if I may coin a phrase) factual twins to make a different choice of moral principle at a certain point in their respective histories and, from that moment, to modify their characters diversely in the light of the choice they have made.

To revert, however, to the point I made at the end of Part I of this paper; the logical oddity still remains. Why should the Egoist want people to choose principles different from his own when the sincere choice of a principle normally entails a desire that other people should choose it too? The quick answer is obvious. It is just an empirical fact that the Egoist must have the field to himself if he is to develop his policy of life with any success. Nevertheless it is still odd, from a logical point of view, that an Egoist of the type we are now considering (i.e. one who does not claim any relevant descriptive or factual differences between himself and others) should insist, for all that, on the importance of the 'I am I' principle for the whole of his moral outlook.

Now a fair amount of work has been done by philosophers on the 'Egocentric Predicament' and related topics. I am therefore by no means breaking entirely new ground. Indeed, Mr. Gellner, in a brief passage in his *Ethics and Logic* (p. 162) has anticipated this part of my paper when he writes 'my "being myself" seems to me independent of the predicates which apply to me and to be something that would survive the replacement of all of them by others . . . (It would also follow that Identity of Indiscernibles does not apply to self-conscious beings)'. This logical peculiarity of 'I' or 'being myself' does, however, deserve closer attention.

Let us take a simple example. Say that I am in pain. I have, for example, burnt my finger. Now, whatever attitude I take to this pain, it would, I suppose, be generally admitted that the fact that it is my pain is of some importance. Even if I ignore my pain to help someone else I am praised for doing so as I would not be for ignoring someone else's burnt finger. Is the fact that it is my pain a reason, however, for a special personal attitude towards it in terms of special distinguishing characteristics or circumstances that mark me off from my fellows? By no means. I might admit that someone else was, in all relevant details and circumstances, my twin and yet have a different attitude towards my own pain. Nor is my attitude based on a concern about myself as a person who can be described in a suitable kind of way. As Mr. Gellner has seen, my 'being myself' would survive the replacement of predicates about myself. Dr. Jekyll would be as concerned with his own pain as Mr. Hyde with his, even although his attitude towards it might be different. Whatever I am and however like someone else I may be, my pain, here and now, is quite different *for me* from his pain. Nor is it just a matter of spatial position in any straightforward sense. A and B can change places. A can take himself and his pain to where B was standing without lessening the pain. One is tempted to say that it is the connection of the pain with *my* body that makes it important for me; and yet one must be careful to point out, at the same time, that it is no more something special about my body than it is about my character that makes the pain important for me. One might indeed say that the more intense the pain, the more any consideration of the type of person one may happen to be fails to arise. In acute pain one can only concentrate on the pain and not on oneself. Yet, for all that, A's feeling excruciating pain is obviously different for A than B's feeling excruciating pain.

Perhaps I have laboured an obvious point, but its very obviousness makes it interesting from a logical point of view. We can, generally speaking, say the same things about any two identical objects, and the only thing that saves the proverbial 'two peas in a pod' from the principle of the Identity of Indiscernibles is their spatial position. When we have, however, two sentient beings, we can make them as much like each other as we wish; they can be 'twins' in every sense and can both be suffering the same degree of toothache. It is true that, like the peas, they are saved from the Identity of Indiscernibles by their spatial position. Whereas, however, this is the *only* difference between the peas, there is the further difference for the sentient being that his relation to his own toothache and to that of his twin must necessarily be different. All this, it might be said, is a lot of fuss about the mere tautology that 'I am I'; but it has at least served to make clear that the distinction between 'I' and 'Thou' cannot be elucidated entirely in terms of *describable* differences between individuals.

To come more closely to the main drift of my argument; it is generally recognised that sensitivity to logical distinctions is a mark not of irrationality but of reason. The Egoist is so often blamed for being completely irrational, for having one rule for himself and a different one for others, even when he has been forced to admit that there are no relevant descriptive differences between himself and others. Might not the Egoist retort in this way: The mere having of personal experiences, irrespective of any descriptive difference, is generally, if tacitly, admitted to be of importance in almost any moral system. If this were not so, why the widespread praise of Moralists for Altruism and self-sacrifice? If ultimate principles are a matter of choice, what exactly is there in my attitude to personal experiences that is basically irrational? Surely, if there is no descriptive difference where a difference is yet *felt*, one is logically entitled to jump either way. One can either say 'B feels the pain in his burnt hand just as much as I would in mine and therefore I should show as much concern for him as I would for myself', or one can say 'B feels the pain in his burnt hand just as much as I would in mine. Aren't I lucky that it isn't in mine? I ought to take steps to avoid hurting my hand in future so that I'll never be in B's unfortunate position'.

These scraps of monologue could of course take place granted the full admission by the speaker that there were no relevant differences in body, character or abilities between himself and B. So that to my earlier suggestions that the Egoist has an over-riding, comprehensive policy, that he can use the word ought' and can claim, with some justification, to be following a rule or principle of life, I now add the suggestion that he is just as sensitive to the distinction between oneself and others as other recognised moralists are. Since many moralists are commended because they advocate that one should care more about an equal pain suffered by someone else than about one's own, can the Egoist be condemned on *formal* grounds if he cares less? One might even be tempted to argue that, if it is reasonable to ignore distinctions of the kind in question (i.e. distinctions based on mere 'otherness' and not on a descriptive difference) the formally correct moralist would be the one who argued that one should care equally about equal pains whether suffered by oneself or others. Yet surely all these attitudes are equally 'reasonable', if one can apply such a word to the choice of ultimate principles. It is indeed true that it is in general irrational to deal differently with cases that are in all relevant details the same. It would be irrational to say of any Euclidean triangle that its angles did not equal two right angles. But are we to call the egocentricity of experiences a relevant difference or not? Surely, the 'rationalist' will say, the mere fact that it is *my* pain is irrelevant. If it is in all respects like someone else's pain it is my duty to give it just so much attention and alleviation as I would give to his and no more. No! the Altruist will say; just because my pain is (*a*) no more acute than my neighbour's pain and yet (*b*) is so much more hard for me to bear than his pain, I, as a moral agent, must try to transcend my immediate feelings, and help my neighbour despite myself. The Egoist will take a third view. Whilst admitting that his neighbour's pain is, *for his neighbour,* as acute as his own, he, the Egoist, will argue that nevertheless the mere location of the pain in another person is a highly relevant factor and sufficient reason for him to adopt a planned policy of avoiding pains for himself.

Why it is difficult to find logical faults in any of these views, can best be explained by the curiously double nature of personal experience. From the point of view of an observer, two experiences of A and B can be in all relevant respects identical; and even A and B can, whilst adopting a 'neutral' view, recognise their identity. From their own point of view, however, there is a relevant difference, namely the fact that they each have their own experiences. Since there are no rules laid down as to whether a 'rational' man should recognise this as a difference or not in his choice of a policy of life, one cannot be dogmatic about the rationality or the irrationality of *any* attitude to this particular problem.

[III]

As I promised at the beginning of my paper, I have not tried to put Egoism either outside or inside the moral pale. Quite clearly what I have called the 'neutrality principle' is generally implied by the use of words like 'principle', 'ought', 'rule', 'reason', etc. Even the consistent Egoist must admit this and cannot logically condemn the acceptance of Egoism by others. What are good rules, reasons, principles for him *could* be good rules, reasons, principles for anyone like himself in similar circumstances. If the Egoist denies this he is being absurd and is thus far outside the moral pale, even if Morality be defined in minimum terms (as for the purposes of this paper it is). I have, however, suggested that, because of the close association of ultimate principles and choice, and because one cannot choose for others, there is no absurdity in the Egoist's denying that others *must* choose his principles or even that they ought to. Indeed there is no absurdity in his wishing that they would not or even in his recommending them against making his choice.[2]

I have tried to strengthen the plausibility of this last point by suggesting, in Part II of my paper, that the non-parallelism in the Egoist's attitude towards himself and others is not only shared, in a different direction, by altruistic moralists, but is also backed by the good sound reason that the logic of personal experiences is in its favour. The Egoist who would try to base his Egoism on characteristic distinction in himself, I suggested, must be either a hypocrite or a fool. The Egoist, however,

---

[2] I indeed admit that, empirically speaking, this would take a deal of cool impudence and would not be likely to succeed. Such a recommendation would not, however, be *logically* absurd.

who realises that the mere having of personal experiences, irrespective of characteristic distinctions, is itself a factor of obvious importance, is entitled to take his own particular stand on this peculiar factor.

I must now, however, turn to the defence of what I have written against charges of frivolity that may be levelled against it. It may very well be said: it is a well known fact that there can be intelligent, self-controlled people, with a plan of life, who care only for themselves. But of what importance is it to state this fact at length?

There are two main things that I want to say about this. First, I should like to draw attention to a point analogous to one made by Mr. Hare in his *The Language of Morals*. If we are to remember the practical force of moral words it is dangerous to ignore this in our linguistic analysis. As Mr. Hare pointed out, it would be dangerous to accept a descriptive analysis of 'good' or 'bad' since the cannibal and the missionary would be unable to commend or condemn their diverse principles if they just *defined* them in descriptive terms. My point is admittedly not quite the same. The Egoist is not being blamed for offering a naturalistic description of moral terms but for a faulty use of these terms (e.g., the word 'ought') themselves. It is, however, worth pointing out, as Mr. Hare admits, that the word 'ought' like the word 'good' has a commending function and the words 'ought not' a condemning function. If we are just to say to the Egoist that he is using words in a queer kind of way, he is likely to retort that he can find no other words to suit his purpose as well. Words like 'want' and 'desire' will certainly not replace 'ought' since the Egoist must somehow distinguish between his settled policy of life and his momentary whims.

But, of course, our quarrel with Egoism is, if partly, certainly not wholly, a complaint that the Egoist does not know the logic of the language he is using. It is indeed true that, ever since Plato's attack on Thrasymachus, it has been popular to consider the Egoist as some kind of illogical fool, and, although Kant distinguished carefully between Theoretical and Practical

Reason, many of Kant's admirers feel that he has shown that, at least in some sense, there is something basically irrational about Egoism. The widespread detestation of Egoism, however, is mainly a detestation of a way of life, not a complaint that the Egoist is lacking in sensitivity for linguistic discrimination. And, if we are not to confuse matters of substance with matters of linguistic analysis, then (as Mr. Hare is always anxious to point out) our linguistic analysis must make allowance for these matters of substance and not strangle them at birth.

Secondly, I should like to go some way towards answering possible complaints about the triviality of the subject of my paper for the issues of everyday life. This is, perhaps, a dangerous thing to do, as it will result in a hybrid performance half concerned with second order issues of linguistic analysis and half with first order practical problems. I take the risk, however, as I have some sympathy with those who find the second order enquiry a little arid and uninspiring.

It *is*, perhaps, academic to treat of pure Egoism, since any analysis of a moral system is always an artificial abstraction from human experience of simplified norms of behaviour. It is, however, true that most of us, perhaps all of us, have an egoistic side to our nature. Now it is also true that when we are being egoistical we often make excuses in terms of particular factors about ourselves and/or our situations; or that we just plainly admit that we are being immoral. But this is not the whole of the story. I do not want to be accused of mixing up observed facts about human behaviour with moral issues, of confusing 'is' with 'ought'. Nevertheless, if it is true that a man's principles are, to a large extent, shown by his behaviour, it is also true that men do not so easily apply the 'neutrality' principle to themselves as to others. Kant knew all about the 'dear self' nor did he underestimate it.

Now it would be quite trivial and unhelpful, for the purposes of this paper, if such people were explicitly aware that they were making an exception of themselves *and always blamed themselves for it.* But do they always say 'I know I ought to act like A, B, C, D, or E on this occasion, but I don't want to, so I am going to be a bad boy'? Let us think of an example where this is not so.

Imagine a meek, little man who surprised a bank-robber with a pistol but has not yet been seen by the robber. He might very well say to himself 'I would be best out of this' or 'I *ought* to get out of this' (not, be it noted, 'I *want* to get out of this'). The very same man might, however, on a visit to the cinema, vigorously applaud and commend a picture of a meek, little man, like himself, hurling himself at a bank-robber and disarming him. We certainly have both prudential and altruistic aspects in our nature and they often live happily side by side. And, if we are to be quite honest, the real 'reason' why we take one attitude to our own actions, our own obligations, and another to those of other people, whom we admit to be in all relevant respects like ourselves, is the strong working in us of the 'Individualistic' axiom based on the logical peculiarity of personal experience. We can argue as much as we like with the meek little man about linguistic usage. We can say 'You ought not to have said "I ought to get out of this", when, at the cinema, you obviously approved of a man like yourself adopting a quite different attitude to an identical situation'. The meek, little man might be discomfited by our discourse, but he would still be prudent for himself and moralistic towards all others like himself, and he might well use words like 'ought' and 'right' in both contexts.

It is indeed true that the 'Neutralistic' or 'Kantian' principle has a deep hold on human nature, whether because of the workings of Reason in us or simply because we are under enormous social pressure to be altruistic, to 'think of the other chap' rather than ourselves. If, however, we are to take sides either for or against Egoism in human nature, it will not do to say that people are really 'Kantian' all the time and that they are always ashamed of making unwarranted exceptions of themselves, after it has been pointed out to them that this is what they have been doing. The plain fact is that few people have the courage, or if it be preferred, the foolhardiness, to be full-blown Egoists. When, therefore, the basic Egoistic principle (the 'Individualistic axiom') is at work in them, influencing their course of action, they prefer to find bogus reasons rather than to recognise its existence, or to recognise it, itself, as a reason. Thus, for instance, the meek, little man, faced with his apparent inconsistency, will perhaps retort on these lines: 'Ah! yes but the Pictures are one thing; Life is another', a remark which would be clearly irrelevant on his own admissions. This non-parallelism in attitude towards ourselves and others runs, in a greater or lesser degree, throughout the human scene. The tremendous problem offered by those who have one rule for themselves and another for people like themselves is not one to be solved solely by pointing out the neutral nature of words like 'ought', 'rule', and 'principle'. It is a problem to be attacked by those who have chosen to be impartial. And their way of attacking it is to fight the Egoists and the principles of Egoism wherever they find them (most of all in themselves) and by whatever methods, Christian or otherwise, may be considered the most appropriate. In this tremendous battle a pointing out of the Egoist's linguistic peculiarities will not take the Non-egoists very far. At the risk of tedious repetition I should like to point out once more that we all have strong tendencies *both* to take an impartial, neutral view of ourselves in our relation to other people *and* to be strongly influenced in our own favour. We do not always, but we certainly can, and do sometimes, use the same *language,* ('ought', 'rule', 'reason', 'principle', etc.) whichever attitude we adopt.

There is one more point, of some importance in establishing the non-triviality of the foregoing enquiry. Although I have concentrated on Egoism I think it is true to say that all my remarks could be transplanted to suit other examples of what Gellner and Hare have called 'E' type as opposed to 'U' type valuations. On page 299 of *Universalisability* Mr. Hare writes, 'If he (the Patriot) thinks that other people do not owe the same duties to their countries, then—unless he points to relevant differences between his country and others—his maxim is not of type "U" '.

Now whether we are to call love of one's country just because it is one's country, or a mother's preference for her own children just because they are her own, an extended, projected kind of Egoism (as, I think, some psychologists would), or whether we are to call it restricted benevolence, is not, for us, of supreme importance. It might be very important, in refuting Psychological Hedonism, to point out that a mother's pleasure in seeing her children happy is not to be confused with a *search* for personal pleasure. Within the context of this paper, however, the important point is to realise that all 'E' type judgements ignore both relevant similarities and relevant differences. They thus would seem to share the logical peculiarities of Egoism. If it be conceded that they embody Egoistic principles in an extended form, all the better. This would show that the points I have made have importance for a far wider area of human behaviour than would appear on the surface. Even if 'E' type valuations are not to be classed as basically egoistic, however, they present much the same logical difficulties, and it is still of interest to see whether, like Mr. Hare, we are to rule them out on formal grounds as non-moral.

I would, first of all, suggest that it is indeed true that most people subscribe to Mr. Hare's view; and this is shown in two ways. First, whenever there is a suggestion of unfair treatment there is a strong tendency, on the part of the accused, to justify himself in terms of relevant differences. The slave-owner, for example, will not put himself in the Negro's place because the Negro 'is not really a human being at all'. And, secondly, when there is no plea for relevant differences, the accused is often shamefaced about his action. The slave-owner who became convinced that the slave was as good as himself would have to free him or suffer a guilty conscience.

But, surely, there is a middle-of-the-way attitude which is highly typical of human standards? The slave-owner might say 'Yes, I see that Uncle Tom is a fine man, just as good as I am, and I should hate to work in the cotton fields all day. But there it is! *There have always been these distinctions* (again, not really a reason at all; compare the "Cinema" example), and it would be morally wrong of me to free the slaves and endanger the welfare of *my own* sons and daughters'. Such a man might very well spend his leisure hours reading books about the freeing of slaves and heartily applauding fictional representations of slave-owners who sacrificed themselves and their families for a noble cause.

Of course my critics will howl me down here and say 'But in your example (and indeed in the "bank-robbery" example) the inconsistency in attitude is obvious. Only one of these attitudes can be the meek, little man's or the slave-owner's *real* moral attitude'.

In answer to this I should say that we must decide whether we are to analyse words like 'moral principle' in a tidy, text-book manner, or whether we are to admit that the use of words like 'ought', 'principle', etc., will conform to the psychological complexities of everyday life. If a man's principles are known by the line he takes in life, then it is perhaps a sad fact, but a fact nevertheless, that, in innumerable cases no real attempt is made, in deciding what ought to be done, to adopt a neutral attitude between oneself and others, one's own children and other people's children, one's own country and other people's countries. Most, or at least many, people unhappily dither in a twilight kingdom inhabiting the region between 'E' type and 'U' type principles, between the 'Individualistic' axiom and the 'Neutrality' principle, and never quite make up their minds to which they owe allegiance.

I do not, therefore, suggest that the innumerable people who are partial to themselves, their family or their country, *without due reason,* are capable of finding a reason for themselves in terms of the arguments presented in Part II of this paper (i.e. in terms of the 'Individualistic' axiom). They would rather appeal to supposed descriptive differences, or to bogus reasons as in the examples above, than to the logical peculiarity of personal experience. And indeed they would find it very odd to regard their irrational (in the sense of biassed) love of child or country as, psychologically, an extension of their love for themselves as centres of experiences.

I do suggest, however, that the bare logical bones of the situation, which serve as a structure for the psychological urge to particularity and self-partiality in conduct, have been uncovered in Part II. And, in conclusion, I would urge, once more, that the fight against Egoism and its extensions cannot, in the main, be waged by pointing out logical inconsistencies. Egoists and their fellow travellers (e.g. doting parents and uncritical patriots), and, indeed, the egoistical part in all of us, will always find rules, reasons, and justifications. (The arguments of Part II of this paper *can* always, that is, serve as an *extra* reason for logically justifying a duality in attitude towards one's own and other people's experiences). We can choose, if we wish, to accept these rules, reasons, and justifications. If, however, we do not like, want, or choose Egoism, we can best fight it by the psychological and persuasive process of trying to get ourselves and others actively to identify ourselves and imaginatively sympathise with other people of all kinds and races.

RIGHTS / *W. D. Ross*

A GENERAL discussion of right or duty would hardly be complete without some discussion, even if only a brief one, of the closely related subject of rights. It is commonly said that rights and duties are correlative, and it is worth while to enquire whether and, if at all, in what sense this is true. The statement may stand for any one, or any combination, of the following logically independent statements:

(1) A right of A against B implies a duty of B to A.
(2) A duty of B to A implies a right of A against B.
(3) A right of A against B implies a duty of A to B.
(4) A duty of A to B implies a right of A against B.

What is asserted in (1) is that A's having a right to have a certain individual act done to him by B implies a duty for B to do *that* act to A; (2) asserts the converse implication; what is meant by (3) is that A's having a right to have a certain act done to him by B implies a duty for A to do *another* act to B, which act

From W. D. Ross, "Rights," The Right and the Good (Oxford: The Clarendon Press, 1930), pp. 48–56. Reprinted by permission of the Clarendon Press, Oxford.

may be either a similar act (as where the right of having the truth told to one implies the duty of telling the truth) or a different sort of act (as where the right to obedience implies the duty of governing well); (4) asserts the converse implication.

Of these four propositions the first appears to be unquestionably true; a right in one being against another is a right to treat or be treated by that other in a certain way, and this plainly implies a duty for the other to behave in a certain way. But there is a certain consideration which throws doubt on the other three propositions. This arises from the fact that we have duties to animals and to infants. The latter case is complicated by the fact that infants, while they are not (so we commonly believe) actual moral agents, are potential moral agents, so that the duty of parents, for instance, to support them may be said to be counterbalanced by a duty which is not incumbent on the infants at the time but will be incumbent on them later, to obey and care for their parents. We had better therefore take the less complicated case of animals, which we commonly suppose not to be even potential moral agents.

It may of course be denied that we have duties to animals. The view held by some writers is that we have duties concerning animals but not to them, the theory being that we have a duty to behave humanely to our fellow men, and that we should behave humanely to animals simply for fear of creating a disposition in ourselves which will make us tend to be cruel to our fellow men. Professor D. G. Ritchie, for instance, implies that we have not a duty to animals except in a sense like that in which the owner of an historic house may be said to have a duty to the house.[1] Now the latter sense is, I suppose, purely metaphorical. We may in a fanciful mood think of a noble house as if it were a conscious being having feelings which we are bound to respect. But we do not really think that it has them. I suppose that the duty of the owner of an historic house is essentially a duty to his contemporaries and to posterity; and he may also think it is a duty to his ancestors. On the other hand, if we think we ought to behave in a certain way to animals, it is out of consideration

[1] *Natural Rights*, p. 108.

primarily for *their* feelings that we think we ought to behave so; we do not think of them merely as a practicing-ground for virtue. It is because we think their pain a bad thing that we think we should not gratuitously cause it. And I suppose that to say we have a duty to so-and-so is the same thing as to say that we have a duty, grounded on facts relating to them, to behave in a certain way towards them.

Now if we have a duty to animals, and they have not a duty to us (which seems clear, since they are not moral agents), the first and last of our four propositions cannot both be true, since (4) implies that a duty of men to animals involves a right of men against animals, and (1) implies that this involves a duty of animals to men, and therefore (4) and (1) together imply that a duty of men to animals involves a duty of animals to men. And since the first proposition is clearly true, the fourth must be false; it cannot be true that a duty of *A* to *B* necessarily involves a right of *A* against *B*. Similarly, the second and third propositions cannot both be true; for (2) and (3) taken together imply that a duty of men to animals involves a duty of animals to men. But here it is not so clear which of the two propositions is true; for it is not clear whether we should say that though we have a duty to animals they have no right against us, or that though they have a right against us they have no duty to us. If we take the first view, we are implying that in order to have rights, just as much as in order to have duties, it is necessary to be a moral agent. If we take the second view, we are implying that while only moral agents have duties, the possession of a nature capable of feeling pleasure and pain is all that is needed in order to have rights. It is not at all clear which is the true view. On the whole, since we mean by a right something that can be justly claimed, we should probably say that animals have not rights, not because the claim to humane treatment would not be just if it were made, but because they cannot make it. But the doubt which we here find about the application of the term 'rights' is characteristic of the term. There are other ways too in which its application is doubtful. Even if we hold that it is our duty not merely to do what is just to others but to promote their welfare beyond what justice requires, it is not at all clear that we should say they have a right to beneficent treatment over and above what is just. We have a tendency to think that not every duty incumbent on one person involves a right in another.

This characteristic of our way of thinking about rights has been fastened upon by theory. Green, for instance, divides the whole region of duty into three parts: (1) moral duties which involve no rights on the other side, (2) obligations involving such rights, both obligations and rights being included in the *jus naturae* and being such as *should* be legally recognised, (3) legal obligations involving legal rights on the other side.[2] He describes the rights in class (2)—what I will for brevity call moral rights—as sharing with legal rights the characteristic of depending for their existence on some form of general recognition. The recognition in the latter case consists in the making of a law; in the former it consists simply in a general state of public opinion. Now it is plainly wrong to describe either legal or moral rights as depending for their existence on their recognition, for to recognize a thing (in the sense in which 'recognize' is here used) is to recognize it as existing already. The promulgation of a law is not the recognition of a legal right, but the creation of it, though it may imply the recognition of an already existing moral right. And to make the existence of a *moral* right depend on its being recognized is equally mistaken. It would imply that slaves, for instance, acquired the moral right to be free only at the moment when a majority of mankind, or of some particular community, formed the opinion that they ought to be free, i.e. when the particular person whose conversion to this view changed a minority into a majority changed his mind. Such a view, of course, cannot be consistently maintained, and we find Green implying in successive sections that social recognition is indispensable to the existence of rights,[3] and that the

---

2 *Principles of Political Obligations*, §§10, 11.

3 'A claim to which reality is given by social recognition, and thus implicitly a right' (§139). Cf. 'This recognition of a power, in some way or other, as that which should be, is always necessary to render it a right' (§23). 'Rights are made by recognition. There is no right "but thinking makes it so"' (§136).

slave has a right to citizenship though this right is not recognized by society.[4] In the latter passage we see the true Green, the passionate lover of liberty, reacting against the theory of the previous page. Some may think that slavery is not wrong; but everyone will admit that there are certain forms of treatment of others which are wrong and which the sufferer has the right to have removed, whether this right is recognized by society or not.

There is, however, to be found in Green another view which is less clearly false. According to this, the existence of a right is made to depend not on the recognition of *it* but on the recognition of a power in the person in question to seek an end common to all the citizens of a community.[5] This avoids the patent error of making the existence of a right depend on its being recognized to exist. Yet like the former view it makes a moral right depend not on the nature of a given person and his relations to his fellows, but on what people think about them, i.e. on what a majority of the community think about them. But though the existence of *legal* rights depends on the degree of enlightenment of the community, the existence of moral rights plainly does not, but on the nature and relations of the persons concerned.

Green's theory seems to have arisen as follows. He starts his historical survey with Hobbes and Spinoza, both of whom identify right with power. A *legal* right *may* be identified with a certain kind of power; it is the power of getting certain things not by one's own brute force but by the aid of the law. Green seems to have tried to get a theory of moral rights by making a similar amendment of the bare identification of right with power; and he accordingly identifies them with the power of getting certain things not by one's own brute force nor by the aid of the law but by the aid of public opinion; instead of saying, what is surely evident, that a moral right is not a power at all. Yet there are elements in his account which point to a truer theory; e.g. 'a "right" is an ideal attribution ("ideal" in the sense of not

---

[4] §140 implies that the slave's right to citizenship is founded on his possessing a common human consciousness with the citizens of the state.

[5] Cf. e.g. §§25, 26.

being sensibly verifiable)'.[6] Now whether a given society recognizes a particular right is, I take it, sensibly verifiable in the sense in which Green here insists that a right is not. What is not sensibly verifiable is whether the society is justified in recognizing the right, and this depends on whether the right is there antecedently to society's recognition of it. Thus the insistence that a right is not sensibly verifiable points to an objective theory of rights; but unfortunately Green follows this clue no farther.

If we eliminate the possibility of holding that animals have rights, by saying that only that which has a moral nature can have a right, our main doubt with regard to the correlation of rights and duties is on the question whether there is a right to beneficence. It is obvious that a man has a right to just treatment, and it is commonly agreed that he has a right to have promises made to him fulfilled; it is less generally agreed that he has a right to beneficent treatment, even when it is admitted that it is our duty to treat him beneficently.

Some would even say that to treat others beneficently is to go beyond our duty. But probably this statement rests on a mere confusion. We usually oppose justice to *benevolence*. But while treating a man justly is commonly understood to mean doing certain things to him (paying our debts to him, and the like), irrespective of the spirit in which we do them, treating him benevolently obviously means doing certain things to him from goodwill. And it is rightly felt that there is a great difference between the two things, and it is found natural to say that the one implies, and the other does not, a right on the other side, and (by some people) even to say that the one is a duty and the other is not. But if we will distinguish between doing what is just and doing it in the spirit of justice, and between doing what is beneficent and doing it in the spirit of beneficence, then (in accordance with the principle that it is always acts, and not acts from a certain motive, that are our duty) it is clear that it is not our duty to act in the spirit of justice, any more than in the spirit of beneficence, and that it *is* our duty to do what is beneficent, as it is our duty to do what is just.

6 §38.

If we are clear on this point, our main objection to saying that the other person has a right to beneficence disappears. I do not say that our whole objection disappears; for there hangs about the notion of a 'right' the notion of its being not only something which one person should in decency respect but also something which the other person can in decency claim, and we feel that there is something indecent in the making of a *claim* to beneficence.

These doubts about the application of the term 'right' appear to spring from the fact that 'right' (the noun) does not stand for a purely moral notion. It began, I suppose, by standing for a legal notion, and its usage has broadened out so as to include certain things that cannot be claimed at law; but its usage has not yet broadened out so much as to become completely correlative to duty. Once we start on the process of broadening it out, however, there seems to be no secure resting-place short of this.

Returning now to the four propositions about the correlativity of duties and rights, it seems that with regard to the second proposition, 'A duty of B to A implies a right of A against B' (which has latterly been the subject of our discussion), we should say (1) that this is not true when A is not a moral agent, and (2) that it is true when A is a moral agent (even if the duty be the duty of beneficent action). And since our only doubt about the third proposition, 'A right of A against B implies a duty of A to B', arises from our doubt whether animals have not rights, if we agree that animals have not rights we need not doubt the truth of this proposition. It is this proposition, above all, that has been maintained by those who have insisted on the correlativity of rights and duties; for this was maintained essentially against the belief that men have 'natural rights' in a state of nature in which they have no duties.

A further problem, however, awaits us, viz. whether a failure to do one's duty involves a corresponding loss of right. Or rather, as we have found the meaning of 'rights' more doubtful than that of 'duties', it will be more profitable to omit any reference to rights, and put our question in the form, 'if A fails in his

duty to B, does that put an end to B's duty to A?' In some cases
we seem to be clear that this is so. If a tradesman sends me
goods inferior to those I chose in his shop, I am not morally, any
more than legally, bound to pay him the full price; I may return
the goods and pay nothing, or (with his consent) keep them and
pay a lower price. And in general any duty arising out of a contract is cancelled by non-fulfilment of the corresponding duty
on the other side. In other cases we are not so clear. It is not so
generally agreed, for instance, that if A tells lies to B, B is
justified in telling lies to A. Two blacks, we say in such a
case, do not make a white. Yet the peculiar stringency of
the duty of veracity seems to spring from an implicit understanding that language shall be used to convey the real opinions
of the speakers, and it would seem that a failure to carry out the
understanding on one side makes it no longer binding on the
other; and we should have small patience with an habitual liar
who insisted on strict veracity in others. It must be admitted that
a man who has deceived me has destroyed what would have
been the main reason for its being my duty to tell him the truth.
But we should probably hesitate to say that by his breach of the
implicit understanding my duty to tell him the truth has been
entirely destroyed, as by the tradesman's breach of contract my
duty to pay him has been destroyed. Various reasons help to account for this. For one thing, it is likely that by deceiving a liar I
may indirectly deceive innocent people; for another, the consequences for my own character are likely to be particularly dangerous. But the main reason probably lies elsewhere. Before the
contract was made between my tradesman and me, there was no
duty incumbent on me of paying him this sum of money. I had a
general duty to promote the good of all men, but there was no
obvious reason for supposing that this could be best done by
transferring this sum of money to him. But even before the implicit undertaking to tell the truth was established I had a duty
not to tell lies, since to tell lies is *prima facie* to do a positive
injury to another person. Since this duty does not rest on contract, it is not abolished by the breach of contract, and therefore
while a person who has been deceived by another is justified in

refusing to answer his questions, he is not justified in telling him lies. Yet that this forms only a small part of the stringency of the duty of truthfulness may be inferred from the leniency with which we should judge deceit, in a case in which no implicit undertaking to tell the truth has been established, e.g. when a civilized man deceives a savage whom he has just met for the first time, or *vice versa*, or when one of two savages belonging to different tribes deceives the other. Deceit is much more venial in such a case, because the offender has no reason to suppose that the other is not deceiving, or going to deceive, *him*.

Taking, then, the obvious division between duties arising out of contract and those that arise otherwise, we must say that while the former are cancelled by breach of the contract on the other side, the latter are not cancelled by the bad behaviour of the other person. It would also seem, from a consideration of our actual moral judgments, that the former type of duty is the more stringent of the two.

Now the distinction between the rights corresponding to duties that arise out of contract, and the rights corresponding to other duties, may be quite suitably expressed as a distinction between contractual and natural rights, and the notion of natural rights as a distinct class may thus be vindicated, if it be cut free from the belief which has been so often bound up with it, that there are rights in a state of nature, i.e. in a state in which there are no duties. Such a belief is made possible for Hobbes only by a complete confusion between rights and powers, amounting to an express identification of the two.

LEGAL RESPONSIBILITY AND EXCUSES /
H. L. A. Hart

[1]

IT IS CHARACTERISTIC of our own and all advanced legal systems
that the individual's liability to punishment, at any rate for
serious crimes carrying severe penalties, is made by law to depend on, among other things, certain mental conditions. These
conditions can best be expressed in negative form as *excusing*
conditions: the individual is not liable to punishment if at the
time of his doing what would otherwise be a punishable act he is,
say, unconscious, mistaken about the physical consequences of
his bodily movements or the nature or qualities of the thing or
persons affected by them, or, in some cases, if he is subjected
to threats or other gross forms of coercion or is the victim of
certain types of mental disease. This is a list, not meant to
be complete, giving broad descriptions of the principal excusing conditions; the exact definition of these and their precise
character and scope must be sought in the detailed exposi-
tion of our criminal law. If an individual breaks the law when
none of the excusing conditions are present, he is ordinarily said
to have acted of "his own free will," "of his own accord," "voluntarily"; or it might be said, "He could have helped doing what he
did." If the determinist[1] has anything to say on this subject, it

From H. L. A. Hart, "Legal Responsibility and Excuses," in Sidney Hook (ed.),
Determinism and Freedom (*New York: New York University Press, 1958*), *pp.*
95–116. Reprinted by permission of the publisher.

1 Earlier papers . . . will doubtless have specified the variety of theories or
claims that shelter under the label "determinism." For many purposes it is

must be because he makes two claims. The first claim is that it may be true—though we cannot at present and may never be able to show that it is true—that human conduct (including in that expression not only actions involving the movements of the human body but its psychological elements or components such as decisions, choices, experiences of desire, effort, etc.) is subject to certain types of law, where law is to be understood in the sense of a scientific law. The second claim is that, if human conduct so understood is in fact subject to such laws (though at the present time we do not know it to be so), the distinction we draw between one who acts under excusing conditions and one who acts when none are present becomes unimportant, if not absurd. Consequently, to allow punishment to depend on the presence or absence of excusing conditions, or to think it justified when they are absent but not when they are present, is absurd, meaningless, irrational, or unjust, or immoral, or perhaps all of these.

My principal object in this paper is to draw attention to

---

necessary to distinguish among them, especially on the question whether the elements in human conduct that are said to be "determined" are regarded as the product of sufficient conditions, or sets of jointly sufficient conditions, which include the individual's character. I think, however, that the defense I make in this paper of the rationality, morality, and justice of qualifying criminal responsibility by excusing conditions will be compatible with any form of determinism that satisfies the two following sets of requirements.

A. The determinist must not deny (*a*) those *empirical* facts that at present we treat as proper grounds for saying, "He did what he chose," "His choice was effective," "He got what he chose," "That was the result of his choice," etc; (*b*) the fact that when we get what we chose to have, live our lives as we have chosen, and particularly when we obtain by a choice what we have judged to be the lesser of two evils, this is a source of satisfaction; (*c*) the fact that we are often able to predict successfully and on reasonable evidence that our choice will be effective over certain periods in relation to certain matters.

B. The determinist does not assert and could not truly assert that we *already know* the laws that he says may exist or (in some versions) *must* exist. Determinists differ on the question whether or not the laws are sufficiently simple (*a*) for human beings to discover, (*b*) for human beings to use for the prediction of their own and others' conduct. But as long as it is not asserted that we know these laws I do not think this difference of opinion important here. Of course if we knew the laws and could use them for the detailed and exact prediction of our own and others' conduct, *deliberation* and *choice* would become pointless, and perhaps in such circumstances there could not (logically) be "deliberation" or "choice."

the analogy between conditions that are treated by criminal law as *excusing* conditions and certain similar conditions that are treated in another branch of the law as *invalidating* certain civil transactions such as wills, gifts, contracts, and marriages. If we consider this analogy, I think we can see that there is a rationale for our insistence on the importance of excusing conditions in criminal law that no form of determinism that I, at any rate, can construct could impugn; and this rationale seems to me superior at many points to the two main accounts or explanations that in Anglo-American jurisprudence have been put forward as the basis of the recognition of excusing conditions in criminal responsibility.

In this preliminary section, however, I want to explain why I shall not undertake the analysis or elucidation of the meaning of such expressions as "He did it voluntarily," "He acted of his own free will," "He could have helped doing it," "He could have done otherwise." I do not, of course, think the analysis of these terms unimportant: indeed I think we owe the progress that has been made, at least in determining what the "free will problem" is, to the work of philosophers who have pursued this analysis. Perhaps it may be shown that statements of the form "He did it of his own free will" or "He could have done otherwise," etc., are not logically incompatible with the existence of the type of laws the determinist claims may exist; if they do exist, it may not follow that statements of the kind quoted are always false, for it may be that these statements are true given certain conditions, which need not include the nonexistence of any such laws.

Here, however, I shall not attempt to carry further any such inquiries into the meaning of these expressions or to press the view I have urged elsewhere, that the expression "voluntary action" is best understood as excluding the presence of the various excuses. So I will not deal here with a determinist who is so incautious as to say that it may be false that anyone has ever acted "voluntarily," "of his own free will," or "could have done otherwise than he did." It will help clarify our conception of criminal responsibility, I think, if I confront a more cautious skeptic who, without committing himself as to the meaning of those expressions or their logical or linguistic dependence on, or independence of, the negation of those types of law to which the determinist refers, yet criticizes our allocation of responsibility by reference to excusing conditions. This more cautious determinist says that, whatever the expressions "voluntary" etc. may mean, unless we have reasonable grounds for thinking there are no such laws, the distinctions drawn by these expressions cannot be regarded as of any importance, and there can be neither reason nor justice in allowing punishment to depend on the presence or absence of excusing conditions.

[II]

In the criminal law of every modern state responsibility for serious crimes is excluded or "diminished" by some of the conditions we have referred to as "excusing conditions." In Anglo-American criminal law this is the doctrine that a "subjective element," or "mens rea," is required for criminal responsibility, and it is because of this doctrine that a criminal trial may involve investigations into the sanity of the accused, into what he knew, believed, or foresaw; into the questions whether or not he was subject to coercion by threats or provoked into passion, or was prevented by disease or transitory loss of consciousness from controlling the movements of his body or muscles. These matters come up under the heads known to lawyers as Mistake, Accident, Provocation, Duress, and Insanity, and are most clearly and dramatically exemplified when the charge is one of murder or manslaughter.

Though this general doctrine underlies the criminal law, no legal system in practice admits without qualification the principle that *all* criminal responsibility is excluded by *any* of the excusing conditions. In Anglo-American law this principle is qualified in two ways. First, our law admits crimes of "strict liability." [2] These are crimes where it is no defense to show that

───────────

[2] For an illuminating discussion of strict liability, see the opinion of Justice Jackson in *Morisetts v. United States* (1952) 342 U.S. 246; 96 L. Ed. 288; 78

the accused, in spite of the exercise of proper care, was ignorant of the facts that made his act illegal. Here he is liable to punishment even though he did not intend to commit an act answering the definition of the crime. These are for the most part petty offenses contravening statutes that require the maintenance of standards in the manufacture of goods sold for consumption; e.g., a statute forbidding the sale of adulterated milk. Such offenses are usually punishable with a fine and are sometimes said by jurists who object to strict liability not to be criminal in any "real" sense. Secondly, even in regard to crimes where liability is not "strict," so that mistake or accident rendering the accused's action *unintentional* would provide an excuse, many legal systems do not accept some of the other conditions we have listed as excluding liability to punishment. This is so for a variety of reasons.

For one thing, it is clear that not only lawyers but scientists and plain men differ as to the relevance of some excusing conditions, and this lack of agreement is usually expressed as a difference of view regarding what kind of factor limits the human *capacity* to control behavior. Views so expressed have indeed changed with the advance of knowledge about the human mind. Perhaps most people are now persuaded that it is possible for a man to have volitional control of his muscles and also to know the physical character of his movements and their consequences for himself and others, and yet be *unable* to resist the urge of temptation to perform a certain act; yet many think this incapacity exists only if it is associated with well-marked physiological or neurological symptoms or independently definable psychological disturbances. And perhaps there are still some who hold a modified form of the Platonic doctrine that Virtue is Knowledge and believe that the possession of knowledge[3] (and

---

S. Ct. 241. Also Sayre, "Public Welfare Offences," 33 *Col. L. Rev.* 58; Hall, *Principles of Criminal Law* (Indianapolis: Bobbs-Merrill Co., 1947), Chap. X.

[3] This view is often defended by the assertion that the mind is an "integrated whole," that if the capacity for self-control is absent, knowledge must also be absent. See Hall, *op. cit.*, p. 524: "Diseased volition does not exist apart from diseased intelligence"; also reference to the "integration theory," Chap. XIV.

muscular control) is per se a sufficient condition of the capacity to comply with the law.[4]

Another reason limiting the scope of the excusing conditions is difficulty of *proof*. Some of the mental elements involved are much easier to prove than others. It is relatively simple to show that an agent lacked either generally or on a particular occasion volitional muscular control; it is somewhat more difficult to show that he did not know certain facts either about present circumstances (e.g., that a gun was loaded) or the future (that a man would step into the line of fire); it is much more difficult to establish whether or not a person was deprived of "self-control" by passion provoked by others, or by partial mental disease. As we consider these different cases, not only do we reach much vaguer concepts, but we become progressively more dependent on the agent's own statements about himself, buttressed by inferences from common-sense generalizations about human nature, such as that men are capable of self-control when confronted with an open till but not when confronted with a wife in adultery. The law is accordingly much more cautious in admitting "defects of the will" than "defect in knowledge" as qualifying or excluding criminal responsibility. Further difficulties of proof may cause a legal system to limit its inquiry into the agent's "subjective condition" by asking what a "reasonable man" would in the circumstances have known or foreseen, or by asking whether "a reasonable man" in the circumstances would have been deprived (say, by provocation) of self-control; and the system may then impute to the agent such knowledge or foresight or control.[5]

For these practical reasons no simple identification of the necessary mental subjective elements in responsibility, with the

---

[4] English judges have taken different sides on the issue whether a man can be said to have "lost self-control," and killed another while in that condition, if he knew what he was doing and killed his victim intentionally. See *Holmes v. D.P.P.* (1946) A. C. 597 (Lord Simon) and *A. G. for Ceylon v. Kumarasinghege v. Don John Perera* (1953) A. C. 200 (Lord Goddard).

[5] But see for a defense of the "reasonable man" test (in cases of alleged provocation) Royal Commission on Capital Punishment, pp. 51–56 (§§139–145). This defense is not confined to the difficulties of proof.

full list of excusing conditions, can be made; and in all systems far greater prominence is given to the more easily provable elements of volitional control of muscular movement and knowledge of circumstances or consequences than to the other more elusive elements.

Hence it is true that legal recognition of the importance of excusing conditions is never unqualified; the law, like every other human institution, has to compromise with other values besides whatever value is incorporated in the recognition of some conditions as excusing. Sometimes, of course, it is not clear, when "strict liability" is imposed, what value (social welfare?) is triumphant, and there has consequently been much criticism of this as an odious and useless departure from proper principles of liability.

Modern systems of law are however also concerned with most of the conditions we have listed as excusing conditions in another way. Besides the criminal law that requires men to do or abstain from certain actions whether they wish to or not, all legal systems contain rules of a different type that provide legal facilities whereby individuals can give effect to their wishes by entering into certain transactions that alter their own and/or others' legal position (rights, duties, status, etc.). Examples of these civil transactions (acts in the law, *Rechtsgeschäfte*) are wills, contracts, gifts, marriage. If a legal system did not provide facilities allowing individuals to give legal effect to their choices in such areas of conduct, it would fail to make one of the law's most distinctive and valuable contributions to social life. But here too most of the mental conditions we have mentioned are recognized by the law as important not primarily as *excusing* conditions but as *invalidating* conditions. Thus a will, a gift, a marriage, and (subject to many complex exceptions) a contract may be invalid if the party concerned was insane, mistaken about the legal character of the transaction or some "essential" term of it, or if he was subject to duress, coercion, or the undue influence of other persons. These are the obvious analogues of mistake, accident, coercion, duress, insanity, admitted by criminal law as excusing conditions. Analogously, the recognition of such conditions as invalidating civil transactions is qualified or limited by other principles. Those who enter in good faith into bilateral transactions of the kind mentioned with persons who appear normal (i.e., not subject to any of the relevant invalidating conditions) must be protected, as must third parties who may have purchased interests originating from a transaction that on the face of it seemed normal. Hence a technique has been introduced to safeguard such persons. This includes principles precluding, say, a party who has entered into a transaction by some mistake from making this the basis of his defense against one who honestly took his words at face value and justifiably relied on them; there are also distinctions between transactions wholly invalidated *ag initio* (void) and those that are valid until denounced (voidable) to protect those who have relied on the transaction's normal form.

[III]

The similarity between the law's insistence on certain mental elements for both criminal responsibility and the validity of acts in the law is clear. Why, then, do we value a system of social control that takes mental condition into account? Let us start with criminal law and its excusing conditions. What is so precious in its attention to these, and what would be lost if it gave this up? What precisely is the ground of our dissatisfaction with "strict liability" in criminal law? To these fundamental questions, there still are, curiously enough, many quite discordant answers, and I propose to consider two of them before suggesting an answer that would stress the analogy with civil transactions.

The first general answer takes this form. It is said that the importance of excusing conditions in criminal responsibility is derivative, and it derives from the more fundamental requirement that for criminal responsibility there must be "moral culpability," which would not exist where the excusing conditions are present. On this view the maxim *actus non est reus nisi mens sit rea* means a morally evil mind. Certainly traces of this view are to be found in scattered observations of English and American judges—in phrases such as "an evil mind with regard to that which he is doing," "a bad mind," "there must be an act done not merely unguardedly or accidentally, without an evil mind." [6] Some of these well-known formulations were perhaps careless statements of the quite different principle that *mens rea* is an intention to commit an act that is wrong in the sense of legally forbidden. But the same view has been reasserted in general terms in England by Lord Justice Denning: "In order that an act should be punishable it must be morally blameworthy, it must be a sin." [7] Most English lawyers would however now agree with Sir James Fitz-James Stephen that the expression *mens rea* is unfortunate, though too firmly established to be expelled, just because it misleadingly suggests that in general moral culpability is essential to a crime, and they would assent to the criticism expressed by a later judge that "the true translation of *mens rea* is an intention to do the act which is made penal by statute or common law." [8] Yet, in spite of this, the view has been urged by a distinguished American contemporary writer on criminal law, Professor Jerome Hall, in his important and illuminating *Principles of Criminal Law*, that *moral* culpability is the basis of responsibility in crime. Again and again in Chapters V and VI of his book Professor Hall asserts that, though the goodness or badness of the *motive* with which a crime is committed may not be relevant, the general principle of liability, except of course where liability is unfortunately "strict" and so any mental element must be disregarded, is the "intentional or reckless doing of a *morally* wrong act." [9] This is declared to be the essential meaning of *mens rea*: "though *mens rea* differs in different crimes there is one common essential element, namely, the *voluntary* doing of a *morally* wrong act for-

6 Lord Esher in *Lee v. Dangar* (1892) 2 Q. B. 337.

7 Denning, *The Changing Law* (London: Stevens, 1953), p. 12.

8 *Allard v. Selfridge* (1925) 1 K. B. 137. (Shearman.) This is quoted by Glanville Williams in *The Criminal Law* (London: Stevens, 1953), p. 29, note 3, where the author comments that the judge should have added "recklessness."

9 Hall, *op. cit.*, p. 166.

bidden by the law." [10] On this view the law inquires into the mind in criminal cases in order to secure that no one shall be punished in the absence of the basic condition of *moral* culpability. For it is just only to "punish those who have intentionally committed *moral* wrongs proscribed by law." [11]

Now, if this theory were merely a theory as to what the criminal law of a good society should be, it would not be possible to refute it, for it represents a moral preference: namely that legal punishment should be administered only where a "morally wrong" act has been done—though I think such plausibility as it would have even as an ideal is due to a confusion. But of course Professor Hall's doctrine does not fit any actual system of criminal law because in every such system there are necessarily many actions (quite apart from the cases of "strict liability") that if voluntarily done are criminally punishable, although our moral code may be either silent as to their moral quality, or divided. Very many offenses are created by legislation designed to give effect to a particular economic scheme (e.g., a state monopoly of road or rail transport), the utility or moral character of which may be genuinely in dispute. An offender against such legislation can hardly be said to be morally guilty or to have intentionally committed a moral wrong, still less "a sin" *proscribed* by law;[12] yet if he has broken such laws "voluntarily" (to use Professor Hall's expression), which in practice means that he was not in any of the excusing conditions, the requirements of *justice* are surely satisfied. Doubts about the justice of the punishment would begin only if he were punished even though he was at the time of the action in one of the excusing conditions; for what is essential is that the offender, if he is to be *fairly* punished, must have acted "voluntarily," and not that he must have

[10] *Ibid.*, p. 167.

[11] *Ibid.*, p. 149.

[12] "The criminal quality of an act cannot be discovered by intuition; nor can it be discovered by any standard but one. Is the act prohibited with penal consequences? Morality and criminality are far from coextensive nor is the sphere of criminality part of a more exclusive field covered by morality unless morals necessarily disapproves of the acts prohibited by the state, in which case the argument moves in a circle." Lord Atkin, *Proprietory Articles Trade Association v. A. G. for Canada* (1931) A. C. 324.

committed some moral offense. In addition to such requirements of justice in the individual case, there is of course, as we
shall see, a different type of requirement as to the *general* character of the laws.

It is important to see what has led Professor Hall and
others to the conclusion that the basis of criminal responsibility
must be moral culpability ("the voluntary doing of a morally
wrong act"), for latent in this position, I think, is a false dilemma. The false dilemma is that criminal liability *must* either
be "strict"—that is, based on nothing more than the outward
conduct of the accused—or *must* be based on moral culpability.
On this view there is no third alternative and so there can be no
reason for inquiring into the state of mind of the accused—"inner facts," as Professor Hall terms them—except for the purpose
of establishing *moral* guilt. To be understood all theories should
be examined in the context of argument in which they are advanced, and it is important to notice that Professor Hall's doctrine was developed mainly by way of criticism of the so-called
objective theory of liability, which was developed, though not
very consistently, by Chief Justice Holmes in his famous essays
on common law.[13] Holmes asserted that the law did not consider,
and need not consider, in administering punishment what in
fact the accused intended, but that it imputed to him the intention that an "ordinary man," equipped with ordinary knowledge,
would be taken to have had in acting as the accused did. Holmes
in advocating this theory of "objective liability" used the phrase
"inner facts" and frequently stressed that *mens rea*, in the sense
of the actual wickedness of the party, was unnecessary. So he
often identified "mental facts" with moral guilt and also identified the notion of an objective standard of liability with the rejection of *moral* culpability as a basis of liability. This terminology was pregnant with confusion. It fatally suggests that there
are only two alternatives: to consider the mental condition of
the accused only to find moral culpability or not to consider it at
all. But we are not impaled on the horns of any such dilemma:
there are independent reasons, apart from the question of moral

13 Holmes, *The Common Law*, Lecture II, "The Criminal Law."

guilt, why a legal system should require a voluntary action as a condition of responsibility. These reasons I shall develop in a moment and merely summarize here by saying that the principle (1) that it is unfair and unjust to punish those who have not "voluntarily" broken the law is a moral principle quite distinct from the assertion (2) that it is wrong to punish those who have not "voluntarily committed a moral wrong proscribed by law."

The confusion that suggests the false dilemma—either "objective" standards (strict liability) or liability based on the "inner fact" of *moral* guilt—is, I think, this. We would all agree that unless a legal system was as a whole morally defensible, so that its existence was better than the chaos of its collapse, and more good than evil was secured by maintaining and enforcing laws in general, these laws should not be enforced, and no one should be punished for breaking them. It *seems* therefore to follow, but does not, that we should not punish anyone unless in breaking the law he has done something morally wrong; for it looks as if the mere fact that a law has been voluntarily broken were not enough to justify punishment; the extra element required is "moral culpability," at least in the sense that we should have done something morally wrong. What we need to escape confusion here is a distinction between two sets of questions. The first is a general question about the moral value of the laws: Will enforcing them produce more good than evil? If they do, then it is morally permissible to enforce them by punishing those who have broken them, unless in any given case there is some "excuse." The second is a particular question concerning individual cases: Is it right or just to punish this particular person? Is he to be excused on account of his mental condition because it would be unjust—in view of his lack of knowledge or control—to punish him? The first, general question with regard to each law is a question for the legislature; the second, arising in particular cases, is for the judge. And the question of responsibility arises only at the judicial stage. One necessary condition of the just application of a punishment is normally expressed by saying that the agent "could have helped" doing what he did, and hence the need to inquire into the "inner facts" is dictated not by the moral principle that only the doing of an *immoral* act may be legally punished, but by the moral principle that no one should be punished who could not help doing what he did. This is a necessary condition (unless strict liability is admitted) for the moral propriety of legal punishment and no doubt also for moral censure; in this respect law and morals are similar. But this similarity as to the one essential condition that there must be a "voluntary" action if legal punishment or moral censure is to be morally permissible does not mean that legal punishment is morally permissible only where the agent has done something morally wrong. I think that the use of the word "fault" in juristic discussion to designate the requirement that liability be excluded by excusing conditions may have blurred the important distinction between the assertions that (1) it is morally permissible to punish only voluntary actions and (2) it is morally permissible to punish only voluntary commission of a moral wrong.

[IV]

Let me now turn to a second explanation of the laws concerned with the "inner facts" of mental life as a condition of responsibility. This is a Benthamite theory that I shall name the "economy of threats" and is the contention that the required conditions of responsibility—e.g., that the agent knew what he was doing, was not subject to gross coercion or duress, was not mad or a small child—are simply the conditions that must be satisfied if the threat to punish announced by the criminal law is to have any effect and if the system is to be efficient in securing the maintenance of law at the least cost in pain. This theory is stated most clearly by Bentham; it is also to be found in Austin and in the report of the great Criminal Law Commission of 1833 of which he was a member. In a refined form it is implicit in many contemporary attempted "dissolutions" of the problem of free will. Many accept this view as a common-sense utilitarian explanation of the importance that we attribute to excusing conditions. It appeals most to the utilitarian and to the determinist, and it is interesting to find that Professor Glanville Williams in his recent admirable work on "The General Principles of Criminal Law," [14] when he wished to explain the exemption of the insane from legal responsibility compatibly with "determinism," did so by reference to this theory.

Yet the doctrine is an incoherent one at certain points, I think, and a departure from, rather than an elucidation of, the moral insistence that criminal liability should generally be conditional on the absence of excusing conditions. Bentham's best statement of the theory is in Chapter XIII of his *Principles of Morals and Legislation:* "Cases in Which Punishment Must be Inefficacious." The cases he lists, besides those where the law is made ex post facto or not adequately promulgated, fall into two main classes. The first class consists of cases in which the penal threat of punishment could not prevent a person from performing an action forbidden by the law *or any action of the same sort;* these are the cases of infancy and insanity in which the agent, according to Bentham, has not the "state or disposition of mind on which the prospect of evils so distant as those which are held forth by the law" has the effect of influencing his conduct. The second class consists of cases in which the law's threat could not have had any effect on the agent in relation to the *particular* act committed because of his lack of knowledge or control. What is wrong in punishing a man under both these types of mental conditions is that the punishment is wasteful; suffering is caused to the accused who is punished in circumstances where it could do no good.

In discussing the defense of insanity Professor Glanville Williams applies this theory in a way that brings out its consistency not only with a wholly utilitarian outlook on punishment but with determinism:

For mankind in the mass it is impossible to tell whom the threat of punishment will restrain and whom it will not; for most it will succeed, for some it will fail. And the punishment must then be applied to those criminals in order to maintain the threat to persons generally. Mentally deranged persons, however, can be separated from the mass by scientific tests, and being a defined class their

14 Williams, *op. cit.*, pp. 346–47.

segregation from punishment does not impair the efficacy of the sanction for people generally.[15]

The point made here is that, if, for example, the mentally deranged (scientifically tested) are exempted, criminals will not be able to exploit this exemption to free themselves from liability, since they cannot bring themselves within its scope and so will not feel free to commit crimes with impunity. This is said in order to justify the exemption of the insane consistently with the "tenet" of determinism, in spite of the fact that from a determinist viewpoint

every impulse if not in fact resisted was in those circumstances irresistible. A so-called irresistible impulse is simply one in which the desire to perform a particular act is not influenced by other factors like the threat of punishment. . . . on this definition every crime is the result of an irresistible impulse.

This theory is designed not merely to fit a utilitarian theory of punishment, but also the view that it is always false, if not senseless, to say that a criminal could have helped doing what he did. So on this theory when we inquire into the mental state of the accused, we do not do so to answer the question, Could he help it? Nor of course to answer the question, Could the threat of punishment have been effective in his case?—for we know that it was not. The theory presents us with a far simpler conceptual scheme for dealing with the whole matter, since it does not involve the seemingly counterfactual speculation regarding what the accused "could have done." On this theory we inquire into the state of mind of the accused simply to find out whether he belongs to a defined class of persons whose exemption from punishment, if allowed, will not weaken the effect on others of the general threat of punishment made by the law. So there is no question of its being unjust or unfair to punish a particular criminal or to exempt him from punishment. Once the crime has been committed the decision to punish or not has nothing to do with any moral claim or right of the criminal to have the features of his case considered, but only with the causal efficacy of

15 Williams, loc. cit.

his punishment on others. On this view the rationale of excuses is not (to put it shortly) that the accused should in view of his mental condition be excused whatever the effect of this on others, but rather the mere fact that excusing him will not harm society by reducing the efficacy of the law's threats for others. So the relevance of the criminal's mental condition is purely the question of the effect on others of his punishment or exemption from it.

This is certainly paradoxical enough. It seems to destroy the entire notion that in punishing we must be just to the particular criminal in front of us and that the purpose of excusing conditions is to protect him from society's claim. But apart from paradox the doctrine that we consider the state of a man's mind only to see if punishment is required in order to maintain the efficacy of threats for others is vitiated by a *non sequitur*. Before a man does a criminal action we may know that he is in such a condition that the threats cannot operate on him, either because of some temporary condition or because of a disease; but it does not follow—because the *threat* of punishment in his case, and in the case of others like him, is useless—that his *punishment* in the sense of the official administration of penalties will also be unnecessary to maintain the efficacy of threats for others at its highest. It may very well be that, if the law contained no explicit exemptions from responsibility on the score of ignorance, accident, mistake, or insanity, many people who now take a chance in the hope that they will bring themselves, if discovered, within these exempting provisions would in fact be deterred. It is indeed a perfectly familiar fact that pleas of loss of consciousness or other abnormal mental states, or of the existence of some other excusing condition, are frequently and sometimes successfully advanced where there is no real basis for them, for the difficulties of disproof are often considerable. The uselessness of a *threat* against a given individual or class does not entail that the *punishment* of that individual or class cannot be required to maintain in the highest degree the efficacy of threats for others. It may in fact be the case that to make liability to punishment dependent on the absence of excusing conditions is the most efficient way of maintaining the laws with the least cost in pain. But it is not *obviously* or *necessarily* the case.

It is clear, I think, that if we were to base our views of criminal responsibility on the doctrine of the economy of threats, we should misrepresent altogether the character of our moral preference for a legal system that requires mental conditions of responsibility over a system of total strict liability or entirely different methods of social control such as hypnosis, propaganda, or conditioning.

To make this intelligible we must cease to regard the law as merely a causal factor in human behavior differing from others only in the fact that it produces its effect through the medium of the mind; for it is clear that we look on excusing conditions as something that *protects* the individual against the claims of the rest of society. Recognition of their excusing force may lead to a lower, not a higher, level of efficacy of threats; yet—and this is the point—we could not regard that as sufficient ground for abandoning this protection of the individual; or if we did, it would be with the recognition that we had sacrificed one principle to another; for more is at stake than the single principle of maintaining the laws at their most efficacious level. We must cease, therefore, to regard the law simply as a system of stimuli goading the individual by its threats into conformity. Instead I shall suggest a mercantile analogy. Consider the law not as a system of stimuli but as what might be termed a *choosing* system in which individuals can find out, in general terms at least, the costs they have to pay if they act in certain ways. This done, let us ask what value this system would have in social life and why we should regret its absence. I do not of course mean to suggest that it is a matter of indifference whether we obey the law or break it and pay the penalty. Punishment *is* different from a mere "tax on a course of conduct." What I do mean is that the conception of the law simply as goading individuals into desired courses of behavior is inadequate and misleading; what a legal system that makes liability generally depend on excusing conditions does is to guide individuals' choices as to behavior by presenting them with reasons for exercising choice in the direction of obedience, but leaving them to choose.

It is at this point that I would stress the analogy between the mental conditions that excuse from criminal responsibility and the mental conditions that are regarded as invalidating civil transactions such as wills, gifts, contracts, marriages, and the like. The latter institutions provide individuals with two inestimable advantages in relation to those areas of conduct they cover. These are (1) the advantage to the individual of determining by his choice what the future shall be and (2) the advantage of being able to predict what the future will be. For these institutions enable the individual (1) to bring into operation the coercive forces of the law so that those legal arrangements he has chosen shall be carried into effect and (2) to plan the rest of his life with a certainty or at least the confidence (in a legal system that is working normally) that the arrangements he has made will in fact be carried out. By these devices the individual's choice is brought into the legal system and allowed to determine its future operations in certain areas, thereby giving him a type of indirect coercive control over, and a power to foresee the development of, official life. This he would not have "naturally"; that is, apart from these legal institutions.

In brief, the function of these institutions of private law is to render effective the individual's preferences in certain areas. It is therefore clear why in this sphere the law treats the mental factors of, say, mistake, ignorance of the nature of the transaction, coercion, undue influence, or insanity as invalidating such civil transactions. For a transaction entered into under such conditions will not represent a real choice: the individual might have chosen one course of events and by the transaction procured another (cases of mistake, ignorance, etc.), or he might have chosen to enter the transaction without coolly and calmly thinking out what he wanted (undue influence), or he might have been subjected to the threats of another who had imposed *his* choices (coercion).

To see the value of such institutions in rendering effec-

tive the individual's considered and informed choices as to what
on the whole shall happen, we have but to conduct the experiment of imagining their absence: a system where no mental
conditions would be recognized as invalidating such transactions and the consequent loss of control over the future that the
individual would suffer. That such institutions *do* render individual choices effective and increase the powers of individuals to
predict the course of events is simply a matter of empirical fact,
and no form of "determinism," of course, can show this to be
false or illusory. If a man makes a will to which the law gives
effect after his death, this is not, of course, merely a case of *post
hoc:* we have enough empirical evidence to show that this was
an instance of a regularity sufficient to have enabled us to predict the outcome with reasonable probability, at least in some
cases, and to justify us, therefore, in interpreting this outcome
as a consequence of making the will. There is no reason why we
should not describe the situation as one where the testator
caused the outcome of the distribution made. Of course the testator's choice in his example is only one prominent member of a
complex set of conditions, of which all the other members were
as necessary for the production of the outcome as his choice.
Science may indeed show (1) that this set of conditions also
includes conditions of which we are at the present moment quite
ignorant and (2) that the testator's choice itself was the outcome of some set of jointly sufficient conditions of which we
have no present knowledge. Yet neither of these two supposi-
tions, even if they were verified, would make it false to say that
the individual's choice did determine the results, or make illusory the satisfaction got (*a*) from the knowledge that this kind
of thing is possible, (*b*) from the exercise of such choice. And if
determinism does not entail that satisfactions (*a*) or (*b*) are
obtainable, I for one do not understand how it could affect the
wisdom, justice, rationality, or morality of the system we are
considering.

If with this in mind we turn back to criminal law and its
excusing conditions, we can regard their function as a mechanism for similarly maximizing within the framework of coercive

criminal law the efficacy of the individual's informed and considered choice in determining the future and also his power to predict that future. We must start, of course, with the need for criminal law and its sanctions as at least some check on behavior that threatens society. This implies a belief that the criminal law's threats actually do diminish the frequency of antisocial behavior, and no doubt this belief may be said to be based on inadequate evidence. However, we must clearly take it as our starting point: if this belief is wrong, it is so because of lack of empirical evidence and not because it contradicts any form of determinism. Then we can see that by attaching excusing conditions to criminal responsibility, we provide each individual with something he would not have if we made the system of criminal law operate on a basis of total "strict liability." First, we maximize the individual's power at any time to predict the likelihood that the sanctions of the criminal law will be applied to him. Secondly, we introduce the individual's choice as one of the operative factors determining whether or not these sanctions shall be applied to him. He can weigh the cost to him of obeying the law —and of sacrificing some satisfaction in order to obey—against obtaining that satisfaction at the cost of paying "the penalty." Thirdly, by adopting this system of attaching excusing conditions we provide that, if the sanctions of the criminal law are applied, the pains of punishment will for each individual represent the price of some satisfaction obtained from breach of law. This, of course, can sound like a very cold, if not immoral, attitude toward the criminal law, general obedience to which we regard as an essential part of a decent social order. But this attitude seems repellent only if we assume that all criminal laws are ones whose operation we approve. To be realistic we must also think of bad and repressive criminal laws; in South Africa, Nazi Germany, Soviet Russia, and no doubt elsewhere, we might be thankful to have their badness mitigated by the fact that they fall only on those who have obtained a satisfaction from knowingly doing what they forbid.

Again, the value of these three factors can be realized if we conduct the *Gedankenexperiment* of imagining criminal law

operating without excusing conditions. First, our power of pre-
dicting what will happen to us will be immeasurably diminished; the likelihood that I shall choose to do the forbidden act
(e.g., strike someone) and so incur the sanctions of the criminal
law may not be very easy to calculate even under our system: as
a basis for this prediction we have indeed only the knowledge of
our own character and some estimate of the temptations life is
likely to offer us. But if we are also to be liable if we strike someone by accident, by mistake, under coercion, etc., the chance
that we shall incur the sanctions are immeasurably increased.
From our knowledge of the past career of our body considered as
a *thing*, we cannot infer much as to the chances of its being
brought into violent contact with another, and under a system
that dispensed with the excusing condition of, say, accident
(implying lack of intention), a collision alone would land us in
jail. Secondly, our choice would condition what befalls us to a
lesser extent. Thirdly, we should suffer sanctions without having
obtained any satisfaction. Again, no form of determinism that I,
at least, can construct can throw any doubt on, or show to be
illusory, the real satisfaction that a system of criminal law incor-
porating excusing conditions provides for individuals in maximizing the effect of their choices within the framework of coercive law. The choices remain choices, the satisfactions remain
satisfactions, and the consequences of choices remain the consequences of choices even if choices are determined and other
"determinants" besides our choices condition the satisfaction arising from their being rendered effective in this way by the structure of the criminal law.

It is now important to contrast this view of excusing conditions with the Benthamite explanation I discussed in Part III
of this paper. On that view excusing conditions were treated as
conditions under which the law's threat could operate with maximum efficacy. They were recognized *not* because they ensured
justice to individuals considered separately, but because sanctions administered under those conditions were believed more
effective and economical of pain in securing the general conformity to law. If these beliefs as to the *efficacy* of excusing con-

ditions could be shown false, then all reasons for recognizing them as conditions of criminal responsibility would disappear. On the present view, which I advocate, excusing conditions are accepted as independent of the efficacy of the system of threats. Instead it is conceded that recognition of these conditions may, and probably does, diminish that efficacy by increasing the number of conditions for criminal liability and hence giving opportunities for pretense on the part of criminals, or mistakes on the part of tribunals.

On this view excusing conditions are accepted as something that may conflict with the social utility of the law's threats; they are regarded as of moral importance because they provide for all individuals alike the satisfactions of a costing system. Recognition of excusing conditions is therefore seen as a matter of protection of the individual against the claims of society for the highest measure of protection from crime that can be obtained from a system of threats. In this way the criminal law respects the claims of the individual as such, or at least as a *choosing being,* and distributes its coercive sanctions in a way that reflects this respect for the individual. This surely is very central in the notion of justice and is *one,* though no doubt only one, among the many strands of principle that I think lie at the root of the preference for legal institutions conditioning liability by reference to excusing conditions.

I cannot, of course, by unearthing this principle claim to have solved everyone's perplexities. In particular, I do not know what to say to a critic who urges that I have shown only that the system in which excusing conditions are recognized protects the individual better against the claims of society than one in which no recognition is accorded to these factors. This seems to me to be enough; yet I cannot satisfy his complaint, if he makes it, that I have not shown that we are justified in punishing anyone *ever,* at all, under any conditions. He may say that even the criminal who has committed his crime in the most deliberate and calculating way and has shown himself throughout his life competent in maximizing what he thinks his own interests will be little comforted when he is caught and punished for some

major crime. At *that* stage he will get little satisfaction if it is
pointed out to him (1) that he has obtained some satisfaction
from his crime, (2) that he knew that it was likely he would be
punished and that he had decided to pay for his satisfaction by
exposing himself to this risk, and (3) that the system under
which he is punished is not one of strict liability, is not one
under which a man who accidentally did what he did would also
have suffered the penalties of the law.

[v]

I will add four observations *ex abundante cautela.*

    1. The elucidation of the moral importance of the men-
tal element in responsibility, and the moral odium of strict liability that I have indicated, must not be mistaken for a psychological theory of motivation. It does not answer the question, Why
do people obey the law? It does not assert that they obey only
because they choose to obey rather than pay the cost. Instead,
my theory answers the question, Why *should* we have a law with
just these features? Human beings in the main do what the law
requires without first choosing between the advantage and the
cost of disobeying, and when they obey it is not usually from
fear of the sanction. For most the sanction is important not because it inspires them with fear but because it offers a guarantee
that the antisocial minority who would not otherwise obey will
be coerced into obedience by fear. To obey without this assurance might, as Hobbes saw, be very foolish: it would be to risk
going to the wall. However, the fact that only a few people, as
things are, consider the question, Shall I obey or pay? does not
in the least mean that the standing possibility of asking this
question is unimportant: for it secures just those values for the
individual that I have mentioned.

    2. I must of course confront the objection the Marxist
might make, that the excusing conditions, or indeed *mutatis
mutandis* the invalidating conditions, of civil transactions are of
no use to many individuals in society whose economic or social
position is such that the difference between a law of strict liabil-

ity and a law that recognizes excusing conditions is of no importance. It is quite true that the fact that criminal law recognizes
excusing mental conditions may be of no importance to a person
whose economic condition is such that he cannot profit from the
difference between a law against theft that is strict and one that
incorporates excusing conditions. If starvation "forces" him to
steal, the values the system respects and incorporates in excusing conditions are nothing to him. This is of course similar to the
claim often made that the freedom that a political democracy of
the Western type offers to its subjects is merely formal freedom,
not real freedom, and leaves one free to starve. I regard this as a
confusing way of putting what may be true under certain conditions; namely, that the freedoms the law offers may be *valueless*
as playing no part in the happiness of persons who are too poor
or weak to take advantage of them. The admission that the excusing conditions may be of no value to those who are below a
minimum level of economic prosperity may mean, of course,
that we should incorporate as a further excusing condition the
pressure of gross forms of economic necessity. This point, though
valid, does not seem to me to throw doubt on the principle
lying behind such excusing conditions as we do recognize at
present, nor to destroy their genuine value for those who are
above the minimum level of economic prosperity, for a difference between a system of strict liability and our present system
plays a part in their happiness.

　　3. The principle by reference to which I have explained
the moral importance of excusing conditions may help clarify an
old dispute, apt to spring up between lawyers on the one hand
and doctors and scientists on the other, about the moral basis of
punishment.

　　From Plato to the present day there has been a recurrent
insistence that if we were rational we would always look on
crime as a disease and address ourselves to its cure. We would
do this not only where a crime has actually been committed but
where we find well-marked evidence that it will be. We would
take the individual and treat him as a patient before the deed

was done. Plato,[16] it will be remembered, thought it superstitious to look back and go into questions of responsibility or the previous history of a crime except when it might throw light on what was needed to cure the criminal.

Carried to its extreme, this doctrine is the program of Erewhon where those with criminal tendencies were sent by doctors for indefinite periods of cure; punishment was displaced by a concept of social hygiene. It is, I think, of some importance to realize why we should object to this point of view, for both those who defend it and those who attack it often assume that the *only* possible consistent alternative to Erewhon is a theory of punishment under which it is justified simply as a return for the moral evil attributable to the accused. Those opposed to the Erewhonian program are apt to object that it disregards moral guilt as a necessary condition of a just punishment and thus leads to a condition in which any person may be sacrificed to the welfare of society. Those who defend an Erewhonian view think that their opponents' objection must entail adherence to the form of retributive punishment that regards punishment as a justified return for the moral evil in the criminal's action.

Both sides, I think, make a common mistake: there *is* a reason for making punishment conditional on the commission of crime and respecting excusing conditions, which are quite independent of the form of retributive theory that is often urged as the only alternative to Erewhon. Even if we regard the over-all purpose of punishment as that of protecting society by deterring persons from committing crimes and insist that the penalties we inflict be adapted to this end, we can in perfect consistency and with good reason insist that these punishments be applied only to those who have broken a law and to whom no excusing conditions apply. For this system will provide a measure of protection to individuals and will maximize their powers of prediction and the efficacy of their choices in the way that I have mentioned. To see this we have only to ask ourselves what in terms of these values we should lose (however much else we might

16 Plato, *Protagoras*, 324; *Laws* 861, 865.

gain) if social hygiene and a *system of compulsory treatment* for those with detectable criminal tendencies were throughout substituted for our system of punishment modified by excusing conditions. Surely the realization of what would be lost, and not a retributive theory of punishment, is all that is required as a reason for refusing to make the descent into Erewhon.

4. Finally, what I have written concerns only *legal* responsibility and the rationale of excuses in a legal system in which there are organized, coercive sanctions. I do not think the same arguments can be used to defend *moral* responsibility from the determinist, if it is in any danger from that source.

OBLIGATION AND ABILITY / *W. K. Frankena*

IT is well-known that we often withdraw such statements as "*A ought to do B*" or "*A ought to have done B rather than C,*" when we become convinced that *A* cannot do or could not have done *B*. This undoubted fact has led many moral philosophers to say, in one way or another, that "ought" implies "can." Indeed, if there is anything on which philosophers are agreed with plain men and with each other, and goodness knows there is very little, it is Kant's dictum, "*Du kannst, denn du sollst!*" Sometimes it is asserted as a separate point of theory, more often simply as a step in some line of argument, but asserted it is. Almost always, however, it is affirmed with little further ado—with little examination, qualification, or explanation. It is asserted cryptically and

From W. K. Frankena, "Obligation and Ability," in Max Black (ed.), Philosophical Analysis: A Collection of Essays (Englewood Cliffs, N. J. : Prentice-Hall, 1963), pp. 148–165. © 1963. Reprinted by permission of the publisher.

unanalytically. This paper is an effort to do something to remedy this state of affairs.

Our dictum has many aspects, uses, and possible interpretations, and we cannot study them all. We shall not discuss nonethical senses of "ought," even though in some of them it seems to imply "can," as in "The train ought to be coming along any moment." We must also limit the scope of "can," partly to avoid the free-will controversy. (a) It has been understood to mean "I am free to choose or not to choose to do A (in the indeterminist sense of 'free')." (b) It may be taken to imply "My doing A is or will be a voluntary action on my part (in Moore's sense of 'voluntary,' according to which an action is voluntary if it is one which the agent would not have done or tried to do if he had chosen otherwise, no question being asked about the possibility of his choosing otherwise[1])." (c) It may be understood to entail "My doing A is or will be a voluntary action, not only in this sense of 'voluntary,' but also in the further sense that I can choose otherwise." [2] (d) Other things that may be meant by "can" are suggested by the fact that "I can't do that!" sometimes means "I have pressing engagements which prevent my doing it," "I should stand to lose too much if I were to do that," etc., and by Luther's *"Ich kann nicht anders."* We shall not be concerned, directly at least, with any of these meanings of "can." (e) In a very ordinary usage, "I can do A" means something that can be roughly expressed by "I know how to do A and am physically capable of doing it" or "I am able to do A, if I choose." Here, says Russell, "I can do A" means "A will occur if I will it." [3] According to Prichard it means "I can bring about a certain state of affairs indirectly," that is, "I can set myself to bring about a certain state of affairs, and my setting myself thus will bring about something which will have that state of affairs as its effect." [4] This is the meaning of "can" which is usually intended

1 See G. E. Moore, *Ethics* (1912), pp. 13–16.
2 See P. A. Schilpp (ed.), *The Philosophy of G. E. Moore* (1942), pp. 623–627.
3 "The Elements of Ethics," *Philosophical Essays* (1910), p. 34.
4 *Duty and Ignorance of Fact* (1932), pp. 4, 22. I am taking "can do" in what he calls the less strict sense.

in our dictum, both by the philosopher and by the man on the street,[5] and the one with which we shall be concerned.

There is an ambiguity in the meaning of "can do" which must be noted before we continue. For we must distinguish between our latent and our active capacities, much as we do between our passive and our active vocabularies. My ability to skate is unfortunately, I am told, merely latent, not active, as is my ability to walk. I can skate in a sense, but not in the same sense in which I can walk; and I cannot, I suppose, run a mile in less than four minutes in either of these senses. Hence "I can do *A*" may mean either that I am actively capable of doing *A*, i.e., I can do *A* in the present stage in the development of my capacities, or that I am latently capable of doing *A*, i.e., I could do *A*, if the latent capacities which I actually have were further developed.

It is clear that "I can do *A*, if I choose" means "I am actively capable of doing *A*"; and we shall, therefore, be dealing with the relation between having an obligation and being actively able to do. Our question, then, is: What are the ethically relevant senses of "ought" and how are they related to "can" in sense (e), that is, in the sense in which it is short for "can do, if I choose" or "am actively able to do"? [6]

We may begin with "ought" as it occurs in general statements or "moral rules." Such statements are of two sorts: rules enjoining certain feelings in certain situations, e.g., "A person ought to feel gratitude toward a benefactor," and rules requiring certain actions in certain circumstances, e.g., "We ought to keep our promises." Consider rules of the former kind. Cambridge philosophers have generally taken the position that "ought" is here used in a "wider" sense, which does not imply "can." Thus Sidgwick writes, "In a wider sense . . . I sometimes judge that I 'ought' to know what a wiser man would know, or feel as a better man would feel, in my place, though I may know that I could not directly produce in myself such knowledge or feeling

[5] At least this is the meaning of "can" intended when our dictum is not associated with the free-will controversy.

[6] Hereafter "can" will be used in this way, unless otherwise specified.

by any effort of will. In this case the word merely implies an ideal or pattern which I 'ought'—in the stricter sense—to seek to imitate as far as possible." [7] The point which these writers have in mind is that feelings are not in control of the will in such a way that one can in a certain situation produce a certain feeling by willing to feel it; I cannot feel gratitude just because I choose to. Therefore in rules of feeling or "ideal rules," as Moore has called them,[8] "ought" does not imply "can" in our sense. If it did, they could not be true. If I have an obligation to feel gratitude toward my benefactors, this must then be an obligation which does not entail my being able to feel it toward them. On the other hand, while agreeing that our feelings are not directly controlled by our will, Sir David Ross maintains that, though the term "right" may properly be applied to feelings, the term "ought" may not—just because "ought" implies "can," and "right" does not. We actually use "ought" in connection with feelings as well as actions, he admits, but this is "an improper use . . . which we could not seriously defend." For we are only justified in saying "A ought to have felt sorrow then," if we are thinking that he might in the past so have disposed himself as to be able to feel sorrow at the time in question, and then the proper thing to say is not "A ought to have felt sorrow then," but "A ought earlier so to have disposed himself as to be able to feel sorrow at the time in question." [9]

It is possible that "We ought to feel gratitude toward our benefactors" means "We ought so to cultivate our feelings that we will feel gratitude toward them," but it seems more plausible to hold that, if we ought so to cultivate our feelings, this is because we first ought to feel gratitude when benefited by others. To argue that, in saying this, we are using "ought" improperly will not do, for, as Ewing points out,[10] the criterion of proper use in such cases as this can only be usage, and we admittedly do

7 *The Methods of Ethics* (1907), p. 33. See also Broad, *Five Types of Ethical Theory* (1930), p. 161.

8 *Philosophical Studies* (1922), p. 317.

9 Ross, *Foundations of Ethics* (1939), pp. 52–55.

10 *The Definition of Good* (1947), p. 131.

apply "ought" to feelings. In fact, it may be a *petitio* to assert that we cannot seriously defend the use of "ought" in ideal rules unless we retranslate them in the manner indicated. For we *can* seriously defend it if we suppose that in this case "ought" does not imply "can," just as we can seriously defend the use of "dear" in "She is very dear to his heart," if we do not assume that "dear" always implies "expensive." In any event, our usage is so fluid that we not only use "right" where we should "more properly" use "ought" (as Ross himself points out[11]), but also use "ought" as a synonym of "right" in the sort of case in which he recognizes that "right" does not imply "can." Hence in *actual* (if not in "proper") usage, there is a sense of "ought" in which ought-judgments do not presuppose possibility.

This, however, means only that to say we ought to feel in a certain way at a certain time is not to say we can so feel at that time if we choose. We should still all agree, I take it, that anyone who is constitutionally cut off from having the feelings in question at any time has not even this ideal duty to feel them at the time stipulated.[12] In the same way we should also admit that "We ought to love our parents" implies that we can cultivate feelings of love toward them and not only toward our fellow children. In other words, even in the present usage, "I ought" implies "I can" in the sense of being latently able.

While "We ought to feel gratitude toward our benefactors" does not entail "We can feel gratitude toward them, if we choose," it does entail "We ought to feel gratitude toward them, *if we can.*" Here enters another sense of "ought," it should be noticed. For what we have is that "We ought (in a sense not implying 'can') to feel A" entails "We ought (in a sense implying 'can') to feel A, if we can." Moore goes farther. He distinguishes these two senses of "ought," and then says that "I ought to do A (in the first sense)" not only entails but means "I ought to do A (in the second sense), if I can." [13] In this he may be

---

11 *Loc. cit.*
12 Cf. Ewing, *op. cit.*, pp. 165–166.
13 *Philosophical Studies*, pp. 317–318.

right, but, as we shall see when we discuss the general question
of the relation of these two senses of "ought," another view is
also tenable.

It is more plausible to hold that rules of action use
"ought" in a sense implying "can, if I choose" than that rules of
feeling do so, for actions seem to be in the control of the will in a
way in which feelings are not. Hence Moore claims that in "rules
of duty" we use "ought" in a can-implying sense, while in "ideal
rules" we do not.[14] Yet Broad contends that, even in some rules
prescribing actions, "ought" occurs in the "wider" usage in which
it does not imply "can," e.g., in "Virtue ought to be rewarded." [15]
To this contention Ross replies,[16] and Kant would certainly
agree, that we can only say this seriously if we are thinking that
some being can and ought so to act to reward virtue. Possibly the
answer to Ross is that, of course, we should not *say seriously*
that virtue ought to be rewarded unless we thought there was
such a being, for our *saying* it would be pointless if there were
not. However, it seems sufficient to remark that "Virtue ought to
be rewarded" does not entail "There is a being who can reward
it" but only "If anyone can reward virtue, he ought to do so,"
observing that in *this* sentence "ought" implies "can," while in
the original it does not.

The Oxford neointuitionists or deontologists commonly
conceive of the more basic rules of action, not as enjoining us
actually to proceed to do certain things, but as asserting what
they variously call claims, *prima facie* duties, responsibilities,
and obligations.[17] For example, they hold that "We ought to keep
our promises" says, not that keeping our promises is always our
actual duty in the relevant circumstances, but that in those circumstances it is our actual duty to keep our promises *if other*

14 *Ibid.*
15 *Loc. cit.*
16 *Op. cit.*, pp. 45–46.
17 For the conception here involved, see Ross, *The Right and the Good*
(1930), Ch. II. For a brief history of the term used to designate it, see Carritt,
Ethical and Political Thinking (1947), p. 3n. I shall use Ross's phrase *"prima
facie* duty."

things are equal.[18] Without committing ourselves to neointuition-
ism, we may make use of this conception. For the opposed principle of utility can be conceived as a *prima facie* duty in the
fortunate situation of having no rivals, so that other things being
always equal, the action which it requires will always be our
actual duty. In fact, an ideal utilitarian may even admit a number of *prima facie* duties, because for him there are many characteristics (besides pleasure) which are ought-implying, where
by an ought-implying characteristic is meant one "such that,
when a state of affairs possesses it, then the fact that an action,
which an agent could do, would produce that state of affairs is
favourably relevant (though only in a very weak degree) to the
hypothesis that that agent ought to do that action." [19]

The point is that statements like "Promises ought to be
kept" and "Pleasure ought to be promoted" may alike be conceived as asserting *prima facie* duties—as affirming that the
characteristics in question are ought-implying in Moore's sense.
Taking them in this way, we may ask whether or not "ought" as
here used implies "can" in the sense of "can do, if I try." Prichard would presumably answer (a) that if a moral rule requires us
even *prima facie* to *do* acts of kind *A* in the relevant situations,
then it presupposes that we can *do* them, if we set ourselves to,
and (b) that moral rules do not require us to do acts of kind *A* in
those situations but only to set ourselves to do them. Point (b)
we shall discuss later. Just now, assuming that moral rules enjoin us to do and not merely to try, we may briefly consider (a).
To justify it Prichard simply says, "We never think that an action can be a man's duty unless he is able to do it." [20] His word-
ing suggests that he is here thinking only of actual, and not of
prima facie duty; and in any case his statement is not obviously

[18] "If other things are equal" means, roughly, "if no other moral features of
the situation prevent its being an actual duty."

[19] Moore, in *The Philosophy of G. E. Moore*, pp. 603–604. I shall neglect
Moore's distinction between saying something is a *prima facie* duty in Ross's
sense and saying a certain characteristic is ought-implying (cf. pp. 565, 596 f.)
as being unimportant for our purposes.

[20] *Op. cit.*, p. 6.

true for the latter, though it may be for the former. It may be that "We ought (*prima facie*) to keep our promises" does not entail "We *can* keep our promises, if we choose" but only "We ought (actually) to keep our promises, *if we can,* and if other things are equal." In fact, this seems to be not only a possible view but a plausible one, especially if we conceive moral rules as stating that certain characteristics are ought-implying in Moore's sense. And it would appear to be almost certainly true, if moral rules require us (*prima facie*), not merely to set ourselves to do, but to do; for then, if they imply that we can do, if we choose, they cannot be true without exception, as they are supposed to be.

There are here two alternatives. One may hold that "We ought (*prima facie*) to do an action of kind *A* in a situation of kind *B*" implies "We can do actions of kind *A*, if we choose," and that, therefore, when one cannot do an action of kind *A*, one has not even a *prima facie* duty to do it, despite the fact that one is in a situation of kind *B*. Or one may contend that one still has a *prima facie* duty to do the action of kind *A* then, though no actual duty, and that "ought (*prima facie*)" does not imply "can." The latter alternative is possible in any case, but it is pretty clearly true on the assumption that (b) is false, unless we admit that moral rules (even as statements of *prima facie* duties) have exceptions, which neointuitionists are reluctant to do. We may add that, on both views, *X*'s being an actual duty will presuppose that it can be done by the agent and that other things are equal. This is all that is essential. It is not essential that "ought" imply "can" in moral rules. We shall, therefore, adopt the latter position.

On this position "ought to do" in the general statements in question implies, not "can do, if I choose," but "ought to do, if I can." Thus, in discussing rules of action, we have come upon two senses of "ought," presumably the same two senses we came upon in dealing with rules of feeling, one implying "can," and one "ought (in the other sense), if I can (and if other things are equal)." Let us call the latter—which occurs in *prima facie* duties—sense (1), and the former sense (2).[21] Then it may be asked, again, whether "ought(1)" not only implies but means "ought(2), if I can (and if other things are equal)." Moore thinks so; Ewing, making use of the concept of "fittingness," thinks not. He admits that some justification for the view in question "is provided by Ross's suggestion that *prima facie* duties are to be viewed as *tendencies* to be absolute duties." "But," he argues, "to say that something is a *prima facie* duty is surely already to say not merely that there is a tendency for it to be fitting that we should adopt a certain attitude to it, but that it is absolutely fitting that we should do so, and also absolutely obligatory on us as far as it is in our power to take up the attitude at all." [22] If Ewing is correct, then "We ought(1) to do *A* (or it is fitting that we do *A*)" does not imply "We can do *A*, if we choose," and does not mean "We ought(2) to do *A*, if we can, and if other things are equal," though it entails this. It should be noted that fittingness may be an indefinable relation, as Ewing and others take it to be, but may also be definable. For all that is said here, "fitting" may mean "optimific," "commanded by God," or "approved by an impartial spectator." Ewing's position is an attractive one, and for a long time seemed to me to be obviously true. It is tempting to think that if something ought to be done if possible, this is because in some sense not involving "can" in its definition, even hypothetically, it already ought to be done. Unfortunately this is not necessarily true. What is obvious is that "I can do *X*" does not entail "I ought(2) to do it." Before I have an obligation to do *X* something more must be true of it than that I am able to do it. This something more may be that *X* is antecedently ("categorically, not merely hypothetically") fitting, but it need not be. It may only be the fact that *X* is pleasant, or keeps a promise, or has some other property which is ought-implying in Moore's sense.

On Ewing's view the situation is this: "being the keeping

21 For reference purposes, the four main senses of "ought" dealt with in this paper are listed below. See final footnote.

22 *Op. cit.*, p. 194.

of a promise" entails "being fitting" and "being fitting" entails "being obligatory(2), if possible, and if other things are equal." On the other, and more economical, view: "being an act of promise-keeping" directly entails "being obligatory (2), if possible, and if other things are equal." Both positions seem to be consonant with common usage, and I now see little ground for choosing one rather than the other, apart from considerations, aesthetic and otherwise, which would take us too far afield for present purposes, since we are not dealing with the problem of trying to define "ought" in its various senses.

So much for "ought(1)," which occurs in our more general judgments of obligation. What of "ought" in particular judgments? Here it may also appear in sense (1). Consider the syllogism:

(a) I ought to make reparations for my wrongful acts.

(b) Doing A will make reparations for my wrongful act B.

(c) Therefore I ought to do A.

"Ought" occurs in sense (1) in the particular conclusion as well as in the general first premise, else the argument is invalid. In neither case, if we are right, does "ought" imply "can, and other things are equal." But one may judge that a certain action is my "actual duty," in the sense in which Ross used this phrase in *The Right and the Good*,[23] as I do when I review my situation and my various *prima facie* duties in an effort to find out what I really ought to do, and conclude that I ought to do action C. Here I use "ought" in sense (2), which presupposes at least that other things are equal and perhaps also that I can do C, and so cannot be identical with sense (1), even though it may be definable in terms of sense (1) or sense (1) in terms of it. The act which I ought(2) to do is the act which actually fulfills most fully my *prima facie* obligations in the situation in question. On the utilitarian theory, of course, this will always be the optimific or optimizing act, but on the neointuitionist view it may not be. This act has often been called the materially or ob-

[23] P. 28.

jectively right act,[24] and has sometimes been referred to as the "fortunate" act, because it is only by luck that we ever do it.[25]

That we use "ought" in sense (2) is clear.[26] When we say that a man ought to do what he thinks he ought to do, we are using "ought" in two senses—in the second case in sense (2). When we say that a man thinks he ought to do *A*, but is mistaken, we are using "ought" in sense (2).[27] In fact, it seems to be admitted by those who deny the objective view of obligation that we actually do use "ought" in this sense, though we should not.[28] Moore even proceeds as if this were the only sense of "ought." [29] To hold this is to hold the objective view of obligation, and is clearly mistaken, as has been shown by Prichard and as we shall see below.[30] But Prichard's arguments show merely that (2) cannot be the only sense of "ought"; they refute the objective *view* of obligation but do not show that "ought" is not actually and defensibly used in an objective *sense*. They seem to show this only because Prichard implicitly assumes "ought" to have but one sense; as soon as it is seen that it has more (especially the three senses recognized by Ewing[31]) it becomes plain that they show nothing of the sort.

Does "ought(2)" imply "can"? We have so far assumed so, as does the usual formula for what ought(2) to be done, viz., "The act which I ought(2) to do is that act, among all those which are possible to me, which will most fully fulfil my obligations(1)." [32] It is, however, possible to find a formula for what ought(2) to be done which does not introduce any reference to what the agent can do, if he chooses. Let "X is open to the agent"

[24] Cf. Sidgwick, *op. cit.*, p. 207; Broad, "Some of the Main Problems of Ethics," *Philosophy*, XXI (1946), pp. 109 ff.

[25] Cf. Russell, *op. cit.*, p. 22; Ross, *The Right and the Good*, p. 31.

[26] See also Carritt, *op. cit.*, Ch. II; Ewing, *op. cit.*, pp. 118–120. On p. 119 Ewing seems to confuse senses (1) and (2).

[27] Or in sense (3), but this presupposes sense (2).

[28] Cf. Prichard, *op. cit.*, p. 24.

[29] So does Lucius Garvin in "Obligation and Moral Agency," *Ethics*, LVIII (1948), 188–194 and "Duty as External," *Jour. of Phil.*, XLV (1948), 549–555.

[30] In *The Right and the Good*, Ross defended the objective view of obligation; in *Foundations* he takes the subjective view.

[31] *Op. cit.*, pp. 118–123.

[32] Cf. Ross, *The Right and the Good*, p. 41.

mean, not "X is possible for him to do, if he chooses," but "X can be chosen and entered upon by the agent." Then we can describe the act which an agent ought(2) to do as the act which, of all those open to him, will most fully fulfill his obligations, without implying that this act is one which he can carry out successfully. Thus there seem to be two possible descriptions of the objectively right act: (a) the usual one, (b) the one just suggested.[33] If we adopt the former, "ought(2)" implies both "can" and "other things are equal"; if we adopt the latter, "ought(2)" implies "other things are equal" but not "can."

It is not easy to see what should be said at this point. Perhaps we should recognize two subsenses of "ought," namely, (2a) and (2b). Discussing this question, Carritt writes, "I think it would be improper to speak of an obligation we *could* not fulfil *if we tried* [as we should if he used "ought" in sense (2b)], such as to move in two directions at once or to learn Chinese in a week. . . ."[34] In so far as Carritt is thinking that "ought(1)" implies "can" [for he fails to distinguish senses (1) and (2)] we may take him to be mistaken; there is no real difficulty about a *prima facie* duty which we cannot carry out. As far as "ought (2)" goes, he may be right. There is little point in recognizing sense (2b) if we have already admitted sense (1), and although it is a possible meaning of "ought," we may well not have adopted it in actual use, not being concerned to say of anything impossible that it is an actual duty in any sense.

Understanding "ought(2)" to imply "can," then, we must ask if "ought(2)" may not be defined in terms of "ought(1)," as well as the other way around. For it would seem that "A ought (2) to be done by me now" may mean "I ought(1) to do A, I can do A, and other things are equal," since it does at least imply this. One who holds Ewing's position might well claim that "ought(2)" is thus definable by reference to "ought(1)," rather than vice versa. So far as I can see, this suggestion may quite well be correct; here again there seems to be little reason for

[33] Russell gives both kinds of descriptions of the objectively right act in *his* sense, *op. cit.*, pp. 25, 36.
[34] *Op. cit.*, p. 24.

choosing between the rival views unless we bring in aesthetic considerations or others which are not within the scope of this paper. Apart from such considerations, it seems to be arbitrary which use of "ought" is taken as basic to the others. Of course, it may also be held that "ought(1)" and "ought(2)" cannot be defined by reference to one another, being either indefinable or definable only in terms of other concepts, ethical or nonethical. Then "ought(1)" will not mean "ought(2), if I can, and if other things are equal," though it will imply this; and "ought(2)" will not mean "ought(1), and can, and other things are equal," though it will imply this.

We may now proceed to study other senses of "ought" in relation to "can." The action which I ought(2) to do is the one which I do and should have before my mind, as the ideal, when I ask, "What should I do in the situation I am now in?" But, as everyone sees, we cannot know what act is right or obligatory in this sense, and we must be and are in a manner morally content with less. Hence moralists have often spoken of the act which will *probably* be most beneficial or which will *probably* most fully fulfil the relevant obligations. Russell, for instance, describes the wise or objectively right act as "that one which, of all that are possible, will probably have the best consequences." [35] They have also spoken of the act which it seems preferable to choose in the light, not of all the evidence available to a wise man with plenty of time, but of the evidence which the agent can reasonably be expected to have, or to get in the time at his disposal. This is the act which Russell calls the subjectively right act, and which Ewing describes as obligatory in his third sense.[36] No doubt there are other possibilities. We have here, in fact, a family of possible senses of "ought," which we might refer to as (3a), (3b), etc., and which all involve the notion of what probably ought to be done relatively to some body of evidence or other, which may not coincide with the body of evidence of which the agent actually makes use. Their differences lie in the way in which this body of evidence is defined. That we use "ought" in

[35] *Op. cit.*, pp. 25, 31–32.
[36] *Loc. cit.*

such senses is shown by the fact that we often say that a man ought not to have done a certain action, which, though successful, could not have been expected to be so.[37]

An action may, therefore, be one which I ought(3) to have done, even if it was wrong(2), though not, of course, if I knew it was wrong(2). Hence senses (2) and (3) are distinct and may be differently related to "can." Yet sense (3) presupposes sense (2), inasmuch as "I ought(3) to do A" presupposes that it is probable, relatively to a given body of evidence, that A ought(2) to be done by me. Perhaps "ought(3)" is definable in terms of "ought(2)," and "I ought(3) to do A" just means "It is probable that I ought(2) to do A." But all that concerns us is the connection between "ought(3)" and "can." "I ought(2) to do A" implies "I can do A." "I ought(3) to do A," however, does not imply "I ought(2) to do A" but only "It is probable on evidence E that I ought(2) to do A," and therefore may not imply "I can do A." In fact, to say that I ought(3) to do A is not to say that of the actions which I *actually* can do A is the one which will probably most fully fulfil my *prima facie* duties. I can no more know, except with probability, what I can do than what I ought(2) to do. Hence, in saying "I ought(3) to do A," I must be implying, not "I can do A," but "I probably can do A"; and it may, then, be that I ought(3) to do A even if I cannot do A, just as it may be that I ought(3) to do A even if it is wrong(2). Suppose it to be probable, relative to the body of evidence in question, that I ought(2) to do A. This will imply that it is probable I can do A. Then I ought(3) to do A. Suppose also that I set out to do it, and it turns out that I am unable to. Then, of course, I no longer have an obligation(3) to do A, and I never had an obligation(2) to do it. But it still remains the case that it was my obligation(3) to do A until the additional evidence came in (because of my setting out to do it) which established my inability to do it. What absolves me from being obliged(3) to do A is not the fact that I am

37 Cf. Carritt, *op. cit.*, p. 15; Ewing, *op. cit.*, pp. 121–122. Ewing answers Prichard's objection to admitting this sense. Cf. pp. 125–128. Ross in effect admits this sense, *Foundations*, pp. 156 f.

unable to do it, but the fact that the body of evidence in question testifies that I am unable.

This brings us to another sense of "ought," often referred to as the peculiarly moral sense, even though it is not the only one which is relevant to ethics.[38] In all of the above senses of "ought," what I am required to do is not simply what I as a matter of fact think I ought to do, but what I objectively ought to do or what some body of evidence, perhaps not possessed or used by me, makes it probable that I objectively ought to do. However, as Russell says, "There is certainly a sense in which a man ought to perform any act which he approves. . . ."[39] A man, we say, ought always to obey his conscience. We may label this use of "ought" sense (4). The act which ought to be done in this sense (i.e., the act which the agent thinks he ought to do) has usually been called the subjectively right act;[40] lately Carritt has called it the putatively right act and Ewing the morally obligatory act. Prichard is right as against Moore in insisting that this subjective sense of "ought" must be recognized, but wrong in implying that there is no more objective sense. For "ought(4)" clearly presupposes another sense of "ought," as is shown by the fact that *A* is my duty(4) only if I already believe it to be my duty in some other sense, viz., (2) or (3).[41]

There is a complexity here which is not always realized. What one thinks right depends partly on his beliefs about the nonethical features of his situation and partly on his beliefs as to its ethical aspects. Hence one may distinguish three cases: (a) the act which one ought to do if the nonethical aspects of the situation are as he thinks they are, (b) the act which the actual situation requires if one's *prima facie* duties therein are what he thinks they are, and (c) the act which one thinks to be required by the situation as he takes it to be. The last is the act

38 See Ewing, *op. cit.*, pp. 128–132, on the relevancy of senses (2) and (3) (his first and third) to ethics.

39 *Op. cit.*, p. 17; cf. Carritt, *op. cit.*, p. 15; Ewing, *op. cit.*, pp. 120 f.

40 E.g., by Sidgwick, *op. cit.*, p. 207.

41 Thinking it to be my duty in sense (2) and thinking it to be my duty in sense (3) will in practice amount to the same thing.

which we have said we ought(4) to do and is, perhaps, the only one of the three with which we need be concerned here.

Obviously, an action may be right in sense (4) and wrong in all of the above senses, or right in those senses and wrong in this. Should one, then, if there is a discrepancy, do the action which is right in sense (4) or the action which is right in some other sense? The answer, in part, is that it depends on the sense in which "should" is being used in the question. If it is used in sense (2), the reply can only be that we should do the action which we ought(2) to do, etc. But the main part of the answer is that one has no choice in the matter; one can (in a sense, not ours) do only what he thinks he ought(2) to do. Further thought may lead him to revise his opinion about this, but he will never *find* a discrepancy between what he finally judges to be right(2) and what is really right(2).[42]

It is often held that if one does what one ought(4) to do one acquires merit and deserves praise and reward and that if one neglects to do it one gains a demerit and deserves blame and punishment. This is not so clearly true as it appears to be, but, in any case, we need not linger over this matter. Our question, as usual, concerns the relation of "ought(4)" and "can." Since it is sometimes regarded as the moral sense of "ought" *par excellence,* one might think that it is the most likely to entail "can." Actually the matter is somewhat complex. "I ought(4)" does not entail "I ought(2)." It entails "I think I ought(2)." Hence it presumably implies, not "I can," but "I think I can." If so, it might appear to follow that, if I think I can and ought(2) to do A, then I ought(4) to do A, even if I cannot. And this seems incredible. To clarify the matter we must distinguish between doing A and trying or setting ourselves to do A. It will, then, be observed that all we are really required to do when we are told that we ought(4) to do A is to try or set ourselves to do it. If I think I ought(2) to do A and try to do it but fail, I may say to you, "I failed my duty," and so I have in sense (2); but you will reply, if you are not unfriendly, "No, you tried, and that is all that can be asked of you," and so it is—in sense (4). It now

42 Cf. Sidgwick, *loc. cit.*

becomes evident (a) that if I cannot do *A*, I have no obligation(4) to do it, but may have an obligation(4) to try, (b) that if I think I can and ought(2) to do *A*, I ought(4) to try to do it, even if I cannot in fact do it, and (c) that if I think or know that I cannot do *A*, I have no obligation(4) even to try to do it. One is also tempted to assert (d) that if I can do *A* and believe I can and ought(2) to do it, I ought(4) to do it and not merely to try. If so, we have here an exception to the rule that our obligation in sense (4) is only to try and not to do. But perhaps this case is not really an exception, for one may claim that even here I am obliged only to try, although if I try I shall succeed in doing, and that, while I am in this case to blame if I do not do, it is only because this means I did not try. Even if it were an exception, of course, it would be true that I have no obligation(4) to do *A* if I cannot do it. In short, "I ought(4) to do *A*" does not entail "I can do *A*," because it does not really ask me to do *A* but only to try, and "I ought(4) to try to do *A*" does not imply "I can do *A*," but only "I think I can do it, and I can try to do it." However, if it did ask me to do *A*, "I ought(4) to do *A*" would entail "I can do *A*." What it asks of me is possible to me; in this respect "ought(4)" implies "can." But it does not ask me to *do*, and therefore does not imply "can do."

Some writers have distinguished yet another sense of "ought," saying that I have not done what I ought if I do what is otherwise right from a wrong or bad or nonmoral motive. They have, therefore, introduced such notions as "the formally right act," "the virtuous act," etc.[43] So far as I can see, however, there is nothing new to be learned from a study of this sense or family of senses (5) of "ought" in its relation to "can." To say "I ought(5) to do from motive *M*, what I think I ought(2) to do," for example, seems to be explicable in terms of other senses of "ought" as follows: "I ought(4) to do what I think I ought(2) to do, *and* I ought(1) to feel motive *M* in situations of this sort." More interesting is "the perfectly right or completely right act,"

[43] See Sidgwick, *op. cit.*, pp. 206–207; Broad, *loc. cit.*; Carritt, *A Theory of Morals* (1928), Ch. XVI.

as it is sometimes called.[44] This may be variously defined by reference to other meanings of "ought" or "right." If "the perfectly right act for me to do here and now" is defined as "the act which I ought here and now to do, in senses (2)–(5)," then "*A* is the perfectly right act for me to do in this situation" implies "I can do *A*, if I choose." For "the perfectly right *A*" is just "the most completely right act of those possible to the agent." On the other hand, if being perfectly right involves, among other things, fulfilling all of the *prima facie* duties relevant to the situation, it may well be impossible for the agent to do the perfectly right act—and so not obligatory(2).

Now that we have studied the senses of "ought" and their relations to "can do, if I choose," it is time to examine Prichard's point (b)—"that an obligation must be an obligation not to do something but to set ourselves to do something."[45] We have admitted this in the case of "ought(4)." But we have also held that one has an obligation(1) to keep promises, for example, and not merely to try to keep them, even when he is unable to do so; and we have affirmed that "ought(2)" implies "can do, if I choose." Both of these conclusions will be false if Prichard is correct, the former because then even obligation(1) is only to try, the latter because then my having an obligation(2) to do *A* does not imply that I can do it, since it does not really enjoin doing, but only that I can set myself.[46] Is Prichard right? The case is turned somewhat in our favor by the fact that we have seen reason for admitting three (plus) senses or families of senses of "ought" in addition to the subjective one (4) which Prichard recognizes. For while it is clear that an obligation in sense (4) is fulfilled by merely trying or setting ourselves, it is not clear that obligations in the other senses are. Moreover, his argument for his position, as well as the one added by Ross, loses its force if these other senses are kept in mind, although this cannot be shown here, for we must limit ourselves to the reasons for believing Prichard and Ross to be mistaken.

[44] See Sidgwick, *loc. cit.;* Broad, *loc. cit.;* Ross, *Foundations*, pp. 52–53.
[45] *Op. cit.*, p. 25.
[46] I do not mean to imply that there are no problems about being able to set oneself. There are, but we are not concerned with them here.

It can, I think, be granted that we may speak of an obligation to try or to set ourselves in senses other than (4).[47] But surely I have no obligation to try if I have no obligation to do. Trying is always trying to do; and, if I have an obligation to try, this is because I first have an obligation to do or think I have. I have an obligation in senses (1) or (2) to try, if and only if I have an obligation in senses (1) or (2) to do; and I have an obligation(4) to try, if and only if I think I ought in senses (1) or (2) to do. To this last point it may be replied that it is enough if I think I ought in senses (1) or (2) to *try*. But thinking this presupposes the thought that I ought in senses (1) or (2) to do. This is shown by the fact that if I know I cannot *do*, I have no obligation to *try* in any sense, and if I think I cannot *do*, I have no obligation(4) to try.

In general, it would seem that, if we were obliged only to *try*, then the fact that we cannot *do*, or know or think we cannot *do*, could not disoblige us, for we can (in our sense) always try. Suppose, however, that we have a straight-out obligation in senses (1) and (2) to try or to exert ourselves to do. What will this mean? It will mean that I ought(1) to perform that act of self-exertion or trying which will bring about, say, the keeping of my promise, and that I ought(2) to perform that act of self-exertion or trying which will come closest to bringing about what would be brought about by the various acts of self-exertion or trying which I ought(1) to perform.[48] For it will not suffice in senses (1) or (2) to perform the act of self-exertion or trying which I think will have the effects in question, since that is the one which I ought in sense (4) to perform. But to ask me to perform the self-exertion which *will* bring about a certain state of affairs is the same as to ask me to *do* a certain action.[49] Thus, asking me to make the self-exertion which will keep my promise is asking me to keep my promise; it is not asking me merely to try to keep it.

There is another line of thought which leads to the con-

---

[47] Carritt denies this for sense (2), *Ethical and Political Thinking*, p. 23.
[48] The term "self-exertion" is Ross's. See *Foundations*, p. 160.
[49] See the account given earlier of Prichard's analysis of being able to do.

clusion that we have obligations to do as well as to try. In an illustration used earlier, we found a man saying, quite naturally, "I failed to do my duty." Now, why did he fail to do his duty in the situation? Not because he did not try, for he did; but because, although he tried, he did not accomplish the required result. We must, therefore, have here a sense, namely (2), in which one ought, not simply to try, but also to accomplish.[50] And, if we have obligations(2) to do, then we have obligations(1) to do, for these two senses must be alike in this matter.

About "ought(3)" I am more doubtful, as it is intermediate between "ought(2)" and "ought(4)." But perhaps it need not be discussed. I have argued that one may have an obligation(3) to do A, even if one cannot in fact do A, although it ceases as soon as one's inability is revealed, and this still seems to me to be the case. In any event, however, Prichard's article (b) is not true for "ought(1)" or "ought(2)," and nothing more than a minor change of doctrine would be required, if it should be that obligation(3) like obligation(4) is merely to try and not to do.

To summarize: We have found the dictum that "ought" in its ethical uses implies "can" (in the sense of "can do, if I choose") not to be true *simpliciter*. "Ought" has several ethically relevant senses, of which four have been particularly discussed.[51] Only in the second of these does "I ought" imply "I can do, if I choose." In the first, it implies "I ought(2) to do, if I can" and "I am latently able to do," but not "I am actively able to do." In the third, "I ought" implies, not "I can," but "I probably can." In both cases, "I ought to do" entails a statement involving "can" in one way or another, but not "I can do, if I choose." In the case of sense (4) the matter is still more complicated. "I ought(4) to *do*

50 Cf. Carritt, *loc. cit.*
51 The following sentences will serve to identify, distinguish, and relate these four senses:

  a. I ought(1) to do what I ought(2) to do, if I can, and if other things are equal.

  b. I ought(2) to do what will most fully fulfil my obligations(1) of the actions which I can do if I choose.

  c. I ought(3) to do what, relatively to evidence E, I probably ought(2) to do.

  d. I ought(4) to [try to] do what I think I ought(2) or ought(3) to do.

A" does imply "I can *do A*, if I choose," for if the latter is false
the former is also. However, it is never true that I ought(4) to *do
A*, but only that I ought(4) to try (though we often say loosely
"*B* ought(4) to 'do' *A*"); and "I ought(4) to try to do *A*" does not
imply "I can *do A*" but only "I think I can do *A* (and I can try to
do *A*)." Therefore, understood in a way in which it may be true,
"I ought(4) to 'do' *A*" does not imply "I can *do A*."

These are our main results. We have also tried to show
two points in Prichard's theory of obligation, accepted by Ross in
his later work, to be false. And we have suggested, somewhat
tentatively, that, with the help of "can" (in our sense),
"ought(1)" and "ought(2)" are interdefinable. We have left for
other occasions such further questions as: (a) Are the various
ethical senses of "ought" all interdefinable, with or without the
help of "can"? (b) Is "ought" in all of its ethical senses definable
in nonethical terms, with or without the help of "can"? (c) What
is meant by "implies" when it is said that "ought" implies "can"?

In arriving at these results we have sought to avoid making any commitments to any particular theory of obligation, naturalistic or nonnaturalistic, neointuitionist or utilitarian. They
may and should, therefore, if we are not mistaken, be accepted
by and incorporated in any ethical theory which is concerned to
accord with common usage.

JUSTICE AS FAIRNESS[1] / *John Rawls*

THE fundamental idea in the concept of justice is that of fair-

From John Rawls, "Justice as Fairness," The Journal of Philosophy, *LIV*
(*1957*) *653–662. Reprinted by permission of the Editors of* The Journal of
Philosophy.

[1] Considerations of space have made it impossible to give appropriate references. I must, however, mention that in the second paragraph of section 3 I am
indebted to H. L. A. Hart. See his paper "Are There Any Natural Rights?,"
Philosophical Review, LXIV (1955), pp. 185 f.

ness. It is this aspect of justice for which utilitarianism, in its classical form, is unable to account, but which is represented, even if misleadingly so, in the idea of the social contract. To establish these propositions I shall develop, but of necessity only very briefly, a particular conception of justice by stating two principles which specify it and by considering how they may be thought to arise. The parts of this conception are familiar; but perhaps it is possible by using the notion of fairness as a framework to assemble and to look at them in a new way.

1. Throughout I discuss justice as a virtue of institutions constituting restrictions as to how they may define offices and powers, and assign rights and duties; and not as a virtue of particular actions, or persons. Justice is but one of many virtues of institutions, for these may be inefficient, or degrading, or any of a number of things, without being unjust. Essentially justice is the elimination of arbitrary distinctions and the establishment, within the structure of a practice, of a proper balance between competing claims. I do not argue that the principles given below are *the* principles of justice. It is sufficient for my purposes that they be typical of the family of principles which might reasonably be called principles of justice as shown by the background against which they may be thought to arise.

The first principle is that each person participating in a practice, or affected by it, has an equal right to the most extensive liberty compatible with a like liberty for all; and the second is that inequalities are arbitrary unless it is reasonable to expect that they will work out for everyone's advantage and unless the offices to which they attach, or from which they may be gained, are open to all. These principles express justice as a complex of three ideas: liberty, equality, and reward for contributions to the common advantage.

The first principle holds, of course, only *ceteris paribus*: while there must always be a justification for departing from the initial position of equal liberty (which is defined by the pattern of rights and duties), and the burden of proof is placed upon him who would depart from it, nevertheless, there can be, and often there is, a justification for doing so. One can view this principle as containing the principle that similar cases be judged similarly, or if distinctions are made in the handling of cases, there must be some relevant difference between them (a principle which follows from the concept of a judgment of any kind). It could be argued that justice requires only an equal liberty; but if a greater liberty were possible for all without loss or conflict, then it would be irrational to settle on a lesser liberty. There is no reason for circumscribing rights until they mutually interfere with one another. Therefore no serious distortion of the concept of justice is likely to follow from including within it the concept of the greatest equal liberty instead of simply equal liberty.

The second principle specifies what sorts of inequalities are permissible, where by inequalities it seems best to understand not any difference between offices and positions, since structural differences are not usually an issue (people do not object to there being different offices as such, and so to there being the offices of president, senator, governor, judge, and so on), but differences in the benefits and burdens attached to them either directly or indirectly, such as prestige and wealth, or liability to taxation and compulsory service. An inequality is allowed only if there is reason to believe that the practice with the inequality will work to the advantage of *every* party. This is interpreted to require, first, that there must normally be evidence acceptable to common sense and based on a common fund of knowledge and belief which shows that this is in fact likely to be the case. The principle does not rule out, however, arguments of a theological or metaphysical kind to justify inequalities (e.g., a religious basis for a caste system) provided they belong to common belief and are freely acknowledged by people who may be presumed to know what they are doing.

Second, an inequality must work for the common advantage; and since the principle applies to practices, this implies that the representative man in *every* office or position of the practice, when he views it as a going institution, must find it reasonable to prefer his condition and prospects with the inequality to what they would be without it. And finally, the various offices to which special benefits and burdens attach are required to be open to all; and so if, for example, it is to the common advantage to attach benefits to offices (because by doing so not only is the requisite talent attracted to them, but encouraged to give its best efforts once there), they must be won in a fair competition in which contestants are judged on their merits. If some offices were not open, those excluded would normally be justified in feeling wronged, even if they benefited from the greater efforts of those who were allowed to compete for them. Assuming that offices are open, it is necessary only to consider the design of the practices themselves and how they jointly, as a system, work together. It is a mistake to fix attention on the varying relative positions of particular persons and to think that each such change, as a once-for-all transaction, must be in itself just. The system must be judged from a general point of view: unless one is prepared to criticize it from the standpoint of a representative man holding some particular office, one has no complaint against it.

2. Given these principles, one might try to derive them from *a priori* principles of reason, or offer them as known by intuition. These are familiar steps, and, at least in the case of the first principle, might be made with some success. I wish, however, to look at the principles in a different way.

Consider a society where certain practices are already established, and whose members are mutually self-interested: their allegiance to the established practices is founded on the prospect of self-advantage. It need not be supposed that they are incapable of acting from any other motive: if one thinks of the members of this society as families, the individuals thereof may be bound by ties of sentiment and affection. Nor must they be mutually self-interested under all circumstances, but only under those circumstances in which they ordinarily participate in their common practices. Imagine also that the persons in this society are rational: they know their own interests more or less accurately; they are capable of tracing out the likely consequences of adopting one practice rather than another and of adhering to a decision once made; they can resist present temptations and attractions of immediate gain; and the knowledge, or the perception, of the difference between their condition and that of others is not, in itself, a source of great dissatisfaction. Finally, they have roughly similar needs and interests and are sufficiently equal in power and ability to assure that in normal circumstances none is able to dominate the others.

Now suppose that on some particular occasion several members of this society come together to discuss whether any of them has a legitimate complaint against their established institutions. They try first to arrive at the principles by which complaints, and so practices themselves, are to be judged. Their procedure for this is the following: each is to propose the principles upon which he wishes his complaints to be tried with the understanding that, if acknowledged, the complaints of others will be similarly tried, and that no complaints will be heard at all until everyone is roughly of one mind as to how complaints are to be judged. They understand further that the principles proposed and acknowledged on this occasion are to be binding on future occasions. Thus each will be wary of proposing principles which give him a peculiar advantage, supposing them to be accepted, in his present circumstances, since he will be bound by it in future cases the circumstances of which are unknown and in which the principle might well be to his detriment. Everyone is, then, forced to make in advance a firm commitment, which others also may reasonably be expected to make, and no one is able to tailor the canons of a legitimate complaint to fit his own special condition. Therefore each person will propose principles of a general kind which will, to a large degree, gain their sense from the various applications to be made of them. These principles will express the conditions in accordance with which each is least unwilling to have his interests limited in the design of practices on the supposition that the interests of others will be limited likewise. The restrictions which would so arise might be thought of as those a person would keep in mind if he were designing a practice in which his enemy were to assign him his place.

In this account of a hypothetical society the character and respective situations of the parties reflect the circumstances in which questions of justice may be said to arise, and the procedure whereby principles are proposed and acknowledged represents constraints, analogous to those of having a morality, whereby rational and mutually self-interested parties are brought to act reasonably. Given all conditions as described, it would be natural to accept the two principles of justice. Since there is no way for anyone to win special advantage for himself, each might consider it reasonable to acknowledge equality as an initial principle. There is, however, no reason why they should regard this position as final; for if there are inequalities which satisfy the second principle, the immediate gain which equality would allow can be considered as intelligently invested in view of its future return. If, as is quite likely, these inequalities work as incentives to draw out better efforts, the members of this society may look upon them as concessions to human nature: they, like us, may think that people ideally should want to serve one another. But as they are mutually self-interested, their acceptance of these inequalities is merely the acceptance of the relations in which they actually stand. They have no title to complain of one another. And so, provided the conditions of the principle are met, there is no reason why they should reject such inequalities in the design of their social practices. Indeed, it would be short-sighted of them to do so, and could result, it seems, only from their being dejected by the bare knowledge, or perception, that others are better situated. Each person will, however, insist on a common advantage, for none is willing to sacrifice anything for the others.

These remarks are not, of course, offered as a proof that persons so circumstanced would settle upon the two principles, but only to show that the principles of justice could have such a background; and so can be viewed as those principles which mutually self-interested and rational persons, when similarly situated and required to make in advance a firm commitment, could acknowledge as restrictions governing the assignment of rights and duties in their common practices, and thereby accept as limiting their rights against one another.

3. That the principles of justice can be regarded in this way is an important fact about them. It brings out the idea that fundamental to justice is the concept of fairness which relates to right dealing between persons who are coöperating with or competing against one another, as when one speaks of fair games, fair competition, and fair bargains. The question of fairness arises when free persons, who have no authority over one another, are engaging in a joint activity and amongst themselves settling or acknowledging the rules which define it and which determine the respective shares in its benefits and burdens. A practice will strike the parties as fair if none feels that, by participating in it, he, or any of the others, is taken advantage of, or forced to give in to claims which he does not regard as legitimate. This implies that each has a conception of legitimate claims which he thinks it reasonable that others as well as himself should acknowledge. If one thinks of the principles of justice as arising in the way described, then they do define this sort of conception. A practice is just, then, when it satisfies the principles which those who participate in it could propose to one another for mutual acceptance under the aforementioned circumstances. Persons engaged in a just, or fair, practice can face one another honestly, and support their respective positions, should they appear questionable, by reference to principles which it is reasonable to expect each to accept. It is this notion of the possibility of mutual acknowledgment which makes the concept of fairness fundamental to justice. Only if such acknowledgment is possible, can there be true community between persons in their common practices; otherwise their relations will appear to them as founded to some extent on force and violence. If, in ordinary speech, fairness applies more particularly to practices in which there is a choice whether to engage or not, and justice to practices in which there is no choice and one must play, the element

of necessity does not alter the basic conception of the possibility of mutual acceptance, although it may make it much more urgent to change unjust than unfair institutions.

Now if the participants in a practice accept its rules as fair, and so have no complaint to lodge against it, there arises a prima facie duty (and a corresponding prima facie right) of the parties to each other to act in accordance with the practice when it falls upon them to comply. When any number of persons engage in a practice, or conduct a joint undertaking, according to rules, and thus restrict their liberty, those who have submitted to these restrictions when required have a right to a similar acquiescence on the part of those who have benefited by their submission. These conditions will, of course, obtain if a practice is correctly acknowledged to be fair, for in this case, all who participate in it will benefit from it. The rights and duties so arising are special rights and duties in that they depend on previous voluntary actions—in this case, on the parties' having engaged in a common practice and accepted its benefits. It is not, however, an obligation which presupposes a deliberate performative act in the sense of a promise, or contract, and the like. It is sufficient that one has knowingly participated in a practice acknowledged to be fair and accepted the resulting benefits. This prima facie obligation may, of course, be overridden: it may happen, when it comes one's turn to follow a rule, that other considerations will justify not doing so. But one cannot, in general, be released from this obligation by denying the justice of the practice only when it falls on one to obey. If a person rejects a practice, he should, as far as possible, declare his intention in advance, and avoid participating in it or accepting its benefits.

This duty may be called that of fair play, which is, perhaps, to extend the ordinary notion; for acting unfairly is usually not so much the breaking of any particular rule, even if the infraction is difficult to detect (cheating), but taking advantage of loopholes or ambiguities in rules, availing oneself of unexpected or special circumstances which make it impossible to enforce them, insisting that rules be enforced when they should be suspended, and, more generally, acting contrary to the intention of a practice. (Thus one speaks of the sense of fair play: acting fairly is not simply following rules; what is fair must be felt or perceived.) Nevertheless, it is not an unnatural extension of the duty of fair play to have it include the obligation which participants in a common practice owe to each other to act in accordance with it when their performance falls due. Consider the tax dodger, or the free rider.

The duty of fair play stands beside those of fidelity and gratitude as a fundamental moral notion; and like them it implies a constraint on self-interest in particular cases. I make this point to avoid a misunderstanding: the conception of the mutual acknowledgment of principles under special circumstances is used to analyze the concept of justice. I do not wish to imply that the acceptance of justice in actual conduct depends solely on an existing equality of conditions. My own view, which is perhaps but one of several compatible with the preceding analysis, and which I can only suggest here, is that the acknowledgment of the duty of fair play, as shown in acting on it, and wishing to make amends and the like when one has been at fault, is one of the forms of conduct in which participants in a common practice show their recognition of one another as persons. In the same way that, failing a special explanation, the criterion for the recognition of suffering is helping him who suffers, acknowledging the duty of fair play is the criterion for recognizing another as a person with similar capacities, interests, and feelings as oneself. The acceptance by participants in a common practice of this duty is a reflection in each of the recognition of the aspirations of the others to be realized by their joint activity. Without this acceptance they would recognize one another as but complicated objects in a complicated routine. To recognize another as a person one must respond to him and act towards him as one; and these forms of action and response include, among other things, acknowledging the duty of fair play. These remarks are unhappily obscure; their purpose here is to forestall the misunderstanding mentioned above.

The conception at which we have arrived, then, is that the principles of justice may be thought of as arising once the constraints of having a morality are imposed upon rational and mutually self-interested parties who are related and situated in a special way. A practice is just if it is in accordance with the principles which all who participate in it might reasonably be expected to propose or to acknowledge before one another when they are similarly circumstanced and required to make a firm commitment in advance; and thus when it meets standards which the parties could accept as fair should occasion arise for them to debate its merits. Once persons knowingly engage in a practice which they acknowledge to be fair and accept the benefits of doing so, they are bound by the duty of fair play which implies a limitation on self-interest in particular cases.

Now if a claim fails to meet this conception of justice there is no moral value in granting it, since it violates the conditions of reciprocity and community amongst persons: he who presses it, not being willing to acknowledge it when pressed by another, has no grounds for complaint when it is denied; whereas him against whom it is pressed can complain. As it cannot be mutually acknowledged, it is a resort to coercion: granting the claim is only possible if one party can compel what the other will not admit. Thus in deciding on the justice of a practice it is not enough to ascertain that it answers to wants and interest in the fullest and most effective manner. For if any of these be such that they conflict with justice, they should not be counted; their satisfaction is no reason for having a practice. It makes no sense to concede claims the denial of which gives rise to no complaint in preference to claims the denial of which can be objected to. It would be irrelevant to say, even if true, that it resulted in the greatest satisfaction of desire.

4. This conception of justice differs from that of the stricter form of utilitarianism (Bentham and Sidgwick), and its counterpart in welfare economics, which assimilates justice to benevolence and the latter in turn to the most efficient design of institutions to promote the general welfare. Now it is said occasionally that this form of utilitarianism puts no restrictions on what might be a just assignment of rights and duties. But this is not so. Beginning with the notion that the general happiness can

be represented by a social utility function consisting of the sum
of individual utility functions with identical weights (this being
the meaning of the maxim that each counts for one and no more
than one), it is commonly assumed that the utility functions of
individuals are similar in all essential respects. Differences are
laid to accidents of education and upbringing, and should not be
taken into account; and this assumption, coupled with that of
diminishing marginal utility, results in a prima facie case for
equality. But even if such restrictions are built into the utility
function, and have, in practice, much the same results as the
application of the principles of justice (and appear, perhaps, to
be ways of expressing these principles in the language of mathematics and psychology), the fundamental idea is very different
from the conception of justice as reciprocity. Justice is interpreted as the contingent result of a higher order administrative
decision whose form is similar to that of an entrepreneur deciding how much to produce of this or that commodity in view of its
marginal revenue, or to that of someone distributing goods to
needy persons according to the relative urgency of their wants.
The choice between practices is thought of as being made on the
basis of the allocation of benefits and burdens to individuals
(measured by the present capitalized value of the utility of these
benefits over the full period of the practice's existence) which
results from the distribution of rights and duties established by a
practice. The individuals receiving the benefits are not thought
of as related in any way: they represent so many different directions in which limited resources may be allocated. Preferences
and interest are taken as given; and their satisfaction has value
irrespective of the relations between persons which they represent and the claims which the parties are prepared to make on
one another. This value is properly taken into account by the
(ideal) legislator who is conceived as adjusting the rules of the
system from the center so as to maximize the present capitalized
value of the social utility function. The principles of justice will
not be violated by a legal system so conceived provided these
executive decisions are correctly made; and in this fact the principles of justice are said to find their derivation and explanation.

Some social decisions are, of course, of an administrative sort; namely, when the decision turns on social utility in the ordinary sense: on the efficient use of common means for common ends whose benefits are impartially distributed, or in connection with which the question of distribution is misplaced, as in the case of maintaining public order, or national defense. But as an interpretation of the basis of the principles of justice the utilitarian conception is mistaken. It can lead one to argue against slavery on the grounds that the advantages to the slaveholder do not counterbalance the disadvantages to the slave and to society at large burdened by a comparatively inefficient system of labor. The conception of justice as fairness, when applied to the offices of slaveholder and slave, would forbid counting the advantages of the slaveholder at all. These offices could not be founded on principles which could be mutually acknowledged, so the question whether the slaveholder's gains are great enough to counterbalance the losses to the slave and society cannot arise in the first place.

The difference between the two conceptions is whether justice is a fundamental moral concept arising directly from the reciprocal relations of persons engaging in common practices, and its principles those which persons similarly circumstanced could mutually acknowledge; or whether justice is derivative from a kind of higher order executive decision as to the most efficient design of institutions conceived as general devices for distributing benefits to individuals the worth of whose interests is defined independently of their relations to each other. Now even if the social utility function is constructed so that the practices chosen by it would be just, at least under normal circumstances, there is still the further argument against the utilitarian conception that the various restrictions on the utility function needed to get this result are borrowed from the conception of justice as fairness. The notion that individuals have similar utility functions, for example, is really the first principle of justice under the guise of a psychological law. It is assumed not in the manner of an empirical hypothesis concerning actual desires and interests, but from sensing what must be laid down if justice is not to be violated. There is, indeed, irony in this conclusion; for utilitarians attacked the notion of the original contract not only as a historical fiction but as a superfluous hypothesis: they thought that utility alone provides sufficient grounds for all social obligation, and is in any case the real basis of contractual obligations. But this is not so unless one's conception of social utility embodies within it restrictions whose basis can be understood only if one makes reference to one of the ideas of contractarian thought: that persons must be regarded as possessing an original and equal liberty, and their common practices are unjust unless they accord with principles which persons so circumstanced and related could freely accept.

Part Three / FREEDOM AND RESPONSIBILITY

I N *many respects, Aristotle's* Ethics *is the classical text most admired by contemporary analysts of ethical issues. In no respect is this more obvious than in their exploration of what may be termed moral psychology—that is, of those aspects of action, volition, and thought that have to do with the responsible conduct of an ethical agent. The revival of a comprehensive philosophical psychology in our own day is largely due to the stimulation of Wittgenstein and Ryle. And the accumulating findings of this now flourishing and very busy branch of philosophy have been freshly and effectively applied to a number of distinct, traditional questions of philosophical ethics.*

The central themes are clear. In the setting of ethical issues, we are concerned primarily with judging human actions, although we also permit our judgments to range over questions of character and intentions. In particular, we are interested in the responsibility of men for the acts they commit and in the conditions of freedom, deliberation, desire, and choice that are presupposed by our concept of responsibility. Finally, we are interested in the conditions and implications of efforts to influence or cause changes in behavior in the direction of acceptable ethical conduct.

Traditionally, many of the relevant debates have centered on the possibility and nature of human freedom. The classic form of this issue has always been occupied with the compatibility of freedom and causality. This is, for instance, the form the issue has taken in the influential discussion of J. S. Mill, which has been either refined or resisted in a variety of ways in our own time (e.g., Schlick, Nowell-Smith, Campbell, Chisholm). More recently, the matter has been construed in more narrowly linguistic terms (e.g., Nowell-Smith, Austin). And the burden of the question has been shifted increasingly on to the analysis of the concept of a human action—which may fairly be regarded as the central theme of the new philosophical psychology (e.g., Ryle, Peters, Melden, Anscombe, Hampshire). The problem here has been to distinguish between full-fledged actions and mere happenings, which has required a refinement of our understanding of the relation between volition and human behavior. The classical puzzles were focused for contemporary study by the early analysis of H. A. Prichard; the discussion has inevitably returned us to an examination of rules and of exception from blame—which are issues very close to the heart of Aristotle's discussion of volition.

The question of punishment has played a somewhat curious role in the history of ethical theory. It enters into the discussion of moral psychology because it is characteristically taken to be involved with the problem of influence or causation, and therefore to raise questions about the nature of freedom (e.g., Schlick, Nowell-Smith). On the other hand, punishment is a prominent feature of ethical and legal practice, and the question of its justifiability provides a most realistic arena within which the contest between broadly utilitarian and deontological approaches may be studied in close detail (e.g., Mabbott, Quinton, Baier, Benn). In fact, the adequacy of a comprehensive ethical principle can be tested quite naturally in terms of the light it throws on the puzzles regarding punishment.

IS 'FREE WILL' A PSEUDO-PROBLEM? / C. A. Campbell

[1]

IN THE days when the Verifiability Principle was accepted by its devotees as a secure philosophical truth, one could understand, though one might not agree with, the sweeping claim that many of the traditional problems of philosophy had been shown to be mere 'pseudo-problems.' It was easy to see how, given the Principle's validity, most of the leading questions which agitated our forefathers in metaphysics, in ethics, and in theology, automatically become nonsensical questions. What is perplexing, however, is that despite the pretty generally acknowledged deterioration in the Principle's status to that of a convenient methodological postulate, the attitude to these same questions seems to have changed but little. To admit that the Verifiability Principle is not an assured truth entails the admission that a problem can no longer be dismissed as meaningless simply on the ground that it cannot be stated in a way which satisfies the Principle. Whether or not a problem is meaningless is now something that can only be decided after critical examination of the particular case on its own individual merits. But the old antipathies seem in large

From C. A. Campbell, "Is 'Free Will' a Pseudo-Problem?" Mind, LX (1951), 686–706. Reprinted by permission of the Editor of Mind.

measure to have survived the disappearance of their logical basis. One gets the impression that for at least many thinkers with Positivist sympathies the 'liquidation' of a large, if unspecified, group of traditional philosophic problems is still established fact. If that impression is mistaken, well and good. One may then hope for an early recrudescence of interest in certain problems that have too long suffered the consequences of an unhappy *tabu*. If the impression is correct, a real service would be done to philosophy if it were plainly stated which of the traditional problems are still regarded as pseudo-problems, and what are the reasons, old or new, for passing this sentence upon them. The smoke of old battles, perhaps understandably, darkens the philosophic air, to the considerable inconvenience of all concerned.

Fortunately, however, the obscurity complained of is not totally unrelieved. We do know of one traditional problem that is definitely on the black list of the *avant garde*—the problem of 'Free Will': and we do have pretty adequate information about the reasons which have led to its being placed thereon. This, so far as it goes, is satisfactory. A plain obligation now lies upon philosophers who still believe that 'Free Will' is a genuine problem to explain just where, in their opinion, the case for the prosecution breaks down. To discharge this obligation is the main purpose of the present paper.

There will be a clear advantage in making our start from the *locus classicus* of the 'pseudo-problem' theory, if *locus classicus* there be. And I think that there must be something of the sort. At any rate, the casual, and indeed slightly bored, tones in which so many contemporary philosophers allude to the traditional problem, and their contentment to indicate in only a sketchy manner the reasons why it no longer exists, strongly suggest that *somewhere* the matter has in their eyes been already effectively settled. At least one important 'document in the case' is, I suspect, Chapter VII of Moritz Schlick's *Problems of Ethics*, first published in 1931. This chapter, the title of which is 'When is a Man Responsible?' and the first section of which bears the heading 'The Pseudo-problem of Freedom of the Will,' presents in concentrated form, but with some show of systematic argument, most of the considerations upon which later writers appear to rely. It will be worth our while, therefore, to try to see just why Professor Schlick is so sure (and he is *very* sure indeed) that 'Free Will,' as traditionally formulated, is a pseudo-problem, begotten by mere confusion of mind.

[II]

I shall first summarise, as faithfully as I can, what I take to be the distinctive points in Schlick's argument.

The traditional formulation of the problem, Schlick points out, is based on the assumption that to have 'free will' entails having a will that is, at least sometimes, exempt from causal law. It is traditionally supposed, quite rightly, that moral responsibility implies freedom in *some* sense: and it is supposed, also quite rightly, that this sense is one which is incompatible with compulsion. But because it is further supposed, quite *wrongly*, that to be subject to causal or natural law is to be subject to compulsion, the inference is drawn that the free will implied in moral responsibility is incompatible with causal continuity. The ultimate root of the error, Schlick contends, lies in a failure to distinguish between two different kinds of Law, one of which does indeed 'compel,' but the other of which does *not*.[1] There are, first, *pre*scriptive laws, such as the laws imposed by civil authority, which presume contrary desires on the part of those to whom they are applied; and these may fairly be said to exercise 'compulsion.' And there are, secondly, *de*scriptive laws, such as the laws which the sciences seek to formulate; and these merely state what does as a matter of fact always happen. It is perfectly clear that the relation of the latter, the natural, causal laws, to human willing is radically different from the 'compulsive' relation of prescriptive laws to human willing, and that it is really an absurdity to talk of a species of natural law like, say, psychological laws, *compelling* us to act in this or that way. The

---

[1] *Problems of Ethics*, Ch. VIII. Section 2. (All references are to the English translation by David Rynin, published in New York in 1939.)

term 'compulsion' is totally inept where, as in this case, there
are no contrary desires. But the traditional discussions of Free
Will, confusing descriptive with prescriptive laws, fallaciously
assume 'compulsion' to be ingredient in Law as such, and it is
contended accordingly that moral freedom, since it certainly implies absence of compulsion, implies also exemption from causal
law.

It follows that the problem of Free Will, as traditionally
stated, is a mere pseudo-problem. The statement of it in terms of
exemption from causal law rests on the assumption that causal
law involves 'compulsion.' And this assumption is demonstrably
false. Expose the muddle from which it arises and the so-called
'problem' in its traditional form disappears.

But is it quite certain that the freedom which moral responsibility implies is no more than 'the absence of compulsion'? This is the premise upon which Schlick's argument proceeds, but Schlick is himself well aware that it stands in need of
confirmation from an analysis of the notion of moral responsibility. Otherwise it might be maintained that although 'the absence
of compulsion' has been shown not to entail a contra-causal type
of freedom, there is nevertheless some *other* condition of moral
responsibility that *does* entail it. Accordingly Schlick embarks
now upon a formal analysis of the nature and conditions of
moral responsibility designed to show that the *only* freedom implied by moral responsibility is freedom from compulsion. It was
a trifle ambitious, however, even for a master of compression
like Professor Schlick, to hope to deal satisfactorily in half-a-
dozen very brief pages with a topic which has been so exten-
sively debated in the literature of moral philosophy: and I cannot pretend that I find what he has to say free from obscurity.
But to the best of my belief what follows does reproduce the gist
of Schlick's analysis.

What precisely, Schlick asks, does the term 'moral responsibility' mean in our ordinary linguistic usage? [2] He begins
his answer by insisting upon the close connection for ordinary

2 *Loc. cit.*, Ch. VII, Section 5.

usage between 'moral responsibility' and *punishment* (strictly speaking, punishment and *reward:* but for convenience Schlick virtually confines the discussion to punishment, and we shall do the same). The connection, as Schlick sees it, is this. In ordinary practice our concern with the responsibility for an act (he tells us) is with a view to determining *who is to be punished for it.* Now punishment is (I quote) 'an educative measure.' It is 'a means to the formation of motives, which are in part to prevent the wrong-doer from repeating the act (reformation), and in part to prevent others from committing a similar act (intimidation).' [3] When we ask, then, 'Who in a given case is to be punished?'—which is the same as the question 'Who is responsible?'—what we are really wanting to discover is some agent in the situation upon whose motives we can bring to bear the appropriate educative influences, so that in similar situations in future his strongest motive will impel him to refrain from, rather than to repeat, the act. 'The question of who is responsible' Schlick sums up, 'is . . . a matter only of knowing who is to be punished or rewarded, in order that punishment and reward function as such—be able to achieve their goal.' [4] It is not a matter, he expressly declares, of trying to ascertain what may be called the 'original instigator' of the act. That might be a great-grand-parent, from the consequence of whose behaviour vicious tendencies have been inherited by a living person. Such 'remote causes' as this are irrelevant to questions of punishment (and so to questions of moral responsibility), 'for in the first place their actual contribution cannot be determined, and in the second place they are generally out of reach.' [5]

It is a matter for regret that Schlick has not rounded off his discussion, as one had hoped and expected he would, by formulating a precise definition of moral responsibility in terms of what he has been saying. I think, however, that the conclusion to which his argument leads could be not unfairly expressed in

[3] *Ibid.*, p. 152.
[4] *Ibid.*, p. 153.
[5] *Ibid.*, p. 153.

some such way as this: 'We say that a man is morally responsible for an act if his motives for bringing about the act are such
as we can affect favourably in respect of his future behaviour by
the educative influences of reward and punishment.'

Given the truth of this analysis of moral responsibility,
Schlick's contention follows logically enough that the only freedom that is required for moral responsibility is freedom from
compulsion. For what are the cases in which a man's motives are
not capable of being favourably affected by reward and punishment?—the cases in which, that is, according to Schlick's analysis, we do not deem him morally responsible? The only such
cases, it would seem, are those in which a man is subjected to
some form of external constraint which prevents him from acting according to his 'natural desires.' For example, if a man is
compelled by a pistol at his breast to do a certain act, or induced
to do it by an externally administered narcotic, he is not 'morally responsible'; or not, at any rate, in so far as punishment
would be impotent to affect his motives in respect of his future
behaviour. External constraint in one form or another seems to
be the sole circumstance which absolves a man from moral responsibility. Hence we may say that freedom from external constraint is the only sort of freedom which an agent must possess
in order to be morally responsible. The 'contra-causal' sort of
freedom which so many philosophers and others have supposed
to be required is shown by a true analysis of moral responsibility
to be irrelevant.

This completes the argument that 'Free Will,' as traditionally formulated, is a pseudo-problem. The only freedom implied by moral responsibility is freedom from compulsion; and
as we have rid ourselves of the myth that subjection to causal
law is a form of compulsion, we can see that the only compulsion which absolves from moral responsibility is the external
constraint which prevents us from translating our desires into
action. The true meaning of the question 'Have we free will?'
thus becomes simply 'Can we translate our desires into action?'
And this question does not constitute a 'problem' at all, for the
answer to it is not in doubt. The obvious answer is 'Sometimes

we can, sometimes we can't, according to the specific circumstances of the case.'

[III]

Here, then, in substance is Schlick's theory. Let us now examine it.

In the first place, it is surely quite unplausible to suggest that the common assumption that moral freedom postulates some breach of causal continuity arises from a confusion of two different types of law. Schlick's distinction between descriptive and prescriptive law is, of course, sound. It was no doubt worth pointing out, too, that descriptive laws cannot be said to 'compel' human behaviour in the same way as prescriptive laws do. But it seems to me evident that the usual reason why it is held that moral freedom implies some breach of causal continuity, is not a belief that causal laws 'compel' as civil laws 'compel,' but simply the belief that the admission of unbroken causal continuity entails a *further* admission which is directly incompatible with moral responsibility; viz. the admission that no man could have acted otherwise than he in fact did. Now it may, of course, be an error thus to assume that a man is not morally responsible for an act, a fit subject for moral praise and blame in respect of it, unless he could have acted otherwise than he did. Or, if *this* is not an error, it may still be an error to assume that a man could not have acted otherwise than he did, in the sense of the phrase that is crucial for moral responsibility, without there occurring some breach of causal continuity. Into these matters we shall have to enter very fully at a later stage. But the relevant point at the moment is that these (not *prima facie* absurd) assumptions about the conditions of moral responsibility have very commonly, indeed normally, been made, and that they are entirely adequate to explain why the problem of Free Will finds its usual formulation in terms of partial exemption from causal law. Schlick's distinction between prescriptive and descriptive laws has no bearing at all upon the truth or falsity of these assumptions. Yet if these assumptions are accepted, it is (I suggest) really inevitable that the Free Will problem should be formu-

lated in the way to which Schlick takes exception. Recognition of
the distinction upon which Schlick and his followers lay so much
stress can make not a jot of difference.

As we have seen, however, Schlick does later proceed to
the much more important business of disputing these common
assumptions about the conditions of moral responsibility. He
offers us an analysis of moral responsibility which flatly contradicts these assumptions; an analysis according to which the only
freedom demanded by morality is a freedom which is compatible
with Determinism. If this analysis can be sustained, there is certainly no problem of 'Free Will' in the traditional sense.

But it seems a simple matter to show that Schlick's analysis is untenable. Let us test it by Schlick's own claim that it
gives us what we mean by 'moral responsibility' in ordinary linguistic usage.

We do not ordinarily consider the lower animals to be
morally responsible. But *ought* we not to do so if Schlick is right
about what we mean by moral responsibility? It is quite possible,
by punishing the dog who absconds with the succulent chops
designed for its master's luncheon, favourably to influence its
motives in respect of its future behaviour in like circumstances.
If moral responsibility is to be linked with punishment as Schlick
links it, and punishment conceived as a form of education, we
should surely hold the dog morally responsible? The plain fact,
of course, is that we don't. We don't, because we suppose that
the dog 'couldn't help it': that its action (unlike what we usually believe to be true of human beings) was simply a link in a
continuous chain of causes and effects. In other words, we do
commonly demand the contra-causal sort of freedom as a condition of moral responsibility.

Again, we do ordinarily consider it proper, in certain circumstances, to speak of a person no longer living as morally
responsible for some present situation. But *ought* we to do so
if we accept Schlick's essentially 'forward-looking' interpretation of punishment and responsibility? Clearly we cannot now
favourably affect the dead man's motives. No doubt they could *at
one time* have been favourably affected. But that cannot be rele-

vant to our judgment of responsibility if, as Schlick insists, the question of who is responsible 'is a matter only of knowing who is to be punished or rewarded.' Indeed he expressly tells us, as we saw earlier, that in asking this question we are not concerned with a 'great-grand-parent' who may have been the 'original instigator,' because, for one reason, this 'remote cause' is 'out of reach.' We cannot bring the appropriate educative influence to bear upon it. But the plain fact, of course, is that we do frequently assign moral responsibility for present situations to persons who have long been inaccessible to any punitive action on our part. And Schlick's position is still more paradoxical in respect of our apportionment of responsibility for occurrences in the distant past. Since in these cases there is no agent whatsoever whom we can favourably influence by punishment, the question of moral responsibility here should have no meaning for us. But of course it has. Historical writings are studded with examples.

Possibly the criticism just made may seem to some to result from taking Schlick's analysis too much *au pied de la lettre*. The absurd consequences deduced, it may be said, would not follow if we interpreted Schlick as meaning that a man is morally responsible where his motive is such as can *in principle* be favourably affected by a reward or punishment—whether or not we who pass the judgment are in a position to take such action. But with every desire to be fair to Schlick, I cannot see how he could accept this modification and still retain the essence of his theory. For the essence of his theory seems to be that moral responsibility has its whole meaning and importance for us in relation to our potential control of future conduct in the interests of society. (I agree that it is hard to believe that anybody *really* thinks this. But it is perhaps less hard to believe to-day than it has ever been before in the history of modern ethics.)

Again, we ordinarily consider that, in certain circumstances, the *degree* of a man's moral responsibility for an act is affected by considerations of his inherited nature, or of his environment, or of both. It is our normal habit to 'make allowances' (as we say) when we have reason to believe that a malefactor

had a vicious heredity, or was nurtured in his formative years in
a harmful environment. We say in such cases 'Poor chap, he is
more to be pitied than blamed. We could scarcely expect him to
behave like a decent citizen with *his* parentage or upbringing.'
But this extremely common sort of judgment has no point at all
if we mean by moral responsibility what Schlick says that we
mean. On *that* meaning the degree of a man's moral responsibility must presumably be dependent upon the degree to which we
can favourably affect his future motives, which is quite another
matter. Now there is no reason to believe that the motives of a
man with a bad heredity or a bad upbringing are either less or
more subject to educative influence than those of his more fortunate fellows. Yet it is plain matter of fact that we do commonly
consider the degree of a man's moral responsibility to be affected
by these two factors.

A final point. The extremity of paradox in Schlick's
identification of the question 'Who is morally blameworthy?'
with the question 'Who is to be punished?' is apt to be partially
concealed from us just because it is our normal habit to include
in the meaning of 'punishment' an element of 'requital for
moral transgression' which Schlick expressly denies to it. On
that account we commonly think of 'punishment,' in its strict
sense, as implying moral blameworthiness in the person punished. But if we remember to mean by punishment what Schlick
means by it, a purely 'educative measure,' with no retributive
ingredients, his identification of the two questions loses such
plausibility as it might otherwise have. For clearly we often
think it proper to 'punish' a person, in *Schlick*'s sense, where we
are not at all prepared to say that the person is morally blameworthy. We may even think him morally commendable. A case
in point would be the unmistakably sincere but muddleheaded
person who at the cost of great suffering to himself steadfastly
pursues as his 'duty' a course which, in our judgment, is fraught
with danger to the common weal. We should most of us feel
entitled, in the public interest, to bring such action to bear
upon the man's motives as might induce him to refrain in future
from his socially injurious behaviour: in other words, to inflict

upon him what Schlick would call 'punishment.' But we should most of us feel perfectly clear that in so 'punishing' this misguided citizen we are not proclaiming his moral blameworthiness for moral wickedness.

Adopting Schlick's own criterion, then, looking simply 'to the manner in which the concept is used,' [6] we seem bound to admit that constantly people do assign moral responsibility where Schlick's theory says they shouldn't, don't assign moral responsibility where Schlick's theory says they should, and assign degrees of moral responsibility where on Schlick's theory there should be no difference in degree. I think we may reasonably conclude that Schlick's account of what we mean by moral responsibility breaks down.

The rebuttal of Schlick's arguments, however, will not suffice of itself to refute the pseudo-problem theory. The indebtedness to Schlick of most later advocates of the theory may be conceded; but certainly it does not comprehend all of significance that they have to say on the problem. There are recent analyses of the conditions of moral responsibility containing sufficient new matter, or sufficient old matter in a more precise and telling form, to require of us now something of a fresh start. In the section which follows I propose to consider some representative samples of these analyses—all of which, of course, are designed to show that the freedom which moral responsibility implies is not in fact a contra-causal type of freedom.

But before reopening the general question of the nature and conditions of moral responsibility there is a *caveat* which it seems to me worthwhile to enter. The difficulties in the way of a clear answer are not slight; but they are apt to seem a good deal more formidable than they really are because of a common tendency to consider in unduly close association two distinct questions: the question "Is a contra-causal type of freedom implied by moral responsibility?" and the question "Does a contra-causal type of freedom anywhere exist?" It seems to me that many philosophers (and I suspect that Moritz Schlick is among them) begin this inquiry with so firm a conviction that the contra-

[6] *Loc. cit.*, Ch. VII, Section 5, p. 151.

causal sort of freedom nowhere exists, that they find it hard to take very seriously the possibility that it is *this* sort of freedom that moral responsibility implies. For they are loath to abandon the common-sense belief that moral responsibility itself is something real. The implicit reasoning I take to be this. Moral responsibility is real. If moral responsibility is real, the freedom implied in it must be a fact. But contra-causal freedom is not a fact. Therefore contra-causal freedom is not the freedom implied in moral responsibility. I think we should be on our guard against allowing this or some similar train of reasoning (whose premises, after all, are far from indubitable) to seduce us into distorting what we actually find when we set about a direct analysis of moral responsibility and its conditions.

[IV]

The pseudo-problem theorists usually, and naturally, develop their analysis of moral responsibility by way of contrast with a view which, while it has enjoyed a good deal of philosophic support, I can best describe as the common view. It will be well to remind ourselves, therefore, of the main features of this view.

So far as the *meaning*, as distinct from the *conditions*, of moral responsibility is concerned, the common view is very simple. If we ask ourselves whether a certain person is morally responsible for a given act (or it may be just "in general"), what we are considering, it would be said, is whether or not that person is a fit subject upon whom to pass moral judgment; whether he can fittingly be deemed morally good or bad, morally praiseworthy or blameworthy. This does not take us any great way; but (*pace* Schlick) so far as it goes it does not seem to me seriously disputable. The really interesting and controversial question is about the *conditions* of moral responsibility, and in particular the question whether freedom of a contra-causal kind is among these conditions.

The answer of the common man to the latter question is that it most certainly *is* among the conditions. Why does he feel so sure about this? Not, I argued earlier, because the common man supposes that causal law exercises 'compulsion' in the sense that prescriptive laws do, but simply because he does not see how a person can be deemed morally praiseworthy or blameworthy in respect of an act which he could not help performing. From the stand-point of moral praise and blame, he would say—though not necessarily from other stand-points—it is a matter of indifference whether it is by reason of some external constraint or by reason of his own given nature that the man could not help doing what he did. It is quite enough to make moral praise and blame futile that in either case there were no genuine alternatives, no open possibilities, before the man when he acted. He could not have acted otherwise than he did. And the common man might not unreasonably go on to stress the fact that we all, even if we are linguistic philosophers, do in our actual practice of moral judgement appear to accept the common view. He might insist upon the point alluded to earlier in this paper, that we do all, in passing moral censure, 'make allowances' for influences in a man's hereditary nature or environmental circumstances which we regard as having made it more than ordinarily difficult for him to act otherwise than he did: the implication being that if we supposed that the man's heredity and environment made it not merely very *difficult* but actually *impossible* for him to act otherwise than he did, we could not properly assign moral blame to him at all.

Let us put the argument implicit in the common view a little more sharply. The moral 'ought' implies 'can.' If we say that A morally ought to have done X, we imply that in our opinion, he could have done X. But we assign moral blame to a man only for failing to do what we think he morally ought to have done. Hence if we morally blame A for not having done X, we imply that he could have done X even though in fact he did not. In other words, we imply that A could have acted otherwise than he did. And that means that we imply, as a necessary condition of a man's being morally blameworthy, that he enjoyed a freedom of a kind not compatible with unbroken causal continuity.

[v]

Now what is it that is supposed to be wrong with this simple piece of argument?—For, of course, it must be rejected by all these philosophers who tell us that the traditional problem of Free Will is a mere pseudo-problem. The argument looks as though it were doing little more than reading off necessary implications of the fundamental categories of our moral thinking. One's inclination is to ask 'If one is to think morally at all, how else than this *can* we think?'

In point of fact, there is pretty general agreement among the contemporary critics as to what is wrong with the argument. Their answer in general terms is as follows. No doubt A's moral responsibility does imply that he could have acted otherwise. But this expression 'could have acted otherwise' stands in dire need of analysis. When we analyse it, we find that it is not, as is so often supposed, simple and unambiguous, and we find that in *some* at least of its possible meanings it implies *no* breach of causal continuity between character and conduct. Having got this clear, we can further discern that only in one of these *latter* meanings is there any compulsion upon our moral thinking to assert that if A is morally blameworthy for an act, A 'could have acted otherwise than he did.' It follows that, contrary to common belief, our moral thinking does *not* require us to posit a contra-causal freedom as a condition of moral responsibility.

So much of importance obviously turns upon the validity or otherwise of this line of criticism that we must examine it in some detail and with express regard to the *ipsissima verba* of the critics.

In the course of a recent article in *Mind*,[7] entitled 'Free Will and Moral Responsibility,' Mr. Nowell-Smith (having earlier affirmed his belief that 'the traditional problem has been solved') explains very concisely the nature of the confusion which, as he thinks, has led to the demand for a contra-causal freedom. He begins by frankly recognising that 'It is evident

7 January, 1948.

that one of the necessary conditions of moral action is that the agent "could have acted otherwise"' and he adds 'it is to this fact that the Libertarian is drawing attention.' [8] Then, after showing (unexceptionably, I think) how the relationship of 'ought' to 'can' warrants the proposition which he has accepted as evident, and how it induces the Libertarian to assert the existence of action that is 'uncaused,' he proceeds to point out, in a crucial passage, the nature of the Libertarian's error:

The fallacy in the argument (he contends) lies in supposing that when we say 'A could have acted otherwise' we mean that A, *being what he was and being placed in the circumstances in which he was placed,* could have done something other than what he did. But in fact we never do mean this.[9]

What then *do* we mean here by 'A could have acted otherwise'? Mr. Nowell-Smith does not tell us in so many words, but the passage I have quoted leaves little doubt how he would answer. What we really mean by the expression, he implies, is not a *categorical* but a *hypothetical* proposition. We mean 'A could have acted otherwise, *if he did not happen to be what he in fact was,* or *if he were placed in circumstances other than those in which he was in fact placed.*' Now, *these* propositions, it is easy to see, are in no way incompatible with acceptance of the causal principle in its full rigour. Accordingly the claim that our fundamental moral thinking obliges us to assert a contra-causal freedom as a condition of moral responsibility is disproved.

Such is the 'analytical solution' of our problem offered (with obvious confidence) by one able philosopher of to-day, and entirely representative of the views of many other able philosophers. Yet I make bold to say that its falsity stares one in the face. It seems perfectly plain that the hypothetical propositions which Mr. Nowell-Smith proposes to substitute for the categorical proposition cannot express 'what we really mean' in this context by 'A could have acted otherwise,' for the simple reason that these hypothetical propositions have no bearing whatsoever

[8] *Loc. cit.,* p. 49.
[9] *Loc. cit.,* p. 49.

upon the question of the moral responsibility of A. And it is A whose moral responsibility we are talking about—a definite person A with a definitive character and in a definitive set of circumstances. What conceivable significance could it have for our attitude to A's responsibility to know that someone with a *different* character (or A with a different character, if that collocation of words has any meaning), or A in a different set of circumstances from those in which A as we are concerned with him was in fact placed, 'could have acted otherwise'? No doubt this supposititious being *could* have acted otherwise than the definitive person A acted. But the point is that where we are reflecting, as we are supposed in this context to be reflecting, upon the question of A's moral responsibility, our interest in this supposititious being is precisely *nil*.

The two hypothetical propositions suggested in Mr. Nowell-Smith's account of the matter do not, however, exhaust the speculations that have been made along these lines. Another very common suggestion by the analysts is that what we really mean by 'A could have acted otherwise' is 'A could have acted otherwise *if he had willed, or chosen, otherwise.*' This was among the suggestions offered by G. E. Moore in the well-known chapter on Free Will in his *Ethics*. It is, I think, the suggestion he most strongly favoured: though it is fair to add that neither about this nor about any other of his suggestions is Moore in the least dogmatic. He does claim, for, I think, convincing reasons, that "we *very often* mean by 'could' merely 'would, *if* so-and-so had chosen.' " [10] And he concludes "I must confess that I cannot feel certain that this may not be all that we usually mean and understand by the assertion that we have Free Will." [11]

This third hypothetical proposition appears to enjoy also the support of Mr. C. L. Stevenson. Mr. Stevenson begins the chapter of *Ethics and Language* entitled 'Avoidability-Indeterminism' with the now familiar pronouncement of his School that 'controversy about freedom and determinism of the will . . . presents no permanent difficulty to ethics, being largely a

10 *Ethics*, p. 212.
11 *Loc. cit.*, p. 217.

product of confusions.' A major confusion (if I understand him rightly) he takes to lie in the meaning of the term 'avoidable,' when we say 'A's action was avoidable'—or, I presume, 'A could have acted otherwise.' He himself offers the following definition of 'avoidable'—"A's action was avoidable" has the meaning of "If A had made a certain choice, which in fact he did not make, his action would not have occurred." [12] This I think we may regard as in substance identical with the suggestion that what we really mean by 'A could have acted otherwise' is 'A could have acted otherwise *if* he had chosen (or willed) otherwise.' For clarity's sake we shall here keep to this earlier formulation. In either formulation the special significance of the third hypothetical proposition, as of the two hypothetical propositions already considered, is that it is compatible with strict determinism. If this be indeed all that we mean by the 'freedom' that conditions moral responsibility, then those philosophers are certainly wrong who hold that moral freedom is of the contra-causal type.

Now this third hypothetical proposition does at least possess the merit, not shared by its predecessors, of having a real relevance to the question of moral responsibility. If, e.g. A had promised to meet us at 2 P.M., and he chanced to break his leg at 1 P.M., we should not blame him for his failure to discharge his promise. For we should be satisfied that he *could not* have acted otherwise, even if he had so chosen; or *could not*, at any rate, in a way which would have enabled him to meet us at 2 P.M. The freedom to translate one's choice into action, which we saw earlier is for Schlick the *only* freedom required for moral responsibility, is without doubt *one* of the conditions of moral responsibility.

But it seems easy to show that this third hypothetical proposition does not exhaust what we mean, and *some*times is not even *part* of what we mean, by the expression 'could have acted otherwise' in its moral context. Thus it can hardly be even part of what we mean in the case of that class of wrong actions (and it is a large class) concerning which there is really no question whether the agent could have acted otherwise, *if* he had

[12] *Ethics and Language*, p. 298.

chosen otherwise. Take lying, for example. Only in some very
abnormal situation could it occur to one to doubt whether A,
whose power of speech was evinced by his telling a lie, was in a
position to tell what he took to be the truth *if* he had so chosen.
Of *course* he was. Yet it still makes good sense for one's moral
thinking to ask whether A, when lying, 'could have acted otherwise': and we still require an affirmative answer to this question
if A's moral blameworthiness is to be established. It seems apparent, therefore, that in this class of cases at any rate one does
not mean by 'A could have acted otherwise,' 'A could have acted
otherwise *if* he had so chosen.'

What then *does* one mean in this class of cases by 'A
could have acted otherwise'? I submit that the expression is
taken in its simple, categorical meaning, without any suppressed
'if' clause to qualify it. Or perhaps, in order to keep before us
the important truth that it is only as expressions of *will* or *choice*
that acts are of moral import, it might be better to say that a
condition of A's moral responsibility is that he could have *chosen*
otherwise. We saw that there is no real question whether A who
told a lie could have acted otherwise *if* he had chosen otherwise.
But there is a very real question, at least for any person who
approaches the question of moral responsibility at a tolerably
advanced level of reflection, about whether A could have *chosen*
otherwise. Such a person will doubtless be acquainted with the
claims advanced in some quarters that causal law operates universally: or/and with the theories of some philosophies that the
universe is throughout the expression of a single supreme principle; or/and with the doctrines of some theologians that the
world is created, sustained and governed by an Omniscient and
Omnipotent Being. Very understandably such world-views
awaken in him doubts about the validity of his first, easy, instinctive assumption that there are genuinely open possibilities
before a man at the moment of moral choice. It thus becomes for
him a real question whether a man could have chosen otherwise
than he actually did, and in consequence, whether man's moral
responsibility is really defensible. For how can a man be morally
responsible, he asks himself, if his choices, like all other events

in the universe, could not have been otherwise than they in fact were? It is precisely against the background of world-views such as these that for reflective people the problem of moral responsibility normally arises.

Furthermore, to the man who has attained this level of reflection, it will in *no* class of cases be a sufficient condition of moral responsibility for an act that one could have acted otherwise *if* one had chosen otherwise—not even in these cases where there *was* some possibility of the operation of 'external constraint.' In these cases he will, indeed, expressly recognise freedom from external constraint as a *necessary condition*, but not as a *sufficient* condition. For he will be aware that, even granted *this* freedom, it is still conceivable that the agent had no freedom to choose otherwise than he did, and he will therefore require that the latter sort of freedom be added if moral responsibility for the act is to be established.

I have been contending that, for persons at a *tolerably advanced level of reflection*, 'A could have acted otherwise,' as a condition of A's moral responsibility, means 'A could have chosen otherwise.' The qualification italicised is of some importance. The unreflective or unsophisticated person, the ordinary 'man in the street,' who does not know or much care what scientists and theologians and philosophers have said about the world, sees well enough that A is morally responsible only if he could have acted otherwise, but in his intellectual innocence he will, very probably, envisage nothing capable of preventing A from having acted otherwise except some material impediment —like the broken leg in the example above. Accordingly, for the unreflective person, 'A could have acted otherwise,' as a condition of moral responsibility, *is* apt to mean no more than 'A could have acted otherwise if he had so chosen.'

It would appear, then, that the view now favoured by many philosophers, that the freedom required for moral responsibility is merely freedom from external constraint, is a view which they share only with the less reflective type of layman. Yet it should be plain that on a matter of this sort the view of the unreflective person is of little value by comparison with the view of the reflective person. There are some contexts, no doubt, in which lack of sophistication is an asset. But this is not one of them. The question at issue here is as to the kind of impediments which might have prevented a man from acting otherwise than he in fact did; and on this question knowledge and reflection are surely prerequisites of any answer that is worth listening to. It is simply on account of the limitations of his mental vision that the unreflective man interprets the expression 'could have acted otherwise,' in its context as a condition of moral responsibility, solely in terms of external constraint. He has failed (as yet) to reach the intellectual level at which one takes into account the implications for moral choices of the world-views of science, religion, and philosophy. If on a matter of this complexity the philosopher finds that his analysis accords with the utterances of the uneducated he has, I suggest, better cause for uneasiness than for self-congratulation.

This concludes the main part of what it seems to me necessary to say in answer to the pseudo-problem theorists. My object so far has been to expose the falsity of those innovations (chiefly Positivist) in the way of argument and analysis which are supposed by many to have made it impossible any longer to formulate the problem of Free Will in the traditional manner. My contention is that, at least so far as these innovations are concerned, the simple time-honoured argument still holds from the nature of the moral ought to the conclusion that moral responsibility implies a contra-causal type of freedom. The attempts to avoid that conclusion by analysing the proposition 'A could have acted otherwise' (acknowledged to be implied in *some* sense in A's moral responsibility) into one or other of certain hypothetical propositions which are compatible with unbroken causal continuity, break down hopelessly when tested against the touchstone of actual moral thinking. It is, I think, not necessary to defend the procedure of testing hypotheses in the ethical field by bringing to bear upon them our actual moral thinking. If there is any other form of test applicable, I should be much interested to learn what it is supposed to be. Certainly 'logical analysis' *per se* will not do. That has a function, but a function that can only be ancillary. For what we are seeking to know is the meaning of the expression 'could have acted otherwise' not *in the abstract,* but in the context of the question of man's *moral responsibility.* Logical analysis *per se* is impotent to give us this information. It can be of value only in so far as it operates within the orbit of 'the moral consciousness.' One may admit, with some qualifications, that on a matter of this sort the moral consciousness without logical analysis is blind: but it seems to me to be true without any qualification whatsoever that, on the same problem, logical analysis without the moral consciousness is empty.

[VI]

There are times when what seems to a critic the very strength of his case breeds mistrust in the critic's own mind. I confess that in making the criticisms that have preceded I have not been altogether free from uncomfortable feelings of this kind. For the arguments I have criticised, and more particularly the analyses of the conditions of moral responsibility, seem to me to be in many cases quite desperately unplausible. Such a state of affairs ought, I think, to give the critic pause. The thought must at least enter his mind (unless he be a total stranger to modesty) that perhaps, despite his best efforts to be fair, he has after all misrepresented what his opponents are saying. No doubt a similar thought will enter, and perhaps find lodgment in, the minds of many readers.

In this situation there is, however, one course by which the critic may reasonably hope to allay these natural suspicions. He should consider whether there may not be certain predisposing influences at work, extrinsic to the specific arguments, which could have the effect of blinding the proponents of these arguments to their intrinsic demerits. If so, he need not be too much disquieted by the seeming weakness of the case against him. For it is a commonplace that, once in the grip of general prepossessions, even very good philosophers sometimes avail themselves of very bad arguments.

Actually, we can, I think, discern at least two such influ-

ences operating powerfully in the case before us. One is sympathy with the general tenets of Positivism. The other is the conviction already alluded to, that man does not in fact possess a
contra-causal type of freedom; whence follows a strong presumption that no such freedom is necessary to moral responsibility.

About the first of these influences I propose to say very
little. I wish merely to indicate how strict adherence to Positivist
tenets precludes one in principle from understanding moral
responsibility as the ordinary man understands it, and how Posi-
tivists are therefore bound, when they attempt to define the conditions of moral responsibility, to say things that seem monstrously unplausible.

That the Positivist—who has certainly not been drawn
initially to this way of philosophising by reflection upon the phenomena of the moral life—should approach the problems of ethical analysis with certain strong prepossessions, is only to be
expected. The most crucial of these is that (nontautologous) statements in this field, as in every other field, can have no meaning
—or at any rate no cognitive meaning—unless they are, at least
in principle, sensibly verifiable. The consequence of that prepos-
session must be to close the mind in advance, more or less absolutely according to the extent to which the Verifiability Principle
is maintained as unshakeable dogma, against the common view
of the moral ought—which happens also to be the view in terms
of which the problem of moral responsibility historically and habitually arises. For on this view the moral ought as apprehended
by the moral consciousness is most certainly an object neither of
'outer' nor of 'inner' sense. One need not wonder, therefore,
that the Positivist should recommend analyses of the conditions
of moral responsibility, such as the hypothetical propositions
offered as the meaning of the expression 'could have acted otherwise,' which to anyone who understands the moral ought in
the ordinary way seem little short of fantastic. By an *a priori*
prejudice he has effectively debarred himself from appreciating
what ordinary men mean by moral obligation and moral responsibility. I cannot forbear adding that in view of the doom which

has so swiftly attended the very various attempts so far made to define moral obligation in Positivist terms, the case for at least a temporary suspension of belief in Positivist presuppositions in the ethical field would appear to be a strong one.

Of far wider and more permanent interest, in my judgment, is the second of the 'predisposing influences'—the conviction that there just *is* no contra-causal freedom such as is commonly alleged to be a condition of moral responsibility. A natural desire to 'save' moral responsibility issues, logically enough, in attempts to formulate its conditions in a manner compatible with unbroken causal continuity. The consequent analyses may be, as I have urged, very unsatisfactory. But there is no doubt that the conviction that motivates the analysis is supported by reasons of great weight: well-known arguments that are the property of no particular school and which most of us learned in our philosophical cradles. A very brief summary of what I take to be the most influential of these arguments will suffice for the comments I wish to make upon them.

A contra-causal freedom, it is argued, such as is implied in the 'categorical' interpretation of the proposition 'A could have chosen otherwise than he did,' posits a breach of causal continuity between a man's character and his conduct. Now apart from the general presumption in favour of the universality of causal law, there are special reasons for disallowing the breach that is here alleged. It is the common assumption of social intercourse that our acquaintances will act 'in character'; that their choices will exhibit the 'natural' response of their characters to the given situation. And this assumption seems to be amply substantiated, over a wide range of conduct, by the actual success which attends predictions made on this basis. Where there should be, on the contra-causal hypothesis, chaotic variability, there is found in fact a large measure of intelligible continuity. Moreover, what is the alternative to admitting that a person's choices flow from his character? Surely just that the so-called 'choice' is not *that person's* choice at all: that, relatively to the person concerned, it is a mere 'accident.' Now we cannot really believe this. But if it *were* the case, it would certainly not help to establish *moral* freedom, the freedom required for *moral* responsibility. For clearly a man cannot be morally responsible for an act which does not express his own choice but is, on the contrary, attributable simply to chance.

These are clearly considerations worthy of all respect. It is not surprising if they have played a big part in persuading people to respond sympathetically to the view that 'Free Will,' in its usual contra-causal formulation, is a pseudo-problem. A full answer to them is obviously not practicable in what is little more than an appendix to the body of this paper; but I am hopeful that something can be said, even in a little space, to show that they are very far from being as conclusive against a contra-causal freedom as they are often supposed to be.

To begin with the less troublesome of the two main objections indicated—the objection that the break in causal continuity which free will involves is inconsistent with the predictability of conduct on the basis of the agent's known character. All that is necessary to meet this objection, I suggest, is the frank recognition, which is perfectly open to the Libertarian, that there is a wide area of human conduct, determinable on clear general principles, within which free will does not effectively operate. The most important of these general principles (I have no space to deal here with the others) has often enough been stated by Libertarians. Free will does not operate in these practical situations in which no conflict arises in the agent's mind between what he conceives to be his 'duty' and what he feels to be his 'strongest desire.' It does not operate here because there just is no occasion for it to operate. There is no reason whatever why the agent should here even contemplate choosing any course other than that prescribed by his strongest desire. In all such situations, therefore, he naturally wills in accordance with strongest desire. But his 'strongest desire' is simply the specific *ad hoc* expression of that system of conative and emotive dispositions which we call his 'character.' In all such situations, therefore, whatever may be the case elsewhere, his will is in effect determined by his character as so far formed. Now when we bear in mind that there are an almost immeasurably greater number of situations in a man's life that conform to *this* pattern than there are situations in which an agent is aware of a conflict between strongest desire and duty, it is apparent that a Libertarianism which accepts the limitation of free will to the *latter* type of situation is not open to the stock objection on the score of 'predictability.' For there still remains a vast area of human behaviour in which prediction on the basis of known character may be expected to succeed: an area which will accommodate without difficulty, I think, all these empirical facts about successful prediction which the critic is apt to suppose fatal to Free Will.

So far as I can see, such a delimitation of the field of effective free will denies to the Libertarian absolutely nothing which matters to him. For it is precisely that small sector of the field of choices which our principle of delimitation still leaves open to free will—the sector in which strongest desire clashes with duty—that is crucial for moral responsibility. It is, I believe, with respect to such situations, and in the last resort to such situations alone, that the agent himself recognises that moral praise and blame are appropriate. They are appropriate, according as he does or does not 'rise to duty' in the face of opposing desires; always granted, that is, that he is free to choose between these courses as genuinely open possibilities. If the reality of freedom be conceded *here,* everything is conceded that the Libertarian has any real interest in securing.

But, of course, the most vital question is, can the reality of freedom be conceded even here? In particular, can the standard objection be met which we stated, that if the person's choice does not, in these situations as elsewhere, flow from his *character,* then it is not *that person's* choice at all?

This is, perhaps, of all the objections to a contra-causal freedom, the one which is generally felt to be the most conclusive. For the assumption upon which it is based, viz. that no intelligible meaning can attach to the claim that an act which is not an expression of the self's *character* may nevertheless be the *self's* act, is apt to be regarded as self-evident. The Libertarian is accordingly charged with being in effect an *Indeterminist,* whose 'free will,' in so far as it does not flow from the agent's charac-

ter, can only be a matter of 'chance.' Has the Libertarian—
who invariably repudiates this charge and claims to be a *Self-
determinist*—any way of showing that, contrary to the assumption of his critics, we *can* meaningfully talk of an act as the
self's act even though, in an important sense, it is not an expression of the self's 'character'?

I think that he has. I want to suggest that what prevents
the critics from finding a meaning in this way of talking is that
they are looking for it in the wrong way; or better, perhaps, with
the wrong orientation. They are looking for it from the stand-
point of the *external observer;* the stand-point proper to, because
alone possible for, apprehension of the physical world. Now
from the external stand-point we may observe processes of
change. But one thing which, by common consent, *cannot* be
observed from without is *creative activity.* Yet—and here lies the
crux of the whole matter—it is precisely creative activity which
we are trying to understand when we are trying to understand
what is traditionally designated by 'free will.' For if there
should be an act which is genuinely the self's act and is nevertheless not an expression of its character, such an act, in which
the self 'transcends' its character as so far formed, would seem
to be essentially of the nature of creative activity. It follows that
to look for a meaning in 'free will' from the external stand-point
is absurd. It is to look for it in a way that ensures that it will not
be found. Granted that a creative activity of any kind is at least
possible (and I know of no ground for its *a priori* rejection),
there is one way, and one way only, in which we can hope to
apprehend it, and that is from the *inner* stand-point of direct
participation.

It seems to me therefore, that if the Libertarian's claim to
find a meaning in a 'free' will which is genuinely the self's will,
though not an expression of the self's character, is to be subjected to any test that is worth applying, that test must be undertaken from the inner stand-point. We ought to place ourselves
imaginatively at the stand-point of the agent engaged in the typical moral situation in which free will is claimed, and ask ourselves whether from *this* stand-point the claim in question does

or does not have meaning for us. That the appeal must be to introspection is no doubt unfortunate. But he would be a very doctrinaire critic of introspection who declined to make-use of it when in the nature of the case no other means of apprehension is available. Everyone must make the introspective experiment for himself: but I may perhaps venture to report, though at this late stage with extreme brevity, what I at least seem to find when I make the experiment myself.

In the situation of moral conflict, then, I (as agent) have before my mind a course of action X, which I believe to be my duty; and also a course of action Y, incompatible with X, which I feel to be that which I most strongly desire. Y is, as it is sometimes expressed, 'in the line of least resistance' for me—the course which I am aware I should take if I let my purely desiring nature operate without hindrance. It is the course towards which I am aware that my *character*, as so far formed, naturally inclines me. Now, as actually engaged in this situation, I find that I cannot help believing that I *can* rise to duty and choose X; the 'rising to duty' being effected by what is commonly called 'effort of will.' And I further find, if I ask myself just what it is I am believing when I believe that I 'can' rise to duty, that I cannot help believing that it lies with me here and now, quite absolutely, which of two genuinely open possibilities I adopt; whether, that is, I make the effort of will and choose X, or, on the other hand, let my desiring nature, my character as so far formed, 'have its way,' and choose Y, the course 'in the line of least resistance.' These beliefs may, of course, be illusory, but that is not at present in point. For the present argument all that matters is whether beliefs of this sort are in fact discoverable in the moral agent in the situation of 'moral temptation.' For my own part, I cannot doubt the introspective evidence that they are.

Now here is the vital point. No matter which course, X or Y, I choose in this situation, I cannot doubt, *qua* practical being engaged in it, that my choice is *not* just the expression of my formed character, and yet *is* a choice made by my *self*. For suppose I make the effort and choose X (my 'duty'). Since my very

purpose in making the 'effort' is to enable me to act against the
existing 'set' of desire, which is the expression of my character
as so far formed, I cannot possibly regard the act itself as the
expression of my *character*. On the other hand, introspection
makes it equally clear that I am certain that it is *I* who choose;
that the act is not an 'accident,' but is genuinely *my* act. Or
suppose that I choose Y (the end of 'strongest desire'). The
course chosen here is, it is true, in conformity with my 'character.' But since I find myself unable to doubt that I *could* have
made the effort and chosen X, I cannot possibly regard the
choice of Y as *just* the expression of my character. Yet here
again I find that I cannot doubt that the choice is *my* choice, a
choice for which *I* am justly to be blamed.

What this amounts to is that I *can* and *do* attach meaning, *qua* moral agent, to an act which is not the self's character
and yet is genuinely the self's act. And having no good reason to
suppose that other persons have a fundamentally different mental constitution, it seems to me probable that anyone else who
undertakes a similar experiment will be obliged to submit a similar report. I conclude, therefore, that the argument against 'free
will' on the score of its 'meaninglessness' must be held to fail.
'Free Will' does have meaning; though, because it is of the nature of a creative activity, its meaning is discoverable only in an
intuition of the practical consciousness of the participating
agent. To the agent making a moral choice in the situation
where duty clashes with desire, his 'self' is known to him as a
creatively active self, a self which declines to be identified with
his 'character' as so formed. Not, of course, that the self's character—let it be added to obviate misunderstanding—either is, or
is supposed by the agent to be, devoid of bearing upon his
choices, even in the 'sector' in which free will is held to operate.
On the contrary, such a bearing is manifest in the empirically
verifiable fact that we find it 'harder' (as we say) to make the
effort of will required to 'rise to duty' in proportion to the extent
that the 'dutiful' course conflicts with the course to which our
character as so far formed inclines us. It is only in the polemics

of the critics that a 'free' will is supposed to be incompatible with recognising the bearing of 'character' upon choice.

"But what" (it may be asked) "of the all-important question of the *value* of this 'subjective certainty'? Even if what you say is sound as 'phenomenology,' is there any reason to suppose that the conviction on which you lay so much stress is in fact *true?*" I agree that the question is important; far more important, indeed, than is always realised, for it is not always realised that the only direct evidence there *could* be for a creative activity like 'free will' is an intuition of the practical consciousness. But this question falls outside the purview of the present paper. The aim of the paper has not been to offer a constructive defence of free will. It has been to show that the problem as traditionally posed is a real, and not a pseudo, problem. A serious threat to that thesis, it was acknowledged, arises from the apparent difficulty of attaching meaning to an act which is not the expression of the self's character and yet *is* the self's own act. The object of my brief phenomenological analysis was to provide evidence that such an act *does* have meaning for us in the one context in which there is any sense in *expecting* it to have meaning.

[VII]

My general conclusion is, I fear, very unexciting. It is merely that it is an error to suppose that the 'Free Will' problem, when correctly formulated, turns out not to be a 'problem' at all. Labouring to reinstate an old problem is dull work enough. But I am disposed to think that the philosophic situation to-day calls for a good deal more dull work of a similar sort.

IFS AND CANS / J. L. Austin

ARE *cans* constitutionally iffy? Whenever, that is, we say that we can do something, or could do something, or could have done something, is there an *if* in the offing—suppressed, it may be, but due nevertheless to appear when we set out our sentence in full or when we give an explanation of its meaning?

Again, if and when there *is* an *if*-clause appended to a main clause which contains a *can* or *could* or *could have*, what sort of an *if* is it? What is the meaning of the *if*, or what is the effect or the point of combining this *if*-clause with the main clause?

These are large questions, to which philosophers, among them some whom I most respect, have given small answers: and it is two such answers, given recently by English philosophers, that I propose to consider. Both, I believe, are mistaken, yet something is to be learned from examining them. In philosophy, there are many mistakes that it is no disgrace to have made: to make a first-water, ground-floor mistake, so far from being easy, takes one (*one*) form of philosophical genius.[1]

Many of you will have read a short but justly admired book written by Professor G. E. Moore of Cambridge, which is called simply *Ethics*. In it, there is a point where Moore, who is engaged in discussing Right and Wrong, says that if we are to

From J. L. Austin, "*Ifs and Cans*," Proceedings of the British Academy, *XLII* (*1956*), *153–180*.

[1] Plato, Descartes, and Leibniz all had this form of genius, besides of course others.

discuss whether any act that has been done was right or wrong then we are bound to discuss what the person concerned *could have* done instead of what he did in fact do. And this, he thinks, may lead to an entanglement in the problem, so-called, of Free Will: because, though few would deny, at least expressly, that a man could have done something other than what he did actually do *if he had chosen,* many people would deny that he *could* (absolutely) have done any such other thing. Hence Moore is led to ask whether it is ever true, and if so in what sense, that a man could have done something other than what he did actually do. And it is with his answer to this question, not with its bearings upon the meanings of *right* and *wrong* or upon the problem of Free Will, that we are concerned.

With his usual shrewdness Moore begins by insisting that there is at least *one* proper sense in which we can say that a man can do something he does not do or could have done something he did not do—even though there may perhaps be *other* senses of *can* and *could have* in which we cannot say such things. This sense he illustrates by the sentence 'I could have walked a mile in 20 minutes this morning, but I certainly could not have run two miles in 5 minutes': we are to take it that in fact the speaker did not do either of the two things mentioned, but this in no way hinders us from drawing the very common and necessary distinction between undone acts that we could have done and undone acts that we could not have done. So it is certain that, at least in *some* sense, we often could have done things that we did not actually do.

Why then, Moore goes on to ask, should anyone try to deny this? And he replies that people do so (we may call them 'determinists') because they hold that everything that happens has a *cause* which precedes it, which is to say that once the cause has occurred the thing itself is *bound* to occur and *nothing else could* ever have happened instead.

However, on examining further the 20-minute-mile example, Moore argues that there is much reason to think that 'could have' in such cases simply means 'could have *if* I had chosen', or, as perhaps we had better say in order to avoid a possible complication (these are Moore's words), simply means 'should have if I had chosen'. And if this *is* all it means, then there is after all no conflict between our conviction that we often could have, in this sense, done things that we did not actually do and the determinist's theory: for he certainly holds himself that I often, and perhaps even always, should have done something different from what I did do *if I had chosen* to do that different thing, since my choosing differently would constitute a change in the causal antecedents of my subsequent act, which would therefore, on his theory, naturally itself be different. If, therefore, the determinist nevertheless asserts that in *some* sense of 'could have' I could *not* ever have done anything different from what I did actually do, this must simply be a second sense[2] of 'could have' different from that which it has in the 20-minute-mile example.

In the remainder of his chapter, Moore argues that quite possibly his first sense of 'could have', in which it simply means 'could or should have if I had chosen', is all we need to satisfy our hankerings after Free Will, or at least is so if conjoined in some way with yet a third sense of 'could have' in which sense 'I could have done something different' means 'I might, for all anyone could know for certain beforehand, have done something different'. This third kind of 'could have' might, I think, be held to be a vulgarism, 'could' being used incorrectly for 'might': but in any case we shall not be concerned with it here.

In the upshot, then, Moore leaves us with only one important sense in which it can be said that I could have done something that I did not do: he is not convinced that any other sense is necessary, nor has he any clear idea what such another sense would be: and he is convinced that, on his interpretation of 'could have', even the determinist can, and indeed must, say that I could very often have done things I did not do. To summarize his suggestions (he does not put them forward with complete conviction) once again:

2 About which Moore has no more to tell us.

1. 'Could have' simply means 'could have if I had chosen'.

2. For 'could have if I had chosen' we may substitute 'should have if I had chosen'.

3. The *if*-clauses in these expressions state the causal conditions upon which it would have followed that I could or should have done the thing different from what I did actually do.

Moore does not state this third point expressly himself: but it seems clear, in view of the connections he alleges between his interpretation of 'could have' and the determinist theory, that he did believe it, presumably taking it as obvious.

There are then three questions to be asked:

1. Does 'could have if I had chosen' mean the same, in general or ever, as 'should have if I had chosen?'

2. In either of these expressions, is the *if* the *if* of causal condition?

3. In sentences having *can* or *could have* as main verb, are we required or entitled always to supply an *if*-clause, and in particular the clause 'if I had chosen'?

It appears to me that the answer in each case is No.

1. Anyone, surely, would admit that in general *could* is very different indeed from *should* or *would*.[3] What a man *could* do is not at all the same as what he *would* do: perhaps he could shoot you if you were within range, but that is not in the least to say that he would. And it seems clear to me, in our present example, that 'I could have run a mile if I had chosen' and 'I should have run a mile if I had chosen' mean quite different things, though unfortunately it is not so clear exactly what either of them, especially the latter, does mean. 'I should have run a mile in 20 minutes this morning if I had chosen' seems to me an unusual, not to say queer, specimen of English: but if I had to interpret it, I should take it to mean the same as 'If I had chosen

---

[3] Since Moore has couched his example in the first person, he uses 'should' in the apodosis: but of course in the third person, everyone would use 'would'. For brevity, I shall in what follows generally use 'should' to do duty for both persons.

to run a mile in 20 minutes this morning, I should (jolly well) have done so', that is, it would be an assertion of my strength of character, in that I put my decisions into execution (an assertion which is, however, more naturally made, as I have now made it, with the *if*-clause preceding the main clause). I should certainly not myself understand it to mean that if I had made a certain choice my making that choice would have caused me to do something. But in whichever of these ways we understand it, it is quite different from 'I *could* have walked a mile in 20 minutes this morning if I had chosen', which surely says something rather about my opportunities or powers. Moore, unfortunately, does not explain why he thinks we are entitled to make this all-important transition from 'could' to 'should', beyond saying that by doing so we 'avoid a possible complication'. Later I shall make some suggestions which may in part explain why he was tempted to make the transition: but nothing can justify it.

2. Moore, as I pointed out above, did not discuss what sort of *if* it is that we have in 'I can if I choose' or in 'I could have if I had chosen' or in 'I should have if I had chosen'. Generally, philosophers, as also grammarians, have a favourite, if somewhat blurred and diffuse, idea of an *if*-clause as a 'conditional' clause: putting our example schematically as 'If p, then q', then it will be said that q follows from p, typically either in the sense that p *entails* q or in the sense that p is a *cause* of q, though other important variations are possible. And it seems to be on these lines that Moore is thinking of the *if* in 'I can if I choose'. But now, it is characteristic of this general sort of *if*, that from 'If p then q' we *can* draw the inference 'If not q, then not p', whereas we can *not* infer either 'Whether or not p, then q' or 'q' simpliciter. For example, from 'If I run, I pant' we *can* infer 'If I do not pant, I do not run' (or, as we should rather say, 'If I am not panting, I am not running'), whereas we can *not* infer either 'I pant, whether I run or not' or 'I pant' (at least in the sense of 'I am panting'). If, to avoid these troubles with the English tenses, which are unfortunately prevalent but are not allowed to matter, we put the example in the past tense, then from 'If I ran, I panted' it *does* follow that 'If I did not pant, I

did not run', but it does *not* follow either that 'I panted whether or not I ran' or that 'I panted' period. These possibilities and impossibilities of inference are typical of the *if* of causal condition: but they are precisely reversed in the case of 'I can if I choose' or 'I could have if I had chosen'. For from these we should not draw the curious inferences that 'If I cannot, I do not choose to' or that 'If I could not have, I had not chosen to' (or 'did not choose to'), whatever these sentences may be supposed to mean. But on the contrary, from 'I can if I choose' we certainly should infer that 'I can, whether I choose to or not' and indeed that 'I can' period: and from 'I could have if I had chosen' we should similarly infer that 'I could have, whether I chose to or not' and that anyway 'I could have' period. So that, whatever this *if* means, it is evidently not the *if* of causal condition.

This becomes even clearer when we observe that it is quite common *elsewhere* to find an ordinary causal conditional *if* in connection with a *can,* and that then there is no doubt about it, as for example in the sentence 'I can squeeze through if I am thin enough', which *does* imply that 'If I cannot squeeze through I am not thin enough', and of course does *not* imply that 'I can squeeze through'. 'I can if I choose' is precisely different from this.

Nor does *can* have to be a very special and peculiar verb for *ifs* which are not causal conditional to be found in connection with it: all kinds of *ifs* are found with all kinds of verbs. Consider for example the *if* in 'There are biscuits on the sideboard if you want them', where the verb is the highly ordinary *are,* but the *if* is more like that in 'I can if I choose' than that in 'I panted if I ran': for we can certainly infer from it that 'There are biscuits on the sideboard whether you want them or not' and that anyway 'There are biscuits on the sideboard', whereas it would be folly to infer that 'If there are no biscuits on the sideboard you do not want them', or to understand the meaning to be that you have only to want biscuits to cause them to be on the sideboard.

The *if,* then, in 'I can if I choose' is not the causal conditional *if.* What of the *if* in 'I shall if I choose'? At first glance,

we see that this is quite different (one more reason for refusing
to substitute *shall* for *can* or *should have* for *could have*). For
from 'I shall if I choose' we clearly cannot infer that 'I shall
whether I choose to or not' or simply that 'I shall'. But on the
other hand, can we infer, either, that 'If I shan't I don't choose
to'? (Or should it be rather 'If I don't I don't choose to'?)
I think not, as we shall see: but even if some such inference can be drawn, it would still be patently wrong to conclude
that the meaning of 'I shall if I choose' is that my choosing to do
the thing is sufficient to cause me inevitably to do it or has as a
consequence that I shall do it, which, unless I am mistaken, is
what Moore was supposing it to mean. This may be seen if we
compare 'I shall ruin him if I choose' with 'I shall ruin him if I
am extravagant'. The latter sentence does indeed obviously state
what would be the consequence of the fulfilment of a condition
specified in the *if*-clause—but then, the first sentence has clearly
different characteristics from the second. In the first, it makes
good sense in general to stress the 'shall', but in the second it
does not.[4] This is a symptom of the fact that in the first sentence
'I shall' is the present of that mysterious old verb *shall*, whereas
in the second 'shall' is simply being used as an auxiliary, without any meaning of its own, to form the future indicative of
'ruin'.

I expect you will be more than ready at this point to hear
something a little more positive about the meanings of these curious expressions 'I can if I choose' and 'I shall if I choose'. Let us
take the former first, and concentrate upon the *if*. The dictionary
tells us that the words from which our *if* is descended expressed,
or even meant, 'doubt' or 'hesitation' or 'condition' or 'stipulation'. Of these, 'condition' has been given a prodigious innings
by grammarians, lexicographers, and philosophers alike: it is
time for 'doubt' and 'hesitation' to be remembered, and these
do indeed seem to be the notions present in 'I can if I choose'.
We could give, on different occasions and in different contexts,

---

[4] In general, though of course in some contexts it does: e.g. 'I may very
easily ruin him, and I *shall* if I am extravagant', where 'shall' is stressed to
point the contrast with 'may'.

many different interpretations of this sentence, which is of a somewhat primitive and *loose-jointed* type. Here are some:

> I can, quaere do I choose to?
> I can, but do I choose to?
> I can, but perhaps I don't choose to
> I can, but then I should have to choose to, and what about *that*?
> I can, but would it really be reasonable to choose to?
> I can, but whether I choose to is another question
> I can, I have only to choose to
> I can, in case I (should) choose to,
> and so on.

These interpretations are not, of course, all the same: which it is that we mean will usually be clear from the context (otherwise we should prefer another expression), but sometimes it can be brought out by stress, on the 'if' or the 'choose' for example. What is common to them all is simply that the *assertion*, positive and complete, that 'I can', is linked to the *raising of the question* whether I choose to, which may be relevant in a variety of ways.[5]

Ifs of the kind I have been trying to describe are common enough, for example the *if* in our example 'There are biscuits on the sideboard if you want them'. I do not know whether you want biscuits or not, but in case you do, I point out that there are some on the sideboard. It is tempting, I know, to 'expand' our sentence here to this: 'There are biscuits on the sideboard *which you can (or may) take* if you want them': but this, legitimate or not, will not make much difference, for we are still left with 'can (or may) if you want', which is (here) just like 'can if you choose' or 'can if you like', so that the *if* is still the *if* of doubt or hesitation, not the *if* of condition.[6]

[5] If there were space, we should consider other germane expressions: e.g. 'I can do it or not as I choose', 'I can do whichever I choose' (*quidlibet*). In particular, 'I can whether I choose to or not' means 'I can, but whether I choose to or not is an open question': it does *not* mean 'I can on condition that I choose and likewise on condition that I don't', which is absurd.

[6] An account on these lines should probably be given also of an excellent ex-

I will mention two further points, very briefly, about 'I can if I choose', important but not so relevant to our discussion here. Sometimes the *can* will be the *can*, and the choice the choice, of legal or other *right*, at other times these words will refer to practicability or feasibility: consequently, we should sometimes interpret our sentence in some such way as 'I am entitled to do it (if I choose)', and at other times in some such way as 'I am capable of doing it (if I choose)'. We, of course, are concerned with interpretations of this second kind. It would be nice if we always said 'I *may* if I choose' when we wished to refer to our rights, as perhaps our nannies once told us to: but the interlocking histories of *can* and *may* are far too chequered for there to be any such rule in practice.[7] The second point is that *choose* is an important word in its own right, and needs careful interpretation: 'I can if I like' is not the same, although the 'can' and the 'if' may be the same in both, as 'I can if I choose'. Choice is always between alternatives, that is between several courses to be weighed in the same scale against each other, the one to be *preferred*. 'You can vote whichever way you choose' is different from 'You can vote whichever way you like'.

And now for something about 'I *shall* if I choose'—what sort of *if* have we here? The point to notice is, that 'I shall' is not an assertion of *fact* but an expression of *intention*, verging towards the giving of some variety of undertaking: and the *if*, consequently, is the *if* not of condition but of *stipulation*. In sentences like:

I shall | marry him if I choose
I intend | to marry him if I choose
I promise | to marry him if he will have me

ample given to me by Mr. P. T. Geach: 'I paid you back yesterday, if you remember'. This is much the same as 'I paid you back yesterday, don't you remember?' It does not mean that your now remembering that I did so is a condition, causal or other, of my having paid you back yesterday.

[7] Formerly I believed that the meaning of 'I can if I choose' was something like 'I can, I have the choice', and that the point of the *if*-clause was to make clear that the 'can' in the main clause was the 'can' of right. This account, however, does not do justice to the role of the 'if', and also unduly restricts in general the meaning of 'choice'.

the *if*-clause is a part of the object phrase governed by the initial verb ('shall', 'intend', 'promise'), if this is an allowable way of putting it: or again, the *if* qualifies the *content* of the undertaking given, or of the intention announced, it does *not* qualify the giving of the undertaking. Why, we may ask, is it perverse to draw from 'I intend to marry him if I choose' the inference 'If I do not intend to marry him I do not choose to'? Because 'I intend to marry him if I choose' is not like 'I panted if I ran' in this important respect: 'I panted if I ran' does not assert anything 'categorically' about me—it does not assert that I did pant, and hence it is far from surprising to infer something beginning 'If I did not pant': but 'I intend to marry him if I choose' (and the same goes for 'I shall marry him if I choose') *is* a 'categorical' expression of intention, and hence it is paradoxical to make an inference leading off with 'If I do *not* intend'.

3. Our third question was as to when we are entitled or required to supply *if* clauses with *can* or *could have* as main verb.

Here there is one thing to be clear about at the start. There are *two* quite distinct and incompatible views that may be put forward concerning *ifs* and *cans*, which are fatally easy to confuse with each other. One view is that wherever we have *can* or *could have* as our main verb, an *if*-clause must always be understood or supplied, if it is not actually present, in order to complete the sense of the sentence. The other view is that the meaning of 'can' or 'could have' can be more clearly reproduced by *some other verb* (notably 'shall' or 'should have') with an *if*-clause appended to *it*. The first view is that an *if* is required to *complete* a *can*-sentence: the second view is that an *if* is required in the *analysis* of a *can*-sentence. The suggestion of Moore that 'could have' means 'could have if I had chosen' is a suggestion of the first kind: but the suggestion also made by Moore that it means 'should have if I had chosen' is a suggestion of the second kind. It may be because it is so easy (apparently) to confuse these two kinds of theory that Moore was tempted to talk as though 'should have' could mean the same as 'could have'.

Now we are concerned at this moment solely with the *first* sort of view, namely that *can*-sentences are not complete without an *if*-clause. And if we think, as Moore was for the most part thinking, about 'could have' (rather than 'can'), it is easy to see why it may be tempting to allege that it always requires an *if*-clause with it. For it is natural to construe 'could have' as a past subjunctive or 'conditional', which is practically as much as to say that it needs a *conditional* clause with it. And of course it is quite true that 'could have' *may* be, and very often is, a past conditional: but it is *also* true that 'could have' may be and often is the *past* (*definite*) *indicative* of the verb *can*. Sometimes 'I could have' is equivalent to the Latin 'Potui' and means 'I *was* in a position to': sometimes it is equivalent to the Latin 'Potuissem' and means 'I *should have been* in a position to'. Exactly similar is the double role of 'could', which is sometimes a conditional meaning 'should be able to', but also sometimes a past indicative (indefinite) meaning 'was able to': no one can doubt this if he considers such contrasted examples as 'I could do it 20 years ago' and 'I could do it if I had a thingummy'. It is not so much that 'could' or 'could have' is ambiguous, as rather that two parts of the verb *can* take the same shape.

Once it is realised that 'could have' can be a past indicative, the general temptation to supply *if*-clauses with it vanishes: at least there is no more temptation to supply them with 'could have' than with 'can'. If we ask how a Roman would have said 'I could have ruined you this morning (although I didn't)', it is clear that he would have used 'potui', and that his sentence is complete without any conditional clause. But more than this, if he had wished to add 'if I had chosen', and however he had expressed that in Latin, he would still not have changed his 'potui' to 'potuissem': but this is precisely what he *would* have done if he had been tacking on some other, more 'normal' kind of *if*-clause, such as 'if I had had one more vote'.[8]

8 If the *if*-clause is 'if I had chosen', then I *was* able, *was* actually in a position, to ruin you: hence 'potui'. But if the *if*-clause expresses a genuine *unfulfilled condition*, then plainly I was *not* actually in a position to ruin you, hence not 'potui' but 'potuissem'. My colleague Mr. R. M. Nisbet has pointed out to me the interesting discussion of this point in S. A. Handford, *The Latin*

That is to say, the 'could have' in 'could have if I had chosen' is a past indicative, *not* a past conditional, despite the fact that there is what would, I suppose, be called a 'conditional' clause, that is an *if*-clause, with it. And this is, of course, why we can make the inferences that, as we saw, we can make from 'I could have if I had chosen', notably the inference to 'I could have' absolutely. Hence we see how mistaken Moore was in contrasting 'I could have if I had chosen' with the 'absolute' sense of 'I could have': we might almost go so far as to say that the addition of the 'conditional' clause 'if I had chosen' makes it certain that (in Moore's language) the sense of 'could have' is the absolute sense, or as I should prefer to put it, that the mood of 'could have' is indicative.

It might at this point be worth considering in general whether it makes sense to suppose that a language could contain any verb such as *can* has been argued or implied to be, namely one that can never occur without an *if*-clause appended to it. At least if the *if* is the normal 'conditional' *if* this would seem very difficult. For let the verb in question be *to X:* then we shall never say simply 'I X', but always 'I X if I Y': but then also, according to the accepted rules, if it is true that 'I X if I Y', and *also* true (which it must surely sometimes be) that 'I do, in fact, Y', it must surely follow that 'I X', simpliciter, without any *if* about it any longer. Perhaps this was the 'possible complication' that led Moore to switch from the suggestion that 'I could have' (in one sense) has always to be *expanded* to 'I could have if' to the suggestion that it has always to be *analysed* as 'I should have if': for of course the argument I have just given does not suffice to show that there could not be some verb which has always to be *analysed* as something containing a conditional *if*-clause: suggestions that this is in fact the case with some verbs are common in philosophy, and I do not propose to argue this point, though I think that doubt might well be felt about it. The only sort of 'verb' I can think of that might always demand a conditional

---

Subjunctive, pp. 130 ff. It is interesting that although this author well appreciates the Latin usage, he still takes it for granted that in English the 'could have' is universally subjunctive or conditional.

clause with it is an 'auxiliary' verb, if there is one, which is used solely to form subjunctive or conditional moods (whatever exactly they may be) of other verbs: but however this may be, it is quite clear that *can*, and I should be prepared also to add *shall* and *will* and *may*, are not in this position.

To summarize, then, what has been here said in reply to Moore's suggestions in his book:

(*a*) 'I could have if I had chosen' does not mean the same as 'I should have if I had chosen'.

(*b*) In neither of these expressions is the *if*-clause a 'normal conditional' clause, connecting antecedent to consequent as cause to effect.

(*c*) To argue that *can* always requires an *if*-clause with it to complete the sense is totally different from arguing that *can*-sentences are always to be analysed into sentences containing *if*-clauses.

(*d*) Neither *can* nor any other verb always requires a conditional *if*-clause after it: even 'could have', when a past indicative, does not require such a clause: and in 'I could have if I had chosen' the verb is in fact a past indicative, not a past subjunctive or conditional.

Even, however, if all these contentions are true so far, we must recognise that it may nevertheless still be the case that *can, could,* and *could have,* even when used as indicatives, are to be analysed as meaning *shall, should,* and *should have,* used as auxiliaries of tense or mood with another verb (i.e. so as to make that other verb into a future or subjunctive), followed by a conditional *if*-clause. There is some plausibility,[9] for example, in the suggestion that 'I can do X' means 'I shall succeed in doing

9 Plausibility, but no more. Consider the case where I miss a very short putt and kick myself because I could have holed it. It is not that I should have holed it if I had tried: I did try, and missed. It is not that I should have holed it if conditions had been different: that might of course be so, but I am talking about conditions as they precisely were, and asserting that I could have holed it. There is the rub. Nor does 'I can hole it this time' mean that I shall hole it this time if I try or if anything else: for I may try and miss, and yet not be convinced that I could not have done it; indeed, further experiments may confirm my belief that I could have done it that time although I did not.

X, if I try' and 'I could have done X' means 'I should have succeeded in doing X, if I had tried'.

It is indeed odd that Moore should have plumped so simply, in giving his account whether of the necessary supplementation or of the analysis of 'could have', for the one particular *if* clause 'if I had chosen', which happens to be particularly exposed to the above objections, without even mentioning the possibility of invoking other *if*-clauses, at least in some cases. Perhaps the reason was that *choose* (a word itself much in need of discussion) presented itself as well fitted to bridge the gulf between determinists and free-willers, which *try* might not so readily do. But as a matter of fact Moore does himself at one point give an analysis of 'I could have done X' which is different in an interesting way from his usual version, although confusible with it. At a crucial point in his argument, he chooses for his example 'The ship could have gone faster', and the suggestion is made that this is equivalent to 'The ship *would* have gone faster *if her officers had chosen*'. This may well seem plausible, but so far from being in line, as Moore apparently thinks, with his general analysis, it differs from it in two important respects:

(*a*) the subject of the *if*-clause ('her officers') is different from the subject of the main clause ('the ship'), the subject of the original sentence:

(*b*) the verb in the *if*-clause following 'chosen' is different from the verb in the main clause, the verb in the original sentence. We do not readily observe this because of the ellipsis after 'chosen': but plainly the verb must be, not 'to go faster', but 'to make her go faster' or, for example, 'to open the throttle'.

These two features are dictated by the fact that a ship is inanimate. We do not wish seriously to ascribe free will to inanimate

---

But if I tried my hardest, say, and missed, surely there *must* have been *something* that caused me to fail, that made me unable to succeed? So that I *could not* have holed it. Well, a modern belief in science, in there being an explanation of everything, may make us assent to this argument. But such a belief is not in line with the traditional beliefs enshrined in the word *can:* according to *them*, a human ability or power or capacity is inherently liable not to produce success, on occasion, and that for no reason (or are bad luck and bad form sometimes reasons?).

objects, and the 'could' of the original sentence is perhaps only justifiable (as opposed to 'might') because it is readily realised that some person's free will is in question.

If we follow up the lines of this new type of analysis, we should have to examine the relations between 'I could have won' and 'I could, or should, have won if I had chosen to lob' and 'I could, or should, have won if he had chosen to lob'. I will do no more here than point out that the difference between 'could' and 'should' remains as before, and that the sense of 'I could have won', if it really is one, in which it means something of the sort 'I should have won if he had chosen to lob' or 'to let me win' (the parallel to the ship example), is of little importance—the 'if' here is of course the conditional *if*.

It is time now to turn to a second discussion of *if*s and *can*s. Quite recently my colleague Mr. Nowell-Smith, in another little book called *Ethics*, also reaches a point in his argument at which he has to examine the sentence 'He could have acted otherwise', that is, could have done something that he did not in fact do. His reason for doing so is that, unless we can truly say this of people, we might find ourselves unable to blame people for things, and this would be generally regretted. This reason is not unrelated to Moore's reason for embarking on his earlier discussion, and Nowell-Smith's views show some resemblances to Moore's: perhaps this is because Nowell-Smith, like Moore at the time he wrote his book, is willing, if not anxious, to come to terms with determinism.

Nowell-Smith begins his discussion by saying (p. 274) that ' "could have" is a modal phrase, and modal phrases are not normally used to make categorical statements'. I am not myself at all sure what exactly a 'modal phrase' is, so I cannot discuss this assertion: but I do not think this matters, because he proceeds to give us two other examples of modal phrases, viz. 'might have' and 'would have',[10] and to tell us first what they are not (which I omit) and then what they are:

10 Also perhaps 'may have', for he discusses 'It *might* have rained last Thursday' in terms that seem really to apply to 'It *may* have rained last Thursday'.

'Would have' and 'might have' are clearly suppressed hypotheticals, incomplete without an 'if . . .' or an 'if . . . not . . . '. Nobody would say 'Jones would have won the championship' unless (*a*) he believed that Jones did not win and (*b*) he was prepared to add 'if he had entered' or 'if he had not sprained his ankle' or some such clause.

Here (*a*) is actually incorrect—we can say 'Jones would (still) have won the championship, (even) if Hagen had entered'—but this does not concern us. (*b*), however, seems to be fairly correct, at least as far as concerns 'would have' (in the case of 'might have' it might well be doubted [11]). So we have it that, when Nowell-Smith says that 'would have' is a 'suppressed hypothetical' he means that it requires the addition of an *if*-clause to complete the sense. And he goes on to say that 'could have' sentences also (though not so obviously) 'express hypotheticals', if not always at least in important cases, such as notably those where we say someone could have done something he did not actually do: in these cases 'could have' . . . is equivalent to 'would have . . . if . . .'.

It will be clear at once that Nowell-Smith, like Moore, is not distinguishing between the contention that 'could have' *requires supplementation by* an *if*-clause and the quite different

[11] I refrain here from questioning it in the case of 'would have'. Yet 'would' is agreed to be often a past indicative of the old verb *will*, requiring no *if*-clause: and I think myself that in, say, 'X would have hanged him, but Y was against it' 'would have' is likewise a past indicative—indeed it is from this sort of example that we can see how the past tenses of *will* have come to be used as auxiliaries of mood for forming the conditionals of other verbs.

To state what seem to be some grammatical facts (omitting all reference to the use of the words concerned in expressing wishes):

Could have is sometimes a past indicative, sometimes a past subjunctive of the verb *can*. When it is the main verb and is a subjunctive, it does require a conditional clause with it. *Can* and its parts are *not* used as auxiliaries of tense or mood to form tenses or moods of other verbs.

Would have, whether or not it is used as a past indicative or subjunctive of the verb *will*, is now commonly used (*should have* in the first person) as an auxiliary for forming the past subjunctive of other verbs: hence if it is the main verb it does in general require a conditional clause with it.

contention that *its analysis contains* an *if*-clause.[12] On the whole it seems plain that it is the second (analysis) view that he wishes to argue for: but the argument he produces is that 'could have' is (in important cases) like 'would have', the point about which is that it needs an *if*-clause to complete it—as though this, which is an argument in favour of the *first* view, told in favour of the second view. But it cannot possibly do so: and in any event *could have* is liable, as we have already seen, to be in important cases a past indicative, so that the contention that it is like *would have* in requiring a conditional *if*-clause is unfounded.

Nevertheless, it must be allowed that Nowell-Smith may still be right in urging that 'could have' *means* 'would have if' and that, as he eventually adds, 'can' means 'will if'. What has he to say in support of this?

He propounds two examples for discussion, which I think do not differ greatly, so I shall quote only the first. Here it is:

He could have read *Emma* in bed last night, though he actually read *Persuasion;* but he could not have read *Werther,* because he does not know German.

This is evidently of the same kind as Moore's 20-minute-mile example. The first thing that Nowell-Smith urges is that such a 'could have' statement is not a categorical, or a 'straightforward' categorical, statement. And his argument in favour of this view is derived from the way in which we should establish its truth or falsity. No inspection of what the man actually did will, he says, verify directly that he could have done something else (here, read *Emma*) which he did not do: rather, we should, to establish this, have to show

12 It is true that he uses two different expressions: 'would have' *is* a (suppressed) hypothetical, while 'could have' sentences *express* hypotheticals. But it does not look as if any distinction is intended, and if it is, the protracted initial analogy between 'could have' and 'would have' seems irrelevant and misleading. Moreover, discussing the (unimportant) case of 'It could have been a Morris', he writes that 'it would be absurd to ask under what conditions it *could or would* have been a Morris' (my italics): this seems to show an indifference to the distinction that I am insisting on.

(*a*) that he has performed tasks of similar difficulty sufficiently often to preclude the possibility of a fluke, and
(*b*) that nothing prevented him on this occasion. For example, we should have to establish that there was a copy
of *Emma* in the house.

To refute it, on the other hand, we should have to show either
'that some necessary condition was absent' (there was no copy
of *Emma*) or 'that the capacity was absent'. That is, let us say,
we have to show on the one hand that he had both the ability and
the opportunity to read *Emma,* or on the other hand that he
lacked either the ability or the opportunity.

Nowell-Smith seems, at least at first, to be less interested
in the matter of opportunity: for he says that we can establish
'directly', i.e. by considering what the facts at the time actually
were, at least that he did *not* have the opportunity, that is, that
something did prevent him, and he does not seem daunted by
the obviously greater difficulty of establishing, in order to establish that he *could* have done it, the general negative that *there
was nothing* to prevent him. At any rate, it is at first upon our
manner of establishing that he had (or had not) the *ability* to do
this thing that he did not do that Nowell-Smith fastens in order
to support his assertion that the 'could have' statement is not
categorical. That the man had the *ability* to read *Emma* can *not,*
he says, be established 'directly', i.e. by observing what happened on that past occasion, but only by considering what prow-
ess he has displayed in the face of similar tasks in the past on
other occasions, or displays now when put to the test: the argument that we have perforce to use is an 'inductive' one (and, he
adds, none the worse for that).

Now let us pass all this, at least for the sake of argument.[13] What interests us is to discover why Nowell-Smith thinks

[13] Yet I think it is not hard to see that we cannot establish 'directly', at least
in many cases, that something 'prevented' him: he was drugged or dazzled,
which prevented him from reading, which establishes that he could not have
read—but how do we know that being drugged or dazzled 'prevents' people
from reading? Surely on 'inductive' evidence? And, in short, to be prevented is
to be rendered unable.

that these considerations show that 'He had the ability to read
Emma' is not a categorical statement. I confess I fail to follow
the argument:

> The very fact that evidence for or against 'could have'
> statements must be drawn from occasions other than that
> to which they refer is enough to show that 'He could have
> acted otherwise' is not a straightforward categorical
> statement.

But do we really know what is meant by a 'straightforward categorical statement'? Certainly it is not the case that statements
made on the strength of inductive evidence are in general not
categorical—for example, the statement that the next mule born
will prove sterile: this seems categorical enough. Perhaps this
example should be ruled out as not in point, on the ground that
here there *will some day* be 'direct' evidence relevant to the assertion, even if it is not available at the moment. Could the same,
I wonder, be said of the inductive conclusion 'All mules are
sterile'? Or is that not categorical? I know that this has been interpreted by some philosophers to mean 'If anything is a mule
then it is sterile', but I see no reason to support that curious interpretation.

The situation becomes still more puzzling when we remember that Nowell-Smith is about to generalise his theory, and
to assert, not merely that 'could have' means 'would have . . .
if', but also that 'can' means 'shall or will . . . if'. Suppose
then that I assert 'I can here and now lift my finger', and translate this as 'I shall lift my finger if . . .': then surely this will be
'directly' verified if the conditions are satisfied and I do proceed
to lift the finger? If this is correct, and if the theory is indeed a
general one, then there seems to be no point in insisting on the
nonavailability of 'direct' evidence, which is only a feature of
certain cases. Incidentally, it is not in fact the case that to say
'He could have done it' is always used in a way to imply that he
did not in fact do it: we make a list of the suspects in a murder
case, all of whom we think could have done it and one of whom
we think did do it. True, this is not Nowell-Smith's case: but

unless we are prepared to assert that the 'could have' in his case differs in meaning from that in the murder case, and so to rule out the latter as irrelevant, we are in danger of having to admit that even 'could have' sentences can be 'directly' verified in favourable cases. For study of the facts of that past occasion can prove to us that he did it, and hence that our original 'He could have' was correct.[14]

However, to proceed. Whether or not we should describe our conclusion here as 'categorical' it seems that it should still be a conclusion of the form 'he *could* have done so and so', and not in the least a conclusion concerning what he *would* have done. We are interested, remember, in his abilities: we want to know whether he could have read *Emma* yesterday: we ascertain that he did read it the day before yesterday, and that he does read it to-day: we conclude that he could have read it yesterday. But it does not appear that this says anything about what he *would* have done yesterday or in what circumstances: certainly, we are now convinced, he *could* have read it yesterday, but *would* he have, considering that he had read it only the day before? Moreover, supposing the view is that our conclusion is not of the 'could have' but of the 'would have if' form, nothing has yet been said to establish this, nor to tell us what follows the 'if'. To establish that he would have read it yesterday if . . . , we shall need evidence not merely as to his abilities and opportunities, but also as to his character, motives, and so on.

It may indeed be thought, and it seems that Nowell-Smith does at least partly think this, that what follows the 'if' should be suppliable from the consideration that to say he could have, in the full sense, is to say not merely that he had the ability, which is what we have hitherto concentrated on, but also that he had the *opportunity*. For to establish *this*, do we not have to establish that certain *conditions* were satisfied, as for instance that there was a copy of *Emma* available? Very well. But here

[14] There are, I should myself think, good reasons for not speaking of 'I can lift my finger' as being directly verified when I proceed to lift it, and likewise for not speaking of 'He could have done it' as being directly verified by the discovery that he did do it. But on Nowell-Smith's account I think that these would count as direct verifications.

there is surely a confusion: we allow that, in saying that he could have, I do assert or imply that certain *conditions*, those of opportunity, *were satisfied:* but this is totally different from allowing that, in saying that he could have, I *assert something conditional.* It is, certainly, entirely possible to assert something conditional such as 'he could have read *Emma* yesterday if there had been a copy available', *could* being then of course a subjunctive: but to say this sort of thing is precisely not to say the sort of thing that we say when we say 'He could have acted otherwise', where 'could have' is an indicative—implying, as we now do, that there was no copy available, we imply that *pro tanto* he could *not* have acted otherwise. And the same will be true if we try saying 'He would have read *Emma* yesterday if there had been a copy available': this too certainly implies that he could not in fact have read it, and so cannot by any means be what we mean by saying that he could have read it.

In the concluding paragraph of his discussion, Nowell-Smith does finally undertake to give us his analysis not merely of 'could have', but also of 'can' (which he says means 'will if'). And this last feature is very much to be welcomed, because if an analysis is being consciously given of 'can' at least we shall at length be clear of confusions connected with the idea that 'could have' is necessarily a subjunctive.[15]

The argument of the last paragraph runs as follows. It is 'logically odd' to say something of this kind (I am slightly emending Nowell-Smith's formula, but only in ways that are favourable to it and demanded by his own argument):

> Smith has the ability to run a mile, has the opportunity to run a mile, has a preponderant motive for running a mile, but does not in fact do so.

[15] It must, however, be pointed out once again that if we are to discuss the assertion that somebody *can* (now) do something, the previous arguments that our assertions are not categorical because they are based on induction and cannot be verified directly, whether they were good or not, must now be abandoned: because of course it *is* possible to verify this 'directly' by the method Nowell-Smith has specified in another connection earlier, viz. by getting the man to try and seeing him succeed.

From this it follows directly, says Nowell-Smith, that 'can' means 'will if', that is, I suppose, that 'Smith can run a mile' *means* 'If Smith has the opportunity to run a mile and a preponderant motive for running it, he will run it'.

It seems, however, plain that nothing of the kind follows.

This may be seen first by setting the argument out formally. Nowell-Smith's premiss is of the form

Not (*p* and *q* and *r* and not -*s*)

that is

Logically odd (ability + opportunity + motive + non-action).

Now from this we can indeed infer

$$p \supset ((q \text{ and } r) \supset s),$$

that is that

If he has the ability, then, if he has the opportunity and the motive, he will do it.

But we can*not infer* the converse

$$((q \text{ and } r) \supset s) \supset p,$$

or in other words that

If, when he has the opportunity and the motive, he does it, he has the ability to do it.

(I do not say this last is not something to which we should, when so put into English, assent, only that it does not follow from Nowell-Smith's premiss: of course it follows merely from the premiss that he does it, that he has the ability to do it, according to ordinary English.) But unless this second, converse implication *does* follow, we can not, according to the usual formal principles, infer that *p* is *equivalent* to, nor therefore that it means the same as, (*q* and *r*) $\supset$ *s*, or in words that ability *means* that opportunity plus motive leads to action.

To put the same point non-formally. From the fact that, if three things are true together a fourth must also be true, we cannot argue that one of the three things *simply means* that if the other two are true the fourth will be true. If we could argue indeed in this way, then we should establish, from Nowell-Smith's premiss, not merely that

> 'He has the ability to do X' *simply means* that 'If he has the opportunity and the motive to do X, he will do X'

but also equally that

> 'He has the opportunity to do X' *simply means* that 'If he has the ability and the motive to do X, he will do X'

and likewise that

> 'He has a preponderant motive to do X' *simply means* that 'If he has the ability and the opportunity to do X, he will do X'.

For clearly we can perform the same operations on *q* and *r* as on *p,* since the three all occupy parallel positions in the premiss. But these are fantastic suggestions. Put shortly, Nowell-Smith is pointing out in his premiss that if a man both can and wants to (more than he wants to do anything else), he will: but from this it does not follow that 'he can' *simply means* that 'if he wants to he will'. Nowell-Smith is struggling to effect a transition from *can* to *will* which presents difficulties as great as those of the transition from *could* to *would:* he puts up his show of effecting it by importing the additional, and here irrelevant, concept of motive, which needless to say is in general very intimately connected with the question of what 'he will' do.

When, in conclusion, Nowell-Smith finally sets out his analysis of 'Smith could have read *Emma* last night', it is this:

> He would have read it, if there had been a copy, if he had not been struck blind, etc., etc., and if he had wanted to read it more than he had wanted to read (this should be 'do') anything else.

But so far from this being what we mean by saying he could have read it, it actually implies that he could *not* have read it, for more than adequate reasons: it implies that he was blind at the time, and so on. Here we see that Nowell-Smith actually does make the confusion I referred to above between a statement which implies or asserts that certain conditions *were* fulfilled and a conditional statement, i.e. a statement about what would have happened if those conditions had been fulfilled. This is unfortunately a confusion of a general kind that is not uncommon: I need only mention the classic instance of Keynes, who confused asserting on evidence h that p is probable with asserting that on evidence h p is probable, both of which can be ambiguously expressed by 'asserting that p is probable on evidence h', but only the former of which asserts that p is (really) probable. Here similarly there is a confusion between asserting on the supposition (or premiss) that he had a copy that he could/would have read it, and asserting that on the supposition that he had a copy he could/would have read it, both of which can be ambiguously expressed by 'asserting that he could/would have read it on the supposition that he had a copy', but only the former of which asserts that he (actually) could have read it.

To some extent, then, we learn from studying Nowell-Smith's arguments lessons similar to those that we learned in the case of Moore. But some are new, as for instance that many assertions about what a man *would have* done or *will do* depend, in critical cases, upon premisses about his *motives* as well as, or rather than, about his abilities or opportunities: hence these assertions cannot be what assertions about his abilities *mean*.[16]

On one point I may perhaps elaborate a little further. It has been maintained that *sometimes* when we say 'He could have done X' this is a conditional: it requires completion by an *if*-clause, typically 'if he had had the opportunity', and so

16 Yet here it must be pointed out once more that it has not been shown that *all* assertions about what he would have done are so dependent, so that this particular argument against the analysis of 'could have' as 'would have if' is not conclusive: in particular, it does not dispose of the possible suggestion that 'could have' means 'would have if he had *tried*', for here considerations of motive may be irrelevant.

does *not* require us, if we are to establish its truth, to establish that he did in fact have the opportunity. Sometimes on the other hand it is a past indicative, implying that he did have the opportunity: in which case we do, to establish its truth, have to establish that certain conditions were satisfied, but the assertion is *not* to be described as a conditional assertion.

Now while I have no wish to retract this account in general or in all cases, I doubt whether it is the whole story. Consider the case where what we wish to assert is that somebody had the opportunity to do something but lacked the ability— 'He could have smashed that lob, if he had been any good at the smash': here the *if*-clause, which may of course be suppressed and understood, relates not to opportunity but to ability. Now although we might describe the whole sentence as 'conditional', it nevertheless manages to assert, by means of its main clause, something 'categorical' enough, viz. that he did have a certain opportunity. And in the same way Nowell-Smith's 'He could have read *Emma,* if he had had a copy', does seem to assert 'categorically' that he had a certain ability, although he lacked the opportunity to exercise it. Looking at it in this way, there is a temptation to say that 'could have' has, besides its 'all-in' *sense* several more *restricted senses:* this would be brought out if we said 'He could have smashed it, *only* he is no good at the smash' or 'He could have read *Emma but* he had no copy', where, we should say, 'could have' is being used in the restricted senses of opportunity or of ability[17] only, and is a past indicative, not a past conditional.

This view might be reinforced by considering examples with the simple 'can' itself. We are tempted to say that 'He can' sometimes means just that he has the ability, with *nothing said* about opportunity, sometimes *just* that he has the chance, with nothing said about ability, sometimes, however, that he really actually *fully can* here and now, having both ability and oppor-

---

[17] I talk here and throughout of 'ability' and 'opportunity' only: but I realise that other abstract nouns like 'capacity', 'skill', and even 'right' are equally involved. All these terms need listing and elucidating before we really get to grips with 'can'.

tunity. Now nobody, I think, would be tempted to say that 'can', where it means one of the two lesser things, for example, 'has the opportunity', i.e. 'can in the full sense if he has the ability', is grammatically a subjunctive or conditional. Perhaps, then, it was not correct to describe 'He could have', either, as always a conditional where it asserts ability or opportunity only, with nothing said about the other, or even where the other is denied to have existed.

The verb *can* is a peculiar one. Let us compare it for a moment with another peculiar verb, *know*, with which it shares some grammatical peculiarities, such as lack of a continuous present tense. When I say that somebody *knows* what the thing in my hand is, I may mean merely that he has the ability to identify it given the opportunity, or that he has the opportunity to identify it if he has the ability, or that he has both. What do we say about *know* here? Certainly we are not prone to invoke the idea of a conditional, but rather that of different senses, or perhaps the still obscure idea of the dispositional. I must be content here merely to say that I do not think that the old armoury of terms, such as 'mood' and 'sense', is altogether adequate for handling such awkward cases. The only point of which I feel certain is that such verbs as *can* and *know* have each an all-in, paradigm use, around which cluster and from which divagate, little by little and along different paths, a whole series of other uses, for many of which, though perhaps not for all, a synonymous expression ('opportunity', 'realize', and so on) can be found.

It is not unusual for an audience at a lecture to include some who prefer things to be important, and to them now, in case there are any such present, there is owed a peroration. Why, in short, does all this matter? First, then, it needs no emphasizing that both *if* and *can* are highly prevalent and protean words, perplexing both grammatically and philosophically: it is not merely worth while, but essential, in these studies to discover the facts about *ifs* and *cans*, and to remove the confusions they engender. In philosophy it is *can* in particular that we seem so often to uncover, just when we had thought some problem

settled, grinning residually up at us like the frog at the bottom of
the beer mug. Furthermore and secondly, we have not here been
dissecting these two words in general or completely, but in a
special connection which perhaps no one will hold trivial. It has
been alleged by very serious philosophers (not only the two I
have mentioned) that the things we ordinarily say about what
we can do and could have done may actually be consistent with
determinism. It is hard to evade all attempt to decide whether
this allegation is true—hard even for those who, like myself, are
inclined to think that determinism itself is still a name for nothing clear, that has been argued for only incoherently. At least I
should like to claim that the arguments considered . . . fail to
show that it *is* true, and indeed in failing go some way to show
that it is *not*. Determinism, whatever it may be, may yet be the
case, but at least it appears not consistent with what we ordinarily say and presumably think. And finally there is a third point.
Reflecting on the arguments in this lecture, we may well ask
ourselves whether they might not be as well assigned to grammar as to philosophy: and this, I think, is a salutary question to
end on. There are constant references in contemporary philosophy, which notoriously is much concerned with language, to a
'logical grammar' and a 'logical syntax' as though these were
things distinct from ordinary grammarian's grammar and syntax: and certainly they do seem, whatever exactly they may be,
different from traditional grammar. But grammar today is itself
in a state of flux; for fifty years or more it has been questioned
on all hands and counts whether what Dionysius Thrax once
thought was the truth about Greek is the truth and the whole
truth about all language and all languages. Do we know, then,
that there will prove to be any ultimate boundary between 'logical grammar' and a revised and enlarged *Grammar*? In the history of human inquiry, philosophy has the place of the initial
central sun, seminal and tumultuous: from time to time it
throws off some portion of itself to take station as a science, a
planet, cool and well regulated, progressing steadily towards a
distant final state. This happened long ago at the birth of mathematics, and again at the birth of physics: only in the last century

we have witnessed the same process once again, slow and at the time almost imperceptible, in the birth of the science of mathematical logic, through the joint labours of philosophers and mathematicians. Is it not possible that the next century may see the birth, through the joint labours of philosophers, grammarians, and numerous other students of language, of a true and comprehensive *science of language*? Then we shall have rid ourselves of one more part of philosophy (there will still be plenty left) in the only way we ever can get rid of philosophy, by kicking it upstairs.

ACTING, WILLING, DESIRING / H. A. Prichard

THE question 'What is acting or doing something?' seems at first
unreal, i.e. a question to which we already know the answer. For
it looks as though everyone knows what doing something is and
would be ready to offer instances. No one, for instance, would
hesitate to say to another 'You ought to go to bed', on the ground
that neither he nor the other knows the kind of thing meant by
'going to bed'. Yet, when we consider instances that would be
offered, we do not find it easy to state the common character
which we think they had which led us to call them actions.

If, as a preliminary, we look for help to the psychologists,
from whom we naturally expect to get it, we find we fail. We find
plenty of talk about reflex actions, ideo-motor actions, instinctive
actions, and so on, but no discussion of what actions are. Instead, they seem to take for granted that our actions are physical
processes taking place within our body, which they certainly are
not.

From H. A. Prichard, "Acting, Willing, Desiring," Moral Obligation (Oxford:
The Clarendon Press, 1949), pp. 187–198. Reprinted by permission of the
Clarendon Press, Oxford.

We should at first say that to do something is to originate or to bring into existence, i.e., really, to cause, some not yet existing state either of ourselves or of someone else, or, again, of some body. But, for clearness' sake, we should go on to distinguish those actions in doing which we originated some new state directly from those in which we did this only indirectly, i.e. by originating directly some other state, by originating which we indirectly originated the final state. As instances of the former we might give moving or turning our head, and as instances of the latter, curing our toothache by swallowing aspirin, and killing another by pressing a switch which exploded a charge underneath him. If challenged, however, we should have to allow that even in instances of the former kind we did not originate directly what the instances suggest that we did, since what we did originate directly must have been some new state or states of our nerve-cells, of the nature of which we are ignorant. We should, however, insist that in doing any action we must have originated *something* directly, since otherwise we could not originate anything indirectly.

The view that to act is to originate something was maintained by Cook Wilson in a paper on *Means and End.* In the course of this paper he also maintained (1) that an action required the desire to do it, and (2) that it is important to avoid the mistake of thinking that the origination of something X is the willing of X, apparently on the ground that if it were, X would exist as soon as we willed it, and yet it usually does not. He also appeared to hold that the origination of X, though not identical with willing the origination, required it, so that when I originated a movement of my hand, this required as an antecedent my willing this origination, and this willing in turn required the desiring to originate the movement.

According to Cook Wilson, then, in considering an action we have to distinguish three things: first, the action itself, the originating something; second, the required willing to originate this; and third, the required desire to originate this. And according to him what we will and what we desire are the same, viz. the action.

Professor Macmurray, in a Symposium[1] on 'What is action?', takes substantially the same view of what an action is. He says: 'An action is not the concomitance of an intention in the mind and an occurrence in the physical world: it is the *producing* of the occurrence by the Self, the *making* of a change in the external world, the *doing* of a deed. No process which terminates in the mind, such as forming an intention, deciding to act, or willing, is either an action or a component of action'. But he goes on to add: 'In certain circumstances such a mental event or process may be followed *necessarily* by action'.

Now, so far as I can see, this account of what an action is, though plausible and having as a truth underlying it that usually in acting we do cause something, is not tenable.

Unquestionably the thing meant by 'an action' is an activity. This is so whether we speak of a man's action in moving his hand, or of a body's action such as that of the heart in pumping the blood, or that of one electron in repelling another. But though we think that some man in moving his hand, or that the sun in attracting the earth, causes a certain movement, we do not think that the man's or the sun's activity *is* or *consists in* causing the movement. And if we ask ourselves: 'Is there such an activity as originating or causing a change in something else?', we have to answer that there is not. To say this, of course, is not to say that there is no such thing as causing something, but only to say that though the causing a change may require an activity, it is not itself an activity. If we then ask: 'What is the kind of activity required when one body causes another to move?', we have to answer that we do not know, and that when we speak of a force of attraction or of repulsion we are only expressing our knowledge that there is some activity at work, while being ignorant of what the kind of activity is. In the case, however, of a man, i.e., really, of a man's mind, the matter is different. When, e.g., we think of ourselves as having moved our hand, we are thinking of ourselves as having performed an activity of a certain kind, and, it almost goes without saying, a *mental* activity of a certain kind, an activity of whose nature we were dimly

1 Aristotelian Society, Supplementary Volume XVII (1938).

aware in doing the action and of which we can become more clearly aware by reflecting on it. And that we are aware of its special nature is shown by our unhesitatingly distinguishing it from other special mental activities such as thinking, wondering, and imagining. If we ask 'What is the word used for this special kind of activity?' the answer, it seems, has to be 'willing'. (I now think I was mistaken in suggesting that the phrase in use for it is 'setting oneself to cause'.) We also have to admit that while we know the general character of that to which we refer when we use the word 'willing', this character is *sui generis* and so incapable of being defined, i.e. of having its nature expressed in terms of the nature of other things. Even Hume virtually admits this when he says: 'By the *will*, I mean nothing but *the internal impression we feel and are conscious of, when we knowingly give rise to any new motion of our body or new perception of our mind'*,[2] and then goes on to add that the impression is impossible to define. Though, however, the activity of willing is indefinable, we can distinguish it from a number of things which it is not. Thus obviously, as Locke insisted, willing is different from desiring, and again, willing is not, as some psychologists would have it, a species of something called conation of which desiring is another species. There is no such genus. Again, it is not, as Green in one passage[3] implies, a species of desiring which is desiring in another sense than that ordinary sense in which we are said to desire while hesitating to act.

In addition, plainly, willing is not resolving, nor attending to a difficult object, as James holds, nor for that matter attending to anything, nor, again, consenting to the reality of what is attended to, as James also maintains, nor, indeed, consenting to anything, nor, once more, identifying ourself with some object of desire, as Green asserts in another passage.[4]

Consequently, there seems to be no resisting the conclusion that where we think of ourselves or of another as having done a certain action, the kind of activity of which we are think-

[2] Hume, *Treatise* (Selby-Bigge, p. 399).
[3] *Prolegomena*, §§140–2.
[4] *Prolegomena*, §146.

ing is that of willing (though we should have to add that we are thinking of our particular act of willing as having been the doing of the action in question, only because we think it caused a certain change), and that when we refer to some instance of this activity, such as our having moved our finger or given some friend a headache, we refer to it thus not because we think it was, or consisted in, the causing our finger to move or our friend's head to ache, but because we think it had a certain change of state as an effect.

If, as it seems we must, we accept this conclusion, that to act is really to will something, we then become faced by the question: 'What sort of thing is it that we will?'

Those who, like Cook Wilson, distinguish between acting and willing, answer that what we will is an action, which according to him is the originating some change. Thus Green says: 'To will an event' (i.e. presumably some change) 'as distinguished from an act is a contradiction'. And by this he seems to mean that, for instance, in the case which he takes of our paying a debt, what we will is the paying of our debt and not our creditor's coming into possession of what we owe him. Again, James and Stout, though they do not consider the question, show by their instances that they take for granted that what we will is an action. Thus James says: 'I will to write, and the act follows. I will to sneeze and it does not'.[5] And Stout illustrates a volition by a man's willing to produce an explosion by applying a lighted match to gunpowder.[6] But, unfortunately, James speaks of what he has referred to as, the act of writing which I will, as certain physiological movements, and similarly Stout speaks of, the production of an explosion which I will, as certain bodily movements. And, of course, the bodily movements to which they are referring are not actions, though they may be the effects of actions. Plainly, then, both are only doing lip-service to the idea that what we will is an action. And James, at least, drops doing even this. For immediately after making the statement just quoted, viz. 'I will to write, and the act follows. I will to sneeze

5 James, *Psychology*, II, p. 560.
6 Stout, *Manual of Psychology*, IV, p. 641.

and it does not', he adds: 'I will that the distant table slide over the floor towards me; it also does not'. Yet no one would say that the sliding of the table, as distinct from my sliding it, was an action.

In this connection it is well for clearness' sake to bear two things in mind. The first is that some transitive verbs used for particular actions are also used intransitively. Thus one not only speaks of turning one's head but also says that one's head turned. And the second is that, while the phrase 'turning one's head' stands for an action and so for an activity of one's mind, yet when I say 'my head turned' I am speaking simply of a movement of my head which is a change of place and not an action. The difference is made clear by considering what is plainly a mistake made by Professor Macmurray. He says that the term 'action' is ambiguous. He says: 'It may refer either to what is done or to the doing of it. It may mean either "doing" or "deed". When we talk of "an action" we are normally referring to what is done. . . . To act is to effect a change in the external world. The deed is the change so effected'. And he emphasises what he considers the ambiguity in order to indicate that it is doings and not deeds that he is considering. Obviously, however, there is no ambiguity whatever. When I move my hand, the movement of my hand, though an effect of my action, is not itself an action, and no one who considered the matter would say it was, any more than he would say that the death of Caesar, as distinct from his murder, was an action or even part of an action.

This difference between, e.g., my moving my hand and a movement of my hand, is one which James and Stout seem to ignore, as becomes obvious when James speaks of the sliding of a table as, like writing, an action. We find the same thing, too, in Locke. For though, e.g., he says that 'we find by experience, that, barely by willing it, we can move the parts of our bodies',[7] yet in contrasting a human with a physical action he implies that what we will is a movement of our body. Probably, if pressed, he would have said that, strictly speaking, what we will is a move-

[7] Locke, *Essay*, II, 21, §4.

ment and so not an action. In addition, James and Stout seem to treat the distinction between an act of willing, or, as they prefer to call it, a volition, and what is willed, as if it were the same as the distinction between an act of willing and its effect, although they are totally different.

It should be clear from what I have just said that those who hold that what we will is an action must, to be successful, mean by an action something which really is an action. They may, of course, maintain that what we will is a physical process, such as a movement of my hand, but if they do they are really denying that what we will is an action.

It should also now be clear that if we face the question 'What sort of thing do we will?', we have only two answers to consider: (1) that it is some change of state of some thing or person; and (2) that it is an action. If, however, we are forced to conclude, as we have been, that doing something is an act of willing, we seem forced to exclude the second answer, simply on the ground that if it were true, then whenever we think of ourselves as having done some action, we must be thinking of ourselves as having willed some action, i.e. as having willed the willing of some change X; and to think this seems impossible. By the very nature of willing, it seems, what we will must be something other than willing, so that to will the willing of a change X must be an impossibility. And if we even try to deny this, we find ourselves forced to admit that the willing of X, which (we are contending) is what we will, must in turn really be the willing the willing of something else, and so on, and thus become involved in an infinite regress. It is true that Cook Wilson, in a long unpublished discussion, tried to vindicate the analogous idea that in certain limiting cases, viz. those in which the desire moving us is not the desire of some change but the desire to cause it ourselves, as happens in playing golf or patience, what we originate is identical with our origination of something. But he never seems to me to succeed in meeting the objection that this identity must be impossible. Similarly, it seems to me, it is impossible for there to be a case in which the willing the willing of X is identical with willing X.

We are thus left with the conclusion that where we think we have done some action, e.g. have raised our arm or written a word, what we willed was some change, e.g. some movement of our arm or some movement of ink to a certain place on a piece of paper in front of us. But we have to bear in mind that the change which we willed may not have been the same as the change we think we effected. Thus, where I willed some movement of my second finger, I may at least afterwards think that the change I effected was a movement of my first finger, and, only too often, where I willed the existence of a certain word on a piece of paper, I afterwards find that what I caused was a different word. Again, in two cases of the act we call trying to thread a needle, what I willed may have been the same, though the changes I afterwards think I effected were very different, being in the one case the thread's going through the needle and in the other its passing well outside it.

Suppose now that it be allowed that so far I have been right. Then the following admissions must be made:

1. An action, i.e. a human action, instead of being the originating or causing of some change, is an activity of willing some change, this usually causing some change, and in some cases a physical change, its doing or not doing this depending on the physical conditions of which the agent is largely ignorant.

2. Sometimes, however, we have performed such an activity without, at any rate so far as we know, having caused any physical change. This has happened when, e.g., we willed a movement of our hand, at a time when it was either paralysed or numb with cold, whether we knew this or not. No doubt in such cases our activity would not ordinarily be called an action, but it is of the same sort as what we ordinarily call and think of as an action.

3. There is no reason to limit the change which it is possible to will to a movement of some part of our body, since, as James says in effect, we can just as much will the sliding of a table towards us as a movement of our hand towards our head. Indeed, we may, in fact, will this in order to convince ourselves

or someone else that by doing so we shall not cause the table to slide. And it looks as though we sometimes will such things in ordinary life, as when in watching a football match we want some player's speed to increase, and will it to increase.

4. Where we have willed some movement of our body and think we have caused it, we cannot have directly caused it. For what we directly caused, if anything, must have been some change in our brain.

5. Where we think that by willing some change we effected some change in the physical world, we are implying the idea that in doing so, we are butting into, or interfering with, the physical system, just as we think of an approaching comet as effecting a breach in the order of the solar system, so long as we do not regard the comet as part of the system. This idea is, of course, inconsistent with our belief in the uniformity of nature unless we include in nature minds as well as bodies; and in any case it is inconsistent with our belief in the conservation of energy. But so long as we think, as we do, that at any rate on some occasions we really effect something in the physical world, we must admit this. And if we knew that such effecting was impossible, we should give up acting.

We have now to face another question, viz. 'Does acting require a desire, and if it does, the desire of what?'

It is at least very difficult to avoid Aristotle's conclusion that acting requires a desire, if only for the reason he gives, viz. that διάνοια αὐτὴ οὐθὲν κινεῖ [intellect itself moves nothing]. It seems that, as Locke maintained, if we never desired something we should never do anything. But what is the desire required?

Here only one or other of two answers seems possible, viz. (1) that it is a desire of the change X which we will, and (2) that it is a desire of the willing of X. And when we try, we do not find it easy to decide between them. For on the one hand, the desire required seems to have to be the desire of X, on the ground that, if we are to will X, we must desire X. And on the other hand, it seems that it must be the desire to will X, since unless we *desired* to will X we could not will X. Indeed, just for

this reason Plato seems to have gone too far in the *Gorgias* when
he maintained that in acting we never desire to do what we do,
but only that for the sake of which we do it. For, if acting is
willing, it seems that the desire required must be a desire of the
willing, even though the desire be a dependent desire, i.e. a desire depending on the desire of something else for its own sake,
viz. that for the sake of which we do the action. And Plato's mistake seems to have been that of restricting desiring to desiring
something for its own sake.

The two answers are, of course, radically different. For if
the desire required is the desire of X, the thing desired and the
thing willed will be the same, as indeed Green implies that they
are when he maintains that willing is desiring in a special sense
of 'desiring'. But if so, while the willing of X will require what
for want of a better term we seem to have to call the thought of
X, as being something involved in the desire of X, it will not
require either the desire of the willing of X or, for that reason,
even the thought of willing X. On the other hand, if the desire
required is the desire to will X, the thing desired and the thing
willed will necessarily be different, and while the willing of X
will require the desire of willing X and so also the thought of
willing X, it will not require the desire of X, though it will require the thought of X, as being something involved in the
thought of willing X. It should, however, be noted that in the
case of the latter alternative, the desire of X may in some cases
be required indirectly as a condition of our desiring the willing
of X.

To repeat here for clearness' sake what is central—if the
desire required is the desire of X, the willing of X will not require
either the desire of the willing of X or even the thought of willing
X, while, if the desire required is the desire of willing X, the
willing of X will not require the desire of X, though it will require the thought of X.

On consideration, however, we have to reject the idea
that the desire required is the desire of X, on three grounds.
First, if it were true, we should always will any change which we
desired to happen, such as the sliding of the table, whether or

not we thought that if we were to will it to happen we should thereby cause it to happen; and obviously we do not. Second, we occasionally will a change to happen without any desire for it to happen. This must occur, e.g., if a man ever does an act moved solely by the desire for revenge, willing, say, the movement of a switch which he is confident will result in the death of another, not from any desire for his death but solely from the desire to cause it by willing the movement. And even if there are no acts animated solely by the desire for revenge, there are certainly actions approximating to this. At all events, in the case of playing a game the desire at work must be not the desire of some change but the desire to cause it. A putter at golf, e.g., has no desire for the ball to fall into the hole; he only desires to cause it to fall in. This contention is, I think, not met by maintaining, as Cook Wilson in fact does, that the player desires the falling into the hole as caused by his action, and so desires the falling as part of, or an element in, his action. Its falling is neither a part of, nor an element in, his action; at best it is only an effect of it. And the player could only be said to desire the falling if, as he does not, he desired it to happen irrespectively of what would cause it to happen. And in this connection it may be added that if the desire required were the desire of X, it would be impossible to do any act as one which we think would or might fulfil some obligation, since *ex hypothesi* the desire required will be a desire for a change X and not a desire to *will* a change X. Then, third, there is a consideration which comes to light if we consider more closely what it is that we will in certain cases, and more especially in those in which we describe an action as one of trying to do so and so. Suppose, e.g., I have done what we describe as having tried to jump a ditch, and so imply that beforehand I was doubtful of success. Obviously I did not will a movement of my body which I was sure would land me, say, two clear yards on the other side, since if I had thought of willing this I should have realized that willing this would not result in my getting across. I willed that movement the willing of which, if I were to will it, I thought the most likely of all the willings of movements in my power to result in my landing on the farther bank. And in this connection it seems worth noting that what we call trying to do something is as much doing something as what we ordinarily call doing something, although the word 'trying' suggests that it is not. It is the willing a change described in the way in which I have just described what I willed in trying to jump a ditch.

It therefore seems that the desire required must be the desire of the willing of a certain change X. Yet this conclusion is exposed to two objections. The first is that if it were true, it would be impossible to will something X for the first time. For in this context we mean by a desire to will X a desire we can only have in consequence of thinking that if we were to will X, our doing so would be likely to cause something else, and ultimately something which we desire for its own sake. But we cannot desire to will something X, unless we at least have a conjecture that if we were to will X, our willing X might cause some change which we desire for its own sake. And this conjecture requires the thought that on some previous occasion we have willed X and thence concluded from what we think followed this willing of X that it may have caused something else Y. Yet *ex hypothesi* we cannot have willed X on this previous occasion from the desire to will X, since then we had no idea of what willing X might cause. James expresses what is really this objection, though in a misleading way, when he says: 'If, in voluntary action properly so-called' (i.e. in what is really an action), 'the act must be foreseen, it follows that no creature not endowed with divinatory power can perform an act voluntarily for the first time'.[8] The statement as it stands is, of course, absurd, because no one before acting *knows* what his act will be, or even that he will act. But it can be taken as an inaccurate way of expressing the thought that an act of will requires an idea of something which we may cause if we perform the act.

To this objection I have to confess that I cannot see an answer. Yet I think that there must be an answer, since, however it has come about, for us as we are now an act of will does seem to require the desire of it, and so some idea of something which it might effect. I need hardly add that it is no answer to maintain

8 James, *Psychology*, II, p. 487.

that the desire immediately required by willing something X is in some cases the desire of X, and in others the desire of willing X.

The second objection is one which seems to me, though insidious, an objection which can be met. It can be stated thus: 'It is all very well to say that the desire immediately presupposed by willing X is the desire to will X. But to say this is not enough. For we often desire to will X, and yet do not, as when we hesitate to get out of bed or out of a warm bath, and when this is so, obviously something else is required, and this something can only be the willing to will X, so that after all there must be such a thing as willing to will'. But to this the reply seems clear. Though it is possible to desire to desire, as when I desire to desire the welfare of my country more than I do, it is impossible to will to will, for the reason already given. And where we hesitate to will X, what is required is not the willing to will X but either a certain increase in our desire to will X or a decrease in our aversion to doing so. Certainly, too, we often act on this idea, hoping, e.g., that by making ourselves think of the coldness of our breakfast if we stay in bed we shall reach a state of desire in which we shall will certain movements of our body. And sometimes we succeed, and when we do, we sometimes, as James puts it, suddenly find that we have got up, the explanation of our surprise apparently being that we, having been absorbed in the process of trying to stimulate our desire to get up, have not reflected on our state of desire and so have not noticed its increase.

There is also to be noticed in this connection a mistake into which we are apt to fall which leads us to think that there must be such a thing as willing to will. We of course frequently want certain changes to happen and also want to will certain changes. But we are apt not to notice that the objects of these desires differ in respect of the conditions of their realisation, and in consequence to carry the account of the process of deliberation described by Aristotle one step too far—as Aristotle did not. According to him, when we want the happening of something Z which is not an action of ours and which we think we cannot cause directly, we often look for something else Y from the hap-

pening of which the happening of Z would result, and then if
necessary for something else X from the happening of which Y
would result, until we come to think of something A from the
happening of which X, Y, and Z would in turn result, and
which we also think it in our power to cause by a certain act
α. And when we have found A the process stops. We, however,
are apt to carry the process one step farther, and apply to the act
α, i.e. the willing of something β, the willing of which we think
likely to cause A, the same process that we applied to Z, Y, X,
and A, thus treating the willing of β as if it were not the willing
of something (which it is), but a change which some act of willing might cause. As a result of doing this we ask 'From what act
of willing would the willing of β result?', and the answer has to
be 'The willing the willing of β'. But the very question is mistaken, because the willing of β is not a change like Z, Y, X,
and A. The only proper question at this stage must be not 'From
what *willing* would the willing of β result?' but 'From what
something would the willing of β result?' And the proper answer must be: 'From a certain increase in our desire to will β'.

THE WILL / *Gilbert Ryle*

[I] FOREWORD

MOST of the mental-conduct concepts whose logical behaviour [is]
examine[d] are familiar and everyday concepts. We all know
how to apply them and we understand other people when they

From Gilbert Ryle, "*The Will*," The Concept of Mind (*London: Hutchinson &*
Co., 1949; New York: Barnes & Noble, 1949), *Ch. III. Reprinted by permission*
of the publishers.

apply them. What is in dispute is not how to apply them, but how to classify them, or in what categories to put them.

The concept of volition is in a different case. We do not now know in daily life how to use it, for we do not use it in daily life and do not, consequently, learn by practice how to apply it, and how not to misapply it. It is an artificial concept. We have to study certain specialist theories in order to find out how it is to be manipulated. It does not, of course, follow from its being a technical concept that it is an illigitimate or useless concept. 'Ionisation' and 'off-side' are technical concepts, but both are legitimate and useful. 'Phlogiston' and 'animal spirits' were technical concepts, though they have now no utility.

I hope to show that the concept of volition belongs to the latter tribe.

[2] THE MYTH OF VOLITIONS

It has for a long time been taken for an indisputable axiom that the Mind is in some important sense tripartite, that is, that there are just three ultimate classes of mental processes. The Mind or Soul, we are often told, has three parts, namely, Thought, Feeling and Will; or, more solemnly, the Mind or Soul functions in three irreducibly different modes, the Cognitive mode, the Emotional mode and the Conative mode. This traditional dogma is not only not self-evident, it is such a welter of confusions and false inferences that it is best to give up any attempt to re-fashion it. It should be treated as one of the curios of theory.

The main object of this [essay] is not, however, to discuss the whole trinitarian theory of mind but to discuss, and discuss destructively, one of its ingredients. I hope to refute the doctrine that there exists a Faculty, immaterial Organ, or Ministry, corresponding to the theory's description of the 'Will' and, accordingly, that there occur processes, or operations, corresponding to what it describes as 'volitions'. I must however make it clear from the start that this refutation will not invalidate the distinctions which we all quite properly draw between voluntary and involuntary actions and between strong-willed and weak-willed persons. It will, on the contrary, make clearer what is meant by 'voluntary' and 'involuntary', by 'strong-willed' and 'weak-willed', by emancipating these ideas from bondage to an absurd hypothesis.

Volitions have been postulated as special acts, or operations, 'in the mind', by means of which a mind gets its ideas translated into facts. I think of some state of affairs which I wish to come into existence in the physical world, but, as my thinking and wishing are unexecutive, they require the mediation of a further executive mental process. So I perform a volition which somehow puts my muscles into action. Only when a bodily movement has issued from such a volition can I merit praise or blame for what my hand or tongue has done.

It will be clear why I reject this story. It is just an inevitable extension of the myth of the ghost in the machine. It assumes that there are mental states and processes enjoying one sort of existence, and bodily states and processes enjoying another. An occurrence on the one stage is never numerically identical with an occurrence on the other. So, to say that a person pulled the trigger intentionally is to express at least a conjunctive proposition, asserting the occurrence of one act on the physical stage and another on the mental stage; and, according to most versions of the myth, it is to express a causal proposition, asserting that the bodily act of pulling the trigger was the effect of a mental act of willing to pull the trigger.

According to the theory, the workings of the body are motions of matter in space. The causes of these motions must then be *either* other motions of matter in space *or,* in the privileged case of human beings, thrusts of another kind. In some way which must forever remain a mystery, mental thrusts, which are not movements of matter in space, can cause muscles to contract. To describe a man as intentionally pulling the trigger is to state that such a mental thrust did cause the contraction of the muscles of his finger. So the language of 'volitions' is the language of the para-mechanical theory of the mind. If a theorist speaks without qualms of 'volitions', or 'acts of will', no further evidence is needed to show that he swallows whole the dogma that a mind is a secondary field of special causes. It can be predicted that he will correspondingly speak of bodily actions as 'expressions' of mental processes. He is likely also to speak glibly of 'experiences', a plural noun commonly used to denote the postulated non-physical episodes which constitute the shadow-drama on the ghostly boards of the mental stage.

The first objection to the doctrine that overt actions, to which we ascribe intelligence-predicates, are results of counterpart hidden operations of willing is this. Despite the fact that theorists have, since the Stoics and Saint Augustine, recommended us to describe our conduct in this way, no one, save to endorse the theory, ever describes his own conduct, or that of his acquaintances, in the recommended idioms. No one ever says such things as that at 10 A.M. he was occupied in willing this or that, or that he performed five quick and easy volitions and two slow and difficult volitions between midday and lunch-time. An accused person may admit or deny that he did something, or that he did it on purpose, but he never admits or denies having willed. Nor do the judge and jury require to be satisfied by evidence, which in the nature of the case could never be adduced, that a volition preceded the pulling of the trigger. Novelists describe the actions, remarks, gestures and grimaces, the daydreams, deliberations, qualms and embarrassments of their characters; but they never mention their volitions. They would not know what to say about them.

By what sorts of predicates should they be described? Can they be sudden or gradual, strong or weak, difficult or easy, enjoyable or disagreeable? Can they be accelerated, decelerated, interrupted, or suspended? Can people be efficient or inefficient at them? Can we take lessons in executing them? Are they fatiguing or distracting? Can I do two or seven of them synchronously? Can I remember executing them? Can I execute them, while thinking of other things, or while dreaming? Can they become habitual? Can I forget how to do them? Can I mistakenly believe that I have executed one, when I have not, or that I have not executed one, when I have? At which moment was the boy going through a volition to take the high dive? When he set foot on the ladder? When he took his first deep breath? When he counted off 'One, two, three—Go', but did not go? Very, very shortly before he sprang? What would his own answer be to those questions?

Champions of the doctrine maintain, of course, that the enactment of volitions is asserted by implication, whenever an overt act is described as intentional, voluntary, culpable or meritorious; they assert too that any person is not merely able but bound to know that he is willing when he is doing so, since volitions are defined as a species of conscious process. So if ordinary men and women fail to mention their volitions in their descriptions of their own behaviour, this must be due to their being untrained in the dictions appropriate to the description of their inner, as distinct from their overt, behaviour. However, when a champion of the doctrine is himself asked how long ago he executed his last volition, or how many acts of will he executes in, say, reciting 'Little Miss Muffet' backwards, he is apt to confess to finding difficulties in giving the answer, though these difficulties should not, according to his own theory, exist.

If ordinary men never report the occurrence of these acts, for all that, according to the theory, they should be encountered vastly more frequently than headaches, or feelings of boredom; if ordinary vocabulary has no non-academic names for them; if we do not know how to settle simple questions about their frequency, duration or strength, then it is fair to conclude that their existence is not asserted on empirical grounds. The fact that Plato and Aristotle never mentioned them in their frequent and elaborate discussions of the nature of the soul and the springs of conduct is due not to any perverse neglect by them of notorious ingredients of daily life but to the historical circumstance that they were not acquainted with a special hypothesis the acceptance of which rests not on the discovery but on the postulation, of these ghostly thrusts.

The second objection is this. It is admitted that one person can never witness the volitions of another; he can only infer from an observed overt action to the volition from which it resulted, and then only if he has any good reason to believe that the overt action was a voluntary action, and not a reflex or habitual action, or one resulting from some external cause. It follows that no judge, schoolmaster, or parent ever knows that the actions which he judges merit praise or blame; for he cannot do better than guess that the action was willed. Even a confession by the agent, if such confessions were ever made, that he had executed a volition before his hand did the deed would not settle the question. The pronouncement of the confession is only another overt muscular action. The curious conclusion results that though volitions were called in to explain our appraisals of actions, this explanation is just what they fail to provide. If we had no other antecedent grounds for applying appraisal-concepts to the actions of others, we should have no reasons at all for inferring from those actions to the volitions alleged to give rise to them.

Nor could it be maintained that the agent himself can know that any overt action of his own is the effect of a given volition. Supposing, what is not the case, that he could know for certain, either from the alleged direct deliverances of consciousness, or from the alleged direct findings of introspection, that he had executed an act of will to pull the trigger just before he pulled it, this would not prove that the pulling was the effect of that willing. The connection between volitions and movements is allowed to be mysterious, so, for all he knows, his volition may have had some other movement as its effect and the pulling of the trigger may have had some other event for its cause.

Thirdly, it would be improper to burke the point that the connection between volition and movement is admitted to be a mystery. It is a mystery not of the unsolved but soluble type, like the problem of the cause of cancer, but of quite another type. The episodes supposed to constitute the careers of minds are assumed to have one sort of existence, while those constituting the careers of bodies have another sort; and no bridge-status is allowed. Transactions between minds and bodies involve links where no links can be. That there should be any causal transactions between minds and matter conflicts with one part, that there should be none conflicts with another part of the theory.

Minds, as the whole legend describes them, are what must exist if there is to be a causal explanation of the intelligent behaviour of human bodies; and minds, as the legend describes them, live on a floor of existence defined as being outside the causal system to which bodies belong.

Fourthly, although the prime function of volitions, the task for the performance of which they were postulated, is to originate bodily movements, the argument, such as it is, for their existence entails that some mental happenings also must result from acts of will. Volitions were postulated to be that which makes actions voluntary, resolute, meritorious and wicked. But predicates of these sorts are ascribed not only to bodily movements but also to operations which, according to the theory, are mental and not physical operations. A thinker may ratiocinate resolutely, or imagine wickedly; he may try to compose a limerick and he may meritoriously concentrate on his algebra. Some mental processes then can, according to the theory, issue from volitions. So what of volitions themselves? Are they voluntary or involuntary acts of mind? Clearly either answer leads to absurdities. If I cannot help willing to pull the trigger, it would be absurd to describe my pulling it as 'voluntary'. But if my volition to pull the trigger is voluntary, in the sense assumed by the theory, then it must issue from a prior volition and that from another *ad infinitum*. It has been suggested, to avoid this difficulty, that volitions cannot be described as either voluntary or involuntary. 'Volition' is a term of the wrong type to accept either predicate. If so, it would seem to follow that it is also of the wrong type to accept such predicates as 'virtuous' and 'wicked', 'good' and 'bad', a conclusion which might embarrass those moralists who use volitions as the sheet-anchor of their systems.

In short, then, the doctrine of volitions is a causal hypothesis, adopted because it was wrongly supposed that the question, 'What makes a bodily movement voluntary?' was a causal question. This supposition is, in fact, only a special twist of the general supposition that the question, 'How are mental-conduct concepts applicable to human behaviour?' is a question about the causation of that behaviour.

Champions of the doctrine should have noticed the simple fact that they and all other sensible persons knew how to decide questions about the voluntariness and involuntariness of actions and about the resoluteness and irresoluteness of agents before they had ever heard of the hypothesis of the occult inner thrusts of actions. They might then have realised that they were not elucidating the criteria already in efficient use, but, tacitly assuming their validity, were trying to correlate them with hypothetical occurrences of a para-mechanical pattern. Yet this correlation could, on the one hand, never be scientifically established, since the thrusts postulated were screened from scientific observation; and, on the other hand, it would be of no practical or theoretical use, since it would not assist our appraisals of actions, depending as it would on the presupposed validity of those appraisals. Nor would it elucidate the logic of those appraisal-concepts, the intelligent employment of which antedated the invention of this causal hypothesis.

Before we bid farewell to the doctrine of volitions, it is expedient to consider certain quite familiar and authentic processes with which volitions are sometimes wrongly identified.

People are frequently in doubt what to do; having considered alternative courses of action, they then, sometimes, select or choose one of these courses. This process of opting for one of a set of alternative courses of action is sometimes said to be what is signified by 'volition'. But this identification will not do, for most voluntary actions do not issue out of conditions of indecision and are not therefore results of settlements of indecisions. Moreover it is notorious that a person may choose to do something but fail, from weakness of will, to do it; or he may fail to do it because some circumstance arises after the choice is made, preventing the execution of the act chosen. But the theory could not allow that volitions ever fail to result in action, else further executive operations would have to be postulated to account for the fact that sometimes voluntary actions are performed. And finally the process of deliberating between alternatives and opting for one of them is itself subject to appraisal-predicates. But if, for example, an act of choosing is describable as voluntary, then, on this suggested showing, it would have in its turn to be the result of a prior choice to choose, and that from a choice to choose to choose. . . .

The same objections forbid the identification with volitions of such other familiar processes as that of resolving or making up our minds to do something and that of nerving or bracing ourselves to do something. I may resolve to get out of bed or go to the dentist, and I may, clenching my fists and gritting my teeth, brace myself to do so, but I may still backslide. If the action is not done, then, according to the doctrine, the volition to do it is also unexecuted. Again, the operations of resolving and nerving ourselves are themselves members of the class of creditable or discreditable actions, so they cannot constitute the peculiar ingredient which, according to the doctrine, is the common condition of any performance being creditable or discreditable.

[3] THE DISTINCTION BETWEEN VOLUNTARY AND INVOLUNTARY

It should be noticed that while ordinary folk, magistrates, parents and teachers, generally apply the words 'voluntary' and 'involuntary' to actions in one way, philosophers often apply them in quite another way.

In their most ordinary employment 'voluntary' and 'involuntary' are used, with a few minor elasticities, as adjectives applying to actions which ought not to be done. We discuss whether someone's action was voluntary or not only when the action seems to have been his fault. He is accused of making a noise, and the guilt is his, if the action was voluntary, like laughing; he has successfully excused himself, if he satisfies us that it was involuntary, like a sneeze. In the same way in ordinary life we raise questions of responsibility only when someone is charged, justly or unjustly, with an offence. It makes sense, in this use, to ask whether a boy was responsible for breaking a window, but not whether he was responsible for finishing his homework in good time. We do not ask whether it was his fault that he got a long-division sum right, for to get a sum right is not a fault. If he gets it wrong, he may satisfy us that his failure was not his fault, perhaps because he had not yet been shown how to do such calculations.

In this ordinary use, then, it is absurd to discuss whether satisfactory, correct or admirable performances are voluntary or involuntary. Neither inculpation nor exculpation is in point. We neither confess to authorship nor adduce extenuating circumstances; neither plead 'guilty' nor plead 'not guilty'; for we are not accused.

But philosophers, in discussing what constitutes acts voluntary or involuntary, tend to describe as voluntary not only reprehensible but also meritorious actions, not only things that are someone's fault but also things that are to his credit. The motives underlying their unwitting extension of the ordinary sense of 'voluntary', 'involuntary' and 'responsible' will be considered later. For the moment it is worth while to consider certain consequences which follow from it. In the ordinary use, to say that a sneeze was involuntary is to say that the agent could not help doing it, and to say that a laugh was voluntary is to say that the agent could have helped doing it. (This is not to say that the laugh was intentional. We do not laugh on purpose.) The boy could have got the sum right which he actually got wrong; he knew how to behave, but he misbehaved; he was competent to tie a reef-knot, though what he unintentionally produced was a granny-knot. His failure or lapse was his fault. But when the word 'voluntary' is given its philosophically stretched use, so that correct as well as incorrect, admirable as well as contemptible acts are described as voluntary, it seems to follow by analogy with the ordinary use, that a boy who gets his sum right can also be described as having been 'able to help it'. It would then be proper to ask: Could you have helped solving the riddle? Could you have helped drawing the proper conclusion? Could you have helped tying a proper reef-knot? Could you have helped seeing the point of that joke? Could you have helped being kind to that child? In fact, however, no one could answer these questions, though it is not at first obvious why, if it is correct to say that someone could have avoided getting a sum wrong, it is incorrect to say that he could have avoided getting it right.

The solution is simple. When we say that someone could have avoided committing a lapse or error, or that it was his fault that he committed it, we mean that he knew how to do the right thing, or was competent to do so, but did not exercise his knowledge or competence. He was not trying, or not trying hard enough. But when a person has done the right thing, we cannot then say that he knew how to do the wrong thing, or that he was competent to make mistakes. For making mistakes is not an exercise of competence, nor is the commission of slips and exercise of knowledge *how;* it is a failure to exercise knowledge *how.* It is true in one sense of 'could' that a person who had done a sum correctly could have got it wrong; in the sense, namely, that he is not exempt from the liability to be careless. But in another sense of 'could', to ask, 'Could you have got it wrong?' means 'Were you sufficiently intelligent and well-trained and were you concentrating hard enough to make a miscalculation?', and this is as silly a question as to ask whether someone's teeth are strong enough to be broken by cracking nuts.

The tangle of largely spurious problems, known as the problem of the Freedom of the Will, partly derives from this unconsciously stretched use of 'voluntary' and these consequential misapplications of different senses of 'could' and 'could have helped'.

The first task is to elucidate what is meant in their ordinary, undistorted use by 'voluntary', 'involuntary', 'responsible', 'could not have helped' and 'his fault', as these expressions are used in deciding concrete questions of guilt and innocence.

If a boy has tied a granny-knot instead of a reef-knot, we satisfy ourselves that it was his fault by first establishing that he knew how to tie a reef-knot, and then by establishing that his hand was not forced by external coercion and that there were no other agencies at work preventing him from tying the correct knot. We establish that he could tie reef-knots by finding out that he had been taught, had had practise, usually got them right, or by finding that he could detect and correct knots tied by others, or by finding that he was ashamed of what he had done and, without help from others, put it right himself. That he was not acting under duress or in panic or high fever or with numb fingers, is discovered in the way in which we ordinarily discover that highly exceptional incidents have not taken place; for such incidents would have been too remarkable to have gone unremarked, at least by the boy himself.

The first question which we had to decide had nothing to do with the occurrence or non-occurrence of any occult episode in the boy's stream of consciousness; it was the question whether or not he had the required higher-level competence, that of knowing how to tie reef-knots. We were not, at this stage, inquiring whether he committed, or omitted, an extra public or private operation, but only whether he possessed or lacked a certain intelligent capacity. What satisfied us was not the (unattainable) knowledge of the truth or falsity of a particular covert cause-overt effect proposition, but the (attainable) knowledge of the truth or falsity of a complex and partially general hypothetical proposition—not, in short, that he did tie a shadowy reef- or granny-knot behind the scenes, but that he could have tied a real one with this rope and would have done so on this occasion, if he had paid more heed to what he was doing. The lapse was his fault because, knowing how to tie the knot, he still did not tie it correctly.

Consider next the case of an act which everyone would decide was not the agent's fault. A boy arrives late for school and on inquiry it turns out that he left home at the usual time, did not dally on his way to the omnibus halt and caught the usual omnibus. But the vehicle broke down and could not complete the journey. The boy ran as fast as he could the rest of the way, but was still late. Clearly all the steps taken by the boy were either the same as those which normally bring him to school in time, or were the only steps open to him for remedying the effects of the breakdown. There was nothing else that he could have done and his teacher properly recommends him to follow the same routine on future occasions. His late arrival was not the result of a failure to do what he was capable of doing. He was prevented by a circumstance which was not in his power to modify. Here again the teacher is judging an action with reference to the capacities and opportunities of the agent; his excuse is accepted that he could not have done better than he did. The whole question of the involuntariness of his late arrival is decided without the boy being asked to report any deliverances of consciousness or introspection about the execution or non-execution of any volitions.

It makes no difference if the actions with which an agent is charged either are or embody operations of silent soliloquy or other operations with verbal or non-verbal images. A slip in mental arithmetic is the pupil's fault on the same grounds as a slip made in written arithmetic; and an error committed in matching colours in the mind's eye may merit the reproach of carelessness in the same way as an error committed in matching colours on the draper's counter. If the agent could have done better than he did, then he could have helped doing it as badly as he did.

Besides considering the ordinary senses of 'voluntary', 'involuntary', 'responsible', 'my fault' and 'could' or 'could not help', we should notice as well the ordinary uses of such expressions as 'effort of will', 'strength of will' and 'irresolute'. A person is described as behaving resolutely when in the execution of difficult, protracted or disagreeable tasks he tends not to relax his efforts, not to let his attention be diverted, not to grumble and not to think much or often about his fatigue or fears. He does not shirk or drop things to which he has set his hand. A weak-willed person is one who is easily distracted or disheartened, apt to convince himself that another time will be more suitable or that the reasons for undertaking the task were not after all very strong. Note that it is no part of the definition of resoluteness or of irresoluteness that a resolution should actually have been formed. A resolute man may firmly resist temptations to abandon or postpone his task, though he never went through a prefatory ritual-process of making up his mind to complete it. But naturally such a man will also be disposed to perform any vows which he has made to others or to himself. Correspondingly the irresolute man will be likely to fail to carry out his often numerous good resolutions, but his lack of tenacity of purpose will be exhibited also in surrenders and slacknesses in courses of action which were unprefaced by any private or public undertakings to accomplish them.

Strength of will is a propensity the exercises of which consist in sticking to tasks; that is, in not being deterred or diverted. Weakness of will is having too little of this propensity. The performances in which strength of will is exerted may be performances of almost any sort, intellectual or manual, imaginative or administrative. It is not a single-track disposition or, for that and other reasons, a disposition to execute occult operations of one special kind.

By 'an effort of will' is meant a particular exercise of tenacity of purpose, occurring when the obstacles are notably great, or the counter-temptations notably strong. Such efforts may, but need not, be accompanied by special processes, often of a ritual character, of nerving or adjuring oneself to do what is required; but these processes are not so much ways in which resoluteness is shown as ways in which fear of irresoluteness manifests itself.

Before we leave the concept or concepts of voluntariness, two further points need to be made. (1) Very often we oppose things done voluntarily to things suffered under compulsion. Some soldiers are volunteers, others are conscripts; some yachtsmen go out to sea voluntarily, others are carried out to sea by the wind and tide. Here questions of inculpation and exculpation need not arise. In asking whether the soldier volunteered or was conscripted, we are asking whether he joined up because he wanted to do so, or whether he joined up because he had to do so, where 'had to' entails 'no matter what he wanted'. In asking whether the yachtsman went out to sea of his own accord or whether he was carried out, we are asking whether he went out on purpose, or whether he would still have gone out as he did, even if he had meant not to do so. Would bad news from home, or a warning from the coastguard, have stopped him?

What is involuntary, in this use, is not describable as an act. Being carried out to sea, or being called up, is something that happens to a person, not something which he does. In this respect, this antithesis between voluntary and involuntary differs from the antithesis we have in mind when we ask whether someone's tying of a granny-knot, or his knitting of his brows, is voluntary or involuntary. A person who frowns involuntarily is not forced to frown, as a yachtsman may be forced out to sea; nor is the careless boy forced to tie a granny-knot, as the conscript is forced to join the army. Even frowning is something that a person does. It is not done to him. So sometimes the question 'Voluntary or involuntary' means 'Did the person do it, or was it done to him?'; sometimes it presupposes that he did it, but means 'Did he do it with or without heeding what he was doing?' or 'Did he do it on purpose or inadvertently, mechanically, or instinctively, etc.?'

(2) When a person does something voluntarily, in the sense that he does it on purpose or is trying to do it, his action certainly reflects some quality or qualities of mind, since (it is more than a verbal point to say) he is in some degree and in one fashion or another minding what he is doing. It follows also that, if linguistically equipped, he can then tell, without research or conjecture, what he has been trying to accomplish. But . . . these implications of voluntariness do not carry with them the double-life corollaries often assumed. To frown intentionally is not to do one thing on one's forehead and another thing in a second metaphorical place; nor is it to do one thing with one's brow-muscles and another thing with some non-bodily organ. In particular, it is not to bring about a frown on one's forehead by first bringing about a frown-causing exertion of some occult non-muscle. 'He frowned intentionally' does not report the occurrence of two episodes. It reports the occurrence of one episode, but one of a very different character from that reported by 'he frowned involuntarily', though the frowns might be photographically as similar as you please.

[4] FREEDOM OF THE WILL

It has been pointed out that in some philosophers' discussions of the voluntariness of actions, the words 'voluntary', 'involuntary' and 'responsible' are used, not with their ordinary restriction to lapses or apparent lapses, but with a wider scope covering all performances which are to be adjudged favourably or unfavourably by any criteria of excellence or admissibility. In their use, a person is described as voluntarily doing the right thing and as voluntarily doing the wrong thing, or as being responsible not only for actions for which he is subject to accusation, but also for actions entitling him to kudos. It is used, that is, as a synonym of 'intentional'.

Now the philosophers who have worked with this stretched usage have had a strong intellectual motive for doing so. They felt the need for an apparatus of terms by which to demarcate those things and occurrences to which *either* plaudits *or* strictures are appropriate from those to which neither are appropriate. Without such an apparatus it would, they felt, be impossible to state what are the qualifications for membership of the realm of Spirit, the lack of which entails relegation to the realm of brute Nature.

The main source of this concern to discover some peculiar element present, wherever Spirit is present, and absent, where it is absent, was alarm at the bogy of Mechanism. It was believed that the physical sciences had established, or were on the way to establishing, that the things and events of the external world are rigidly governed by discoverable laws, laws the formulations of which admit no appraisal-words. It was felt that all external happenings are confined within the iron grooves of mechanical causation. The genesis, the properties and the courses of these happenings were, or would be, totally explained in terms of measurable and, it was supposed, therefore purposeless forces.

To salve our right to employ appraisal-concepts, the field of their proper application had to be shown to lie somewhere else than this external world, and an internal world of unmeasurable but purposeful forces was thought to do the trick. 'Volitions' being already nominated as the required outputs of internal forces, it was then natural to suppose that voluntariness, defined in terms of propagation by volitions, was the common and peculiar element which makes occurrences spiritual. Scientific propositions and appraisal-propositions were accordingly distinguished as being respectively descriptions of what takes place in the external world and descriptions of what takes place in the internal world—at least until psychologists claimed that their assertions were scientific descriptions of what takes place in the inner world.

The question whether human beings can merit praise or blame was consequently construed as the question whether volitions are effects.

[5] THE BOGY OF MECHANISM

Whenever a new science achieves its first big successes, its enthusiastic acolytes always fancy that all questions are now soluble by extension of its methods of solving its questions. At one time theorists imagined that the whole world was nothing more than a complex of geometrical figures, at another that the whole world was describable and explicable in the propositions of pure arithmetic. Chemical, electrical, Darwinian and Freudian cosmogonies have also enjoyed their bright but brief days. 'At long last', the zealots always say, 'we can give, or at least indicate, a solution of all difficulties and one which is unquestionably a scientific solution'.

The physical sciences launched by Copernicus, Galileo, Newton and Boyle secured a longer and a stronger hold upon the cosmogony-builders than did either their forerunners or their successors. People still tend to treat laws of Mechanics not merely as the ideal type of scientific laws, but as, in some sense, the ultimate laws of Nature. They tend to hope or fear that biological, psychological and sociological laws will one day be 'reduced' to mechanical laws—though it is left unclear what sort of a transaction this 'reduction' would be.

I have spoken of Mechanism as a bogy. The fear that theoretically minded persons have felt lest everything should turn out to be explicable by mechanical laws is a baseless fear. And it is baseless not because the contingency which they dread happens not to be impending, but because it makes no sense to speak of such a contingency. Physicists may one day have found the answers to all physical questions, but not all questions are physical questions. The laws that they have found and will find may, in one sense of the metaphorical verb, govern everything that happens, but they do not ordain everything that happens. Indeed they do not ordain anything that happens. Laws of nature are not fiats.

An illustration may elucidate this point. A scientifically trained spectator, who is not acquainted with chess or any other game, is permitted to look at a chessboard in the intervals between the moves. He does not yet see the players making the moves. After a time he begins to notice certain regularities. The pieces known to us as 'pawns', normally move only one square at a time and then only forwards, save in certain special circumstances when they move diagonally. The pieces known to us as 'bishops' only move diagonally, though they can move any number of squares at a time. Knights always make dog-legged moves. And so on. After much research this spectator will have worked out all the rules of chess, and he is then allowed to see that the moves of the pieces are made by people whom we know as 'players'. He commiserates with them upon their bondage. 'Every move that you make', he says, 'is governed by unbreakable rules; from the moment that one of you puts his hand on a pawn, the move that he will make with it is, in most cases, accurately predictable. The whole course of what you tragically dub your "game" is remorselessly pre-ordained; nothing in it takes place which cannot be shown to be governed by one or other of the iron rules. Heartless necessity dictates the play, leaving no room in it for intelligence or purpose. True, I am not yet competent to explain every move that I witness by the rules that I have so far discovered. But it would be unscientific to suppose that there are inexplicable moves. There must therefore be further rules, which I hope to discover and which will satisfactorily complete the explanations which I have inaugurated'. The players, of course, laugh and explain to him that though every move is governed, not one of them is ordained by the rules.

'True, given that I start to move my bishop, you can predict with certainty that it will end on a square of the same colour as that from which it started. That can be deduced from the rules. But that, or how far, I shall move my bishop at this or that stage of the game is not stated in, or deducible from, the rules. There is plenty of room for us to display cleverness and stupidity and to exercise deliberation and choice. Though nothing happens that is irregular, plenty happens that is surprising, ingenious and silly. The rules are the same for all the games of chess that have ever been played, yet nearly every game that has ever been played has taken a course for which the players can recall no close parallels. The rules are unalterable, but the games are not uniform. The rules prescribe what the players may not do; everything else is permitted, though many moves that are permitted would be bad tactics.

'There are no further rules of the game for you to discover and the "explanations" which you hope to find for the particular moves that we make can, of course, be discovered, but they are not explanations in terms of rules but in terms of some quite different things, namely, such things as the player's consideration and application of tactical principles. Your notion of what constitutes an explanation was too narrow. The sense in which a rule "explains" a move made in conformity with it is not the same as the sense in which a tactical principle explains a move, for all that every move that obeys a tactical principle also obeys a rule. Knowing how to apply tactical principles involves knowing the rules of the game, but there is no question of these principles being "reducible" to rules of the game'.

This illustration is not intended to suggest that the laws of physics are very much like the rules of chess; for the course of Nature is not a game and its laws are not human inventions or conventions. What the illustration is meant to bring out is the fact there is no contradiction in saying that one and the same process, such as the move of a bishop, is in accordance with two principles of completely different types and such that neither is 'reducible' to the other, though one of them presupposes the other.

Hence there derive two quite different sorts of 'explanation' of the moves, neither of which is incompatible with the other. Indeed the explanation in terms of tactical canons presupposes that in terms of the rules of chess, but it is not deducible from those rules. This point can be expressed in another way. A spectator might ask, in one sense of 'why', why the bishop always ends a move on a square of the same colour as that on which it began the game; he would be answered by being referred to the rules of chess, including those prescribing the design of the board. He might then ask, in another sense of 'why', why a player at a certain stage of the game moved one of his bishops (and not some other piece) to one square (and not to another); he might be answered that it was to force the opposing Queen to cease to threaten the player's King.

Words like 'explanation', 'law', 'rule', 'principle', 'why', 'because', 'cause', 'reason', 'govern', 'necessitate', etc., have a range of typically different senses. Mechanism seemed to be a menace because it was assumed that the use of these terms in mechanical theories is their sole use; that all 'why' questions are answerable in terms of laws of motion. In fact all 'why' questions of one type are perhaps answerable in those terms and no 'why' questions of other types are answerable merely in those terms.

It may well be that throughout the whole length of *The Decline and Fall of the Roman Empire* Gibbon never once infringes the rules of English grammar. They governed his entire writing, yet they did not ordain what he should write, or even the style in which he should write; they merely forbade certain ways of conjoining words. Knowing these rules and Gibbon's obedience to them, a reader can predict from the fact that a particular sentence has for its subject a plural noun that its verb will be a plural verb. His predictions will be uniformly correct, yet we feel no inclination to lament that Gibbon's pen ran in a fatal groove. Grammar tells the reader that the verb must be a plural verb, but not which verb it will be.

An argumentative passage from *The Decline and Fall*

might be examined for the grammatical rules which its word-ar-rangements observe, the stylistic canons which its word-arrange-ments observe, and the logical rules which its word-arrangements observe. There is no conflict or competition between these differ-ent types of principles; all alike are applied in the same material; all alike can supply licences for correct predictions; all alike may be referred to for answers to questions of the same verbal pat-tern 'Why did Gibbon write this and not something else?'

The discoveries of the physical sciences no more rule out life, sentience, purpose or intelligence from presence in the world than do the rules of grammar extrude style or logic from prose. Certainly the discoveries of the physical sciences say nothing of life, sentience, or purpose, but nor do the rules of grammar say anything about style or logic. For the laws of phys-ics apply to what is animate as well as to what is inanimate, to intelligent people as well as to idiots, just as the rules of gram-mar apply to *Whitaker's Almanac* as well as to *The Decline and Fall*, to Mrs. Eddy's as well as to Hume's reasonings.

The favourite model to which the fancied mechanistic world is assimilated is that of billiard balls imparting their mo-tion to one another by impact. Yet a game of billiards provides one of the simplest examples of a course of events for the de-scription of which mechanical terms are necessary without being sufficient. Certainly from accurate knowledge of the weight, shape, elasticity and movements of the balls, the consti-tution of the table and the conditions of the atmosphere it is in principle possible, in accordance with known laws, to deduce from a momentary state of the balls what will be their later state. But it does not follow from this that the course of the game is predictable in accordance with those laws alone. A scientific forecaster, who was ignorant of the rules and tactics of the game and of the skill and plans of the players, could predict, perhaps, from the beginning of a single stroke, the positions in which the balls will come to rest before the next stroke is made; but he could predict no further. The player himself may be able to fore-see with modest probability the sort of break that he will make, for he knows, perhaps, the best tactics to apply to situations like this and he knows a good deal about his own skill, endurance, patience, keenness and intentions.

It must be noticed that in so far as the player has any skill in getting the balls where he wishes, he must have knowledge, of a rule-of-thumb sort, of the mechanical principles which govern the accelerations and decelerations of the balls. His knowledge how to execute his intentions is not at loggerheads with his knowledge of mechanical laws; it depends on that knowledge. In applying appraisal-concepts to his play we are not worried by the fact that the motions imparted by him to the balls are governed by mechanical laws; for there could not be a game of skill at all if, *per impossibile*, the instruments of the game behaved randomly.

The modern interpretation of natural laws as statements not of necessities but of very, very long odds is sometimes acclaimed as providing a desiderated element of non-rigourousness in Nature. Now at last, it is sometimes felt, we can be scientific while reserving just a very few occasions in which appraisal-concepts can be properly applied. This silly view assumes that an action could not merit favourable or unfavourable criticism, unless it were an exception to scientific generalisations. But the billiards player asks for no special indulgences from the laws of physics any more than he does from the rules of billiards. Why should he? They do not force his hand. The fears expressed by some moral philosophers that the advance of the natural sciences diminishes the field within which the moral virtues can be exercised rests on the assumption that there is some contradiction in saying that one and the same occurrence is governed both by mechanical laws and by moral principles, an assumption as baseless as the assumption that a golfer cannot at once conform to the laws of ballistics *and* obey the rules of golf *and* play with elegance and skill. Not only is there plenty of room for purpose where everything is governed by mechanical laws, but there would be no place for purpose if things were not so governed. Predictability is a necessary condition of planning.

Mechanism then is a mere bogy and while there is much

to be elucidated in the special concepts of biology, anthropology, sociology, ethics, logic, aesthetics, politics, economics, historiography, etc., there is no need for the desperate salvage-operation of withdrawing the applications of them out of the ordinary world to some postulated other world, or of setting up a partition between things that exist in Nature and things that exist in non-Nature. No occult precursors of overt acts are required to preserve for their agent his title to plaudits or strictures for performing them, nor would they be effective preservatives if they did exist.

Men are not machines, not even ghost-ridden machines. They are men—a tautology which is sometimes worth remembering. People often pose such questions as 'How does my mind get my hand to make the required movements?' and even 'What makes my hand do what my mind tells it to do?' Questions of these patterns are properly asked of certain chain-processes. The question 'What makes the bullet fly out of the barrel?' is properly answered by 'The expansion of gases in the cartridge'; the question 'What makes the cartridge explode?' is answered by reference to the percussion of the detonator; and the question 'How does my squeezing the trigger make the pin strike the detonator?' is answered by describing the mechanism of springs, levers and catches between the trigger and the pin. So when it is asked 'How does my mind get my finger to squeeze the trigger?' the form of the question presupposes that a further chain-process is involved, embodying still earlier tensions, releases and discharges, though this time 'mental' ones. But whatever is the act or operation adduced as the first step of this postulated chain-process, the performance of it has to be described in just the same way as in ordinary life we describe the squeezing of the trigger by the marksman. Namely we say simply 'He did it' and not 'He did or underwent something else which caused it'.

In conclusion, it is perhaps worth while giving a warning against a very popular fallacy. The hearsay knowledge that everything in Nature is subject to mechanical laws often tempts people to say that Nature is either one big machine, or else a conglomeration of machines. But in fact there are very few machines in Nature. The only machines that we find are the machines that human beings make, such as clocks, windmills and turbines. There are a very few natural systems which somewhat resemble such machines, namely, such things as solar systems. These do go on by themselves and repeat indefinitely the same series of movements. These do go, as few unmanufactured things go, 'like clock-work'. True, to make machines we have to know and apply Mechanics. But inventing machines is not copying things found in inanimate Nature.

Paradoxical though it may seem, we have to look rather to living organisms for examples in Nature of self-maintaining, routine-observing systems. The movements of the heavenly bodies provided one kind of 'clock'. It was the human pulse that provided the next. Nor is it merely primitive animism which makes native children think of engines as iron horses. There is very little else in Nature to which they are so closely analogous. Avalanches and games of billiards are subject to mechanical laws; but they are not at all like the workings of machines.

MOTIVES AND MOTIVATION[1] / R. S. Peters

'I am therefore going to commit a final and incorrigible lewdness. I am going to assess certain of the broad requirements for analyses of human motivation by examining human motivational phenomena'.   S. KOCH.

INTRODUCTORY

THERE are two good reasons for dwelling on the use of the term

From R. S. Peters, "*Motives and Motivation*," The Concept of Motivation (*New York: Humanities Press, 1958; London: Routledge & Kegan Paul, 1958*), Ch. II. Reprinted by permission of the publishers.

1 The main arguments of this essay first appeared in an article bearing the same title in *Philosophy*, XXXI (1956).

'motive' and 'motivation' before proceeding to a detailed analysis of psychological theories. In the first place, as I have argued elsewhere (Peters, 1956), the term 'motive' is used in specific sorts of contexts in ordinary language. The generalized use of this term by psychologists, some of whom hold that we have a motive for *everything* that we do, has therefore a rather bizarre effect, which it is the philosopher's task to make explicit.

Secondly the term 'motive' is not distinctive in that it does a quite different explanatory job from 'his reason' or 'the reason why'; rather it marks off certain sorts of reasons in certain types of contexts. Motives, in other words, are a particular class of reasons, which are distinguished by certain logical properties. My thesis is that the concept of 'motivation' has developed from that of 'motive' by attempting a causal interpretation of the logical force of the term. This is made possible by the failure to distinguish different levels of questions.

THE ORDINARY USE OF THE TERM 'MOTIVE'

Motives are a particular class of reasons. Many sorts of things can be reasons for actions, but motives are reasons of a particular sort. We can ask of a reason for an action 'Was that his motive?' But we cannot ask of a motive, without in some way repeating ourselves 'Was that the reason why he did it?' Our preliminary problem about the concept of 'motive' is to specify its delimiting criteria within the general class of 'reasons for action'.

In certain contexts, instead of asking 'Why did Jones do that?' we may ask what Jones' motive was. Often this is in a context where it is appropriate to ask 'What made Jones do that?'—when there is a departure from the conventional expectations. We ask, for instance, what a man's motive is for committing a murder or for joining a party with whose aims he is not in sympathy. The implication is that these actions are not characteristic of him or ones which conform to any standard rule-following purposive pattern. But to ask for a man's motive is

very different from asking what made him do it in that it
strengthens rather than rules out the suggestion that there was
some point in what he did. When we say 'What made Jones
cross the road?' we are most likely implying that he had no objective in mind. We are suggesting that something has happened
to him rather than that he is aiming at something. But to ask for
his motive is to suggest that this is very much a case of a directed action though the man's objective may be hidden from us
as well as being pursued according to no standard pattern of
rules.

There are, I would suggest, three characteristics shared
by explanations in terms of motives which account for the difficulty in fitting them neatly into the framework of types of explanation which has been outlined. In the first place we only ask
about a man's motives when we wish, in some way, to hold his
conduct up for assessment. The word is used typically in moral
or legal discourse where actions have to be *justified* and not simply explained. We ascribe or impute motives to others and avow
them or confess to them in ourselves. This explains why we
often ask for motives when there is a breach of conventional
expectations; for it is in just these sorts of contexts that men
have to justify their actions. It also explains the too easy connection of the term 'motive' with early psycho-analytic explanations of the odd and unusual. Ordinary language can convey
such subtle suggestions; for one way in which it differs from
scientific language is that its use is not simply to describe and
explain. It may command, condemn, guide, express states of
mind, announce, provoke, exhort, and perform countless other
such social functions. Often a different word is used precisely
because such a specific social function is to be performed. Scientific language, almost by definition, has no such subtleties; and
this is one of the difficulties which confront the theorist who
uses a term like 'motive' in a special theory. The social implications of using the term haunt the theory.

This explains the sense of outrage which the ordinary
man has when the psychologist gets busy on his motives. For

psychologists tend to use the term indiscriminately and to ignore the contextual confinement of the use of the word in ordinary language. Some of them, indeed, suggest that we have a motive for *everything* that we do. The effect of such a suggestion is to put all actions up for assessment. We don't mind being asked our motive for effecting an entry into our neighbour's house without his permission; for this is the sort of action which obviously requires some sort of justification. But we take it amiss when our motives are questioned for getting married, playing chess, or giving Xmas presents to our friends. For in such cases we are doing the done thing and there should be no necessity for justification. Of course we probably have reasons for doing these sorts of things; people don't get married through force of habit or in a fit of absent-mindedness. But if we are asked about our motives the suggestion is that we may not have such obvious reasons. We may be up to no good. We may be marrying the girl for her money or giving Xmas presents to court popularity. When we are asked about our motives we may produce one that is a perfectly satisfactory justification, perhaps one that is usual in the circumstances. We might say, for instance, that we entered our neighbour's house to turn off the kettle which he had left boiling on the stove or that we were getting married in order to have a family. Similarly we can say that our neighbour is a man of the highest motives or that his motives in giving presents to his friends were unimpeachable. A motive is not necessarily a discreditable reason for acting, but it is a reason asked for in a context where there is a suggestion that it *might* be discreditable. The demand is for justification, not simply explanation.

From the point of view of ordinary usage it is bad enough for psychologists to suggest that we might have a motive for everything which we do. But matters become even worse when it is added that such motives may be unconscious. For the implication is that we may be up to no good and do not know it. This is a rather unnerving aspersion to have cast on our conduct. For the feeling of insecurity created by the suggestion that we may be at the mercy of unknown forces is aggravated by the implication

that we may also be to blame for seemingly innocent acts. Fits of
forgetfulness come to seem like intentional insults. And, in *some*
respects they may be. But they are obviously not like them in
that we could reasonably be said to be to *blame* for both. Yet the
indiscriminate and extended use of the term 'motive' conveys
just this suggestion. It has the unfortunate effect of blurring distinctions which are essential for practical life.

Motives, then, are reasons for action which are asked for
when there is an issue of justification as well as of explanation.
The question then arises as to the type of explanation that is
offered when a motive is suggested. For not all reasons for action
are motives. This is obvious enough; for we can ask whether a
reason for an action is a motive. This brings us to the second
characteristic of motives, that they are reasons of the directed
sort. We may give a motive by alluding to a directive disposition
like hunger, greed, or ambition. We say, for instance, 'His motive for marrying the girl was greed', or 'That politician's motive
is ambition'. Or we can answer a question about a man's motive
by quoting an exercise of such a directive disposition, as when
we say 'He married her *for the sake* of her money', 'he went into
politics in *order to* advance himself'. All such explanations assign a goal to the individual whose motives are in question. Now,
as I have shown, not all reasons for action are of this directed
sort. We can explain a man's action in terms of traits of character, like considerateness, and punctuality. These may be reasons
why people act; but they are not motives. For such terms do not
indicate any definite sort of goals towards which a man's actions
are directed. Motives, of course, may be mixed; but this only
means that a man aims at a variety of goals by means of the
same course of action. Similarly a man may have a strong motive or a weak one, an ulterior motive or an ostensible one. Such
distinctions relate only to the influence of the goal on him or to
the extent to which it is hidden. If he has a motive he must have
a goal of some sort, however weak its influence or however obvious or attainable it may be.

It seems to me most important to insist on the directedness of motive explanations. For this aspect of motives has been

sadly neglected in recent years both by philosophers and psychologists. The classic philosophical discussion of motives in recent years occurred in Ch. IV of Ryle's *Concept of Mind*. But, as I stressed on a previous occasion Ryle's treatment of motives is very confusing because he uses the term 'motive' too much as a blanket term. In his eagerness to refute the thesis that motives are mental occurrences—ghostly thrusts, to use his rather striking terminology—he claims that motive explanations always involve reference not to inner occurrences but to dispositions; but he groups together, quite indiscriminately, vanity, considerateness, patriotism, and interest in symbolic logic as examples of motives. Now these may well be dispositions, but they cannot all be appealed to as motives; for they do not all imply directedness. In rejecting the thesis that motives refer to inner emotional states, he fails to distinguish between the various types of disposition which he parades to take the place of the mythical emotional states. Psychologists, too, . . . have been guilty of a similar oversight. For in their interest in causes they have tended to equate motives with drives or initiating states of tension and have failed to stress the directedness of behaviour which is the cash value of assigning a motive to it.

This second characteristic of motive explanations links, to a certain extent, with features of the first. If we ask for a man's reason for doing something, the implication is that he is acting in no untoward way. His behaviour is within the framework of some rule-following purposeful pattern, but it is not clear which rule or which purpose it falls under. To ask for his motive, on the other hand, is only to ask for the end which explains his behaviour. The implication is that it is, to some extent, a departure from a habit or a purpose for the attainment of which there are conventions of appropriateness. We just want to know the goal which explains the sequence of his acts and the various moves he is making. The implication is that he is not sticking to standard moves. If we ask a man's motive for getting married we imply that this is, for him, merely an *efficient* way of getting to some end—e.g. the girl's money. It is not one of the standard or conventional ways of getting money. We are looking at what he is doing purely from the point of view of its being an efficient way of attaining an end. We cannot accept that the usual reasons for getting married fit his case. So we look around for some other reason that is operative.

This introduces naturally the third characteristic of motives as a class of reasons for action: they must be reasons why a person acts. By this is meant that the goal which is quoted to justify a man's action must also be such that reference to it actually explains what a man has done. The motive, in other words, must not be simply 'his reason'; indeed, in the case of 'unconscious motives' his motive cannot be *his* reason. The motive must be *the* reason why he did whatever he did. I have shown that we can also give *the* reason why a man acts in terms of nondirectional dispositions (traits) or in terms of a *causal* theory. Motives are therefore only one particular type of answer to the question 'What was *the* reason why he did it?' They involve the postulation of a type of goal towards which his behaviour was *actually* directed. We might, for instance, contrast the reasons which a man who is careless about his clothes gives for buying a new suit with his underlying motives. The implication of this contrast is that the objective which he pictures to himself or parades in public is not the one towards which his conduct is actually directed. This, it is implied, cannot be the reason why he bought the suit; it cannot therefore be his motive. But his reason might coincide with his motive. He might say that he bought the suit in order to impress his employer and this might also be the reason why he bought it. This would be an example of a conscious motive. If his motive was unconscious, then the reason why he bought the suit would be something likely to attract the notice of his secretary, and the implication of saying that it was unconscious would be that he did not entertain this goal as a conscious objective. The intermediary case would be when his motive was equivalent to his *real* reason. In such a case he would put up a façade of impressing his employer but would not be deluding or deceiving himself about the actual reason for buying the suit. Of course he might have bought the suit both to impress his employer and to attract the attention of his secretary. If both reasons were in fact operative we would say that his motives in buying the suit were mixed. In other words, the distinction between conscious and unconscious, though important in some contexts, does not really affect the logical force of the term 'motive', which is to imply that, whatever he says or thinks about it, his behaviour is actually directed towards a certain type of goal.

My contention is therefore that there are three main characteristics of 'motive' as an explanatory concept in ordinary language:

(*a*) It is used in contexts where conduct is being assessed and not simply explained, where there is a breakdown in conventional expectations.

(*b*) It is used to refer to a reason of a directed sort and implies a directed disposition in the individual whose conduct is being assessed,

(*c*) It must state *the* reason why a person acts, a reason that is *operative* in the situation to be explained. The motive *may* coincide with *his* reason but it *must* be *the* reason why he acts.

Given this sort of analysis, further higher-order questions suggest themselves very easily. We might want to know, for instance, why certain types of reason are operative. Why are we inclined to accept sex, greed, ambition and hunger as motives, but would be incredulous if an anti-social man says that his motive for going to a party is to study his friend's furniture? Many would give the answer in terms of culture and knowledge of the individual in question. They would say that we only cite as motives those directed dispositions which are widespread, and dependable in a given culture. Indeed motives refer to those goals which exert so much influence on men that they will depart from their routines and flout social convention to attain them. To get on in the world is, in our culture, a widespread and insistent aim. Training and example exert a constant pressure on men to pursue this aim. Therefore if the evidence suggests that Jones is not lacking in ambition and if we can explain a piece of his behaviour in terms of his ambition, we are quite satisfied in claiming that ambition is his motive. But this would be but an elaboration of what could be called a structural theme—an indication of the structure of dependable goals in a given culture and of the organization of the character of the individual in relation to them. It would be of interest to anthropologists and sociologists, but of little interest to psychologists. For they would be looking for a different sort of answer to the question 'Why are such goals operative?'

The Oxford English dictionary, as a matter of fact, throws out hints about the sorts of things which have been of interest to psychologists. It defines 'motive' as

That which 'moves' or induces a person to act in a certain way; a desire, fear, or other emotion, or a consideration of reason, which influences or tends to influence a person's volition; also often applied to a contemplated result or object the desire of which tends to influence volition.

This definition indicates well enough the directive aspect of the term 'motive'—the 'contemplated result or object' or the 'consideration of reason' which influences volition. But it also stresses the notion of 'moving' which is the etymological suggestion of the word, and its connection with emotion and desire. And many would suggest that it is this connection with emotion and movement which makes a reason a motive. It is an operative reason because of a causal connection between directedness and some inner springs in the individual. A motive, it would be argued, is an emotively charged reason. The directedness of behaviour is set off by an emotional state. Motives, on this view, inhabit a hinterland between reasons and causes. They refer not only to the goal towards which behaviour is directed but also to emotional states which set it off.

Whether or not, in ordinary language, there is any such necessary connection between giving the motive for an action and making any assertions of a causal kind about a man's emotional state before or when he does it, is difficult to say. My guess is that in general there is no such necessary connection. Psychologists have developed quasi-causal theories to *explain* the directedness of behaviour, to answer the question 'Why are certain sorts of reasons operative?' and these theories may well have insinuated themselves into ordinary language as part of the meaning of 'motive'. It might well be, therefore, that people who are slightly sophisticated by psychological theories assume some such necessary connection. But it would seem odd, when a question of motive is raised in a court of law, to ferret around for answers to questions about the emotions of the man whose conduct was being assessed. Evidence would be collected about what he was aiming at. But surely there would be little speculation about what *initiated* his purposeful behaviour.

. . .

ON PUNISHMENT / *A. M. Quinton*

[I] INTRODUCTORY

THERE is a prevailing antinomy about the philosophical justification of punishment. The two great theories—retributive and utilitarian—seem, and at least are understood by their defenders, to
stand in open and flagrant contradiction. Both sides have arguments at their disposal to demonstrate the atrocious conse-
quencies of the rival theory. Retributivists, who seem to hold
that there are circumstances in which the infliction of suffering
is a good thing in itself, are charged by their opponents with
vindictive barbarousness. Utilitarians, who seem to hold that
punishment is always and only justified by the good consequences it produces, are accused of vicious opportunism. Where
the former insists on suffering for suffering's sake, the latter
permits the punishment of the innocent. Yet, if the hope of justifying punishment is not to be abandoned altogether, one of
these apparently unsavory alternatives must be embraced. For
they exhaust the possibilities. Either punishment must be self-
justifying, as the retributivists claim, or it must depend for its

*From A. M. Quinton, "On Punishment," Analysis, XIV (1954), 512–517. Re-
printed by permission of Basil Blackwell.*

justification on something other than itself, the general formula of "utilitarianism" in the wide sense appropriate here.

In this paper I shall argue that the antinomy can be resolved, since retributivism, properly understood, is not a moral but a logical doctrine, and that it does not provide a moral justification of the infliction of punishment but an elucidation of the use of the word. Utilitarianism, on the other hand, embraces a number of possible moral attitudes toward punishment, none of which necessarily involves the objectionable consequences commonly adduced by retributivists, provided that the word "punishment" is understood in the way that the essential retributivist thesis lays down. The antinomy arises from a confusion of modalities, of logical and moral necessity and possibility, of "must" and "can" with "ought" and "may." In brief, the two theories answer different questions: retributivism the question "when (logically) *can* we punish?", utilitarianism the question "when (morally) *may* we or *ought* we to punish?" I shall also describe circumstances in which there is an answer to the question "when (logically) *must* we punish?" Finally, I shall attempt to account for this difference in terms of a distinction between the establishment of rules whose infringement involves punishment from the application of these rules to particular cases.

[II] THE RETRIBUTIVE THEORY

The essential contention of retributivism is that punishment is only justified by guilt. There is a certain compellingness about the repudiation of utilitarianism that this involves. We feel that whatever other considerations may be taken into account, the primary and indispensable matter is to establish the guilt of the person to be punished. I shall try to show that the peculiar outrageousness of the rejection of this principle is a consequence, not of the brutality that such rejection might seem to permit, but of the fact that it involves a kind of lying. At any rate the first principle of retributivism is that it is necessary that a man be guilty if he is to be punished.

But this doctrine is normally held in conjunction with some or all of three others which are logically, if not altogether psychologically, independent of it. These are that the function of punishment is the negation or annulment of evil or wrongdoing, that punishment must fit the crime (the *lex talionis*) and that offenders have a right to punishment, as moral agents they ought to be treated as ends not means.

The doctrine of "annulment," however carefully wrapped up in obscure phraseology, is clearly utilitarian in principle. For it holds that the function of punishment is to bring about a state of affairs in which it is as if the wrongful act had never happened. This is to justify punishment by its effects, by the desirable future consequences which it brings about. It certainly goes beyond the demand that only the guilty be punished. For, unlike this demand, it seeks to prescribe exactly what the punishment should be. Holding that whenever wrong has been done it must be annulled, it makes guilt—the state of one who has done wrong—the sufficient as well as the necessary condition of punishment. While the original thesis is essentially negative, ruling out the punishment of the innocent, the annulment doctrine is positive, insisting on the punishment and determining the degree of punishment of the guilty. But the doctrine is only applicable to a restricted class of cases, the order of nature is inhospitable to attempts to put the clock back. Theft and fraud can be compensated, but not murder, wounding, alienation of affection, or the destruction of property or reputation.

Realizing that things cannot always be made what they were, retributivists have extended the notion of annulment to cover the infliction on the offender of an injury equal to that which he has caused. This is sometimes argued for by reference to Moore's theory of organic wholes, the view that sometimes two blacks make a white. That this, the *lex talionis*, revered by Kant, does not follow from the original thesis is proved by the fact that we can always refrain from punishing the innocent but that we cannot always find a punishment to fit the crime. Some indeed would argue that we can never fit punishment to wrongdoing, for how are either, especially wrongdoing, to be measured?

(Though, as Ross has pointed out, we can make ordinal judgments of more or less about both punishment and wrongdoing.)

Both of these views depend on a mysterious extension of the original thesis to mean that punishment and wrongdoing must necessarily be somehow equal and opposite. But this is to go even further than to regard guilt and punishment as necessitating one another. For this maintains that only the guilty are to be punished and that the guilty are always to be punished. The equal and opposite view maintains further that they are to be punished to just the extent that they have done wrong.

Finally retributivism has been associated with the view that if we are to treat offenders as moral agents, as ends and not as means, we must recognize their right to punishment. It is an odd sort of right whose holders would strenuously resist its recognition. Strictly interpreted, this view would entail that the sole relevant consideration in determining whether and how a man should be punished is his own moral regeneration. This is utilitarian and it is also immoral, since it neglects the rights of an offender's victims to compensation and of society in general to protection. A less extreme interpretation would be that we should never treat offenders merely as means in inflicting punishment but should take into account their right to treatment as moral agents. This is reasonable enough; most people would prefer a penal system which did not ignore the reformation of offenders. But it is not the most obvious correlate of the possible view that if a man is guilty he ought to be punished. We should more naturally allot the correlative right to have him punished to his victims or society in general and not to him himself.

[III] THE RETRIBUTIVIST THESIS

So far I have attempted to extricate the essentials of retributivism by excluding some traditional but logically irrelevant associates. A more direct approach consists in seeing what is the essential principle which retributivists hold utilitarians to deny. Their crucial charge is that utilitarians permit the punishment of the innocent. So their fundamental thesis must be that only the guilty are to be punished, that guilt is a necessary condition of punishment. This hardly lies open to the utilitarian counter-charge of pointless and vindictive barbarity, which could only find a foothold in the doctrine of annulment and in the *lex talionis*. (For that matter, it is by no means obvious that the charge can be sustained even against them, except in so far as the problems of estimating the measure of guilt lead to the adoption of a purely formal and external criterion which would not distinguish between the doing of deliberate and accidental injuries.)

Essentially, then, retributivism is the view that only the guilty are to be punished. Excluding the punishment of the innocent, it permits the other three possibilities: the punishment of the guilty, the nonpunishment of the guilty, and the nonpunishment of the innocent. To add that guilt is also the sufficient condition of punishment, and thus to exclude the nonpunishment of the guilty, is another matter altogether. It is not entailed by the retributivist attack on utilitarianism and has none of the immediate compulsiveness of the doctrine that guilt is the necessary condition of punishment.

There is a very good reason for this difference in force. For the necessity of not punishing the innocent is not moral but logical. It is not, as some retributivists think, that we *may* not punish the innocent and *ought* only to punish the guilty, but that we *cannot* punish the innocent and *must* only punish the guilty. Of course, the suffering or harm in which punishment consists can be and is inflicted on innocent people, but this is not punishment, it is judicial error or terrorism or, in Bradley's characteristically repellent phrase, "social surgery." The infliction of suffering on a person is only properly described as punishment if that person is guilty. The retributivist thesis, therefore, is not a moral doctrine, but an account of the meaning of the word "punishment." Typhoid carriers and criminal lunatics are treated physically in much the same way as ordinary criminals; they are shut up in institutions. The essential difference is that no blame is implied by their imprisonment, for there is no guilt to which the blame can attach. "Punishment" resembles the word "murder"; it is infliction of suffering on the guilty

and not simply infliction of suffering, just as murder is wrongful killing and not simply killing. Typhoid carriers are no more
(usually) criminals than surgeons are (usually) murderers.
This accounts for the flavor of moral outrage attending the notion of punishment of the innocent. In a sense a contradiction in
terms, it applies to the common enough practice of inflicting the
suffering involved in punishment on innocent people and of sen-
tencing them to punishment with a lying imputation of their responsibility and guilt. Punishment *cannot* be inflicted on the innocent; the suffering associated with punishment *may* not be
inflicted on them, firstly, as brutal and secondly, if it is represented as punishment, as involving a lie.

This can be shown by the fact that punishment is always
for something. If a man says to another "I am going to punish
you" and is asked "what for?" he cannot reply "nothing at all" or
"something you have not done." At best, he is using "punish" here
as a more or less elegant synonym for "cause to suffer." Either
that or he does not understand the meaning of "punish." "I am
going to punish you for something you have not done" is as absurd a statement as "I blame you for this event for which you
were not responsible." "Punishment implies guilt" is the same
sort of assertion as "ought implies can." It is not *pointless* to
punish or blame the innocent, as some have argued, for it is
often very useful. Rather the very conditions of punishment and
blame do not obtain in these circumstances.

[IV] AN OBJECTION

But how can it be useful to do what is impossible? The innocent
can be punished and scapegoats are not logical impossibilities.
We do say "they punished him for something he did not do." For
A to be said to have punished B it is surely enough that A
thought or said he was punishing B and ensured that suffering
was inflicted on B. However innocent B may be of the offense
adduced by A, there is no question that, in these circumstances,
he has been punished by A. So guilt cannot be more than a *moral*
precondition of punishment.

The answer to this objection is that "punish" is a member of that now familiar class of verbs whose first-person-present use is significantly different from the rest. The absurdity of "I am punishing you for something you have not done" is analogous to that of "I promise to do something which is not in my power." Unless you are guilty I am no more in a position to punish you than I am in a position to promise what is not in my power. So it is improper to say "I am going to punish you" unless you are guilty, just as it is improper to say "I promise to do this" unless it is in my power to do it. But it is only *morally* improper if I do not *think* that you are guilty or that I can do the promised act. Yet, just as it is perfectly proper to say of another "he promised to do this," whether he thought he could do it or not, provided that he *said* "I promise to do this," so it is perfectly proper to say "they punished him," whether they thought him guilty or not, provided that they *said* "we are going to punish you" and inflicted suffering on him. By the first-person-present use of these verbs we prescribe punishment and *make* promises; these activities involve the satisfaction of conditions over and above what is required for *reports* or *descriptions* of what their prescribers or makers represent as punishments and promises.

Understandably "reward" and "forgive" closely resemble "punish." Guilt is a precondition of forgiveness, desert—its contrary—of reward. One cannot properly say "I am going to reward you" or "I forgive you" to a man who has done nothing. Reward and forgiveness are always *for* something. But, again, one can say "they rewarded (or forgave) him for something he had not done." There is an interesting difference here between "forgive" and "punish" or "reward." In this last kind of assertion "forgive" seems more peculiar, more inviting to inverted commas, than the other two. The three undertakings denoted by these verbs can be divided into the utterance of a more or less ritual formula and the consequences authorized by this utterance. With punishment and reward the consequences are more noticeable than the formula, so they come to be sufficient occasion for the use of the word even if the formula is inapplicable and so improperly used. But, since the consequences of forgiveness are negative, the absence of punishment, no such shift occurs. To reward involves giving a reward, to punish inflicting a punishment, but to forgive involves no palpable consequence, e.g., handing over a written certificate of pardon.

Within these limitations, then, guilt is a *logically* necessary conditions of punishment and, with some exceptions, it might be held, a morally necessary condition of the infliction of suffering. Is it in either way a sufficient condition? As will be shown in the last section there are circumstances, though they do not obtain in our legal system, nor generally in extralegal penal systems (e.g., parental), in which guilt is a logically sufficient condition of at least a sentence of punishment. The parallel moral doctrine would be that if anyone is guilty of wrongdoing he ought morally to be punished. This rather futile rigorism is not embodied in our legal system with its relaxations of penalties for first offenders. Since it entails that offenders should never be forgiven it is hardly likely to commend itself in the extralegal sphere.

[v] THE UTILITARIAN THEORY

Utilitarianism holds that punishment must always be justified by the value of its consequences. I shall refer to this as "utility" for convenience without any implication that utility must consist in pleasure. The view that punishment is justified by the value of its consequences is compatible with any ethical theory which allows meaning to be attached to moral judgments. It holds merely that the infliction of suffering is of no value or of negative value and that it must therefore be justified by further considerations. These will be such things as prevention of and deterrence from wrongdoing, compensation of victims, reformation of offenders, and satisfaction of vindictive impulses. It is indifferent for our purposes whether these are valued as intuitively good, as productive of general happiness, as conducive to the survival of the human race or are just normatively laid down as valuable or derived from such a norm.

Clearly there is no *logical* relation between punishment

and its actual or expected utility. Punishment *can* be inflicted when it is neither expected, nor turns out, to be of value and, on the other hand, it can be foregone when it is either expected, or would turn out, to be of value.

But that utility is the morally necessary or sufficient condition, or both, of punishment are perfectly reputable moral attitudes. The first would hold that no one should be punished unless the punishment would have valuable consequences; the second that if valuable consequences would result punishment ought to be inflicted (without excluding the moral permissibility of utility-less punishment). Most people would no doubt accept the first, apart from the rigorists who regard guilt as a morally sufficient condition of punishment. Few would maintain the second except in conjunction with the first. The first says when you may not but not when you ought to punish, the second when you ought to but not when you may not.

Neither permits or encourages the punishment of the innocent, for this is only logically possible if the word "punishment" is used in an unnatural way, for example as meaning any kind of deliberate infliction of suffering. But in that case they cease to be moral doctrine about punishment as we understand the word and become moral doctrines (respectively, platitudinous and inhuman) about something else.

So the retributivist case against the utilitarians falls to the ground as soon as what is true and essential in retributivism is extracted from the rest. This may be unwelcome to retributivists since it leaves the moral field in the possession of the utilitarians. But there is a compensation in the fact that what is essential in retributivism can at least be definitely established.

[VI] RULES AND CASES

So far what has been established is that guilt and the value or utility of consequences are relevant to punishment in different ways. A further understanding of this difference can be gained by making use of a distinction made by Sir David Ross in the appendix on punishment in *The Right and the Good*. This will also help to elucidate the notion of guilt which has hitherto been applied uncritically.

The distinction is between laying down a rule which attaches punishment to actions of a certain kind and the application of that rule to particular cases. It might be maintained that the utilitarian theory was an answer to the question "What kinds of action should be punished?" and the retributive theory an answer to the question "On what particular occasions should we punish?" On this view both punishment and guilt are defined by reference to these rules. Punishment is the infliction of suffering attached by these rules to certain kinds of action, guilt the condition of a person to whom such a rule applies. This accounts for the logically necessary relation holding between guilt and punishment. Only the guilty can be punished because unless a person is guilty, unless a rule applies to him, no infliction of suffering on him is properly called punishment, since punishment is infliction of suffering as laid down by such a rule. Considerations of utility, then, are alone relevant to the determination of what in general, what *kinds* of action, to punish. The outcome of this is a set of rules. Given these rules, the question of whom in particular to punish has a definite and necessary answer. Not only will guilt be the logically necessary but also the logically sufficient condition of punishment or, more exactly, of a sentence of punishment. For declaration of guilt will be a declaration that a rule applies and, if the rule applies, what the rule enjoins—a sentence of punishment—applies also.

The distinction between setting up and applying penal rules helps to explain the different parts played by utility and guilt in the justification of punishment, in particular the fact that where utility is a moral, guilt is a logical, justification. Guilt is irrelevant to the setting up of rules, for until they have been set up the notion of guilt is undefined and without application. Utility is irrelevant to the application of rules, for once the rules have been set up, punishment is determined by guilt; once they are seen to apply, the rule makes a sentence of punishment necessarily follow.

But this account is not an accurate description of the

very complex penal systems actually employed by states, institutions, and parents. It is, rather, a schema, a possible limiting case. For it ignores an almost universal feature of penal systems (and of games, for that matter, where penalties attend infractions of the rules)—discretion. For few offenses against the law is one and only one fixed and definite punishment laid down. Normally only an upper limit is set. If guilt, the applicability of the rule, is established no fixed punishment is entailed but rather, for example, one not exceeding a fine of forty shillings or fourteen days' imprisonment. This is even more evident in the administration of such institutions as clubs or libraries and yet more again in the matter of parental discipline. The establishment of guilt does not close the matter; at best it entails some punishment or other. Precisely how much is appropriate must be determined by reference to considerations of utility. The variety of things is too great for any manageably concise penal code to dispense altogether with discretionary judgment in particular cases.

But this fact only shows that guilt is not a logically *sufficient* condition of punishment; it does not affect the thesis that punishment entails guilt. A man cannot be guilty unless his action falls under a penal rule and he can only be properly said to be punished if the rule in question prescribes or permits some punishment or other. So all applications of the notion of guilt necessarily contain or include all applications of the notion of punishment.

PUNISHMENT / *S. I. Benn and R. S. Peters*

TO DO justice is to treat men unequally only according to the degree of their relevant inequalities. . . . Men differ in so many ways that no two are ever alike in all respects; yet to do justice we must disregard all differences except those that accord with the appropriate criteria in each field. And these criteria must be justified by showing that beneficent consequences can be expected to follow their operation as general rules. Earlier we considered those governing income distribution, and inquired how they might be justified, and how they applied to particular cases. Punishment, or retributive justice, presents a similar set of problems, but it is further complicated by the fact that to punish a man is deliberately to do something unpleasant to him, not as a dentist does, as a regrettable accompaniment to the long-term betterment of his condition, but as a matter of deliberate principle. We did not feel called upon to ask 'What can justify distributing any income at all?' because we need make no apology for giving people things they want. But since people would generally prefer not to be punished, we are bound to ask 'What can justify ever punishing anyone at all?', before going on to consider the criteria for punishing in particular cases.

From S. I. Benn and R. S. Peters, "Punishment," Social Principles and the Democratic State *(London: George Allen & Unwin, 1959), pp. 173–195. Printed in paperback edition as* Principles of Political Thought *(New York: Free Press of Glencoe, 1959), pp. 201–227. Copyright © 1959 by George Allen & Unwin. Reprinted by permission of the publishers.*

[1] THE JUSTIFICATION OF PUNISHMENT

(a) 'Punishment' Defined

'What can justify punishment?' is a moral, not a linguistic, question, not therefore to be answered by analysing concepts. Nevertheless, some of the confusions which have made the question seem unnecessarily difficult in the past may be avoided by clarifying the way in which the word 'punishment' is most generally used. For instance, many people have insisted on the close connection between punishment and guilt for a crime already committed. It would therefore be wrong, they say, to justify it as a deterrent to crime in the future. But they have often failed to recognize that this reference back to a crime is part of the *meaning* of 'punishment'. (We deal with this point more fully later on.)

Professor Flew[1] has suggested five criteria for the use of the word 'punishment' in its primary sense, i.e. five conditions satisfied by an ordinary or standard case to which the word would be applied:

i. it must involve an 'evil, an unpleasantness, to the victim';

ii. it must be for an offence (actual or supposed);

iii. it must be of an offender (actual or supposed);

iv. it must be the work of personal agencies (i.e. not merely the natural consequences of an action);

v. it must be imposed by authority (real or supposed), conferred by the system of rules against which the offence has been committed.

To these criteria another might be added: that the unpleasantness should be an essential part of what is intended and not merely incidental to some other aim. While it is not a misuse of the word to talk, for example, about 'punishing the innocent', or of a boxer 'punishing his opponent', these usages, though re-

[1] A. Flew 'The Justification of Punishment', in *Philosophy*, Vol. XXIX, 1954, pp. 291–307.

lated to the primary one, disregard one or more of the criteria ordinarily satisfied, and must be treated accordingly as extended or secondary usages. In considering the justification of punishment, we are confining the word to its primary sense, except where otherwise stated.

(b) The Two Main Approaches to Justification— Utilitarian and Retributive

The problem has been approached from two standpoints. One, the utilitarian, is typified by Bentham:

> All punishment is mischief: all punishment in itself is evil. Upon the principle of utility, if it ought at all to be admitted, it ought only to be admitted in as far as it promises to exclude some greater evil.[2]

> The immediate principal end of punishment is to control action. This action is either that of the offender, or of others: that of the offender it controls by its influence, either on his will . . . in the way of *reformation;* or on his physical power . . . by *disablement:* that of others it can influence no otherwise than by its influence over their wills . . . in the way of *example.*[3]

The other, the retributive approach, is exemplified in its most thoroughgoing form by Kant:

> Judicial punishment . . . can never be inflicted simply and solely as a means to forward a good, other than itself, whether . . . of the criminal, or of civil society; but it must at all times be inflicted on him, for no other reason than *because he has acted criminally.* A man can never be treated simply as a means for realizing the views of another man . . . He must first of all be found to be *punishable,* before there is even a thought of deriving from the punishment any advantage for himself or his fellow-citizens. The penal law is a categorical imperative; and woe to that man who crawls through the sepentine turnings of the happiness-doctrine, to find out some consideration, which, by its promise of advantage, should free the criminal from his penalty, or even from any degree thereof. That is the maxim of the Pharisees, 'it is expedient that one man should die for

---

[2] *Introduction to the Principles of Morals and Legislation* (ed., W. Harrison, 1948), Ch. XIII, Sec. I, 2, p. 281.
[3] *Ibid., loc. cit.,* n. 1.

the people, and that the whole nation perish not'; but if justice per-
ishes, then it is no more worth while that man should live upon the
earth.[4]

There appears to be a serious difference of view here, the one
looking for justifications to the beneficent consequences of punishment, the other exclusively to the wrongful act. It remains to
be seen whether the gulf can be bridged.

(c) Distinction Between Justification of Punishment in General and in Particular

It is important, first, to distinguish between a rule, or an institution constituted by rules, and some particular application of it.
We can ask what can justify punishment in general, i.e. why we
should have rules that provide that offenders against them
should be made to suffer. But this is quite different from asking
how to justify a particular application of such rules, in punishing a given individual. Though retributivist and utilitarian have
tried to answer both questions, each in his own terms, the
strength of the former's case rests on his answer to the second,
of the latter's on his answer to the first. And their difficulties
arise from trying to make one answer do for both questions.

(d) Justifying Punishment in General

The retributivist refuses to look to the consequences of punishment for its justification. It is therefore virtually impossible for
him to answer the question 'What justification could there be for
rules requiring that those who break them should be made to
suffer?' except perhaps in theological terms. For appeals to authority apart, we can justify rules and institutions only by showing that they yield advantages. Consequently retributivist answers to the problem can be shown, on analysis, to be either
mere affirmations of the desirability of punishment, or utilitarian
reasons in disguise. To the first class belong assertions of the
type 'it is fitting (or justice requires) that the guilty should
suffer'. For to say 'it is fitting' is only to say that it ought to be

4 Quoted by F. H. Bradley: *Ethical Studies* (2nd edn., 1927), p. 28 n.l. (and
see also p. 57 n.l.), from I. Kant *Die Metaphysik der Sitten*.

the case, and it is just this that is in question. To say, with Kant, that punishment is a good in itself, is to deny the necessity for justification; for to justify is to provide reasons in terms of something else accepted as valuable. But it is by no means evident that punishment needs no justification, the proof being that many people have felt the need to justify it. Again it might be argued that the concept 'a legal system' necessarily implies punishment; but even so, one might still ask why we should have systems of just that sort.

Some concession, however, might be made to Kant's point of view of a type which would be consistent with denying that punishment is a good in itself. For, although it might be argued, as by utilitarians, that the pain of punishment is something that requires justification, some grounds must also be produced for stipulating that such pain, if justifiably inflicted, should be confined to those who have committed offences. For it might be the case that the infliction of pain on the relatives of offenders or on their employers was a more effective deterrent than inflicting it on the offenders themselves. In 'it is fitting that the guilty should suffer' stress should be put on 'the guilty' rather than on 'suffer'. It would then be a re-iteration of the principle of justice which, we have insisted,* must always go along with the consideration of interests affected by rules. For laws, by their very nature, are directed against people who actually do or are likely to do certain sorts of things. And these sorts of things are things like murder or theft which people can reasonably be said to *choose* to do; they are not things like measles that just happen to them. To inflict pain on people who have not, by their choice, put themselves into the category in question (e.g. of thieves or murderers) would be to discriminate against them on irrelevant grounds. It would be to disregard their claims and to treat them merely as tools for discouraging others. In so far, then, as the retributivists insist on the principles of justice, they have an element of a case in that they stress the injustice of treating people as guilty when they are in fact innocent. But what cannot be

* See S. I. Benn and R. S. Peters, *Social Principles and the Democratic State* (London: Allen & Unwin, 1959), Ch. 2, Sections IV and V, and Ch. 5, passim.

granted to them is their thesis that the infliction of pain on anyone at all is ever desirable without any further justification being
given.

Some retributivists argue that while punishment is a
prima facie evil, and thus in need of justification, it is less objectionable than that the wicked should prosper. This is to subsume
the rule 'Crimes ought to be punished' under a more general
rule: either 'The wicked ought to be less well off than the virtuous' or 'The wicked ought not to profit from their crimes'. But
'wickedness' involves assessment of character; we do not punish
men for their wickedness, but for particular breaches of law.
There may be some ignoble but prudent characters who have
never broken a law, and never been punished, and noble ones
who have—our system of punishment is not necessarily the
worse for that. We may have to answer for our characters on the
Day of Judgment, but not at Quarter Sessions. The State is not
an agent of cosmic justice; it punishes only such acts as are
contrary to legal rules, conformity to which, even from unworthy
motives like fear, is considered of public importance. And if we
offer the narrower ground, that the wicked ought not to profit
from their *crimes,* we are bound to justify the distinction between crimes and offences against morals in general. What is
the special virtue of legal rules, that a breach of them alone warrants punishment? It seems that the wicked are to be prevented
from prospering only if their wickedness manifests itself in selected ways; but how is the selection made, unless in terms of its
consequences? In any case, if we permit the subsumption of
'Crime ought to be punished' under the more general 'The
wicked ought not to prosper', it would still be proper to seek justification for the latter. It would not help to say 'Justice requires
punishment'; for this is but to reiterate that there is no need for
further justification. It might be argued that in such a universe,
where the wicked prospered, there would be no inducement to
virtue. But this move would merely defer the utilitarian stage of
justification; it would not render it superfluous.

A similar veiled utilitarianism underlies Hegel's treatment of punishment, as an annulment of the wrong.[5] It is not easy to see how a wrong can be annulled: what is done cannot, in a literal sense, be undone. It is possible to make restitution for some wrongs, but this is beside the point, for punishment is the infliction of suffering not the exaction of compensation or restitution. A man may be sent to prison for injuring another, and *also* be liable for damages. Punishment is not intended to restore the fortunes of the victim. But if it were, the justification would be in terms of the better condition of the victim, or of society in general which would result from the punishment, and, like all utilitarianism, this is forward looking. So also is another Hegelian argument, that the idea of right, which law embodies, would be denied, unless it were re-affirmed through the machinery of punishment. But why should it be re-affirmed in precisely this form? Would not formal condemnation of the wrong principle which the crime exemplified, be sufficient? In evidence to the Royal Commission on Capital Punishment, Lord Justice Denning declared: 'The ultimate justification of any punishment is not that it is a deterrent, but that it is the emphatic denunciation by the community of a crime'.[6] But 'punishment' does not mean 'denunciation', nor does the necessity for denunciation, which may coincide with that for punishment, imply a right or duty to inflict suffering on those denounced. Even if it did, the justification would be utilitarian, since the need for denunciation rests presumably on the need to uphold law for the general advantage.

Others have treated punishment as if it were a sort of automatic reflex, a response of the social order to the crime, following in the nature of things like a hang-over.[7] But this is to

---

[5] See *Philosophy of Right* (trans. by T. M. Knox, 1942). Secs. 97 and 99, and Addition No. 61. A. M. Quinton in his 'On Punishment', in *Philosophy, Politics, and Society* (ed. P. Laslett, 1956), p. 84 comments: 'The doctrine of "annulment" . . . is clearly utilitarian in principle. For it holds that the function of punishment is to bring about a state of affairs in which it is as if the wrongful act had never happened. This is to justify punishment by its effects, by the desirable future consequences which it brings about'. See also the discussion in A. C. Ewing: *The Morality of Punishment* (1929), pp. 24–25.

[6] Cmd. 8932, Sec. 53 (1953).

[7] Thus Sir Ernest Barker, in *Principles of Social and Political Theory* (1951),

confuse rules with scientific laws. It is in the nature of things that certain physical acts have certain unavoidable physical consequences; but the penal consequences of a breach of legal rules follow only because human beings have made that sort of a rule. We do not need to justify the laws of nature, because there is no way of making them other than they are; social rules must be justified because they are different in precisely this way. To treat punishment as a natural, unwilled response to a breach of law is to class it with natural phenomena, about which questions of justification do not arise; it is not to justify it.[8] It is of course true that once we have agreed on the need for penal laws, any particular act of punishment might be justified (though not necessarily sufficiently justified) by reference to a rule that has been broken. This may explain how it comes about that people think that punishment is a sort of social reflex. But it is a point of view that presupposes a system of punishment that has already been accepted.

Lastly, among so-called retributive justifications, we must consider one advanced by Bosanquet:

Compulsion through punishment and the fear of it, though primarily acting on the lower self, does tend, when the conditions of true punishment exist (i.e. the reaction of systems of rights violated by one who shares in it), to a recognition of the end by the person punished, and may so far be regarded as his own will, implied in the maintenance of a system to which he is a party, returning upon himself in the form of pain. And this is the theory of punishment as retributive

---

p. 182: 'the mental rule of law which pays back a violation of itself by a violent return, much as the natural rules of health pay back a violation of themselves by a violent return'. The persuasive pun on 'violation' and 'violence' is misleading—the relation is one of sound, not of sense.

8 For J. D. Mabbott, too, punishment is a kind of automatic response though in a different sense. 'Punishment is a corollary not of law but of lawbreaking. Legislators do not *choose* to punish. They hope no punishment will be needed . . . The criminal makes the essential choice; he "brings it on himself".' ('Punishment', in *Mind*, Vol. 48, 1939, p. 161. He reaffirms the position in 'Freewill and Punishment', in *Contemporary British Philosophy*, 3rd Series [ed. H. D. Lewis, 1956], p. 303.) But legislators choose to make *penal* rules, and it is this choice that needs justification.

. . . The punishment is, so to speak, his right, of which he must not be defrauded.[9]

Now it must be admitted that few criminals seek to destroy the entire social order, and the average burglar would no doubt feel indignant if his own house were burgled. He might even agree, in principle, that law-breakers should be punished. Yet his efforts to elude the police are evidence enough that he does not will his own punishment, in any ordinary sense of the phrase. He may be unreasonable and immoral in making a special exception in his own favour—but that does not justify constructing a theory of punishment on a hypothetical will (which Bosanquet calls his 'real will') that would be his were he reasonable and moral; for then he might not be a burglar. To treat punishment as if it were self-imposed is to offer a spurious account, in terms of consent, of something that, in the nature of the case, most criminals will always do their best to avoid.

To say, with Bosanquet that punishment is the 'right' of the criminal is to disregard one of the usual criteria governing the use of the word 'right', namely, that it is something which will be enforced only if the subject so chooses, the corollary being that it operates to his advantage. Only by pretending that punishment is self-imposed can we think of the criminal as exercising a choice, and only by treating it as reformative can we regard it as to his advantage. Indeed, Bosanquet does introduce a reformative justification in saying that punishment tends 'to a recognition of the end by the person punished'. But that is a utilitarian, not a retributive justification.[10] The acceptable part of

---

[9] B. Bosanquet: *The Philosophical Theory of the State* (1923 edn.). p. 211. Cf. Hegel, *op. cit.*, Sec. 100: 'The injury which falls on the criminal is not merely *implicitly* just—as just, it is *eo ipso* his implicit will, an embodiment of his freedom, his right . . .' 'Punishment is regarded as containing the criminal's right and hence by being punished he is honoured as a rational being. He does not receive this due honour unless the concept and measure of his punishment are derived from his own act. Still less does he receive it if he is treated either as a harmful animal who has to be made harmless, or with a view to deterring and reforming him'. And see Sec. 220.

[10] Cf. Bosanquet, *op. cit.*, pp. 209–210: 'If a man is told that the way he works his factory . . . is rendering him liable to fine or imprisonment, then, if

Bosanquet's view is connected with a point which we have made
earlier. Men put themselves into the category of offenders by
choice; it is not something that just happens to them. It is odd to
say that people choose to be punished; but it is their choice
which has put them into a special category. In this respect they
are relevantly different from other people who have not so
chosen.

Retributive justifications of punishment in general are
unsatisfactory, we have suggested, for the very reason that they
refuse to look to the consequences of rules of this sort, denying
thereby a necessary part of the procedure for justifying rules.
And there is no reason why we should limit ourselves to the consequences for the criminal. It would be an odd sort of theory that
was ready to accept punishment in principle, because of the
good it did to criminals, but refused to consider possible benefits
or damage to the rest of the community. We need not be put off
by Kant's injunction that the criminal must be treated as an end,
providing that in weighing advantages and disadvantages to
everyone we do not lose sight of his welfare altogether; we are
not bound to treat it as our sole legitimate concern. There is
nothing in the utilitarian approach, as Bentham understood it,
that denies this principle. The criminal must, like anyone else,
'count for one'; but he must not count for 'more than one'.

Bentham's case is that punishment is a technique of social control which is justified so long as it prevents more mischief than it produces. At the point where the damage to the
criminal outweighs the expected advantage to the rest of society,
it loses that justification. As a technique, it operates advanta-
geously in three ways (though these need not exhaust the possibilities): by reforming the criminal, by preventing him (e.g. by
death or imprisonment) from repeating the offence, and by deterring others from like offences.

i. *Reformation.* Not all theories dealing with the reform

---

he is an ordinary, careless, but respectable citizen, he will feel something of a
shock, and recognise that he was getting too neglectful of the rights of others,
and that, in being pulled up, he is brought back to himself'. This is plainly a
utilitarian argument.

of criminals are theories of punishment, in our sense. We must distinguish theories dealing with reformative measures to *accompany* the punishment from those which hold that the suffering intrinsic to the idea of punishment is itself reformative. Detention in a mental hospital may not be in itself an essential part of the process of curing mental disorders, though it may provide a convenient opportunity for psycho-therapy. Similarly, prison reformers concerned with the moral re-education of criminals are offering theories of punishment in a strict sense only if they expect the suffering involved in loss of liberty, prison discipline, etc. itself to lead to reformation. This is important, for though reformative treatment might cure criminal inclinations by relaxing the rigours of punishment, it might still defeat the ends of punishment, if it reduced the deterrent effects for others.

'Reformation' is in any case ambiguous. A prison sentence may persuade a man that 'crime does not pay'; but in that case he is as much deterred by example as anyone who learns the lesson at second hand. He would be a 'reformed character' only if he showed remorse for his past misdeeds, and resolved not to repeat them, not through fear of further punishment, but simply because they were wrong. It is questionable whether punishment produces this sort of moral reformation in very many cases. Some offenders may be shaken by imprisonment into reflecting on their behaviour and resolve to do better; it is at least as likely, however, that the blow to self-respect, and criminal associations, may lead to moral deterioration. We attempt to reform first offenders by passing them over to the probation officer, rather than to the prison warder. There is, however, the further point that, no matter how humane the intentions of the officials providing reformative treatment, it will almost certainly be accompanied by some compulsion and carry some elements of stigma and rebuke, which would tend to act as deterrents.

This is not to say that punishment is never justifiable as reformative; but it is questionable, on utilitarian grounds, whether the reformative benefits alone of the institution would justify it.

ii. *Prevention.* Similarly, though we should not regard it

as the *main* purpose of punishment to prevent crime by removing or otherwise disabling the potential criminal, this aim is recognised, in long terms of 'preventive detention' for hardened criminals, and in sentences of transportation and deportation. The death penalty is thought by some to be similarly justified. It is clear, however, that the case for punishment as prevention is convincing only for criminals with several convictions; for in other cases we are not entitled to assume that the offender would repeat his crime.

iii. *Deterrence.* The strongest utilitarian case for punishment is that it serves to deter potential offenders by inflicting suffering on actual ones. On this view, punishment is not the main thing; the technique works by threat. Every act of punishment is to that extent an admission of failure, and we punish only that the technique may retain some effectiveness in the future. The problem of justifying punishment arises only because the technique is not completely effective; if it were, there would be nothing to justify.

Retributivists do not of course deny that punishment can act in these ways, nor that it has these advantages. They maintain only that they are incidental, and that a system of punishment devised solely on these principles would lead to monstrous injustices, which we shall consider in the next section. However that may be, it is evident that while the utilitarian can provide *some* sort of justification, the retributivist is either offering utilitarian arguments in disguise, or virtually denying that punishment in general needs any justification at all. Of course there is no arguing with him if he *consistently* takes his stand on the intuition that there ought to be punishment. If a retributivist just insists that it is morally repugnant that a man should do an injury to another man without suffering injury himself there is little more to be said. For by standing on such an 'intuition' he is claiming that there are no further reasons for his principle. The utilitarian can only point out to the retributivist that a great many people think that punishment requires some justification; that he can provide good reasons for punishing people; and that, though it is intolerable that there should be murder, rape, and

dope-peddling, punishment is just one way of reducing the inci-
dence of such admitted evils. He sees nothing intrinsically fitting about this particular way, which itself involves increasing
the misery in the world. The strength of the retributivist position
lies, however, in his approach to the justification of the particular act of punishment, which we must now consider.

(e) Justifying Particular Punishments

i. *Retributivist Criticisms of Utilitarianism*. Critics of
the utilitarian approach contend that it would justify punishing
not only the guilty but the innocent too. For if punishment is
justified solely by its effects, would it not be permissible to manufacture evidence against an innocent man, in order to provide
an example to others? If there were an outbreak of crimes particularly difficult to detect, and if people generally could be persuaded that an innocent man had in fact committed such a
crime, would not the utilitarian conditions for punishment be
adequately satisfied? Alternatively, if the advantages of deterrence could be achieved by merely *seeming* to punish a criminal,
would it not be wrong to do more than pretend to punish him,
since the advantages could then be had without the disadvantages? [11] Again, to the extent that the utilitarian relies on reformative or preventive benefits, would he not seem justified in punishing before a crime had been committed? If a man were
thought to be contemplating, or even capable of, an offence,
might he not be sent to prison and a crime thereby prevented,
with the prospect of a reformed character thrown in for good
measure?

If utilitarianism could really be shown to involve punishing the innocent, or a false parade of punishment, or punish-

[11] This criticism is prompted by Bentham's assertion: 'It is the idea only of
the punishment (or, in other words, the *apparent* punishment) that really acts
upon the mind . . . It is the apparent punishment, therefore, that does all the
service, I mean in the way of example, which is the principal object' (*Op. cit.*,
Ch. XV, 9, p. 303). Some 'indirect utilitarians' have maintained that rules must
be observed, and punishment inflicted, even when the immediate effects are not
on balance beneficial, in order that the over-all advantage of respect for law
shall be preserved. J. D. Mabbott contends that this argument could always be
met by the injunction to 'keep the exception dark' (*Punishment*, pp. 155–157).

ment in anticipation of an offence, these criticisms would no doubt be conclusive. They are, however, based on a misconception of what the utilitarian theory is about. We said at the beginning of this [essay] that 'punishment' implied, in its primary sense, not the inflicting of *any* sort of suffering, but inflicting suffering under certain specified conditions, one of which was that it must be for a breach of a rule. Now if we insist on this criterion for the use of the word, 'punishment of the innocent' becomes a logical impossibility. For it follows from the definition of 'punishment' that suffering inflicted on the innocent cannot be *'punishment'*. It is not a question of what is morally justified, but of what is logically possible.*

When we talk of 'punishing the innocent', we may mean: (i) 'pretending to punish', in the sense of manufacturing evidence or otherwise imputing guilt, while knowing a man to be innocent. This would be to treat him *as if* he were guilty, and involve the lying assertion that he was. It is morally objectionable, not only as a lie, but because it involves treating an innocent person differently from others without justification, or for an irrelevant reason, the reason offered being falsely grounded.[12] (ii) We may mean, by 'punish', 'cause to suffer'; we might use it, for example, of a case in which suffering is inflicted where there is no offence in question, and so where no guilt, actual or pretended, is implied. Further, suffering might not be the main intention, but only incidental to some other aim. In that case, it could not be said that as a matter of *logical necessity*, it is wrong to punish the innocent. To imprison members of a subversive political party, treating them *in that respect* like criminals, though no offence had been proved or even charged, would not necessarily be immoral, especially if the intention were not primarily that they should suffer, but to prevent them causing mischief. Persons believed by the Secretary of State 'to be of hostile origin or association' were detained, under wartime Defence Regulation 18b, though technically guiltless of an

---

* An analogous relation between 'guilt' and 'pardon' accounts for the oddness of 'granting a free pardon' to a convicted man later found to be innocent.
12 Cf. A. Quinton, *op. cit.*

offence. Critics of the Regulation might have attacked this as 'punishment of the innocent'—but they would have been borrowing implications of the primary sense of 'punishment' to attack a type of action to which these did not apply. For it is only *necessarily* improper to 'punish the innocent' if we pretend they are guilty, and if suffering is essential to the intention, i.e. if we accept all the primary usage criteria. If we use the word in some looser sense, there might be a case for acting in this way in special circumstances.

We are arguing that in exceptional conditions it may be legitimate to inflict suffering as a technique of social control or policy, without relation to offences under rules, just as we detain lunatics or enemy aliens. Such suffering is not, however, in the primary sense of the word, 'punishment', and is not *therefore* objectionable as 'punishment of the innocent' (though it may be on other grounds). It is only when it is deliberately inflicted on the pretext of guilt that it is open to the retributivist objections. The short answer to the critics of utilitarian theories of punishment, is that they are theories of 'punishment', not of *any* sort of technique involving suffering.

It might be objected that we are seeking to answer a moral objection with a definition. For why should we stop short at inflicting suffering on *offenders*? Supposing we could protect society yet further by having a rule that authorised inflicting suffering on, say, the relatives of offenders, if the actual offenders had vanished or escaped abroad? Though it might be strictly inaccurate to describe such a system as 'punishment' it might well serve the same purpose as punishment. Such a system would be highly objectionable, at any rate in any ordinary circumstances; but could it not be justified by the utilitarian procedure of appealing to the net advantage of having such a system?

On a crude understanding of utilitarianism, it could; but it would leave out of account the considerations of impartiality and respect for persons which we have argued are as necessary to the idea of morality as regard for consequences. It is not inconsistent with regarding a man as a source of claims, with ends of his own deserving of respect, to have a system of punishment which lays it down that people who choose to break rules suffer penalties. In a sense, to have *rules* forbidding certain types of conduct commits us to doing *something* to discourage people from breaking them. As a responsible person, the potential offender can decide whether to put himself in the class of persons liable to punishment. But this is not the case if the victims of the suffering to be inflicted are not themselves offenders. They would be made to suffer only as instruments for inflicting suffering on the real offender. Their own claims would have received no consideration at all; nor would they have *put themselves* in the class of people liable to punishment. They would be passive levers employed by society to bring pressure to bear upon potential offenders, without themselves being offenders. This would be morally intolerable.*

ii. *The Retributive Theory.* We are now able to examine the strength and the weakness of the retributive position itself.

If there is any opinion to which the man of uncultivated morals is attached (wrote F. H. Bradley) it is the belief in the necessary connection of punishment and guilt. Punishment is punishment, only where it is deserved. We pay the penalty, because we owe it, and for no other reason; and if punishment is inflicted for any other reason whatever than because it is merited by wrong, it is a gross immorality, a crying injustice, an abominable crime, and not what it pretends to be.[13]

What is misleading in this way of putting the case, is that it overlooks the extent to which this is a definition of 'punishment'. The 'necessary connection of punishment and guilt' is a logical connection. It would be more accurate to write 'Punishment is "punishment", only when it is deserved'—for the inverted com-

---

* It might be, however, that in very exceptional conditions one might take the claims of such people into account, but decide, nevertheless, that it was so important that the law should be upheld that they must be put aside. It is impossible to say, without reference to any particular context, that such a choice would be wrong. But it would have to be a *choice:*—maintaining the law would have to be quite deliberately chosen as more important than the claims of the innocents not to be made to suffer without having committed an offence. On occasion, a schoolmaster may feel justified in punishing a whole class of boys, if he cannot find the actual offenders and feels that it is vital for discipline that the guilty shall not escape unpunished.

13 *Ethical Studies* [2nd edn., 1927], pp. 26–27.

mas indicate that the sentence is about the way a word is to be used, not about the qualities of the act. A. M. Quinton has put this point succinctly: 'It is not, as some retributivists think, that we *may* not punish the innocent and *ought* only to punish the guilty, but that we *cannot* punish the innocent and *must* only punish the guilty . . . The infliction of suffering on a person is only properly described as punishment if that person is guilty. The retributivist thesis, therefore, is not a moral doctrine, but an account of the meaning of the word "punishment".' [14] This is strictly true, but it presupposes the moral principle, which we have already allowed, that inflicting suffering on *offenders* is the only systematic way of inflicting suffering to maintain law which is morally defensible in most circumstances.

So long, then, as the retributive thesis is limited to saying that no act of punishment is justified that is not the consequence of a breach of law, it is unobjectionable—but its truth depends on the meaning of the words used. This is not however the only interpretation that could be put on retributive theory. For it might be held that the theory points to a close connection between punishment and *moral* guilt.[15] The connection however cannot be very close. For moral guilt is not a *sufficient* condition of punishment, there being many offences like lying, which are moral offences, but which are not dealt with as punishable offences, like making false declarations of income to the Inspector of Taxes. It is difficult to maintain even that moral guilt is a *necessary* condition for punishment. For since it is the duty of the judge to apply law as it is, not to question its morality, from his point of view at least it would be right to punish a purely legal offence. It would also be open to the utilitarian to argue that, though one might be morally guiltless in disobeying a mischievous law, punishment would be unjustifiable, not because of the absence of moral guilt, but because no mischievous law

[14] *Op. cit.*, p. 86.

[15] Cf. C. W. K. Mundle: 'Punishment and Desert', in *Philosophical Quarterly*, Vol. 4, 1954: 'the retributive theory implies that punishment of a person by the State is morally justifiable, if and only if he has done something which is both a legal and a moral offence, and only if the penalty is proportionate to the moral gravity of his offence' (p. 227).

could justify the further mischief of punishment. It is not a question of what conditions a particular act of punishment must satisfy, but of the conditions that a *rule* must satisfy if punishment is to be properly attached to a breach of it.

It remains, however, to consider how the utilitarian approach should deal with the question of justifying the particular act of punishment. To ask, in respect of every particular case, that it be justified as preventing more mischief than it causes would be to miss the point of punishment as an institution. Once we agree that rules are desirable, and that they ought to take a particular form, there is always a *prima facie* case for applying them whenever appropriate occasions arise. For there would be no point in having rules if, on every separate occasion, we were required to balance the probable consequences of keeping them or ignoring them. Such a process would defeat the very purpose of the rule, which is to introduce regularity and predictability into human intercourse.[16] It would be especially self-defeating in respect of punishment. Punishment would not be an effective deterrent unless it could be relied upon to follow every breach of law, except in circumstances sufficiently well-understood for the exceptions not to constitute a source of uncertainty, diminishing the effectiveness of the threat. This is not to say that guilt should be a sufficient condition, nor even that no discretion should be permitted to judges in deciding whether a particular case called for punishment or not. It means only that guilt once established, there is a case for punishment which has to be defeated. Proof of an offence is sufficient to overcome the initial utilitarian presumption against causing suffering, and the onus of proof then rests on whoever would set the punishment aside.

[II] DETERMINING THE APPROPRIATE DEGREE OF PUNISHMENT

The characteristic of a retributive theory of punishment, we have said, is that it looks backward to the crime, not forward to the consequences of the punishment. And this approach is

16 Cf. Hume, in App. III to *Enquiry concerning the Principles of Morals*.

linked by some, though not all, retributivists to a belief that liability to punishment ought to be related to moral guilt, i.e. that men ought to be punished for their wickedness, or at least, that only wicked men deserve punishment. The utilitarian, on the other hand, regards punishment purely as a way of maintaining rules, and judges it according to the degree that the suffering it prevents outweighs the suffering it inflicts. These two attitudes are carried over into discussions of the degree of severity of the punishments which ought to be inflicted for different offences.

One of the criticisms levelled against utilitarianism is that by relating the justification of punishment to its expected consequences, rather than to the crime itself, it would seem to justify penalties divorced from the relative seriousness of crimes. Thus, if the only way to deter people from trivial offences were to impose major penalties, it would appear justifiable, on a utilitarian view, to punish parking offences more severely than, say, robbery with violence. Bentham held that where detection is difficult, and the risk of punishment accordingly diminished, greater severity ought to compensate for the uncertainty. On this view, a serious but easily detected crime might warrant lesser penalties than a minor but secret one. This conclusion being to the retributivist intolerable, he contends that to escape it we must seek the measure of punishment in the crime itself, relating it to the degree of wickedness involved in committing it.

Once again it is important to distinguish criteria for the justification of rules from those for justifying their application in particular cases. To ask 'How much punishment is appropriate to a given offence?' is ambiguous; for the question may refer either to the punishment allotted by a rule to a particular *class* of acts, or to *one particular* act within that class. Penal laws generally emphasize the distinction; they rarely prescribe one precise punishment for every offence of a given type, but rather stipulate a maximum (and occasionally a minimum) penalty, leaving determination of particular penalties to the judge's discretion. Two questions emerge: one, the legislator's, asks 'What principles are relevant to the determination of maximum (or

standard) punishments for offences of different classes?'; the
second, the judge's, asks 'By what criteria, in addition to the
maximum (and perhaps the minimum) penalty prescribed by
the law, ought I decide the punishment appropriate to a given
criminal action?'

(a) Principles Relevant to the Determination of Penalties for Different Classes of Offences

'The only case' said Kant, 'in which the offender cannot complain that he is being treated unjustly is if his crime recoils upon
himself and he suffers what he has inflicted on another, if not
in a literal sense, at any rate according to the spirit of the law.'
'It is only *the right of requital* (jus talionis) which can fix definitely the quality and quantity of the punishment.' [17] This is the
most extreme retributive position, but its essential weakness is
discernible in any more moderate attempt to relate the punishment directly to the nature of the crime.

The retaliatory principle of 'an eye for an eye' will work
literally only in a few special cases, and in some of these it
would be rejected as intolerably cruel. But if we are to take it in
some other sense, 'in the spirit of the law', it involves a sort of
arithmetical equation of suffering as impracticable as Bentham's
hedonistic calculus. Suffering of one sort cannot be *equated* with
another, though it may be possible to prefer one to another (or to
be indifferent as between one and another). I can certainly say
that I would rather see A suffer in one way than B in another; or
that there is really nothing to choose between the two. But this is
quite different from saying that A ought to be made to suffer in
exactly the same degree as B, whom he has injured; for this
involves not a preference enunciated by some third person, but a
quasi-quantitative comparison of the sufferings of two different
people, treated as objective facts. And there is no way of making
this comparison, even though the external features of their
suffering may be identical. It is even more evidently impossible
when the suffering of one is occasioned by, say, blackmail, and

17 *Op. cit.*

of the other by imprisonment.* Short of literal retaliation, there is no way in which the crime can be made the measure of the punishment, unless reference can be made to some predetermined scale. But the question then becomes that of drawing up the scale. This difficulty remains in the retributive theory as presented by Mr. J. D. Mabbott. While admitting that there can be no direct relation between the offence and the penalty, he maintains that by comparing one crime with another we can make an estimate of the punishments *relatively* appropriate: 'We can grade crimes in a rough scale and penalties in a rough scale, and keep our heaviest penalties for what are socially the most serious wrongs regardless of whether these penalties . . . are exactly what deterrence would require.' [18] What, however, are we to understand by 'socially the most serious wrongs'? Part at least of what we should mean by that phrase is that we ought to do our utmost to prevent them. The most serious wrongs are the ones we are least ready to tolerate. Consequently, these are not only the ones we blame most severely; they are also the ones we feel justified in penalizing most heavily, in order to deter people from committing them. It is difficult to see, then, how deterrence could be left out in constructing or justifying such a scale. Again, there is surely no doubt that in allocating penalties for offences against, say, currency or import regulations, what is most relevant is not the severity with which we *blame* the offence in any moral sense, but the profit that the offender might expect to make on such a transaction. Crime must not *pay*, however mildly we might blame it. It is not easy, with offences of this sort, to know what degree of blame is appropriate, because they are offences against morality only because there is a *prima facie* moral duty to obey the law. It is difficult to feel very deeply about breaches of rules which might be quite different in six

---

* Hegel virtually admits the impossibility of a rational answer to these questions (*Philosophy of Right*, §101), but insists that there must be a right answer (§214), to which we must try, empirically, to approximate. But by what test shall we judge whether our shots at justice are approaching, or receding from the target?

18 *Op. cit.*, p. 162.

months' time; but that is not a reason for punishing them leniently, if that would destroy the effectiveness of the rules.

The retributivist's difficulty is that he wants the crime itself to indicate the amount of punishment, which it cannot do unless we first assume a scale of crimes and penalties. But on what principles is the scale to be constructed, and how are new offences to be fitted into it? These difficulties admit of no solution unless we agree to examine the consequences to be expected from penalties of different degrees of severity; i.e. unless we adopt a utilitarian approach. It remains to be seen whether this can be done without our having to concede the retributivist case that this might involve severe penalties for trivial offences.

For the utilitarian, arguing in deterrent terms, it is the threat rather than the punishment itself which is primary. Could we rely on the threat being completely effective, there could be no objection to the death penalty for every offence, since *ex hypothesi* there would be no occasion ever to inflict it. Unhappily, since no detection system is perfect, punishment can never be utterly certain, and we must reckon on some offenders taking the risk, and therefore upon the need to inflict *some* punishments, if the threat is to remain effective for others. We must suppose, therefore, for each type of crime, a scale of possible penalties, to each of which would correspond a number of probable occasions on which it would be necessary to carry out the threat, the number presumably decreasing (though at a diminishing rate) as the penalty increases. Ultimately, however, we should almost certainly reach a hard core of offenders who, by reason perhaps of a misguided certainty that they would never be caught, would remain undeterred whatever the penalty. We should then choose, for each class of offence, a penalty which will prevent too much damage to the community, without inflicting an intolerable amount of suffering on offenders. A little more, and we might prefer more crimes to inflicting it; a little less, and we should reduce the number of crimes by increasing it. (This is Bentham's principle of 'frugality'.)[19]

This statement of the case might appear to suffer from

19 *Op. cit.*, Ch. XV, 11–12, pp. 303–304.

precisely the same weakness as the retaliatory theories, namely, that it involves a quantitative comparison of harm done to the community on the one hand, and the criminal on the other. But this is not so. We say something like this: To increase the penalty for parking offences to life imprisonment would reduce congestion on the roads by making people more careful where they parked. Nevertheless, the inconvenience of a larger number of offences would not justify so sweeping a disregard for the liberty even of a very few offenders. With blackmail or murder, the mischief of the offence is so great that the possibility of averting further instances defeats to a far greater extent the claims of the offender. One parking offence more or less is of no great moment; one murder more or less is.* We should consequently feel justified in inflicting heavier penalties.

This type of assessment does not involve the quantitative computations of retributivist theory. Whereas in that case we were asked to estimate the damage done by the crime, and then to inflict that amount on the criminal, here we are required only to choose between one combination of circumstances and another —between, say, a certain degree of congestion on the roads plus a certain amount of suffering to a given number of offenders, and a lesser congestion plus more suffering, though to fewer offenders. This type of choice may not always be easy to make— but many moral choices *are* difficult. The point is that there is nothing theoretically impossible, or even unusual, about asking people to make it. We are accustomed to expressing *preferences* between things incapable of quantitative comparison; what is impossible is to assess how much one man has suffered by being blackmailed, and to inflict a similar amount of suffering on the blackmailer in terms of a prison sentence.

It is apparent that the criticism levelled at utilitarianism,

* If the difference between the death penalty and imprisonment for life could be shewn to involve even a small difference in the number of murders likely to be committed, the case for the former would be accordingly stronger. But the Royal Commission on Capital Punishment (1949–53), having weighted the statistical evidence, concluded that it was important 'not to base a penal policy in relation to murder on exaggerated estimates of the uniquely deterrent force of the death penalty'. Cmd. 8932, §790 (3).

that it would justify severe penalties for relatively trivial offences, is groundless. For part of what we mean when we call an offence 'relatively trivial' is that we do not care so much about people committing that one as we do about others; and that, in turn, implies that we should be unwilling to inflict so much suffering to prevent it. Similarly, 'relatively serious' crimes are those that are relatively intolerable; and to describe them in this way is to say that we feel justified in going to much greater lengths to prevent them. If this is so, the proposition 'Trivial crimes do not deserve severe penalties' is analytic, being necessarily the consequence of the way we use 'trivial' in this context. Like the other retributive criticisms of utilitarianism discussed, it rests on a definition.*

(b) *Criteria Governing the Allocation of Penalties to Particular Offenders*

We distinguished earlier between the legislator's question, which seeks criteria for determining maximum (and perhaps minimum) penalties for different classes of crime, and the judge's question, which seeks criteria for determining the penalty appropriate to a particular offender. Two men guilty of what is technically the same offence are not necessarily awarded the same punishment. On the principle that justice requires that equals be treated equally, this would seem *prima facie* unjust, unless we can suggest criteria, other than legal guilt, by which they might properly be considered unequal. Now judges do employ such criteria; it makes a difference whether a man has previous convictions, whether he has acted under strong provocation, or temptation, or duress. These considerations would be relevant not only to the determination of punishment, but also of blame, and the coincidence of criteria certainly lends colour to the retributive view

---

* There are people who would rather suffer any crimes than inflict certain penalties, e.g. torture or death, which they regard as absolutely wrong. This need not mean that such penalties can *never* be right, but only that there are no *imaginable* circumstances in which their consequences could justify them. But some absolutists altogether deny that consequences are relevant; they are then making an ultimate judgment which cannot be discussed, and for which justification can be neither offered nor sought.

that the degree of moral guilt, or blameworthiness, is relevant to the determination of punishment. If we are to continue to maintain the mainly utilitarian position that we have adopted hitherto, we must meet two possible objections arising from these considerations:

(*i*) Is it consistent with utilitarianism that we look to the particular conditions of the crime, and of the criminal, for the measure of punishment? From the point of view of deterrence, does it make any difference that X acted under temptation, or provocation? Should we not look forward to the exemplary advantage of the maximum penalty, rather than backward to the extenuating circumstances of the crime? And if we do not do this, is it not because we accept the relevance of criteria of moral guilt to the determination of penalties?

We argued earlier that once rules are accepted, there is no need to justify every particular application of them in terms of its beneficent consequences. What is necessary, then, in this case, is to justify in utilitarian terms the criteria of extenuation, not each application of them.

Now there are some conditions, like unavoidable ignorance or mistake of fact, lunacy, infancy, or irresistible duress, which completely exonerate an offender, both in morals and in law. We neither blame nor punish a person for breaking a rule unless the act is intentional and the offender a responsible person, who knows what he is doing and knows that it is wrong. For it is only in such a case that a man could be said to *put himself* in the category liable to blame or punishment. In the cases we are considering a person might be said, *prima facie*, to have broken the law and therefore to have placed himself in the normal category of law-breaker. But this case is defeated by any of the considerations mentioned which would make a relevant difference between this and the normal law-breaker. And justice demands a distinction in treatment. Consequently, no act committed under the conditions mentioned would be either punishable or blameworthy.

The recognition of such criteria, however, could also be defended in strictly utilitarian terms. If the principal object of punishment is to act as a deterrent, it can be effective only in respect of *deliberate* acts. Accordingly, if it is waived on any of the grounds mentioned, its effectiveness is not impaired. The same man contemplating murder gets no encouragement if a homicidal maniac escapes punishment, since the defence of insanity would not be open to *him*. It would be a pointless mischief, then, to make men suffer for any but deliberate offences.

Again, there are conditions like strong temptation or provocation which mitigate the degree of blame and would also justify a milder penalty. Unlike the conditions just discussed these extenuate rather than exonerate. They are, however, sufficiently like those conditions for us to feel, on rather vague grounds of fairness, that a distinction ought properly to be drawn between offences committed under them and the normal case. A utilitarian, however, would be reluctant to make such concessions unless he were assured that there would be no weakening of the threat. An offence committed under such conditions would be exceptional, and leniency could be expected only under similar conditions. And though these might not be such as to warrant saying that a person acting under them was not responsible, in such a state of mind he would be unlikely to take much account of the threat of punishment. If that were so, it would be pointless to inflict the full measure of suffering provided for the offence.* Suppose, however, that it could be shown that crimes of passion could as a matter of fact be successfully discouraged by very severe penalties, such that the extra suffering inflicted on actual offenders was more than justified by the extra protection given to society, there would be a conflict between the vague notion of fairness which makes us talk of passion as an extenu-

* Cf. Bosanquet, *op. cit.*, pp. 214–215. 'The true reason for allowing circumstances which change the character of the act to influence the sentence is that, in changing its character, they may take it out of the class of offences to which it *prima facie* belongs, and from which men need to be deterred by a recognised amount of severity. If a man is starving and steals a turnip, his offence, being so exceptionally conditioned, does not threaten the general right of property, and does not need to be associated with any high degree of terror in order to protect that right. A man who steals under no extraordinary pressure of need does what might become a common practice if not associated with as much terror as is found by experience to deter men from theft.'

ating circumstance and the purely utilitarian considerations of prevention and deterrence.

(*ii*) The second possible objection is that since the criteria tending to mitigate blame and punishment coincide in so many particulars, should we not be justified in saying that men deserve punishment only to the extent that they are morally guilty (or wicked, or blameworthy)?

This would be so if there were a complete correspondence of criteria—but this is not the case. The question of motive is crucial. We generally regard a man as less blameworthy if, in breaking a rule, he does so 'from the highest motives', instead of selfishly or maliciously. A traitor prompted by conscientious political convictions might be blamed for wrongheadedness, but we might still respect his integrity, and blame him less than a merely mercenary one. Now this type of consideration is sometimes important in mitigating punishment (e.g. in the case of 'mercy-killing'), but by no means always. Sincere fifth-columnists cannot expect to be treated less severely than merely disgruntled or ambitious ones. A man's motives are frequently so obscure and so difficult to establish objectively, that leniency on this account might well invite the insincere to counterfeit sincerity, with no way of unmasking the cheat.* A man's high motives may sometimes be a reason for not punishing him at all; but in other cases they may be a reason for punishing him as severely as the law allows. For the conscientious offender may be the stubbornest of all: his scruples may be far less easily overborne by threats of punishment than more selfish motives. Only the

---

* Consider, in this connection, the difficulty of distinguishing the genuine survivor of a suicide pact, who has been unable to carry out his side of the bargain, from the 'cheat' who relies on a counterfeit pact to evade the maximum penalty for murder. (See the Report on Capital Punishment, §§163–176.) The same applies to 'mercy-killings': 'How, for example, were the jury to decide whether a daughter had killed her invalid father from compassion, from a desire for material gain, from a natural wish to bring to an end a trying period of her life, or from a combination of motives?' (*Ibid.* §179). Nevertheless, where we feel reasonably sure that the motive was merciful, we expect leniency. Bosanquet's account is probably sufficient justification: a mercy-killing is not really in the same class as a brutal murder for profit, and we may feel justified in tolerating a few examples rather than inflict the maximum penalty on this type of offender.

man of weak conviction is likely to be put off by threats of punishment. The effectiveness of government, if not its very survival, could well depend on its success in coercing conscientious but recalcitrant minorities. In that case, conscientious motives could scarcely be admitted in extenuation of the offence. On the other hand, the severity of the penalty necessary to secure a high degree of conformity might be a mischief outweighing the advantage gained. It might then be reasonable to give up punishing conscientious offenders altogether, if they can be discerned from the fakes. We no longer punish conscientious objectors to military service, having learnt by experience that they are rarely amenable to threats, that they are unsatisfactory soldiers if coerced, and that, given a rigourous test of conscientiousness, there will not be enough of them to frustrate the community's purpose. In this instance, the motive has been formally embodied into the rule, such that anyone who breaks it conscientiously, and in accordance with recognized procedures, does not in fact break it at all.

Though there is a considerable overlapping of the criteria for awarding blame and punishment, the case of motive seems to indicate that they are not necessarily identical. The wide area of coincidence seems nevertheless to demand explanation. Morality, like law, is a system of rules for guiding behaviour, and blame is to the one what punishment is to the other. Many rules supported by blame (including self-blame, or remorse) appear also as legal rules upheld by punishments; for the ends of moral guidance are largely similar to those of legal control. But qualities of character, and therefore the motives for actions, count for more in moral than in legal judgments; for morality operates not merely by prescribing or prohibiting certain classes of action, but also by training character (and therefore conduct in general) by praise and blame of 'the whole man'. We blame men for being bad-tempered; we punish only for assault. Praise and blame, reward and punishment, are nevertheless closely analogous, and since their functions are broadly alike, it is not surprising that the criteria for allocating them should largely correspond. But because we usually blame the criminal we punish, it does not follow that we therefore do, or ought to, punish according to the criteria of moral guilt. Analogous techniques are likely to employ analogous criteria: but since punishment is administered through formal machinery of investigation, proof, sentence, and execution, according to established rules, the criteria governing its operation are likely to differ in some important respects from those implicit in the informal and personal procedures by which we blame.

The very closeness of the analogy, however, leads us to slip easily in thought from one system to the other. Judges often speak and act as if the criteria of moral guilt were directly relevant to the determination of penalties in particular cases.[20] Conversely, the ordinary man may exclaim in indignation against an offence against morals, 'He deserves to be punished', though no law has been broken. We learn to obey rules in childhood by a mixture of praise and blame, reward and punishment, and we easily assume that the same criteria are appropriate to both types of sanction. But the legal process is a technique for controlling large numbers of people; it necessarily requires different criteria from parental and pedagogical discipline.

Nevertheless, law depends for its effectiveness on public confidence and support. In the nineteenth century, many people came to feel that penalties for trivial offences were often excessive. This led to a perversion of justice in the contrary direction, since juries would refuse to convict on clear evidence of guilt. In the twentieth century, the McNaghten Rules, which define 'insanity' as a legal defence against a murder charge, have been widely criticized, and judges have been known to encourage juries to bring in verdicts of insanity in cases clearly outside the Rules, but to which the death sentence seemed inappropriate on moral grounds.[21] A penal system which has to be applied by judges and juries, and which invites public criticism of its deci-

[20] Cf. the discussion of the relative guilt of accomplices in *Capital Punishment Report*, Sec. 118.

[21] *Ibid.*, Secs. 289–295.

sions, cannot remain effective if it departs too radically from conventional standards apportioning blame.

[III] CONCLUSION

It has not been the purpose of this [essay] to advocate or defend any particular set of penal arrangements, nor to suggest that those currently operating in this country are necessarily rationally justifiable. Instead, we have tried to indicate how to go about defending or attacking punishments, in general or in particular. We have asked, not whether this or that arrangement is justified, but what would be the appropriate procedure for justifying it; not, primarily, what criteria are, or ought to be, employed in fixing penalties, but how to go about choosing, or criticizing such criteria. Our main contention has been that punishment is a technique for preventing breaches of rules; like any technique, it must be judged by its results. On the other hand, like any system of rules, once adopted, it implies a *prima facie* case for implementation in particular instances, so that in any normal case it is sufficient to point to a breach of a rule of the appropriate type to justify a penalty. That is not to say that guilt is always a sufficient condition for punishment. There are other reasonably relevant criteria. These, however, must be compatible with the overriding conception of punishment as a technique for upholding rules. Not indeed that *any* penalty could be justified that upheld the rules—for the efficiency of a technique must be judged not only by its achievements but also by its cost. Whatever criteria we employ must satisfy the condition that, while upholding rules, they do not entail so great a measure of suffering that the rules are no longer worth upholding. We have seen that in allocating punishment to a class of offences, we are, in a sense, deciding how much crime of that type we are ready to tolerate, in preference to the alternative of a stricter penalty.

We have provided no short way to a decision on, say, capital punishment as a penalty for murder; we have only indicated the lines on which discussion must go. But if, as some maintain, to abolish it would not impair the effective deterrence or prevention of that crime, there would seem, on our analysis, no further argument by which to defend it.[22]

Finally; punishment is not the sole technique for ensuring that laws are kept. More people obey laws because they respect them than do so because they fear the consequences of breaking them. It is better to create conditions in which there are fewer potential offenders than to keep down the numbers of actual ones by punishing them. As a technique employing deliberate suffering, it must be counted, in moral terms, as costly, to be considered rather as a last resort than as the obvious and natural way of maintaining the social order intact.

[22] See H. L. A. Hart, 'Murder and the Principles of Punishment: England and the United States' in *Northwestern University Law Review*, Vol. 52, 1957, pp. 433–461.

Books and articles either much-discussed or particularly useful on a given topic are followed by Roman numerals in parentheses, corresponding to the principal divisions of the text. Items not marked thus are often relevant to several issues or not conveniently classified under the headings here preferred.

BOOKS

Adams, E. M. *Ethical Naturalism and the Modern World-View*. Chapel Hill: University of North Carolina Press, 1960. (I)

Aiken, Henry David. *Reason and Conduct*. New York: Alfred A. Knopf, 1962.

Anscombe, G. E. M. *Intention*. Oxford: Basil Blackwell, 1957. (III)

Ayer, A. J. *Language, Truth and Logic*. London: Victor Gollancz, 1948, Ch. 6, and pp. 20–22. (I)

Baier, Kurt. *The Moral Point of View*. Ithaca: Cornell University Press, 1958. (I)

Blanshard, Brand. *Reason and Goodness*. London: George Allen & Unwin, 1961.

Braithewaite, R. B. *Theory of Games as a Tool for the Moral Philosopher*. Cambridge, Eng.: Cambridge University Press, 1955. (III)

Brandt, R. *Hopi Ethics*. Chicago: University of Chicago Press, 1954.

Brandt, Richard. *Ethical Theory*. Englewood Cliffs, N. J.: Prentice-Hall, 1961.

Carnap, R. *Philosophy and Logical Syntax*. London: Kegan Paul, Trench, Trubner and Co., 1935, Secs. 1, 2, 4. (I)

D'Arcy, Eric. *Human Acts*. Oxford: The Clarendon Press, 1963. (III)

Dewey, John. *Theory of Valuation*. Chicago: University of Chicago Press, 1939.

Edel, Abraham. *Ethical Judgment*. Glencoe, Ill.: Free Press, 1955.

————. *Method in Ethical Theory*. London: Routledge & Kegan Paul, 1963.

Edwards, Paul. *The Logic of Moral Discourse*. Glencoe, Ill.: Free Press, 1955. (I)

Ewing, A. C. *The Definition of Good*. New York: The Macmillan Company, 1947. (I)

————. *Ethics*. London: English Universities Press, 1953.

————. *Second Thoughts in Moral Philosophy*. New York: The Macmillan Company, 1959.

Farrer, Austin. *The Freedom of the Will*. New York: Charles Scribner's Sons, 1958. (III)

Findlay, J. N. *Language, Mind and Value*. London: George Allen & Unwin, 1963.

Frankena, W. K. *Ethics*. Englewood Cliffs, N. J.: Prentice-Hall, 1963.

Gauthier, D. *Practical Reasoning*. London: Oxford University Press. 1963. (II)

Ginsberg, Morris. *On the Diversity of Morals*. New York: The Macmillan Company, 1956.

Hall, E. *What Is Value?* London: Routledge & Kegan Paul, 1952.

Hall, Jerome. *General Principles of Criminal Law*. Indianapolis: Bobbs-Merrill Co., 1947.

Hampshire, Stuart. *Thought and Action*. London: Chatto & Windus, 1959. (III)

Hare, R. M. *The Language of Morals*. Oxford: The Clarendon Press, 1952. (I)

————. *Freedom and Reason*. Oxford: The Clarendon Press, 1963.

Hart, H. L. A. *The Concept of Law*. Oxford: The Clarendon Press, 1961. (II)

Hartland-Swann, John. *An Analysis of Morals*. London: George Allen & Unwin, 1960.

Hay, William H., Marcus G. Singer, and Arthur E. Murphy (eds.). *Reason and the Common Good. Selected Essays of Arthur E. Murphy*. Englewood Cliffs, N. J.: Prentice-Hall, 1963.

Hill, T. E. *Contemporary Ethical Theories*. New York: The Macmillan Company, 1951.

Hook, Sidney (ed.). *Determinism and Freedom*. New York: New York University Press, 1958. (III)

Hospers, John. *Human Conduct*. New York: Harcourt, Brace & World, 1961.

Kemp, G. *Reason, Action and Morality*. London: Routledge & Kegan Paul, 1964.

Ladd, John. *The Structure of a Moral Code*. Cambridge: Harvard University Press, 1957.

Lamont, W. D. *The Principles of Moral Judgment*. Oxford: The Clarendon Press, 1946.

Lepley, Ray (ed.). *Value: A Cooperative Inquiry*. New York: Columbia University Press, 1949.

Lewis, C. I. *An Analysis of Knowledge and Valuation*. La Salle, Ill.: Open Court Publishing Co., 1946.

———. *The Ground and Nature of the Right*. New York: Columbia University Press, 1955.

Lyons, David. *Forms and Limits of Utilitarianism*. Oxford: Oxford University Press, 1965. (II)

Mackinnon, D. M. *A Study in Ethical Theory*. London: Black, 1957.

Mandelbaum, Maurice. *The Phenomenological Moral Experience*. Glencoe, Ill.: Free Press, 1955.

Margolis, Joseph. *Psychotherapy and Morality*. New York: Random House, 1966.

Mayo, Bernard. *Ethics and the Moral Life*. London: Macmillan and Co., 1958.

Melden, A. I. (ed.). *Essays in Moral Philosophy*. Seattle: University of Washington Press, 1958.

———. *Rights and Right Conduct*. Oxford: Basil Blackwell, 1959. (II)

———. *Free Action*. London: Routledge & Kegan Paul, 1961. (III)

Montefiore, Alan. *A Modern Introduction to Moral Philosophy.* London: Routledge & Kegan Paul, 1958. (I)

Moore, G. E. *Principia Ethica.* Cambridge, Eng.: Cambridge University Press, 1903.

————. *Ethics.* Oxford: Oxford University Press, 1912.

Morris, Herbert (ed.). *Freedom and Responsibility.* Stanford, Calif.: Stanford University Press, 1961. (III)

Murphy, Arthur E. *The Theory of Practical Reason.* La Salle, Ill.: Open Court Publishing Co., 1964.

Nakhnikian, G., and H. Castañeda (eds.). *Morality and the Language of Conduct.* Detroit: Wayne State University Press, 1961.

Nowell-Smith, P. H. *Ethics.* Harmondsworth: Penguin Books, 1954. (I)

Pepper, Stephen. *The Sources of Value.* Berkeley: University of California Press, 1959.

Perry, R. B. *General Theory of Value.* New York: Longmans, Green, 1926.

————. *Realms of Value.* Cambridge: Harvard University Press, 1954.

Peters, R. S. *The Concept of Motivation.* London: Routledge & Kegan Paul, 1958. (III)

Prichard, H. A. *Moral Obligation.* Oxford: Clarendon Press, 1949. (II)

Prior, A. N. *Logic and the Basis of Ethics.* New York: Oxford University Press, 1949, Ch. 1. (I)

Raphael, D. D. *The Moral Sense.* London: Oxford University Press, 1947.

————. *Moral Judgment.* London: George Allen & Unwin, 1955.

Rice, Philip Blair. *On the Knowledge of Good and Evil.* New York: Random House, 1955.

Ross, W. D. *The Right and the Good.* Oxford: Clarendon Press, 1930. (I)

————. *Foundations of Ethics.* Oxford: Clarendon Press, 1939. (I)

Russell, B. *Religion and Science.* New York: Henry Holt and Co., 1935, Ch. 9.

Ryle, Gilbert. *The Concept of Mind.* London: Hutchinson & Co., 1949.

————. *Dilemmas.* Cambridge, Eng.: Cambridge University Press, 1954, Ch. 4.

Schilpp, Paul Arthur (ed.). *The Philosophy of G. E. Moore.* Evanston, Ill.: Northwestern University Press, 1942.

Schlick, Moritz. *Problems of Ethics.* Englewood Cliffs, N. J.: Prentice-Hall, 1939.

Sellars, Wilfrid, and John Hospers (eds.). *Readings in Ethical Theory.* New York: Appleton-Century-Crofts, 1952.

Sesonske, Alexander. *Value and Obligation.* Berkeley: University of California Press, 1957. (I)

Shirk, Evelyn. *The Ethical Dimension.* New York: Appleton-Century-Crofts, 1965.

Singer, Marcus George. *Generalization in Ethics.* New York: Alfred A. Knopf, 1961. (II)

Smart, J. J. C. *An Outline of a System of Utilitarian Ethics.* Melbourne: Melbourne University Press, 1961. (II)

Sparshott, F. E. *An Enquiry into Goodness.* Chicago: University of Chicago Press, 1958.

Stace, W. T. *The Concept of Morals.* New York: The Macmillan Company, 1937.

Stevenson, C. L. *Ethics and Language.* New Haven, Conn.: Yale University Press, 1944. (I)

———. *Facts and Values.* New Haven, Conn.: Yale University Press, 1963. (I)

Taylor, Paul. *Normative Discourse.* Englewood Cliffs, N. J.: Prentice-Hall, 1961. (I)

Toulmin, Stephen. *The Place of Reason in Ethics.* Cambridge, Eng.: Cambridge University Press, 1950. (I)

Vivas, Eliseo. *The Moral Life and the Ethical Life.* Chicago: University of Chicago Press, 1950.

von Wright, G. H. *The Varieties of Goodness.* London: Routledge & Kegan Paul, 1963.

———. *Norm and Action.* London: Routledge & Kegan Paul, 1963.

Warnock, Mary. *Ethics Since 1900.* Oxford: Oxford University Press, 1960. (I)

Wellman, Carl. *The Language of Ethics.* Cambridge: Harvard University Press, 1961.

Westermarck, Edward. *Ethical Relativity.* New York: Harcourt, Brace & World, 1932.

Williams, Glanville. *Criminal Law.* London: Stevens and Sons, 1953.
————. *The Sanctity of Life and the Criminal Law.* New York: Alfred A. Knopf, 1957.
Wilson, J. *Reason and Morals.* Cambridge, Eng.: Cambridge University Press, 1961.
Ziff, Paul. *Semantic Analysis.* Ithaca, N. Y.: Cornell University Press, 1960, Ch. 6. (I)
Zink, S. *The Concepts of Ethics.* New York: St. Martin's Press, 1962.

ARTICLES

Acton, H. B., and J. W. N. Watkins, "Negative Utilitarianism," *Proceedings of the Aristotelian Society,* Suppl. XXXVII (1963), 83–114. (II)
Aiken, Henry David, "Emotive 'Meanings' and Ethical Terms," *Journal of Philosophy,* XLI (1944), 456–470. (I)
————, "Evaluation and Obligation: Two Functions of Judgments in the Language of Conduct," *Journal of Philosophy,* XLVII (1950), 5–22. (I)
Aune, Bruce, "Abilities, Modalities and Free Will," *Philosophy and Phenomenological Research,* XXIII (1962–1963), 397–413.
Austin, J. L., "A Plea for Excuses," in J. O. Urmson and G. J. Warnock (eds.), *Philosophical Papers* (Oxford: Oxford University Press, 1961).
Ayer, A. J., "Freedom and Necessity," in *Philosophical Essays* (New York: St. Martin's Press, 1954). (III)
————, "On the Analysis of Moral Judgments," in *Philosophical Essays* (New York: St. Martin's Press, 1954). (I)
————, "The Principle of Utility," in *Philosophical Essays* (New York: St. Martin's Press, 1954). (II)
Baier, K., "Doing my Duty," *Philosophy,* XXVII (1952), 253–260. (II)
————, "Good Reasons," *Philosophical Studies,* IV (1953), 1–15. (I)
————, "Proving a Moral Judgment," *Philosophical Studies,* IV (1953), 33–44. (I)
————, "Is Punishment Retributive?" *Analysis,* XVI (1955), 25–32. (III)

Barnes, W. H. F., "Ethics without Propositions," *Proceedings of the Aristotelian Society*, Suppl. XXII (1948), 1–30. (I)

——, W. D. Falk, and A. Duncan-Jones, "Intention, Motive, and Responsibility" (Symposium), *Proceedings of the Aristotelian Society*, Suppl. XIX (1945), 230–288. (III)

Baylis, C. A., "Grading, Values, and Choice," *Mind*, LXVII (1958), 485–501.

Beardsley, E. L., "Moral Worth and Moral Credit," *Philosophical Review*, LXVI (1957), 304–328. (II)

——, "Determinism and Moral Perspectives," *Philosophy and Philosophical Research*, XXI (1960), 1–20. (III)

Beardsley, Monroe C., "Intrinsic Value," *Philosophy and Phenomenological Research*, XXVI (1965), 1–17.

Beck, Lewis White, "Apodictic Imperatives," *Kant-Studien*, XLIX (1957), 7–24. (II)

Bennett, J., "Moral Argument," *Mind*, LXIX (1960), 544–549.

Benson, John, "The Characterisation of Actions and the Virtuous Agent," *Proceedings of the Aristotelian Society*, LXIII (1962–1963), 251–266.

Black, Max, "The Gap Between 'Is' and 'Should,'" *Philosophical Review*, LXXIII (1964), 165–181. (II)

Blackstone, W. T., "Are Metaethical Theories Normatively Neutral?" *Australasian Journal of Philosophy*, XXXIX (1961), 65–74.

——, "On Justifying a Metaethical Theory," *Australasian Journal of Philosophy*, XLI (1963), 57–66. (II)

Bradley, R. D., "Free Will: Problem or Pseudo-problem?" *Australasian Journal of Philosophy*, XXXVI (1958), 33–45.

——, " 'Ifs,' 'Cans' and Determinism," *Australasian Journal of Philosophy*, XLI (1963), 146–158. (III)

Brandt, R. B., "The Emotive Theory of Ethics," *Philosophical Review*, LIX (1950), 305–318. (I)

——, "The Status of Empirical Assertion Theories in Ethics," *Mind*, LXI (1952), 458–479. (I)

——, "The Definition of an 'Ideal Observer' Theory in Ethics," *Philosophy and Phenomenological Research*, XV (1955), 407–413. (I)

Braybrooke, David, "How Are Moral Judgments Connected with Displays of Emotion?" *Dialogue,* IV (1965), 206–223.

Britton, Karl, "Utilitarianism: the Appeal to a First Principle," *Proceedings of the Aristotelian Society,* LX (1959–1960), 141–154. (II)

Broad, C. D., "On the Function of False Hypotheses in Ethics," *Ethics,* XXVI (1916), 377–397. (II)

————, "Is 'Goodness' a Name of a Simple Non-natural Quality?" *Proceedings of the Aristotelian Society,* XXXIV (1933–1934), 249–268. (I)

————, "Some Reflections on Moral-Sense Theories in Ethics," *Proceedings of the Aristotelian Society,* XLV (1944–1945), 131–166. (I)

————, "Determinism, Indeterminism and Libertarianism," in *Ethics and the History of Philosophy* (London: Routledge & Kegan Paul, 1952). (III)

————, "Egoism as a Theory of Human Motives," in *Ethics and the History of Philosophy* (London: Routledge & Kegan Paul, 1952). (II)

————, "G. E. Moore's Latest Published Views on Ethics," *Mind,* LXX (1961), 435–457. (I)

Brown, D. G., "Evaluative Inference," *Philosophy,* XXX (1955), 214–228. (II)

Campbell, C. A., "Moral and Non-Moral Values," *Mind,* XLIV (1935), 237–299.

Canfield, John V., "The Compatibility of Free Will and Determinism," *Philosophical Review,* LXXI (1962), 352–368. (III)

Castañeda, Hector-Neri, "Imperative Reasonings," *Philosophy and Phenomenological Research,* XXI (1960), 21–49.

————, "The Logic of Change, Action, and Norms," *Journal of Philosophy,* LXII (1965), 333–344.

Caton, Charles E., "In What Sense and Why 'Ought'-Judgments Are Universalisable," *Philosophical Quarterly,* XIII (1963), 48–55. (II)

Cohen, M. F., "Knowledge and Moral Belief," *Australasian Journal of Philosophy,* XLII (1965), 168–188.

Danto, A., and S. Morgenbesser, "Character and Free Will," *Journal of Philosophy*, LIV (1957), 493–505. (III)

Davidson, D., J. M. McKinsey, and P. Suppes, "Outlines of a Formal Theory of Value," *Philosophy of Science*, XXII (1955), 140–160.

Dumont, R. G., "Promising," *Australasian Journal of Philosophy*, XLI (1963), 44–56.

Duncan-Jones, A., "Kant and Universalisation," *Analysis*, XVI (1955), 12–14.

————, "Utilitarianism and Rules," *Philosophical Quarterly*, VII (1957), 364–367. (II)

Duncker, K., "Ethical Relativity," *Mind*, XLVIII (1939), 39–47.

Durrant, R. G., "Moral Neutrality and the Analysis of Morality," *Australasian Journal of Philosophy*, XXXVI (1958), 169–188. (II)

Ebbinghaus, Julius, "Interpretation and Misinterpretation of the Categorical Imperative," *Philosophical Quarterly*, IV (1954), 97–108.

Edgley, R., "Practical Reason," *Mind*, LXXIV (1965), 174–191.

Ewing, A. C., "Utilitarianism," *Ethics*, LVIII (1947), 100–111. (II)

————, "What Would Happen if Everybody Acted Like Me?" *Philosophy*, XXVIII (1953), 16–29. (II)

Falk, W. D., " 'Ought' and Motivation," *Proceedings of the Aristotelian Society*, XLVIII (1947–1948), 111–138.

————, "Guiding and Goading," *Mind*, LXII (1953), 145–169. (I)

————, "Morality and Convention," *Journal of Philosophy*, LVII (1960), 675–685.

Field, G. C., "The Place of Definition in Ethics," *Proceedings of the Aristotelian Society*, XXXII (1931–1932), 79–94. (I)

Firth, R., "Ethical Absolutism and the Ideal Observer," *Philosophy and Phenomenological Research*, XII (1952), 317–345. (I)

Flew, Antony, "The Justification of Punishment," *Philosophy*, XXIX (1954), 291–307. (III)

————, "On Not Deriving 'Ought' from 'Is,' " *Analysis*, XXV (1964), 25–32.

Foot, P. R., "Free Will as Involving Determinism," *Philosophical Review*, LXVI (1957), 439–450. (III)

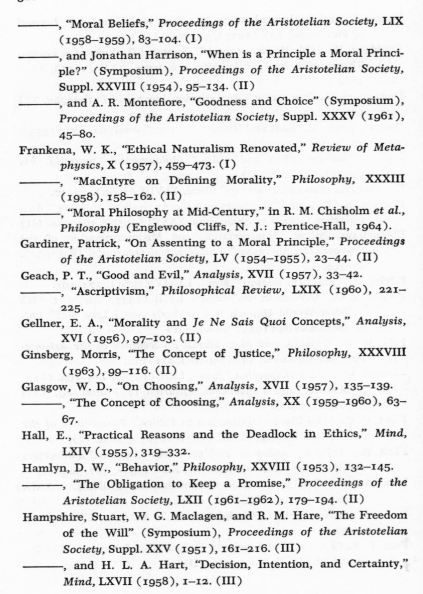

————, "Moral Beliefs," *Proceedings of the Aristotelian Society,* LIX (1958–1959), 83–104. (I)

————, and Jonathan Harrison, "When is a Principle a Moral Principle?" (Symposium), *Proceedings of the Aristotelian Society,* Suppl. XXVIII (1954), 95–134. (II)

————, and A. R. Montefiore, "Goodness and Choice" (Symposium), *Proceedings of the Aristotelian Society,* Suppl. XXXV (1961), 45–80.

Frankena, W. K., "Ethical Naturalism Renovated," *Review of Metaphysics,* X (1957), 459–473. (I)

————, "MacIntyre on Defining Morality," *Philosophy,* XXXIII (1958), 158–162. (II)

————, "Moral Philosophy at Mid-Century," in R. M. Chisholm *et al.,* *Philosophy* (Englewood Cliffs, N. J.: Prentice-Hall, 1964).

Gardiner, Patrick, "On Assenting to a Moral Principle," *Proceedings of the Aristotelian Society,* LV (1954–1955), 23–44. (II)

Geach, P. T., "Good and Evil," *Analysis,* XVII (1957), 33–42.

————, "Ascriptivism," *Philosophical Review,* LXIX (1960), 221–225.

Gellner, E. A., "Morality and *Je Ne Sais Quoi* Concepts," *Analysis,* XVI (1956), 97–103. (II)

Ginsberg, Morris, "The Concept of Justice," *Philosophy,* XXXVIII (1963), 99–116. (II)

Glasgow, W. D., "On Choosing," *Analysis,* XVII (1957), 135–139.

————, "The Concept of Choosing," *Analysis,* XX (1959–1960), 63–67.

Hall, E., "Practical Reasons and the Deadlock in Ethics," *Mind,* LXIV (1955), 319–332.

Hamlyn, D. W., "Behavior," *Philosophy,* XXVIII (1953), 132–145.

————, "The Obligation to Keep a Promise," *Proceedings of the Aristotelian Society,* LXII (1961–1962), 179–194. (II)

Hampshire, Stuart, W. G. Maclagen, and R. M. Hare, "The Freedom of the Will" (Symposium), *Proceedings of the Aristotelian Society,* Suppl. XXV (1951), 161–216. (III)

————, and H. L. A. Hart, "Decision, Intention, and Certainty," *Mind,* LXVII (1958), 1–12. (III)

Hardie, W., "My Own Free Will," *Philosophy,* XXXII (1957), 21–38. (III)

Hare, R. M., "Universalizability," *Proceedings of the Aristotelian Society,* IV (1954–1955), 295–312. (II)

————, and P. M. Gardiner, "Pain and Evil" (Symposium), *Proceedings of the Aristotelian Society,* XXXVIII (1964), 91–124.

Harrison, J., "Can Ethics do without Propositions?" *Mind,* LIX (1950), 358–371. (I)

————, "Empiricism in Ethics," *Philosophical Quarterly,* II (1952), 289–306. (I)

————, "Utilitarianism, Universalization, and Our Duty to be Just," *Proceedings of the Aristotelian Society,* LIII (1952–1953), 105–134. (II)

————, "Kant's Four Examples of the First Formulation of the Categorical Imperative," *Philosophical Quarterly,* VII (1957), 50–62. (II)

————, "Knowing and Promising," *Mind,* LXXI (1962), 443–457.

Hart, H. L. A., "The Ascription of Responsibility and Rights," in Antony Flew (ed.), *Logic and Language,* First Series (Oxford: Basil Blackwell, 1951). (II)

————, "Prolegomenon to the Principles of Punishment," *Proceedings of the Aristotelian Society,* LX (1959–1960), 1–26. (III)

————, "Negligence, *Mens Rea,* and Criminal Responsibility," in A. G. Guest (ed.), *Oxford Essays in Jurisprudence* (New York: Oxford University Press, 1961). (II)

Hartman, R. S., "General Theory of Values," in R. Klibansky (ed.), *Philosophy in the Mid-Century,* Vol. III (Florence: La Nuova Italia Editrice, 1958).

Henson, R. G., "On Being Ideal," *Philosophical Review,* LXV (1956), 389–400.

Holland, R., and H. D. Lewis, "The Autonomy of Ethics" (Symposium), *Proceedings of the Aristotelian Society,* Suppl. XXXII (1958), 25–74.

Horsburgh, H. J. N., "Criteria of Assent to a Moral Rule," *Mind,* LXIII (1954), 345–368. (II)

Hungerland, Isabel C., "Contextual Implication," *Inquiry,* III (1960), 211–258.

Jarvis, J., "In Defense of Moral Absolutes," *Journal of Philosophy*, LV (1958), 1043–1053.

———, "Practical Reasoning," *Philosophical Quarterly*, XII (1962), 316–328. (II)

Jeffrey, Richard C., Carl G. Hempel, and J. Sayer Minas, "Ethics and Decision Theory" (Symposium), *Journal of Philosophy*, LXII (1965), 528–544. (II)

Johnson, O. A., "Ethical Intuitionism—a Restatement," *Philosophical Quarterly*, VII (1957), 193–203. (I)

Kading, Daniel, "Are There Really No Duties to Oneself?" *Ethics*, LXX (1960), 155–157.

Kaplan, A., "Are Moral Judgments Assertions?" *Philosophical Review*, LI (1942), 280–303. (I)

———, "Logical Empiricism and Value Judgments," in P. A. Schilpp (ed.), *The Philosophy of Rudolf Carnap* (La Salle, Ill.: Open Court Publishing Co., 1964).

Kerner, George C., "Approvals, Reasons and Moral Argument," *Mind*, LXXI (1962), 474–486.

Kretzmann, N., "Desire as a Proof of Desirability," *Philosophical Quarterly*, VIII (1958), 246–258.

Ladd, John, "Value Judgments, Emotive Meaning and Attitudes," *Journal of Philosophy*, XLVI (1949), 119–129. (I)

———, "Free Will and Voluntary Action," *Philosophy and Phenomenological Research*, XII (1952), 392–405. (III)

———, Kurt Baier, and J. B. Schneewind, "Ethics and the Concept of Action" (Symposium), *Journal of Philosophy*, LXII (1965), 633–650. (III)

Lemmon, E. J., "Moral Dilemmas," *Philosophical Review*, LXXI (1962), 139–158.

Lewis, H. D., "Obedience to Conscience," *Mind*, LIV (1945), 227–253. (II)

———, J. W. Harvey, and G. A. Paul, "The Problem of Guilt" (Symposium), *Proceedings of the Aristotelian Society*, Suppl. XXI (1947), 175–218. (II)

Locke, Don, "Ifs and Cans Revisited," *Philosophy*, XXXVII (1962), 245–256. (III)

SELECTED READINGS 529

Lucas, J. R., "The Lesbian Rule," *Philosophy*, XXX (1955), 195–213.
(II)
——, "On Not Worshipping Facts," *Philosophical Quarterly*, VIII
(1958), 144–156. (II)
Mabbott, J. D., "Punishment," *Mind*, XLCIII (1939), 152–167. (III)
——, "Moral Rules," *Proceedings of the British Academy*, XXXIX
(1953), 97–117. (II)
——, "Free-will and Punishment," in H. D. Lewis (ed.), *Con-
temporary British Philosophy*, 3rd Series (London: George
Allen & Unwin, 1956). (III)
Macdonald, Margaret, "Natural Rights," *Proceedings of the Aris-
totelian Society*, XLVII (1947–1948), 225–250. (II)
——, "Ethics and the Ceremonial Use of Language," in Max Black
(ed.), *Philosophical Analysis* (Ithaca, N. Y.: Cornell University Press, 1950). (I)
MacIntyre, Alasdair, "What Morality is Not," *Philosophy*, XXXII
(1957), 325–335. (II)
——, D. S. Schwayder, and Joseph Margolis, "Ethics and Lan-
guage" (Symposium), *Journal of Philosophy*, LXII (1965),
513–528. (I)
Mackinnon, D. M., "Ethical Intuition," in H. D. Lewis (ed.), *Con-
temporary British Philosophy*, 3rd Series (London: George
Allen & Unwin, 1956).
Maclagen, W. G., "Respect for Persons as a Moral Principle," *Philos-
ophy*, XXXV (1960), 193–217, 289–305. (II)
Mandelbaum, Maurice, "Determinism and Moral Responsibility,"
Ethics, LII (1960), 204–219. (III)
Margolis, Joseph, "Intention, Consciousness, and Action," *Methodos*,
XIV (1962), 41–46. (III)
——, "Classification and the Concept of Goodness," *Australasian
Journal of Philosophy*, XLI (1963), 21–23. (I)
——, " 'Lying Is Wrong' and 'Lying Is Not Always Wrong,' " *Phi-
losophy and Phenomenological Research*, XXIII (1963), 414–
418. (II)
Matson, W. I., "The Irrelevance of Free-will to Moral Responsibility,"
Mind, LXV (1956), 489–497. (III)

Matthews, G. M., "Evaluative and Descriptive," *Mind*, LXVII (1958), 335–343.

McCloskey, H. J., "An Examination of Restricted Utilitarianism," *Philosophical Review*, LXVI (1957), 466–485. (II)

———, "The Complexity of the Concept of Punishment," *Philosophy*, XXXVII (1962), 307–325. (III)

———, "Problems Arising from Erroneous Moral Judgments," *Philosophy*, XXXIX (1964), 283–300.

———, "Rights," *Philosophical Quarterly*, XV (1965), 115–127. (II)

———, "A Critique of the Ideals of Liberty," *Mind*, LXXIV (1965), 485–508.

McLaughlin, R. N., "Obligation and Ability," *Dialogue*, IV (1965), 323–335.

McNeilly, F. S., "Competing Criteria," *Mind*, LXVI (1957), 289–307.

Medlin, B., "Ultimate Principles and Ethical Egoism," *Australasian Journal of Philosophy*, XXXV (1957), 111–118. (II)

Melden, A. I., and W. K. Frankena, "Human Rights" (Symposium), *American Philosophical Association* (Eastern Div.), I (1952), 167–207. (II)

Miller, Leonard G., "Rules and Exceptions," *Ethics*, LXVI (1956), 262–270. (II)

Montague, Roger, " 'Ought' from 'Is,' " *Australasian Journal of Philosophy*, XLIII (1965), 144–167. (II)

Moore, G. E., "The Conception of Intrinsic Value," in Moore, *Philosophical Studies* (London: Routledge & Kegan Paul, 1922). (I)

———, "The Nature of Moral Philosophy," in Moore, *Philosophical Studies* (London: Routledge & Kegan Paul, 1922).

———, "Is Goodness a Quality?" in Moore, *Philosophical Papers* (London: George Allen & Unwin, 1959). (I)

Moser, S., "Utilitarian Theories of Punishment and Moral Judgments," *Philosophical Studies*, VII (1957), 15–19. (III)

Mothersill, Mary, "Anscombe's Account of the Practical Syllogism," *Philosophical Review*, LXXI (1962), 448–461. (II)

Mundle, C. W. K., "Punishment and Desert," *Philosophical Quarterly*, IV (1954), 216–228. (III)

Monro, D. H., "Are Moral Problems Genuine?" *Mind*, LXV (1956), 166–183.

Narveson, Jan, "Utilitarianism and Formalism," *Australasian Journal of Philosophy*, XLIII (1965), 58–72.

Nielsen, Kai, "Justification and Moral Reasoning," *Methodos*, IX (1957), 1–35. (I)

――――, "The Functions of Moral Discourse," *Philosophical Quarterly*, VII (1957), 236–248. (I)

――――, "The 'Good Reasons' Approach and 'Ontological Justification' of Morality," *Philosophical Quarterly*, IX (1959), 116–130. (I)

――――, "Conventionalism in Morals and the Appeal to Human Nature," *Philosophy and Phenomenological Research*, XXIII (1962–1963), 217–231.

――――, "On Human Needs and Moral Appraisals," *Inquiry*, VI (1963), 170–183.

――――, "Ethical Naturalism Once Again," *Australasian Journal of Philosophy*, XLI (1963), 313–317.

Nowell-Smith, P. H., "Freedom and Moral Responsibility," *Mind*, LVII (1948), 45–61. (III)

――――, "Determinists and Libertarians," *Mind*, LVIII (1954), 317–337. (III)

――――, "Choosing, Deciding and Doing," *Analysis*, XVIII (1958), 63–69. (III)

――――, "Ifs and Cans" *Theoria*, XXVI (1960), 85–101.

――――, and E. J. Lemmon, "Escapism," *Mind*, LXIX (1960), 289–300.

――――, "Contextual Implication and Ethical Theory," *Proceedings of the Aristotelian Society*, Suppl. XXXVI (1962), 1–18.

Nystedt, H., "The Problem of Duty and Knowledge," *Philosophy*, XXVI (1951), 333–346. (II)

O'Connor, D. J., "Possibility and Choice," *Proceedings of the Aristotelian Society*, Suppl. XXXIV (1960), 1–24.

Passmore, J. A., and P. L. Heath, "Intentions" (Symposium), *Proceedings of the Aristotelian Society*, XXIX (1955), 131–164. (III)

Paton, H. J., and R. C. Cross, "The Emotive Theory of Ethics," *Pro-*

ceedings of the Aristotelian Society, Suppl. XXII (1948), 107–140. (I)

Penelhum, T., "The Logic of Pleasure," *Philosophy and Phenomenological Research,* XVII (1957), 488–503. (II)

Peters, R. S., "Cause, Cure and Motive," *Analysis,* X (1950), 103–109. (III)

———, "Moral Education and the Psychology of Character," *Philosophy,* XXXVII (1962), 37–56. (III)

———, D. J. McCracken, and J. O. Urmson, "Motives and Causes" (Symposium), *Proceedings of the Aristotelian Society,* Suppl. XXVI (1952), 139–194. (III)

Phillips Griffiths, A., "Justifying Moral Principles," *Proceedings of the Aristotelian Society,* LVIII (1957–1958), 103–124. (II)

———, "Acting with Reason," *Philosophical Quarterly,* VIII (1958), 289–299. (II)

———, and R. S. Peters, "The Autonomy of Prudence," *Mind,* LXXI (1962), 161–180.

Pitcher, G., "On Approval," *Philosophical Review,* LXVII (1958), 195–211.

Prior, A. N., "The Autonomy of Ethics," *Australasian Journal of Philosophy,* XXXVIII (1960), 199–206.

Raab, F., "Free Will and the Ambiguity of 'Could,'" *Philosophical Review,* LXIV (1955), 60–77. (III)

Raphael, D. D., and B. Mayo, "Human Rights" (Symposium), *Proceedings of the Aristotelian Society,* Suppl. XXXIX (1965), 205–236. (II)

Rawls, J., "Outline of a Decision Procedure for Ethics," *Philosophical Review,* LX (1951), 177–197. (II)

———, "The Sense of Justice," *Philosophical Review,* LXXII (1963), 281–305. (II)

Rees, W. J., "The General Nature of a Moral Duty," *Philosophy,* XXVIII (1952), 41–57. (II)

———, "Moral Rules and the Analysis of 'Ought,'" *Philosophical Review,* LXII (1953), 23–40. (II)

Rhees, R., "Some Developments in Wittgenstein's View of Ethics," *Philosophical Review,* LXXIV (1965), 17–26.

Robinson, R., "The Emotive Theory of Ethics," *Proceedings of the Aristotelian Society*, Suppl. XXII (1948), 79–106. (I)

Ross, A., "Imperatives and Logic," *Philosophy of Science*, XI (1944), 30–46.

Runciman, W. G., and A. K. Sen, "Games, Justice and the General Will," *Mind*, LXXIV (1965), 554–562. (II)

Russell, Bertrand, "The Elements of Ethics," in *Philosophical Essays* (London: George Allen & Unwin, 1910).

Russell, L. J., "Ideals and Practice," *Philosophy*, XVII (1942), 99–116, 195–209. (III)

Ryle, Gilbert, and W. B. Gallie, "Pleasure" (Symposium), *Proceedings of the Aristotelian Society*, Suppl. XXVIII (1954), 135–164. (II)

Rynin, D., "The Autonomy of Ethics," *Mind*, LXVI (1957), 308–317.

———, "Non-Cognitive Synonymy and the Definability of 'Good,' " in *Logic and Language* (Dordrecht: D. Riedel, 1962).

Samek, Robert, "Performative Utterances and the Concept of Contract," *Australasian Journal of Philosophy*, XLIII (1965), 196–210.

Searle, J. R., "How to Derive 'Ought' from 'Is,' " *Philosophical Review*, XLIII (1964), 43–58.

Shwayder, D. S., "Moral Rules and Moral Maxims," *Ethics*, LXVII (1957), 269–285. (II)

———, "The Sense of Duty," *Philosophical Quarterly*, VII (1957), 116–125. (II)

Singer, Marcus G., "Negative and Positive Duties," *Philosophical Quarterly*, XV (1965), 97–103. (II)

Smart, J. J. C., "Extreme and Restricted Utilitarianism," *Philosophical Quarterly*, VI (1956), 344–354. (II)

———, "The Methods of Ethics and the Methods of Science," *Journal of Philosophy*, LXII (1965), 344–349.

Stevenson, C. L., "Brandt's Questions about Emotive Ethics," *Philosophical Review*, LIX (1950), 528–534. (I)

Stone, R., "Ratiocination not Rationalisation," *Mind*, LXXIV (1965), 463–482. (II)

Stout, A. K., "Motive and the Rightness of an Act," *Australasian Journal of Philosophy*, XVIII (1940), 18–37.

————, "But Suppose Everybody Did the Same," *Australasian Journal of Philosophy*, XXXII (1954), 1–29. (II)

Strawson, P. F., "Social Morality and Individual Ideal," *Philosophy*, XXXVI (1961), 1–17.

Taylor, Paul, "Social Science and Ethical Relativism," *Journal of Philosophy*, LV (1953), 32–44.

————, "Four Types of Ethical Relativism," *Philosophical Review*, LXIII (1954), 500–516.

————, "Prescribing and Evaluating," *Mind*, LXXI (1962), 213–230.

Tomas, V., "Ethical Disagreements and the Emotive Theory of Values," *Mind*, LX (1951), 205–222. (I)

Toulmin, S. E., "Principles of Morality," *Philosophy*, XXXI (1956), 142–153. (II)

Urmson, J. O., "On Grading," *Mind*, LIX (1950), 145–159. (I)

von Wright, G. H., "Practical Inference," *Philosophical Review*, LXXII (1963), 159–179. (II)

Waismann, Friedrich, "Notes on Talks with Wittgenstein," *Philosophical Review*, LXXIV (1965), 12–16.

Wasserstrom, Richard A., "Strict Liability in the Criminal Law," *Stanford Law Review*, XII (1960), 730–745. (II)

Weiler, Gershon, "Universalizability by Me," *Philosophical Quarterly*, X (1960), 167–170. (II)

Wellman, Carl, "The Ethical Implications of Cultural Relativity," *Journal of Philosophy*, LX (1963), 169–183.

Wheatley, Jon, "The Logical Status of Meta-ethical Theories," *Theoria*, XXVI (1960), 71–82.

White, A. R., "The Language of Motives," *Mind*, LXVII (1958), 258–263. (III)

Wick, Warner, "More about Duties to Oneself," *Ethics*, LXX (1960), 158–162.

Williams, B. A. O., and R. F. Atkinson, "Consistency in Ethics" (Symposium), *Proceedings of the Aristotelian Society*, Suppl. XXXIX (1965), 103–138. (II)

Wittgenstein, L., "A Lecture on Ethics," *Philosophical Review*, LXXIV (1965), 3–12.

Wollheim, Richard, and Isaiah Berlin, "Equality," *Proceedings of the Aristotelian Society*, LVI (1955–1956), 281–326. (II)

Joseph Margolis is Professor of Philosophy and Head of the Department of Philosophy at the University of Western Ontario. He has previously taught at Columbia University, University of California at Berkeley, University of Minnesota, Northwestern University, and the University of Cincinnati. His published works include *Philosophy Looks at the Arts* (1962), *Psychotherapy and Morality* (1965), and *The Language of Art and Art Criticism* (1965) as well as numerous contributions to the professional journals.

J. L. Austin Late White's Professor of Moral Philosophy, Oxford University. Author, *Philosophical Papers* (edited by J. O. Urmson and G. J. Warnock, 1961), *How to do Things with Words* (1962), *Sense and Sensibilia* (reconstructed by G. J. Warnock, 1962).

S. I. Benn Senior Fellow in Philosophy, Australian National University. Co-author, *Social Principles and the Democratic State* (1959).

J. A. Brunton Lecturer in Philosophy, University College, Cardiff.

C. A. Campbell Professor Emeritus, University of Glasgow. Author, *Scepticism and Construction* (1931), *Selfhood and Godhood* (1957).

Philippa Foot Fellow of Somerville College, Oxford University.

W. K. Frankena Professor of Philosophy, University of Michigan. Author, *Ethics* (1963) and several influential papers in ethical theory, in particular, "The Naturalistic Fallacy" (1939).

E. A. Gellner Professor of Philosophy, London School of Economics. Author, *Words and Things* (1959).

Stuart Hampshire Professor of Philosophy, Princeton University. Author, *Spinoza* (1951), *Thought and Action* (1959), and *Freedom of the Individual* (1965). Edited *Philosophy of Mind* (1966).

R. M. Hare Fellow of Balliol College, Oxford University. Author, *The Language of Morals* (1952), and *Freedom and Reason* (1963).

H. L. A. Hart Professor of Jurisprudence, Oxford University. Author, *The Concept of Law* (1961), *Law, Liberty and Morality*

(1963), and, with A. M. Honoré, *Causation in the Law* (1959).

G. E. Moore   Late Professor of Philosophy, Cambridge University. Author, *Principia Ethica* (1903), *Ethics* (1912), *Philosophical Studies* (1922), *Some Main Problems of Philosophy* (1953), *Philosophical Papers* (1959), *The Commonplace Book* (edited by Casimir Lewy, 1962), *Lectures on Philosophy* (edited by Casimir Lewy, 1966).

P. H. Nowell-Smith   Professor of Philosophy, University of Kent. Author, *Ethics* (1954). Editor, *Philosophical Books*.

R. S. Peters   Professor of Philosophy of Education, University of London Institute of Education. Author, *Hobbes* (1956), *The Concept of Motivation* (1958), and, with S. I. Benn, *Social Principles and the Democratic State* (1959). Revised and brought up to date Brett's *History of Psychology*.

H. A. Prichard   Late White's Professor of Moral Philosophy, Oxford University. Author, *Kant's Theory of Knowledge* (1909), *Moral Obligation* (1949), and *Knowledge and Perception* (1950).

A. M. Quinton   Fellow of New College, Oxford University.

John Rawls   Professor of Philosophy, Harvard University. Author of several influential papers in ethical theory, in particular, "Two Concepts of Rules" (1955) and "Justice as Fairness" (1958).

W. D. Ross   Formerly, Professor of Philosophy and Provost, Oriel College, Oxford University. Author, *Aristotle* (1923), *The Right and the Good* (1930), *Foundations of Ethics* (1939), *Plato's Theory of Ideas* (1951), and *Kant's Ethical Theory* (1954).

Gilbert Ryle   Waynflete Professor of Metaphysical Philosophy, Oxford University. Author, *The Concept of Mind* (1949) and *Dilemmas* (1954). Editor, *Mind*.

C. L. Stevenson   Professor of Philosophy, University of Michigan. Author, *Ethics and Language* (1944) and *Facts and Values* (1963).

P. F. Strawson   Fellow of University College, Oxford University. Author, *Introduction to Logical Theory* (1952) and *Individuals* (1959).